THE THEORY AND
EMPIRICAL ANALYSIS
OF PRODUCTION

NATIONAL BUREAU OF ECONOMIC RESEARCH
CONFERENCE ON RESEARCH IN INCOME AND WEALTH

THE THEORY AND EMPIRICAL ANALYSIS OF PRODUCTION

MURRAY BROWN, *editor*

GEORGE WASHINGTON UNIVERSITY

Studies in Income and Wealth

VOLUME THIRTY-ONE

*by the Conference
on Research in Income
and Wealth*

NATIONAL BUREAU OF ECONOMIC RESEARCH

NEW YORK

Distributed by COLUMBIA UNIVERSITY PRESS

NEW YORK AND LONDON 1967

PREFATORY NOTE

This volume of *Studies in Income and Wealth* contains the papers presented at the Conference on Production Relations held in October 1965 at the Carnegie International Center in New York City. The Program Committee consisted of Alfred Conrad, Evsey Domar, S. A. Goldberg, James F. Knowles, and Murray Brown, who served as chairman and conference editor. In addition we are indebted to Ester Moskowitz for editorial work and H. Irving Forman for charting.

CONTENTS

Production Analysis and Economic Policy

THE THEORY AND

EMPIRICAL ANALYSIS

OF PRODUCTION

INTRODUCTION

MURRAY BROWN

SOME conferences are constructive, not in having solved any major out-standing problems, but in producing dissatisfaction with received knowl-edge, by articulating the unresolved problems, and by airing new approaches. The conference on production functions which provided the papers for this volume was of that type. For it did provide a forum for new ideas, yet a significant part of it—indeed for some participants, the memorable part—was characterized by dissatisfaction and dissidence.

A stock-taking of the developments in the field of production since the mid-1950s could not have been the direct source of this dissatisfac-tion. For in that period, we have witnessed the breakthrough of Abramo-vitz, Solow, Kendrick, and Schmookler, who startled us by describing the enormous range of our ignorance concerning the sources of economic growth. Then, Solow, in the first part of the 1960s, taught us some of the implications for growth and production of dealing with layers upon layers of fixed assets. About the same time, the CES production function was discovered. All of these developments stimulated sufficient research to justify the belief that the field had progressed relatively far since the previous way station, which can be dated in 1948 with Paul Douglas's classic presidential address to the American Economic Association. In-deed, if these made the sum of the recent developments in production economics, then one could justifiably question the vexation expressed at the conference.

But more had occurred; there was real dissatisfaction as a result, and it was intensely expressed—in fact, the day and a half conference seemed like a winter of discontent with production economics. I would say that its sources were the following: the inability to derive in the recent past acceptable production function estimates from engineering data and, hence, in some people's opinion, to obtain structural or stable estimates; the wide and unreconciled disparities of estimates of the elasticity of substitution taken from intercountry, interregional, inter-industry, cross-section, and time series data, and between small differ-

ences in time periods, thus casting doubt on the specification and results of production studies; the uncertainty that the elasticity of substitution is even pertinent to growth analysis in the short and medium
run; the role of two new "impossibility" theorems which place certain
restrictions on the estimation of production functions and on their interpretation; the inability to evaluate from empirical studies of production
functions whether an increase in technological change since World War
II has actually occurred; and the asserted lack of usefulness of the
empirical results for policy purposes. We shall return to these in a
moment.

In itself, dissatisfaction or controversy is not sufficient to justify a
conference. The problems must be important. These issues are, for not
only do they lie close to the heart of production economics, they affect
as well the areas of economic growth, the distribution of income, and
employment. The payoff of effective results would be quite substantial,
which probably explains the considerable efforts devoted to the field in
spite of the inherent difficulty of coming up with something that will
satisfy scientific requirements.

Paul Douglas, in his contribution to this volume, tells us of the efforts
he devoted to production economics and the various types of difficulties,
professional as well as intellectual, he encountered. He recalls the very
beginning; this occurred even before his collaboration with Charles Cobb
that resulted in the development of the celebrated and frequently used
production function bearing their names. Indeed, these experiences
were the beginning of the subject itself, since he was the first to explore
the problems in theory and estimation that are associated with con-
temporary production function analysis. Ostensibly, it may appear that
we have not come very far from that period in which Paul Douglas's
work generated intense controversy and unsympathetic reactions. But
that is not the case, for though the controversy may be as intense as
ever, it proceeds on a different basis, on the assumption that the task
Paul Douglas began is salient work, and that we require more rather
than less efforts toward obtaining acceptable empirical and theoretical
results.

There were three sessions at the conference, the first dealing with a
review of the past and the other two containing papers which presented
newly developed work. It is not feasible to summarize the contents of
the papers in either neat categories or succinct conclusions. In what

follows, I shall merely try to highlight the contents of the papers and the more important points of dissent and to indicate where additional work is required, though this is done at the risk of belaboring the obvious.

The first substantive point of controversy of the conference arose in connection with the use of engineering data in the estimation of production functions. Robert Solow notes in his paper that if we ignore some programming applications, little progress was made in using that type of data after the initial attempts of Chenery and Clark. Then the Kurtz-Manne study appeared, which implemented in an ingenious manner a relatively new body of engineering data for production function estimation. But Furubotn's criticism of that study, to which Solow adds his agreement, holds that the production function estimates are unstable, that they depend on relative factor prices. Though the Furubotn and Solow criticisms went unchallenged at the conference, some participants—the oral remarks of Chenery, Easterlin, and Leontief could be interpreted in this way—voiced the feeling that even though previous efforts to estimate engineering production functions encountered aggregation and other unresolved problems, researchers should attempt to obtain such estimates. Indeed, notwithstanding these very difficult problems, severe skeptics of the aggregate production function approach maintained that we would succeed in obtaining structural estimates of production functions only with engineering-type data. In his paper, Solow takes a compromise position between the engineering and aggregate approach. Also, a compromise is offered by the Gort-Boddy and Eisner papers, which employ individual-firm data. But no consensus was reached as to the desirable research strategy, though it is safe to say that engineering production function studies would receive wide support and encouragement.

Solow reviews a number of theoretical devices—some old, some new—which he believes offer promising research leads. Underlying the new device, the invention possibility frontier, is the notion of factor-augmenting technical change. This assumes that technical knowledge augments the efficiency of one or the other inputs within a stable production function. Solow emphasizes that the advantage of this scheme is that it gives "something" to estimate or talk about. But there is a cost in its use; the scheme does not encompass changes in the elasticity of substitution or in the exponents of the Cobb-Douglas production function as a result of changes in technical knowledge. Both Solow and Tobin indicate that the factor-augmentation representation of technical change, though perhaps useful in empirical work as well as in growth theory, may be misleading if improvements apparently embodied in a factor are identified as augmenting it. The idea turned up again in empirical discussions at the conference when it was noted that education probably augmented both capital and labor; hence, in the specification of production functions, education should not only multiply the labor input, but other factors should be adjusted as well for quality change in labor.

In Kennedy's pioneering paper on induced technical change and in the subsequent work by Drandakis-Phelps, Samuelson, and Weizsäcker, the factor-augmentation scheme and the invention possibility frontier are used to great advantage. For, given the frontier, a choice can be made of the degree of augmentation of each factor, and hence the degree of technical bias is determined within the system. If a saving function and an assumption concerning the growth of labor is added, factor shares and growth paths are determined. This is a considerable bounty of results. Yet, though Solow noted some shortcomings, Tobin asked the really basic question—essentially, how does it work for the individual firm? Is it operationally meaningful in a microdecision setting?

Additional research openings are discussed by Solow—namely, Kaldor's technical progress function, Arrow's learning-by-doing model, extensions of the CES model, and Houthakker's aggregation theorem. Tobin contributes to the list by pointing to two omitted problems that he feels merit further work, the treatment of depreciation and the role of short-run fluctuations in production analysis.

Marc Nerlove commences his review of the recent empirical studies of production with a discussion of the proposition, derived by Richard Nelson, concerning the implications of the elasticity of substitution for medium-run growth. Zvi Griliches also cites the Nelson result. The result can be stated as follows: No matter what reasonable values the elasticity may be taken to be, increases in the capital-labor ratio explain only a small fraction of the growth in productivity in the postwar period. If this is indeed the case, then for growth analysis one may not need to worry himself about specifying and estimating the relatively complex CES production function; one need only use the Cobb-Douglas function, which is considerably simpler. Nerlove challenges this from two points of view: Over long periods, it is certainly important to know the value of the elasticity of substitution; and, moreover, when capital and labor are measured in efficiency units one cannot say that elasticity is *a priori* irrelevant. Brown goes even further and attempts to show that the elasticity of substitution is really a first-order parameter and hence is relevant to medium-run growth analysis. As with most of the controversies that took place in the conference, this had no conclusive ending.

It was Nerlove's review of the recent attempts to estimate the elasticity of substitution from various types and bodies of data that detonated the most resounding reaction of the conference. For there are significant differences among these many estimates, and there is no clear-cut explanation of their diversity. With respect to the cross-section estimates (interindustry, intercountry, and interregion), Nerlove presents the Liu-Hildebrand generalization of the CES model, employing it in his search for an explanation of the diversity of the estimates. It does not turn the trick. However, Griliches suggests an alternative interpretation of that model, which, if valid, implies that it may not be the appropriate model, after all, on which one should base such an explanation. Nerlove takes note, as does Mansfield and many others, of the sensitivity of the results to variations in the specification of the equation fitted and to the data used.

No relief from unreconciled discrepancies is forthcoming from Nerlove's review of time series studies of the elasticity of substitution, either. This section is prefaced by Arrow's formulation of the Diamond-McFadden "impossibility" theorem which sets out conditions for estimating the elasticity of substitution and the bias of technical change from time series. In Arrow's formulation these conditions are not excessively restrictive, although Nerlove criticizes some studies for violating them. Brown relaxes their restrictiveness even more, the result being that on most reasonable assumptions it is not "impossible" to estimate these two characteristics.

One strong impression received from the review of time series and cross-section studies is that biases and technical difficulties in the various studies make it difficult to square the results with each other. Nevertheless, a pattern emerges of differences between cross-section and time series estimates of the elasticity of substitution—namely, the former are generally larger than the time series estimates. This is reinforced if one considers the elasticities computed by Griliches in the introduction to his paper for the conference. After reviewing his cross-section estimates

and those contained in time series studies, Griliches throws his support
to the cross-section side of the controversy. Boddy addresses some
pertinent remarks to the discussion. For him, both time series and cross-
section estimates are biased, but the latter type are probably more so.
The bias in cross-section elasticities derives from the relationship used
in the estimation procedure, which specifies fixed assets constructed in
the past (and based upon factor prices in the past) as a function of
current factor prices. Clearly, there are some open questions here, but
one can say, on the basis of the participants' reactions to the disparate
estimates and to the controversy—some "shuddered," some "despaired,"
and one observer to the conference quipped to me in the hall: "You
should go into a respectable field, like astrology"—one can assert that
these problems represent a major obstacle that must be removed before
significant progress can be made.

Mansfield's comments are really complementary to the Nerlove paper;
he discusses Jorgenson's new "impossibility" theorem, focuses on the
consistency between estimated rates of technological advance in various
industries, and whether it has increased from the pre- to the post-World
War II period. Intransigence appears to characterize this important area,
also. In particular, about half of the industries Mansfield reviews showed
a higher rate of technological change in the postwar period than the prewar period and about half showed a lower rate. No unambiguous conclusion can be drawn.

The paper contributed by the Canadian authors—Lithwick, Post, and
Rymes—served to introduce the newly developed work presented at the
conference. As noted by their discussant, Derek White, this may well
be a landmark on the recent economic scene in Canada; but no provincial
conclusions should be drawn from this, since the theoretical and empirical
results, especially with respect to their work on total factor productivity,
transcend the Canadian economy. With the aid of new capital stock data,
similar in concept and scope to the U.S. capital data produced by the
Office of Business Economics, the authors compute total factor productivity, measured in two ways: by means of proportionate rates of changes
in the prices of inputs and outputs and by the conventional real method.
The former method constitutes an innovation in productivity measurement. They find that as in the United States and many other countries,
most of the change in output per man-hour is attributable to some
residual influence. In another part of their paper the authors review the

Cobb-Douglas production function studies of Canadian data and derive a major conclusion: Intersectoral movements of resources are relatively more important in Canada than in the United States in promoting growth. The authors enter the controversy centered around the use of net or gross stock in production functions—a controversy that reappears in somewhat different guise in the discussion of the Griliches paper—and come down heavily on the net stock side. Their statement of the problem and their rationale for selection of the appropriate stock concept is an excellent representative of the traditional approach.

The principal purpose of Zvi Griliches' paper is to explain the major sources of productivity growth in United States manufacturing in the postwar period. He employs the Cobb-Douglas production function, and presents cross-section estimates of the CES productivity equation to show that the assumption of unitary elasticity of substitution is not inappropriate for his data. Two important conclusions are drawn: Labor quality emerges as a significant explanatory variable, and mild increasing returns to scale with respect to capital and labor appear to be present. Bodkin takes up a point noted earlier in the conference—that the factor-augmenting properties of the labor quality variable, which is essentially educational attainments of the labor force, imply that this variable may not enter multiplicatively with raw labor (especially after Griliches introduces industry and state dummy variables into his cross-section analysis). For a different reason—namely, the measurement of the labor quality variable itself—Popkin feels that the effect of labor quality is overestimated. This, together with the discussion of the same issue by Weisbrod and by Brown and Conrad, leave one with the decided opinion that the measurement and specification of labor quality in production function analysis requires considerably more work.

Bodkin raises a very interesting point with respect to the calculation of the effect of economies of scale upon productivity measures. Griliches, in his calculation, corrects for the changing number of firms, but Bodkin suggests that this may be unjustified if the aggregate production function measures Marshallian external economies rather than economies of scale specific to the individual firms. Clearly, not only does the technique of measuring gross economies of scale require additional attention, but the external-internal returns problem is ripe for examination.

It is difficult for a paper that has the audacity to use a capital stock concept to escape challenge, and Griliches' paper is no exception. Neisser and Brown maintain, for different reasons, that his treatment of capital is inconsistent, that his concept of rent is incompatible with a service concept of capital, and that the use of depreciation allowances introduces an element of embodied technological change via the obsolescence component which also is inconsistent with his service concept of capital. Griliches' reply adds several interesting dimensions to the discussion, but this problem and the one covered by Lithwick-Rymes-Post deserve more extensive treatment. Finally, a general and valuable point raised by Domar is that one must be careful to adjust the output side when one adjusts inputs for embodiment or quality change; Griliches notes that this does not apply to his study.

Though the main objective of the Brown-Conrad paper is similar to the Griliches study—namely, the explanation of the sources of productivity in postwar United States—they differ in several respects. The former study uses the CES framework, it employs a covariance analysis on pooled time series and cross-section data, and it includes a research variable as well as education as a source of productivity change. Its principal conclusions are: A given percentage increase in education and research in durables goods industries produces a substantially larger percentage increase in productivity than does the same percentage increase in research and education in the productivity of nondurable goods industries; there is a suggestion that a malallocation occurred in the period under consideration, that the system did not allocate education and research resources between the two types of industries in an efficient manner.

The discussants challenged the data and its transformations. Terleckyj focused on the author's input-output specification of research, which was an attempt to quantify the external benefits to an industry of the research conducted in other industries. The rationale behind the author's specification is that research resulting in new or improved products is not reflected in output as measured in the national income accounts. Terleckyj felt that Brown and Conrad should have separated the internal and external benefits of research in their estimation procedure. Weisbrod raises some additional questions concerning the possibility of biases in the treatment of this variable, but his main attack is reserved for the education variable. There is no reason to reproduce the arguments against, and in defense of, the treatment of education, for as noted above in the discussion of Griliches' paper, this is an area in which a consensus is quite a way off and certainly requires more detailed study.

A serious technical criticism is raised by Griliches to the Brown-Conrad analysis, which employed a modified stepwise estimation procedure. This procedure is inefficient and inconsistent (in the statistical sense), but the authors use the reply to include additional tests which do not have those properties and find that both sets of results yield the same conclusions. Other criticisms were directed to the Brown-Conrad study, perhaps the one of note being their assumption of competition (see Weisbrod's discussion). Although the authors do not accept the implied criticism, it opens up a very difficult area in the field of production which must be added to the list of those that require exploration.

Both the Gort-Boddy and Eisner studies utilize the Cobb-Douglas production function (though Eisner does experiment with direct estimates of the CES function in an appendix), and focus on individual-firm data. The latter aspect of these studies is an auspicious one, for, as noted above, it represents a compromise between the aggregative approach and the requirements of engineering production functions. An innovation of the Eisner paper is the explicit introduction of a capacity utilization variable that is measured independently of the output which is to be explained. This plays a major role in the time series tests and in reconciling the disparate cross-section and time series estimates he obtains. With respect to the cross-section tests, Eisner finds that constant returns to scale are present (compare this with Griliches' findings of slightly increasing returns to scale and with Hickman's comments), and that the labor and capital elasticities of production are precisely those found by Paul Douglas in his pioneering studies for the United States. This is emphasized by Jorgenson, who feels that Eisner's model, by and large, explains the data.

Hickman does not concur with his fellow discussant. He challenges the time series experiments performed by Eisner, the utilization variable used in the study, and the particular specification of that variable. In general, he would be unwilling to accept at face value the economic implications of the Eisner study. He has praise for the general approach though, and joins Tobin in calling for more work on the problem of short-run production movements. With Domar, he also notes that Eisner uses gross output as a dependent variable but fails to include materials among the factors of production. However, since Eisner's paper is a progress report on a continuing research project, it may well be that he will confirm in time Douglas's major findings, provided that it can be shown that the elasticity of substitution is approximately unity, and also that one can reconcile the disparate estimates in the manner he indicates.

Gort and Boddy pose a difficult and fundamental problem concerning the effects of interactions between past and present investment. Suppose, they say, that each vintage capital item is associated with a unique production function so that their aggregate is a production function of the embodied type; this may be a serious misspecification if the different vintage capital items are interdependent, i.e., if the investment today depends, say, on the capital items put in place yesterday. In short, they assert that to a large extent a firm's investment decisions depend on its investment biography. The authors present a scheme for handling the interdependence of vintage capital items which specifies a production function (for simplicity, they use the Cobb-Douglas type) in which the capital variable is a distributed lag in investment flows. This permits a representation of the interactions between successive investments, since the coefficients on the vintage investment terms are allowed to differ. The main results of their tests of a simplified version of the model on cross-section data for the electric power industry tend to support the interaction hypothesis. There were several expressions of support for pursuing the type of analysis proposed by Gort and Boddy, and though Anne Carter voiced serious reservations about the empirical results, both discussants endorsed it. There is little doubt that the micro-orientation of the Eisner and Gort-Boddy studies, and the interaction property of investment in the latter study will receive considerable attention in future work.

Richard Nelson's paper ventures to initiate a dialogue between the fields of policy and production functions. Though little formal work in effectuating a dialogue has been attempted, Nelson's paper and the discussion by Knowles and Chenery indicate that this is a legitimate research field in its own right. After critically examining the conventional methods of formalizing and measuring technological change in a production function framework, Nelson discusses the instruments that can influence production, with special reference to research activities and education. He maintains that, even abstracting from the indirect and perhaps tenuous connection between research expenditures and production, it is unlikely that the government can significantly increase research spending in nonmilitary areas. The situation is somewhat better with respect to education because the government can spend directly in this sphere. Yet, Nelson argues that simply providing more money to educational institutions may not result in a real increase in relevant education imparted to students. He is slightly more encouraging with respect to theoretical developments and policy formation, for, at the minimum, these developments have articulated the list of relevant variables that influence production and that can be employed as instruments.

The discussion of Knowles and Chenery is complementary to Nelson's paper. Both discussants suggest other fields in production function research that have important policy implications. Knowles urges additional work on the relation of average hours worked to productivity and between education training programs and productivity. Chenery points out that sector production functions may indicate differences in wage policy between sectors if the elasticities of substitution differ between them. He also emphasizes the important insights for the growth policies of the United States and the developing countries that can derive from intercountry analyses of production functions.

As a final note to this introduction, it might be said that the conference unequivocally demonstrated that we really know very little about production relative to what we would wish. This gap between attainments and desiderata, a natural state of affairs in all research fields, is particularly large here. But when we consider the amount of dissatisfaction with the present condition of production economics, the commitment to the belief that it is a fundamental and important area, and the growing number of people working on its problems, we must view our position, perhaps not quite as a beginning but certainly not as an end.

COMMENTS ON THE COBB-DOUGLAS
PRODUCTION FUNCTION

PAUL H. DOUGLAS

I AM delighted to offer, at your invitation, some comments on the origin and development of the so-called Cobb-Douglas production function to the second and third generation of production theorists here assembled. The inspiration for this function began nearly forty years ago, in the spring of 1927, when I was temporarily lecturing at Amherst College and working simultaneously on two books which were published some years later, namely, *Real Wages in the United States* and *The Theory of Wages*. I had charted on logarithmic paper (1) the numbers employed in manufacturing in the United States from 1899 to 1922, and (2) the best estimates which I could compute of fixed capital in manufacturing deflated to dollars of constant purchasing power. We, of course, also had (3) the Federal Reserve Board's index of physical production in manufacturing during this period.

Previously I had been working on the theory of wages primarily in terms of relative elasticities of supply. But I was not at all satisfied with this facile approach to the subject, and I realized that we had to obtain some approximation of the slopes or elasticities of the marginal productivity curves of labor and capital, if we were to develop a satisfactory explanation both of wage rates and of the share which labor and capital had in the distribution of the total product.

As I have said, I had charted these three curves logarithmically on a common base and found that, in general, the production curve for manufacturing lay from one-third to one-quarter of the distance between the labor curve, which had the slowest rate of growth, and the capital curve, which had the greatest rate of growth. There were, of course, differences in the rates of growth over the years, and the depression years were characterized by decreases both in production and in labor employed. But since the capital index was one of capital available and not capital actually used, there was a marked deficiency in it.

I am not a mathematician, so I then went to my friend, Charles W. Cobb, who was on the mathematics faculty of Amherst, and asked him if he could devise a mathematical function which could be used to measure the comparative effect of each of the two factors upon the total product. Almost immediately he remembered the Euler theorem of a simple homogeneous function of the first degree and suggested it as a first approximation

$$P = bL^kC^{1-k}$$

Here the exponent for labor would be independently determined, while the assumption would be made that to increase both labor and capital by an equal percentage would increase the product by that percentage. Therefore the exponent for capital would be dependently derived as $1 - k$. We remembered that this simple function had been suggested and indeed laid down over thirty years before by that extraordinary genius, Philip H. Wicksteed, in his *Coordination of the Laws of Production and Distribution* and, later, in his *Common Sense of Political Economy*. To my mind, Wicksteed was the greatest English economist of his day and, incidentally, a most versatile man. He was not only a Unitarian minister of distinction but also the translator of Dante, the author of a series of monographs on the Italian cities of the Renaissance, and he concluded his life with a translation of the Icelandic sagas into English poetry. The same theorem had also been treated very elegantly by Leon Walras.

Cobb and I agreed on this formula and started to find the value of k by the method of least squares. This we discovered to be approximately .75 and, therefore, the exponent of capital $(1 - k)$ was taken as .25. We also found that the computed annual values were very close to the actual values, and that the standard errors of estimate were less than one would expect from the sampling error based on normal distribution. Such deviations as did occur could have been largely explained by business cycle changes and by errors in the estimates of the quantities of capital, because our measurement of capital was, as I have said, one of availability rather than of utilization. This overestimated the amount of capital used during periods of depression and slightly underestimated the relative stock of capital used during prosperity. Consequently, this tended to give a theoretical product in excess of actual product in the depression years and to understate product slightly in the prosperity years.

Assuming that these results were approximately correct, we could then find the slope of the marginal productivity curves. But before I go into that may I say that this follows from the simple logic of the formula: If we assume that an increase of 1 per cent in both labor and capital seems to cause an increase of 1 per cent in total product, and if an increase of 1 per cent in labor alone carries with it an increase of three-quarters of 1 per cent in total product and an increase of 1 per cent in capital brings about an increase of one-fourth of 1 per cent in total product, then from this you can derive the slopes of the marginal productivity curves, or what may be called the elasticity curve of labor of -4.0, and of capital of about $1\frac{1}{3}$. From these relationships, under perfect competition, we would expect labor and capital each to receive as its share of the value of product the proportion indicated by its exponent.

We had available the National Bureau of Economic Research studies on income. They seemed to show that for the period 1909–19, labor's share of the value added in manufacturing was 74.1 per cent, or an almost precise coincidence with the value of 75 per cent which we would get from the productivity theory and from the production function under perfectly competitive labor and capital markets. On the basis of all this, Cobb and I prepared a paper for the December 1927 meeting of the American Economic Association. This was forty years after John Bates Clark and Stuart Wood had read their seminal papers on marginal productivity at one of the earliest meetings of the American Economic Association.

Our paper met with a very hostile reception, and the next few years were full of the most caustic criticism. I think no one said a good word about what we had tried to do, and the attacks came from the most diverse quarters. The neoclassicists were very irate at our attempt to quantify the theory which they had contemplated in the abstract as unquantified. The institutionalists were highly indignant that anyone should attempt to find order in what they believed to be an essentially disorderly universe. The econometricians—and there were a few then—were very grieved that one should try to attach specific values to the elaborate models which they were even then constructing. The statisticians resented very much the attempt to say that this rough series had any degree of inner meaning or relationship. So, the views and personal comments for many years were very hostile. Ragnar Frisch and Horst

Mendershausen, as I remember, said that our study should be thrown in the waste basket and all future research on it discontinued. My friends thought that the better part of valor was to ignore the whole subject and never mention it, but others were not so kind.

Very frankly, I was tempted to give up and try to establish scientific respectability in other fields. But a perverse streak led me to decide not to do this, and so I incorporated not only the earlier paper in my book *The Theory of Wages,* which I published in 1934, but included also a later study based on Massachusetts manufacturing, and one on New South Wales made by Aaron Director. They seemed to bear out the general, although not the precise, results of the earlier study on the United States.

After *The Theory of Wages* appeared and my own energies began to be absorbed in other fields, such scientific time as I had available was spent almost entirely on the theory of production. I worked very closely not only with time series but also with cross-section studies of the American censuses from 1889 on to 1919, in which I would take each industry in a census year as an observation and measuring product, not in terms of physical product but value added by manufacturing. I went on to study the best statistics in this field in the world; namely, those of the British Commonwealth countries. Australia had a great statistician then in G. H. Knibbs. Starting in one of the Australian states and later continuing in the Commonwealth, he built up annual censuses of production, employment, and capital. Those series, I believe, continue to the present day and are literally a treasure trove of available material. With assistants, I published studies in the next eight years on a variety of cross-section studies and time series for New South Wales, the Commonwealth of Australia, and for New Zealand. In the process of time the values of k and $(1 - k)$ seemed to settle at about two-thirds and one-third respectively.

In the meantime, David Durand of Cornell published a very able paper in which he pointed out that the original Cobb-Douglas function had assumed what should have been the objective of research to try to prove; namely, that the sum of the exponents of labor and capital is indeed equal to unity—i.e., that constant returns to scale are actually the case. He therefore suggested that the formula be rewritten as

$$P = bL^k C^j$$

so that the exponents would be independently derived. I am deeply indebted to Mr. Durand for this suggestion.

Beginning in 1938 we therefore began to revise our statistical studies and to recompute them on the basis of the Durand modification. We published papers from time to time on the subject, but other engagements occupied me for some years, particularly during the years from 1942 to 1946. I was only able to return to the subject in the latter year when with Miss Grace Gunn we worked for a year, full time, on this matter. Very roughly, what we learned was that in practice the sum of the exponents k and j was found to be very close to one. There seemed to be some statistical evidence to indicate that production was explained by these two variables, at least so far as it was described by the marginal production theory. The values of k tended to be about .65 while those of j tended to be approximately .35 though, of course, some variation from study to study was revealed.

By this time we had accumulated about 2,100 observations for the United States and about 1,400 for countries other than the United States. We found that the deviations of the actual observations from the theoretical values for the United States were relatively minor. They were much less than one would expect from the normal distribution measures of statistical error, and this was true also of the British Commonwealths. We also found that if we analyzed the deviations of more than two standard errors of estimate, there seemed to be good theoretical reasons for them; namely, that for industries characterized by a degree of monopoly the actual value of product exceeded the theoretical values. This, we thought, was an actual corroboration of the theory. For what one could call industries characterized by excessive competition, where the labor was drawn from the most culturally deprived sections of population (which is notably true in the processing of fibers), the actual product was less than we would expect from the theoretical model. We therefore considered the deviations as basically corroborations rather than the reverse.

In the meantime, the National Bureau of Economic Research had been revising its own estimates of the distribution of the national product, and the share of W/P was lower than in their earlier study. Indeed, it was coming down to somewhere around 65 per cent, so it corresponded to our studies. Roughly the same thing was borne out, although with differences in the values, in the Commonwealth countries, and the

Commonwealth figures are much better, of course, than ours. I read a summary of all these investigations in my presidential address to the American Economic Association in December 1947, which was published in the *American Economic Review* for March 1948, and Kelley and Milman later republished it in a revised edition of *The Theory of Wages.*

I have been compelled to drop this work since then. I had in mind a book on the theory of production and was working with Miss Gunn upon it. Just as I started to go down and read the presidential address to the AEA, the telephone rang in the hotel where my wife and I were staying. I was told that I had been nominated by my party as the candidate for United States senator from Illinois. As I went down to the assembly room, I said to my wife, "Emily, this may be the end of the line for my scientific studies," and I quoted to her the line from Othello, "Oh, farewell forever now the tranquil life."

It was not until years later that I discovered that my partial rehabilitation had been started. In Russia they only rehabilitate a man after he has been shot, but ten years later I found that my rehabilitation had commenced. In Oxford, of all places, *The Theory of Wages* was required reading for an honor's degree, although I believe it is still subject to dubiety. I understand it has also been a text at Cambridge. I think all this gave a certain patina of respectability to the idea. As a result, Commonwealth and American students at Oxford and Cambridge read this book as prescribed and discussed by the dons. Others now felt that it was perhaps respectable for them to take up the subject.

I have not been able to keep in touch with all the literature since then, but I make periodic soundings into it as I am greatly interested in what is going on, and I came here to hear something about it.

I'd like to take just a minute or two, if I may, for some observations. I have never maintained that labor and capital were the sole independent variables which influenced production. Certain errors in the capital formula should be modified to get some measurement of capital actually used rather than capital available. I am quite prepared to admit that the introduction of an explicit measure of technological change, which we assumed and perhaps included under b, is an improvement. I am not so certain that it has been accurately identified or quantified. Then, my friend and former colleague, Theodore W. Schultz, started to work on education as an independent variable and explained some of the movement on this ground. But I never felt that the production function should be confined to the simple two variables, or at most three variables, which were used in the early studies. I have subscribed to many of the improvements developed in these articles which I can understand. I am also greatly interested in the development of the newer theoretical models. I have nothing to say against the development of these new models, but I would like to tell you a story about two friends of mine.

One friend did not know how to swim and wanted to learn how. He bought books on all the correct strokes, and every morning he would get on a large bed and try these strokes out, and he developed marvelous swimming form, but I could never get him to enter the water. So far as I know, he never actually swam. Another friend wanted to take up tennis, and he developed fine serves and lobs, but I could never get him to a play a game. I have felt the same thing about some of the inquiries into politics by the political scientists. I don't want to discount for one minute the tremendous importance of theoretical concepts and assumptions which one must make, but I do say there is a time in the development of science when one should learn to swim by getting into the water, and to play tennis by playing the game.

It is very difficult to convince some to do this. I therefore hope that building on the Australian and Canadian—possibly the South African —figures, we can erect a structure of studies so that we can progress in this work and actually develop studies utilizing not merely time series but what I call cross-section series with each industry as an observation. You can get many tens of thousands of observations now dating back sixty years, and with modern computers it is relatively easy to do this, whereas in my day we cranked out our limited studies by hand. I hope some—I don't say all—will make experiments in this field.

Let me say also, and I think Dr. Knowles will have some comments on this, that while in the United States we have on the whole the best statistics in the world, we've been very backward in developing capital statistics, and this is a very important point. We did collect capital statistics once upon a time, but in 1921 the Joint Committee of the American Economic Association and the American Statistical Association recommended, unanimously, that all future collection of capital statistics be discontinued by the United States Census. This was a proof of the remarkable foresight of the pundits of the two professions. We have suffered for their mistake ever since. Drs. Kendrick and Goldsmith have done very valuable work in this field, and I hope very much that we can begin to collect these capital figures again. The Joint Economic Committee, of which I am alternately chairman and vice chairman, recommended this step under the very able stimulus of Senator Proxmire, who is himself an economist. I hope very much that this can be done. Then we may have more material for these empirical studies of the production function.

I personally have faith that there is a fundamental unity in economic as in physical life, and that the world does not move haphazardly, and that we can begin to find the inner laws and tendencies of production and distribution. There is law and relative regularity everywhere else —why not in production and distribution?

REVIEW OF RECENT
THEORETICAL AND EMPIRICAL
DEVELOPMENTS
IN THE FIELD OF PRODUCTION

SOME RECENT DEVELOPMENTS IN THE
THEORY OF PRODUCTION

ROBERT M. SOLOW

MASSACHUSETTS INSTITUTE OF TECHNOLOGY

ONLY two or three years ago, Walters published a long survey of "Cost
and Production Function" (38).[1] Its bibliography listed 345 items, from
Alchian to Zellner. It is true that Walters gave much of his space to
econometric work (this is a field in which theory and empirical work are,
happily, hard to separate). It is true also that one has the casual impression of having seen another 345 items go sailing by since 1963.
Nevertheless, I do not intend to attempt another rounded survey of
even the pure theory of production. Instead, what follows is merely a
brief summary of a handful of new ideas that seem to me especially
worth attention. Any such selection is bound to be idiosyncratic. It in-
vites difference of opinion about what is useful or interesting and what
is merely neat. That may be inevitable; in any case, these are a few
theoretical leads that seem to me to be worth following up, perhaps to
establish their full utility, perhaps eventually to dismiss them as dead
ends.

Before I begin, I must justify some exclusions. Despite the substantial
volume of recent work on the static theory of production, it seems to
me that little has occurred to alter the standard textbook accounts. If
one were rewriting now the chapter on cost and production in Samuelson's *Foundations of Economic Analysis* or the corresponding parts in
the standard texts of Boulding or Stigler, there is not much one would
have to change. There has been, in fact, one major advance in the pure
theory of production in the past twenty years, and that is the development of the linear model of production under the heading Activity
Analysis or Linear Programming. The texts I read as a student were at
home only under the assumption that different inputs were smoothly

---

[1] Figures in parentheses refer to the bibliography at the end of this paper.

substitutable for one another in production. (Samuelson's *Foundations* is only a partial exception.) Today one can handle with ease and elegance the case of a finite number of joint production activities. Indeed, if it comes to that, computational possibilities are better for this case than for the older one.

As I have said, I take the development of linear theory to be a major advance in the theory of production. I think it is fair to say, however, that the results of activity analysis and linear programming have gone to confirm and considerably to deepen the main insights of the smooth theory of production. They have not changed the results in any sharp or unpredictable way. In any case, I shall not discuss activity analysis further. There have already been several full expositions of linear theory in the context of the theory of production: Dorfman, Samuelson, and Solow (9), and Boulding and Spivey (4); and the material is beginning to be included in textbooks, e.g., Davidson, Smith, and Wiley (6), and Dorfman (8).

The pure theory of production is fundamentally microeconomic in character; it deals with physically identifiable inputs and outputs. In the classroom one usually says that the economic theory of production takes for granted the "engineering" relationships between inputs and outputs and goes on from there. By contrast, much (though not quite all) of the recent interest in the theory of production has been macro-economic in character. Since the "inputs" and "outputs" are statistical aggregates like "labor," "plant," "equipment," "durable manufactures," there is no possibility of finding engineering relationships. Econometric methods have to do duty instead. Still, it remains an intriguing idea to deduce economically useful production functions from raw technological information. I had hoped to say something on that subject; but it appears that very little of general interest has been done since the early paper of Chenery (5). I do not mean to deprecate the extensive work on agricultural input-output relations, summarized in Heady and Dillon (18), or the process analysis of Manne, Markowitz, and others (26), but they seem to me to be mainly interesting as empirical rather than theoretical enterprises.

I had hoped to find an exception in the interesting idea of Kurz and Manne (24). They begin with some "engineering" estimates of the capabilities of 115 different types of machine tools (e.g., "boring machine, horizontal, under 3″ spindle, under 36″ bed") to perform each of 129 different metalworking tasks, defined in terms of geometrical shape, size of piece, tolerance, and size of lot (e.g., "flat surface—no contours, small size, semiprecision, long run"). Obviously, some combinations of machine tool and task will be hopeless, but for the rest Kurz and Manne use process-analysis estimates of output per worker and machine tool in number of pieces per daily eight-hour shift, and capital investment per worker and machine tool. From this raw material they try ingeniously to estimate a production function which will adequately summarize the possibilities of substituting one machine for another on different tasks and the more general possibility of substituting capital investment for labor in metalworking tasks. Unfortunately, the execution seems to be faulty and the criticism of Furubotn (14) justified. To get on with the job, Kurz and Manne eliminate as "inefficient" all those task-machine combinations that require higher investment costs per machine tool and worker without yielding higher output per machine tool and worker. But for this sort of step to make sense, capital costs have to be "annualized" or, in this case, "diurnalized"; depreciation rates and maintenance costs need not be equal or proportional for machine tools with different initial costs. Even if that were accomplished, it would remain true that changes in the relative prices of alternative machine tools would change the shape of the Kurz-Manne "production function" and even the composition of the set of efficient machine-task combinations. This means that the Kurz-Manne production function is less like an "engineering" relationship and more like a macroeconomic relation than might casually appear. I do not find this conclusion so very disturbing. The problems are not different in principle from those arising in any attempt to construct a conglomerate measure of input or output; and perhaps machine-tool prices move more or less together in fact. If aggregation is inevitable, relax and enjoy it.

It will come as no surprise to any reader of the current literature that many of the topics I do intend to mention have to do with the representation and analysis of technological change. I propose to begin with the idea of describing shifts in the production function as "factor-augmenting," and go on, as an application, to summarize briefly some first steps toward a theory of induced bias in technical progress. I then turn to Kaldor's notion of replacing the production function altogether by a "technical progress function" and to Arrow's extension of the production function to include "learning by doing." Then I want to call attention to some recent work on the definition and significance of the elasticity of substitution when there are more than two inputs, to the construction of models of production in which the choice of input intensities is once and for all with no further variation possible, and finally to a neglected paper of Houthakker's (19) on aggregation.

The microeconomic theory of production merges imperceptibly into the theory of distribution; it is hard to write about one without trespassing on the other. Analogously, when the theory of production is cast in macroeconomic terms it merges imperceptibly with the theory of economic growth. I shall try hard to avoid poaching, if only because this territory has recently been so superbly surveyed by Hahn and Matthews (17). To stay clear of growth theory I must limit myself so far as possible to the descriptive aspects of the theory of production, and I must avoid discussing equilibrium conditions to the extent that is possible.

Factor-augmenting Technical Change

Leave aside for the moment all fancy considerations about the possible "embodiment" of technological change in capital goods, trained labor, or anything else. Then a general way to represent technological change in a single-product production function is:

$$(1) \qquad\qquad Q = F(X, Y; T)$$

where Q is output, X and Y are inputs (all measured in natural physical units), and T is a parameter or even, for extra generality, a vector of parameters, each value of which corresponds to a different level of technology. It is natural to think of T as changing in time, perhaps smoothly, as knowledge accumulates; in that case F should be a non-decreasing function of T. But there is no reason why T should not change by discrete jumps, or from place to place, or climate to climate, or from entrepreneur to entrepreneur. Then there is no need for F to be monotone in T. In principle, the production functions corresponding to two different T's can be *any* two production functions. If we assume constant returns to scale in X and Y, so that everything is summed up in the unit isoquant, then corresponding to T_1 and T_2 may be any pair of isoquants for $Q = 1$. If the change from T_1 to T_2 is intended to be unambiguous technical progress, then the only restriction is that the later isoquant should never pass outside of the earlier. If in fact the shift from T_1 to T_2 has occurred continuously, then any continuous deformation of the first isoquant to the second is a possible path, provided only that the movement is always inward.

This is rather too general for use, and some specialization is in order. It seems to be helpful in theory and in empirical practice to represent technical change as factor augmenting:

$$(2) \qquad\qquad Q = F[a(T)X, b(T)Y]$$

It must be realized that this is a genuine specialization; not every (1) can be written as (2). The loss of generality is indicated by the fact that (1) makes output a function of three variables, while (2) is a function of two, only the variables themselves are $a(T)X$ and $b(T)Y$, which bear a natural interpretation as inputs of X and Y in "efficiency units." Obviously if a increases by 5 per cent and b by 10 per cent, then one unit of X and one of Y can do exactly what 1.05 units of X and 1.10 units of Y could do before the change. It is tempting to think that because a change in a is X-augmenting it must be, so to speak, X-specific; for example, if X is homogeneous labor one might expect an improvement in its quality to be reflected in an increase in a. But this is an error. An improvement highly specific to X may be reflected in a or b or both.

It is well known that (2) is itself a generalization of the definitions of "neutral" technological change proposed by Hicks and Harrod. Hicks's definition was that the marginal rate of substitution between X and Y should be independent of T for each fixed X and Y; Harrod's was that the average product of X should be independent of T for fixed marginal product of X. It has been often shown that Hicks-neutrality is equivalent to (2) and $a(T)/b(T) = $ constant, while Harrod-neutrality is equivalent to (2) and $a(T) = $ constant. (All this is under constant returns to scale.) One asks immediately: On what grounds is the requirement $a(T) = $ constant to be preferred to the perfectly symmetrical alternative $b(T) = $ constant? The answer is that the Harrod definition is framed particularly with the idea in mind that X is a produced factor of production—capital—and Y is a primary factor of production—labor. Then Harrod-neutral, or purely labor-augmenting, technical progress is an especially convenient vehicle for the study of steady economic growth, though there is room for argument about its factual plausibility. The symmetric assumption of purely capital-augmenting technical progress has certain nice properties of its own, mainly in connection with aggregation [see Fisher (13), Gorman (15), and Samuelson (33)].

One of the advantages of formulation (2) is that it gets away from these unnecessarily tight restrictions to "neutrality" of one kind or another, without going all the way back to (1). Diamond (7), Fei and Ranis (11), and no doubt others have proposed to describe the course of technical progress by an index, say R, of the rate of progress, and an index, say B, of its bias. As applied to the general formulation (1), Diamond suggests

$$R = \partial \log F / \partial T$$

$$B = \frac{\partial}{\partial T} \log \left(\frac{\partial F / \partial X}{\partial F / \partial Y} \right) = \frac{\partial}{\partial T} \left(\frac{F_x}{F_y} \right) \bigg/ \left(\frac{F_x}{F_y} \right)$$

This particular index of bias is obviously Hicks-oriented. It shows what happens to the marginal rate of substitution between X and Y for fixed X and Y as the level of technology T changes; Hicks-neutrality means $B = O$. One could easily define a Harrod-oriented index of bias, as I shall show in a moment. Calculation shows that

$$B = \left[\frac{a'(T)}{a(T)} - \frac{b'(T)}{b(T)} \right] \left(1 - \frac{1}{\sigma} \right)$$

$$R = \eta_X \frac{a'(T)}{a(T)} + \eta_Y \frac{b'(T)}{b(T)}$$

where σ is the elasticity of substitution between X and Y, and η_X and $\eta_Y = 1 - \eta_X$ are the elasticities of output with respect to X and Y respectively. (Observe that $B = O$ when either a/b is constant, even momentarily, or $\sigma = 1$, in which case a and b cannot be distinguished.) I leave it to the reader to reason out why the direction of bias depends on whether σ is greater or less than one.

Fei and Ranis (11) and Sheshinski (34) have introduced a Harrod-oriented index of bias through the formula

$$C = \frac{\partial}{\partial T} \log \frac{Q}{X}$$

evaluated with F_X constant. The same sort of calculation for the factor-augmenting formulation yields

$$C = (1 - \sigma)\frac{a'(T)}{a(T)},$$

so that $C = O$ if and only if a is constant or $\sigma = 1$. By symmetry there is an analogous measure of bias which vanishes when b is constant:

$$D = (1 - \sigma)\frac{b'(T)}{b(T)}$$

There is, of course, a lot of redundancy here. As Diamond, Fei and Ranis, and Sheshinski have shown, the conventional analysis of the production side of economic growth can be carried on in terms of η_X, σ, and any two of R, B, C, D. For example,

$$D - C = \sigma B$$

and

$$\eta_X C + \eta_Y D = (1 - \sigma)R.$$

It should be kept in mind that neither η_X nor σ is a constant, independent of X and Y, except in special cases.

I want to emphasize that the value of the factor-augmenting representation is not in such taxonomic identities as these. It is that in empirical as in theoretical work it gives "something" to estimate or talk about, namely, the functions $a(T)$ and $b(T)$. It does this, as I have mentioned, only at the cost of some generality; the factor-augmenting representation is not broad enough to encompass changes in the elasticity of substitution or in Cobb-Douglas exponents, for example. On the other hand it does free the discussion from the straitjacket of "neutrality" of one kind or another; this is an advantage if, as seems to be the case, neutrality is too restrictive to fit the facts.

The extra flexibility is especially valuable if one has to account for more than two factors of production. Of course, the whole analysis becomes more complicated; one needs an index of the rate of technological progress plus two indexes of bias plus three elasticities of substitution, and there is even some choice about how to define the elasticity of substitution. Besides, if the context is economic growth, the only possible extension of the underlying idea of Harrod-neutrality turns out to be extremely limiting. One must suppose that there is only one primary factor, all the rest being themselves produced. If one requires that the average products of the produced factors all be constant and independent of the level of technology when all their marginal products are constant, then technological progress must augment only the single primary factor. This seems rather too special. Hicks-neutrality extends more easily, but still seems special. The factor-augmenting representation $Q = F[a(T)X, b(T)Y, c(T)Z, . . .]$ generalizes easily and may yet be usable.

Induced Bias in Technical Progress

As an example of the theoretical convenience of the factor-augmenting assumption, I shall cite some very recent progress with an old and worrisome problem: the notion of induced bias in invention. The main papers are by Kennedy (23), Samuelson (32), and Drandakis and Phelps (10); Samuelson gives references to earlier literature, particularly Fellner (12). Before Kennedy, the discussion suffered from lack of an explicit representation of the set of inventions or lines of invention among which inventors choose (or at least along which they choose to search). The factor-augmentation functions $a(T)$ and $b(T)$ provide sufficiently—but, one hopes, not laughably—concrete "objects" for the theory to be about.

The basic device of the newer theory is an "invention possibility frontier" which can be written

$$I(a'/a, b'/b) = 0$$

Technical change is still taken to be autonomous, in the sense that there is no accounting for the resources used up in research. There is, however, an opportunity cost, in the sense that only a limited improvement in technology is possible per unit of time, and only one "direction" of improvement can be pursued at a time. Directions of technological progress are described by the factor-augmentation functions, which are now taken as functions of time rather than of some latent level of technology. It is natural to assume that the invention possibility frontier describes a curve in the plane of $a'(t)/a(t) = g_a$ and $b'(t)/b(t) = g_b$ which is falling and concave, like any transformation curve. Drandakis and Phelps insist that we consider only the quadrant where g_a and g_b are both nonnegative. Their reason is that if either is negative there will be some factor proportions for which the new production function is "worse" than the old. I am inclined to think this is unwise. For a particular pair g_a and g_b to represent unambiguous technical progress at every factor ratio, what is required is that the quantity R defined above be nowhere negative. This condition may be satisfied even with one of g_a or g_b negative, if the relative shares happen not to run the full gamut from zero to one; Cobb-Douglas is an extreme example. If all relative shares are possible, then of course Drandakis and Phelps are right. Even so, it is probably better then to step a bit outside the pure factor-augmentation assumption and allow either g_a or g_b to be negative at least where it does not imply technological regress. The reason is that empirical work might conceivably throw up indications of negative factor augmentation; rationally aimed research might do this on the sensible presumption that it need only worry about relative shares not too far from the current ones.

The new theories of induced technical progress operate on the assumption that the economy "chooses" among the combinations satisfying $I(g_a, g_b) = 0$ a best pair. "Best" is usually defined to mean maximizing the instantaneous rate of technical progress R at the going factor shares; if factor-price imputation is competitive, this is the same thing as maximizing the instantaneous rate of decrease of unit costs at going factor prices. (Fellner and Samuelson discuss some longer-sighted criteria.) Maximization of $\eta_X g_a + \eta_Y g_b$ subject to $I(g_a, g_b) = 0$ yields the necessary condition

$$\frac{\eta_X}{\eta_Y} = \frac{\eta_X}{1 - \eta_X} = \frac{I_a}{I_b},$$

where I_a and I_b are partial derivatives. It is to be remembered that η_X and η_Y are, under constant returns to scale, functions of aX/bY. Thus, given the current values of a, b, X, and Y, the rates of growth of a and b are determined.

This is only half the story. Add a mechanism governing the evolution of X and Y (if X is capital and Y labor this amounts to a determinate theory of investment and an assumption about the growth of the labor force) and the story is complete. At the next instant we have determinate values for a, b, X, and Y and therefore enough information to determine the new g_a and g_b, and carry the story further forward. To tell in detail how it comes out would carry me across that narrow line into the theory of growth and distribution. It is useful, however, to say this much. If the elasticity of substitution between X and Y (which is the same as the elasticity of substitution between aX and bY) is less than one, the dynamic process usually tends to a stable limit in which g_a and g_b are constant and therefore relative shares are constant. The reason is that when $\sigma < 1$, an increase in aX/bY decreases η_X; given the concavity of the invention possibility frontier, a decrease in η_X decreases g_a and increases g_b. Suppose, to take an uncomplicated case, that X and Y have different but exogenous rates of growth. If aX/bY is initially growing, η_X will fall, so will g_a, and this process must continue until aX/bY is constant. (If X is capital and Y is labor, this seems to establish a presumption in favor of labor augmentation.) Clearly, if $\sigma > 1$ everywhere this steady state is unstable, and the system will diverge to an extreme of distribution and/or biased technical change.

This particular episode in the theory of production and technical progress has only just begun; there is plenty of room for refinement and improvement. For the fairly short run one probably wants some version of "embodiment." For the long run one can hardly take the invention possibility frontier as stationary; it can itself be shifted by devoting resources to research, and one expects the internal logic of science itself to create a variable "natural" drift of technical change in one direction or another. This might make the invention possibility frontier a function of calendar time, or perhaps of its own past. Samuelson has pointed to a deeper problem [see also Salter (31)]: factor proportions themselves may enter the invention possibility function, if only through the relative shares. The idea is that if labor represents 70–80 per cent of total costs, it offers a larger target to shoot at than capital or other factors. In one version at least, as Samuelson shows, this formulation eliminates the presumption in favor of labor augmentation mentioned above.[2] It is depressing to think how hard it will be to get any empirical light at all on these questions.

It is easy formally to extend this theory of induced invention to three or more factors. But as so often happens it loses transparency. In this case it happens for two reasons: It is hard to capture what is captured by the (single) two-factor elasticity of substitution by any definition of $[n\,(n-1)/2]$ n-factor elasticities of substitution; and the dynamics de-

---

[2] One symmetrical way to capture this idea is to write (with Samuelson) the invention possibility curve as $I(g_a, g_b, \eta_X) = 0$ with $I_a(g, g, \eta_X)/I_b(g, g, \eta_X)$ identically equal to $\eta_X/(1 - \eta_X)$ where $I(g, g, \eta_X) = 0$. Then the theory yields $g_a = g_b$ all the time, their common value depending on η_X, which itself depends on factor supplies in the conventional way.

pends on a much more complicated interaction of the various substitution possibilities and the various trade-offs along the invention possibility surface.

Kaldor's Technical Progress Function

It is a recurrent theme of modern production theory that technological progress is somehow embodied in or otherwise bound up with investment in capital goods. Incorporation of this hypothesis into a production function like (1) or (2) has led to so-called vintage models of production. These have been so widely analyzed and discussed that I shall not try to survey them here. In an attempt to get at the same phenomenon, Kaldor (21) has proposed a rival formulation. He argues that the connections among production, investment, and technical change cannot be expressed by any kind of reversible relation between inputs and outputs, but can be described by what he calls a technical progress function. This alternative formulation seems to have attracted very little attention and to have inspired no empirical work. I am half inclined to conclude this reflects the Darwinian process at work. On the other hand, the notion of a technical progress function has recently been refined in Kaldor and Mirrlees (22) to the point where it is not really so different from "conventional" formulations based on the vintage model of production. The refinement, however, has not been carried far enough.

In the original version the technical progress function was superimposed on a setting of homogeneous capital and labor. Let me adapt my earlier noncommittal notation by taking X as capital and Y as labor. Let $q = Q/Y$ and $x = X/Y$ and represent relative time rates of growth by $g_q = q'(t)/q(t)$, etc. Kaldor's proposal was to write

$$(3) \qquad\qquad g_q = K(g_x);$$

he assumed $K(0) \geqq 0$, $K' > 0$, $K'' \leqq 0$. Thus, with capital intensity constant, productivity would increase through general technological drift, but an increase in capital intensity would be associated with a still faster increase in productivity subject to a kind of diminishing returns. I do not find this wholly nonsensical, though it is rather implausible that the relation between the rate of growth of productivity and the rate of growth of capital intensity should necessarily be independent of the degree of capital intensity already achieved.

Many people have remarked that a relation like (3) can be deduced from (1) or (2), but only on the assumption that the production function is Cobb-Douglas. See, for example, Black (3). From (2), for instance, under constant returns to scale, follows

$$g_q = \eta_x g_x + R$$

In general, of course, η_x is a function of x, which does not appear in Kaldor's technical progress function. If (2) is Cobb-Douglas, however, then η_x is constant and we have a technical progress function which is linear, or at least linear at each instant of time; and conversely. But this coincidence seems to me to be uninteresting. It is a factual question how one can legitimately represent production relations when technological knowledge is changing. The interesting analytical questions arise only after we have an acceptable description of technically feasible possibilities, when we introduce a mechanism by which the individual or the economy chooses among them. As Weizsäcker has shown (39), this part of the story is defective both in Kaldor and Kaldor and Mirrlees even if one accepts the technical progress function. Weizsäcker goes on to introduce a criterion of choice and works out a distribution theory on general supply-demand principles. In the same spirit, but without going that far, I think it will be useful to suggest by a simple example what sort of technically feasible choices are implicit in the Kaldor formulation.

To do so, it is simpler to work in discrete time. The analogue of (3) is:

$$\frac{q_t - q_{t-1}}{q_{t-1}} = K\left(\frac{x_t - x_{t-1}}{x_{t-1}}\right)$$

More compactly,

$$q_t/q_{t-1} = 1 + K\left(\frac{x_t}{x_{t-1}} - 1\right) = J(x_t/x_{t-1})$$

Thus, by iteration

$$q_t = q_{t-1}J(x_t/x_{t-1}) = q_{t-2}J(x_{t-1}/x_{t-2})J(x_t/x_{t-1}) = \cdots =$$
$$= q_0 \prod_{k=1}^{t} J(x_k/x_{k-1}).$$

This illustrates that production possibilities at any one point of time depend on the whole path the firm or economy has followed in the past. Arrow's "learning by doing" (1) shares this characteristic; so does the model of Solow *et al.* (36), which has strictly exogenous technical progress.

Imagine a central planning board which has just inherited an economy and its past at time zero; the board looks ahead for, say, two periods, during which time the supply of labor is given. Then production possibilities are

$$Q_1 = Y_1 \frac{Q_0}{Y_0} J\left(\frac{X_1 Y_0}{X_0 Y_1}\right); \ Q_2 = \frac{Y_2}{Y_0} Q_0 J\left(\frac{X_1 Y_0}{X_0 Y_1}\right) J\left(\frac{X_2 Y_1}{X_1 Y_2}\right)$$

In particular, if the supply of labor is constant,

$$Q_1 = Q_0 J(X_1/X_0); \ Q_2 = Q_0 J(X_1/X_0) J(X_2/X_1)$$

Various elementary questions can be answered. For example, suppose there is no depreciation and the planning board has already decided how much it intends to invest over the next two years, so that X_2 is fixed: How should it allocate the total of investment ($= X_2 - X_0$) between the two years to make end-period output Q_2 as large as possible? A necessary condition for a solution with positive investment in both years is

$$(X_1/X_0)\frac{J'(X_1/X_0)}{J(X_1/X_0)} = (X_2/X_1)\frac{J'(X_2/X_1)}{J(X_2/X_1)}$$

This condition is obviously satisfied if the stock of capital is made to grow at the same geometric rate in the two periods; if the *elasticity* of J is monotone the condition is satisfied only then. But at the steady growth solution the sign of the appropriate second derivative is positive if the elasticity of J is increasing with its argument, negative if decreasing. Only in the latter case is steady growth of capital the maximizing strategy. Otherwise (I stick to monotone elasticity to avoid a tiresome catalog) the best strategy is to pile all the investment into one year, no matter which. Black seems to have believed that steady growth was optimal here so long as K was concave, but that is erroneous. It is amusing that if J has a constant elasticity, i.e., $J(u) = ku^j$, then even with varying labor Q_t is proportional to $k^t X_t^j Y_t^{1-j}$, independent of the intervening path. So it is equivalent to the original conventional vintage model. The reader can easily work out the similar case when the planning board wants to maximize $P_1 Q_1 + P_2 Q_2$ or a similar weighted sum of consumption in the two periods and terminal capital.

The Kaldor-Mirrlees version restricts the technical progress function to a vintage model of production and then asserts that the rate of change of output per man as between last year's equipment and this year's equipment is an increasing concave function of the rate of change of investment per man as between those employed using last year's and this year's equipment. In obvious notation,

$$Q_t = Q_0(L_t/L_0) \prod_{k=1}^{t} J\left(\frac{I_k L_{k-1}}{I_{k-1} L_k}\right)$$

where L_k is to be identified as the labor actually employed operating the kth period's investment. One should ask and answer the same sort of planning questions for this version. I do not take the time to do so because the problem is now a bit more complicated. The difference is that before one could legitimately take total labor as exogenous, but now L_t can be made to exceed the natural increase of the labor force by discretionary scrapping of old, unproductive plant. That there is a family resemblance between the two formulations is revealed by the special case of constant-elasticity J; for then Q_t is proportional to $k^t I_t^j L^{1-j}$ regardless of what has happened since $t = 0$. It is thus equivalent to the standard "putty-clay" vintage model.

Arrow's Learning by Doing

The notion that technical progress could be "embodied" in capital goods was invented to give expression to the common sense picture that many advances in technical knowledge can affect production only when they are designed into new capital goods through gross investment. (I take it as a major intellectual puzzle, by the way, to explain why a notion that seems so self-evident in micro terms should contribute so little additional explanatory power in econometric macromodels. Can we be that close to a steady state?) In such models more investment means higher over-all productivity. But even in such models, the accumulation of technical knowledge is assumed to be autonomous. Many economists have had the idea that technological progress itself has an endogenous aspect, not simply in the sense that society can devote scarce resources to research, but in the somewhat vaguer sense that what happens in production itself has an important effect on the generation of new knowledge about production. Something like learning or exploration may occur. (The development of consumer preferences can be approached the same way, requiring modification of the standard picture of consistent, given tastes defined over the whole commodity space.)

I suppose that Kaldor's technical progress function is an attempt to capture this idea of the endogenous generation of technological knowledge. It seems to me to be defective: Why on earth should the rate of increase of productivity depend only on the rate of increase of investment per man? Arrow (1) has proposed a better thought-out alternative way of capturing much the same notion. His results have been generalized and extended by Levhari (25). Otherwise, apart from mere footnote references, there has been no further development along the lines opened by Arrow. Whether "learning by doing" is a blind alley or merely awaits some concentrated theoretical and empirical effort, I have no way of knowing. It seems at least to be getting at an aspect of reality.

Arrow's particular assumption is that technological change grows out of "experience," and cumulated experience is measured by cumulated gross investment. At any given level of technology there are fixed coefficients in the production of aggregate output from labor and existing capital goods. I adapt my earlier notation so that Y_t now represents cumulated gross investment since the economy began. If $m(Y)$ represents the fixed complement of labor with a unit of capital constructed at a moment when cumulative gross investment is Y (i.e., with serial number Y), and $n(Y)$ is the capacity embodied in a unit of capital of serial number Y, then the fixed coefficient technology implies at each instant of time

$$Q_t = \int_{Y_{t'}}^{Y_t} n(Y)dY$$

$$X_t = \int_{Y_{t'}}^{Y_t} m(Y)dY$$

Where $Y_{t'}$ is the serial number of the oldest capacity actually in use at time t. (The assumptions will be enough to guarantee that the serial numbers of the capacity in use form an interval.) Now if M and N are the indefinite integrals of m and n, one can eliminate $Y_{t'}$ to get

$$Q_t = N(Y_t) - N\{M^{-1}[M(Y_t) - X_t]\}$$

This can serve as a sort of aggregate production function. It is a novel one because its arguments are current labor input and cumulative gross investment, including some capital goods no longer surviving. The last remark is an important one; it is the essence of this model that even the "Titanic" is still contributing to maritime productivity. Even if it can no longer carry passengers, the fact that it was once built makes all current serial numbers a little bigger than they would otherwise be and therefore all current capital more productive than it would have been if the "Titanic" had never existed.

The Arrow "production function" may be a little more transparent in the special case he analyzed, where $n(Y) = n = $ constant and $m(Y) = mY^{-h}$. With fixed coefficients all technical change is factor-augmenting; this is the Harrod-neutral or pure labor-augmenting case, with the difference that the degree of labor augmentation depends on cumulative gross investment. Carrying out the calculation gives

$$Q = nY\left[1 - \left(1 - \frac{1-h}{m}\frac{X}{Y^{1-h}}\right)^{1/1-h}\right], \quad h \neq 1$$

$$= nY(1 - e^{-X/m}), \quad h = 1$$

In this form one sees easily what is true in general, that there are increasing returns to scale in the variables X and Y, though the microscopic technology has constant returns to scale—is, in fact, linear. This fact directs attention to what is probably the most interesting consequence of the model for general economic analysis. Under these assumptions about technology, smoothly functioning competitive markets would impute to fully employed labor a wage equal to its social marginal product. The residual quasirents yield a private return to capital which is definitely less than the social rate of return on investment. The builders of the "Titanic" have no way of earning anything corresponding to its posthumous contribution to output (nor to some part of its contribution even before it sank).

Levhari is able to extend the analysis beyond the fixed coefficient case. Let $I(v) = Y'(v)$ be the rate of gross investment at time v, $Q(v, t)$ be the output produced with its use at time t, and $L(v, t)$ be the labor allocated to it at time t. Then Levhari treats the case of an arbitrary constant-returns-to-scale technology with

$$Q(v, t) = F[I(v), Y^n(v) L(v, t)]$$

Note that the endogenously generated technical progress is still purely labor-augmenting in this formulation. But factor proportions are now variable, both at the planning stage and after concrete capital already exists. The broad qualitative properties of the model are not much changed, but are somewhat enriched. Levhari treats both the case where $F_2(1, 0)$ is bounded and the case where it is not. In the first case, old capital is eventually retired for economic reasons; in the second case, it is not.

One can think of other generalizations that ought to be carried out. The restrictive assumption of Harrod-neutrality may be necessary if the analysis is to center on steady states, but there is every reason to go further. Advances in technique may be generated as much by employment as by investment; on the other hand one might imagine that the "learning" associated with a given amount of investment might be less if it has to be diffused over a larger number of workers.

The Elasticity of Substitution

In any two-factor production function like (1) or (2) it is handy to have a measure of the ease with which X and Y can be substituted for one another. The standard measure is the elasticity of substitution, defined as

$$(4) \quad \sigma = \frac{F_X F_Y}{F F_{XY}} = \frac{F_X(X, Y, T) F_Y(X, Y, T)}{F(X, Y, T) F_{XY}(X, Y, T)} = \frac{F_X(X/Y, 1, T) F_Y(X/Y, 1, T)}{F(X/Y, 1, T) F_{XY}(X/Y, 1, T)},$$

with the subscripts indicating partial derivatives. (The last step depends on homogeneity or "homotheticity.") It is well known that, thus defined, σ is the (positive) elasticity of X/Y with respect to P_X/P_Y along an isoquant. That is, corresponding to a 1 per cent change in the price ratio or slope or marginal rate of substitution (with output constant) is a σ per cent change in the opposite direction in the ratio of the factors. Thus, for example, if $\sigma = 2$, a fall of 1 per cent in P_X/P_Y is associated with a 2 per cent increase in the ratio of X to Y, and therefore with a 1 per cent increase in $P_X X/P_Y Y$. In other words, the competitively imputed share in output of the more rapidly growing factor rises. Vice versa, if $\sigma < 1$. In general the elasticity of substitution varies from one point on the unit isoquant (and therefore on every isoquant, under constant returns to scale or even slightly more general assumptions) to another. It can oscillate from one side of unity to the other without violating the usual convexity conditions. The cases where the elasticity of substitution is in fact constant all along the isoquant have been much studied for convenience.

Most discussion of the elasticity of substitution has originated in its significance for competitive distribution (because capital grows faster than labor, usually). But there is something to be said for its purely descriptive utility. For example, it will be remembered that the particular parameter σ turned up quite naturally in the earlier discussion of biased technical progress. If competitive imputation were wholly irrelevant, one might still want to have some neat way of describing the degree of complementarity or substitutability between factors, if only for empirical work.

Unfortunately, as soon as one recognizes three or more factors of production it is no longer so clear how one ought to measure the degree of substitutability among them. There are alternative reasonable definitions of "the" elasticity of substitution, each answering a slightly different question. This multiplicity has been known for a long time, but has come to the surface again in the course of the exploration of production functions for which the elasticities of substitution—however defined— are constant. The basic references are Arrow *et al.* (2) for the two-factor case, and Uzawa (37) and McFadden (27) for the *n*-factor case.

All the problems show up in the three-factor case, so assume constant returns to scale and $Q = F(X, Y, Z)$. I suppose the most straightforward definition of the elasticity of substitution between X and Y is what McFadden calls the direct (partial) elasticity of substitution: Apply the two-factor definition to X and Y, holding fixed the other factor(s) Z. That is to say, fix Q and Z and thus define a curve in the XY plane which can play the role of a two-dimensional isoquant; along that curve calculate the elasticity of X/Y with respect to $P_X/P_Y = dx/dy$. The formula (4) cannot be applied directly because it involves a use of Euler's theorem, which is of course improper when there are other factors. One does find, however,

$$\sigma_{XY}{}^1 = \frac{(XF_X + YF_Y)F_XF_Y}{-F_{XX}F_Y{}^2 + 2F_{XY}F_XF_Y - F_{YY}F_X{}^2} = \frac{(XF_X + YF_Y)F_XF_Y}{\begin{vmatrix} 0 & F_X & F_Y \\ F_X & F_{XX} & F_{XY} \\ F_Y & F_{YX} & F_{YY} \end{vmatrix}}$$

This is true without any assumption about returns to scale; if F is homogeneous of any degree, however, $\sigma_{XY}{}^1$ depends only on factor proportions. It is clear from the definition, though, that for the competitive constant-returns situation $\sigma_{XY}{}^1$ is the appropriate concept for answering this question: If X and Y are available at given prices while the other factors are fixed in amount, will a rise in p_X relative to p_Y be associated with an increase or a decrease in the ratio of outlays on X to outlays on Y? Or, as the question more often arises in a macroeconomic vein: If the input of X rises relative to the input of Y, all other inputs constant, will outlays on X rise or fall relative to outlays on Y? Note that this is not the same thing as asking about distributive shares, since X and Y are not the only factors and all factors' shares may change; thus the share of X may rise relative to Y but fall relative to the total.

An alternative definition, reducing to the first (and indeed to the standard two-factor σ) when $n = 2$, is Allen's partial elasticity of substitution between X and Y

$$\sigma_{xy}{}^2 = \frac{XF_x + YF_y + ZF_z}{XY} \frac{D_{xy}}{D}$$

where D is the determinant

$$\begin{vmatrix} 0 & F_x & F_y & F_z \\ F_x & F_{xx} & F_{xy} & F_{xz} \\ F_y & F_{yx} & F_{yy} & F_{yz} \\ F_z & F_{zx} & F_{zy} & F_{zz} \end{vmatrix}$$

and D_{xy} is the cofactor of F_{XY}. Under constant returns to scale the first numerator factor is simply $F(X, Y, Z)$. There are several ways of describing the economic meaning of $\sigma_{XY}{}^2$. Standard transformations in the theory of production show that

$$\sigma_{XY}{}^2 = \frac{C}{XY} \frac{\partial X}{\partial p_Y} = \frac{E(p_X X)/Ep_Y}{p_Y Y/C}$$

where the notation Ex/Ey stands for the elasticity of x with respect to y and C is the minimum cost of producing a unit of output. C, X, and Y are to be treated as functions of the factor prices. Suppose p_Y goes up by 1 per cent, output and all other factor prices constant. Then, to terms of first order, unit cost will rise by $p_Y Y/C$ per cent and $p_X X$ will rise by a larger or smaller percentage according as $\sigma_{XY}{}^2$ is larger or smaller than one. Thus if $\sigma_{XY}{}^2$ is larger (smaller) than one, an increase in the price of Y, other prices constant, will increase (decrease) the share of X in total costs (or proceeds). But notice that this is not the same thing as holding all other factor inputs constant and increasing the input of Y; it is the same thing, under homogeneity, when there are only two factors, but not when there are three or more. Which is the right assumption depends on the frame of reference; to a firm or small industry, it is more likely to be factor prices that are constant, though output may change, but to the economy as a whole, under maintained full employment, it is more likely to be input totals.

McFadden has introduced a third definition, which he calls the "shadow elasticity of substitution." In concept it is a sort of hybrid of the two mentioned so far; he applies the two-factor definition—the elasticity of input ratio with respect to marginal rate of substitution along an isoquant—holding fixed the prices of the other factors and the unit cost.

Finally, one can seek a definition which does answer the typical macroeconomic question: What happens to the competitively imputed relative share of X if the input of X rises, other factor inputs held constant and all prices permitted to float. (I have seen the concept used this way in an unpublished paper by R. Sato, and in the MIT lectures of Paul Samuelson.) Note that this is a "one-subscript" elasticity of substitution, which we can call σ_X. A natural formula can be found in the following way. Define the elasticity of derived demand for X, θ_X say, as $-EX/Ep_X$, where Y, not p_Y, is constant. Then, in the two-factor case, it is easily verified that $\theta_X = -F_X/XF_{XX}$ and $\sigma_X = \sigma_Y = \sigma = \theta_X(1 - \eta_X) = \theta_Y(1 - \eta_Y)$. In the three- or n-factor situation, it remains true that $\theta_X = -F_X/XF_{XX}$ and that η_X, the competitive share of X increases or decreases with X according as $\theta_X(1 - \eta_X)$ is larger or smaller than one. One can then define

$$\sigma_X = \theta_X(1 - \eta_X)$$

and know that it gives the right answer to the question being asked.

I have mentioned that the immediate objective of most recent work on the elasticity of substitution has been the search for production functions whose elasticities of substitution are constant for all input bundles. In turn, the objective of this search is added flexibility in empirical work; there can be no other objective, except perhaps curiosity, because there is no reason in principle why elasticities of substitution by any definition should be constant. The results have been discouraging. In the two-factor case, the situation is now well known. The various definitions of σ coincide (no subscripts, because there is only one pair of factors) and the production functions with constant σ are of the form

$$F(X, Y) = (aX^\rho + bY^\rho)^{1/\rho}$$

where $\rho = 1 - \dfrac{1}{\sigma}$.

The work of Uzawa and McFadden has shown that the three- or *n*-factor case is unrewarding. The natural extension of the two-factor function

$$F(X, Y, Z) = (aX^\rho + bY^\rho + cZ^\rho)^{1/\rho}$$

still has constant elasticity of substitution, and the various definitions coincide. The trouble is that all factors (or all pairs of factors) have the *same* elasticity of substitution. That is unsatisfactory, but it seems that very little additional flexibility is possible. For the "direct" and "shadow" definitions the situation is as follows: The factors must be divided into classes; between any pair of factors in the same class, the elasticity of substitution must be unity; and indeed their competitive shares must be identical; for *any* pair of factors in different classes, the elasticity of substitution has the *same* common value. For the Allen partial elasticity of substitution the situation is a little more flexible: Again the factors are partitioned into classes; between any pair from different classes the elasticity of substitution is unity; each pair from the same class has a common elasticity of substitution, the same for each pair from a given class, but possibly different for each class. For the fourth definition given above, the Arrow-Chenery-Minhas-Solow function has constant σ, but necessarily the same for each factor. It is not known if any other function admits constant σ by that definition.

Since the search for three-factor production functions with constant elasticities of substitution has yielded so little, one may seek a wider class of production functions. Mrs. V. Mukerji (28) has observed that the natural generalization of (5)

$$F(X, Y, Z) = (aX^{\rho_1} + bY^{\rho_2} + cZ^{\rho_3})^{1/\rho}$$

has the property

$$\frac{\sigma_{xy}{}^1}{\sigma_{xz}{}^1} = \frac{1 - \rho_3}{1 - \rho_2}, \text{ etc.}$$

In general, for these production functions, the Allen elasticities of substitution may vary, but their *ratios* are constant. [Note that the only homogeneous functions in this class are the powers of (5).] Something a bit stronger is actually true, namely that $\sigma_{ij}{}^1/\sigma_{mn}{}^1 = c_i c_j / c_m c_n$ with the c's constant. But Gorman (16) has proved that, apart from some generalizations to allow for limitational factors and to exploit a little more fully the departure from homogeneity, the proportionality of Allen elasticities of substitution implies that the technology is either of the Uzawa or the Mukerji type.

So if anyone wants to estimate more-than-three-factor production functions to study substitution possibilities, his choice is still pretty limited.

A Theorem of Houthakker's on Aggregation

I have not reviewed any of the recent work on formal aggregation, but I cannot resist mentioning a result due to Houthakker (19), in the hope that someone will take it up and push it further. The assumption is that production within some aggregate, like an industry or even an economy, is carried on in cells, which may be firms or establishments or even places. Within each cell there are fixed factor proportions. Factors are divided into fixed and variable inputs; the variable ones are available to each cell at common fixed prices, while the fixed factors are peculiar to each cell. The fixed factors may represent capital equipment or entrepreneurial ability or locational advantage or anything; they need never by aggregated. Although there are fixed proportions within each cell, different cells may have different requirements for the variable factors. Under competitive assumptions, at any constellation of prices for output and the variable inputs, those cells will produce which can earn nonnegative quasirents after paying the variable inputs, and those cells will produce at capacity. (If there are a lot of cells just breaking even, there will be some indeterminacy. Competitive assumptions can be replaced by any definite alternative assumptions.)

Houthakker's analysis is good for any number of variable inputs; he calculates explicitly for two; I will take the case of one, just to give the idea. Let Y be the variable factor and p_Y its price in terms of product; let y be the requirement of Y per unit of output in an arbitrary cell. That cell will produce to capacity if $p_y Y \leq 1$, else it will not produce. Imagine there are so many cells, with such fine gradations, that it is reasonable to think of them as a continuum. (This is not essential; indeed for practical work one would want a computer and discrete cells anyway, but integrating is neater than summing.) Let $g(y)$ be the density function giving the capacity of cells with labor requirement y, so that $g(y)dy$ is the capacity of cells whose labor requirements per unit of output lie between y and $y + dy$. At any price p_Y, the aggregate output produced will be

$$Q = \int_0^{1/p_Y} g(y)dy$$

and the total input of the variable factor will be

$$Y = \int_0^{1/p_y} yg(y)dy.$$

Elimination of p_y between these equations yields an aggregate production function giving Q as a function of Y or, in the more general case, of all the variable inputs. In this one-variable-input case, the relation between Q and Y is formally identical to an ordinary Lorenz curve.

For instance, as Houthakker shows, if $g(y)$ is the Pareto-like density Ay^{h-1} (one would want to have h greater than one if one would like to have the density tend to zero with y, but not too much greater or else the integrals would not converge), then the result is $Q =$ constant times $Y^{(h/h+1)}$, which is, of course, a one-factor Cobb-Douglas. The remaining fraction $(1/h + 1)$ of output is imputed as quasirents to the fixed factors.

A slightly different interpretation can be imposed on this structure. Suppose that y has been changing monotonically in time under the influence of technical progress and changing economic conditions; the normal presumption is that $y(t)$ has been decreasing. Suppose that investment, measured in net additions to capacity has been $I(t)$. Then $g(y)$ is found by inverting $y(t)$ to give t as a function of y, and substituting in $I(t)$. If both $y(t)$ and $I(t)$ are exponentials, one comes back to the Houthakker case. It is easy to introduce sudden-death depreciation, or any other simple mechanism for physical mortality. When there is more than one variable factor, this interpretation of the Houthakker procedure allows the desirable property that more than one set of factor proportions be embodied in each year's capacity; different cells may face different conditions or have different expectations.

Houthakker himself treats only the Pareto distribution, which gives rise to the Cobb-Douglas. The calculations can also be carried out with exponential or gamma-type distributions; they lead to a legitimate but not especially convenient aggregate production function. Can anyone think of other interesting cases? Even some numerical calculations would be worth having.

"Putty-Clay" Models

Finally, I want to mention, but not really to discuss, the so-called putty-clay model of production. The name was coined by Phelps to describe technologies in which factor proportions are variable *ex ante,* before capital has been committed to concrete form, but fixed *ex post.* A new nickname is needed; and so is an extension to the (presumably more realistic?) case where some *ex post* variability remains, but with an elasticity of substitution smaller than the *ex ante* one. The idea was pioneered by Johansen (20) in a paper that left aside the value-theory implications entirely. Subsequent work by Phelps (29), Pyatt (30), and Solow (35) has filled in some of the gaps, but there is a lot more to be done. Almost no empirical work has been based on the putty-clay idea: Pyatt's attempt is not very successful, perhaps because it relies on a convenient but unsatisfactory assumption about the choice of technique: that first-year quasirents per unit of investment be maximized.

The importance of the putty-clay model is that it gives prominence to obsolesence—the erosion of quasirents through the competition of newer and more efficient plant. It also poses very sharply some important questions about behavior in the short run: What is maximized, the value of the competitive approximation, the degree of monopoly when aggregate effective demand is deficient. One of the useful functions of theory is the suggestion of new kinds of data it would be interesting to collect. In this model, as I have said, the key concept is the stream of quasirents yielded by a capital investment from the time it is made until it expires either from physical wear and tear or because it can no longer cover prime costs (or some noncompetitive alternative). Can we get such "life cycle" data on revenues and costs?

References

1. Arrow, K. J., "The Economic Implications of Learning by Doing," *Review of Economic Studies,* 29 (1962), 155–73.
2. Arrow, K. J., H. Chenery, B. Minhas, and R. Solow, "Capital-Labor Substitution and Economic Efficiency," *Review of Economics and Statistics,* 63 (1961), 225–50.

3. Black, J., "The Technical Progress Function and the Production Function," *Economica*, 29 (1962), 166–70.
4. Boulding, K., and W. Spivey, *Linear Programming and the Theory of the Firm*, New York, 1960.
5. Chenery, H. B., "Engineering Production Function," *Quarterly Journal of Economics*, 63 (1949), 507–31.
6. Davidson, R. K., V. Smith, and J. Wiley, *Economics, an Analytical Approach*, Homewood, Ill., 1958.
7. Diamond, P. A., "Disembodied Technical Change in a Two-Sector Model," *Review of Economic Studies*, 32 (1965), 161–68.
8. Dorfman, R., *The Price System*, Englewood Cliffs, N.J., 1964.
9. Dorfman, R., P. A. Samuelson, and R. M. Solow, *Linear Programming and Economic Analysis*, New York, 1958.
10. Drandakis, E. M., and E. S. Phelps, "A Model of Induced Invention, Growth, and Distribution," unpublished, July 1965.
11. Fei, J. C. H., and G. Ranis, "Innovational Intensity and Factor Bias in the Theory of Growth," *International Economic Review*, 6 (1965), 182–98.
12. Fellner, W., "Two Propositions in the Theory of Induced Innovations," *Economic Journal*, 71 (1961), 305–08.
13. Fisher, F. M., "Embodied Technical Change and the Existence of an Aggregate Capital Stock," *Review of Economic Studies*, forthcoming.
14. Furubotn, E. G., "Engineering Data and the Production Function," *American Economic Review*, 55 (1965), 512–16.
15. Gorman, W. M., "Capital Aggregation in Vintage Models," *Review of Economic Studies*, forthcoming.
16. ———, "Production Functions in which the Elasticities of Substitution Stand in Fixed Proportion to Each Other," *Review of Economic Studies*, 32 (1965), 217–24.
17. Hahn, F. H., and R. C. O. Matthews, "The Theory of Economic Growth: A Survey," *Economic Journal*, 74 (1964), 779–902.
18. Heady, E. O., and J. L. Dillon, *Agricultural Production Functions*, Ames, Iowa, 1962.
19. Houthakker, H. S., "The Pareto Distribution and the Cobb-Douglas Production Function in Activity Analysis," *Review of Economic Studies*, 23 (1955), 27–31.
20. Johansen, L., "Substitution versus Fixed Production Coefficients in the Theory of Economic Growth: A Synthesis," *Econometrica*, 27 (1959), 157–76.
21. Kaldor, N., "A Model of Economic Growth," *Economic Journal*, 67 (1957).
22. Kaldor, N., and J. Mirrlees, "A New Model of Economic Growth," *Review of Economic Studies*, 29 (1962), 174–92.
23. Kennedy, C., "Induced Bias in Innovation and the Theory of Distribution," *Economic Journal*, 74 (1964), 541–47.

24. Kurz, M., and A. S. Manne, "Engineering Estimates of Capital-Labor Substitution in Metal Machinery," *American Economic Review,* 53 (1963), 662–81.

25. Levhari, D., "Extensions of Arrow's 'Learning by Doing,'" *Review of Economic Studies,* forthcoming.

26. Manne, A. S., and H. M. Markowitz (ed.), *Studies in Process Analysis,* New York, 1963.

27. McFadden, D., "Further Results on CES Production Functions," *Review of Economic Studies,* 30 (1963), 73–83.

28. Mukerji, V., "A Generalized SMAC Function with Constant Ratios of Elasticities of Substitution," *Review of Economic Studies,* 30 (1963).

29. Phelps, E. S., "Substitution, Fixed Proportions, Growth and Distribution," *International Economic Review,* 4 (1963), 265–88.

30. Pyatt, G., "A Production Functional Model of United Kingdom Manufacturing Industry," in *Econometric Analysis for Economic Planning,* Colston Research Society Symposium, Bristol, 1965.

31. Salter, W. E. G., *Productivity and Technical Change,* Cambridge, Mass., 1960.

32. Samuelson, P. A., "Notes on Weizsäcker-Kennedy Theories of Induced Invention," unpublished, 1965.

33. ——, "Simple Intuitive Proofs of Neoclassical Functions Admitting of Capital Aggregation," *Review of Economic Studies,* forthcoming.

34. Sheshinski, E., "Factor-Augmenting, Disembodied, Technical Change," unpublished, 1965.

35. Solow, R. M., "Substitution and Fixed Proportions in the Theory of Capital," *Review of Economic Studies,* 29 (1962), 207–18.

36. Solow, R. M., J. Tobin, C. C. von Weizsäcker, and M. E. Yaari, "A Model of Fixed Capital without Substitution," *Review of Economic Studies,* forthcoming.

37. Uzawa, H., "Production Functions with Constant Elasticities of Substitution," *Review of Economic Studies,* 30 (1962), 291–99.

38. Walters, A. A., "Production and Cost Functions: An Econometric Survey," *Econometrica,* 31 (1963), 1–66.

39. Weizsäcker, C. C. von, "Zur ökonomischen Theorie des technischen Fortschritts," unpublished, 1964.

COMMENT

JAMES TOBIN, Yale University

Professor Solow's survey is a valuable and lucid short course in recent production theory. He claims neither completeness nor representativeness in his coverage. I will not try to judge this claim. But I do think that the topics and contributions that have excited his interest can be taken as indicative of the state of the subject. The generalization which his selective survey provokes is that analytical convenience in related branches of theory has been the main influence shaping the theory of production in recent years. The concepts, assumptions, and formulations which sustain theoretical interest are those which lend themselves easily to getting results in the theory of capital accumulation and growth. The shape of production theory would be different had it been aimed instead at providing a convenient theoretical framework for estimating technological relationships.

The principal exception in Solow's catalogue is activity analysis, a development motivated principally to approximate the complexity of production processes. But its very flexibility and generality seem to confine it to the role of a specific problem-solving technique or to use in abstract models of competitive equilibrium. Anyway it plays little part in the ferment about capital and growth to which so much current work on production is oriented.

Two-factor aggregation. Of the many aspects of theorizing geared directly to this interest, the most prominent is the aggregation of inputs into two factors, capital and labor. (Ghosts from the nineteenth century as, "What happened to land?") One reason for two-factor aggregation is that blackboards are two-dimensional. But the main reason certainly is that growth models focus attention on how these two aggregates differ in the mechanisms determining their supply. Capital is generated by saving from current production, labor by demographic factors usually assumed to proceed exogenously at a natural rate.

This motivation, however, has lost some of its force by recognition that saving can be embodied in human beings, through expenditures on education and health, as well as in physical goods. In any case it is not obvious that classifying inputs by origin should also be the appropriate way to aggregate them in describing the technology of production. That requires various capital goods to be better substitutes for each other, and various kinds of labor better substitutes for each other, than capital goods are for kinds of labor. In a two-factor production function robots would be better thrown with human labor than with floor space, even though they are "produced means of production" resulting from saving.

The embodiment of technical progress in successive vintages of gross investment is certainly a brilliant and seminal idea, for which the profession is greatly indebted to Professor Solow himself. But its appealing simplicity does depend on the aggregation of all the investment of one vintage into one homogeneous productive factor. The model becomes very complicated if a variety of capital goods, obsolescing at different rates, is allowed—plant, equipment, inventories, houses, consumer durables.

Factor-augmenting technical change. The assumption that technical progress augments one or the other input within a stable production function is a powerful simplification, no doubt useful in empirical work as well as in growth theory. But as Solow points out, the approach can be misleading if improvements apparently embodied in a factor are identified as augmenting it. Innovations embodied in new machinery may be labor-augmenting, of course, and the education of farmers may be land-augmenting. The spirit of the Phelps-Nelson approach to the productivity of education—that education enlarges choice of technology —seems more promising than the assumption, made by Denison among others, that it stretches man-hours.

Induced innovation. The notion of factor-augmenting progress is the basis for the new theories of induced innovation reviewed by Solow. The principal interest of these theories, perhaps their principal motivation, is the explanation they give for the stability of distributive shares over time. Unfortunately, although there are plausible versions of these theories which imply such stability, there are equally plausible assumptions which do not. The trouble is that the opportunity locus describing the terms of trade-off for the economy between labor augmentation and capital augmentation is a *deus ex machina.* How does the process work for the individual firm? What explains the concavity of the locus? What scarce resources determine its position? Why cannot it be moved by increasing these resources? Do they get paid, and if so how does their payment affect the theory of distribution?

Learning by doing. As Solow remarks, the Arrow model is most interesting and merits further work. Earlier contributions on the same subject, notably by Hirsch, have related learning to cumulative production. Arrow assumes that we learn only from investment; this indeed is the reason that investment has a higher social than private return. Saving and investment would not carry this extra benefit if production of consumer goods were equally instructive. Here again a priori reasoning cannot choose between plausible assumptions which have quite diverse implications.

Omitted problems. Solow's survey does not report any recent theoretical work in some areas where it is badly needed. I think, for one example, of the theory of depreciation. The assumption of exponential decay contradicts common sense and casual observation. It owes its popularity not to any evidence that this is the way capital goods wear out but to the abundant evidence that it fits smoothly into growth models. The idea that depreciation depends on intensity of use as well as on passage of time is so outmoded that the term "user cost" has been appropriated to mean a cost that does not depend on use at all but only on time.

I find more surprising the omission from Solow's survey of an important challenge which he himself has taken up. This is to provide a theory which will explain input-output relations observed in short-run fluctuations as well as in long-run growth. Perhaps our failure to reconcile these two kinds of observations should lead us, among other things, to question the complacency Solow expresses regarding the basic general neoclassical production function. It is a static function, a relationship among simultaneous steady flows of outputs and inputs. We dodge the difficult problem of specifying the timing of inputs and related outputs by assuming stationary conditions. But we have no right to assume that the relations of outputs to employment and other inputs which would hold when outputs are stationary will also hold when outputs are changing. Nor should we assume, as current growth models generally do, that there is no lag between investment expenditures and the availability of the resulting capital formation as productive input.

I too am greatly interested in growth theory. But I do think that the theory of production deserves a life of its own, with the purpose of providing models which better represent and simplify the facts of technology. This is a worthy purpose in itself, and it may be that pursuing it will also advance in the long run the related theories of capital accumulation and growth.

RECENT EMPIRICAL STUDIES OF THE CES

AND RELATED PRODUCTION FUNCTIONS

MARC NERLOVE

> ". . . this bottle was *not* marked 'poison,' so
> Alice ventured to taste it, and finding it very
> nice (it had, in fact, a sort of mixed flavour of
> cherry-tart, custard, pine-apple, roast turkey,
> toffee, and hot buttered toast), she very soon
> finished it off."
>
> —*Alice's Adventures in Wonderland*

IN their paper which first popularized the now famous constant-elastic-ity-of-substitution production function, Arrow, Chenery, Minhas, and Solow (ACMS) suggest three important areas in which knowledge of the elasticity of substitution plays a crucial role: [1] (1) The stability or instability of certain growth paths implied by some models, notably the Harrod-Domar model, depends on the value of the elasticity of substitution. (2) The effects of varying factor endowments on the pattern of trade and relative factor prices depends crucially on the nature of variation in the elasticity of substitution between factors among different industries.[2] Finally, (3) ACMS reiterate the traditional importance of the elasticity of substitution for relative shares over time. The last point has been stressed by Kravis (1959) and more elaborately by Solow

NOTE: This paper is based on research done under Grant NSF-GS-142 from the National Science Foundation to Stanford University and with the partial support of NSF-GS-818 to Yale University. I am indebted to G. Chow, Zvi Griliches, G. S. Maddala, and Peter Mieszkowski for helpful comments, although they are not, of course, responsible for errors.

[1] Arrow *et al.* (1961; see References at end of paper for bibliographic details). Although no Russian has yet stepped forward to claim credit for discovery of the CES function, it is safe to say that ACMS first *popularized* the function in the English-language literature. They mention its earlier use by Solow (1956) and Swan (1956). Whitaker (1964) attributes its first use to Dickinson in a 1954 paper in the *Review of Economic Studies*. In any case, the claim of Brown and de Cani (1963) to have derived the function independently seems well sub-stantiated.

[2] See especially Minhas (1962).

(1964). It seems clear, however, that the most important implication of any aggregate production function will be in the linking of changes in factor supplies and output, in the aggregate, over time and thus to the understanding of economic growth.

Nelson (1965) has recently questioned the relevance of the CES production function in this connection. He shows that the rate of growth in total output is approximately given in the two-factor case by

$$(1) \quad \frac{\dot{V}}{V} = \frac{\dot{A}}{A} + b_0 \frac{\dot{L}}{L} + (1 - b_0) \frac{\dot{K}}{K} + \frac{1}{2} b_0 (1 - b_0) \frac{\sigma - 1}{\sigma} \left[\frac{\dot{K}}{K} - \frac{\dot{L}}{L} \right]^2,$$

where b_0 denotes the initial share of labor in total output. The final term shows the effect of the CES function as opposed to the Cobb-Douglas form on growth, i.e., of assuming a constant but nonunitary elasticity of substitution. Note that when either the rates of growth in capital and labor are equal or when $\sigma = 1$, the expression for the rate of growth in total output reduces to that implied by the Cobb-Douglas function. $\dot{A}/A$ here represents the effects of *neutral* technical change. What Nelson shows is that ". . . for the analysis of growth over short periods of time, and in situations where the growth of capital stock is not greatly different from that of the labor supply . . . little is to be gained from going to the CES model." [3] For example, between 1947 and 1960, capital stock grew about 3 per cent a year faster than the labor force. Assuming labor's share at about two-thirds and an elasticity of substitution of one-half rather than 1 would reduce the annual rate of growth less than 3 per cent per year below the rate predicted by the Cobb-Douglas model, i.e., by

$$\frac{1}{2} \cdot \frac{2}{3} \cdot \frac{1}{3} \cdot \left(\frac{-\frac{1}{2}}{\frac{1}{2}} \right) (.03)^2 = -\frac{1}{9} \cdot \frac{9}{10,000} = -.0001.$$

The implication which Nelson draws from this is that, no matter what the elasticity of substitution may be taken to be, increases in capital per worker or per man-hour explain only a small fraction of the growth in productivity in the postwar period and that the low degree of expla-

---

[3] Nelson (1965, p. 6).

nation is not sensitive to the choice of any particular value of the elasticity of substitution.

Three points might be made in partial reply to Nelson's assertion of the irrelevance of the elasticity of substitution: First, as Nelson recognizes, over long periods or when the capital grows much more rapidly than the labor force, differences of the elasticity of substitution from 1 may play a much more significant role in determining the final outcome. Second, the result refers to capital and labor inputs as conventionally measured and makes no allowance for growth in the *effective* stock of capital or labor force due to improvements in quality or investment in human capital. If technical change is primarily of the capital-embodied type and there is little or no change in the quality of the labor force, conventional measures of inputs may greatly understate the discrepancy between the rates of growth of the two inputs and thus lend unwarranted support to Nelson's contention. On the other hand, investment in human capital and the consequent growth in the quality of the labor force tend to offset embodied technical change and to return us to Nelson's position. The net outcome, it seems, is an empirical question; to argue the irrelevance of the elasticity of substitution a priori contains elements of prejudgment. Third, the analysis refers only to the aggregate relationship between outputs and inputs. As aggregate output and therefore income grow, we would expect a shift of demand from primary goods to manufactures and services. Differences in the elasticities of substitution among industries may lead to significant effects on the rate of growth possible with given growth in factor supplies.[4] High elasticities of substitution in primary production and lower elasticities in secondary and tertiary industries coupled with the assumed shift in demand will lead to a redistribution of the labor force along the lines observed in developed economies in recent decades. Unless, however, technical change is biased in the tertiary sector, or there are other offsetting effects leading to increased elasticities of substitution between capital and labor, the aggregate elasticity of substitution must fall and ultimately growth must be slowed by even a relatively small discrepancy between the rates of growth of capital stock and labor force.

One may conclude, then, that despite Nelson's persuasive argument, the elasticity of substitution is not a priori essentially irrelevant to the problem of growth. In particular, differences in the elasticity of substi-

[4] See Arrow *et al.* (1961, p. 241).

tution among industries may profoundly affect the pattern and rate of development. There are, of course, numerous other applications in which the elasticity of substitution plays a crucial role. All this is well known and has been said many times before; its repetition here is to set recent empirical work on measurement of the elasticity of substitution in proper perspective.

In subsequent pages, we consider a selection of recent cross-section and time-series studies of the CES and related production functions. The major finding of this survey is the diversity of results: Even slight variations in the period or concepts tend to produce drastically different estimates of the elasticity. While there seems little rhyme or reason for most of these differences, a number of possible sources of bias exist and may account for at least some of the discrepancies. In addition to these effects, simultaneous equations difficulties also arise; they are discussed both within the traditional profit-maximizing framework [following Kmenta (1964) and Maddala-Kadane (1965)] and to a limited extent within the framework of an aggregate model. Finally the question of identifying biased technical change and a nonunitary elasticity of substitution is discussed. It is shown that the "impossibility theorem" of Diamond and McFadden (1965) does not invalidate most of the recent work of David and van de Klundert (1965). The impressive and useful work of Dhrymes and Kurz (1964) and McFadden (1965), extending and modifying the CES function in application to the electric power industry, must regretfully be left to one side in the present paper. In addition, the unpublished work of D. M. O'Neill, which came to my attention after completion of this paper, is not discussed.

Cross-Section Studies

Since publication of the 1961 ACMS paper, there have been a number of attempts to estimate CES or related production functions from cross-section data. Minhas (1960–63) describes in detail the data and methods used to arrive at the intercountry CES functions presented in Arrow *et al.* (1961), and the estimates he gives are identical. Fuchs (1963) has recomputed these same regressions with a shift variable, 1 for what he calls the developed countries, and zero for what he calls the underdeveloped countries. Independently of ACMS, Minasian (1961) estimated the elasticity of substitution between capital and labor from logarithmic regressions of values added per unit of labor on the wage rate for two-digit manufacturing industries in the United States using *Annual Survey of Manufactures* data for 1957 by state. Solow (1964), using identical data for 1956 by Census regions, has derived an alternative set of elasticities for most of the same two-digit industries. Liu and Hildebrand (1965) have estimated a production function which includes the CES as a special case, again from *Annual Survey of Manufactures* data for 1957 by states. All employees and production workers only are considered separately. Dhrymes (1965) has calculated elasticities of substitution from two different estimating equations derived from the CES formulation for two-digit industries in 1957. He finds corresponding estimates significantly different. Finally, Murata and Arrow (1965) have repeated the earlier intercountry comparisons of Minhas and ACMS using United Nations and International Labor Organization data for two periods: 1953–56 and 1957–59. These results are more comparable with those of Minasian, Solow, and Liu and Hildebrand as they refer to two-digit industries or combinations thereof rather than the three-digit industries considered originally by ACMS. Arrow *et al.* (1961) also include a number of results comparable with those for two-digit industries based on an analysis of United States and Japanese data alone.

Findings of the major studies are summarized in Table 1. The findings of Murata and Arrow (1965) are reported in Table 2. Table 11 below repeats the summary for corresponding two-digit industries in more convenient form and gives analogous results based on time series data.

Before turning to the interpretation of the Liu-Hildebrand results, which require some rather extensive explanation, let us compare the results obtained by Arrow *et al.* (1961), Fuchs (1963), and Arrow-Murata (1965), on the one hand with those of Minasian (1961) and Solow (1964), on the other.

The results reported by Arrow *et al.* (1961) comprise multicountry comparisons for a number of three-digit industries and U.S.-Japanese comparisons for a number of two-digit industries. The data for the first were developed on the basis of censuses of manufactures for nineteen countries in different years between 1950 and 1955. The second comparison is made on the basis of data derived from input-output studies.[5] Fuchs

[5] See Minhas (1960–63, pp. 24–25 mimeo. version); and Arrow *et al.* (1961, p. 239).

TABLE 1

Cross-Section Estimates of the Elasticity of Substitution Between Capital and Labor in Manufacturing Industries

Industry	Arrow, et al. (1961)	Fuchs[a] (1963)	Minasian (1961)	Solow (1964)	Liu-Hildebrand (1965)[b] All Employees	Liu-Hildebrand (1965)[b] Production Workers	Dhrymes (1965)[c] Elasticity of Substitution from Regression I	Dhrymes (1965)[c] Elasticity of Substitution from Regression II
Food and kindred products			0.58 (.16)	0.69 (.22)	2.15[d]	1.29[d]	.560 (.122)	0.972 (.132)
Dairy products	0.72 (.07)	0.90 (.08)						
Fruit and vegetable canning	0.86 (.08)	1.09 (.10)						
Grain and mill products	0.91 (.10)	1.32 (.17)						
Bakery products	0.90 (.07)	1.07 (.11)						
Sugar	0.78 (.12)	0.90 (.18)						
Tobacco	0.75 (.15)	1.22 (.21)	3.46 (.52)	1.96 (.30)				
Textile mill products			1.58 (.35)	1.27 (.15)	1.65	2.08	.676 (.115)	1.033 (.153)
Spinning and weaving	0.81 (.07)	0.98 (.10)						

(continued)

TABLE 1 *(continued)*

Industry	Arrow, et al. (1961)	Fuchs[a] (1963)	Minasian (1961)	Solow (1964)	Liu-Hildebrand (1965)[b]		Dhrymes (1965)[c]	
					All Employees	Production Workers	Elasticity of Substitution from Regression I	Elasticity of Substitution from Regression II
Knitting mills	0.79 (.06)	0.95 (.08)						
Apparel and related products	0.86 (.07)			1.01 (.13)	1.43	2.38[d]	.538 (.134)	1.029 (.181)
Lumber and wood products	0.89 (.04)	1.08 (.14)	0.94 (.11)	0.99 (.09)	1.00	0.91	.779 (.076)	1.101 (.111)
Furniture and fixtures	0.97 (.10)	1.04 (.09)	1.09 (.23)	1.12 (.11)	0.92[d]	0.96[e]	.696 (.079)	1.394 (.060)
Pulp, paper, and products	0.87 (.06)	0.91 (.18)	1.60 (.35)	1.77 (1.01)	1.06[d]	0.72[d]	.203 (.062)	0.638 (.078)
Printing and publishing		1.02 (.09)		1.02 (.21)			.681 (.125)	1.106 (.061)
Chemicals and products				0.14 (.95)	1.24	0.88	.309 (.096)	1.030 (.063)
Basic chemicals	0.83 (.07)	1.11 (.10)						
Misc. chemicals	0.90 (.06)	1.06 (.09)						
Fats and Oils	0.84 (.09)	1.06 (.18)						

(continued)

TABLE 1 *(continued)*

Industry	Arrow, et al. (1961)	Fuchs[a] (1963)	Minasian (1961)	Solow (1964)	Liu–Hildebrand (1965)[b] All Employees	Production Workers	Dhrymes (1965)[c] Elasticity of Substitution from Regression I	Elasticity of Substitution from Regression II
Petroleum and coal products			-0.54 (1.06)	1.45 (.71)	Not calculated		.113 (.111)	1.311 (.083)
Rubber products			0.82 (.29)	1.48 (.88)	1.44	1.39	.403 (.088)	1.037 (.144)
Leather and leather goods	0.86 (.06)	0.98 (.10)	0.96 (.29)	0.89 (.27)	0.79	0.93	.508 (.149)	1.126 (1.117)
Stone, clay, and glass products			0.59 (.25)	0.32 (.46)	1.28[d]	1.44[d]	.491 (.110)	0.887 (.077)
Clay products	0.92 (.10)	0.66 (.20)						
Glass	1.00 (.08)	1.27 (.10)						
Ceramics	0.90 (.04)	1.08 (.13)						
Cement	0.92 (.15)	1.31 (.22)						
Primary metal products			0.92 (.24)	1.87 (1.25)	0.99[d]	1.00[d]	.095 (.061)	0.968 (.136)
Iron and steel	0.81 (.05)	0.76 (.11)						

(continued)

TABLE 1 (concluded)

Industry	Arrow, et al. (1961)	Fuchs[a] (1963)	Minasian (1961)	Solow (1964)	Liu-Hildebrand (1965)[b]		Dhrymes (1965)[c]	
					All Employees	Production Workers	Elasticity of Substitution from Regression I	Elasticity of Substitution from Regression II
Nonferrous metals	1.01 (.12)	0.94 (.20)						
Fabricated metal products	0.90 (.09)	1.01 (.17)		0.80 (.29)	0.70[d]	0.45[e]	.401 (.135)	0.950 (.149)
Nonelectrical machinery			0.31 (.21)	0.64 (.45)	0.60[d]	0.44[e]	.121 (.071)	0.245 (.702)
Electrical machinery	0.87 (.12)	1.03 (.21)	1.26 (.33)	0.37 (.54)	0.79[d]	1.10[d]	.194 (.109)	0.620 (.350)
Transportation equipment			2.04 (.49)	0.06 (.82)	2.01[d]	1.91[d]		
Instruments and related products				1.59 (.15)	1.24[e]	1.65[d]		

[a]Countries broken into two groups; shift variable − 1 for Group I, 0 for Group II introduced. Group I: United States, Canada, New Zealand, Australia, Denmark, Norway, United Kingdom, Ireland, Puerto Rico. Group II: Colombia, Brazil, Mexico, Argentina, El Salvador, Southern Rhodesia, Iraq, Ceylon, Japan, India.

[b]Computed at 1957 share of capital in value added. See Tables 4–6 for the method and results.

[c]Regression I is logarithmic regression of value added per unit of labor on the wage rate; regression II is logarithmic regression of value added per unit of capital on the rate of return to capital; state data from 1957 *Census of Manufactures*.

[d]Capital-labor ratio coefficient in regression is more than twice its standard error.

[e]Coefficient of capital-labor ratio nearly twice its standard error.

TABLE 2

Intercountry Estimates of the Elasticity of Substitution for Two-Digit Manufacturing Industry, Murata-Arrow (1965)[a]

Industry	Data for 1953-56:				Data for 1957-59:			
	Estimate Based on:				Estimate Based on:			
	Log Regression of Value Added per Employee on Wage Rate	Log Regression of Wage Rate on Value Added per Employee[b]	R^2	Degrees of Freedom	Log Regression of Value Added per Employee on Wage Rate	Log Regression of Wage Rate on Value Added per Employee[b]	R^2	Degrees of Freedom
Food, beverages and tobacco	.722 (.054)	.799 (.075)	.903	19	.725 (.054)	.801 (.074)	.906	19
Textiles	.793 (.049)	.851 (.062)	.932	19	.827 (.069)	.931 (.084)	.888	18
Clothing, footwear, and made-up textiles	.660 (.067)	.775 (.102)	.851	17	.804 (.043)	.841 (.054)	.956	16
Wood products and furniture	.818 (.068)	.920 (.083)	.890	18	.919 (.074)	1.025 (.080)	.896	18
Paper and paper products	.904 (.050)	.955 (.055)	.947	18	.788 (.061)	.874 (.078)	.901	18
Printing and publishing	.836 (.075)	.951 (.090)	.879	17	.926 (.063)	.999 (.068)	.927	17
Leather and leather goods	.711 (.059)	.801 (.083)	.888	18	.699 (.050)	.761 (.072)	.919	17

(continued)

TABLE 2 (concluded)

Industry	Data for 1953-56: Estimate Based on:				Data for 1957-59: Estimate Based on:			
	Log Regression of Value Added per Employee on Wage Rate	Log Regression of Wage Rate on Value Added per Employee [b]	R^2	Degrees of Freedom	Log Regression of Value Added per Employee on Wage Rate	Log Regression of Wage Rate on Value Added per Employee [b]	R^2	Degrees of Freedom
Rubber products	.829 (.058)	.889 (.069)	.933	15	.768 (.106)	1.000 (.137)	.768	16
Chemicals, petroleum, and coal	.838 (.050)	.887 (.060)	.946	16	.834 (.087)	0.988 (.104)	.844	17
Stone, clay, glass	.847 (.046)	.896 (.054)	.945	20	.859 (.051)	0.920 (.060)	.934	20
Primary metals	.856 (.066)	.943 (.077)	.909	17	.873 (.063)	0.946 (.072)	.923	16
Metal products	.917 (.052)	.970 (.056)	.945	18	.922 (.069)	1.011 (.076)	.912	17

Source: Exchange rate from *Year Book of Labor Statistics, 1963*, International Labor Organization, Geneva, 1963. Value added (local currency), wages and salary payments (local currency), number of employees from *The Growth of World Industry, 1938-1961*, United Nations, 1963.

[a] Countries used were selected from the following list in each case: Australia, Belgium, Canada, Denmark, El Salvador, Finland, India, Iraq, Ireland, Japan, Luxembourg, Mexico, New Zealand, Norway, Pakistan, Philippines, Portugal, Puerto Rico, Singapore, Sweden, United Arab Republic, United Kingdom, and United States.

[b] Approximate standard errors based on Taylor's series expansion; see L. R. Klein, *A Textbook of Econometrics*, Evanston, Ill. 1953, p. 258.

(1963) has simply re-used the three-digit industry data but calculated new regressions, introducing a shift variable to account for differences in intercept between two groups of countries:

Group I	*Group II*
United States	Colombia
Canada	Brazil
New Zealand	Mexico
Australia	Argentina
Denmark	El Salvador
Norway	Southern Rhodesia
United Kingdom	Iraq
Ireland	Ceylon
Puerto Rico	Japan
	India

Aside from the fact that it seems improbable to find Japan in Group II and Puerto Rico in Group I, the two groups might be taken to reflect differences in development. Note that in every case but clay products, iron and steel, and nonferrous metals, the elasticity of substitution estimated allowing for a shift exceeds that obtained originally by Arrow *et al.* (1961) and in only two cases (glass, and iron and steel) can the estimate be considered significantly different from 1.

If we write the CES production function as

$$(2) \qquad y = \gamma[\delta x^{-\rho} + (1 - \delta)]^{-1/\rho},$$

where y = value added per unit labor and x = the capital-labor ratio, the equation estimated by Arrow *et al.* (1961) is

$$(3) \qquad \log y = -\frac{1}{1 + \rho} \log \gamma^{-\rho}(1 - \delta) + \frac{1}{1 + \rho} \log w.$$

Now Fuchs' modification amounts to saying that the constant term in (3) varies in a systematic way depending on how developed a country one is considering. However, a very curious result emerges from Fuchs' calculations: The shift variable is 1 for Group I, mainly developed countries, and zero for Group II, mainly underdeveloped countries. Furthermore, the estimated coefficients for the shift variable in the various regressions are nearly all *negative!* If we think of the grouping of countries as reflecting essentially differences in efficiency, this is a most peculiar result, as it would seem to imply lower value added per unit of labor for a given wage rate the more highly developed the country. Fuchs' explanation for this result is that observed wages in less developed countries more often fail fully to reflect labor costs than they do in more highly developed economies. Thus the *observed* wage rate (but not the true unit labor cost) is negatively correlated with efficiency. As shown in the lower panel of Figure 1, this results in an underestimate of the elasticity of substitution. As can be seen it is not even necessary that there be any differences in efficiency at all; the errors of observation in the wage rate would be sufficient to account for Fuchs' result.

FIGURE 1

*Effects of Varying Efficiency on the Estimated
Elasticity of Substitution*

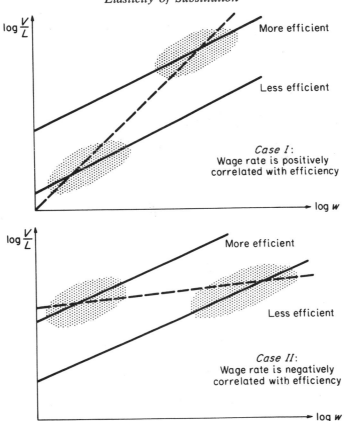

More realistically, however, one might wish to allow far differences in efficiency *positively* correlated with the observed wage rate. In this case, an overestimate of the elasticity of substitution will result, as illustrated in the top panel of Figure 1. In order to test for variations in efficiency, ACMS used capital data (conventionally measured) for four industries and five countries (United States, Canada, United Kingdom, Japan, and India).[6] On the basis of very rough estimates of the relation between the efficiency parameter γ and the wage rate, ACMS argue that the two are positively related, the elasticity of the former with respect to the latter being about 0.3. On the basis of a constant elasticity relation between γ and w, the wage rate, ACMS work out a correction factor for finding the elasticity of substitution, σ, from the regression coefficiant of log w in the regression of log V/L, value added per unit labor, on log w.[7] Let b be the regression coefficient and e the elasticity of γ with respect to w; then

(4) $$\sigma = \frac{b - e}{1 - e}.$$

As long as $e < b < 1$, $\sigma < b$, so that the estimated elasticity of substitution is biased toward 1 (if it is less to start with) if wages and efficiency are positively corrected. This is illustrated in the top half of Figure 1.

The results obtained by Arrow and Murata (1965) may be used to shed light on the question of whether a broadening of the commodity classification tends to increase the estimated elasticity of substitution as Solow (1964) argued.[8] Table 3 compares the range of the findings of ACMS for three-digit industries with the corresponding results of Arrow and Murata. The table shows that a finer classification has very little effect; if anything, the elasticities of substitution are somewhat higher for the more narrowly defined groups! While one cannot definitely reject Solow's very plausible contention, it seems that we cannot account for differences on the basis he suggested.

Minasian (1961), Solow (1964), and Liu and Hildebrand (1965) have used *Survey of Manufactures* data for 1956 and 1957. Solow uses regional aggregates, and the others use state data to investigate

[6] Arrow *et al.* (1961, p. 235).
[7] Arrow *et al.* (1961, p. 237).
[8] Solow (1964, p. 118): "It seems plausible that, in general, elasticities of substitution should be smaller the more narrowly defined the industrial classification, and the larger the degree of aggregation."

TABLE 3

Comparison of Corresponding Elasticities of Substitution for
Two-Digit and Three-Digit Industry Classifications

Industry	Two-Digit Results, Range, Murata-Arrow (1965)	Three-Digit Results, Range, Arrow *et al.* (1961)
Food and kindred products;		
tobacco	.72 - .73	.72 - 0.91
Textiles	.79 - .83	.79 - 0.81
Apparel	.66 - .80	
Lumber and products	.82 - .92	.86 - 0.89
Paper	.79 - .90	.97
Printing and publishing	.84 - .93	.87
Chemicals, coal, etc.	.83 - .84	.83 - 0.90
Rubber, etc.	.77 - .83	
Leather, etc.	.70 - .71	.86
Stone, clay, glass	.85 - .86	.92 - 1.00
Primary metals	.86 - .87	.81 - 1.01
Fabricated metal products	.92	.90

the elasticities of substitution. The Liu-Hildebrand results are actually based on a production function of which the CES is a special case; therefore, we consider the Minasian and Solow results first. One important difference between the two is that Solow's results are based on a very few regional aggregates while Minasian's utilize the greater number of observations supplied by state data. Another difference is that 1957, the year used by Minasian, was one of recession, whereas 1956, Solow's year, was not.[9] There are a number of cases in which the results differ markedly:

[9] Gordon (1961, pp. 492–501): "By the beginning of 1956 the economy was operating close to full capacity, with bottlenecks appearing in various durable-goods industries . . ." (p. 494). "In the industrial sphere prices rose . . . wages rose rapidly throughout the economy" (p. 496). ". . . Industrial production failed to rise any further after the beginning of 1957; the economy entered into what we have called a turning point zone; and a cumulative contraction developed in the latter half of the year" (p. 496). "A number of deflationary forces were already at work in the first half of the year. Manufacturers' new orders for durable goods were declining. . . . Temporarily offsetting these deflationary

| | Elasticity of Substitution ||
Industry	Minasian	Solow
Tobacco manufactures	3.46	1.96
Petroleum and coal	−0.54	1.45
Rubber and plastics	0.82	1.48
Primary metals	0.92	1.87
Nonelectrical machinery	0.31	0.64
Electrical machinery	1.26	0.37
Transportation equipment	1.04	2.04

The remaining results are more consistent with one another. These differences must either be accounted for by the difference in the level of regional aggregation or by the differential effects of full-capacity operation (1956) as compared with partial utilization (1957). The level of regional aggregation affects the results because of differences in the product mix compared: The mix is likely to be more heterogeneous across states than across Census regions. For example, when we compare Delaware and Ohio in the category rubber and plastics we are getting largely plastics in Delaware and rubber in Ohio. On the other hand, regional aggregation tends to obscure these differences and produce a more homogeneous product mix across regions. There seems to be somewhat more localization in the industries for which Solow and Minasian obtained very different estimates, but it does not seem possible to account for the peculiar pattern of results in this way. Nor does it seem possible to account in detail for the differences found in terms of the differential effect of the 1957 recession which was concentrated primarily in the durable goods area. Certainly one can say that the category "food and kindred products" will be more comparable between the two years than, say, "electrical machinery." But why should "tobacco manufactures" differ so, or "lumber and timber" not? Perhaps all one can conclude is that, when there is a lot of noise in the system, apparently small changes can produce substantial variation in the results.

In his review of Minhas (1960–63), Leontief (1964) wrote (pp. 343–44):

---

forces were the continued expansion in consumers' expenditures on nondurables and on services. . ." (p. 497). ". . . Though brief, the decline [after the middle of 1957] was very rapid; and in terms of the decline in GNP, industrial production, and employment, it was the most severe (although the shortest) of the recessions experienced since World War II." Durable goods expenditures and expenditures on plant and equipment declined most severely (pp. 497–98).

Minhas . . . proceeded on the assumption that only the variable . . . [value added per unit labor] is subject to random errors, while the [wage rate] . . . is not. Had he instead, in fitting the slopes of these regression lines, allowed also for errors affecting the observed magnitudes of [the wage rate] . . . , all estimated elasticities would necessarily turn out to be larger, since in 23 out of 24 industries examined by him, the magnitude of the . . . [elasticities of substitution] turn out to be less—although in most instances only slightly less—than 1.

The inverse proportionality . . . [implied by an elasticity of substitution less than 1] between the number of workers employed per unit of output of a particular industry and the wage rate paid to them by that industry in different countries can be explained in entirely different terms. The assumption that a man-year of labor in one part of the world is equivalent to a man-year in any other part . . . can be questioned.

The elasticity which Minhas estimates . . . measures . . . not the substitution between capital and labor but the substitution between different grades of labor.

Leontief's point is illustrated by Figure 2.

FIGURE 2

*Illustration of the Possible Bias in Estimating a
CES Production Function from Intercountry Data*

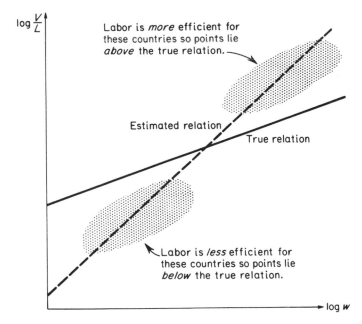

According to Leontief's argument, then, high-wage countries are those with more efficient labor and so the estimated elasticity of substitution is biased toward unity. We would expect far more variation in labor quality among countries than among regions or states within the United States. Consequently, the results obtained by Solow and Minasian for the elasticities of substitution should be *less* than the corresponding estimates obtained by Arrow and Murata (1965), which, as we saw earlier, are little different from those obtained by Minhas and also presented in Arrow *et al.* (1961). Unfortunately, this does not prove to be the case. Only in the category "stone, clay, glass" do the estimated elasticities of Minasian and Solow seem unambiguously less than the corresponding result obtained by Arrow and Murata. The other two cases are "food and kindred products" and "chemicals, etc.," but the former has been combined with "tobacco" and the latter with "petroleum and coal" by Arrow and Murata. The Solow-Minasian results bracket the Arrow-Murata results. The U.S.-Japanese comparisons presented in Arrow *et al.* (1961) alter this finding little. Once again the expected differences do not turn out to be the ones observed.

Solow (1964) suggests a possible explanation (p. 118):

> . . . the earlier observations [used by ACMS] come from a list of countries which included the United States and Canada at the high-wage end and Ceylon, India and Iraq at the low-wage end. Within any one industry the range of wage rates was always very wide, the highest running at least ten or twenty times the lowest. Within my interregional samples, the wage variation is much smaller; never in any industry is the highest wage as much as twice the lowest and almost always the range is much narrower.

But it is difficult to see that the narrow range of wage variation in the interregional or interstate studies explains more than large standard errors; the explanation does not seem to account for *higher* estimated elasticities.

In an unpublished paper, McKinnon (1963b) suggests an alternative possibility, namely, that the differences may be due to the systematic variation of product prices.[10] In all of the cross-section studies considered so far, the assumption has been made that the prices of final commodities across regions or countries were constant while money wages varied. This, of course, must imply variations in the rate of return on

---

[10] A similar idea is contained in V. Smith (1963), who, however, does not systematically explore its implications.

capital. Certainly, such variations are not plausible *within* a country such as the United States. Furthermore, Minhas (1960–63) shows that among the five countries he considered (United States, Canada, United Kingdom, Japan, and India) there is remarkably little variation in the average rate of return on capital in manufacturing; there are, however, marked differences in the rates of return among countries in individual industrial categories. Suppose, then, we tentatively accept the hypothesis of constant product prices internationally, but reject this hypothesis within the United States. Grounds for this position might be that the product mix within each two-digit category varies less across countries than within the United States, where there is a good deal of regional specialization. (This, of course, is not to deny that product prices do vary internationally. There is considerable evidence that they do. The question is whether or not an explanation of the differences between the United States and intercountry results can be explained on the hypothesis that product prices vary less internationally than interregionally because product mix varies less internationally than interregionally at the two-digit level.)

In order to explain the higher estimates of the elasticity of substitution Solow and Minasian obtain on the basis of the use of money values rather than real values, we need only assume that prices are positively correlated with money wages—eminently plausible. In the case of Solow, he intends to estimate

$$(5) \qquad \log \frac{V}{L} = a + b \log w,$$

where V is real value added and w is the real wage rate. Instead, however, he estimates

$$(5') \qquad \log \frac{pV}{L} = a' + b' \log pw,$$

where p is the price index for output. Estimating (5') rather than (5) is tantamount to leaving out the term $-(b-1) \log p$ in

$$(5'') \qquad \log \frac{pV}{L} = a + b \log pw - (b-1) \log p.$$

Now if the true elasticity of substitution is less than 1, the coefficient of $\log p$ will be positive. Hence, the omission of $\log p$ will bias the slope of log *pw* upward if log *pw* and log *p* are positively correlated. Indeed the bias is

$$(6) \qquad E[\text{est. } b - b] = (1 - b) \frac{\text{cov } [\log pw, \log p]}{\text{var } [\log p]}$$

$$= (1 - b) \frac{\text{var } [\log p] + \text{cov } [\log w, \log p]}{\text{var } [\log p]}.$$

Unless, therefore, the logarithms of real wages and prices are actually negatively correlated, the estimated elasticity of substitution will be biased upward. Although Minasian actually estimates a logarithmic regression of labor's share in the wage rate, exactly the same argument goes through. The argument thus accounts for the differences between the intercountry and the interregional results.[11]

The final two columns of Table 1 present results obtained by Dhrymes (1965). Those presented in the first of the two columns are based on logarithmic regressions of value added per unit of labor on the wage rate across states in 1957. Even though these results appear to be based on substantially the same data (individual states, 1957) as those obtained by Minasian, it is clear from the table that they differ very substantially from corresponding estimates obtained by Minasian. For example, Minasian's estimate of σ for pulp, paper, and products is nearly eight times Dhrymes', while his estimate of σ for primary metal products is nearly ten times Dhrymes'. Conversely, Minasian's estimate for rubber products is double Dhrymes'. The only explanation for these gross differences appears to be the slight variation in the basic series employed.

In the second of the two columns in which Dhrymes' results are reported, elasticities of substitution based on logarithmic regressions of value added per unit of capital stock (essentially book value) on the rate of return to capital (computed as a residual) are presented. These estimates are uniformly higher than those based on the more usual estimation procedure. While it is possible to account for these results in terms of errors in the measurement of capital stock (as Dhrymes shows in the first section of his paper), Dhrymes prefers to regard the divergence as a test of the perfect-competition and constant-returns-to-scale hypothesis

---

[11] Eisner's explanation of the possible reasons for an upward bias in Solow's estimates is closely related to the discussion here. Eisner, however, views the matter somewhat more generally in terms of "permanent" and "transitory" components. See his discussion of Solow (1964, pp. 128–37).

of the standard formulation. In view, however, of the extreme sensitivity of nearly all estimates of elasticities of substitution it is moot whether any such elaborate conclusions might be drawn from the differences among these estimates.

The Liu-Hildebrand results are most interesting, for together with some unpublished work of Bruno (1962), they suggest a production function which is neither the Cobb-Douglas nor its generalization, the CES function, but which includes both as special cases.

What Liu and Hildebrand do is to fit a logarithmic relationship containing the capital-labor ratio as well as the wage rate to explain value added per unit labor. Thus, letting

$$y = \frac{V}{L}$$

$$x = \frac{K}{L}$$

we write the production function $V = F(K, L)$, which we assume is homogeneous of degree 1, as

$$V = LF\left(\frac{K}{L}, 1\right) = Lf(x)$$

or

$$y = f(x).$$

Assuming the wage rate w equals the marginal product of labor (output prices held constant),

$$w = y - xf',$$

we find the relationship fitted by Liu and Hildebrand as

(7) $$\log y = \log a + b \log\left(y - x\frac{dy}{dx}\right) + g \log x.$$

As is well known, the assumption $g = 0$ leads to the CES function. Following Bruno, we integrate (7) to uncover the production function implied:

Equation (7) may be rewritten

$$y = a\left(y - x\frac{dy}{dx}\right)^b x^g.$$

Thus

$$y = a\left(y^2\frac{dz}{dx}\right)^b x^g,$$

where $z = x/y$. After some manipulation we find

$$x^{(1-2b-g)/b}dx = a^{1/b}z^{(1-2b)/b}dz,$$

so that integrating one obtains

$$\frac{x^{(1-g-b)/b}}{(1-g-b)/b} = \frac{a^{1/b}z^{(1-b)/b}}{(1-b)/b} + c,$$

where c is a constant of integration. Substituting $z = x/y$ and simplifying we obtain finally

(8)
$$y = [\beta x^{-\rho} + \alpha x^{-m\rho}]^{-1/\rho}$$

where
$$\rho = \frac{1-b}{b}$$

$$m = \frac{g}{1-b}$$

$$\alpha = \frac{1-b}{(1-b-g)a^{1/b}}$$

$$\beta = \frac{-c(1-b)}{a^{1/b}b}.$$

Note that (8) corresponds exactly to the CES formulation when $m = 0$, and this occurs if and only if $g = 0$; i.e., when the capital-labor ratio does not enter the estimating equation.

To obtain the elasticity of substitution for the Bruno function (8), we simply fill in the appropriate derivatives in the formula

(9)
$$\sigma = -\frac{f'(f-xf')}{xff''}.$$

Differentiating (8) we obtain

$$f' = y^{1+\rho}[\beta x^{-(1+\rho)} + \alpha m x^{-(1+m\rho)}],$$

whence

(10)
$$f - xf' = y - y^{1+\rho}[\beta x^{-\rho} + \alpha m x^{-m\rho}].$$

Now the wage rate is assumed to be equal to $f - xf' =$ the marginal product of labor; hence, raise (8) to the power $-\rho$ and multiply by $y^{1+\rho}$; we obtain

$$y = y^{1+\rho}[\beta x^{-\rho} + \alpha x^{-m\rho}].$$

Substituting in (10),

(11) $$w = y^{1+\rho}\alpha(1 - m)x^{-m\rho},$$

—which of course is really just the form we started with since (11) implies

$$\log y = \frac{-1}{1 + \rho}\log \alpha(1 - m) + \frac{1}{1 + \rho}\log w + \frac{m\rho}{1 + \rho}\log x.$$

Differentiating a second time

(12) $$f'' = (1 + \rho)\frac{f'}{xf}[xf' - f] + (1 - m)\rho\alpha m y^{1+\rho}x^{-(2+m\rho)}$$

$$= -(1 + \rho)\frac{f'}{xf}w + \rho m w x^{-2}.$$

Substituting from (10) and (12) in (9) we obtain

(13) $$\sigma = \frac{f'w}{\left[(1 + \rho)\dfrac{f'}{xf}w - \rho m w x^{-2}\right]xf} = \frac{1}{(1 + \rho) - \rho m \dfrac{f}{xf'}}.$$

Since, however,

$$f = w + xf',$$

so that

$$\frac{f}{xf'} = \frac{w}{xf'} + 1 = \frac{w}{\dfrac{K}{L}r} + 1 = \frac{wL/V}{rK/V} + 1 = \frac{s_L}{s_K} + 1$$

$$= \frac{s_L + s_K}{s_K} = \frac{1}{s_K}$$

where $s_K =$ capital's share, we arrive finally at the simple formula

(14) $$\sigma = \frac{1}{1 + \rho - \dfrac{\rho m}{s_K}}.$$

TABLE 4

Summary of Liu-Hildebrand (1965) Regressions for Two-Digit Industries[a]

Industry	All Employees				Production Workers Only			
	b	g	$\tilde{R}^2$	N	b	g	$\tilde{R}^2$	N
Food and kindred products	0.407 (.177)	.446 (.139)	.548	35	0.282 (.144)	.430 (.148)	.464	35
Textile mill products	0.975 (.175)	.160 (.109)	.695	18	1.427 (.299)	.122 (.156)	.641	18
Apparel and related products	1.071 (.263)	.097 (.086)	.669	18	1.094 (.374)	.211 (.102)	.617	18
Lumber and wood products	0.990 (.135)	.002 (.070)	.943	14	0.989 (.165)	−.033 (.090)	.920	14
Furniture and fixtures	1.258 (.128)	−.154 (.072)	.859	19	1.402 (.177)	−.191 (.102)	.807	19
Pulp, paper, and products	0.386 (.322)	.331 (.050)	.730	28	0.298 (.340)	.304 (.069)	.657	28
Chemicals and products	0.866 (.231)	.201 (.085)	.424	31	0.780 (.254)	.076 (.109)	.309	31
Petroleum and coal products	0.180 (.716)	.282 (.224)	.152	18	−0.027 (.951)	.309 (.283)	.213	18
Rubber products	1.278 (.553)	.018 (.217)	.523	16	1.231 (.286)	−.052 (.132)	.738	16
Leather and leather goods	0.890 (.457)	−.050 (.113)	.368	15	0.926 (.528)	.0003 (.118)	.434	15
Stone, clay, and glass products	0.539 (.177)	.295 (.065)	.611	25	0.568 (.175)	.309 (.069)	.627	25
Primary metal products	0.298 (.704)	.321 (.141)	.234	28	0.187 (.683)	.374 (.154)	.250	28
Fabricated metal products	0.401 (.207)	.178 (.068)	.336	32	0.189 (.208)	.243 (.080)	.298	32
Machinery except electrical	0.222 (.263)	.258 (.100)	.343	25	0.222 (.226)	.204 (.104)	.262	25
Electrical machinery	0.300 (.210)	.278 (.071)	.483	22	0.606 (.233)	.202 (.089)	.494	22
Transportation equipment	1.008 (.448)	.214 (.060)	.504	26	0.998 (.545)	.205 (.073)	.441	26
Instruments and related products	0.601 (.294)	.217 (.116)	.681	12	0.874 (.264)	.196 (.098)	.805	12

N = number of observations.

[a]Summary of estimates of regressions of the form

$$\log V/L = a + b \log w + g \log K/L$$

for two-digit industries from *Census of Manufactures, 1957,* in Liu-Hildebrand (1965, pp. 36-39).

Table 4 gives a summary of the Liu-Hildebrand regressions. Tables 5 and 6 show the details of the calculation of the elasticity of substitution obtained from these regressions by applying (14) together with the share of capital figures given by Solow (1964). These are not strictly comparable for two reasons: First, they refer to 1956 rather than 1957; and, second, as they are based on the relative share of all wage payments, not just those to production workers, the calculations in Table 5 contain a slight error. On the whole, however, the use of Solow's figures is not thought to lead to any substantial difficulty.

If $\rho \geq 0$ and if $m \geq 0$ (as it will be if $g \geq 0$ under the condition that ρ is non-negative), then, clearly, the elasticity of substitution will be greater than the coefficient of log w in the estimating equation corresponding to (7):

(15) $\qquad y = \log a + b \log w + g \log x$

$$= \frac{-1}{1+\rho} \log [(1-m)\alpha] + \frac{1}{1+\rho} \log w + \frac{\rho m}{1+o} \log x.$$

However, if the "apparent elasticity of substitution," b, is greater than unity (corresponding to a negative value of ρ) then the coefficient of log x will be negative unless m is also negative. Indeed, the true elasticity of substitution, σ, can be shown to be less, equal, or greater than the "apparent elasticity," b, according as g is negative, zero, or positive. In most cases, we may expect g to be positive (it is except for lumber and furniture in the Liu-Hildebrand regressions); hence, the direction of the discrepancy is unaltered. In any event, a simple calculation will serve to obtain the corrected elasticity whatever the slope of log x. The formula illustrates, moreover, that generally the elasticities of substitution tend to decrease as the share of capital rises.

When the value of ρ is positive, so that the slope of log w is less than unity, (15) shows that the coefficient of log w in a regression of log y on log w alone will tend to overstate the true slope of log w because this slope will be biased upward if wages and the capital-labor ratio are positively correlated. However, in this case the slope of log w will understate the *true* value of σ. Thus, assuming the Bruno function to be the correct model, we see that omissions of the capital-labor ratio lead to two offsetting effects. However, when the ratio is included the implied elastic-

TABLE 5

Capital Share in Value Added and Computation of Adjusted
Elasticities of Substitution Between Capital and Total
Employment Implied by the Liu-Hildebrand Results

Industry (1)	Share of Capital[a] (2)	$1 + \rho = \frac{1}{b}$ (3)[b]	$m\rho = \frac{g}{b}$ (4)[b]	Elasticity of Substitution in 1957[c] (5)
Food products	.55	2.4570	1.0958	2.1524
Textile products	.39	1.0256	0.1640	1.6526
Apparel	.39	0.9337	0.0905	1.4253
Lumber	.36	1.0101	0.0020	0.9955
Furniture	.42	0.7949	−0.1224	0.9206
Pulp, paper, etc.	.52	2.5906	0.8574	1.0618
Chemicals	.66	1.1547	0.2320	1.2450
Rubber	.45	0.7824	0.0410	1.4465
Leather	.38	1.1235	−0.0561	0.7867
Stone, clay, glass	.51	1.8552	0.5472	1.2783
Primary metals	.46	3.3557	1.0771	0.9860
Fabricated metals	.42	2.4937	0.4438	0.6959
Nonelectrical machinery	.41	4.5045	1.1621	0.5988
Electrical machinery	.45	3.3333	0.9266	0.7848
Transportation equipment	.43	0.9920	0.2122	2.0060
Instruments	.42	1.6638	0.3610	1.2433

[a]From (1964, p. 117). Solow gives the relative share of wage payments from which this column was computed. Strictly speaking, the share of total payroll should have been used. Thus, the capital share is somewhat larger than it should be, and the use of more appropriate figures would tend to increase all the elasticities of substitution except furniture and leather, which would be decreased by the change.

[b]From Liu-Hildebrand (1965, pp. 36 - 37).

[c]Equals the reciprocal of column 3 minus (column 4 divided by column 2).

TABLE 6

Capital Share in Value Added and Computation of Adjusted Elasticities of Substitution Between Capital and Production Workers Implied by the Liu-Hildebrand Results

Industry (1)	Share of Capital[a] (2)	$1+\rho=\dfrac{1}{b}$ (3)[b]	$m\rho=\dfrac{g}{b}$ (4)[b]	Elasticity of Substitution in 1957[c] (5)
Food products	.55	3.5460	1.5247	1.2923
Textile products	.39	0.7007	0.0854	2.0760
Apparel	.39	0.9140	0.1928	2.3832
Lumber	.36	1.0111	−0.0333	0.9060
Furniture	.42	0.7132	−0.1362	0.9639
Pulp, paper, etc.	.52	3.3557	1.0201	0.7174
Chemicals	.66	1.2820	0.0974	0.8815
Rubber	.45	0.8123	0.0422	1.3918
Leather	.38	1.0799	0.0003	0.9267
Stone, clay, glass	.51	1.7605	0.5439	1.4409
Primary metals	.46	5.3475	1.9999	1.0001
Fabricated metals	.42	5.2910	1.2857	0.4485
Nonelectrical machinery	.41	4.5045	0.9189	0.4418
Electrical machinery	.45	1.6501	0.3333	1.0996
Transportation equipment	.43	1.0020	0.2054	1.0073
Instruments	.42	1.1441	0.2242	1.6499

[a]From Solow (1964, p. 117).

[b]From Liu-Hildebrand (1965, pp. 38 - 39).

[c]Equals the reciprocal of column 3 minus (column 4 divided by column 2).

ity of substitution turns out to be much greater in most cases than the slope of log w. In many instances, the Liu-Hildebrand regression produces elasticities of substitution larger than those obtained by Solow and Minasian but in other cases not. What remains striking is the diversity of results and their sensitivity to small changes in the specification of the equation fitted or of the data used.

A possible explanation for the extreme variability of the results obtained by Liu and Hildebrand has been suggested by Griliches and Mieszkowski: If the true relation were in fact Cobb-Douglas, say,

$$V = aK^{\alpha}L^{1-\alpha},$$

K/L and w would be connected by the log-linear relation

$$\log w = \log a' + \alpha \log \frac{K}{L}$$

where $a' = a(1 - \alpha)$. Thus we would expect a good deal of collinearity between log w and log K/L if the true relation were Cobb-Douglas. This effect, if present, should tend to show up in large standard errors for the estimated coefficients of both variables, as indeed there are.

The results of all of the studies discussed in this section are summarized in Table 11, below. The diversity, as we have remarked, is striking. A number of possible reasons for such apparent inconsistencies have been advanced in the present section. A number of additional comments on sources of bias are discussed below in connection with the work of Maddala and Kadane (1965) and Kmenta (1964). It seems clear that a number of conflicting factors are operating, perhaps simultaneously, to produce the differences observed. The mixed flavor of the contents of *this* bottle does not seem quite so nice as Alice's.

Time-Series Studies

Even before ACMS published their paper in 1961, there had been considerable interest in the elasticity of substitution and in obtaining estimates of it especially for the economy as a whole. However, as in the case of cross-section work, studies utilizing time series have been greatly stimulated by ACMS. Recent studies of the aggregate elasticity of substitution have been made by Kravis (1959), Arrow *et al.* (1961),

Diwan (1963), Kendrick and Sato (1963), Brown and de Cani (1963), Kendrick (1964), Ferguson (1965a), David and van de Klundert (1965). Estimates of the elasticity of substitution for two-digit U.S. manufacturing industries based on time-series data have been obtained by McKinnon (1962 and 1963a), Lucas (1963), Kendrick (1964), Maddala (1965), and Ferguson (1965b). Mention should also be made of the work of McKinnon (1963a) and Maddala (1963) on the elasticity of substitution in certain extractive industries. Solow (1964) reports estimates of the rate of embodied technological progress based on his cross-section estimates of the elasticity of substitution, but these will not be discussed here.

Nearly all time-series studies make some attempt to allow for, and estimate, technological change. Some studies attempt to allow for variations in capacity utilization from year to year, although not with much success.[12] Recently, Diamond and McFadden (1965) have raised serious questions as to the possibility of identifying the production function under technological change. A simplified discussion of their "impossibility theorem" along lines developed by K. J. Arrow is given in this section together with some results indicating under what sort of assumptions identification is possible. The possible bias due to lack of attention to the problem of capacity utilization is also discussed.

Table 7 summarizes recent time-series studies of the elasticity of substitution and technical change in two-digit U.S. manufacturing industries.

Both Ferguson (1965) and McKinnon (1962) use annual data for the postwar period. However, Ferguson uses *Census of Manufactures* and *Annual Survey of Manufactures* material while McKinnon's data are derived from secondary sources. McKinnon allows for a distributed lag in the relationship he estimates, while Ferguson does not. Both allow for technical change; however, McKinnon assumes it must be neutral, whereas Ferguson appears to allow for non-neutral varieties. This last is entirely spurious, and although we have reported in the final column of the section of Table 7 dealing with Ferguson's results what he purports to have found, it can be shown that these results are meaningless (see below): On the whole, Ferguson's estimates of the elasticities of substitution are high, being greater than 1 in nine of nineteen cases

---

[12] I have argued elsewhere that such allowance is exceedingly important to make: Nerlove (1965, pp. 10–17).

TABLE 7

Time-Series Results on the Elasticity of Substitution, Two-Digit Manufacturing Industries, United States

Industry	Ferguson (1965b), 1949-61				
	Elasticity of Substitution	Estimated Coefficient of Trend	$\bar{R}^2$	Rate of Neutral Technological Progress[a] (per cent)	Biased Technical Change[b]
Food and kindred products	0.24 (.20)	.018 (.003)	.995	2.3	None
Tobacco manufactures	1.18 (.46)	.008 (.01)	.99	−4.4[a]	Capital using
Textile mill products	1.10 (.44)	.003 (.005)	.995	−3.0[a]	Capital using
Apparel and related products	1.08 (.16)	.003 (.001)	.99	−3.8[a]	Capital using
Lumber and timber basic	0.91 (.07)	*	.94	None	None
Furniture and fixtures	1.12 (.05)	*	.98	None	Capital saving
Paper and allied products	1.02 (.06)	*	.96	None	Mixed
Printing and publishing	1.15 (.31)	.001 (.004)	.99	−0.7[a]	Capital saving
Chemicals and allied products	1.25 (.07)	*	.97	None	Mixed
Petroleum and coal	1.30 (.15)	*	.87	None	Mixed
Rubber and plastic	0.76 (.56)	.005 (.007)	.96	2.1	Capital using
Leather and leather products	0.87 (.14)	.005 (.002)	.99	0.4	Capital using
Stone, clay, and glass	0.67 (.47)	.007 (.005)	.97	2.1	Capital using
Primary metals	1.20 (.11)	*	.94	None	Mixed
Fabricated metal products	0.93 (.26)	.002 (.005)	.98	2.9	Mixed
Machinery except electrical	1.04 (.04)	*	.98	None	Mixed
Electrical machinery	0.64 (.36)	.007 (.007)	.99	1.9	Capital saving
Transportation equipment	0.24 (.56)	.018 (.013)	.97	2.4	None
Instruments	0.76 (.29)	.011 (.006)	.99	4.6	Capital using

(continued)

TABLE 7 *(continued)*

Industry	McKinnon (1962), 1947-58				
	Long-run Elasticity of Substitution	Coefficient of Adjustment	Estimated Coefficient of Trend	$\bar{R}^2$	Rate of Neutral Technological Progress[c] (per cent)
Food and kindred products	0.373	0.581 (.326)	0.379 (.378)	.977	2.4
Tobacco manufactures	0.921	0.655 (.297)	−0.240 (.556)	.902	−10.7
Textile mill products	0.162	0.691 (.323)	0.860 (.568)	.988	3.4
Apparel and related products	0.694	0.875 (.215)	0.024 (.203)	.927	0.2
Lumber and timber basic	0.802	0.764 (.322)	−0.016 (.909)	.962	−0.3
Furniture and fixtures	1.021	0.704 (.178)	−0.158 (.313)	.959	24.2
Paper and allied products	0.094	0.822 (.577)	0.907 (1.161)	.911	2.8
Printing and publishing	0.844	0.756 (.284)	−0.051 (.294)	.922	−1.0
Chemicals and allied products	−1.109	0.556 (.310)	2.602 (.886)	.948	4.0
Petroleum and coal	n.o.	n.o.	n.o.	n.o.	n.o.
Rubber and plastic	0.354	0.628 (.091)	0.422 (.099)	.994	2.4
Leather and leather products	0.251	0.669 (.294)	0.470 (.351)	.959	2.2
Stone, clay, and glass	−1.124	0.377 (.349)	0.798 (.382)	.943	2.3
Primary metals	0.033	1.233 (.503)	0.838 (.665)	.526	1.6
Fabricated metal products	0.328	0.704 (.173)	0.104 (.092)	.904	0.5
Machinery except electrical	0.754	0.509 (.245)	−0.103 (.260)	.764	−1.9
Electrical machinery	0.432	0.940 (.398)	0.627 (.741)	.924	2.7
Transportation equipment	0.182	0.863 (.360)	0.954 (.292)	.800	3.1
Instruments	0.379	1.371 (.158)	1.439 (.283)	.989	3.9

(continued)

TABLE 7 *(continued)*

| Industry | McKinnon (1963a), 1899-1957[d] | | Kendrick (1964), 1953-57 | Maddala (1965)[e] | |
	Elasticity of Substitution	Rate of Neutral Technological-Progress (per cent)	Elasticity of Substitution	Elasticity of Substitution Estimated Using Stigler's Data	Elasticity of Substitution Estimated Using Residual Share of Capital
Food and kindred products	n.o.	n.o.	0.25	.033- 0.142	.088- 0.423
Tobacco manufactures	n.o.	n.o.	0.88	.089- 0.463	-.142- -0.525
Textile mill products	0.44 (.10)	2.6	0.59	.058- 0.099	.138- 0.216
Apparel and related products	1.44 (.51)	3.5	0.09	-.045- -0.134	-.024- -1.030
Lumber and timber basic	0.56 (.23)	2.0	0.40	.171- 0.262	.251- 0.309
Furniture and fixtures	0.91 (.18)	2.1	1.86	.109- 0.206	.184- 0.442
Paper and allied products	0.94 (.17)	4.4	0.55	.170- 0.225	.260- 0.389
Printing and publishing	0.94 (.51)	0.0	0.18	-.037- -0.102	-.079- -0.400
Chemicals and allied products	1.12 (.24)	2.7	0.65	.101- 0.221	.106- 1.139
Petroleum and coal	n.o.	n.o.	0.51	.273- 0.374	.359- 0.486
Rubber and plastic	n.o.	n.o.	0.35	.186- 0.339	.041- 0.224
Leather and leather products	0.52 (.11)	1.4	0.47	-.010- -1.318	-.052- -0.307
Stone, clay, and glass	1.08 (.30)	-4.0	0.89	.266- 0.400	.539- 1.418
Primary metals	n.o.	n.o.	0.81	.215- 0.266	.327- 0.463
Fabricated metal products	n.o.	n.o.	0.78	.038- 0.405	.062- 0.713
Machinery except electrical	n.o.	n.o.	0.50	.147- 0.247	.334- 0.671
Electrical machinery	0.64 (.19)	2.8	0.80	.108- 0.224	-.026- -4.305
Transportation equipment	n.o.	n.o.	0.65	.052- 0.460	-.008- -2.270
Instruments	n.o.	n.o.	-0.14	.416- 0.583	.577- 1.048

(continued)

TABLE 7 *(concluded)*

	Lucas (1963)[f]		
Industry	Elasticity of Substitution	Estimated Coefficient of Trend	R^2
Food and kindred products	.397 (.056)	.010 (.001)	.934
Tobacco manufactures	.152 (.050)	.031 (.003)	.956
Textile mill products ⎫ ⎬ Apparel and related products ⎭	.131 (.063)	.017 (.001)	.957
Lumber and timber basic ⎫ ⎬ Furniture and fixtures ⎭	.480 (.068)	.009 (.001)	.800
Paper and allied products	.505 (.098)	.008 (.001)	.793
Printing and publishing	.488 (.069)	.008 (.001)	.921
Chemicals and allied products	.678 (.089)	.012 (.003)	.975
Petroleum and coal	.375 (.068)	.011 (.002)	.852
Rubber and plastic	.323 (.062)	.018 (.002)	.927
Leather and leather products	.407 (.095)	.007 (.001)	.798
Stone, clay, and glass	−.205 (.107)	.029 (.002)	.956
Primary metals ⎫ ⎬ Fabricated metal products ⎭	.641 (.193)	.008 (.002)	.600
Machinery except electrical ⎫ ⎬ Electrical machinery ⎭	.476 (.152)	.013 (.003)	.780
Transportation equipment	Automobiles only		
	.730 (.094)	.018 (.004)	.796
Instruments	n.o.	n.o.	n.o.

Notes to Table 7

Source: McKinnon (1962) uses annual data 1947-58. Labor share wL/V from Schultze and Tryon, *Prices and Cost in Manufacturing Industries*, Study Paper No. 17, in *The Study of Employment, Growth and Price Levels*, Joint Economic Committee, U.S. Congress, Washington: 1960. L and V are from Levinson: *Postwar Movements of Prices and Wages in Manufacturing Industries*, Study Paper No. 21, in *Study of Employment, Growth and Price Levels*,

Mckinnon (1963a) uses John W. Kendrick: *Productivity Trends in the United States*, Princeton for NBER, 1961. Labor's share times output/$mh = w$.

Ferguson (1965) uses *Census of Manufactures*, 1954 and 1958, and *Annual Survey* volumes for other years. V = value added, current dollars; L = number of employees; $wL/L = W$ = compensation of employees per employee. Capital data used to compute bias in technical change are from Daniel Creamer, "Capital Expansion and Capacity in Postwar Manufacturing" and "Recent Changes in Manufacturing Capacity," in *Studies in Business Economics*, National Industrial Conference Board, New York, 1962.

Maddala (1965) uses time series data 1947-58. V = Federal Reserve Board index of industrial production for the industry in question. L = man-hours worked = persons engaged times average hours worked, Department of Commerce figures. K = Total capital by industry from George J. Stigler, *Capital and Rates of Return in Manufacturing Industries*, Princeton for NBER, 1963, adjusted for capacity utilization by average hours worked. Labor's share is obtained by multiplying employee compensation by ratio of persons engaged in production to the total of full-time equivalent employees and dividing by V. Average wage may then be obtained by dividing by L. Rate of return on capital either from Stigler, *op. cit.*, or by dividing capital's share obtained as a residual from V by K.

Lucas (1963) uses time series data 1931-58. Physical output is given as an index, component of Federal Reserve Board index of industrial production. Labor input was derived from number of full-time equivalent employees (Department of of Commerce) times average hours worked per week, (Kendrick, *op. cit.*). Output price was obtained by dividing gross value added (Department of Commerce) by physical output series. Wage rate was obtained by dividing employee compensation (Department of Commerce) by the labor input series.

n.o. = not obtained.

*Not significantly different from zero and negative. Trend therefore dropped.

[a]These estimates differ from Ferguson's by a factor of $1/(1-\sigma)$ where σ is the elasticity of substitution. Since σ is greater than 1 in some cases an estimate of negative technological progress results. This point seems to have been overlooked by Ferguson.

[b]Value of distribution parameter in CES function is computed directly from the marginal rate of substitution = factor-price-ratio relationship using the estimated value of the elasticity of substitution. An increasing weight attached to capital is equated with "capital-using" innovations; a decreasing weight with "capital-saving" innovations. Many series show a mixed behavior.

[c]Computed by dividing estimated coefficient of trend by $\gamma(1-\sigma)$, where γ is the estimated coefficient of adjustment and σ is the estimated elasticity of substitution. Estimates are scaled by a factor of $2.3026/100$ to make results comparable to those using natural logarithms.

[d]Years covered: 1899, 1909, 1919, 1929, 1937, 1948, 1953, 1957.

Notes to Table 7 (concluded)

[e]First estimate of each pair based on regression of log K/L on log w/r, where r is the rate of return on capital either as estimated by George Stigler *(Capital and Rates of Return in Manufacturing Industries,* Princeton for NBER, 1963)or as a residual by deducting labor's share from the total value added. The second estimate of each pair is based on the regression of log w/r on log K/L. It can be shown that if both variables are subject to error (or both endogenous in some larger system) the two estimates bracket the consistent estimate [Maddala (1965, p. 8, Table 1)].

[f]Based on a logarithmic regression of output per unit of labor on the deflated wage rate and (linear) trend, 1931-58 [Lucas (1963, p. 63, Table 5.1, cols. 1-3)].

and insignificantly different from 1 in all but one of the remaining ten cases. McKinnon (1962), using data for a slightly different period and of a slightly different sort, provides a more varied assortment. His long-run elasticities of substitution range from 0.033 to 1.021 not counting the negative values obtained for chemicals and allied products and for stone, clay, and glass. It is extremely unlikely that the slight variation in period could account for the substantial differences between McKinnon's and Ferguson's results; furthermore, McKinnon's allowance for a dis-tributed lag tends to increase the long-run elasticities which he measures rather than reducing them. However, there is an extremely significant difference between McKinnon's regressions and Ferguson's: McKinnon uses deflated data, Ferguson, current-dollar values. As we saw in the previous section, the use of dollar values when capital costs vary re-latively little and real wages are not highly negatively correlated with prices tends to bias the estimated elasticities of substitution upward. Thus the differences between the two sets of results may be attributed to Ferguson's failure to deflate.

Maddala (1965) presents direct estimates of the elasticity of substitu-tion based upon two different logarithmic regressions using two types of information on the rate of return to capital: the first of the regressions is that of log K/L on log w/r ,whereas the second reverses the roles of the two variables. It can be argued that the two estimates of the elastic-ity of substitution tend to bracket the true value as the sample size in-creases. In most instances, however, the bracketing values are rather far apart. The estimates differ quite considerably in most cases from McKinnon's results (1962) for roughly the same period and illustrates the great sensitivity of the estimated elasticity of substitution to the form of the relationship fitted.

Lucas (1963) uses the ACMS method but applies it to data over the long period 1931–58. In most instances the resulting estimates of the elasticity of substitution obtained are higher than the previously cited results of McKinnon and Maddala, if only the "short-run" elasticities of McKinnon are considered.

The estimates in both McKinnon (1963a) and Kendrick (1964) differ from the ones discussed above in being based on data for widely separated points in time: Kendrick's results are based on only two points, 1953 and 1957; McKinnon's on eight points, 1899, 1909, 1919, 1929, 1937, 1948, 1953, and 1957. McKinnon's estimates are obtained from a logarithmic regression of real values added per unit of labor on the real wage rate, while Kendrick simply computes an arc elasticity of substitution by comparing the capital-labor ratio with the relative price ratio in the two years 1953 and 1957. Being based on only two years, Kendrick's estimates are subject to a great deal of uncertainty; further-more, both 1953 and 1957 were recession years, a downturn occurring about the middle of the year in each case.[13] On the other hand, by com-paring the capital-labor ratio with the movement of relative prices directly, Kendrick achieves estimates which are free of the assumption that the elasticity of substitution is constant. Of the years chosen by McKinnon, only the last two were periods of relatively low economic activity. Thus, in comparison with the other results reported in Table 7, those of McKinnon (1963a) are relatively less dominated by recession phenomena, Kendrick's less dominated by special assumptions as to the form of the production function. It is perhaps not surprising that there seems to be relatively little consistency between these results and the others. Maddala's estimates, like those of Lucas and Ferguson, are heavily dominated by recession phenomena.

In this connection, however, it is worthwhile giving some indication of the probable results of little or no adjustment for the effects of varia-tions in aggregate demand. In an earlier paper which was to have been part of this survey, the probable effects of variations in the level of aggregate activity upon estimates of the elasticities of output with re-spect to various factor inputs were discussed.[14] The effects, however,

[13] Gordon (1961, pp. 486–89 and 492–501).
[14] Nerlove (1965).

on the estimates of the elasticity of substitution between capital and labor as estimated by ACMS or related methods is much more subtle and difficult to specify a priori. Ferguson (1965b, p. 142), for example, argues that

. . . the use of time-series data to estimate the elasticity of substitution imparts a downward bias that is basically attributable to changes in the quality of labor service, especially during periods of expansion and contraction. . . . In recession periods, an increase in unemployment is normally accompanied by an increase in the quality of labor services because the more efficient workers (at each wage rate) are the ones retained. . . . Thus value added per man-year tends to increase in recession periods. . . . The opposite tends to occur in periods of expansion; so on balance the observed slope is less than the true slope.

In order for Ferguson's argument to be valid, it is necessary that real or money wages, depending on which is used in the regression, be negatively correlated with the errors attributable to changing quality of labor. Thus, wages would have to fall in recessions and rise in expansions. There is some evidence that *real* wages (as deviations from trend) did just this; however, Ferguson's argument suggests that under these circumstances his estimate should be lower in contrast to the cross-section results and to those of McKinnon (1963a), which are based largely on full-capacity years. They are higher.

An additional effect of cyclic phenomena on the estimated elasticity of substitution is the "vintage capital" effect. In a downswing the older, less efficient plants are shut down, and in the upswing they are reopened. Hence, product per worker tends to increase in recessions and fall during recoveries. A similar effect due to the quasi-fixity of labor inputs has been noted by Oi, Okun, and others.[15] Labor is a quasi-fixed factor and not freely variable over the course of the relatively short and mild recessions experienced in the postwar period. On the other hand, output does vary over the course of the cycle so that productivity tends to rise in booms and fall in slumps, i.e., output per unit of labor varies directly with the level of aggregate activity. If money wages are rather rigid in the short run, real wages will tend to rise in recessions and fall in recoveries. The net effect would be to bias downward the estimated short-run elasticity in regressions based upon real value added and real wages. On the other hand, evidence to the contrary for the postwar period

[15] Oi (1962); Okun (1962).

would suggest an upward bias. Apparently, therefore, such explanations cannot account for all the differences observed.

Unfortunately, variations in the price level produce even more complicated effects in regressions based upon current-dollar data. In general, as we saw, price variation tends to bias the estimates upward in comparison with the supposedly true values which occur in the real relationship. If, however, errors of the type described in the preceding paragraph also occur, it is difficult to judge the net outcome.

Table 8 summarizes recent studies of the aggregate elasticity of substitution and rate of technical change. While most of the studies are restricted to the measurement of neutral technological change and constant returns to scale, a number of investigations, notably Brown–de Cani (1963) and David–van de Klundert (1965) attempt estimates of technical change which may be either capital- or labor-augmenting. Ferguson (1965a) allows both nonconstant returns to scale and the possibility of labor-augmenting technical change. For comparison, the early results obtained by Solow (1957) are given at the bottom of the table.

Recently, Diamond and McFadden (1965) have questioned the possibility of identifying both the production function and arbitary forms of technical change. Before discussing the results presented in Table 8, therefore, it seems well to examine the Diamond-McFadden "impossibility theorem" in some detail so as to avoid spending time trying to make sense out of results which may in fact be purely arbitrary. The result demonstrated by Diamond and McFadden (p. 1) is that

. . . it is, in fact, impossible to measure either the bias or the elasticity [of substitution]; i.e., given the time series of all observable market phenomena for a single economy which has a neo-classical production function, these same time series could have been generated by an alternative function having an arbitrary elasticity or arbitrary bias at the observed points. This statement is subject to the limitations that in the absence of technical change one can measure the elasticity of substitution (and trivially the bias, which is zero) while in the absence of a change in the capital-labor ratio one can determine the bias.

The Diamond-McFadden result is also, as we shall show, subject to the qualification that certain "smoothness" assumptions about the nature of technical change may also produce identification. In what follows, we give a simplified and more transparent derivation of the Diamond-

TABLE 8

Summary of Time Series Results on the U.S. Aggregate Production
Function: Elasticity of Substitution and Technical Change

Reference and Period	Estimated Elasticity of Sub-stitution	Assumption as to Nature of Technical Change	Estimated Increase in Efficiency (per cent per annum)		
			Neutral	Labor Augmenting	Capital Augmenting
Kravis (1959), 1900-57	0.64	Restricted: Hicks neutral	Not esti-mated		
Arrow *et al.* (1961), 1909-49	0.57	Restricted: Hicks neutral	1.83		
Diwan (1963) by ACMS method 1919-58	0.37	Restricted: Hicks neutral	1.4		
From regression of log factor ratio on log factor price ratio, 1919-30 and 1935-58.	.068	Restricted: Hicks neutral	Not esti-mated		
Kendrick-Sato (1963), 1919-60.	0.58	Restricted: Hicks neutral	2.10		
Brown-de Cani (1963) 1890-1918	{ 0.35SR 0.55LR	Assumed zero within periods; unrestricted between periods.	Numerical estimates not given. Predominantly labor saving.		
1919-1937	{ 0.08SR 0.31LR		Predominantly capital saving.		
1938-58	{ 0.11SR 0.47LR		(This does not agree with the finding of David-van de Klundert.)		
Kendrick (1964), 1953-57	0.62	Assumed zero			
Ferguson (1965a), Assuming con-stant returns to scale 1929-63	0.67	Restricted: Hicks neutral	1.5		
		Restricted: Harrod neutral		1.5	
1948-63	1.16	Restricted: Hicks neutral	1.9		
		Restricted: Harrod neutral		1.9	

(continued)

TABLE 8 *(concluded)*

Reference and Period	Estimated Elasticity of Sub- stitution	Assumption as to Nature of Technical Change	Estimated Increase in Efficiency (per cent per annum)		
			Neutral	Labor Augmenting	Capital Augmenting
Allowing non-constant returns to scale, 1929-63[a]	0.49	Restricted: Hicks neutral	−0.1		
		Restricted: Harrod neutral		−0.1	
1948-63[b]	0.64	Restricted: Hicks neutral	0.1		
		Restricted: Harrod neutral		0.1	
David-van de Klundert (1965), 1899-1960					
Regression with distributed lag	0.11SR 0.32LR	Unrestricted: Factor aug- menting		2.23-2.30[c]	1.51-1.58[c]
Regression without dis- tributed lag	0.16	Unrestricted: Factor aug- menting		2.30-2.34[c]	1.44-1.48[c]
For comparison: Solow (1957), 1909-49	Assumed 1.0	Unrestricted[d]	1.5		

SR = short run.

LR = long run.

[a]Estimated return to scale equals 2.53.

[b]Estimated return to scale equals 1.45.

[c]Different estimates use different values of labor's share.

[d]With a Cobb-Douglas function and constant returns to scale nonneutral techno-logical change cannot be distinguished.

McFadden result for CES production functions which is due to K. J. Arrow.

Technological change may be considered to be of the capital-augment-ing or the labor-augmenting type if it is equivalent to a change in the units in which capital and labor are measured; thus, instead of the arguments K and L in the function F, we write $E_K K$ and $E_L L$. We assume that factors are paid their marginal products and that the shares of capital and labor S_K and S_L respectively exhaust the total product Y. We observe the following variables:

(1)
$$Y = \text{total output.}$$
$$K = \text{measured capital input.}$$
$$L = \text{measured labor input.}$$
$$S_K = \text{total payment to capital.}$$
$$S_L = \text{total payment to labor.}$$

The importance of the constant returns assumption is that, with it, we can identify the factor payments as the marginal factor products times the "true," not the measured, factor inputs. Without the assumption, still assuming competition, some factors would be earning rents (which might be negative) over and above their marginal productivities. Two neoclassical production functions, F and G, both homogeneous of degree 1, will be said to be "consistent with the data" if

(2) $$Y = F(E_K{}^F \cdot K, E_L{}^F \cdot L, t) = G(E_K{}^G \cdot K, E_L{}^G \cdot L, t)$$
$$S_K = F_1 E_K{}^F K = G_1 E_K{}^G K$$
$$S_L = F_2 E_L{}^F L = G_2 E_L{}^G L,$$

where F_i and G_i, $i = 1, 2$, are the marginal productivities. Note that for CES production functions, equality of the partial derivatives of F and G with respect to each of their arguments implies that all the parameters of the functions are identical. What the Diamond-McFadden result amounts to is that with no further restrictions on the "errors" $E_i{}^F$, $E_i{}^G$, $i = K, L$, there exists more than one neoclassical production function consistent with any given set of observations (1) provided: (a) the capital-labor ratio does vary over time, and (b) the elasticity of substitution is not in fact equal to unity, so that factor shares remain constant over time.

Differentiating the first of equations (2) with respect to t we obtain

(3) $$\dot{Y} = F_1\{\dot{E}_K{}^F K + E_K{}^F \dot{K}\} + F_2\{\dot{E}_L{}^F L + E_L{}^F \dot{L}\} + F_3$$
$$= G_1\{\dot{E}_K{}^G K + E_K{}^G \dot{K}\} + G_2\{\dot{E}_L{}^G L + E_L{}^G \dot{L}\} + G_3$$

where F_3 and G_3 are the derivatives of F and G with respect to the third argument, t. Let

$$(4) \quad \begin{cases} e_i{}^F = \dfrac{\dot{E}_i{}^F}{E_i{}^F}, \\[3mm] e_i{}^G = \dfrac{\dot{E}_i{}^G}{E_i{}^G}, \end{cases} \qquad i = K, L,$$

be the rates of capital- and labor-augmenting technical progress, and let

$$(5) \quad \begin{cases} \mu^F = F_3/Y \\[2mm] \mu^G = G_3/Y \end{cases}$$

be the rates of non-factor-augmenting technical progress. Making use of the second and third of equations (2) and (4) and (5) we may re-write (3) as

$$(6) \quad \begin{aligned} y = \dot{Y}/Y &= s_K\{e_K{}^F + k\} + s_L\{e_L{}^F + l\} + \mu^F \\ &= s_K\{e_K{}^G + k\} + s_L\{e_L{}^G + l\} + \mu^G, \end{aligned}$$

where k and l are the rates of growth of the *measured* capital stock and labor force. The functions F and G are "consistent with the data" so the factor shares s_K and s_L are the same in both equations as are k and l. Thus

$$(7) \quad s_K\{e_K{}^F - e_K{}^G\} + s_L\{e_L{}^F - e_L{}^G\} + \mu^F - \mu^G = 0,$$

is the fundamental relation connecting the rates of technical change.

First note that if we assume no technical change is factor-augmenting, so that

$$\begin{cases} E_i{}^F \equiv E_i{}^G \equiv 1 \\[2mm] e_i{}^F \equiv e_i{}^G \equiv 0, \end{cases} \qquad i = K, L,$$

then (7) implies

$$\mu^F \equiv \mu^G.$$

Referring back to (2) we see this implies all the corresponding par-tials of F and G are identical, and the data therefore "identifies" the pro-duction function.

On the other hand, suppose we assume that the only technical change is factor-augmenting, so that $\mu^F \equiv \mu^G \equiv 0$. Then (7) becomes

$$(7') \quad s_K\{e_K{}^F - e_K{}^G\} + s_L\{e_L{}^F - e_L{}^G\} = 0.$$

If s_K and s_L are not constant, then we can always find numbers $e_i{}^F$ and $e_i{}^G$, $i = K, L$, such that $(7')$ holds *unless we also require that the differences* $e_i{}^F - e_i{}^G$, $i = K, L$, *be constant as well*. This is practically tantamount to requiring that technological change be describable by exponentially smooth growth in E_K and E_L, but not quite. What it does do is to impose a smoothness condition on technological change which may be best understood in terms of smooth exponential growth in the effectiveness of measured capital and labor inputs. If this condition is imposed, $(7')$ implies

$$e_i{}^F = e_i{}^G, \qquad\qquad i = K, L,$$

which in turn implies, as $e_i{}^F$ and $e_i{}^G$ are also assumed to be constant, that

$$E_i{}^F = E_i{}^G.$$

It follows at once from (2), that the corresponding partials of F and G must be identical. If the "smoothness" of E_K and E_L, or some other restriction, is not assumed, then by suitable choice of these numbers we can make some other CES production function consistent with the observed variables; in particular, given any series $E_K{}^F$ and $E_L{}^F$ we can find $E_K{}^G$ and $E_L{}^G$ such that G, with some other elasticity of substitution, also explains the observable data.

Absence of non-factor-augmenting technical change or the assumption of exponential factor-augmenting change is sufficient for identification. Suppose, however, we drop the assumption that there is no non-factor-augmenting technical change. We are then back to the general formula (7); only now nonconstancy of the shares no longer implies the equalities $e_i{}^F = e_i{}^G$, $i = K, L$, even if $e_i{}^F$ and $e_i{}^G$ are assumed to be constant. However, if μ^F and μ^G are also assumed to be constant we have

$$s_K \{e_K{}^F - e_K{}^G\} + (1 - s_K)\{e_L{}^F - e_L{}^G\} + \mu^F - \mu^G = 0$$

or

$$(e_L{}^F + \mu^F) - (e_L{}^G + \mu^G) + s_K \{(e_K{}^F - e_L{}^F) - (e_K{}^G - e_L{}^G)\} = 0,$$

whence

$$\begin{cases} e_L{}^F + \mu^F = e_L{}^G + \mu^G \\ e_K{}^F - e_L{}^F = e_K{}^G - e_L{}^G \end{cases}$$

Thus the *bias* of technical change is determined uniquely, but neither the technical change itself nor the production function is. It follows that the assumption that all technical change is factor augmenting is quite essential to identification unless we assume it is absent altogether.

Finally, we must show that variation in the factor shares and in the capital-labor ratio is also essential for identification. First, observe that constancy of s_K and s_L allows (7') to be satisfied for an infinite number of pairs $(e_K^F - e_K^G, e_L^F - e_L^G)$ the ratio of which is $-s_L/s_K$. Thus, given this restriction we cannot identify the production function. But this should be intuitively clear in any case, since if the factor shares are constant we could not distinguish any production function from the Cobb-Douglas. It is well known that factor-augmenting and neutral technological change are quite equivalent for this function, and the bias is therefore indeterminate.

Next, suppose that the capital-labor ratio does not change over time. This implies

$$L\dot{K} - K\dot{L} = 0$$

or

$$k = l,$$

so that for either F or G we have

$$y = s_K e_K + s_L e_L + \mu.$$

It is not possible to assume e_K, e_L, and μ constant if the observed shares and rate of growth in output do not behave in exactly the right fashion. A fortiori, the production function cannot be identified.

In his paper on two-digit manufacturing industries, Ferguson (1965b) first estimates the elasticity of substitution and the rate of neutral technological change; he then uses his results to compute a nonsmooth estimate of the bias in factor-augmenting technical change (the only other kind permitted in CES functions). This is clearly nonsense on the basis of the Diamond-McFadden impossibility theorem. David and van de Klundert (1965) attempt the same fallacious computation in the second half of their paper. The results reported in Table 8, however, are from the first half of this paper and based on the assumption that all technical change is factor-augmenting and exponential. These assumptions, as we saw, are sufficient to identify the production function and technical change. Ferguson (1965a) assumes either neutral or labor-augmenting exponential technical change; these assumptions are sufficient to identify the production function if constant returns to scale are assumed. If constant returns are not assumed, but the production function is supposed to be homogeneous of degree greater than 1, paying factors their marginal products will more than exhaust the total product, and it is therefore difficult to interpret the factor shares. Under the restrictions imposed by Ferguson, however, identification is achieved.

Brown and de Cani (1963) attempt to estimate all types of technical change (factor-augmenting and nonneutral, non-factor-augmenting change) by estimating different production functions for different "technological epochs." It is only by employing the extreme assumption that there is no technological change of any sort within technological epochs that they can identify all of these factors. In a sense, this is the opposite of our smoothness assumption which "lets us out" of the implications of the impossibility theorem.[16] Brown and de Cani, in effect, assume that everything changes abruptly the instant one passes over from one technological epoch to another. It is moot just how reasonable an assumption this is.

If technical change is not neutral but biased, factor-augmenting, and exponential, then the following results are obtained:

The ACMS estimating equation becomes

$$(8) \qquad \log y = -\log E_L(0) + \sigma \log w + e_L(1 - \sigma)t$$

where $E_L(0)$ is the initial value of labor efficiency. Alternatively, the method used by Kravis (1959), Diwan (1963), and Kendrick-Sato (1963), relies on determination of the relationship between the capital-labor ratio and the factor-price ratio. With biased technical change of a factor-augmenting sort, the appropriate estimating equation becomes

$$(9) \qquad \log x = (1 - \sigma) \log \frac{E_L(0)}{E_K(0)} + \sigma \log \frac{w}{r} + (1 - \sigma)[e_L - e_K]t$$

where w is the wage rate and r the rate of return on capital. Thus, if the true elasticity of substitution is less than 1, if technical change is biased toward the labor-augmenting type, and if the relative price of labor is rising over time, the estimates of σ obtained by means of (9) will be biased upward if only neutral technical change is assumed ($e_L = e_K$). On the other hand, no bias results from the ACMS method as long as neutral technical change occurs. It follows that the high values of σ

---

[16] Lest any misinterpretation result, recall that the argument above referred only to *sufficient* conditions for identification.

TABLE 9

*Time Series Results on the Elasticity of Substitution in
Three Extractive Industries, McKinnon (1963a),
Census Years 1870 - 1958*

Industry	Estimated Elasticity of Substitution	Estimated Coefficient of Trend	Rate of Neutral Technical Change	$\bar{R}^2$
Bituminous coal	0.92 (.34)	.17 (.22)	4.8%	.93
Anthracite coal	1.23 (.63)	−.03 (.25)	0.3	.79
Iron ore	1.06 (.22)	.29 (.23)	−12.1	.96

obtained by Kravis, Kendrick and Sato, and by Diwan (his second method), in relation to the low values obtained by Diwan (his first method) and David and van de Klundert, are explicable. The high value obtained by Arrow *et al.,* however, cannot be explained on these grounds. Indeed, the only difference between the result reported by Arrow *et al.* and Diwan (his first method) appears to be in the choice of period. Why a shift of nine or ten years in the period of estimation should produce such a large effect is difficult to surmise.

In closing this section, the time-series studies of McKinnon (1963a) and Maddala (1963) of certain extractive industries are presented without comment in Tables 9 and 10.

Table 11 summarizes the time-series and cross-section results for U.S. two-digit manufacturing industries which have been considered in the above review.

Estimation and Identification Problems

In this section we discuss various simultaneous-equations difficulties which may arise in the estimation of CES production functions along the lines explored by Kmenta (1964) and Maddala and Kadane (1965).

TABLE 10

Estimates of the Elasticity of Substitution in Bituminous
Coal Mining Based on Time Series of Cross Sections,
Maddala (1963), Census Years, 1919-54

Year	Using Data on Physical Output	Using Data on Deflated Value Added
1919	1.092	1.124
	(.053)	(.051)
1929	1.044	1.042
	(.076)	(.070)
1935	1.141	1.103
	(.083)	(.068)
1939	1.145	1.159
	(.080)	(.068)
1954	1.343	1.326
	(.191)	(.169)
Pooled:		
With year shifts	1.118	1.120
	(.044)	(.038)
Without year shifts	1.213	1.205
	(.046)	(.039)

The form of the CES function usually given is

$$(1) \qquad V = \gamma[\delta K^{-\rho} + (1 - \delta)L^{-\rho}]^{-1/\rho}.$$

A slightly more general version allows nonconstant returns to scale while still restricting the function to homogeneity of some degree: [17]

$$(1') \qquad V = \gamma[\delta K^{-\rho} + (1 - \delta)L^{-\rho}]^{-\mu/\rho}.$$

Suppose that V has been defined in real terms. As before, let w and r be the wage rate and rate of return on capital, respectively, and let p be the price of final output. We also introduce the multiplicative resid-

[17] See Kmenta (1964, p. 2), and Brown (1962, p. 10).

TABLE 11

Summary of Time Series and Cross-Section Estimates of the Elasticity of Substitution Between Capital and Labor for Two-Digit Manufacturing Industries

	Time Series Estimates					
Industry	McKinnon (1962)	McKinnon (1963a)	Kendrick (1964)	Ferguson (1965b)	Maddala (1965)	Lucas (1963)
Food and kindred products	0.37	n.o.	0.25	0.24	.03- 0.14	.40
Tobacco manufactures	0.92	n.o.	0.88	1.18	.09- 0.46	.15
Textile mill products	0.16	0.44	0.59	1.10	.06- 0.10⎫	
Apparel, etc.	0.69	1.44	0.09	1.08	−.05--0.13⎭	.13
Lumber and timber	0.80	0.56	0.40	0.91	.17- 0.26⎫	
Furniture and fixtures	1.02	0.91	1.86	1.12	.11- 0.21⎭	.48
Paper, etc.	0.09	0.94	0.55	1.02	.17- 0.23	.51
Printing and publishing	0.84	0.94	0.18	1.15	−.04--0.10	.49
Chemicals, etc.	−1.11	1.12	0.65	1.25	.10- 0.22	.68
Petroleum and coal	n.o.	n.o.	0.51	1.30	.27- 0.37	.38
Rubber and plastics	0.35	n.o.	0.35	0.76	.19- 0.34	.32
Leather, etc.	0.25	0.52	0.47	0.87	−.01--1.32	.41
Stone, clay, glass	−1.12	1.08	0.89	0.67	.27- 0.40	−.21
Primary metals	0.03	n.o.	0.81	1.20	.22- 0.27⎫	
Fabricated metal products	0.33	n.o.	0.78	0.93	.04- 0.41⎭	.64
Nonelectric machinery	0.75	n.o.	0.50	1.04	.15- 0.25⎫	
Electrical machinery	0.43	0.64	0.80	0.64	.11- 0.22⎭	.48
Transportation equipment	0.18	n.o.	0.65	0.24	.05- 0.46	.73[b]
Instruments	0.38	n.o.	−0.14	0.76	.42- 0.58	n.o.

n.o. = not obtained.

[a]Based on a comparison of the United States and Japan only.

[b]Automobiles only.

TABLE 11

				Cross-Section Estimates				
				Liu-Hildebrand (1965)		Murata-Arrow (1965), Intercountry Data		
Industry	Arrow et al. (1961)[a]	Minasian (1961)	Solow (1964)	All Employees	Production Workers	1953-56	1957-59	Dhrymes (1965)
Food and kindred products	0.93	0.58	0.69	2.15	1.29 ⎫	.72	.73	.56 - 0.97
Tobacco manufactures	n.o.	3.46	1.96	n.o.	n.o. ⎭			n.o.
Textile mill products	0.80	1.58	1.27	1.65	2.08	.79	.83	.68 - 1.03
Apparel, etc.	n.o.	n.o.	1.01	1.43	2.38	.66	.80	.54 - 1.03
Lumber and timber	0.84	0.94	0.99	0.99	0.91 ⎫	.82	.92	.78 - 1.1
Furniture and fixtures	n.o.	1.09	1.12	0.92	0.96 ⎭			.70 - 1.39
Paper, etc.	1.14	1.60	1.77	1.06	0.71	.90	.79	.20 - 0.64
Printing and publishing	1.21	n.o.	1.02	n.o.	n.o.	.84	.93	.68 - 1.11
Chemicals, etc.	0.90	n.o.	0.14	1.25	.88 ⎫	.84	.83	.31 - 1.03
Petroleum and coal	n.o.	-0.54	1.45	n.o.	n.o. ⎭			.11 - 1.31
Rubber and plastics	0.98	0.82	1.48	1.45	139	.83	.77	.40 - 1.04
Leather, etc.	0.72	0.96	0.89	0.79	0.93	.71	.70	.51 - 1.13
Stone, clay, glass	1.08	0.59	0.32	1.28	1.44	.85	.86	.49 - 0.89
Primary metals	n.o.	0.92	1.87	0.99	1.00	.86	.87	.10 - 0.97
Fabricated metal products	n.o.	n.o.	0.80	0.70	0.45	.92	.92	.40 - 0.95
Nonelectric machinery	0.97	0.31	0.64	0.60	0.41	n.o.	n.o.	.12 - 0.25
Electrical machinery		1.26	0.37	0.78	1.10	n.o.	n.o.	.19 - 0.62
Transportation equipment	1.04	2.04	0.06	2.01	1.91	n.o.	n.o.	n.o.
Instruments	n.o.	n.o.	1.59	1.24	1.65	n.o.	n.o.	n.o.

ual u_0 into (1'). This is equivalent to using γu_0 instead of γ in (1'), and for the sake of simplicity, we do not introduce the residual explicitly until the ends of various derivations. The system consists of six variables: V, L, K, p, w, and r. If we suppose that entrepreneurs maximize profits

$$(2) \qquad\qquad pV - wL - rK$$

subject to (1'), and taking p, w, and r as given, we can obtain two more equations connecting the six variables. The marginal conditions are

$$(3) \qquad \begin{cases} p = \lambda \\ w = \lambda\mu(1 - \delta)L^{-(1+\rho)}V^{1+\rho/\mu}\gamma^{-\rho/\mu}, \\ r = \lambda\mu\delta K^{-(1+\rho)}V^{1+\rho/\mu}\gamma^{-\rho/\mu} \end{cases}$$

where λ is marginal cost holding factor prices constant; i.e.,

$$(4) \qquad\qquad \lambda = \frac{\partial C}{\partial V} = \frac{\partial\{wL + rK\}}{\partial V}$$

where L and K are the equilibrium values satisfying (1')–(3). Equations (1')–(3) may be rewritten in a variety of suggestive forms. Note, too, that imperfections in profit maximization may be treated as equivalent to the multiplication of p, w, and r by factors u_1, u_2, and u_3. Again, such factors will be suppressed in what follows until they are needed.

One suggestive form of (1')–(3) may be obtained directly from the profit-maximizing conditions and the production function by simple manipulation:

$$(5) \qquad \begin{cases} \dfrac{V}{L} = a\left(\dfrac{w}{p}\right)^{1/1+\rho} V^{-\rho(1-\mu)/\mu(1+\rho)} \\[4mm] \dfrac{V}{K} = b\left(\dfrac{r}{p}\right)^{1/1+\rho} V^{-\rho(1-\mu)/\mu(1+\rho)} \end{cases}$$

where $a = \mu^{-1/1+\rho}\gamma^{\rho/\mu(1+\rho)}(1 - \delta)^{-1/1+\rho}$ and
$b = \mu^{-1/1+\rho}\gamma^{\rho/\mu(1+\rho)}\delta^{-1/1+\rho}$.

When there are constant returns to scale $\mu = 1$ and the first of equations (5) becomes the one estimated by ACMS. Not having capital data or information on the rate of return, they did not attempt to estimate the second equation.

If $\mu = 1$ and if w, r, and p are independent of the residuals in (5), which turn out to both be

$$u_0{}^{p/\mu(1+\rho)}$$

and if there are no imperfections in profit maximization, then it will be appropriate to estimate either equation by least squares and so obtain an estimate of $1/(1 + \rho) = \sigma$, the elasticity of substitution.[18] Actually, if data are available, it is even simpler to combine the two equations of (5) by dividing one by the other, to obtain

(6)
$$\frac{K}{L} = \left[\frac{\delta}{1 - \delta}\right]^{1/1+\rho} \left(\frac{w}{r}\right)^{1/1+\rho}.$$

However, this equation does not involve γ and so must hold exactly unless there are imperfections in profit maximization. These in turn might make it impossible to estimate (6) by ordinary least squares.

Equation (6) suggests an alternative method of estimation: If we are considering a particular industry over time in an economy subject to fluctuations in aggregate demand, and thus in the demand for the product of the industry, the output of the industry might be considered as independent of the random effects which cause equations (3) to hold with an error and, hence, of the residuals in (6). Using log V as an instrumental variable would then allow us to obtain consistent estimates of $\sigma = 1/(1 + \rho)$ and of $\delta/(1 - \delta)$, and hence of δ and ρ. Inserting these estimates in (1') we obtain

(7)
$$V = \gamma z^\mu,$$

where

$$z = [\hat{\delta}K^{-\hat{\rho}} + (1 - \hat{\delta})L^{-\hat{\rho}}]^{-1/\hat{\rho}}$$

Unfortunately, unless K and L are independent of the residual in the production function, it does not follow that we are able to obtain consistent estimates of μ and γ from a least-squares regression of log V on log z. Kmenta (1964) suggests that this might be the case. Then, however, direct methods for estimating the production function seem more useful.

Although nonlinear, the production function may still be estimated by

[18] An iterative procedure for estimating a similar set of two related equations based on a production function closely related to the CES has been suggested by Hilhorst (1961); see Brown (1962, p. 19).

least-squares.[19] Alternatively, one may follow the procedure outlined by Kmenta and approximate (1′) by the first- and second-order terms in the Taylor series expansion. Write (1′) as

$$(8) \qquad \log V = \log \gamma - \frac{\mu}{\rho} f(\rho) + \log u_0$$

where $f(\rho) = \log [\delta K^{-\rho} + (1 - \delta) L^{-\rho}]$. Following Kmenta, who relies on the empirical findings of ACMS, we expand $f(\rho)$ around the value $\rho = 0$ which corresponds to the value $\sigma = 1$, i.e., the Cobb-Douglas case:

$$(9) \quad f(\rho) = -\rho[\delta \log K + (1 - \delta) \log L] + \frac{1}{2} \rho^2 \delta(1 - \delta)[\log K - \log L]^2$$

$$+ \text{ higher-order terms.}$$

Discarding terms of higher order than the second in ρ, we obtain a logarithmic approximation to (1′) in the form

$$(10) \qquad \log V = \log \gamma - \frac{\mu}{\rho} \{-\rho[\delta \log K + (1 - \delta) \log L]$$

$$+ \frac{1}{2} \rho^2 \delta(1 - \delta)[\log K - \log L]^2\} + v$$

$$= \log \gamma + \mu\delta \log K + \mu(1 - \delta) \log L$$

$$- \frac{\mu\rho}{2} \delta(1 - \delta)[\log K - \log L]^2 + v,$$

where $v = u_0 - (\mu/\rho)$ — the neglected higher-order terms in the Taylor series expansion of $f(\rho)$. If estimates of the coefficients in (10) are available γ, μ, δ, and ρ may be estimated as functions of these in the obvious way. Asymptotic standard errors of the resulting estimates may be obtained along the lines suggested by Klein (1953, p. 258). In this formulation, the term involving the squared logarithm of the capital-labor ratio indicates the departure from the Cobb-Douglas situation (it drops out when $\rho = 0$). Numerical calculations of Kmenta (1964, p. 7), show that, *provided the second-order term is included,* the error resulting from neglect of the higher-order terms is not serious unless *both* the capital-labor ratio and the elasticity of substitution are either very high or very

[19] See the references to Kenney and Keeping and to Davidon cited by Kmenta (1964).

low.[20] If the second-order term is not included, I would surmise that the errors will be substantial even for moderate departures. Thus, even if capital and labor inputs are not correlated with u_0, they will be correlated with v. Since the coefficient of the left-out term will normally be negative, it follows that ordinary least-squares estimates of the Cobb-Douglas will tend to yield an estimate of the elasticity of output with respect to capital which is too low and an estimate of the elasticity with respect to labor which is too high. This is apart from difficulties resulting from the lack of independence between capital and labor and the residual of the production function.

Suppose we are dealing with a sample of firms. Under certain circumstances, it might be plausible to assume that labor and capital were uncorrelated with the residual in the production. If, for example, the residual were a stochastic element from the standpoint of the entrepreneurial decision makers who were forced to decide upon input levels *in advance* of any knowledge of the residual element, then the assumption would follow from expected profit maximization. Outside of agriculture, however, these circumstances seem rather implausible. In a cross section of firms, it is generally more reasonable to assume that the residuals reflect differences among firms, such as the possession of nonmeasured amounts of other factors, and so are known to the decision makers, who then allow for such differences in optimizing input levels, thus producing a correlation between these and the residuals. In other contexts, for example, an industry observed over time, the residual may represent left-out variables, imperfect specification of the production function, or other factors, some of which are likely to be taken account of in the determination of input levels. Thus, in general, one would not expect the conditions for direct estimation of the production function to obtain.

If factor prices and output price are fixed over all observations, such as would be the case if we were to observe a sample of firms in a perfectly competitive industry with perfect factor mobility, then the production function (1′) and the profit-maximizing conditions as given by (5) determine the output and factor input levels as functions of the produc-

---

[20] "Very high or very low" means far from 1 in the case of the elasticity of substitution. A very high or very low capital-labor ratio is defined in terms of the value which would make output equal to 1 if the function were Cobb-Douglas (i.e., $\sigma = 1$).

tion function residual u_0 (attached to the parameter γ) and imperfections in profit maximization, say u_1 and u_2 (attached to w/p and r/p, respectively). In logarithmic form, equations (10), the approximate form of (1'), and (5), become

$$(11) \begin{cases} x_0 - \mu\delta x_1 - \mu(1-\delta)x_2 + \dfrac{1}{2}\rho\mu\delta(1-\delta)(x_1 - x_2)^2 \\ \qquad\qquad\qquad\qquad\qquad\qquad = k_0 + v_0 \\[2mm] \left(1 + \dfrac{\rho}{\mu}\right)x_0 - (1+\rho)x_1 \qquad\quad = k_1 + v_1 \\[2mm] \left(1 + \dfrac{\rho}{\mu}\right)x_0 \qquad\qquad - (1+\rho)x_2 = k_2 + v_2 \end{cases}$$

where $x_0 = \log V$.

$x_1 = \log L$.

$x_2 = \log K$.

$v_i = \log u_i, i = 0, 1, 2$.

$k_0 = \log \gamma$.

$k_1 = -\log\left(\dfrac{w}{p}\right)^{-1}\mu(1-\delta)\gamma^{\rho/\mu}$.

$k_2 = -\log\left(\dfrac{r}{p}\right)^{-1}\mu\delta\gamma^{\rho/\mu}$.

In general, the parameters of (11) are not identified. However, provided one is willing to make sufficiently stringent assumptions regarding the joint distribution of the random variables v_0, v_1, and v_2, one can, as Kmenta (1964) shows, estimate them.

The most statistically convenient assumption that one can make is that the residuals v_0, v_1, and v_2 are independent from observation to observation and that their contemporaneous variance-covariance matrix is diagonal. The econometric content of these assumptions is not clear. If, for example, we are dealing with a cross section of firms, it seems highly unlikely that imperfections in profit maximization as represented by v_1 and v_2 should not be correlated. If we are examining an industry over time, the factors left out of the production function represented by v_0 are likely to be reflected also in the marginal productivity conditions. Furthermore, they are likely to be serially correlated. With no exogenous variables in the system, identification becomes a complex matter, and is only possible by means of rather unrealistic assumptions. When the above assumptions are made, a full-information maximum-likelihood procedure is possible. Kmenta (1964, pp. 24–26), shows that this is equivalent to the following two-stage least-squares procedure:

Define

$$z_1 = \varphi x_0 - x_1$$
$$z_2 = \varphi x_0 - x_2$$
$$z_3 = (x_1 - x_2)^2$$

where $\varphi = (1 + \rho/\mu)(1 + \rho)$.

Since v_1 and v_2 are assumed to be independent, the second and third of equalities (11) imply

(12) $$\text{cov}(v_1, v_2) = 0 = \varphi^2 \text{ var}(x_0) - \varphi[\text{cov}(x_0, x_1) + \text{cov}(x_0, x_2)] + \text{cov}(x_1, x_2).$$

If the covariances on the right are replaced by their sample values, a consistent estimate of φ may be obtained by solving (12). It can be shown that the roots of (12) are real; the question is which of the two should be used. This may be resolved by reference to the likelihood function: If $\rho > 0$, $0 < \delta < 1$, and $0 < \mu < 1$, it can be shown that the smaller of the two roots will yield the higher value of the likelihood function. Having obtained a consistent estimate $\hat{\varphi}$ of φ, we may form the z_1, z_2, and z_3 defined above and the equation

(13) $$x_0 = a_0 + a_1 z_1 + a_2 z_2 + a_3 z_3 + \epsilon$$

where
$$a_0 = k_0/(1 - \mu\varphi)$$
$$a_1 = -\mu\delta/(1 - \mu\varphi)$$
$$a_2 = -\mu(1 - \delta)/(1 - \mu\varphi)$$
$$a_3 = \rho\mu\delta(1 - \delta)/2(1 - \mu\varphi)$$
$$\epsilon = v_0/(1 - \mu\varphi)$$

Thus, if we had estimates of a_i, $i = 0, 1, 2, 3$, we could obtain estimates of ρ, μ, δ and k_0. Since, by the second and third of equations (11)

(14) $$z_i = \frac{k_i + v_i}{1 + \rho}, \quad i = 1, 2,$$

and

(15) $$z_3 = (x_1 - x_2)^2$$
$$= \frac{(k_1 - k_2 + v_1 - v_2)^2}{(1 + \rho)^2},$$

it follows, by the assumption that v_0, v_1, and v_2 are independent, that z_i, $i = 1, 2, 3$, are independent of ϵ. Hence, the ordinary least-squares estimates of a_i, $i = 0, 1, 2, 3$, in (13) are consistent. Indeed, Kmenta (1964) shows they are precisely the maximum-likelihood estimates if $\hat{\varphi}$ as determined by (12) is used.

If prices vary from observation to observation a wider variety of estimation possibilities is opened up, and with the choice comes a greater risk of error. Equations (1′) and (3) may be used to determine any three of the six variables V, L, $\dot{K}$, p, w, and r except in the degenerate case when $\mu = 1$ which implies that supply is perfectly elastic so that the scale of operation must be indeterminate under conditions of perfect competition.

To obtain various useful formulations from (1′) and (3), it is convenient to proceed by finding first the cost function, then equating marginal cost to price, and finally inserting the result in (3) to obtain the supply function and two derived demand functions for factors of production. These, in fact, will be the reduced form when p, w, and r are treated as exogenous, with V, L, and K endogenous. From (3) and the definition of total factor costs we have

$$(16) \quad \frac{C}{pV} = \frac{w}{p}\frac{L}{V} + \frac{r}{p}\frac{K}{V} = \frac{w}{p}\left\{ a^{-1}\left(\frac{w}{p}\right)^{-1/1+\rho} V^{\rho(1-\mu)/\mu(1+\rho)}\right\}$$

$$+ \frac{r}{p}\left\{ b^{-1}\left(\frac{r}{p}\right)^{-1/1+\rho} V^{\rho(1-\mu)/\mu(1+\rho)}\right\}$$

$$= \left\{ a^{-1}\left(\frac{w}{p}\right)^{\rho/1+\rho} + b^{-1}\left(\frac{r}{p}\right)^{\rho/1+\rho}\right\} V^{\rho(1-\mu)/\mu(1+\rho)}.$$

Thus, marginal cost is

$$(17) \quad \lambda = \frac{\partial C}{\partial V} = p\left\{ a^{-1}\left(\frac{w}{p}\right)^{\rho/1+\rho} + b^{-1}\left(\frac{r}{p}\right)^{\rho/1+\rho}\right\} V^{\rho(1-\mu)/(1+\rho)}$$

$$\left\{ 1 + \frac{\rho(1-\mu)}{\mu(1+\rho)}\right\}$$

$$= \frac{C}{V}\frac{\mu - \rho}{\mu(1+\rho)}.$$

Setting marginal cost equal to price we obtain the supply function in implicit form:

$$\left\{ a^{-1}\left(\frac{w}{p}\right)^{\rho/1+\rho} + b^{-1}\left(\frac{r}{p}\right)^{\rho/1+\rho} \right\} V^{\rho(1-\mu)/\mu(1+\rho)} = \frac{\mu + \rho}{\mu(1 + \rho)}.$$

Solving for p with $\mu = 1$, constant returns to scale, shows that supply is perfectly elastic at a price

$$p = [a^{-1} w^{\rho/1+\rho} + b^{-1} r^{\rho/1+\rho}]^{1+\rho/\rho},$$

in this case. In general, with $\mu \neq 1$,

(18) $$V = \left[\alpha\left(\frac{w}{p}\right)^{\rho/1+\rho} + \beta\left(\frac{r}{p}\right)^{\rho/1+\rho} \right]^{(1+\rho)/\rho(1-\mu)}$$

where $\alpha = \dfrac{\mu + \rho}{\mu(1+ \rho)}\, a^{-1}$

$$\beta = \frac{\mu + \rho}{\mu(1+ \rho)}\, b^{-1}.$$

Substituting for V from (18), and $\lambda = p$, in the second and third equations of (3), we obtain the derived demand functions for capital and labor:

(19)
$$
\begin{cases}
L = \dfrac{\mu(1 + \rho)}{\mu + \rho}\, \alpha\left[\dfrac{w}{p}\right]^{-1/1+\rho} \\[4pt]
\quad\quad \left[\alpha\left(\dfrac{w}{p}\right)^{\rho/1+\rho} + \beta\left(\dfrac{r}{p}\right)^{\rho/1+\rho} \right]^{(1+\rho)(\mu+\rho)/\rho(1-\mu)} \\[12pt]
K = \dfrac{\mu(1 + \rho)}{\mu + \rho}\, \beta\left[\dfrac{r}{p}\right]^{-1/1+\rho} \\[4pt]
\quad\quad \left[\alpha\left(\dfrac{w}{p}\right)^{\rho/1+\rho} + \beta\left(\dfrac{r}{p}\right)^{\rho/1+\rho} \right]^{(1+\rho)(\mu+\rho)/\rho(1-\mu)}
\end{cases}
$$

If p, w, and r are exogenous, equations (18) and (19) represent the appropriate reduced form; least-squares estimates have all the well-known desirable properties. Of course, the equations are highly non-linear; so either iterative procedures or a linearization along the lines suggested by Kmenta (1964) and outlined above must be employed. Furthermore, only three parameters enter the equations, and there are more than that number of coefficients; hence, restrictions apply within and across equations. The only way in which the across-equation restrictions may be properly imposed is by specifying the nature of the dependence (or that there is none) between the disturbances in the several equations.

If there are no imperfections in profit maximization, the residual entering all three equations is the same, namely, the residual in the production function itself. In this case, it is useful to combine all three equations into a single estimation equation expressing equilibrium net revenue as a function of the prices

(20) $\pi = pV - wL - rK$

$$= \left\{ p - \frac{\mu(1+\rho)}{\mu+\rho} [Q]^{\rho/\rho(1-\mu)} \left[\alpha w \left(\frac{w}{p} \right)^{-1/1+\rho} \right. \right.$$

$$\left. \left. + \beta r \left(\frac{r}{p} \right)^{-1/1+\rho} \right] \right\} [Q]^{\mu(1+\rho)/\rho(1-\mu)},$$

where $Q = \alpha(w/p)^{\rho/1+\rho} + \beta(r/p)^{\rho/1+\rho}$. The terms α and β contain the residual element, which may be factored out. An assumption concerning its distribution then permits maximum-likelihood methods to be employed. The nonlinear equations resulting must, in general be solved by numerical methods.

That there are no imperfections in profit maximization, or, to put the matter more accurately, other factors which cause the marginal conditions to hold only inexactly, seems somewhat implausible. If we allow residual elements in all of the equations (1′) and (3), the residuals in (18) and (19) will all be different. If we maintain the assumption that prices are all exogenous, specifying the joint distribution of the residual elements in (18) and (19) permits employment of maximum-likelihood methods. It is no longer necessary to specify independence, and, indeed, assuming the residuals follow a multivariate normal distribution and are independent, we could compute estimates of covariances of residuals in the supply and derived demand equations. Kmenta (1964, pp. 17–19), suggests a two-stage least-squares procedure which is computationally simpler than the maximum-likelihood procedure described above. It involves first estimating the elasticity of substitution from a logarithmic regression of the capital-labor ratio on the factor-price ratio and using the result in other equations of the system to obtain estimates of the other parameters. I would conjecture that Kmenta's two-stage procedure is asymptotically as efficient as the full maximum-likelihood procedure described above only when the residuals in all three equations may be assumed to be independent; if they are not, the full maximum-likelihood method would appear to offer some advantages which might offset, at least partly, the computational complexity.

Suppose now that output and factor prices are exogenous. We may either suppose that output price is determined endogenously and make use of all three equations (18) and (19), or we may take output price as given as well, so that *real* factor prices are exogenous, and assume that firms minimize costs for a given output rather than maximize profits. This last set of assumptions leads to a model which has applications in the study of regulated industries and seems worth exploring.[21] In this case, we dispense with the supply function altogether; our system now consists of the production function (1') and quasi-derived-demand functions for the factors which show the dependence of their equilibrium levels on the exogenously determined level of output, e.g., (5). Once again, these equations involve the same parameters, and restrictions must be imposed both within and across equations. A simple way to do this is to consider the cost function rather than the three individual equations. The cost function may be obtained from (16) by substitution of $p = \lambda$ from (17):

$$(21) \quad C = p^{1/1+\rho}\{a^{-1}w^{\rho/1+\rho} + b^{-1}r^{\rho/1+\rho}\}V^{(\mu+\rho)/\mu(1+\rho)}$$

$$= \left[\frac{C}{V}\frac{\mu+\rho}{\mu(1+\rho)}\right]^{1/1+\rho}\{a^{-1}w^{\rho/1+\rho} + b^{-1}r^{\rho/1+\rho}\}V^{(\mu+\rho)/\mu(1+\rho)}$$

$$= \frac{\mu(1+\rho)}{\mu+\rho}[\alpha w^{\rho/1+\rho} + \beta r^{\rho/1+\rho}]^{(1+\rho)/\rho}V^{(1-\mu)/\mu}.$$

The function is highly nonlinear; either iterative procedures must be employed directly or an approximation to the function must be devised along the lines suggested by Kmenta (1964) in connection with the CES function itself. We have

[21] Cf. Nerlove (1963).

(22) $\log C = A^* + \left(\dfrac{1-\mu}{\mu}\right)\log V + \left(\dfrac{1+\rho}{\rho}\right)f(\rho) + v^*$

where $A^* = \log \dfrac{\mu(1+\rho)}{\mu+\rho} + \dfrac{1+\rho}{\rho}\log\left\{\dfrac{\mu+\rho}{\mu(1+\rho)}\mu^{1/1+\rho}\gamma^{-\rho/\mu(1+\rho)}\right\}$

$f(\rho) = \log\{\delta^{1/1+\rho}w^{\rho/1+\rho} + (1-\delta)^{1/1+\rho}r^{\rho/1+\rho}\}$

and $v^* = \log$ {residual occurring in (21)}.

Expanding $f(\rho)$ in a Taylor's series about $\rho = 0$

(23) $f(\rho) = \rho[\delta \log w + (1-\delta)\log r - \delta \log \delta - (1-\delta)\log(1-\delta)]$

$\qquad + \dfrac{\rho^2}{2}\{\delta(1-\delta)[\log w - \log r]^2 + \delta[1 + 2\delta \log \delta$

$\qquad + 2(1-\delta)\log(1-\delta)]\log w + (1-\delta)[1 + 2\delta \log \delta$

$\qquad + 2(1-\delta)\log(1-\delta)]\log r - [\delta \log \delta + (1-\delta)\log(1-\delta)]^2$

$\qquad - [(1-\delta)\log(1-\delta)[1 - \log(1-\delta)] + \delta \log \delta[1 - \log \delta]\}$

$\qquad + \text{(higher-order terms)}.$

Hence

(24) $\log C = A + \left(\dfrac{1-\mu}{\mu}\right)\log V + (1+\rho)\delta\{1 + \rho[1 + 2\delta \log \delta$

$\qquad + 2(1-\delta)\log(1-\delta)]\}\log w + (1+\rho)(1-\delta)\{1 + \rho[1$

$\qquad + 2\delta \log \delta + 2(1-\delta)\log(1-\delta)]\}\log r$

$\qquad + \dfrac{(1+\rho)\rho\delta(1-\delta)}{2}[\log w - \log r]^2 + v.$

where A *is* A^* plus the appropriate function of δ and ρ and v is v^* plus higher-order terms of the Taylor's series expansion. Unfortunately, from the standpoint of estimation, (24) is not as simple a form as (10); indeed, we have three coefficients (of $\log w$, of $\log r$, and of [$\log w -\log r]^2$) to determine only two coefficients ρ and δ so that (24) overidentifies the parameters of the production function. To obtain unique estimates would probably almost be as difficult as estimating (21) directly by iterative methods.

Thus far we have explored the cases in which (a) all prices are taken as exogenous, leaving output and factor input levels to be determined endogenously; and (b) factor prices and output are taken to be exogenous, leaving factor inputs to be determined endogenously on the assumption that the supply function is suppressed. Another interesting case is that in which labor input, the rate of return on capital, and output price are taken as exogenous. This condition might plausibly be assumed in an intercountry comparison in which one assumed immobile labor, mobile capital, and unfettered trade in commodities. (Consideration of more than one industry, however, causes some difficulty with the labor immobility hypothesis, since, while it is plausible to assume immobility among countries, it is harder to swallow immobility among industries in the same country.) In this case, we must solve (1') and (3) for V, K, and w in terms of L, r, and p. Clearly, the elasticity of substitution is most easily estimated by regressing $\log V/K$ on $\log r/p$ when returns to scale are assumed to be constant. If the constant returns assumption is not made, however, or if data on capital stock and rate of return are not available, matters become more complicated. In this first instance, a full maximum-likelihood procedure seems to be called for, although doubtless some approximate procedures might be devised. Unfortunately, lack of data is far more serious; even if there are constant returns to scale, lack of capital stock and rate-of-return data will prevent satisfactory estimation of the elasticity of substitution except under other exogenicity assumptions.

One possible approach to the problem of estimation with insufficient data is to ask not what the correct method of estimation should be, but rather how much of a difference it makes if an incorrect method is used. This is the approach taken by Maddala and Kadane (1965). They assume constant returns to scale and suppress the output price level. In addition, they consider only the linear terms of the approximation to the production function, (10), i.e., they consider a system in which a Cobb-Douglas function is used to approximate the CES for purposes of analyzing simultaneous equations effects only. Their system thus consists of only three equations:

$$(25) \quad \begin{cases} \log V = \log \gamma + \delta \log K + (1 - \delta) \log L + v_0 \\ \log \dfrac{V}{L} = - \dfrac{1}{1 - \rho} \log \gamma^\rho (1 - \delta) + \dfrac{1}{1 + \rho} \log \dfrac{w}{p} + v_1 \\ \log \dfrac{V}{K} = - \dfrac{1}{1 + \rho} \log \gamma^\rho \delta + \dfrac{1}{1 + \rho} \log \dfrac{r}{p} + v_2 \end{cases}$$

Since w/p is endogenous in the case under consideration, estimation of the elasticity of substitution from the second of equations (25) will be subject to simultaneous equations bias.

To assess the effects of simultaneous equations bias analytically, one may proceed as follows: First express w/p and V/L in terms of L and r/p; the two variables considered as exogenous. This may be done by solving (25) for V, K, and w/p. Next, write down the least squares estimates of $\sigma = 1/(1 + \rho)$ from the second of equations (25), i.e.,

$$
(26) \qquad \hat{\sigma} = \frac{\mathrm{cov}\left[\log\dfrac{V}{L}, \log\dfrac{w}{p}\right]}{\mathrm{var}\left[\log\dfrac{w}{p}\right]}
$$

where the covariances are the sample values. Replacing these by the population values tells us what the least-squares estimates will be asymptotically and this in comparison with the true σ will reveal the asymptotic bias. Finally, we express the population covariance and variance in (26) by the corresponding values expressed in terms of the true parameters and the population variances and covariances of the exogenous variables and the residuals in the problem. Unfortunately, one does not come out with very neat answers to the question in this way. Furthermore, the dependence of the simultaneous-equations bias on the population moments of the exogenous variables and residuals in this case means in effect that we cannot ever hope to give a general answer to the question. An alternative approach is to assume various plausible values for the parameters and generate values of the exogenous variables and the residuals according to some stochastic scheme.[22] Maddala and Kadane (1965) have done just this for three cases:

(i) L and r/p exogenous;
(ii) K and L exogenous;
(iii) r/p and x exogenous;

[22] Clearly, this amounts to specifying a distribution for both the exogenous variables and the residuals. Such a specification also makes it possible to complete the analytical treatment of simultaneous-equations bias. Thus, given sufficient energy, I could reproduce analytically all the results obtained by Kadane and Maddala (1965) including those presented below. Furthermore, I could, if I had even more energy, try out alternative distributional assumptions. But electronic computers have nearly infinite energy and the "capital-intensive" approach of Maddala and Kadane seems, after all, the path of least resistance.

and for a variety of assumptions about the contemporaneous variance-covariance matrix of the residuals in equations (25). They assumed serial independence throughout. In case (i) they assumed L was uniformly distributed in the interval (0, 1,000) and r/p in the interval (0, 5), rejecting those values which would have entailed the calculation of the logarithm of a negative number.

The assumptions made about the contemporaneous residual variance-covariance matrix were as follows:

A. All the disturbances are uncorrelated with "technical" disturbances (those in the production function itself) having a higher variance than the "economic" disturbances [those in the second and third equations of (25)].

B. As in A, except the relative variances of the "technical" and "economic" disturbances are reversed.

C. All disturbances are positively correlated and the variance of the "technical" disturbance is greater than the variances of the "economic" disturbances.

D. As in C except the relative variances of the "technical" and "economic" disturbances are reversed.

E. The "economic" disturbances are highly correlated but independent of the "technical" disturbance. The "economic" disturbances have higher variance than that of the "technical" disturbance.

All residuals were assumed to follow a multivariate normal distribution. For each of three values of the true elasticity of substitution, $\sigma = 0.4$, $\sigma = 0.9$, and $\sigma = 1.6$, and values of $\gamma = 1$ and $\delta = .3$, samples were drawn (how many, they don't say) and two alternative estimates of the elasticity of substitution were computed, one from the regression of log V/L on log w/p (the ACMS case) and the other from the regression of log w/p on log V/L. The results they obtained for L and r/p exogenous are reproduced in Table 12.

Table 12 shows that the true elasticity of substitution seems to be seriously underestimated by the ACMS method except when σ is actually rather close to one. The alternative regression tends to overestimate in most cases, but not as seriously. Simultaneous equations difficulties were aggravated, as we might expect, by dependence among the residuals in the various equations. On the basis of their findings in this and other cases, Maddala and Kadane recommend the regression of log w/p on

TABLE 12

Mean Estimates of the Elasticity of Substitution and Mean Variance of Estimate[a]

(various values of true elasticity of substitution and residual variance-covariance matrix assumed)

True Elasticity of Substitution and Type of Regression	Assumption about Residual Variance-Covariance Matrix				
	A	B	C	D	E
$\sigma = 0.4$					
(i) Log $\frac{V}{L}$ dependent					
Mean estimated $\hat{\sigma}$	0.32	0.10	0.31	0.15	0.11
Mean variance of estimate	(.0018)	(.0034)	(.0027)	(.0038)	(.0009)
(ii) Log $\frac{w}{p}$ dependent					
Mean estimated $\hat{\sigma}$	0.41	0.43	0.51	0.63	0.38
Mean variance of estimate	(.0040)	(.0061)	(.0018)	(.0462)	(.0363)
$\sigma = 0.9$					
(i) Log $\frac{V}{L}$ dependent					
Mean estimated $\hat{\sigma}$	0.88	0.83	0.86	0.77	0.76
Mean variance of estimate	(.0012)	(.0040)	(.0015)	(.0026)	(.0023)
(ii) Log $\frac{w}{p}$ dependent					
Mean estimated $\hat{\sigma}$	0.89	0.91	0.89	0.82	0.80
Mean variance of estimate	(.0010)	(.0050)	(.0035)	(.0028)	(.0030)
$\sigma = 1.6$					
(i) Log $\frac{V}{L}$ dependent					
Mean estimated $\hat{\sigma}$	1.36	0.60	1.29	0.76	0.58
Mean variance of estimate	(.0243)	(.1037)	(.0357)	(.0711)	(.0947)
(ii) Log $\frac{w}{p}$ dependent					
Mean estimated $\hat{\sigma}$	1.62	1.81	1.81	2.12	1.53
Mean variance of estimate	(.0283)	(.2025)	(.0930)	(.2442)	(.1982)

[a]Obtained by Maddala and Kadane (1965) in Monte Carlo studies when labor force and rate of return on capital are assumed to be exogenous

log V/L, rather than the other way around, since these estimates seem to be more robust in the face of simultaneous equations misspecification.

On the whole, there is little that can be done about difficulties in estimation due to lack of relevant data. On the other hand, as we have seen in the course of this section, simultaneous-equations problems and problems of nonlinearity do arise even when all relevant data are available. In general, the best method for attacking the estimation problem in such situations seems to be the maximum-likelihood approach. Although this method typically leads to simultaneous nonlinear equations which must be solved for the estimates, computational techniques are available and may definitely be considered feasible on modern electronic computers.[23] In short, the estimation of the CES production function in a simultaneous-equations context is just one further illustration of the computer revolution underway in the field of econometric methods.

References

Arrow, K. J., H. B. Chenery, B. S. Minhas, and R. M. Solow (1961), "Capital-Labor Substitution and Economic Efficiency," *Review of Economics and Statistics*, August, pp. 225–250.

Brown, M. (1962), "The Constant Elasticity of Substitution Production Function," Report No. 6219, *Econometric Institute*, Rotterdam, Holland, June.

Brown, M., and J. S. de Cani (1963), "Technological Change and the Distribution of Income," *International Economic Review*, September, pp. 289–309.

Bruno, M. (1962), "A Note on the Implications of an Empirical Relationship between Output per Unit of Labour, the Wage Rate, and the Capital-Labour Ratio," Stanford University, July (mimeo.).

David, P. A., and Th. van de Klundert (1965), "Non-Neutral Efficiency Growth and Substitution between Capital and Labor in the U.S. Economy, 1899–1960," *American Economic Review*, June, pp. 356–394.

Dhrymes, P. J. (1965), "Some Extensions and Tests for the CES Class of Production Functions," *Review of Economics and Statistics*, November, pp. 357–366.

————, and M. Kurz (1964), "Technology and Scale in Electricity Generation," *Econometrica*, July, pp. 287–315.

Diamond, P. A., and D. McFadden (1965), "Identification of the Elasticity of Substitution and the Bias of Technical Change: An Impossibility Theorem," unpublished.

[23] See, for example, Traub (1964).

Diwan, R. K. (1963), "An Empirical Estimate of the Constant Elasticity of Substitution Production Function," paper presented at meeting of Econometric Society, Copenhagen, July 1963; abstract in *Econometrica,* October 1964, pp. 662–663.

Ferguson, C. E. (1965a), "Substitution, Technical Progress, and Returns to Scale," *American Economic Review, Proceedings,* May, pp. 296–305.

——— (1965b), "Time-Series Production Functions and Technological Progress in American Manufacturing Industry," *Journal of Political Economy,* April, pp. 135–147.

Fuchs, V. R. (1963), "Capital Labor Substitution, A Note," *Review of Economics and Statistics,* November, pp. 436–438.

Gordon, R. A. (1961), *Business Fluctuations,* New York.

Hilhorst, J. G. M. (1961), "Production Functions for Manufacturing Industry," *Statistische en Econometrische Onderzoekingen,* Central Bureau of Statistics, Den Haag, pp. 180–204.

Kendrick, J. W. (1964), Comment on Solow (1964), in *The Behavior of Income Shares,* Princeton for NBER, pp. 140–142.

Kendrick, J. W., and R. Sato (1963), "Factor Prices, Productivity, and Economic Growth," *American Economic Review,* December, pp. 974–1003.

Klein, L. R. (1953), *A Textbook of Econometrics,* Evanston, Ill.

Kmenta, J. (1964), "On Estimation of the CES Production Function," *Social Systems Research Institute, University of Wisconsin, Paper No. 6410,* October.

Kravis, I. (1959), "Relative Income Shares in Fact and Theory," *American Economic Review,* December, pp. 917–949.

Leontief, W. (1964), "An International Comparison of Factor Costs and Factor Use" [review of Minhas (1960–63)], *American Economic Review,* June, pp. 335–345.

Liu, T. C., and G. H. Hildebrand (1965), *Manufacturing Production Functions in the United States, 1957,* Ithaca, N.Y.

Lucas, R. E. (1963), "Substitution Between Labor and Capital in U.S. Manufacturing, 1929–58," unpublished Ph.D. dissertation, University of Chicago.

McFadden, D. (1964), "Notes on Estimation of the Elasticity of Substitution," Institute of Business and Economic Research, University of California, Berkeley, November (mimeo.).

McKinnon, R. I. (1962), "Wages, Capital Costs, and Employment in Manufacturing: A Model Applied to 1947–58 U.S. Data," *Econometrica,* July, pp. 501–521.

——— (1963a), "The CES Production Function Applied to Two-Digit Manufacturing and Three Mining Industries for the United States," unpublished.

——— (1963b), "Factor Price Changes and Production Function Estimation," Stanford University (mimeo.).

Maddala, G. S. (1963), "Technological Change in the Bituminous Coal Industry, 1919–54," unpublished Ph.D. dissertation, University of Chicago.

———— (1965), "Differential Industry Effects and Differential Factor Effects of Technological Change," Memo. 36, Research Center in Economic Growth, Stanford University, March.

Maddala, G. S., and J. B. Kadane (1965), "Specification Errors in the Context of the CES Production Function," paper presented at meeting of the Econometric Society, New York, December.

Minasian, J. R. (1961), "Elasticities of Substitution and Constant-Output Demand Curves for Labor," *Journal of Political Economy,* June, pp. 261–270.

Minhas, B. S. (1962), "The Homohypallagic Production Function, Factor-Intensity Reversals, and the Heckscher-Ohlin Theorem," *Journal of Political Economy,* April, pp. 138–156.

———— (1960–63), "An International Comparison of Factor Costs and Factor Use." (Ph.D. dissertation, Stanford University, November 1960), *Contributions to Economic Analysis No. 31,* Amsterdam: North-Holland, 1963.

Murata, Y., and K. J. Arrow (1965), unpublished results of estimation of elasticities of substitution for two-digit industries from intercountry data for two periods, June.

Nelson, R. R. (1965), "The CES Production Function and Economic Growth Projections" (mimeo.).

Nerlove, M. (1963). "Returns to Scale in Electricity Supply," pp. 167–198, in C. Christ *et al.* (ed.), *Measurement in Economics: Studies in Mathematical Economics and Econometrics in Memory of Yehuda Grunfeld,* Stanford.

———— (1965), "Notes on the Production Relations Included in Macro-Econometric Models," Stanford University, June (mimeo.).

Oi, W. Y. (1962), "Labor as a Quasi-Fixed Factor," *Journal of Political Economy,* December, pp. 538–555.

Okun, A. M. (1962), "Potential GNP: Its Measurement and Significance," *Proceedings of the Business and Economic Statistics Section of the American Statistical Association.*

Smith, V. (1963), "On Production Functions of Constant Elasticity of Substitution," Purdue University (mimeo.).

Solow, R. M. (1956), "A Contribution to the Theory of Economic Growth," *Quarterly Journal of Economics,* pp. 65–94.

———— (1957), "Technical Change and the Aggregate Production Function," *Review of Economics and Statistics,* pp. 312–320.

———— (1964), "Capital, Labor and Income in Manufacturing," in *The Behavior of Income Shares,* Princeton for NBER, pp. 101–128.

Swan, T. W. (1956), "Economic Growth and Capital Accumulation," *Economic Record,* pp. 334–361.

Traub, J. L. (1964), *Iterative Methods for the Solution of Equations*, Englewood Cliffs, N.J.

Whitaker, J. K. (1964), "A Note on the CES Production Function," *Review of Economic Studies*, April, pp. 166–167.

COMMENT

EDWIN MANSFIELD

The past decade has witnessed an enormous increase in the amount of attention devoted by economists to the study of production functions. Faced with the large number of studies that have resulted, Nerlove, in this very interesting and useful review article, has chosen to concentrate his attention primarily on the recent work on the CES production function. His paper consists largely of a description of the findings and limitations of recent studies of the elasticity of substitution. His major finding is the diversity of the results; small differences in period and concept seem to produce markedly different estimates. Nerlove makes an attempt to account for some of these discrepancies, but does not get very far. The net impression one obtains from the paper is that there are a large number of biases, none very well understood, which are operating simultaneously to produce very inconsistent and untrustworthy results.

Turning from the elasticity of substitution, I want to take up two questions regarding the rate of technological change. First, to what extent are the estimated rates of technological change in various industries consistent from one study to another. Although Nerlove shows that the estimates of the elasticity of substitution vary greatly, he says nothing in this regard about the estimated rates of technological change. Despite the well-known and important deficiencies in these estimates,[1] they are all that are available for many purposes, and it is important to know whether there is considerable agreement from one study to another, the estimated rate of technological change being consistently higher in some industries than in others.

To find out, I looked first at the studies by Ferguson[2] and McKin-

---

[1] The rate of technological change is measured by the rate of growth of the residual, which, as Nerlove points out, absorbs various specification errors. For example, besides technological change, the residual contains the effects of inputs not explicitly included in the production function.

[2] C. E. Ferguson, "Time-Series Production Functions and Technological Progress in American Manufacturing Industry," *Journal of Political Economy*, April 1965.

non [3] cited by Nerlove. Then I added the results obtained by Solow,[4] Massell,[5] and myself.[6] The findings, shown in Table 1, indicate that there is considerable diversity in the results, despite the fact that all the studies pertain to much the same period. An extreme case of this diversity is the tobacco industry, where the estimated annual rate of technological change varied from −10.7 per cent to 39.2 per cent. Moreover, the furniture industry is only slightly less unstable, the estimated annual rate of technological change varying from zero to 24.2 per cent.

Some of the factors responsible for these differences are easy to find. Solow's estimates are rates of *capital-augmenting* technological change; consequently, they would be expected to be two or three times as large as the others. My estimates and Massell's are based on the Cobb-Douglas production function, whereas the others use the CES. Solow's estimates and mine assume that technological change is capital-embodied whereas the others assume that it is disembodied. Ferguson uses current-dollar values, whereas the others use deflated data. Massell and I, and to some extent Solow, attempt to correct for underutilization of capital whereas the others do not. Ferguson tries to include nonneutral technological change, whereas the others assume all technological change is neutral.[7]

Although the estimates for a particular industry vary considerably, their rank ordering may remain much the same. To see whether this is so, I ran rank correlations between the estimates in each pair of studies. The results, shown in Table 2, indicate that there generally is some positive correlation between an industry's rank in one study and its rank in another, but that the correlation is never high. The closest agreement seems to exist among Ferguson, McKinnon, and me. Solow and Massell agree with nobody else—including one another.

Having said this, I must add a few words of caution. It is important that we put these findings in perspective and that we refrain from drawing unduly pessimistic conclusions. The results are not as discouraging

[3] R. I. McKinnon, "Wages, Capital Costs, and Employment in Manufacturing: A Model Applied to 1947–58 U.S. Data," *Econometrica*, July 1962.

[4] R. M. Solow, "Capital, Labor, and Income in Manufacturing," in *The Behavior of Income Shares*, Princeton for NBER, 1964.

[5] B. Massell, "A Disaggregated View of Technical Change," *Journal of Political Economy*, 1961.

[6] E. Mansfield, "Rates of Return from Industrial Research and Development," *American Economic Review*, May 1965.

[7] Also, McKinnon allows for a distributed lag in the relationship he estimates, while the others do not.

TABLE 1

Rates of Neutral Technological Change, U.S. Manufacturing,
Postwar Period, Results of Five Studies

(per cent)

Industry	McKinnon, 1949-61	Ferguson,[a] 1949-61	Massell, 1946-57	Solow,[b] 1949-58	Mansfield, 1946-62
Food	2.4	2.3	1.4	8.2	4.7
Tobacco	−10.7	−4.4	0.8	39.2	n.a.
Textiles	3.4	−3.0	1.6	7.9	n.a.
Apparel	0.2	−3.8	0.9	n.a.	3.0
Lumber	−0.3	None	3.8	0.0	n.a.
Furniture	24.2	None	1.0	9.0	1.9
Paper	2.8	None	2.3	8.3	3.4
Chemicals	4.0	None	3.5	5.9	3.7
Petroleum and coal	n.a.	None	1.9	n.a.	n.a.
Rubber	2.4	2.1	1.0	7.4	n.a.
Leather	2.2	0.4	1.1	7.3	n.a.
Glass	2.3	2.1	2.5	5.2	1.5
Primary metals	1.6	None	0.4	n.a.	n.a.
Fabricated metals	0.5	2.9	0.3	3.2	n.a.
Machinery	−1.9	None	2.0	0.0	c
Electrical machinery	2.7	1.9	3.7	3.9	3.6
Transportation equipment	3.1	2.4	2.4	n.a.	n.a.
Instruments	3.9	4.6	1.0	0.0	8.3
Printing	−1.0	−0.7	2.4	4.3	n.a.

n.a. = not available.

Source: See footnotes 2-6.

[a]Unlike the others, Ferguson tries to include nonneutral technological change as well in his paper.

[b]Rates of capital-augmenting technological change.

[c]Less than zero.

as they may seem. As noted above, several of these studies contain important defects, which are recognized by their authors and which can be overcome by disaggregation, deflation, correction for underutilization of capacity, etc. Perhaps the principal conclusion to be drawn from Tables 1 and 2 is that these defects can cause more havoc than is commonly recognized.

TABLE 2

Coefficients of Rank Correlation Between Estimates of
Rates of Technological Change, U.S. Manufacturing

	Ferguson	McKinnon	Mansfield	Massell	Solow
Ferguson	1.00	0.37	0.54	0.05	−0.34
McKinnon		1.00	0.47	0.18	0.25
Mansfield			1.00	0.00	−0.03
Massell				1.00	−0.33
Solow					1.00

Source: Table 1.

Finally, I want to turn to an important question bearing on the work of the National Commission on Automation and others concerned with policy in the area of technological change. To what extent has there been an increase since World War II in the rate of technological change? It is easy to find statements by economists and others asserting that the rate of technological change in the postwar period is much more rapid than that before the war. It is also possible to find statements asserting the opposite. Although there is considerable evidence that the rate of increase of output per man-hour has been higher than before the war, the evidence with respect to total factor productivity has been less clear cut. For example, Kendrick and Sato find that the average annual rate of increase of total factor productivity in the private domestic economy was 2.14 per cent during 1948–60, as contrasted with 2.08 per cent during 1919–60.[8]

Nerlove's Table 7 seems to provide a small amount of new evidence on this score. It contains estimates of the rate of technological change in various two-digit manufacturing industries during 1899–1957 and 1947–58. The results, taken from published and unpublished work by McKinnon,[9] provide no evidence that the rate of technological change has been higher in most industries in the postwar period. Table 7 shows

[8] J. Kendrick and R. Sato, "Factor Prices, Productivity, and Growth," *American Economic Review,* December 1963.
[9] McKinnon, *op. cit.,* and "The CES Production Function Applied to Two-Digit Manufacturing and Three Mining Industries for the United States," unpublished, 1963.

that the estimated postwar rate of technological change was lower than that during 1899–1957 in five of the ten industries for which a comparison can be made. These industries are apparel, lumber, paper, printing, and electrical machinery. In the remaining five industries—furniture, chemicals, leather, textiles, and glass—the estimated postwar rate of technological change was higher than that for 1899–1957.

Moreover, if the results for the postwar period that Ferguson, Massell, or I obtained are used in place of McKinnon's, the results are the same.[10] In at least one-half of the industries for which a comparison can be made, the estimated postwar rate of technological change was lower than that for 1899–1957. These results are suggestive, but extremely tentative. Without a more complete description of McKinnon's unpublished study, one cannot be sure that it is entirely comparable with any of the studies of the postwar period, including his own.

EVSEY D. DOMAR

If it was found by Nelson, as quoted by Nerlove, that sizable changes in the elasticity of substitution produce very small effects on the other variables, it should follow that relatively small changes in the other variables should exert strong effects on the elasticity of substitution. The data being what they are, why is it surprising then that the magnitude of the elasticity of substitution derived in the several studies jumps all over the place?

ZVI GRILICHES

There is an alternative statistical interpretation of the Hildebrand and Liu results. The basic point to note is that there is an identification problem here. There are two equations in the system, say

(1) $$y = ak + u$$
(2) $$y = sw + v$$

where y is the logarithm of output per man, k is the logarithm of capital per man, w is the logarithm of the wage rate, and u and v are disturbances. The first equation is the approximate production function (for σ

[10] Because Solow's results are rates of capital-augmenting technological change, it would be incorrect to compare them with McKinnon's results for 1899–1957.

$s \neq 1$, we could add a k^2 term without affecting the rest of the argument). The second equation is the marginal productivity or ACMS relation. Now fitting a combined relation

$$(3) \qquad\qquad y = b_1 w + b_2 k + e$$

and finding a significant b_2 coefficient does not contradict the above model [equation (2)]. In fact if k is measured without error, u is independent of v, and the variance of v is not identically zero and if the model [(1) and (2)] is correct, one would expect the b_1 coefficient in (3) to be insignificant (rather than the b_2 coefficient as suggested by Hildebrand and Liu) since *all* the effects of w are contained in k. Moreover, k incorporates also the relevant variance of v. Thus, if k is the correct measure of capital it should not only be significant in (3) but should actually swamp the effect of w. Since, however, k is rarely measured without error and w is related to the "systematic" component of k, the latter variable may perform as a proxy for the correct k measure and not be forced out from (3). The final effect will depend on the relative variances of v, the error in the marginal conditions, and the error of measurement in k. But there is no need to interpret these results as implying a more complicated production function.

RAFORD BODDY, State University of New York at Buffalo

I wish to offer an important reason for the usual but perplexing differences among estimates of the elasticity of substitution, σ. My interpretation of the disparities among the estimates of σ is based on the premise that factor proportions for old plants cannot be varied as easily after the plant is built as at the time of the original investment decision. Only the factor proportions of the newest plants are fully adjusted to current expectations of wage rates and to current capital costs. Over time, factor costs change, and give rise to changes in expectations of future costs. The factor proportions of the newest, best-practice plants change as these costs change. The practice in cross-section and in time series analyses has been to regress aggregate factor proportions, or average-practice coefficients, against recent costs. This leads to biases in estimates of σ which depend on the relation of *average-practice and best-practice* factor proportions.

My interpretation is limited to estimates based upon marginal productivity conditions as distinct from those based on the direct approximations of the production function. In fact, few estimates have yet come from the more direct approach. Most estimates of σ have been related to the equation:

(1)
$$\frac{X}{L} = (1 - \kappa)^{-\sigma} \gamma^{\sigma\rho} \left(\frac{w}{p}\right)^{\sigma}$$

I will not develop the argument in terms of (1) but rather in terms of the alternative equation:

(2)
$$\frac{K}{L} = \left(\frac{\kappa}{1 - \kappa}\right)^{\sigma} \left(\frac{w}{q}\right)^{\sigma}$$

where q is the price of capital and w is the wage rate.

Consider plants with identical products, but built at different times in one metropolitan area. Assume that there has been no nonneutral technical change. When building a particular plant, some enterpreneur compared the mean expected wage rates to current capital cost and chose some capital-labor proportion. Assume that expected wage rates depend on past wage rates. With increasing relative wage rates over the period, the coordinates of the logs of the initial factor proportions and expected relative factor prices would lie along the line, R of Figure 1, section A with the coordinates of the newest plant furthest from the origin. The older plants have the lower capital-labor ratios. The slope of the line is σ, the elasticity of substitution.

Given that the older plants are still producing, what will be the average-practice coefficient, $\Sigma K / \Sigma L$, and the average factor prices of the area for the year in which the last plant was built? If all of the capital decisions are analyzed as if they were current ones, the nominal price of capital will be equal for all the plants. For plants in the same business in the single metropolitan area, the current wage rates will tend to be equal, also. The capital-labor ratios are likely to be unequal, with the older plants having the lower values. Variations in the factor proportions of existing plants fall far short of those possible at the time of initial construction. It follows that the average-practice coefficient for the area, $\Sigma K / \Sigma L$, will be less than the capital-labor ratio of the newest plant. The relative size of the two coefficients depends on the relative sizes of the older and newer plants. The logs of the plant factor ratios are the set ($\bullet$)

FIGURE 1

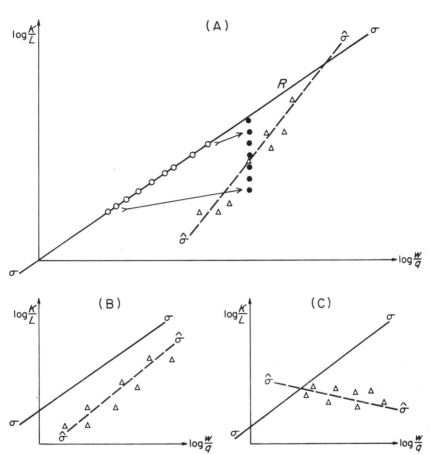

of Figure 1, section A. The log of the average-practice coefficient for the area is Δ.

The practice in cross-section and time series analyses has been to estimate σ from the regression of average-practice coefficients against recent costs. It is clear from Figure 1, section A that the relation of $\hat{\sigma}$ to σ depends on the relation of average-practice coefficients to the best-practice coefficients of the newest plants.

In cross-section studies for industries in which resources have moved to lower-wage geographic areas, and little new investment has occurred in the higher-wage areas, the estimate of σ is likely to be biased downward. For the same discrepancies on a log scale between average-practice and best-practice coefficients the bias will be greater when there is a narrower spread among regions in recent wage rates. An extreme case arises when the wage rates that determined the average factor proportions of the lower-wage areas are higher than those which would elicit the average-practice coefficient of the high-wage area. The estimate of σ will then be negative (cf. Figure 1, section C).

If the industry is old in all areas and the relative price differences have a long history, the relation of average-practice to best-practice coefficients is likely to be such that $E(\hat{\sigma})$ will be approximately equal to σ. There may be slightly higher standards of obsolescence in the higher-wage areas which would impart a slight upward bias to $\hat{\sigma}$ (cf. Figure 1, section B).

If the recent percentage growth of capacity has been greater in the high-wage areas, or if the wage differences have narrowed, the bias will be upward (cf. Figure 1, section A). Within an economy such as that of the United States, upward biases could occur for a number of reasons. When the workers of an industry are attracted to the higher wages in the expanding areas, the older areas will find themselves faced with higher than expected wage costs and lower quasi-rents. For industries subjected to the recent introduction of regionwide or nationwide wage bargaining the narrowing of the wage differentials would be unfavorable to the areas with the historically lower capital-labor ratios. Again, for the same relative discrepancies between best-practice and average-practice coefficients, the bias will be greater if there is a narrower spread in wage rates.

In Figure 2 below we assess time series estimates through successive cross-section scatters.

Assume that technological change has been neutral. The best-practice coefficients of T_0, T_1, and T_2 would lie along the line with slope σ. Best-practice proportions regressed against the ratio of expected wage rates and current capital costs would provide unbiased estimates of the elasticity of substitution.

Most time series estimates, however, have been for aggregative data. The factor proportions are ratios of total capital to total labor, i.e., average-practice coefficients. Therefore, the aggregate time series estimates of the elasticity of substitution will be unbiased only if the ratio of average-practice to best-practice proportions has not changed systematically. Comparison of best-practice and average-practice coefficients for a

FIGURE 2

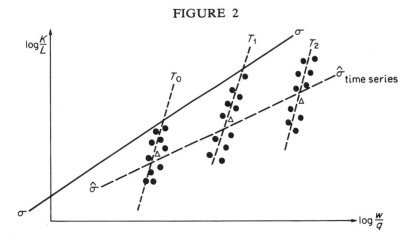

number of industries over extended intervals of time suggests that there has been little systematic change in the ratio.[1] There are some instances, however, where the bias might be significant. If the first observation is of the industry at the time of its inception, and subsequent observations relate to successive periods of growth, the ratio of average-practice to best-practice coefficients will fall over time. There will be a downward bias to $\hat{\sigma}$. Prior to the time when a relatively constant age of capital is achieved, fixed proportions, a constant rate of investment, I_0, and an exponential rate of growth of relative labor costs, w/q, would result in a $\hat{\sigma}$ approximately $(\frac{1}{2})$ σ.

When the industry has begun to decay, the ratio of best-practice to average-practice coefficients again rises as wage costs increase and few, if any, new plants are built. The estimate, $\hat{\sigma}$, is then an estimate of the *ex post* elasticity of substitution that measures the ease of substitution after the plant is built. For time series, the *ex post* elasticity of substitution serves as the lower bound of $\hat{\sigma}$.

The above discussion suggests that not only the standard errors, but the biases to the estimates of $\hat{\sigma}$ are increased for observations with narrow variations in wage rates. Whereas variations in the ratio of average-practice to best-practice coefficients are likely to have little impact on $\hat{\sigma}$ for observations that include high and low wage rates, such variations will lead to significant biases where the sample areas have very similar wage rates. Similarly, time series variations in the average age of the

[1] W. E. G. Salter, *Productivity and Technical Change*, Cambridge, Mass., 1960.

FIGURE 3

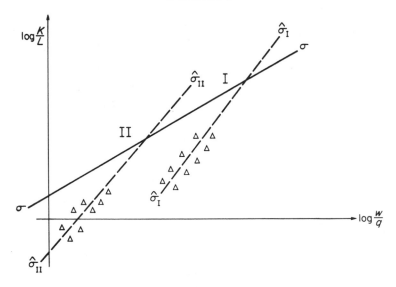

capital stock are likely to bias $\hat{\sigma}$ very little if there have been extensive changes in real wage rates, but the bias can be sizable if the variation in wages over the period has been small.

While I do not offer it as the sole explanation, the theory resolves in a simple manner some paradoxical results. We would expect that long-run time series, and cross-section estimates for very diverse countries, would be least subject to the above biases. Generally these estimates of $\hat{\sigma}$ are less than 1. The estimates of $\hat{\sigma}$ for cross sections with less variation in wage rates tend to be greater than 1 and to increase inversely with the narrowness of differences in wage rates. It seems likely that more narrowly defined industries have more narrowly defined regional bases. This may explain why Solow's reasonable deduction,[2] that the elasticity of substitution for two-digit industries should be higher than for three-digit industries, is not borne out by U.S. cross-section estimates. The theory and these results suggest that estimates of $\hat{\sigma}$ from such samples have positive biases.

From the representation in Figure 3 of two cross sections where the wage differences *within* each are small, note the implicit estimates of the relative capital intensity of the "technologies." Because of the bias to $\hat{\sigma}$

[2] Solow, R. M., "Capital, Labor and Income in Manufacturing," *The Behavior of Income Shares,* Studies in Income and Wealth 27, Princeton University Press for National Bureau of Economic Research, 1964.

the intercept is larger for the sample with the lower-capital labor ratios and lower wage rates. The intercept would be the estimate of $\sigma \log \kappa/(1 - \kappa)$. Increases in κ are increases in the capital-using nature of the technology. Cross-section 2, with the lower capital-labor ratios and lower real wage costs appears to have a more capital-using technology! If $\hat{\sigma}$ is biased upward this somewhat paradoxical result should arise for cross-section regressions of one industry at different points in time and for cross sections at one point in time for observations with equally narrow wage differentials. The implications for the simultaneous cross sections explain the estimates of Fuchs [3] and Arrow.[4] The Fuchs estimates for more homogeneous subsamples are represented by cross-sections 1 and 2. The original Arrow estimate (not shown in the figure) corresponds to the regression on all of the observations.

MURRAY BROWN

There are two points I would like to make on Professor Nerlove's excellent review.

1. In the present volume, both Marc Nerlove and Zvi Griliches state that the elasticity of substitution is a second-order parameter in the analysis of middle-range growth. The inference is drawn that if we were living in a world in which the values of this elasticity were 0.5, say, but we analyze the world as if the elasticity were 1.0, the effect on the middle-range rate of growth of such a misspecification would scarcely be noticed. It can be shown, within the same framework used by Nerlove, Griliches, and Richard Nelson,[1] that the elasticity of substitution is a first-order parameter, and hence the misspecification is potentially serious in the analysis of middle-range growth.

There are two relevant equations in the Nelson derivation:

(2a) $d(\dot{O}/O)/dt = b(1 - b)[(e - 1)/e][(\dot{L}/L) - (\dot{K}/K)]^2,$

(3) $\Delta O/O \sim \Delta A/A + (b_0 \Delta L/L) + (1 - b_0)(\Delta K/K)$
    $+ \frac{1}{2}b_0(1 - b_0)[(e - 1)/e][(\Delta K/K) - (\Delta L/L)]^2,$

[3] V. R. Fuchs, "Capital-Labor Substitution, A Note," *Review of Economics and Statistics,* November 1963.

[4] K. J. Arrow, H. B. Chenery, B. S. Minhas, and R. M. Solow, "Capital-Labor Substitution and Economic Efficiency," *Review of Economics and Statistics,* August 1961.

[1] *Aggregate Production Functions and Medium-Range Growth Projections,* Santa Monica, Cal., The Rand Corporation, December 1963, pp. 49 ff.

where O is output, L is labor, K is capital, b is the elasticity of production with respect to labor, and e is the elasticity of substitution between capital and labor.[2] Equation (2a) "indicates the rate of change of the output growth equation . . . assuming given and constant $\dot{L}/L$ and $\dot{K}/K$. . . ."[3] Equation (3) depicts the rate of growth of output as a function of the growth of labor; and capital, as a function of technological progress, $\Delta \dot{A}/A$, and as a function of the elasticities of substitution and production. The second equation implies that the rate of growth of output will be greater, the greater the elasticity of substitution.

"With the long run elasticity of substitution equal to about 0.5, Equation (2) suggests that the drag of less than unitary elasticity of substitution should have reduced the annual growth rate of output by $<.001$ percentage points a year below what a Cobb-Douglas model would have predicted. The effect would scarcely have been noticed."[4]

The difficulty with this is that not only is equation (2) and the last term in equation (3) affected by the misspecification, but all terms in equation (3) are affected. For b, the elasticity of production with respect to labor, is a function of e, the elasticity of substitution, so that when we misspecify, we misspecify not only second-order terms but first-order terms as well. From the CES production function, we find for b:

(4) $$b = h(O/L)^{(1/e)-1},$$

where h is a constant. Now, combine this with (3), and ignore the second-order term:

(5)
$$\Delta O/O \sim (\Delta A/A) + h(O/L)^{(1/e)-1}(\Delta L/L) + [1 - h(O/L)]^{(1/e)-1}(\Delta K/K).$$

Note that e appears in all terms on the right-hand side except the first. If we assume that $e = 1$, and ignore the second-order term still, equation (5) becomes

(6) $$\Delta O/O \sim (\Delta A'/A') + a(\Delta L/L) + (1 - a)(\Delta K/K),$$

where all variables are as before but a is the constant production elasticity with respect to labor and $A' \neq A$. Suppose we focus on the rate of growth in the base period; then (5) becomes

(7) $$\Delta O/O \sim (\Delta A/A) + h(\Delta L/L) + (1 - h)(\Delta K/K).$$

---

[2] Ibid., p. 52.   [3] Ibid.   [4] Ibid., p. 53.

Clearly, if $a = h$, then the misspecification would not affect the first-order terms and the Nelson-Nerlove-Griliches conclusion would hold. But—and this is the heart of the story—$a \neq h$ when e is taken as 1.0 rather than 0.5, or any value other than unity for that matter.

It is evident that $a \neq h$ whenever $e \neq 1$, but it can be shown simply as follows. Under the above assumptions, $h \rightarrow a$ as $e \rightarrow 1$; i.e., h becomes the labor production elasticity in the Cobb-Douglas world. In other CES worlds, h must differ from a. Hence the rate of growth forecasted by the specification of $e = 1$ would differ from that forecasted by a specification of $e \neq 1$, and the difference in specifications would affect the first-order terms.

Since b in (3) and (4) is the elasticity of production with respect to labor that is independent of the time period—i.e., it applies to short-run, medium-run, and long-run growth—these results show that the elasticity of substitution is a first-order parameter in the analysis of all three types of growth situations. This controverts the assertion that the elasticity of substitution is a second-order parameter, and hence of negligible importance.

2. The condition that technological change be describable by smooth growth in the factor-augmenting terms in order to identify the elasticity of substitution is inferred by Nerlove from the Diamond-McFadden "impossibility" theorem. This condition is unnecessarily restrictive.[5] There is another kind of technological change that is permitted, which together with the smoothness condition accounts for most of the types of technological change that one would be likely to encounter. To see this, suppose that the growth equation (3) on page 95 is sectionally continuous; i.e., suppose that it can be subdivided into a finite number of parts, in each of which F and G are continuous and F and G have finite limits as the arguments approach either endpoint of the subinterval from the interior. This is a modification of the necessary conditions for identification, and it means that the values of the growth equations are permitted to take on finite jumps. In economic terms, these jumps are structural breaks in the growth equation, and can be estimated by a straightforward application of Chow's analysis of covariance.

[5] An alternative method of deriving an "impossibility" theorem was developed by Ryuzo Sato, "The Estimation of Biased Technical Progress and the Production Function," paper presented to the Econometric Society, December 1964.

Returning to equation (3) and remembering that it is continuous by subregions, Nerlove's results then hold by subregions; i.e., the smoothness condition for identification need only hold within subregions. Hence, if there are structural breaks in the growth equation which are ordinary discontinuities, and if that function is sectionally continuous, and if factor-augmenting technological change is smooth within regions, we obtain different elasticities of substitution (these differences may be interpreted as technological changes, also), and we can identify the production function within regions.

NEW APPROACHES TO PRODUCTION FUNCTION ANALYSIS

POSTWAR PRODUCTION RELATIONSHIPS
IN CANADA

N. H. LITHWICK
CARLETON UNIVERSITY

GEORGE POST
BANK OF CANADA

T. K. RYMES
CARLETON UNIVERSITY

Preface

ON May 25, 1966, the Dominion Bureau of Statistics published substantial revisions in its indexes of constant-dollar gross domestic product at factor cost by industry (DBS 61-005, *Annual Supplement to the Monthly Index of Industrial Production*). Time limitations prevented the recalculation of our data to include these revisions. Readers are warned that for a number of major groups in manufacturing, the findings on the investment-output relationship and total factor productivity increase presented in the text of this paper require substantial revision. At the time of publication we were able to include the revised series in several of our key tables. These are presented at the end of our Statistical Appendix, and a brief analysis of the effects these revisions have on our results is carried out. Reworking of our material with the revised data is continuing, and copies of the revised tables will be obtainable from the authors upon request toward the end of 1966.

Introduction

This study attempts to examine postwar production relationships in Canadian manufacturing from several perspectives, reflecting our view that no single approach can adequately explain the complexities involved.

Our initial task has been to try to determine the nature of the capital formation process in manufacturing. This was followed by a calculation of the contributions of labor, capital, and technical change to the growth of manufacturing output. Finally, an attempt was made to set these findings for manufacturing into a longer-run, economy-wide context by reference to several relevant studies.

The analysis of investment behavior employed three models. The first model related net investment directly to net capital stock, whereas the second used the net stock to estimate a capacity series, and the gap between capacity and expected output then was introduced to explain gross investment. The second equation resulted in a generally better fit, but the possibility of trends in investment renders these findings somewhat less significant. Estimates of the adjustment coefficients in these models reveal that it takes several years to arrive at the desired capital output relationship through adjustments in the stock of capital. The final function involved an attempt to estimate whether technological advance had in part been embodied in new capital. Our findings for Canadian manufacturing lend no support to the embodiment hypothesis.

Our second section was devoted to estimating the contribution of measured factor inputs and their productivity advance to the growth of output in the thirteen major groups in manufacturing. In conducting the analysis, we introduced a number of different assumptions about our variables, including such things as the lives of the capital goods, various labor measures, different allocations of the income of incorporated enterprises and different measures of output. The results suggest such great variability in the growth rate of "total factor productivity" under the various assumptions that we conclude that much more refined concepts and more reliable data are required to enable us to choose the most accurate variables from the bewildering variety we have found necessary to consider. The final part of this section contains an attempt to check on the growth rate of total factor productivity by inverting the usual procedure which uses deflated "real" values and replacing it with a model using factor and product prices. While our results were not entirely satisfactory, the technique developed should be considered as a necessary check on the more customary procedure.

The final section surveys several Cobb-Douglas type functions which have been applied to the total economy as well as the major sectors. They suggest that while manufacturing's growth performance was not spectacular in the postwar period, it did contribute substantially to the growth of aggregate productivity. Also, the higher growth rate of aggregate output and productivity in Canada as compared to the United States is not the result of faster growth in any single industry, but rather reflects the very sharp decline of agriculture in Canada in the postwar period. This interindustry shift from an industry with low productivity levels to more efficient ones, has been a once-and-for-all event, however, suggesting that the past growth rate in aggregate productivity will not be easily attained in the future.

We have presented a rather lengthy statistical appendix, which includes most of the data developed for this study. Finally, a technical appendix has been added, which gives the theoretical arguments that underlie the procedures we have followed.

1. Capital Inputs and Investment Decisions

In this section of the paper we analyze the investment expenditures by Canadian manufacturing establishments in the postwar period. We are interested in the investment process because it is the means by which businessmen adjust the existing capital stock to attain the optimum stock. By analyzing investment expenditures we attempt to make inferences about what capital stock the business planners regard as the equilibrium stock at any given time. We do not know actual retirements and use the perpetual inventory estimates of stock in our calculations. This procedure does not, of course, give us an independent estimate of the size of the stock, but we can derive a view about the desired relationship between actual output and actual stock as measured by the perpetual inventory method.

We must recognize at once that in planning production over any immediate period like a month or a quarter the businessman has very limited scope for adjusting his capital stock. For a major change of the capital stock, it is only in the longer time context of a year or two years that redundant assets can be sold or scrapped and new assets can be ordered, constructed, installed, and started up. Hence the relationship between output and capital input during any particular year is determined by historical factors and may not correspond closely to the relationship that would represent an optimum in the light of relative factor prices from the planner's point of view. This result is particularly to be expected where output is subject to large variations that are inherently difficult to forecast.

The relationship which, in a sense, is under the control of the business planner is the one between expected output and the capital stock in some future period. The expected volume of output is the sum of expected sales plus desired inventory changes; therefore, its actual realization is influenced by price policies, advertising expenditures, and actual inventory buildups. Nevertheless, for most manufacturing firms and industries it appears that the principal determinant of output variation is the fluctuation of the level of aggregate demand and variations in the elasticity of demand for the product through changes in substitute products—both elements which are largely beyond the control of the planner. The desired capital stock at some future time is within the control of the planner subject to financial and physical constraints as to how rapidly the existing stock can be reduced or augmented. These constraints impose themselves on planners as sharply rising marginal costs so that at any specific time there is an optimum rate at which to change the capital stock. This optimum rate is achieved when the increment to expected profit from having a more rapid adjustment of the capital stock is equal to the marginal cost of hastening the adjustment.[1]

Many economists have attempted to find empirical evidence of the influence of the availability of investment goods and financial resources on investment expenditures. These investigations have been hampered by lack of relevant data on the marginal costs of funds and assets to individual firms. In this study we have not attempted to include considerations of the supply of investment goods in our investigation, nor have we been able to include the impact of new products and new processes which render existing equipment obsolete and require an enlargement of the physical capital stock.

We have used two simple models of the investment expenditure process in our attempt to derive inferences about the desired capital stock in the postwar period. One model uses net capital expenditures as the dependent variable, and the other model uses gross expenditures. The net investment figure is arrived at by deducting from gross capital

---

[1] An interesting analysis of the determinants of the speed of the capital stock adjustment process is given by R. Eisner and R. Strotz, "Determinants of Business Investment," in *Impacts of Monetary Policy,* a series of research studies prepared for the Commission on Money and Credit, Princeton, N.J., 1963, pp. 64–87.

expenditures the estimated annual depreciation charge used in calculating the net capital stock estimates.

We suppose that

(1) $$I_{nt} = \alpha(N_t^* - N_{t-1})$$

where I_{nt} is net investment, N_t^* is the net capital stock that would be optimal at the end of period t, N_{t-1} is the actual capital stock at the beginning of period t, and α is the adjustment coefficient. The capital stock data used are perpetual inventory estimates prepared by the DBS using the Set I assumptions about asset lives.[2] All these data are expressed in 1949 dollars. The desired capital stock N_t^* is assumed to depend on the quantity of output that is expected in future periods. The equation is

(2) $$N_t^* = f(O_{t+1}^*, O_{t+2}^*, \cdots, O_{t+n}^*)$$

where O_{t+1}^* is the level of output that it is anticipated can be profitably sold in period $t + 1$. This level of anticipated profitable output depends, of course, on the level and elasticity of demand at expected prices and the expected prices for material and labor inputs, as well as on the current costs of financing and capital goods. If the desired stock can be attained in a single period, then the desired stock this period will be influenced only by expected output next period. To the extent that capital stock changes this year are part of a long-term adjustment that cannot be completed in a single period, then the output expected two or more periods in the future will influence the stock that is currently desired. Because we believe that O_{t+1}^*, O_{t+2}^*, and so on will be formulated on the basis of the currently available information they will be strongly correlated. Hence we assume

(2a) $$N_t^* = \beta O_{t+1}^*$$

where β is the optimal capital-output ratio.

A more realistic and detailed model of investment decisions might explicitly recognize that O_{t+1}^* is subject to uncertainty, and attempt to take its distribution into account perhaps by introducing an expected loss function that would weight the costs of too large a stock against those of too small a stock.

The difficult step for us, as for the business planner, is to relate ex-

---

[2] The basic data underlying this paper are described in the attached Statistical Appendix. The alternative life assumptions used in the estimation of the capital stock are given in Table SA–9.

pected output to currently available information. We suppose that this estimate will be based primarily on the past performance of the output series itself.

(3) $O_{t+1}^* = g(O_{t-1}, O_{t-2}, \cdots, O_{t-m})$

Ideally we should like to make expected output depend upon the whole history of past output and in particular to take account of past discrepancies between expected and actual levels of output. We are restrained here by the relatively few observations available in the postwar period and by the fact that the level of sales in one year is related to the level in earlier years.

We have assumed the simple relationship

(3a) $O_{t+1}^* = a + bO_{t-1} + c\Delta O_t$

The inclusion of ΔO_t assumes that the planner has some knowledge of the level of actual output during the current year, but this does not seem unlikely given knowledge of advance orders and market data.

In our analysis we have explored two different measures of output; the gross value of shipments by manufacturing establishments in 1949 dollars and the gross domestic product originating in these manufacturing industries in 1949 dollars. The two concepts gave broadly similar results when the relative magnitudes of the two series are taken into account. We shall report here only the results derived when O_t measured gross domestic product.

Substituting (3a) and (2a) into (1) we have

(4) $I_{nt} = \alpha[\beta(a + bO_{t-1} + c\Delta O_t) - N_{t-1}]$
$$= A + BO_{t-1} + c\Delta O_t - \alpha N_{t-1}$$

We anticipated that the sign of O_{t-1} and ΔO_t would be positive and the sign for N_{t-1} would be negative. For only one of the thirteen industries was the coefficient of ΔO_t significantly positive at the 95 per cent level. Hence this variable was deleted, and the regression coefficients re-estimated. The results of the regressions based on this simple capital stock adjustment model are presented in Table 1.

It may be noted from Table 1 that this very simple regression has the signs we anticipated for all industries except clothing and miscellaneous manufacturing.[3] In six of the thirteen regressions, however, R^2 adjusted

---

[3] There is reason to believe that underestimation of output in the clothing industry may account for the unexpected results there.

TABLE 1

Estimated Regression Coefficients (millions of 1949 dollars)

	O_{t-1}	N_{t-1}	Constant	$\bar{R}^2$	$\bar{S}$	Durbin-Watson Ratio	Mean Net Investment	Stand. Deviation I_n
Food and beverages	0.520 (5.878)	−0.303 (−5.763)	−41.464	0.709	4.334	2.132	44.715	8.363
Tobacco, rubber, and leather products	0.135 (1.508)	−0.128 (−0.989)	−2.547	0.070	2.861	0.943	4,631	3.088
Textile products	0.078 (0.985)	−0.282 (−4.476)	78.344	0.657	4.675	1.244	6.369	8.311
Clothing	−0.101 (−4.474)	−0.081 (−0.850)	40.256	0.677	1.569	2.211	0.408	2.875
Wood products	0.157 (1.767)	−0.170 (−1.707)	7.821	0.011	4.726	2.085	10.285	4.945
Paper products	1.301 (3.244)	−0.380 (−3.269)	−191.144	0.377	29.276	1.136	55.085	38.605
Printing, publishing, and allied industries	0.184 (1.215)	−0.156 (−1.088)	1.672	0.000	4.585	2.263	10.285	4.512
Iron and steel products	0.265 (2.179)	−0.082 (−1.158)	−81.718	0.274	20.016	1.910	45.985	24.443
Transportation equipment	0.193 (4.264)	−0.123 (−2.816)	−28.317	0.539	10.797	2.098	19.439	16.549
Nonferrous metal products and electrical apparatus and supplies	0.584 (5.573)	−0.375 (−5.087)	−2.627	0.684	14.686	2.256	32.639	27.200
Nonmetallic minerals and products of petroleum and coal	1.351 (3.071)	−0.422 (−2.782)	−34.366	0.432	20.480	1.684	66.239	28.286
Chemical products	0.921 (1.390)	−0.424 (−1.369)	−8.775	0.000	30.871	1.371	40.331	30.784
Miscellaneous manufacturing	−0.011 (−0.226)	0.152 (0.990)	−6.073	0.268	1.173	2.262	2.315	1.427
Total manufacturing	0.565 (4.197)	−0.290 (−3.891)	−668.579	0.540	86.270	2.238	338.715	132.384

Note: The observations cover the period 1948 to 1960. The *t*-values of the estimated regression coefficients are given in parentheses. The 5 per cent significance level for *t* in a one-tailed test is 1.81. The 5 per cent significance for $\bar{R}^2$ is .340. The lower and upper 5 per cent significance points for the Durbin-Watson test for positive serial correlation with 15 observations are 0.95 and 1.54.

for degrees of freedom is not significantly different from zero. The co-efficient of N_{t-1}, which is $-\alpha$, the adjustment coefficient, lies between .08 and .42 for those industries where the regression plane is significant. A value for α of 0.30 implies the actual capital stock will be 76 per cent adjusted to a once-and-for-all shift in the desired stock at the end of four years.

In an effort to explain a greater part of the variation of net investment, alternative hypotheses were specified. On the presumption that financial factors influence ideas about the desired capital stock, a corporate interest rate variable was introduced. Alternatively, an estimated rate of return to capital series was included. Both of these variables had significant coefficients with the expected signs for only a few industries and were deleted.

In an effort to discover the influence of technological change on the desired capital stock an explicit vintage variable, the average age of capital in the net stock, was included in equation (4). Again, the coefficient of this variable behaved erratically, and the variable was deleted. Equation (4) was also formulated into a Koyck-type distributed lag, but the estimated lag coefficient was greater than unity for some industries, and this equation was dropped.

Although the regression equation that has been fitted is a stochastic rather than an exact relation one may estimate a value for $N_t{}^*$ for each year using the estimated values of the parameters in (4).[4] As an example we take the estimated equation for total manufacturing investment:

$$I_{nt} = -668.6 + 0.565\, O_{t-1} - 0.290\, N_{t-1}$$

From (2) and (3)

$$N_t{}^* = \beta(a + bO_{t-1})$$
$$= \beta a + \beta bO_{t-1}$$

Therefore from (4)

$$\beta a = \frac{A}{\alpha} = \frac{-668.6}{.290} = -2305.445$$

$$\beta b = \frac{B}{\alpha} = \frac{.565}{.290} = 1.948$$

so that $N_t{}^* = -2305.4 + 1.948\, O_{t-1}$.

---

[4] See B. G. Hickman, "On a New Method of Capacity Estimation," *Journal of the American Statistical Association,* June 1964, pp. 529–49, where the capacity of the existing capital stock is inferred by a similar procedure.

The values of N_t^* for total manufacturing for the period 1948 to 1960 are given in Table 2 and compared with the original series for N_t. This is obviously not an independent estimate of the net capital stock but is rather an inference about the discrepancies which existed over this period between actual and desired net capital stock drawn from the series of net investment and our hypotheses about the nature of the investment process.

There seems little doubt that the desired capital stock for total manufacturing is underestimated by this method for the years 1948–50. These were years when many types of consumer goods were in relatively short supply and when prices were rising rapidly. Business planners may have had relatively pessimistic expectations in these early years, but it is more likely that the actual volume of investment was constrained by the availability of capital goods. The desired capital stock for each industry may be calculated by a similar procedure. The average of the annual percentage differences for each industry is presented in Table 3. The mean discrepancies are large in those industries, like iron and steel and miscellaneous manufacturing, where the regressions are not a good fit to the observed investment series.

In the second set of regressions we used gross investment (I_{gt}) as the dependent variable. Instead of introducing the net stock of capital as an explanatory variable we used it to calculate an estimate of capacity and made investment depend on the difference between expected output and actual capacity.

$$(5) \qquad I_{gt} = \delta(U_{t-1} - O_{t+1}^*) + EG_{t-1}$$

where U_{t-1} is capacity output at the middle of the preceding year, and G_{t-1} is gross capital stock at the beginning of the period. We shall refer to the difference U_{t-1} minus O_{t+1}^* as expected excess capacity. We suppose that replacement is a constant proportion, E, of the gross capital stock, G_t, regardless of age or technical change and wish to estimate this proportion directly. One reason for using this equation was to estimate the parameters of a regression equation that had already been fitted to data for U.S. manufacturing by Alice Bourneuf.[5]

In her article Bourneuf uses the direct estimates of capacity collected by the McGraw-Hill Company to derive the excess capacity variable.

---

[5] "Manufacturing Investment, Excess Capacity and the Rate of Growth of Output," *American Economic Review*, September 1964, pp. 607–25.

TABLE 2

Net Capital Stock, Total Manufacturing, 1948-60

	Desired Capital Stock N_t^*	Actual Capital Stock N_t	Percentage Difference $\dfrac{N_t^* - N_t}{N_t}$
1948	5,091.3	4,604.6	10.6
1949	5,416.6	4,818.6	12.4
1950	5,630.9	4,968.0	13.3
1951	6,123.0	5,317.1	15.2
1952	6,821.3	5,774.8	18.1
1953	7,099.1	6,187.4	14.7
1954	7,726.2	6,457.1	19.7
1955	7,448.4	6,782.3	9.8
1956	8,384.8	7,367.9	13.8
1957	9,210.2	7,937.3	16.0
1958	9,035.6	8,197.6	10.2
1959	8,860.9	8,460.8	4.7
1960	9,583.2	8,717.6	9.9
Mean percentage difference			13.0

Note: Method of calculating N_t^* is described in the text.

TABLE 3

Mean Percentage Difference Between Desired and Actual Stock,
By Industries, 1948-60

	Per Cent
Food and beverages	11.4
Tobacco, rubber, and leather	18.2
Textile products	5.4
Clothing	4.6
Wood products	14.6
Paper products	9.3
Printing and publishing	26.2
Iron and steel	66.0
Transportation equipment	30.9
Nonferrous metals	6.5
Nonmetallic minerals	12.4
Chemical products	13.6
Miscellaneous manufacturing	−26.5
Total manufacturing	13.0

We have used the estimate of net capital stock to derive estimates of capacity output. This will make a comparison of the coefficients of the excess capacity variables based on the different sets of data of some interest to us.

For these regressions we derived an estimate of capacity output, U_t, by making very simple assumptions about the output-capital ratio at capacity. After examining the ratios of actual output to net capital stock for the postwar period, it was decided that this ratio appeared to be quite stable for seven industries and that 1955 or 1956 was a year that represented full capacity utilization.[6] The output-capital ratio for the chosen year was multiplied by the net stock value in each year to obtain a capacity series. For six industries [7] and total manufacturing there appeared to be a persistent trend in this ratio, and so a trend line was fitted to the output-capital ratios for the two years 1948 and 1956, and the values along this trend were used to transform the stock series into a capacity output series.[8]

(6) $$U_t = k_t N_t$$

where k_t is the output-capital stock ratio. To make U_t comparable with O_t, net stock at midyear was used in this calculation.[9]

Substituting (3a) and (6) into (5) we have

(7) $$I_{gt} = \delta[k_{t-1}N_{t-1} - (a + bO_{t-1} + c\Delta O_t)] + EG_{t-1}$$
$$= -\delta a + \delta k_{t-1}N_{t-1} - \delta bO_{t-1} - \delta c\Delta O_t + EG_{t-1}$$

It is clear when the equation is specified this way that this model is basically the same as the stock adjustment hypothesis we postulated above. Because we wish to estimate depreciation directly, problems can be expected from the inclusion of both the net and the gross capital

[6] The 1955 ratio was used for the tobacco, rubber, and leather products major group and for the nonferrous metal products and electrical apparatus major group.

[7] These six industries were food and beverages, textiles, paper products, iron and steel, chemicals, and miscellaneous manufacturing. The trend through the ratios for 1947 and 1956 was used for the miscellaneous manufacturing industry.

[8] To the extent that capacity was not utilized to the same degree in 1948 as in 1956 this trend line will be biased. The trend for all industries except miscellaneous manufacturing was one of falling output per dollar of net capital stock. Looking at the components of the estimated stock, one notes for most industries that the amount of output for each dollar of machinery and equipment fell considerably over the 1948–56 period, while the output per dollar of building and construction rose slightly.

[9] The estimates of capacity output and excess capacity are presented in Table SA–1.

stock variables. Since both capital stock measures are accumulated totals of past capital expenditures with relatively long lives we can expect the levels of these two series to follow similar patterns.[10] We considered the inclusion of the average age variable to explain replacement demand, but found that it was also collinear with the net stock variable, and so decided to adopt Bourneuf's model, in which the net capital variable is incorporated in the excess capacity variable—the difference between capacity and actual output. This variable, $U_t - O_t$, is not collinear with G_{t-1}. We have, in effect, constrained the coefficient b in (3a) and (7) to equal 1.0. This implies that future output is expected to be equal to lagged output plus some fraction of the current change in output. The regression to be estimated becomes

$$(8) \qquad I_{gt} = D + EG_{t-1} + F(U_{t-1} - O_{t-1}) + H\Delta O_t$$

We expect F to be a negative coefficient ($F = \delta$) and E and H to be positive. The coefficients estimated for this equation are given in Table 4.

For nine of the thirteen industries and for total manufacturing F is significantly negative while E is significantly positive for ten industries and the total. E is, however, rather larger than expected in most equations.[11] The coefficient of ΔO_t is significantly positive for only four industries, although it has the wrong sign in only two cases.

When interpreting the coefficients of this second set of regressions the reader should recall that the k_t parameter was also estimated from these same data and hence used additional degrees of freedom.[12]

The coefficient of $(U_{t-1} - O_{t-1})$ for the total manufacturing regression implies that if the difference between capacity output and actual output falls by a million dollars gross investment would increase by $664,000. This coefficient is over twice as large as that estimated by Bourneuf using the U.S. excess capacity series. This is to be expected since the direct estimate of excess capacity for the United States is larger

---

[10] Griliches has argued that both the net and gross measures should be included (see "Capital Stock in Investment Functions: Some Problems of Concept and Measurement," in C. Christ *et al.* (ed.), *Measurement in Economics, Studies in Mathematical Economics and Econometrics in Memory of Yehuda Grunfeld,* Stanford, 1963, pp. 115–37).

[11] In interpreting the coefficient E it should be noted that this is an estimate of replacement expenditures which corresponds to a straight-line depreciation procedure.

[12] The $\bar{R}^2$, $\bar{S}$, and t estimated in Table 4 have not been adjusted for the loss of degrees of freedom in estimating k_t.

TABLE 4

Estimated Regression Coefficients

	$(U_{t-1}-O_{t-1})$	G_{t-1}	ΔO_t	Constant	$\bar{R}^2$	$\bar{S}$	Durbin-Watson Ratio	Mean Gross Investment	Standard Deviation I_g
Food and beverages	-0.373 (-6.296)	0.024 (3.948)	0.018 (0.131)	61.146	0.883	3.755	2.139	91.215	11.443
Tobacco, rubber, and leather products	-0.278 (2.762)	0.066 (3.505)	0.144 (1.899)	-1.318	0.639	2.474	1.391	17.277	4.288
Textile products	-0.069 (-0.631)	-0.133 (-3.160)	-0.010 (-0.118)	108.562	0.483	5.332	1.314	28.777	7.721
Clothing	0.009 (0.296)	-0.118 (-4.785)	0.045 (1.062)	39.119	0.708	1.318	2.567	11.085	2.538
Wood products	-0.191 (-2.348)	0.066 (2.520)	0.154 (1.953)	-2.681	0.261	4.383	1.731	34.908	5.308
Paper products	-1.699 (-4.857)	0.157 (4.617)	0.405 (0.883)	-124.826	0.655	22.629	1.523	117.815	40.101
Printing, publishing, and allied industries	-0.206 (-1.137)	0.085 (1.649)	0.151 (0.689)	-7.941	-0.104	4.928	2.187	22.385	4.881
Iron and steel products	-0.427 (-5.157)	0.181 (8.019)	0.268 (4.026)	-101.912	0.829	12.666	1.171	100.600	31.894

(continued)

TABLE 4 (concluded)

	$(U_{t-1}-O_{t-1})$	G_{t-1}	ΔO_t	Constant	$\bar{R}^2$	$\bar{S}$	Durbin-Watson Ratio	Mean Gross Investment I_g	Standard Deviation I_g
Transportation equipment	-0.196 (6.294)	0.214 (5.266)	0.147 (3.145)	-114.858	0.751	7.849	2.016	45.200	16.375
Nonferrous metal products and electrical apparatus and supplies	-0.547 (-6.020)	0.084 (5.085)	0.104 (0.770)	9.380	0.762	14.112	2.072	83.385	30.114
Nonmetallic minerals and products of petroleum and coal	-1.326 (-5.332)	0.173 (7.683)	0.924 (3.848)	-85.399	0.847	13.010	1.726	104.485	34.663
Chemical products	-2.751 (-3.728)	0.085 (2.756)	2.111 (1.925)	-26.667	0.499	22.533	1.363	72.377	33.122
Miscellaneous manufacturing	0.132 (1.532)	0.129 (5.405)	-0.074 (-0.982)	-5.228	0.687	1.247	2.235	8.685	2.319
Total manufacturing	-0.664 (-7.762)	0.148 (9.848)	0.364 (4.368)	-747.561	0.878	54.257	1.270	738.231	161.951

Note: All variables are measured in millions of 1949 dollars. The observations cover the period 1948 to 1960. t-values of the estimated regression coefficients are given in parentheses. The 5 per cent significance level for t in a one-tailed test is 1.83. The 5 per cent significance level for $\bar{R}^2$ is .416. The lower and upper 5 per cent significance points for the Durbin-Watson test for positive serial correlation with 15 observations are 0.82 and 1.75.

than the estimate we devised by assuming 100 per cent utilization of capacity in 1948 and 1956. If we had assumed, say, that only 95 per cent of total capacity was used in these years excess capacity in absolute terms would have been higher over the entire period; and the coefficient F, correspondingly lower.

What can we conclude from these two sets of simple regressions? We have very strong evidence that the existing net capital stock, as we have measured it, is significantly related to the investment expenditures over this period, as we expected it would be. In general the second equation explaining gross investment gave a better fit. This might suggest that our estimate of replacement investment is too mechanical and hence leaves the net investment series with relatively large variations to be explained. In total manufacturing, for example, mean net investment is less than one-half of mean gross investment, but the standard deviation of net investment is 82 per cent of the standard deviation of gross investment. On the other hand, the direct estimate of the depreciation appears too high, suggesting that there may be a trend component of investment that is contributing to the coefficient of G_{t-1}. When a trend variable was explicitly included in equation (8) the coefficient of G_{t-1} was reduced in all but four major groups and was estimated to be significant at the 95 per cent level in only two regressions.

INVESTMENT AND TECHNICAL CHANGE

In our investment regressions we measured the capital stock at its costs in 1949 dollars less accumulated straight-line depreciation. We made no attempt to adjust the stock for quality changes. The question naturally arises: Is there any way we can use these data to determine the extent to which technological change has operated to make new additions to the capital stock more productive than earlier additions? One technique that is possible is to relate output per unit of labor input to additions to the capital stock. This procedure assumes that some components of this partial productivity measure are systematically related to the size of the capital stock and to the replacement of old assets by new ones. That is

(9)
$$\frac{O_t}{L_t} = f(N_{t-1}, A_{t-1})$$

where L_t is the number of workers employed in year t and A_{t-1} represents the average age of assets at the beginning of the period. Because age and net stock tend to be highly correlated it was decided to specify this relation in a first-difference form and to use gross investment and drop the age variable. To recognize that output per worker is subject to strong short-term cyclical variation as the level of production deviates from the optimum level of capacity utilization, the change in the level of output was included as an explanatory variable. The equation that was fitted to the data for each industry was

(10) $$\Delta \frac{O_t}{L_t} = R + SI_{gt-1} + T\Delta O_t$$

Gross capital expenditures were used as the independent variable in this regression because both the net addition of assets and the replacement of old assets would be expected to embody technical change. The coefficients estimated in these regressions are summarized in Table 5.

It is surprising that there appears to be no significant relationship between investment this year and the change in output per employee next year. At the same time there is a significantly positive relationship between changes in output and output per worker in ten of the regressions. This implies that, in the short run at least, the business cycle, rather than improved capital equipment, tends to be the dominant influence on labor productivity measures.

In his recent study, Hickman has used a trend variable to measure the influence of steady technical progress on the capital-output ratio.[13] By introducing a time trend into our equation (2a) we can similarly hypothesize that the relation between desired stock and expected sales is

$$N_t^* = \beta O_{t+1}^* + Et$$

Hickman finds that for most of the industries he studied the coefficient of the trend was negative, indicating that technical progress was sufficiently rapid to reduce the equilibrium amount of capital per unit of output. When a time trend was added to the first regression equation summarized in Table 1 the coefficient of this trend variable was significantly different from zero at the 95 per cent level in only four cases when it

---

[13] Bert G. Hickman, *Investment Demand and U.S. Economic Growth*, Washington, D.C., 1965. The basic regression model used in this study is specified as a log-linear relation which is, in our notation,

$$\log N_t - \log N_{t-1} = \log a + b_1 \log O_t^* + b_2 \log P_t^* + b_3 t - b_4 \log N_{t-1}$$

and P_t^* refers to the "normal" level of relative prices.

TABLE 5

Estimated Regression Coefficients, Change in Output per Worker Employed

	I_{gt-1}	ΔO_t	Constant	$\bar{R}^2$	$\bar{S}$	Durbin-Watson Ratio	Mean Change Output per Worker	Standard Deviation of Change
Food and beverages	−0.192 (−0.092)	6.787 (3.341)	−62.290	0.422	73.824	1.745	77.541	101.065
Tobacco, rubber, and leather products	4.454 (0.913)	9.407 (6.795)	−16.339	0.773	64.763	2.648	92.344	141.386
Textile products	−1.749 (−0.369)	6.589 (3.667)	134.595	0.463	142.788	2.288	115.351	202.853
Clothing	−0.915 (−0.174)	4.467 (3.200)	30.696	0.370	56.945	2.148	34.393	74.668
Wood products	−2.190 (−0.409)	2.406 (1.492)	133.121	0.173	77.609	2.354	78.120	88.829
Paper products	0.953 (0.929)	9.201 (3.713)	−173.913	0.560	101.176	2.015	103.187	158.675
Printing, publishing, and allied industries	5.949 (0.903)	7.076 (1.613)	−132.613	−0.031	99.090	1.944	63.979	101.589
Iron and steel products	−0.162 (−0.096)	2.383 (3.333)	28.440	0.551	134.758	1.814	61.142	209.220
Transportation equipment	−2.705 (−0.679)	0.515 (0.415)	197.201	−0.160	212.500	2.162	83.721	205.354

(continued)

TABLE 5 (concluded)

	I_{gt-1}	ΔO_t	Constant	$\bar{R}^2$	$\bar{S}$	Durbin–Watson Ratio	Mean Change Output per Worker	Standard Deviation of Change
Nonferrous metal products and electrical apparatus and supplies	2.129 (1.342)	3.340 (2.095)	−130.106	0.111	159.616	1.661	127.264	176.218
Nonmetallic minerals and products of petroleum and coal	1.015 (1.000)	6.921 (3.013)	32.987	0.334	124.776	1.457	285.449	159.159
Chemical products	−0.275 (−0.177)	18.852 (3.164)	−87.929	0.420	159.114	1.930	271.469	217.489
Miscellaneous manufacturing	−12.719 (−1.266)	15.823 (5.337)	62.384	0.662	64.211	2.023	59.593	114.988
Total manufacturing	0.143 (0.842)	0.366 (2.770)	−65.889	0.298	79.410	2.111	102.484	98.619

Note: The dependent variable is the change in dollars of gross domestic product (in constant 1949 prices) per worker. Gross investment and output are measured in millions of 1949 dollars. The regressions are based on the period 1948 to 1960. t-values for the regression coefficients are given in parentheses. The 5 per cent level of significance for t in a one-tailed test is 1.81. The 5 per cent level of significance for $\bar{R}^2$ is .340. The lower and upper 5 per cent significance points for the Durbin–Watson test for positive serial correlation with 15 observations are 0.95 and 1.54.

had a positive sign. We conclude that these regressions do not supply any evidence of embodied technological improvement which has reduced the capital-output ratio in Canadian manufacturing. One of the essential differences between our results and those of Hickman is that the two measures of net stock differ. In general, Hickman's life assumptions are shorter than those underlying the DBS Set I estimates and are based on declining balance depreciation while the Canadian estimates use straight-line depreciation assumptions. He assumes further that average useful lives have been shorter since 1946 than they were in the prewar period.

We also inserted a time trend in our second regression model summarized in Table 4. In only two cases was the partial regression coefficient significantly different from zero. In eight regressions the coefficient was positive and in six, negative. We have already mentioned that this time variable appeared to be collinear with the gross stock variable in this second model.

CONCLUSIONS

We want now briefly to summarize Part I. Our objective in this section of the paper was to throw light indirectly on the role of capital stock in Canadian manufacturing by studying the capital stock adjustment process, i.e., net investment. We demonstrated in our first set of regressions that investment decisions for most industries are related by a very simple model to current levels of output. Our estimates of the adjustment coefficient imply that several years will be required to attain a desired level of capital stock under conditions of real world uncertainty. Our second model, which uses the net capital stock estimate to derive a series for capacity and then relates investment to the gap between capacity and actual output, explains a larger part of the total variation of investment. This model too implies that a period of several years will be required before the optimum relation between capacity and actual output will be attained. This second model does suggest the importance of capacity utilization variables to explain capital expenditures. Our hope to estimate replacement investment directly was probably doomed to failure because the life assumptions of the perpetual inventory method are reflected in the gross capital stock series.

We might conceivably have used these investment regressions as a device to evaluate the alternative estimates of the capital stock that have been prepared by the DBS. Before doing this, however, one would have to be confident that the regression relation was fully and correctly specified. It is conceivable that the set of capital stock estimates that would give the "best fit" with one model might not give the "best fit" with some alternative model. The difficult task of evaluating the life assumptions underlying the alternative capital stock estimates still lies in the future. We have a very great need in Canada for more detailed first-hand knowledge of asset lives and the economic forces that affect them.

Finally, we sought evidence in the investment experience that output per unit of labor had been increasing over time due to the embodiment of technical change in newer capital goods. In Table 5 we summarized a set of regressions which failed to attribute increments of output per worker to recent investment and hence threw doubt on the assertion that output increases result from embodied technical change. The inclusion of time trends in both of our earlier regression models also failed to present any clear evidence that the equilibrium amount of capital (unadjusted for quality) per unit of output was falling over time. This latter contrasts with Hickman's findings which he interpreted as indicating the presence of smooth disembodied technical change. Further work is required to decide if the difference between the measure of the net capital stock we used and that used by Hickman could have accounted for this different conclusion. The difference between the two measures of net stock is basically a matter of the asset life assumptions and depreciation rates assumed.

II. *Total Measured Factor Productivity, 1946–60*

In this section we examine "total measured factor productivity" at a disaggregated level within the Canadian manufacturing sector. In the Technical Appendix attached to this paper, we set forth our reasons for the various output and input measures which we use. The main set of our estimates are for the period 1946 to 1956; deal with thirteen combined major groups in Canadian manufacturing; use constant-1949-dollar gross domestic product at factor cost as the output measure, employees and paid man-hours as alternate labor input measures, and constant dollar net stock of fixed capital, inventories, and capital consumption allowances as the relevant capital input measures.

In this section, we are in particular concerned with the effects which different assumptions about the average economic lives of fixed capital goods have upon estimates of "total measured factor productivity."

Constant-dollar gross domestic product in manufacturing rose over the period from $3.5 billion to $6.1 billion. This expansion in output was interrupted in 1954 and in 1957 and 1958 when output fell from its 1956 level of $5.9 billion to $5.8 billion and $5.7 billion respectively, rose again in 1959 to $6.1 billion and showed a very moderate decline in 1960. As Chart SA-1 indicates, the interruption in the advance in output which occurred after 1956 was more widely shared among the major groups than was the minor interruption which occurred in 1954.

Even more striking is the sharp decline in gross fixed capital formation measured in constant 1949 dollars which accompanied the decline in output in 1957 and 1958. Total gross fixed capital formation in manufacturing fell from a 1956–57 level of slightly more than $1 billion to about $750 million in 1958–59. The food and beverages major group was exceptional in that a steady increase in capital formation prevailed over the period while every other major group suffered interruptions or declines.

The sharp break in the advance of economic activity in Canadian manufacturing in 1956–57 suggests that changes in estimated total measured factor productivity in the latter part of the 1946-to-1960 period would require careful interpretation. Clearly, in the late 1950s a part of the capital stock in Canadian manufacturing was in some sense underemployed. Yet, as is discussed in the Technical Appendix, it is hard to see how our capital input measures (the net stock and capital consumption allowances) could be satisfactorily adjusted to reflect this phenomenon. For this reason, we prefer to focus attention on the 1946–56 period. The estimates for the longer period, 1946 to 1960, are presented largely to show the cyclical sensitivity of estimates of total measured factor productivity.

The format in which our estimates are presented is the identity [14]

$$\frac{\dot{A}}{A} \equiv \frac{\dot{Q}}{Q} - \left[\sum \frac{W_j L_j}{PQ} \left(\frac{\dot{L}_j}{L_j} \right) + \sum_k \frac{r_k P_k{}^N N_k}{PQ} \left(\frac{\dot{N}_k}{N_k} \right) + \sum_l \frac{r_l P_l{}^I I_l}{PQ} \left(\frac{\dot{I}_l}{I_l} \right) \right. $$
$$\left. + \sum_k \frac{P_k D_k}{PQ} \left(\frac{\dot{D}_k}{D_k} \right) \right]$$

---

[14] The derivation of this and other identities which we use is provided in the Technical Appendix.

where
$$\dot{A}/A,\ \dot{Q}/Q,\ \dot{L}_j/L_j,\ \dot{N}_k/N_k,\ \dot{I}_l/I_l,\ \text{and}\ \dot{D}_k/D_k$$

are the proportionate rates of change of total measured factor productivity; constant-dollar gross domestic product at factor cost; the jth component of the labor input; the kth component of the constant-dollar midyear net stock of fixed capital; the lth component of the constant-dollar midyear inventory, and the kth component of the constant-dollar capital consumption allowances. The weights given to the proportionate rates of growth of the measured factor inputs are their respective shares in current-dollar gross domestic product at factor cost in 1949. A full discussion of our output and input measures and factor weights is provided in the Statistical Appendix, but four points about our data should now be made. First, our labor input data are basically of two types, persons employed and paid man-hours. Ideally we would have preferred measures of labor inputs weighted together by market labor prices. In the Statistical Appendix, we provide measures of the labor input where some account is taken of the fact that the labor force is not as homogeneous as a count of persons employed or man-hours paid implies. Second, in constructing our input weights, we have arbitrarily split the net income of unincorporated businesses between returns to labor and returns to capital. Little of the manufacturing activity in Canada is carried on by unincorporated business, and when we replace the arbitrary split used (50:50) in our estimation procedures by different arbitrary divisions, the estimates of total measured factor productivity are affected only negligibly. Third, we have been unable to account for the role of land as a factor input in our estimates. Fourth, in preparing the estimates of the stock of fixed capital in Canadian manufacturing the DBS was confronted by the virtual absence of reliable estimates of the average economic life of capital goods. To investigate what biases the initial set of life assumptions would have had on the levels and rates of growth of the resulting stock estimates if the initial life estimates had been, in fact, too long or too short, four additional sets of capital stock estimates were prepared, based on a range of average economic lives which, it was felt, would bracket the actual lives of capital goods being used.[15] We have included only three sets in our tables and the effects on our total meas-

---

[15] See Table SA–9 in the Statistical Appendix and forthcoming DBS reference paper, *Estimates of Fixed Capital Flows and Stocks, Manufacturing, Canada, 1926–1960.*

ured factor productivity estimates are quite significant. The rates of growth of the capital inputs (both the net stock and capital consumption allowances estimates) are affected by the different average economic lives used to prepare them. The weights for the net stock, inventories, and capital consumption allowances are also affected as different lives are used. Longer lives used in the perpetual inventory estimation of the stock of net fixed capital lead to higher levels of the current-dollar net stock for the year in which the factor weights are constructed and, therefore, relatively lower weights for inventories. Current-dollar capital consumption allowances in the base year may fall or rise as longer lives are used in the "perpetual inventory" method of estimation. Thus the factor input weights for the net midyear stock, midyear inventories, and capital consumption allowances will alter in different directions as different lives are used in estimating fixed capital flows and stocks in Canadian manufacturing.

ESTIMATES OF TOTAL MEASURED FACTOR PRODUCTIVITY

In Table 6, we present the first set of estimates of total measured factor productivity for the periods 1946–56 and 1946–60. The output measure is constant-1949-dollars gross domestic product at factor cost. The estimates reveal (1) the expected cyclical sensitivity of total measured factor productivity, (2) substantial intermajor group variations in measured productivity advance, and (3) considerable sensitivity with respect to assumptions about the average economic lives of fixed capital goods.

The cyclical sensitivity of our estimates shows more clearly in Table 7 and Chart SA-1. It would appear that if 1949 had been chosen as the initial year for the food and beverages and tobacco, rubber, and leather products major groups estimates the recorded advances in total measured factor productivity would have been greater in those major groups. It is interesting to note that the tobacco, rubber, and leather products major group is the only one in manufacturing where the data suggests an absolute decline in the inputs used. If 1949 had been chosen as the initial year for the textiles and clothing major groups as well, the measured productivity performance would again have been more impressive. The textiles major group recorded most uneven productivity advance over the period, and the average advances shown by our estimates do not reveal the disturbances to which the major group was clearly subject. The

TABLE 6

Total Measured Factor Productivity (Gross Domestic Product Basis)
Total Manufacturing and Major Groups, 1946-56 and 1946-60•
(continuous annual rates of change)

Set of Lives	Gross Domestic Product at Factor Cost[a]	Labor Input		Midyear Net Stock of Fixed Capital[a]	Midyear Inventories[a]	Capital Consumption Allowances[a]	Total Measured Factor Input		Total Measured Factor Productivity	
		Employees	Paid Man-Hours				Employees	Paid Man-Hours	Employees	Paid Man-Hours
Total Manufacturing										
1946-56										
I	5.3	2.5	2.0	5.8	4.3	2.8	3.2	2.9	2.1	2.4
III				5.3		2.2	3.1	2.8	2.2	2.5
V				6.4		4.7	3.4	3.1	1.9	2.2
1946-60										
I	4.0	1.4	1.0	5.6	3.8	3.4	2.5	2.2	1.5	1.8
III				5.1		3.0	2.4	2.1	1.6	1.9
V				5.9		4.9	2.7	2.3	1.4	1.7
Food and Beverages										
1946-56										
I	3.1	1.3	0.9	6.4	3.3	3.0	2.5	2.3	0.5	0.8
III				5.9		2.9	2.5	2.2	0.6	0.8
V				7.2		5.0	2.8	2.5	0.3	0.6
1946-60										
I	3.0	1.3	0.9	5.8	3.2	3.3	2.5	2.2	0.6	0.8
III				5.4		3.2	2.4	2.2	0.6	0.9
V				6.2		5.0	2.6	2.4	0.4	0.7

(continued)

TABLE 6 (continued)

Set of Lives	Gross Domestic Product at Factor Cost[a]	Labor Input		Midyear Net Stock of Fixed Capital[a]	Midyear Inventories[a]	Capital Consumption Allowances[a]	Total Measured Factor Input		Total Measured Factor Productivity	
		Employees	Paid Man-Hours				Employees	Paid Man-Hours	Employees	Paid Man-Hours
Tobacco, Rubber and Leather Products										
1946-56	2.6	-0.9	-1.2		2.7					
I				3.5		3.6	0.1	-0.1	2.5	2.8
III				3.4		3.0	0.1	-0.2	2.6	2.8
V				3.1		4.9	0.1	-0.1	2.5	2.7
1946-60	2.0	-1.2	-1.4		1.9					
I				3.3		4.0	-0.2	-0.4	2.2	2.4
III				3.4		3.6	-0.2	-0.4	2.2	2.4
V				2.9		4.3	-0.3	-0.4	2.2	2.4
Textile Products (excl. clothing and fur)										
1946-56	2.8	0.5	0.1		12.3					
I				4.2		1.6	2.1	1.9	0.7	0.9
III				3.8		1.2	2.0	1.7	0.8	1.1
V				5.4		2.3	2.5	2.2	0.3	0.6
1946-60	2.3	-0.6	-1.0		9.4					
I				3.1		1.2	0.9	0.7	1.4	1.6
III				2.8		1.0	0.9	0.6	1.5	1.7
V				3.5		2.2	1.2	0.9	1.1	1.4
Clothing										
1946-56	2.1	0.5	0.4		2.2					
I				2.0		2.1	0.9	0.8	1.2	1.3
III				1.9		0.8	0.8	0.7	1.3	1.4
V				1.3		2.2	0.8	0.7	1.3	1.4

(continued)

TABLE 6 (continued)

Set of Lives	Gross Domestic Product at Factor Cost [a]	Labor Input		Midyear Net Stock of Fixed Capital [a]	Midyear Inventories [a]	Capital Consumption Allowances [a]	Total Measured Factor Input		Total Measured Factor Productivity	
		Employees	Paid Man-Hours				Employees	Paid Man-Hours	Employees	Paid Man-Hours
Clothing (continued)										
1946-60										
I	0.9	0.2	0.0	1.0	1.9	0.9	0.5	0.3	0.4	0.6
III				1.1		1.0	0.5	0.3	0.4	0.6
V				-0.2		1.8	0.3	0.2	0.5	0.7
Wood Products										
1946-56										
I	4.7	2.5	2.0	3.8	3.6	0.9	2.6	2.3	2.0	2.4
III				3.1		-0.7	2.4	2.1	2.2	2.6
V				4.3		3.1	2.8	2.5	1.8	2.2
1946-60										
I	3.2	0.9	0.5	3.4	2.8	1.2	1.3	1.0	1.9	2.2
III				2.9		0.2	1.2	0.9	2.0	2.3
V				3.4		3.1	1.5	1.2	1.7	2.0
Paper Products										
1946-56										
I	5.3	3.3	2.1	6.9	2.7	3.8	4.3	3.6	1.1	1.7
III				6.1		3.0	4.0	3.4	1.3	1.9
V				7.6		7.1	4.8	4.2	0.5	1.2
1946-60										
I	4.3	2.4	1.4	6.3	2.7	4.5	3.7	3.2	0.6	1.1
III				5.8		3.9	3.6	3.0	0.8	1.3
V				6.5		6.8	4.0	3.5	0.3	0.8

(continued)

TABLE 6 (continued)

Set of Lives	Gross Domestic Product at Factor Cost[a]	Labor Input		Midyear Net Stock of Fixed Capital[a]	Midyear Inventories[a]	Capital Consumption Allowances[a]	Total Measured Factor Input		Total Measured Factor Productivity	
		Employees	Paid Man-Hours				Employees	Paid Man-Hours	Employees	Paid Man-Hours
Printing, Publishing, and Allied Industries										
1946-56										
I	5.8	4.0	3.5	4.8	4.4	1.8	4.0	3.7	1.8	2.1
III				4.2		1.4	3.9	3.6	1.9	2.2
V				7.0		3.1	4.4	4.1	1.4	1.7
1946-60										
I	4.6	3.1	2.6	5.0	3.7	2.2	3.3	3.0	1.3	1.6
III				4.4		2.0	3.2	2.9	1.4	1.7
V				6.7		3.7	3.7	3.4	0.9	1.2
Iron and Steel Products										
1946-56										
I	5.9	2.6	2.2	5.8	5.4	2.4	3.3	3.0	2.6	2.9
III				5.3		2.3	3.2	2.9	2.6	2.9
V				6.1		3.7	3.4	3.1	2.4	2.8
1946-60										
I	3.8	1.7	1.2	5.8	4.4	3.5	2.7	2.3	1.1	1.5
III				5.5		3.6	2.6	2.3	1.2	1.5
V				6.1		4.7	2.8	2.4	1.0	1.4
Transportation Equipment										
1946-56										
I	6.7	3.4	3.1	4.2	1.5	-1.1	3.2	2.9	3.6	3.8
III				3.3		-1.5	3.0	2.7	3.8	4.0
V				5.5		1.7	3.5	3.2	3.3	3.5

(continued)

TABLE 6 (continued)

Set of Lives	Gross Domestic Product at Factor Cost[a]	Labor Input		Midyear Net Stock of Fixed Capital[a]	Midyear Inventories[a]	Capital Consumption Allowances[a]	Total Measured Factor Input		Total Measured Factor Productivity	
		Employees	Paid Man-Hours				Employees	Paid Man-Hours	Employees	Paid Man-Hours
Transportation Equipment (continued)										
1946-60	3.4	0.6	0.4		0.4					
I				3.9		-0.2	1.1	0.9	2.3	2.5
III				3.1		-0.2	1.0	0.8	2.4	2.6
V				4.6		2.0	1.3	1.1	2.2	2.3
Nonferrous Metal Products and Electrical Apparatus and Supplies										
1946-56	7.6	5.0	4.5		4.5					
I				3.4		1.1	4.2	3.9	3.3	3.6
III				3.3		0.5	4.1	3.8	3.4	3.7
V				2.7		2.3	4.3	4.0	3.3	3.6
1946-60	5.5	2.6	2.3		5.3					
I				3.6		2.3	2.8	2.6	2.7	3.0
III				3.6		1.9	2.8	2.5	2.8	3.0
V				3.0		3.2	2.9	2.6	2.7	2.9
Nonmetallic Mineral Products and Products of Petroleum and Coal										
1946-56	10.2	4.6	4.3		7.6					
I				10.4		6.9	6.6	6.4	3.6	3.7
III				9.5		6.1	6.3	6.2	3.8	4.0
V				11.7		9.0	7.1	6.9	3.1	3.2
1946-60	8.1	3.5	3.2		6.9					
I				9.8		7.0	5.8	5.6	2.3	2.5
III				9.1		6.2	5.6	5.4	2.5	2.7
V				10.7		8.5	6.1	5.9	2.0	2.2

(continued)

TABLE 6 (concluded)

Set of Lives	Gross Domestic Product at Factor Cost[a]	Labor Input Employees	Labor Input Paid Man-Hours	Midyear Net Stock of Fixed Capital[a]	Midyear Inventories[a]	Capital Consumption Allowances[a]	Total Measured Factor Input Employees	Total Measured Factor Input Paid Man-Hours	Total Measured Factor Productivity Employees	Total Measured Factor Productivity Paid Man-Hours
				Chemical Products						
1946-56										
I	7.0	3.3	2.8	8.8	4.6	7.6	5.2	5.0	1.7	2.0
III				8.2		7.2	5.1	4.8	1.9	2.2
V				10.0		8.9	5.6	5.3	1.4	1.7
1946-60										
I	6.6	2.6	2.2	8.2	3.5	7.4	4.6	4.3	2.0	2.3
III				7.8		7.0	4.5	4.2	2.2	2.4
V				9.0		8.5	4.8	4.6	1.8	2.0
				Miscellaneous Manufacturing Industries						
1946-56										
I	6.1	4.6	4.3	3.2	8.0	2.8	4.6	4.4	1.4	1.6
III				3.2		2.2	4.6	4.4	1.5	1.7
V				2.9		2.8	4.6	4.4	1.4	1.6
1946-60										
I	6.2	4.8	4.6	3.6	8.1	3.4	4.9	4.7	1.4	1.5
III				3.6		3.3	4.8	4.7	1.4	1.6
V				3.6		3.9	4.9	4.8	1.3	1.4

Note: See Table SA-12 for the same series recalculated using the revised output data.

Source: See Statistical Appendix. The three different rates of change of midyear net stock and capital consumption allowances are based on the sets I, III, and V of average economic lives used by the DBS in the forthcoming reference paper, *Estimates of Fixed Capital Flows and Stocks, Manufacturing, Canada, 1926-1960*. For five of the combined major groups (foods and beverages; tobacco, rubber, and leather products; paper products; printing, publishing, and allied industries; and chemical products), the average economic lives used in sets I and II were the same. Continuous annual rates of change in this and subsequent tables are calculated as $(\ln \text{GDP}_{56} - \ln \text{GDP}_{46})/10$.

[a]Measured in constant 1949 dollars.

TABLE 7

Indexes of Constant 1949 Gross Domestic Product and Total Measured Factor Productivity,
Total Manufacturing and Major Groups, 1946-60

(1949 = 1.000)

Year	Total Manufacturing GDP	Total Manufacturing Factor Productivity Employees	Total Manufacturing Factor Productivity Man-Hours	Food and Beverages GDP	Food and Beverages Factor Productivity Employees	Food and Beverages Factor Productivity Man-Hours	Tobacco, Rubber, and Leather Products GDP	Tobacco, Rubber, and Leather Products Factor Productivity Employees	Tobacco, Rubber, and Leather Products Factor Productivity Man-Hours	Textiles GDP	Textiles Factor Productivity Employees	Textiles Factor Productivity Man-Hours
1946	0.852	0.956	0.947	0.980	1.100	1.097	1.045	1.033	1.015	0.887	1.063	1.043
1947	0.932	0.989	0.983	0.972	1.043	1.048	1.124	1.099	1.090	0.940	1.025	1.017
1948	0.973	1.002	0.999	0.985	1.019	1.019	1.026	1.034	1.040	0.973	1.008	1.008
1949	1.000	1.000	1.000	1.000	1.000	1.000	1.000	1.000	1.000	1.000	1.000	1.000
1950	1.062	1.053	1.053	1.038	1.039	1.038	1.049	1.053	1.062	1.125	1.091	1.085
1951	1.150	1.075	1.084	1.068	1.038	1.045	1.038	1.048	1.072	1.131	1.055	1.080
1952	1.185	1.066	1.078	1.135	1.077	1.085	1.089	1.111	1.117	1.029	1.049	1.074
1953	1.264	1.085	1.102	1.174	1.084	1.102	1.179	1.167	1.183	1.079	0.998	1.021
1954	1.229	1.067	1.091	1.206	1.094	1.116	1.122	1.148	1.174	0.943	0.944	0.963
1955	1.347	1.150	1.171	1.268	1.135	1.158	1.252	1.268	1.277	1.140	1.101	1.109
1956	1.451	1.179	1.201	1.331	1.157	1.183	1.358	1.330	1.340	1.173	1.095	1.108
1957	1.429	1.124	1.154	1.356	1.127	1.159	1.368	1.338	1.364	1.176	1.109	1.133
1958	1.407	1.126	1.159	1.419	1.166	1.196	1.349	1.345	1.372	1.096	1.079	1.103
1959	1.498	1.178	1.204	1.476	1.182	1.211	1.476	1.451	1.473	1.244	1.224	1.241
1960	1.493	1.162	1.191	1.502	1.184	1.217	1.379	1.383	1.400	1.225	1.209	1.231

(continued)

TABLE 7 (continued)

Year	Clothing			Wood Products			Paper Products			Printing, Publishing and Allied Industries		
		Factor Productivity			Factor Productivity			Factor Productivity			Factor Productivity	
	GDP	Employees	Man-Hours	GDP	Employees	Man-Hours	GDP	Employees	Man-Hours	GDP	Employees	Man-Hours
1946	0.953	1.068	1.058	0.868	0.981	0.956	0.810	0.962	0.948	0.769	0.952	0.938
1947	0.922	0.990	0.985	0.982	1.000	0.986	0.891	0.981	0.968	0.836	0.980	0.971
1948	0.976	1.004	1.010	1.006	1.004	1.007	0.949	0.995	0.987	0.926	1.030	1.030
1949	1.000	1.000	1.000	1.000	1.000	1.000	1.000	1.000	1.000	1.000	1.000	1.000
1950	1.013	1.023	1.022	1.082	1.050	1.049	1.093	1.085	1.082	1.015	0.987	0.991
1951	1.012	1.023	1.046	1.148	1.078	1.079	1.175	1.097	1.098	1.051	0.989	0.998
1952	1.114	1.107	1.111	1.158	1.078	1.074	1.134	1.015	1.035	1.075	1.006	1.024
1953	1.150	1.114	1.119	1.254	1.125	1.118	1.181	1.034	1.067	1.147	1.043	1.062
1954	1.089	1.121	1.149	1.242	1.140	1.146	1.241	1.055	1.100	1.216	1.069	1.085
1955	1.128	1.174	1.186	1.364	1.210	1.209	1.310	1.075	1.123	1.271	1.096	1.112
1956	1.176	1.204	1.206	1.383	1.206	1.214	1.378	1.062	1.109	1.373	1.139	1.160
1957	1.168	1.177	1.199	1.273	1.152	1.172	1.355	0.982	1.033	1.382	1.104	1.124
1958	1.144	1.195	1.212	1.320	1.249	1.265	1.356	0.960	1.013	1.344	1.086	1.113
1959	1.131	1.182	1.188	1.366	1.267	1.273	1.447	1.010	1.062	1.432	1.123	1.148
1960	1.079	1.126	1.143	1.360	1.267	1.285	1.484	1.023	1.074	1.465	1.129	1.160

(continued)

TABLE 7 (continued)

Year	Iron and Steel Products			Transportation Equipment			Nonferrous Metal Products and Electrical Apparatus and Supplies			Nonmetallic Mineral Products and Products of Petroleum and Coal		
		Factor Productivity			Factor Productivity			Factor Productivity			Factor Productivity	
	GDP	Employees	Man-Hours	GDP	Employees	Man-Hours	GDP	Employees	Man-Hours	GDP	Employees	Man-Hours
1946	0.808	0.888	0.879	0.806	0.802	0.806	0.752	0.820	0.815	0.729	0.929	0.932
1947	0.936	0.956	0.949	0.953	0.927	0.929	0.896	0.922	0.921	0.838	1.001	0.998
1948	1.015	0.996	0.988	0.972	0.975	0.979	0.956	0.966	0.968	0.913	1.001	1.000
1949	1.000	1.000	1.000	1.000	1.000	1.000	1.000	1.000	1.000	1.000	1.000	1.000
1950	1.025	1.029	1.035	1.083	1.089	1.085	1.080	1.058	1.062	1.114	1.069	1.069
1951	1.170	1.070	1.084	1.313	1.148	1.159	1.172	1.041	1.052	1.232	1.087	1.091
1952	1.189	1.030	1.047	1.491	1.122	1.138	1.180	1.011	1.028	1.296	1.083	1.094
1953	1.153	0.978	0.999	1.652	1.162	1.180	1.346	1.072	1.090	1.448	1.100	1.111
1954	1.062	0.936	0.964	1.373	1.054	1.082	1.333	1.060	1.088	1.535	1.096	1.111
1955	1.238	1.065	1.090	1.451	1.124	1.159	1.504	1.166	1.191	1.779	1.245	1.259
1956	1.453	1.147	1.170	1.579	1.148	1.183	1.604	1.158	1.183	2.011	1.314	1.334
1957	1.396	1.066	1.098	1.512	1.062	1.105	1.539	1.094	1.125	2.039	1.247	1.267
1958	1.283	1.045	1.083	1.325	1.034	1.075	1.499	1.096	1.133	2.102	1.234	1.254
1959	1.472	1.126	1.157	1.315	1.089	1.122	1.582	1.150	1.179	2.304	1.289	1.307
1960	1.317	1.021	1.054	1.300	1.088	1.118	1.633	1.200	1.229	2.265	1.236	1.258

(continued)

TABLE 7 *(concluded)*

Year	Chemical Products			Miscellaneous Manufacturing Industries		
		Factor Productivity			Factor Productivity	
	GDP	Employees	Man-Hours	GDP	Employees	Man-Hours
1946	0.870	1.002	0.999	0.802	0.997	0.992
1947	0.908	1.017	1.020	0.841	0.962	0.968
1948	0.957	1.038	1.039	0.814	0.937	0.942
1949	1.000	1.000	1.000	1.000	1.000	1.000
1950	1.077	1.059	1.063	1.048	1.018	1.017
1951	1.200	1.084	1.091	1.190	1.110	1.120
1952	1.223	1.031	1.046	1.218	1.086	1.102
1953	1.399	1.045	1.061	1.411	1.166	1.172
1954	1.521	1.077	1.097	1.343	1.124	1.139
1955	1.655	1.171	1.193	1.364	1.135	1.147
1956	1.748	1.176	1.201	1.470	1.154	1.168
1957	1.834	1.153	1.180	1.533	1.139	1.159
1958	1.980	1.198	1.227	1.663	1.191	1.210
1959	2.084	1.243	1.272	1.832	1.246	1.260
1960	2.197	1.280	1.311	1.916	1.208	1.223

Note: See Table SA-13 for the same series recalculated using the revised output data.

Source: Indexes of constant 1949 dollar gross domestic product at factor cost: From DBS 61-505, *Indexes of Real Domestic Product by Industry of Origin 1935-61*, Table 1.

Indexes of total measured factor productivity. See Statistical Appendix. These indexes are based on Set I of the average economic lives of capital goods and correspond to row I in Table 6. The indexed total measured factor productivity is the gross-domestic-product-at-factor-cost version.

rates of productivity advance shown by the clothing major group are biased downward because of an understatement in the increase in output in the latter part of the period which we were unable to correct.[16]

Productivity advance in the paper products major group was also uneven and, on average, surprisingly low. With the exception of the combined nonmetallic mineral products and products of petroleum and

[16] In DBS 61-005, *Annual Supplement to the Monthly Industrial Production*, May 1964, p. 3, it is reported that the constant-dollar gross domestic product index for clothing from ". . . the mid-fifties . . ." has been badly biased downward. There is thus on this account alone also a slight downward bias in the index of constant-dollar gross domestic product for total manufacturing. Confirmation of these suspicions has resulted in our revisions contained in the Statistical Appendix.

coal major group and the chemical products major groups, the paper products major group exhibits the highest rate of advance of fixed capital input in manufacturing. Yet it also exhibits one of the lowest rates of advance in total measured factor productivity. As would be expected from the nature of their products, the productivity performance of the iron and steel products and transportation equipment major groups exhibits marked cyclical sensitivity. Particularly striking are the recorded rates of increase of total measured factor inputs shown by the combined nonmetallic mineral products and products of petroleum and coal major group and the rather high rates of increase in total measured factor productivity. It would appear that the ranking of the major groups, in terms of increased total measured factor productivity is only moderately affected by cyclical variations, with the range of increases in total measured factor productivity exhibited by the different major groups in Tables 6 and 7 being quite wide.

It is well known that estimates of rates of change of total measured factor productivity require careful interpretation. Our method does not take any account of possible changes in returns to scale and the nonneutrality of technological advance, and suffers from all the limitations of the labor input data and difficulties involved in capital measurement in a world of changes in degrees of competition, unsteady technological advance, and an obvious absence of anything like equilibrium prices, wage rates, and rates of return to capital. Moreover, our estimates would not appear to be invariant to changes in the assumed economic lives of capital goods which enter the estimation of stocks of fixed capital and capital consumption allowances.

The data indicate the difficulty clearly. In Table 6 the rates of growth of the midyear net stock of fixed capital and capital consumption allowances shown in the I rows are based on the initial Set I of average economic lives used by DBS in preparing the fixed capital stock and flow estimates in manufacturing. The data in rows III are based, in general, on the longest lives assumed and in V, in general, on the shortest lives assumed.[17] The changes in the estimates of total measured factor

---

[17] We calculated but have not reported the effects on our estimates of using the two intermediate Sets II and IV of assumed lives used by DBS in the forthcoming reference paper, *Estimates of Fixed Capital Flows and Stocks, Manufacturing, Canada, 1926–1960*. Again, with rows I as standard, the variations in the rates of increase of total measured factor productivity when the sets of intermediate lives are used are less than when the sets of extreme lives are used but are nevertheless substantial.

productivity for the period 1946–56 are generally such that, as assumed lives are longer, it is increased while, as assumed lives are shorter, it is decreased. The reverse relationship would appear to hold with respect to the rates of growth of the net stock of capital and capital consumption allowances. These results are by no means uniform.

Such alterations in observed results are of particular concern when we remember that the average lives of capital goods and the time pattern of depreciation probably change cyclically and secularly. As previously indicated, we have no data about life distributions and, given our findings, conclude that the short-run estimates of total measured factor productivity presented here must be viewed with considerable skepticism.

Even when a longer period is taken, though the variations emanating from different assumed lives of capital goods are sharply reduced, they still introduce some ambiguity into the results. Thus, for total manufacturing over the period 1926–56, we have the estimates presented in Table 8.

As can be seen from a comparison of Table 6 and Table 8 the differences among the growth rates of the two capital inputs and the measured factor inputs and total factor productivity are reduced substantially. However, the secular changes, which have, in all likelihood, been occurring in the average economic lives of capital goods, and on which we have no data, serve to detract from any additional confidence with which such longer-term analysis may be conducted.

The effects of different assumed lives of fixed capital goods are reduced when the estimates of total measured factor productivity are prepared on the net domestic product at factor cost output basis. Slight variations occur in the recorded rates of growth of net domestic product (these variations are implied in the rates of growth of gross domestic product per unit of capital consumption allowances as shown in Table 6) but the variation in the rates of change of total factor inputs and productivity is reduced as the assumed lives are altered.

In the case of the net domestic product variant, the reduction in the variation of the estimates of total measured factor productivity is brought about, of course, by the elimination of capital consumption allowances as one of the inputs and the consequent increased weight given to the labor input. Nonetheless, as Table 9 shows, the differences in the estimates are still considerable for some major groups as stock and capital consumption allowances data based on different assumed average economic lives of fixed capital goods are used.

TABLE 8

Total Measured Factor Productivity (Gross Domestic Product Basis), Total Manufacturing, 1926-56

(continuous annual rates of change)

	Gross Domestic Product at Factor Cost[a]	Employees	Midyear Net Stock of Fixed Capital[a]	Midyear Inventories[a]	Capital Consumption Allowances[a]	Total Measured Factor Input (employees)	Total Measured Factor Productivity (employees)
I	4.4	3.0	2.6	3.7	2.4	3.0	1.4
III			2.5		2.5	2.9	1.5
V			2.9		2.9	3.1	1.4

Source: See Statistical Appendix. No reliable man-hours data are available back to 1926 for total manufacturing.

[a]Measured in constant 1949 dollars.

TABLE 9

Total Measured Factor Productivity (Net Domestic Product Basis), Total Manufacturing and Major Groups, 1946-56

(continuous annual rates of change)

	Set of Lives	Net Domestic Product at Factor Cost[a]	Labor Input		Midyear Net Stock of Fixed Capital[a]	Midyear Inventories[a]	Total Measured Factor Input		Total Measured Factor Productivity	
			Employees	Paid Man-Hours			Employees	Paid Man-Hours	Employees	Paid Man-Hours
Total manufacturing	I	5.5	2.5	2.0	5.8	4.3	3.2	2.9	2.3	2.6
	III	5.6			5.3		3.2	2.8	2.4	2.8
	V	5.4			6.4		3.3	3.0	2.1	2.4
Food and beverages	I	3.1	1.3	0.9	6.4	3.3	2.7	2.4	0.4	0.7
	III	3.1			5.9		2.5	2.2	0.6	0.9
	V	2.9			7.2		2.6	2.3	0.3	0.6
Tobacco, rubber, and leather products	I	2.6	-0.9	-1.2	3.5	2.7	-0.1	-0.4	2.7	3.0
	III	2.6			3.4		-0.1	-0.4	2.7	3.0
	V	2.5			3.1		-0.2	-0.4	2.7	2.9
Textile products	I	2.9	0.5	0.1	4.2	12.3	2.2	1.9	0.8	1.0
	III	2.9			3.8		2.1	1.8	0.9	1.2
	V	2.8			5.4		2.5	2.2	0.3	0.6
Clothing products	I	2.1	0.5	0.4	2.0	2.2	0.9	0.7	1.2	1.4
	III	2.1			1.9		0.8	0.7	1.3	1.4
	V	2.1			1.3		0.8	0.6	1.3	1.5

(continued)

TABLE 9 (continued)

	Set of Lives	Net Domestic Product at Factor Cost [a]	Labor Input		Midyear Net Stock of Fixed Capital [a]	Midyear Inventories [a]	Total Measured Factor Input		Total Measured Factor Productivity	
			Employees	Paid Man-Hours			Employees	Paid Man-Hours	Employees	Paid Man-Hours
Wood products	I	5.0	2.5	2.0	3.8	3.6	2.8	2.4	2.2	2.6
	III	5.1			3.1		2.7	2.3	2.4	2.8
	V	4.8			4.3		2.8	2.4	2.0	2.3
Paper products	I	5.5	3.3	2.1	6.9	2.7	4.3	3.6	1.2	1.9
	III	5.6			6.1		4.1	3.4	1.5	2.2
	V	5.0			7.6		4.4	3.7	0.6	1.3
Printing, publishing, and allied industries	I	6.0	4.0	3.5	4.8	4.4	4.1	3.8	1.9	2.3
	III	6.0			4.2		4.0	3.7	2.0	2.4
	V	5.9			7.0		4.5	4.0	1.5	1.9
Iron and steel products	I	6.1	2.6	2.2	5.8	5.4	3.4	3.0	2.7	3.1
	III	6.1			5.3		3.3	3.0	2.8	3.2
	V	6.0			6.1		3.4	3.1	2.6	3.0
Transportation equipment	I	7.1	3.4	3.1	4.2	1.5	3.4	3.1	3.8	4.0
	III	7.2			3.3		3.2	3.0	4.0	4.3
	V	6.9			5.5		3.5	3.3	3.4	3.7

(continued)

TABLE 9 (concluded)

| | | Labor Input | | | | Total Measured Factor Input | | Total Measured Factor Productivity | |
Set of Lives	Net Domestic Product at Factor Cost[a]	Employees	Paid Man-Hours	Midyear Net Stock of Fixed Capital[a]	Midyear Inventories[a]	Employees	Paid Man-Hours	Employees	Paid Man-Hours
Nonferrous metal products and electrical apparatus and supplies									
I	8.5			3.4		4.7	4.4	3.8	4.2
III	8.6	5.0	4.5	3.3	4.5	4.7	4.3	4.0	4.3
V	8.6			2.7		4.6	4.3	3.9	4.3
Nonmetallic mineral products of petroleum and coal									
I	10.6			10.4		6.5	6.4	4.1	4.3
III	10.7	4.6	4.3	9.5	7.6	6.4	6.2	4.3	4.5
V	10.3			11.7		6.7	6.6	3.6	3.8
Chemical products									
I	6.9			8.8		5.0	4.7	1.9	2.2
III	7.0	3.3	2.8	8.2	4.6	4.9	4.6	2.1	2.4
V	6.7			10.0		5.1	4.8	1.6	1.9
Miscellaneous manufacturing industries									
I	6.3			3.2		4.7	4.5	1.5	1.7
III	6.3	4.6	4.3	3.2	8.0	4.7	4.5	1.6	1.8
V	6.3			2.9		4.8	4.6	1.5	1.7

Source: See Statistical Appendix and notes to Table 6.

[a] Measured in constant 1949 dollars.

At the component (i.e., plant and machinery and equipment) level of detail for the capital stock and flow inputs in our estimates of total measured factor productivity, the variations in the rates of growth for the period 1946 to 1956, introduced by using different assumed average economic lives in producting such flow and stock estimates, are substantial and nonuniform. Given the perpetual inventory procedure by which the capital stock and flow estimates have been prepared, different assumed lives interact with the historical pattern of constant-dollar gross fixed capital formation to produce substantial variations in the resulting estimates. In Table 10, rows I give average annual rates of growth of the two components of the net stock and capital consumption allowances, which are based on Set I of the assumed economic lives of capital goods adopted by the Dominion Bureau of Statistics. In rows III, 20 per cent longer lives, compared to rows I, were used for all components. In rows V, 20 per cent shorter lives were used for the construction-type components and 40 per cent shorter lives were used for the machinery and equipment components (excluding capital items charged to operating expenses).

The type of complexity introduced may be seen by examining the estimates for total manufacturing. As is seen in comparing rows III with rows I, the rate of growth of the machinery and equipment component of both the net stock and capital consumption allowances falls sharply although, because of the changed relative importance of the components, the rate of growth of the total net stock is affected to a lesser degree. When shorter lives are used, the rates of growth of both components of the net stock are increased whereas when the capital consumption allowances are examined, for plant it is shown reduced and for machinery and equipment it is shown increased. For total manufacturing, from Table 10 it would appear that when shorter lives are used, the rates of increase of both components and of the total net stock are raised as compared to the results when Set I or Set III lives are used. An examination of the estimates for the major groups reveals, however, that such uniformity is by no means the case.

Since the cyclical and secular history of gross fixed capital formation by component will differ for each major group, it follows that only tentatively can it be argued that shorter lives increase the recorded rates of growth of the capital stock and flow inputs and vice versa. These

TABLE 10

Midyear Net Stock and Capital Consumption Allowances, 1946-56

(continuous annual rates of change)

| | | Constant 1949 Dollars | | | | | |
| | | Net Midyear Stock of Fixed Capital | | | Capital Consumption Allowances | | |
	Set of Lives	Plant	Machinery and Equipment	Total	Plant	Machinery and Equipment	Total
Total manufacturing	I	3.6	8.4	5.8	2.9	2.8	2.8
	III	3.5	6.2	5.3	2.9	1.9	2.2
	V	4.1	9.6	6.4	2.5	5.7	4.7
Food and beverages	I	4.6	8.0	6.4	3.9	2.6	3.0
	III	4.5	7.1	5.9	4.2	2.4	2.9
	V	4.9	9.8	7.2	4.1	5.3	5.0
Tobacco, rubber, and leather products	I	1.1	7.7	3.5	2.0	4.2	3.6
	III	1.3	6.9	3.4	2.3	3.2	3.0
	V	0.7	8.4	3.1	1.5	6.2	4.9
Textiles (except clothing and fur)	I	1.9	5.3	4.2	0.2	1.8	1.6
	III	1.7	5.2	3.8	1.6	1.1	1.2
	V	3.1	7.0	5.4	0.0	3.0	2.3
Clothing	I	-3.5	8.9	2.0	0.0	3.8	2.1
	III	-2.6	8.1	1.9	-1.3	2.6	0.8
	V	-4.2	9.0	1.3	-4.1	6.3	2.2

(continued)

TABLE 10 (continued)

		Constant 1949 Dollars					
		Net Midyear Stock of Fixed Capital			Capital Consumption Allowances		
	Set of Lives	Plant	Machinery and Equipment	Total	Plant	Machinery and Equipment	Total
Wood products	I	0.1	9.4	3.8	0.5	1.2	0.9
	III	-0.7	7.7	3.1	-1.1	-0.3	-0.7
	V	-1.4	12.3	4.3	-0.8	5.7	3.1
Paper products	I	2.5	13.0	6.9	2.6	4.3	3.8
	III	2.6	10.8	6.1	2.9	3.1	3.0
	V	2.8	15.5	7.6	1.2	9.8	7.1
Printing, publishing, and allied industries	I	3.6	5.7	4.8	3.0	1.4	1.8
	III	3.4	4.7	4.2	3.4	0.9	1.4
	V	4.2	9.6	7.0	2.1	3.5	3.1
Iron and steel products	I	4.2	7.0	5.8	2.5	2.4	2.4
	III	3.9	6.4	5.3	3.5	1.9	2.3
	V	5.5	6.6	6.1	1.7	4.2	3.7
Transportation equipment	I	2.6	5.8	4.2	-0.1	-1.6	-1.1
	III	2.3	4.2	3.3	2.4	-3.5	-1.5
	V	4.4	6.8	5.5	1.4	1.9	1.7

(continued)

TABLE 10 (concluded)

		Constant 1949 Dollars					
		Net Midyear Stock of Fixed Capital			Capital Consumption Allowances		
	Set of Lives	Plant	Machinery and Equipment	Total	Plant	Machinery and Equipment	Total
Nonferrous metal products and electrical apparatus and supplies	I	3.1	3.7	3.4	4.1	0.1	1.1
	III	3.3	3.3	3.3	3.8	-0.6	0.5
	V	2.8	2.6	2.7	4.5	1.3	2.3
Nonmetallic mineral products and products of petroleum and coal	I	8.6	14.9	10.4	6.2	7.6	6.9
	III	7.9	13.5	9.5	5.6	6.7	6.1
	V	9.6	17.8	11.7	7.3	10.8	9.0
Chemical products	I	4.5	15.6	8.8	3.8	9.9	7.6
	III	4.4	14.5	8.2	4.1	8.8	7.2
	V	5.5	17.9	10.0	1.1	13.2	8.9
Miscellaneous manufacturing industries	I	1.5	5.9	3.2	2.3	3.0	2.8
	III	1.7	5.6	3.2	1.5	2.6	2.2
	V	1.5	6.1	2.9	0.9	3.8	2.8

Note: Based on data in forthcoming DBS reference paper *Estimates of Fixed Capital Flows and Stocks, Manufacturing, Canada, 1926-1960.*

substantial differences imply considerable variations in recorded capital-output ratios (compare Table 6 and Table 10) and consequent differences in the importance which one attaches to capital accumulation as a contributor to growth. It is our conclusion that much better data on the lives of capital goods are required before much progress can be made in Canada in economic investigations concerned with the relationship over time between capital and output. As we have indicated, for longer periods of comparison, the uncertainties introduced by lack of knowledge about the economic lives of capital goods are reduced; but clearly, the possibility of secular changes in the lives of capital goods should make us cautious in interpreting the reduction in differences in calculated estimates of total measured factor productivity advance. Indeed, when observed historical relationships between output and capital are used for short-run projections of such relationships, the lack of adequate knowledge about the lives of capital goods and actual depreciation patterns weighs against the reliability of these projections.

As the factor weighting diagram reproduced in our Statistical Appendix shows, it is of critical importance to take account of the changes in inventories in estimating total measured factor productivity in Canadian manufacturing. For some major groups inventories would appear to be as significant an input as fixed capital. Failure to take them into account would have led to quite erroneous impressions as to improvements in economic efficiency and a substanial overstatement of the significance of the net stock of fixed capital as a factor input within Canadian manufacturing.

SOME ALTERNATIVE MEASURES

In the Technical Appendix accompanying this paper, we argue that total measured factor productivity estimates can be prepared, at industry levels of detail, with output taken as gross output and with intermediate inputs being handled as inputs (rather than negative outputs) along with the primary factors of production. The gross output version of total measured factor productivity shown for selected major groups in Table 11 are for the shorter period 1946 to 1953 and are based only on the initial Set I of average economic lives of fixed capital goods. The analysis cannot be extended beyond 1953 because reliable estimates of constant-dollar gross output and intermediate inputs by major group are not available. Even for the period shown in Table 11 the gross output and intermediate input data are unsatisfactory.

The rates of growth of total measured factor productivity are reduced when the gross output, rather than the gross domestic product, basis is used, as the comparison offered in Table 11 indicates. In such a short period, it is not surprising that the rates of growth of gross output and intermediate inputs are different. When the rates of growth of gross output and intermediate inputs are similar, the only difference in estimates of total measured factor productivity between the gross output and gross domestic product version will arise from the changed weights attached to the inputs. Data constraints prevent us from ascertaining how different the rates of growth of gross output and intermediate inputs would be in the longer run.

Differences which exist, however, suggest that in comparing the rates of improvement which various major groups have made in transforming inputs into output, the gross output version may be equally as useful as the gross domestic product version. The ranking of the major groups (in terms of the rates of growth of total measured factor productivity) alters as the different output versions are used, and the interpretation of the results would correspondingly be affected. Unfortunately, we are at present unable to press further with such comparisons.

As is indicated in the Technical Appendix, the estimation of total measured factor productivity can also be carried out in terms of the proportionate rates of changes in the prices of inputs and outputs.

In Table 12, we show some very tentative estimates of the rates of growth of prices of outputs and inputs on a gross domestic product basis for all major groups and total manufacturing. Again, these estimates are based on the initial set of assumed lives of capital goods and therefore correspond to rows I in Table 6.

The recorded rates of increase of total measured factor productivity shown in columns (10) and (11) of Table 12, because of data problems, are not as satisfactory as those shown in columns (12) and (13), which are repeated from Table 6. In general, the estimates derived by working with the prices of inputs and outputs would appear to be lower than those derived by working with the constant-dollar output and input measures. The differences amongst the rates of growth of "own-product"

TABLE 11

*Total Measured Factor Productivity Gross Output Basis and Gross
Domestic Product Basis, Selected Major Groups, 1946-53*

(continuous annual rates of change)

| | Gross Output[a] | Labor Input | | Midyear Stock of Fixed Capital[a] | Mid- year Inven- tories[a] | Capital Con- sumption Allowances[a] |
		Employ- ees	Paid Man- Hours			
Textile products	3.2	1.2	0.4	5.5	17.3	2.1
Clothing products	2.4	1.8	1.5	3.3	3.0	2.4
Wood products	5.0	3.4	3.1	3.9	4.9	0.0
Printing, publishing, and allied industries	5.7	4.4	3.8	4.9	6.4	1.4
Iron and steel products	5.4	3.1	2.4	6.0	7.3	0.4
Transportation equipment	10.2	6.3	6.1	3.1	3.0	-3.7
Nonferrous metal products and electrical apparatus and supplies	8.3	6.0	5.5	2.6	7.8	-1.4
Nonmetallic mineral products and products of petroleum and coal	9.9	4.9	4.7	10.0	13.7	6.3
Chemical products	6.4	4.0	3.5	10.2	1.8	8.0
Miscellaneous manufacturing industries	8.1	6.0	5.8	3.3	10.4	2.1

Source: See Statistical Appendix. Calculations in last five columns are comparable, except for time period, with those in Table 6.

[a]Measured in constant 1949 dollars.

Inter- mediate Input[a]	Total Measured Factor Input		Total Measured Factor Productivity		Gross Domestic Product[a]	Total Measured Factor Input		Total Measured Factor Productivity	
	Employ- ees	Paid Man- Hours	Employ- ees	Paid Man- Hours		Employ- ees	Paid Man- Hours	Employ- ees	Paid Man- Hours
3.5	3.4	3.1	−0.2	0.0	2.8	3.2	2.7	−0.4	0.1
2.1	2.1	2.0	0.2	0.3	2.7	2.1	1.9	0.6	0.8
4.1	3.8	3.7	1.3	1.4	5.3	3.4	3.1	1.9	2.2
5.7	5.0	4.7	0.7	1.0	5.7	4.4	3.9	1.3	1.8
5.6	4.7	4.5	0.6	0.8	5.1	3.7	3.3	1.3	1.8
10.2	8.0	7.9	2.3	2.3	10.2	5.0	4.8	5.3	5.4
8.3	6.7	6.6	1.6	1.8	8.3	4.6	4.3	3.7	4.0
9.9	9.3	9.2	0.6	0.6	9.8	7.4	7.3	2.4	2.5
6.2	6.0	5.9	0.4	0.5	6.8	5.7	5.4	1.1	1.4
8.1	7.0	6.9	1.1	1.1	8.1	5.9	5.7	2.2	2.3

TABLE 12

Total Measured Factor Productivity (Gross Domestic Product Basis), Total Manufacturing and Major Groups, Prices of Inputs and Outputs, 1946-56

(continuous annual rate of change)

	Persons Employed Price	Paid Man-Hours Price	Net Rate of Return to Capital	Midyear Net Stock of Capital Price	Midyear Inventory Price
	(1)	(2)	(3)	(4)	(5)
Total manufacturing	7.1	7.5	1.3	5.9	−0.4
Food and beverages	6.5	6.9	−2.3	5.6	2.2
Tobacco, rubber, and leather products	6.9	7.2	−0.6	6.0	1.5
Textile products	6.8	7.2	−8.1	5.6	−7.7
Clothing	5.0	5.2	−4.8	5.3	1.1
Wood products	7.1	7.6	−5.6	5.4	4.5
Paper products	7.2	8.3	−5.6	6.1	4.2
Printing, publishing, and allied industries	6.8	7.2	3.8	5.8	2.0
Iron and steel products	7.3	7.8	3.4	5.9	3.0
Transportation equipment	6.7	7.0	4.1	6.1	3.9
Nonferrous metal products and electrical apparatus and supplies	7.5	8.0	15.5	6.0	1.5
Nonmetallic mineral products and products of petroleum and coal	7.9	8.2	5.4	6.4	2.8
Chemical products	7.4	8.0	−5.3	6.0	4.4
Miscellaneous manufacturing	7.0	7.2	4.3	6.0	1.8

Source: See Statistical Appendix. Data in column (10): columns (8) minus (7); column (11): columns (9) minus (7); columns (12) and (13) from Table 6.

Capital Consumption Allowances Price	Gross Domestic Product Price	Total Measured Factor Input Price		Total Measured Factor Productivity		Total Measured Productivity From Table 6	
		Employ-ees	Man-Hours	Employ-ees	Man-Hours	Employ-ees	Man-Hours
(6)	(7)	(8)	(9)	(10)	(11)	(12)	(13)
5.8	4.9	6.4	6.7	1.5	1.8	2.1	2.4
5.6	4.7	5.1	5.4	0.4	0.7	0.5	0.8
5.8	3.6	6.1	6.3	2.5	2.7	2.5	2.8
5.6	3.4	3.4	3.7	0.0	0.3	0.7	0.9
5.4	2.6	3.6	3.7	1.0	1.1	1.2	1.3
5.5	4.7	5.6	5.9	0.8	1.2	2.0	2.4
6.0	4.6	4.5	5.2	-0.1	0.5	1.1	1.7
5.7	5.2	7.1	7.4	1.9	2.2	1.8	2.1
5.8	5.5	7.4	7.7	1.9	2.3	2.6	2.9
5.9	5.3	7.3	7.6	2.0	2.3	3.6	3.8
5.9	7.6	9.6	9.9	2.1	2.4	3.3	3.6
6.3	5.5	8.5	8.7	3.0	3.2	3.6	3.7
5.8	2.8	4.7	5.0	1.9	2.2	1.7	2.0
6.2	5.5	7.3	7.5	1.8	2.0	1.4	1.6

prices [18] of labor, as shown in Table 13, would appear to be of sufficient interest to warrant further study of total measured factor productivity in Canadian manufacturing over this period, using the relationship between prices of inputs and output as well as the more customary constant-dollar inputs-and-output approach.

CONCLUSIONS

In the third section of this paper, some additional conclusions based on the results of this section are drawn. At this point, however, we may say that in the postwar period, by whatever output variant it is measured, total measured factor productivity grew at substantially different rates over the various major groups making up Canadian manufacturing. The different rates are, of course, cyclically sensitive. We offer some further comparisons, when additional variants of the labor inputs are used, in the Statistical Appendix. Our results would appear to confirm the suspicion that lack of knowledge about the average economic lives of capital goods, secular and cyclical changes in those lives, and the pattern of depreciation of capital goods rule out at present the testing of any simple hypothesis connecting the rate of growth and the changing average age of the net stock of capital and the rate of growth of total measured factor productivity. From our estimates, there is no readily discernible relationship between the rate of growth of the net stock of capital and total measured factor productivity.

Given the crudity of our concepts and data, it was not possible to say anything definitive about the way in which total measured factor productivity increases were shared by the primary inputs in each major group. We suggest, however, that the estimation of total measured factor productivity should be used to cast light on such a phenomenon. Looking at total measured factor productivity changes by means of proportionate rates of change in the prices of inputs and outputs not only gives some idea of the distribution of the fruits of increasing efficiency, but when changes in own-product factor prices are examined, under admittedly restrictive assumptions, we may then gain some knowledge about the changing marginal productivities of the various factors. These are extremely important topics of investigation and much further refine-

---

[18] The rate of change of the own-product price of labor is defined simply as the proportionate rate of change of the price of labor less the proportionate rate of change in the price of the product it produces.

TABLE 13

Output Per Unit of Labor Input, Own-Product Price of Labor, 1946-56

(continuous annual rates of change)

	Output per Person Employed (1)	Own-Product Price (employees) (2)	Output per Paid Man-Hours (3)	Own-Product Price (paid Man-Hours) (4)
Total manufacturing	2.8	2.2	3.3	2.6
Food and beverages	1.8	1.8	2.2	2.2
Tobacco, rubber, and leather products	3.5	3.3	3.8	3.6
Textiles (except clothing and fur)	2.3	3.4	2.7	3.8
Clothing products	1.6	2.4	1.7	2.6
Wood products	2.2	2.4	2.7	2.9
Paper products	2.0	2.6	3.2	3.7
Printing, publishing, and allied industries	1.8	1.6	2.3	2.0
Iron and steel products	3.3	1.8	3.7	2.3
Transportation equipment	3.3	1.4	3.6	1.7
Nonferrous metal products and electrical apparatus and supplies	2.6	−0.1	3.1	0.4
Nonmetallic mineral products and products of petroleum and coal	5.6	2.4	5.9	2.7
Chemical products	3.7	4.6	4.2	5.2
Miscellaneous manufacturing industries	1.5	1.5	1.8	1.7

Source: Column (1): Table 6, gross domestic product at factor cost minus labor input, employees; column (3): Table 6, gross domestic product at factor cost minus labor input, paid man-hours; column (2): Table 12, column (1) minus column (7): column (4): Table 12, column (2) minus column (7).

ment of concepts and data is necessary before satisfactory results can be obtained.

III. Long-Run Aggregate Economic Performance in Canada

Our study of production relations in Canada in the postwar years has been concentrated upon manufacturing activity. In this section we intend to provide some background for our findings by presenting evidence on the entire economy's progress, and the role of manufacturing therein, together with a longer view of the process of growth in Canada.

The initial major study of growth in Canada was undertaken by Hood and Scott for the Royal Commission on Canada's Economic Prospects.[19] Surveying past economic performance in Canada, the authors were impressed with the stability in certain key relationships among economic variables.[20] These include

1. The ratio of saving to income
2. The ratio of capital to output [21]
3. The share of labor earnings in national income
4. The rate of return on capital.

Since these regularities are consistent with equilibrium conditions derived from simple models of economic growth, the authors conclude that "in a broad way the economic system in the long run is stable and moves toward equilibrium. . . ." [22]

On the basis of this conclusion, a forecast of the level of economic activity in 1980 was made. This involved estimating the growth of labor input and labor productivity and, thereby, the growth of output. From this, it was possible to infer the level of capital required, and hence the savings and investment requirements of the system to validate this program.

For our purposes, their summary of past growth with their strong emphasis on stability of basic relationship is of major interest. In Table 14 we summarize their findings.

[19] William C. Hood and Anthony Scott, *Output, Labour and Capital in the Canadian Economy*, Ottawa, 1957.

[20] This finding parallels Lawrence Klein's in his article "Great Ratios in Economics," *Quarterly Journal of Economics*, May 1961.

[21] Their development of capital stock estimates at the major industry level for the years 1945–55, on both a net and a gross basis, were the first of their kind for Canada.

[22] *Ibid.*, p. 118.

TABLE 14

Basic Relationships Among Economic Variables,

Canadian Economy, Selected Years, 1926-55

	Savings as Per Cent of GNE (1)	Ratio, Capital to Output		Labor Share in National Income (4)	Rate of Return to Capital	
		Industrial (2)	Total (3)		Government Bond Yields (5)	Index of Long-Term Yields (6)
1926	20.1	1.5	n.a.	78.1	n.a.	141.3
1935	11.5	1.5	n.a.	68.3	3.0[a]	98.1[a]
1941	19.6	0.9	n.a.	68.4	3.1	100.6
1947	24.5	1.0	2.2	65.1[b]	2.6	84.4
1953	26.3	1.2	2.3	73.6	3.6[c]	116.2[c]
1955	26.4	1.2	2.4	72.9	3.1[d]	101.7[d]

Source: Data are from William C. Hood and Anthony Scott, *Output, Labour and Capital in the Canadian Economy,* Ottawa, 1957: Column (1): Table 2.16, p. 42, in current dollars, savings measured on a gross domestic basis. Columns (2) and (3): Table 2.17, p. 44, in 1949 dollars, net fixed capital to gross domestic product at factor cost; total capital is equal to industrial plus social. Column (4): Table 2.20, p. 57, wages, salaries, and supplementary labor incomes plus estimates of labor income for unincorporated business. Column (5): Table 2.23, pp. 62-63, 15-year Government of Canada theoretical bond yield. Column (6): Table 2.23, pp. 62-63, DBS index of Government of Canada long-term bond yields, 1936-39 = 100.

[a]For 1936.

[b]For 1945.

[c]For 1952.

[d]For 1954.

These data have been utilized in a study of postwar growth supervised by Professor Domar.[23] Following the techniques of Solow and Kendrick, the growth rate of output is allocated to capital, labor, and residual sources, and the results are presented in Table 15. Unfortunately, the lack of capital stock data by industry prior to 1946 led to the use of a rather short period. In an effort to obtain as long a view of growth as

[23] Evsey D. Domar *et al.,* "Economic Growth and Productivity in the United States, Canada, United Kingdom, Germany and Japan in the Post-War Period," *Review of Economics and Statistics,* February 1964.

TABLE 15

Economic Growth in Canada in the Postwar Period, 1949-60

(average annual rates of growth)

Industry	| 1949-60				| 1949-56	
	Output	Man-Hours	Capital	Combined Factor Input	Total Factor Productivity	Output	Total Factor Productivity
Agriculture	1.7	−3.7	3.7	−0.3	2.0	4.0	3.5
Forestry, fishing, and trapping	3.1	1.1	4.7	2.4	0.7	5.4	−0.2
Mining, quarrying, and oil wells	8.5	0.5	11.5	7.6	0.9	10.8	1.1
Manufacturing	3.7	0.7	4.8	2.3	1.4	5.3	2.7
Construction	3.8	2.6	6.8	3.2	0.6	6.7	1.9
Public utilities	9.9	4.0	9.3	7.9	2.0	10.3	1.4
Trade	4.1	3.3	7.2	4.7	−0.6	5.3	−0.2
Finance, insurance, and real estate	4.9	4.1	4.4	4.3	0.6	5.0	0.6
Transportation, storage, and communication	3.8	1.3	4.7	2.3	1.5	5.3	2.8
Services (including government)	3.8	4.4	5.7	4.6	−0.8	4.3	0.5
Total economy	4.0	1.2	5.5	2.8	1.2	5.4	2.4

Source: Evsey D. Domar *et al.*, "Economic Growth in the United States, Canada, United Kingdom, Germany, and Japan in the Post-War Period," *Review of Economics and Statistics,* February 1964, Tables 1, 2, 4, and 6, and their unpublished manuscript, Table 2-2, Canada.

possible, the period 1949–60 was selected. This final year, however, was one of significant underutilization of capacity in the Canadian economy.[24] Since no attempt was made to evaluate the potential level of output and resource use in 1960, the measures in Table 15, reflecting actual performance, are dominated by cyclical influences. To indicate this, the growth rates of output and the factor productivity that obtain for a shorter but more comparable period are also presented. It is clear that the elimination of differences in cyclical phases for the two end years yields a more impressive picture of growth in Canada; for in most sectors, the growth of output and the growth rate of factor productivity are substantially increased. These data can be compared to those for the present study by examining the manufacturing sector alone. We find that between 1946 and 1956, manufacturing output grew at a rate of 5.3 per cent per annum and that total factor productivity grew at between 2.2 and 2.5 per cent.[25] This is close to the 1949–56 rates of 5.3 per cent and 2.7 per cent in Domar, and presents a very different picture of growth in Canada than does their published data for the longer period 1949–60, where in manufacturing output grew at 3.7 per cent and total factor productivity at 1.4 per cent.

The implications to be drawn from these findings are limited, however, for they are dominated by the rather unique features of the early postwar years. A second study of growth in Canada [26] has used the same degree of industry detail but has extended the analysis over a longer period. In addition, growth in potential output was considered in order to remove swings in output due primarily to short-run fluctuations. This was obtained by considering the growth rate between years of similar, high-capacity utilization levels. The selected years were 1926 and 1956, when the unemployment rate stood at approximately 3 per cent. If other similar years covering roughly the same span of time are examined, the growth rate does not change significantly, and thus the selected period does give a relatively unbiased estimate of potential growth. While this period enabled examination of growth in the aggregate economy, at the industry level of detail, lack of data necessitated the selection of a slightly shorter period.

An attempt was made to allocate the sources of growth not only to

[24] DBS, *Canadian Statistical Review:* 7 per cent of the labor force was unemployed in 1960. In 1949, the rate was less than one-half of this.
[25] Table 6.
[26] N. H. Lithwick, "Economic Growth in Canada: A Quantitiative Analysis," forthcoming, University of Toronto Press.

conventionally measured factors of production but also to those changes in their quality which could be measured.[27] These findings are presented in Table 16 together with Lithwick's revisions of Denison's results to conform to his definitions. These include a rejection of both the need to correct for extra days of schooling, together with Denison's proposed offset to the decline in hours, neither of which were felt to be warranted. Adjustments for years of schooling, the rent component in the income of the more educated, and age and sex composition of the labor force were made and are included in the labor contribution to growth.

Despite a more rapid increase in man-hours than in the United States, the quality improvement has been very minor indeed, due primarily to the relative backwardness in Canada's investment in education. The greater increase in physical capital input has offset this in part; so the total factor input has grown at approximately the same rate in the two countries. Thus, the much higher growth rate in aggregate output in Canada must be due to the higher growth rate of its factor productivity. This finding is at first surprising, given the relatively much greater allocation of resources to technological advance in the United States.[28]

The second phase of Lithwick's study offers some explanation of this discrepancy. An investigation into growth at the sectoral level was undertaken for a somewhat shorter period.[29] Capital stock estimates for this level of detail were made, and they proved to be consistent both with the estimates made from the aggregate for the longer period, and with Hood and Scott's.[30] Once again the labor input series was adjusted for quality change. The findings are presented in Table 17.

[27] Following the technique developed by E. F. Denison in *The Sources of Economic Growth in the United States and the Alternatives Before Us,* Washington, D.C., 1962.

[28] For example, U.S. research and development expenditures per capita over the period 1955–61, were about ten times as high as in Canada (cf. forthcoming study for the Royal Commission on Taxation by T. Wilson and N. H. Lithwick).

[29] Due primarily to the lack of output data prior to 1935 at the industry level (cf. DBS, *Indexes of Real Domestic Product by Industries of Origin, 1935–61,* Ottawa, 1963).

[30] Lithwick, *op. cit.,* Appendix Table B-11, p. 188. In the postwar period, the growth rates of manufacturing capital on both a net and gross basis are remarkably alike for the DBS, Hood-Scott, and Lithwick series. The *levels* of stock are different, however, with DBS showing the greatest volume, Hood-Scott the lowest, and Lithwick an intermediate amount on both bases. For a longer period, significant differences in the growth rates do emerge. Lithwick's growth rates over the longer period are below the DBS estimates, and Hood-Scott's are greater. This stems

TABLE 16

Contributions to Potential Growth,

Canada, 1926-56, and United States, 1929-57

		Canada, 1926-56		U.S., 1929-57
Labor input		0.62		0.82
Labor force	1.21		1.00	
Average annual hours	−0.62		−0.53	
Man-hours		.59	.47	
Education	+0.12		0.35	
Age-sex composition	−0.09		0.01	
Quality change		.03	.36	
Gross domestic capital Input		0.55[a]		0.41
Land	.03		.00	
Residential construction	.04		.05	
Other construction and machinery and equipment	.42		.28	
Inventories	.06		.08	
Foreign capital owned by nationals		0.02		0.02
Domestic capital owned by foreigners		−0.05		0.00
Total factor input		1.15		1.25
Contribution of total measured factor productivity		2.74		1.68
Average annual growth rate, GNP		3.89		2.93

Source: N. H. Lithwick, "Economic Growth in Canada: A Quantitative Analysis," unpublished Ph.D. dissertation, Harvard University, 1963, Table 12, p. 37, and Table 13, p. 39; and E. F. Denison, *The Sources of Economic Growth in the United States and the Alternatives Before Us,* Washington, D.C., 1962, Table 32, p. 266.

[a]The gross capital measure is used here to permit comparability with Denison. If net stock is used, the contribution is slightly lower (0.52). due to the slower growth rate of net stock in this period.

The main discrepancy between Lithwick's growth rate of factor productivity in manufacturing of 2.3 per cent and that of the present study

from the respective estimates of early-year capital stock, which differ substantially due to the very weak data used to compile these estimates. (Once again our
thanks to Mr. White for suggesting this comparison.)

TABLE 17

Growth Rates in Canada, By Industry, 1937-61

Industry	Gross Domestic Product	Adjusted Labor Input	Net Capital Stock — Construction	Net Capital Stock — Machinery and Equipment	Total Measured Factor Input	Total Measured Factor Productivity
Agriculture	1.2	-1.8	3.3	5.2	-0.4	1.6
Forestry, fishing, and trapping	1.8	-1.1	5.9	4.4	0.2	1.5
Mining, quarrying, oil wells	5.2	0.5	7.7	6.4	3.3	1.9
Manufacturing[a]	4.8	2.2	2.3	4.6	2.6	2.3
Construction	5.7	3.3	4.1	8.7	3.6	2.1
Electric power and gas utilities	8.4	3.7	5.9	6.0	5.0	3.3
Trade, wholesale and retail	4.7	3.0	3.3	8.0	3.3	1.4
Finance, insurance, and real estate	4.5	3.6	3.5	8.2	3.6	1.0
Transportation storage and communication	5.3	1.8	1.1	5.8	2.0	3.3
Commercial and community services	3.8	3.8	2.9	7.6	3.8	0.1
Total private economy	4.3	0.8	3.2	5.1	1.5	2.8

Source: N. H. Lithwick, "Economic Growth in Canada: A Quantitative Analysis," unpublished Ph.D. dissertation, Harvard University, 1963, Table 19, p. 52.

[a]With the revised manufacturing output data, gross domestic product for manufacturing shows an annual growth rate of 5.2 per cent, and productivity grows at 2.7 per cent.

of 2.2 to 2.5 per cent [31] is removal in the former of quality changes that are attributable to labor. This adjustment has been made to the present data in Appendix Table SA-7, and the quality-adjusted growth rate of factor productivity for total manufacturing is estimated to be 2.2 per cent.

There appeared to be some inconsistency between the high growth rate of factor productivity in the aggregate and the rates for the majority of the component industries. Since the aggregate is a weighted average of the productivity advance in the various individual industries, apparently some process was occurring which is not detected when simple aggregates are used.

The explanation of this phenomenon is the interindustry shifts in relative importance.[32] Thus, shifts out of agriculture, where factors of production have relatively low productivity, into industries where it is somewhat higher will serve to raise aggregate productivity.

An evaluation of the importance of these shifts between industries was made for both Canada and the United States, and this factor turned out to explain much of the difference in factor productivity, as can be seen in Table 18.

The discrepancy in the influence of these shifts is largely explained by the fact that in the United States, shifts from agriculture began earlier and extended over a much longer period than in Canada, where this shift was concentrated largely in the decade of the forties.

These findings were confirmed by a variety of tests.[33] During the course of conducting these tests, it was found that at the industry level, the factor productivity growth rates for Canada and the United States were quite similar, as can be seen by comparing Tables 17 and 19.

This similarity in rates of technological advance offers some support for the contention that Canada has been able to borrow not only capital

[31] Table 6.

[32] This was calculated in two ways. The first was to divide the change in output into interindustry and intraindustry growth of product per man-hour. This was calculated as

$$\Delta a = (a_0 \cdot \Delta l) + (l_1 \cdot \Delta a)$$

where a is the product per adjusted man-hour and l is the share of an industry in the labor force. The second was to assume that capital could also be shifted between industries over the long run and to calculate the interindustry share in the growth of output per combined factor input. The results were not very different using the two procedures.

[33] The tests involved an attempt to derive each industry's contribution to the aggregate total measured factor productivity indirectly. Summing these yielded a growth rate in the aggregate factor productivity close to the one calculated directly.

TABLE 18

Sources of Growth, United States and Canada, Private Domestic Economy,
1937-61 and 1929-57

	Canada, 1937-61 (ten industries)		U.S., 1929-57 (five industries)	
Growth Rate of Output		4.3		2.9
Measured factor inputs				
Labor	.6		.5	
Capital	.8	1.5	.5	0.9
Interindustry shifts		0.7		0.1
Net factor productivity		2.2		1.8

Source: N. H. Lithwick, "Economic Growth in Canada: A Quantitative
Analysis," unpublished Ph.D. dissertation, Harvard University, Table 37, p. 91.

TABLE 19

Growth Rates in the United States, by Industry, 1927-57

Industry	Gross Domestic Product	Adjusted Labor Input	Net Capital Stock	Total Measured Factor Input	Total Measured Factor Productivity
Agriculture	0.9	-1.1	1.5	-0.7	1.7
Mining	1.5	-0.7	-0.1	-0.5	2.0
Manufacturing	3.5	1.4	2.1	1.6	2.0
Transportation, communications, and public utilities	4.1	-0.2	1.3	0.1	4.0
All other industries	2.4	1.2	2.2	1.4	1.0
Total private economy	2.9	0.6	2.0	0.9	2.0

Source: N. H. Lithwick, "Economic Growth in Canada: A Quantitative
Analysis," unpublished Ph.D. dissertation, Harvard University, 1963,
Table 34, p. 83.

from the United States, but also the particularly important inputs concealed within measured factor productivity, such as new ideas and new techniques.[34] It also reveals that the difference between the two economies lies largely in the interaction between industrial sectors, rather than within any particular sector or group of sectors.

Further attempts to discover possible sources of interaction led to a decomposition of the manufacturing sectors which contributed one-third of the aggregate measured factor productivity. For the United States, shifts within manufacturing were found to explain .05 percentage points of the net factor productivity.[35] The availability of new data for this study, particularly the DBS capital stock estimates [36] permitted us to evaluate the same interaction effect within Canadian manufacturing which contributes one-half of the aggregate measured factor productivity. This amounted to approximately .07 percentage points in Canada's net factor productivity. Thus, after these effects have been removed, the growth rates of net factor productivity in Canada and the United States are 2.11 and 1.80 respectively. This difference likely reflects specification errors in the simple Cobb-Douglas model used, especially since it was found necessary to neglect returns to scale, and since these will show up in the measured factor productivity.

The main conclusions that may be inferred from this study are that agriculture has played a unique role in Canada's recent growth, and that any attempt to extrapolate aggregate productivity advance on the basis of past experience must keep this condition in mind. As for manufacturing, its growth performance has been rather unspectacular, with output and technical advance proceeding at an average rate.

More comprehensive studies of potential growth in Canada have been recently completed but are not yet available for publication. One, by T. Wilson for the Royal Commission on Taxation, has utilized the Knowles technique [37] to estimate the nature of potential growth. While we are unable to present his findings, he does indicate that his results are not significantly different from Lithwick's aggregative findings.

[34] Insofar as the periods chosen are not strictly comparable, this hypothesis must remain tentative.

[35] Lithwick, *op. cit.*, Table 43, p. 100.

[36] *Estimates of Fixed Capital Flows and Stocks, Manufacturing, Canada, 1926–60*, forthcoming.

[37] James W. Knowles, *The Potential Economic Growth in the United States*, Joint Economic Committee Study of Employment, Growth, and Price Levels, Study Paper No. 21, Washington, D.C., 1960.

One further study may also be referred to, which was available in unpublished form at the time of writing. Professor T. M. Brown has produced a study of Canadian economic growth for the Royal Commission on Health Services, in which econometric tools are used. We were unable to obtain permission to cite his findings prior to publication, however, and are therefore not in a position to report on this work.

Statistical Appendix

CONSTANT-1949-DOLLAR OUTPUT ESTIMATES

The rates of growth of constant-dollar gross domestic product at factor cost for total manufacturing and our thirteen 1948 DBS Standard Industrial Classification major groups are derived from DBS 61-505, *Indexes of Real Domestic Product by Industry of Origin, 1935–61,* Table 1, pages 67–68, and of gross output (for the years where obtainable) from DBS 61-502, *Revised Index of Industrial Production, 1935–1957,* Appendix C. We used DBS 13-513, *Supplement to the Inter-Industry Flow of Goods and Services, Canada, 1949,* Table 1, to obtain approximations to gross output and intermediate inputs (excluding intramajor group consumption) in 1949, in order to obtain the 1946–53 rate of change of constant-1949-dollar intermediate inputs. Minor differences in industrial coverage between the 13-513 and 61-502 indexes of gross output reduce the validity of the estimates of rates of change of constant-dollar gross output and intermediate input presented in Table 11. The various indexes of output purport to relate to manufacturing activity only.

CONSTANT-1949-DOLLAR CAPACITY OUTPUT ESTIMATES

The ratios of gross domestic product in 1949 dollars to the net stock of capital in 1949 dollars based on Set I lives were calculated. By inspection it was determined that there were no persistent trends in the capital-output ratios for seven major groups. For these groups the year 1955 or 1956 was assumed to represent capacity output from the capital stock. The net stock for each group in each postwar year was divided by the selected capital-output ratio to give an estimate of the output that might have been produced if the capital stock had been utilized to the same extent as in 1955 or 1956.

For those major groups for which there appeared to be a trend in the capital-output ratio a straight line was fitted through the ratios of 1948 and 1956. The ratios for each year were calculated from this line, and the net stock for each year was divided by this trend value of the capital-output ratio. This gives the capacity output in each year, on the assumption that the degree of utilization was the same in 1948 as in 1956 and that the capital-output ratio corresponding to capacity did follow a linear trend over the period. The capacity estimates are presented in Table SA–1.

THE LABOR INPUT

The DBS has recently released annual indexes of output per person employed and per man-hour for total manufacturing, based on persons employed and man-hours data which are superior to ours. The labor input we used in Part II of this paper are of two kinds. First, the rates of growth (and indexes) of the number of administrative and office (including working owners and partners) employees and production and related workers are taken from DBS 31-201, *General Review of the Manufacturing Industries of Canada* (various annual issues), and data prepared for the Canadian Political Science Association Historical Statistics project.[1] The number of employees purports to include only those engaged in manufacturing activities and matches the purported activity coverage of the output indexes. As an alternative measure of the labor input, we calculated the rate of growth (index) of administrative and office employees separately from those for production and related workers and weighted the rates of growth (indexes) together by the 1949 proportions between salaries and wages.

In Table SA–2, we compare the two rates of growth and the resulting effects on the estimated rates of change of total measured factor productivity.

As can be seen from Table SA–2, the two series on labor inputs yield only negligible differences for most major groups, though the differences for the tobacco, rubber, and leather and the textiles major groups are substantial.

For man-hours data, we had an even wider choice. Average paid weekly man-hours for both wage earners and salaried employees by major group were obtained from various issues of DBS 72-204, *Earnings and Hours of Work in Manufacturing*. These data are based on an annual survey conducted one week in late October or November and include full-time, short-time, and overtime hours worked and any hours of paid absence in the week. The data pertain to establishments employing fifteen or more persons and include working owners and partners. Data on annual averages of paid weekly man-hours for *wage earners only* in establishments employing fifteen or more persons by major group in manufacturing were obtained from various issues of DBS 72-202, *Review of Man-hours and Hourly Earnings*.

The man-hours statistics include hours worked by full-time and part-time wage earners, including overtime hours actually worked; premium or penalty hours credited for purposes of computing overtime payment are not included. Hours credited to wage-earners absent on leave with pay in the reported pay periods are included in the statistics as though the hours had been worked. The averages are obtained by dividing the aggregated hours reported for the week by the number of full-time and part-time wage earners working such hours.[2]

[1] M. C. Urquhart and K. A. H. Buckley (ed.), *Historical Statistics of Canada,* Toronto, 1965.

[2] DBS 72–202, *Review of Man-hours and Hourly Earnings, 1945–62*, p. 45.

TABLE SA-1

Estimates of Excess Capacity, Total Manufacturing and Major Groups,

1946 - 60

(millions of constant 1949 dollars)

	Capacity Output	Capacity Minus Actual Output	Capacity Output	Capacity Minus Actual Output	Capacity Output	Capacity Minus Actual Output
	Food and Beverages		*Tobacco, Rubber, and Leather Products*		*Textile Products*	
1946	465.3	−91.6	162.9	−21.9	196.7	−17.9
1947	508.4	−44.0	177.0	−21.8	215.0	−12.4
1948	559.8	0.0	187.6	6.1	235.4	0.0
1949	599.1	30.8	191.2	14.4	249.8	7.9
1950	626.5	36.6	192.1	6.6	257.6	−14.5
1951	648.8	41.9	193.0	9.4	266.0	− 7.6
1952	667.2	22.2	196.0	3.4	274.9	26.0
1953	684.4	17.2	203.4	− 5.2	278.1	17.1
1954	708.1	22.7	213.1	14.7	279.5	51.4
1955	734.0	13.4	221.4	0.0	280.4	4.6
1956	756.4	0.0	230.7	− 9.5	283.7	0.0
1957	777.4	6.8	241.3	− 0.5	289.7	5.2
1958	800.4	− 6.0	247.9	9.3	290.1	24.3
1959	819.0	−19.8	250.7	−10.2	284.4	−16.5
1960	841.6	−12.0	257.8	14.0	279.0	−17.3
	Iron and Steel Products		*Transportation Equipment*		*Nonferrous Metal Products and Electrical Apparatus and Supplies*	
1946	569.8	85.0	409.7	91.2	513.1	174.9
1947	584.8	23.2	400.4	23.9	504.8	101.7
1948	609.0	0.0	392.1	8.1	506.4	76.4
1949	625.2	25.2	390.5	− 4.6	513.9	64.0
1950	630.8	15.8	396.2	−31.7	519.5	33.6
1951	653.9	−48.1	415.4	−103.4	533.6	6.3
1952	716.9	3.5	450.5	−138.6	569.9	39.1
1953	780.1	88.3	508.5	−144.2	614.5	9.1
1954	812.6	175.4	565.7	23.2	647.8	48.1
1955	831.1	88.3	597.9	24.6	676.5	0.0
1956	871.8	0.0	623.9	0.0	722.3	0.7
1957	934.8	97.2	649.7	52.3	783.6	91.2
1958	971.9	202.1	669.9	146.4	828.4	153.8
1959	997.3	114.1	689.7	170.1	840.5	128.6
1960	1,040.4	216.6	705.4	191.8	843.4	108.8

Capacity Output	Capacity Minus Actual Output	Capacity Output	Capacity Minus Actual Output	Capacity Output	Capacity Minus Actual Output	Capacity Output	Capacity Minus Actual Output
Clothing Products		*Wood Products*		*Paper Products*		*Printing, Publishing, and Allied Industries*	
259.3	3.5	297.4	24.8	322.7	3.0	160.4	14.5
274.2	26.7	313.3	4.9	345.5	− 6.2	164.9	6.3
291.0	29.0	331.0	15.0	374.6	0.0	176.7	1.0
303.3	34.9	341.2	27.1	398.0	3.3	190.3	0.6
311.7	39.8	351.2	11.3	413.7	−17.7	201.9	9.4
317.3	45.7	366.2	5.6	435.8	−28.0	214.0	14.6
321.9	22.9	380.6	16.9	465.4	17.8	222.5	18.6
326.7	18.0	390.9	− 3.0	485.7	19.6	226.0	8.4
327.2	34.9	401.1	11.0	493.2	3.4	237.0	6.3
321.9	19.1	414.2	−14.2	504.6	−12.5	250.8	9.7
315.6	0.0	434.4	0.0	543.9	0.0	260.5	0.0
310.8	− 2.7	451.1	51.3	598.2	63.4	275.5	13.3
304.5	− 2.5	453.8	39.2	621.5	86.3	292.2	37.2
299.7	− 3.9	462.0	32.9	616.3	45.2	308.1	36.4
298.7	9.1	477.4	50.2	614.1	28.4	321.6	43.7

Capacity Output	Capacity Minus Actual Output	Capacity Output	Capacity Minus Actual Output	Capacity Output	Capacity Minus Actual Output	Capacity Output	Capacity Minus Actual Output
Nonmetallic Mineral Products and Products of Petroleum and Coal		*Chemical Products*		*Miscellaneous Manufacturing Industries*		*Total Manufacturing*	
137.8	− 4.1	166.9	− 9.3	59.7	− 2.9	3,564.3	93.2
150.1	−13.0	177.4	− 6.5	65.6	0.0	3,726.5	−70.6
173.9	− 3.9	193.8	0.0	71.5	8.0	3,964.1	0.0
192.8	− 1.9	208.2	5.7	76.5	− 1.5	4,157.4	83.3
204.5	−12.3	214.8	− 3.3	80.6	− 0.5	4,284.9	−41.8
222.1	−17.8	224.1	−18.9	85.2	− 7.6	4,468.7	−216.5
249.2	− 3.1	261.0	13.3	90.4	− 4.6	4,782.0	−45.8
278.4	− 3.5	311.0	27.7	96.2	−13.9	5,117.3	−32.4
309.6	10.7	331.0	23.0	100.8	− 4.0	5,366.8	359.7
345.8	− 0.5	331.8	− 3.3	106.4	0.0	5,575.2	87.4
391.6	0.0	354.0	0.0	114.7	0.0	5,911.5	0.0
442.2	45.1	392.1	20.7	124.6	5.0	6,343.1	521.2
483.8	74.6	419.6	18.6	133.3	3.6	6,633.3	901.1
520.3	71.7	430.4	8.4	142.4	− 0.5	6,792.5	689.5
546.4	105.4	437.4	− 7.5	154.8	5.4	6,947.0	864.4

TABLE SA-2

Unweighted and Weighted Persons Employed, Total Measured Factor Input and Total Measured Factor Productivity, Total Manufacturing and Major Groups, 1946-56 and 1946-60

(continuous annual rates of change)

	Persons Employed		Total Measured Factor Input		Total Measured Factor Productivity	
	(1)	(2)	(3)	(4)	(5)	(6)
Total manufacturing						
1946-56	2.5	2.6	3.2	3.3	2.1	2.0
1946-60	1.4	1.6	2.5	2.6	1.5	1.4
Food and beverages						
1946-56	1.3	1.3	2.5	2.6	0.5	0.5
1946-60	1.3	1.3	2.5	2.5	0.6	0.6
Tobacco, rubber, and leather products						
1946-56	−0.9	−0.7	0.1	0.2	2.5	2.4
1946-60	−1.2	−0.9	−0.2	0.0	2.2	1.9
Textile products						
1946-56	0.5	1.0	2.1	2.5	0.7	0.3
1946-60	−0.6	−0.2	0.9	1.2	1.4	1.1
Clothing products						
1946-56	0.5	0.5	0.9	0.9	1.2	1.2
1946-60	0.2	0.2	0.5	0.5	0.4	0.4
Wood products						
1946-56	2.5	2.5	2.6	2.6	2.0	2.0
1946-60	0.9	0.9	1.3	1.3	1.9	1.9
Paper products						
1946-56	3.3	3.4	4.3	4.3	1.1	1.0
1946-60	2.4	2.5	3.7	3.8	0.6	0.5
Printing, publishing, and allied industries						
1946-56	4.0	4.0	4.0	4.0	1.8	1.8
1946-60	3.1	3.1	3.3	3.3	1.3	1.3

(continued)

TABLE SA-2 *(concluded)*

	Persons Employed		Total Measured Factor Input		Total Measured Factor Productivity	
	(1)	(2)	(3)	(4)	(5)	(6)
Iron and steel products						
1946-56	2.6	2.8	3.3	3.4	2.6	2.4
1946-60	1.7	1.9	2.7	2.8	1.1	1.0
Transportation equipment						
1946-56	3.4	3.7	3.2	3.3	3.6	3.4
1946-60	0.6	0.8	1.1	1.2	2.3	2.2
Nonferrous metal products and electrical apparatus and supplies						
1946-56	5.0	5.2	4.2	4.4	3.3	3.2
1946-60	2.6	2.8	2.8	3.0	2.7	2.6
Nonmetallic mineral products and products of petroleum and coal						
1946-56	4.6	4.8	6.6	6.7	3.6	3.5
1946-60	3.5	3.6	5.8	5.9	2.3	2.2
Chemical products						
1946-56	3.3	3.4	5.2	5.3	1.7	1.7
1946-60	2.6	2.7	4.6	4.6	2.0	2.0
Miscellaneous manufacturing industries						
1946-56	4.6	4.9	4.6	4.8	1.4	1.2
1946-60	4.8	5.0	4.9	5.1	1.4	1.2

Note: Columns (1), (3), and (5) refer to the unweighted persons-employed labor input and are reproduced from Table 6 while columns (2), (4), and (6) refer to persons employed weighted by wages and salaries proportions in 1949.

The measured total factor input and total measured factor productivity rates of change are on a gross domestic product basis. Factor inputs and factor productivity estimates are based on Set I of the average economic lives used by DBS in preparing the manufacturing capital stock estimates.

Charts for each major group were drawn comparing annually:

1. The number of salaried employees from 31-201 and 72-204;
2. The number of wage earners from 31-201, 72-202 and 72-284;
3. Annual averages of paid weekly hours of wage earners from 72-202 and 72-204.

In some instances, significant differences in trend in these comparisons were noted. For purposes of Part II of our paper, the paid man-hours series for which rates of growth and indexes were calculated were based on the number of salaried employees from DBS 31-201 times average weekly hours from DBS 72-204 and the number of wage earners from DBS 31-201 times average weekly hours from DBS 72-202. The two components were added together to derive the paid man-hours input used throughout Part II. To obtain an appraisal of how different selection procedures would have affected our estimates, additional variants of the paid man-hours input were prepared.

As is shown in Table SA–3, differences in estimated rates of change in total measured factor productivity are only negligibly affected when the average weekly hours data for wage-earners is taken from DBS 72-204 rather than DBS 72-202. Greater differences emerge, however, when the hours data are weighted together, using wages and salaries as weights.

We also compared our labor input data with that recently published by DBS for total manufacturing. With respect to persons employed, the variant we used in Part II of this paper, compared to the more refined DBS data, would suggest a slight downward bias in our data. It would appear that our growth rate for persons employed in total manufacturing may be biased downward by one-tenth of one percentage point. Given the weight for labor (see below) in our estimation of total measured factor productivity, an increase in the growth rate of our persons employed input of 0.1 would lead to a decrease in the rate of growth of total measured factor productivity in total manufacturing of approximately two-thirds of 0.1, a variation substantially below that introduced by variations in the different capital inputs when the average economic lives of the capital goods were changed. Moreover, the foregoing tables suggest that the use of market prices to weight the labor inputs together would lead to higher rates of growth of the labor input than are shown in Part II of our paper.

We are somewhat surprised at the close correspondence between the DBS man-hours worked series and our man-hours paid series used in Part II. We have tentative evidence which would suggest that our man-hours paid series should be running ahead of the DBS man-hours worked series more than it does. The relatively close match between our crude labor input data and the better data from DBS for total manufacturing does not ensure that a similarly close match would exist at the major group level of detail.

In addition to the differences between hours paid and hours worked, differences in the quality of the labor input in the various industries may lead to total measured factor productivity growth rates that are not really

TABLE SA-3

Unweighted and Weighted Variants of Man-Hours, Total Measured Factor Input, and Total Measured Factor Productivity, Total Manufacturing and Major Groups, 1946-56 and 1946-60

(continuous annual rates of change)

	Paid Man-Hours				Total Measured Factor Input				Total Measured Factor Productivity			
	(1)	(2)	(3)	(4)	(5)	(6)	(7)	(8)	(9)	(10)	(11)	(12)
Total manufacturing												
1946-56	2.0	2.0	2.2	2.2	2.9	2.9	3.0	3.0	2.4	2.4	2.3	2.3
1946-60	1.0	1.0	1.2	1.2	2.2	2.2	2.3	2.3	1.8	1.9	1.7	1.7
Food and beverages												
1946-56	0.9	0.8	0.9	0.8	2.3	2.2	2.3	2.2	0.8	0.9	0.8	0.8
1946-60	0.9	0.8	0.9	0.8	2.2	2.1	2.2	2.2	0.8	0.9	0.8	0.8
Tobacco, rubber, and leather products												
1946-56	-1.2	-1.5	-1.1	-1.3	-0.1	-0.4	-0.0	-0.2	2.8	3.0	2.7	2.8
1946-60	-1.4	-1.6	-1.3	-1.4	-0.4	-0.5	-0.3	-0.4	2.4	2.5	2.2	2.4
Textile products												
1946-56	0.1	0.3	0.6	0.8	1.9	2.0	2.2	2.3	0.9	0.8	0.6	0.5
1946-60	-1.0	-0.9	-0.6	-0.4	0.7	0.8	1.0	1.0	1.6	1.6	1.4	1.3
Clothing products												
1946-56	0.4	0.2	0.3	0.2	0.8	0.6	0.7	0.6	1.3	1.5	1.4	1.5
1946-60	0.0	-0.2	-0.1	-0.2	0.3	0.2	0.2	0.3	0.6	0.7	0.7	0.6

(continued)

TABLE SA-3 (continued)

	Paid Man-Hours				Total Measured Factor Input				Total Measured Factor Productivity			
	(1)	(2)	(3)	(4)	(5)	(6)	(7)	(8)	(9)	(10)	(11)	(12)
Wood products												
1946-56	2.0	2.1	2.0	2.0	2.3	2.3	2.3	2.3	2.4	2.4	2.4	2.4
1946-60	0.5	0.4	0.5	0.4	1.0	1.0	1.0	1.0	2.2	2.2	2.2	2.2
Paper products												
1946-56	2.1	2.2	2.3	2.4	3.6	3.7	3.7	3.8	1.7	1.6	1.6	1.5
1946-60	1.4	1.6	1.6	1.7	3.2	3.3	3.3	3.4	1.1	1.0	1.0	1.0
Printing, publishing, and allied industries												
1946-56	3.5	3.4	3.6	3.5	3.7	3.6	3.7	3.6	2.1	2.2	2.1	2.2
1946-60	2.6	2.6	2.7	2.6	3.0	3.0	3.0	3.0	1.6	1.6	1.6	1.6
Iron and steel products												
1946-56	2.2	2.0	2.3	2.2	3.0	2.9	3.1	3.0	2.9	3.0	2.8	2.9
1946-60	1.2	1.1	1.4	1.3	2.3	2.2	2.5	2.4	1.5	1.6	1.3	1.4
Transportation equipment												
1946-56	3.1	3.0	3.3	3.3	2.9	2.9	3.1	3.1	3.8	3.8	3.6	3.6
1946-60	0.4	0.3	0.6	0.5	0.9	0.9	1.1	1.0	2.5	2.6	2.3	2.4
Nonferrous metal products and electrical apparatus and supplies												
1946-56	4.5	4.6	4.8	4.9	3.9	4.0	4.1	4.2	3.6	3.6	3.4	3.6
1946-60	2.3	2.2	2.5	2.5	2.6	2.6	2.7	2.7	3.0	3.0	2.8	2.8

(continued)

TABLE SA-3 (concluded)

	Paid Man-Hours				Total Measured Factor Input				Total Measured Factor Productivity			
	(1)	(2)	(3)	(4)	(5)	(6)	(7)	(8)	(9)	(10)	(11)	(12)
Nonmetallic mineral products and products of petroleum and coal												
1946-56	4.3	4.1	4.6	4.4	6.4	6.3	6.6	6.5	3.7	3.8	3.6	3.7
1946-60	3.2	3.0	3.4	3.3	5.6	5.5	5.7	5.7	2.5	2.6	2.4	2.4
Chemical products												
1946-56	2.8	2.7	2.9	2.8	5.0	4.9	5.0	5.0	2.0	2.1	1.9	2.0
1946-60	2.2	2.1	2.3	2.2	4.3	4.3	4.4	4.4	2.3	2.3	2.2	2.3
Miscellaneous manufacturing industries												
1946-56	4.3	4.4	4.6	4.6	4.4	4.5	4.7	4.7	1.6	1.6	1.4	1.4
1946-60	4.6	4.5	4.9	4.9	4.7	4.7	4.9	4.9	1.5	1.5	1.3	1.3

Source: Columns (1), (5), and (9): Based on persons-employed data from DBS 31-201, *General Review of the Manufacturing Industries of Canada*, average weekly hours for salaried employees from DBS 72-204, *Earnings and Hours of Work in Manufacturing*, and average weekly hours for wage earners from DBS 72-202, *Review of Man-hours and Hourly Earnings 1945-62*, and are reproduced from Table 6. Columns (2), (6), and (10): Based on persons-employed data from DBS 31-201, average weekly hours for salaried employees and wage earners from DBS 72-204. Columns (3), (7), and (11): Same as column (1) with hours data for two components weighted together using 1949 wages and salaries proportions. Columns (4), (8), and (12): Same as column (2) with hours data for two components weighted together using 1949 wages and salaries proportions.

The total measured factor input and total measured factor productivity rates of changes are on the gross domestic product basis. Data refer only to Set I of the average economic lives used by DBS in preparing the capital stock estimates.

TABLE SA-4

Comparison of Indexes of Labor Input,

Total Manufacturing, 1947-60

(1949 = 100.0)

	Persons Employed			Man-Hours Worked,	Man-Hours Paid			
	DBS	Our Indexes		DBS		Our Indexes		
	(1)	(2)	(3)	(4)	(5)	(6)	(7)	(8)
1947	96.3	96.6	95.9	97.7	97.4	97.6	96.6	96.7
1948	98.5	98.7	98.1	100.4	99.1	99.4	98.4	98.7
1949	100.0	100.0	100.0	100.0	100.0	100.0	100.0	100.0
1950	101.7	101.0	101.3	100.8	101.0	101.1	101.1	101.3
1951	107.9	107.4	107.7	104.9	106.0	104.4	106.3	104.9
1952	110.8	110.0	110.6	106.6	108.1	108.0	108.7	108.7
1953	114.2	113.3	114.0	110.5	110.6	109.2	111.4	110.1
1954	109.3	108.3	109.4	103.9	104.4	103.8	105.7	105.3
1955	112.1	110.9	112.1	107.0	107.6	107.4	109.0	108.9
1956	116.8	115.5	116.8	112.3	112.0	111.3	113.5	112.9
1957	117.3	116.0	117.7	111.4	111.0	108.9	112.9	111.0
1958	111.5	110.1	112.0	105.9	104.8	104.4	106.9	106.6
1959	112.9	111.3	113.1	107.8	107.0	106.2	108.9	108.3
.1960	111.4	110.3	112.2	105.6	105.4	104.4	107.6	106.7
		(continuous annual rates of change)						
1947-56	2.1	2.0	2.2	1.5	1.6	1.5	1.8	1.7
1947-60	1.1	1.0	1.2	0.6	0.6	0.5	0.8	0.8

Note: See revisions using new GDP data in Table SA-14.

Source: Columns (1) and (4): DBS 14-501, *Indexes of Output Per Person Employed and Per Man-Hour in Canada, Commercial Non-Agricultural Industries, 1947-63,* Table 2. These DBS series are not available prior to 1947. Column (2): Unweighted persons employed. Column (3): Persons employed with wages and salaries as weights. Column (5): See source note to column (1), Table SA-3. Column (6): See source note to column (2), Table SA-3. Column (7): See source note to column (3), Table SA-3. Column (8): See source note to column (4), Table SA-3.

indicators of the differences in rates of technological advance. We have attempted to adjust our data to indicate the results of not correcting for these factors.

The first adjustment undertaken was to try to estimate the number of hours worked per week. Since the published DBS data which we have used are on a paid basis, and since wages have included a rising component of paid time off, there has been a growing gap between the number of hours actually worked and the number of hours for which workers have received payment. Our procedure was to use some sample evidence on the value of paid time off between 1953 and 1960 in selected manufacturing industries of Canada.[3]

These data are certainly not completely satisfactory, the sampling unit being "companies." Eighty-eight manufacturing companies were sampled in the first survey, having just under a quarter million employees or one-sixth of the total number of employees in manufacturing in that year. No evidence is presented on the sampling procedures, so no estimate of the degree of bias or the size of the sampling error can be determined.

With these serious problems in mind, let us nevertheless consider their findings and the implications of these for our own results. Table SA–6 presents the effect of removing hours paid but not worked upon the growth rate of man-hours. In all cases, the effect is very substantial indeed, with labor input showing a much slower growth rate than on the paid basis.

It is clear that a slower-growing labor input will have the effect of increasing the rate of growth of total measured factor productivity. To get a rough idea of the extent of that increase, we take the growth rate of the total measured factor productivity in the period 1946–60 and calculate the effect of our adjustment. These data are presented in Table SA–7.

The effect of this adjustment is to raise total measured factor productivity by about one-third on the average, with a very great degree of variability between industries. This suggests that a large part of the increase in productivity has been concealed through the use of hours paid data in studies of Canadian growth.[4]

If the orders of magnitude suggested here are correct, it is essential, for any accurate evaluation of growth in Canada, that data on hours worked be obtained.

The second aspect of labor input which we wish to consider is the changing quality as reflected in amount of education and changes in age and sex composition. The treatment follows that of Denison[5] with the adjustment for days of schooling neglected. The results, summarized in Table SA–8, reveal that for all but one major group (tobacco, rubber, and leather

[3] *Fringe Benefit Costs in Canada*, Toronto, Industrial Relations Counsellors Service, Inc., No. 1, December 1954. Recent studies have been conducted by the Thorne Group, but reasonable consistency has been maintained.

[4] This leads to an overstatement of labor's role in growth to the same extent.

[5] E. F. Denison, *The Sources of Economic Growth in the United States and the Alternatives Before Us*, Washington, D.C., 1962.

TABLE SA-5

Indexes of Output Per Labor Input, Total Manufacturing, 1947-60
(1949 = 1.000)

| | Output Per Person Employed | | | Output Per Man-Hour Worked, | | Output Per Man-Hour Paid | | |
| | DBS | Our Indexes | | DBS | | | Our Indexes | | |
	(1)	(2)	(3)	(4)	(5)	(6)	(7)	(8)
1947	0.968	0.965	0.972	0.954	0.957	0.955	0.965	0.964
1948	0.988	0.986	0.992	0.969	0.982	0.979	0.989	0.986
1949	1.000	1.000	1.000	1.000	1.000	1.000	1.000	1.000
1950	1.044	1.051	1.048	1.054	1.051	1.050	1.050	1.048
1951	1.066	1.071	1.068	1.096	1.085	1.102	1.082	1.096
1952	1.069	1.077	1.071	1.112	1.096	1.097	1.090	1.090
1953	1.107	1.116	1.109	1.144	1.143	1.158	1.135	1.148
1954	1.124	1.135	1.123	1.183	1.177	1.184	1.163	1.117
1955	1.202	1.215	1.202	1.259	1.252	1.254	1.236	1.237
1956	1.242	1.256	1.242	1.292	1.296	1.304	1.278	1.285
1957	1.218	1.232	1.214	1.283	1.287	1.312	1.266	1.287
1958	1.262	1.278	1.256	1.329	1.343	1.348	1.316	1.320
1959	1.327	1.346	1.324	1.390	1.400	1.411	1.376	1.383
1960	1.340	1.354	1.331	1.414	1.416	1.430	1.388	1.399
	(continuous average annual rates of change)							
1947-56	2.8	2.9	2.7	3.4	3.4	3.5	3.1	3.2
1947-60	2.5	2.6	2.4	3.0	3.0	3.1	2.8	2.9

Note: See revisions using the revised output data in Table SA-15.

Source: Columns (1) and (4): DBS 14-501 (see source note, Table SA-4); columns
(2), (3), and (5)-(8) derived by dividing index of constant 1949 dollar gross domestic
product at factor cost for total manufacturing, DBS 61-505, *Indexes of Real Domestic
Product by Industry of Origin 1935-61,* by respective indexes in Table SA-4.

products) the quality of the labor input increased at an average rate for all
manufacturing of one-third of 1 per cent over the decade 1946–56. If we
allocate this increase to labor input, then its contribution to growth increased
by about one-quarter of 1 per cent per year, and the growth rate of factor productivity declines by that much. Once again there is great variability
between the quality gains in the different industries with only weak association between the rate of quality gain and the growth rate of total factor pro-

TABLE SA-6

Correction of Labor Input for Hours Paid But Not Worked, Canada, 1953-60

	Average Hourly Wage (1)	Average Annual Hours Paid (2)	Paid Time Off Per Year (3)	Hours Paid But Not Worked (4)	Average Annual Hours Worked (5)	Number of Employees (6)	Man-Hours Worked Per Year (7)	Man-Hours Paid Per Year (8)	Continuous Annual Rates of Change	
									Hours Worked (9)	Hours Paid (10)
Total manufacturing										
1953	$1.44	2,137	$205	142	1,995	1,327	2,613	2,837		
1960	2.01	2,101	523	260	1,841	1,292	2,328	2,724	-1.53	-0.58
Food and beverages										
1953	1.22	2,189	207	170	2,020	177	357	387		
1960	1.73	2,106	535	309	1,797	193	347	417	-0.38	1.08
Textile products										
1953	1.23	2,127	167	136	1,991	73	146	156		
1960	1.63	2,163	373	229	1,934	62	120	134	-2.82	-2.16
Paper products										
1953	1.72	2,122	205	119	2,002	84	169	187		
1960	2.38	2,064	410	172	1,892	95	179	202	0.85	1.08

(continued)

TABLE SA-6 *(concluded)*

	Average Hourly Wage (1)	Average Annual Hours Paid (2)	Paid Time Off Per Year (3)	Hours Paid But Not Worked (4)	Average Annual Hours Worked (5)	Number of Employees (6)	Man-Hours Worked Per Year (7)	Man-Hours Paid Per Year (8)	Continuous Annual Rates of Change — Hours Worked (9)	Continuous Annual Rates of Change — Hours Paid (10)
Chemical products										
1953	$1.60	2,116	$211	132	1,984	50	100	106	0.07	0.84
1960	2.39	2,049	545	228	1,821	55	100	113		
Nonmetallic minerals and products of petroleum and coal										
1953	1.59	2,075	291	183	1,892	17	32	36	−1.73	−0.73
1960	2.25	2,012	682	303	1,709	17	29	34		
Iron and steel products										
1953	1.64	2,153	201	123	2,030	188	382	405	−0.71	−0.08
1960	2.28	2,096	464	204	1,892	192	364	403		

Note: Column (3): Expressed in dollars, includes vacations with pay and holidays with pay together with other time paid off (Studies in Industrial Relations "Fringe Benefit Costs in Canada," 1953, Table 7, p. 23; 1959, Table 7, p. 29; and 1961, Table 7, p. 29) Column 4: Column (3) divided by column (1). Column 5: Column (2) minus column (4). Column 6: Expressed in thousands of persons. Column 7: Column (5) times column (6) expressed in millions of man-hours. Column 8: Column (2) times column (6) expressed in millions of man-hours. Column (9) and (10) are derived from columns (7) and (8).

TABLE SA-7

Growth Rate of Total Measured Factor Productivity Based on Hours Worked, Canada, 1953-60

| | Difference in Growth Rate of Man-Hours (1) | Labor Coefficient (2) | Increase in Growth Rate of Factor Productivity (3) | Measured Factor Productivity | | Percentage Increase Due to Adjustment (6) |
| | | | | Growth Rate | | |
				Man-Hours Paid (4)	Man-Hours Worked (5)	
Total manufacturing	−0.95	.676	.6	1.8	2.5	35
Food and beverages	−1.46	.644	.9	0.8	1.8	115
Textile products	−0.66	.678	.4	1.6	2.1	27
Paper products	−0.23	.531	.1	1.1	1.2	111
Chemical products	−0.77	.548	.4	2.3	2.7	18
Nonmetallic mineral products and products of petroleum and coal	−1.00	.518	.5	2.5	3.0	21
Iron and steel products	−0.63	.700	.4	1.5	1.9	30

Source: Column (1): Table SA-6, column (9) minus column (10). Column (3): Column (2) times minus column(1). Column (4): Table 6, 1946 to 1960 Set III. Column (5): Column (3) plus column (4). Column (6): Percentage increase, column (5) over column (4).

TABLE SA-8

The Effect of Changing Labor Quality

	Rate of Growth of Factor Productivity (1946–56) (1)	Rate of Growth of Education (2)	Age-Sex Quality (3)	Labor Weight (4)	Contribution of Education (5)	Contribution of Age-Sex (6)	Total Quality Contribution (7)	Factor Productivity Net of Quality Change (8)	Percentage Decrease of Factor Productivity After Quality Adjustment (9)
Food and beverages	0.85	0.07	.03	.63	.05	.02	.07	0.78	7.9
Tobacco, rubber and leather products	3.00	−0.48	.01	.76	−.36	.01	−.35	3.35	17.9[a]
Textile products	0.82	0.10	.60	.67	.06	.41	.47	0.35	57.4
Clothing products	1.48	0.16	.16	.77	.13	.13	.25	1.23	17.0
Wood products	2.37	0.08	.07	.74	.06	.05	.11	2.26	4.5
Paper products	1.63	0.09	.20	.53	.05	.11	.15	1.48	9.4
Printing, publishing, and allied industries	2.20	1.03	−.31	.76	.78	−.24	.55	1.66	24.8
Iron and steel products	2.98	0.12	.37	.70	.08	.26	.34	2.64	11.3
Transportation equipment	3.83	0.04	.46	.69	.02	.31	.34	3.49	8.8

(continued)

TABLE SA-8 (concluded)

	Rate of Growth of Factor Productivity (1946–56) (1)	Rate of Growth of Education (2)	Age–Sex Quality (3)	Labor Weight (4)	Contribution of Education (5)	Contribution of Age–Sex (6)	Total Quality Contribution (7)	Factor Productivity Net of Quality Change (8)	Percentage Decrease of Factor Productivity After Quality Adjustment (9)
Nonferrous metal products and electrical apparatus and supplies	3.60	0.16	.01	.69	.11	.01	.11	3.49	3.1
Nonmetallic mineral products and products of petroleum and coal	3.82	0.15	.13	.52	.08	.07	.14	3.67	3.8
Chemical products	2.14	0.26	.35	.55	.14	.19	.34	1.81	15.7
Miscellaneous manufacturing industries	1.62	0.20	.25	.71	.14	.18	.32	1.30	19.6
Total manufacturing	2.46	0.11	.23	.67	.08	.15	.23	2.24	9.2

Source: Column (4): Set I lives, row b of column (1), Table SA-10. Column (5): column (4) times column (2). Column (6): column (4) times column (3). Column (7): column (5) plus column (6). Column (8): column (1) minus column (7). Column (9): column (7) divided by column (1).

[a]Increase.

ductivity. Some stronger association was found between the level of quality in the various industries in 1951 and the growth rate of factor productivity.[6]

These findings may be briefly summarized. The use of hours paid data yields a rather large downward bias in the growth rate of factor productivity of about one-third. On the other hand, failure to attribute quality improvements to labor leads to an overstatement of factor productivity by about one-tenth on the average. What is evident is that rather large swings in the size of total measured factor productivity can be obtained by making quite straightforward adjustments to our labor input series.

FIXED CAPITAL INPUT

Preliminary data on constant-1949 and current-dollar gross fixed capital formation, midyear net stock, and capital consumption allowances by major group and total manufacturing were obtained from preliminary worksheets lying behind the forthcoming DBS reference paper, *Estimates of Fixed Capital Flows and Stocks, Manufacturing, Canada, 1926–1960*. Historical gross fixed capital formation data were not adequate to permit DBS to make these estimates for the seventeen major groups in the 1948 DBS Standard Industrial Classification Manufacturing Division, with the result that the estimates are prepared for the combined tobacco, rubber, and leather products; the nonferrous metal products and electrical apparatus and supplies; and nonmetallic mineral products and products of petroleum and coal major groups. As indicated in Part II the estimates were prepared using five different sets of average economic lives of fixed capital goods. The five different sets are reproduced here in Table SA–9.

The estimates of current-dollar gross fixed capital formation by industry, which provide the basic source data for the DBS capital stock measurement program, have been shifted, for 1961 and all subsequent years, from the 1948 DBS SIC to the 1960 DBS SIC.[7] The break in the investment series that results necessitates further work before the capital stock estimates in manufacturing can be extended beyond 1960.

INVENTORIES

Estimates of rates of change of constant-1949 and current-dollar end-of-second-quarter inventories by major group in manufacturing were computed from confidential data kindly supplied by the National Accounts and Balance

---

[6] We fitted the function

$$A = -15.4 + 9.2S + 9.3E$$
$$\quad\quad\quad (2.7)\quad (1.6)$$

The t .95 values for the b coefficients is 2.23. $R_c = .630$, and a variance test yielded a significant regression plane at the 95 per cent level. A is the growth rate of factor productivity, S is the level of the age-sex index, and E is the level of the education index.

[7] See Department of Trade and Commerce, *Private and Public Investment in Canada, Outlook, 1962.*

TABLE SA-9

Five Sets of Average Economic Lives of Capital Goods, Used in DBS Estimates of Fixed Capital Stocks and Flows in Canadian Manufacturing

Set	Building Construction	Engineering Construction	Machinery and Equipment	Capital Items Charged to Operating Expenses
	Food and Beverages			
I	50	55	29	5
II	50	55	29	5
III	60	66	35	7
IV	40	44	23	3
V	40	44	17	3
	Clothing Products			
I	30	0	21	5
II	50	0	21	5
III	36	0	25	7
IV	24	0	17	3
V	24	0	13	3
	Printing, Publishing and Allied Industries			
I	50	55	30	5
II	50	55	30	5
III	60	66	36	7
IV	40	44	24	3
V	40	44	18	3

Set	Building Construction	Engineering Construction	Machinery and Equipment	Capital Items Charged to Operating Expenses
	Tobacco, Rubber and Leather Products			
I	50	55	15	5
II	50	55	15	5
III	60	66	18	7
IV	40	44	12	3
V	40	44	9	3
	Wood Products			
I	30	35	26	5
II	50	55	26	5
III	36	42	31	7
IV	24	28	21	3
V	24	28	16	3
	Iron and Steel Products			
I	45	50	21	5
II	50	55	21	5
III	54	60	25	7
IV	36	40	17	3
V	36	40	13	3

Set	Building Construction	Engineering Construction	Machinery and Equipment	Capital Items Charged to Operating Expenses
	Textile Products			
I	45	50	26	5
II	50	55	26	5
III	54	60	31	7
IV	36	40	21	3
V	36	40	16	3
	Paper Products			
I	50	55	22	5
II	50	55	22	5
III	60	66	26	7
IV	40	44	18	3
V	40	44	13	3
	Transportation Equipment			
I	40	45	30	5
II	50	55	30	5
III	48	54	36	7
IV	32	36	24	3
V	32	36	18	3

(continued)

TABLE SA-9 (concluded)

Nonferrous Metal Products and Electrical Apparatus and Supplies

Set	Building Construction	Engineering Construction	Machinery and Equipment	Capital Items Charged to Operating Expenses
I	40	45	22	5
II	50	55	22	5
III	48	54	26	7
IV	32	36	18	3
V	32	36	13	3

Nonmetallic Mineral Products and Products of Petroleum and Coal

Set	Building Construction	Engineering Construction	Machinery and Equipment	Capital Items Charged to Operating Expenses
I	35	40	26	5
II	50	55	26	5
III	42	48	31	7
IV	28	32	21	3
V	28	32	16	3

Miscellaneous Manufacturing Industries

Set	Building Construction	Engineering Construction	Machinery and Equipment	Capital Items Charged to Operating Expenses
I	30	35	13	5
II	50	55	13	5
III	36	42	16	7
IV	24	28	10	3
V	24	28	8	3

Chemical Products

Set	Building Construction	Engineering Construction	Machinery and Equipment	Capital Items Charged to Operating Expenses
I	50	55	22	5
II	50	55	22	5
III	60	66	26	7
IV	40	44	18	3
V	40	44	13	3

Source: Forthcoming DBS reference paper, on *Estimates of Fixed Capital Flows and Stocks, Manufacturing, Canada, 1926-1960.* Negligible engineering construction occurred in the clothing products major group. Row headings (I, II, III, IV, V) correspond with those in tables in Part II of this paper.

of Payments Division of DBS. Estimates for 1946 were obtained by us by graphical interpolation.

LAND

The only data on the stock of land used in manufacturing are those of the Department of National Revenue, in *Taxation Statistics*. The data suffer from a number of conceptual and classification problems, and we were unable to use them. Thus, the weights for the net stock of capital are overstated and, if land was a significant factor in any major group, our estimates of total measured factor productivity suffer from the failure to take land into account. While for an aggregate economy of fixed territorial boundaries, it can be argued that the constant-price stock of land, and other natural agents, remains unchanged, it is clearly not defensible to make such an assumption in any disaggregated analysis of total measured factor productivity.

FACTOR WEIGHTS

The weighting diagram for the year 1949 was obtained from DBS 13-513, *Supplement to the Inter-Industry Flow of Goods and Services, Canada, 1949*, Table 1. Estimates of current-dollar gross domestic product are provided for 29 two- and three-digit 1948 DBS SIC industries in manufacturing, broken down into wages, salaries and supplementary labor income; investment income; net income of unincorporated business; and capital consumption allowances and inventory valuation adjustments. These data were combined into our thirteen major groups, and the last item was replaced by the estimates of current-dollar capital consumption allowances derived from the DBS fixed capital stocks and flows study for manufacturing. We were not able to deal with the inventory valuation adjustment satisfactorily, and our weights have some slight ambiguity in this respect. In addition, as previously mentioned, the DBS 13-513 industry and activity coverage in manufacturing is slightly different than that for manufacturing in DBS 61-505. We arbitrarily split the net income of unincorporated enterprises three ways: 25:75; 50:50, and 75:25 to labor and net returns to capital, respectively. The net returns to capital were split between the net stock of fixed capital and inventories on the basis of their respective current-dollar values in mid-1949. Each time a different set of life assumptions for fixed capital goods were used, the weights for capital consumption allowances, the net stock of capital, and inventories were revised. The resulting weighting diagram for the gross domestic product version of our estimates of total measured factor productivity is reproduced below in Table SA–10.

The weighting diagram for the net domestic product version was derived by expressing the weights for labor net stock of fixed capital and inventories as a fraction of one minus the weight for capital consumption allowances in Table SA–10.

Differences in the handling of net income of unincorporated businesses appear to have little effect. Table SA–11 presents the total measured factor productivity estimates contained in Table 6 as well as the variants just described. As can be seen from Table SA–11, the three alternative allocations have little effect upon the resulting estimates.

ALTERNATIVE MEASURES

As indicated in the text, our data for the right-hand side of the basic identity developed in the Technical Appendix are far from satisfactory.

Two principal statistics for manufacturing were required to estimate the rate of change of the price of gross domestic product at factor cost. We needed the estimates of census value added based on historical data developed within DBS and brought up to date to 1960 by examining various DBS 31-201, *General Reviews of the Manufacturing Industries of Canada,* and special conversion statements supplied by DBS to permit the conversion of 1960 data based on the DBS 1960 Standard Industrial Classification to the DBS 1948 Standard Industrial Classification. The conversion is not wholly satisfactory and reduces the validity of those of our estimates for which 1960 is a terminal year. We also needed expenditures on repair to capital goods by major group from the DBS Capital Expenditures Survey.[8] These latter data, when subtracted from the Census value-added data, yielded our first approximation to current-dollar gross domestic product. The 1949 current-dollar gross domestic product by major group from DBS 13-513 was extrapolated to 1946 and 1960 on the basis of the movement of our approximation. The procedure has two grave drawbacks. The DBS 13-513 and 61-505 industry and activity coverage are slightly different, and our approximation is weak owing to imperfections in the repair expenditures data, and the failure to account for the remaining intermediate inputs may well bias our approximation to current-dollar gross domestic product upward over time. The rate of growth of our approximation was calculated, and from it was subtracted the rate of growth of constant-1949 gross domestic product to derive the rate of growth of the price of gross domestic product. Accordingly, the latter estimate may be too high, which may impart the general downward bias we observed in our estimates of total measured factor productivity shown in Table 12.

From our approximation of current-dollar gross domestic product, we subtracted an estimate, at the major group level, of wages and salaries and supplementary labor income, the latter derived for total manufacturing from DBS 72-502, *Labour Income, 1926–1958,* and subsequent monthly bulletins and allocated over major groups by shares of wages and salaries, and current-dollar capital consumption allowances to derive an estimate of the current-dollar net returns to capital. Again, we were unable to make the inventory valuation adjustment or to adjust for net income of unincorporated enterprises. The remaining portion when divided by the sum of the current-dollar midyear net stock of fixed capital and end-of-second-quarter inventories yielded a very weak estimate indeed of the net rate of return to capital.

[8] DBS 610-504, *Private and Public Investment in Canada, 1946–1957,* and subsequent Department of Trade and Commerce *Outlooks.*

TABLE SA-10

1949 Weighting Diagram for Gross Domestic Product Version of Total Measured Factor Productivity

Set of Lives	Split of Unincorporated Income[a]	Total Manufacturing				Food and Beverages				Tobacco, Rubber, and Leather Products			
		Labor	Net Stock of Fixed Capital	Inventories	Capital Consumption Allowances	Labor	Net Stock of Fixed Capital	Inventories	Capital Consumption Allowances	Labor	Net Stock of Fixed Capital	Inventories	Capital Consumption Allowances
I	a	.657	.168	.095	.080	.623	.183	.120	.074	.741	.089	.112	.060
	b	.666	.162	.092		.633	.177	.115		.757	.082	.102	
	c	.676	.156	.088		.644	.170	.111		.773	.074	.093	
III	a		.178	.088	.078		.196	.113	.069		.097	.108	.054
	b		.171	.084			.189	.109			.090	.100	
	c		.164	.081			.182	.105			.082	.091	
V	a		.150	.109	.084		.166	.135	.076		.077	.118	.065
	b		.145	.105			.160	.130			.070	.108	
	c		.139	.100			.154	.126			.064	.098	

Set of Lives	Split of Unincorporated Income[a]	Textile Products				Clothing Products				Wood Products			
		Labor	Net Stock of Fixed Capital	Inventories	Capital Consumption Allowances	Labor	Net Stock of Fixed Capital	Inventories	Capital Consumption Allowances	Labor	Net Stock of Fixed Capital	Inventories	Capital Consumption Allowances
I	a	.670	.156	.082	.092	.745	.088	.132	.034	.722	.125	.080	.073
	b	.674	.154	.081		.766	.082	.120		.738	.116	.074	
	c	.678	.151	.079		.786	.072	.107		.757	.104	.066	
III	a		.170	.077	.084		.096	.124	.034		.133	.072	.073
	b		.167	.076			.087	.113			.123	.066	
	c		.164	.074			.078	.101			.110	.060	
V	a		.139	.100	.092		.124	.090	.041		.113	.092	.073
	b		.136	.098			.112	.081			.104	.085	
	c		.134	.096			.100	.072			.094	.076	

(continued)

TABLE SA-10 (continued)

Top half:

Set of Lives	Split of Unincorporated Income[a]	Paper Products				Printing, Publishing, and Allied Industries				Iron and Steel Products			
		Labor	Net Stock of Fixed Capital	Inventories	Capital Consumption Allowances	Labor	Net Stock of Fixed Capital	Inventories	Capital Consumption Allowances	Labor	Net Stock of Fixed Capital	Inventories	Capital Consumption Allowances
I	a	.531	.265	.086	.118	.757	.158	.027	.058	.693	.135	.104	.068
	b					.762	.154	.026		.696	.134	.102	
	c									.700	.132	.101	
III	a		.275	.077	.118		.166	.024	.053		.144	.095	.068
	b						.162	.023			.142	.094	
	c										.140	.093	
V	a		.244	.100	.125		.153	.038	.053		.118	.117	.073
	b						.148	.037			.116	.115	
	c										.114	.113	

Bottom half:

Set of Lives	Split of Unincorporated Income[a]	Transportation Equipment				Nonferrous Metal Products and Electrical Apparatus and Supplies				Nonmetallic Mineral Products and Products of Petroleum and Coal			
		Labor	Net Stock of Fixed Capital	Inventories	Capital Consumption Allowances	Labor	Net Stock of Fixed Capital	Inventories	Capital Consumption Allowances	Labor	Net Stock of Fixed Capital	Inventories	Capital Consumption Allowances
I	a	.665	.180	.104	.051	.685	.143	.044	.128	.513	.216	.139	.132
	b	.687	.166	.096		.692	.138	.042		.518	.213	.137	
	c	.709	.152	.088		.702	.131	.040					
III	a		.187	.088	.060		.144	.040	.131		.234	.132	.122
	b		.172	.081			.138	.039			.231	.130	
	c		.157	.074			.131	.036					
V	a		.163	.130	.042		.115	.043	.157		.196	.154	.137
	b		.151	.120			.110	.041			.194	.152	
	c		.138	.110			.103	.038					

(continued)

TABLE SA-10 *(concluded)*

Set of Lives	Split of Unincor-porated Income[a]	Labor	Net Stock of Fixed Capital	Inven-tories	Capital Con-sumption Allowances	Labor	Net Stock of Fixed Capital	Inven-tories	Capital Con-sumption Allowances
			Chemical Products				*Miscellaneous Manufacturing Industries*		
I	a	.543	.246	.111	.100	.683	.145	.111	.061
	b	.548	.242	.109		.707	.131	.100	
	c					.744	.111	.084	
III	a		.261	.106	.090		.155	.101	.061
	b		.257	.105			.140	.092	
	c						.118	.077	
V	a		.211	.126	.121		.123	.120	.073
	b		.208	.124			.111	.108	
	c						.092	.090	

Note: Data will not necessarily add to 1.000 in all cases owing to rounding.

[a]Rows labeled a, b, and c correspond to three alternative allocations of the net income of unincorporated businesses. The assumed share of labor and net capital are: (a) 25:75, (b) 50:50, and (c) 75:25.

We derived an estimate of the rate of change of the price of the net stock of fixed capital by subtracting the rate of growth of the constant-1949-dollar net stock of fixed capital from its current-dollar counterpart, and the rate of growth of the price of capital consumption allowances and inventories by the same procedure. The rate of growth of the "price" of the labor inputs, which is no more than the rate of growth of the unit value of the labor inputs, was derived by subtracting the rates of growth of the two labor inputs used in Part II of our paper from the rates of growth of wages, salaries, and supplementary labor income. Obviously, these estimates are weak, and, as we stated in the text, further research is required before the estimates presented in Table 12 can be accepted with any confidence.

REVISION OF OUTPUT DATA

As was pointed out in the introductory preface, the publication of substantial revisions in the constant-dollar GDP series by DBS in mid-1966 has invalidated much of our analysis. In this section we present several tables based on the revised data. Table SA–12 corresponds to text Table 6; Table SA–13 is the revision of Table 7; Table SA–14 is the revision of Table SA–4; and Table SA–15 is the revision of Table SA–5. The effect of the revisions is presented in Chart SA–1, which compares the old and the revised GDP and GDP-per-man-hours series.

TABLE SA-11

Total Measured Factor Productivity (Gross Domestic Product Basis), Alternative Allocation of Net Income of Unincorporated Businesses, Total Manufacturing and Major Groups, 1946-56

(continuous annual rates of change)

Set of Lives	Split of Unincorporated Income[a]	Total Manufacturing		Food and Beverages		Tobacco, Rubber, and Leather Products		Textile Products		Clothing Products	
		Employees	Paid Man-Hours	Employees	Paid Man-Hours	Employees	Paid Man-Hours	Employees	Paid Man-Hours	Employees	Paid Man-Hours
I	a	2.1	2.4	0.5	0.7	2.5	2.7	0.6	0.9	1.2	1.3
	b	2.1	2.4	0.5	0.8	2.5	2.8	0.7	0.9	1.2	1.3
	c	2.1	2.4	0.6	0.8	2.6	2.8	0.7	1.0	1.2	1.4
III	a	2.2	2.5	0.5	0.8	2.5	2.7	0.8	1.0	1.2	1.3
	b	2.2	2.5	0.6	0.8	2.6	2.8	0.8	1.1	1.3	1.4
	c	2.3	2.6	0.6	0.9	2.6	2.9	0.8	1.1	1.3	1.4
V	a	1.9	2.2	0.2	0.5	2.4	2.7	0.3	0.5	1.3	1.4
	b	1.9	2.2	0.3	0.6	2.5	2.7	0.3	0.6	1.3	1.4
	c	1.9	2.2	0.3	0.6	2.6	2.8	0.3	0.6	1.3	1.4

(continued)

TABLE SA-11 (continued)

Set of Lives	Split of Unincorporated Income[a]	Wood Products		Paper Products[b]		Printing, Publishing and Allied Industries[c]		Iron and Steel Products		Transportation Equipment	
		Employees	Paid Man-Hours	Employees	Paid Man-Hours	Employees	Paid Man-Hours	Employees	Paid Man-Hours	Employees	Paid Man-Hours
I	a	2.0	2.4			1.8	2.1	2.6	2.9	3.6	3.8
	b	2.0	2.4	1.1	1.7			2.6	2.9	3.6	3.8
	c	2.1	2.4			1.8	2.1	2.6	2.9	3.6	3.8
III	a	2.2	2.6			1.9	2.2	2.6	2.9	3.8	4.0
	b	2.2	2.6	1.3	1.9			2.6	2.9	3.8	4.0
	c	2.3	2.6			1.9	2.2	2.6	3.0	3.7	4.0
V	a	1.8	2.1			1.4	1.7	2.4	2.7	3.3	3.5
	b	1.8	2.2	0.5	1.2			2.4	2.8	3.3	3.5
	c	1.9	2.2			1.4	1.7	2.5	2.8	3.3	3.5

(continued)

TABLE SA-11 (concluded)

Set of Lives	Split of Unincorporated Income[a]	Nonferrous Metal Products and Electrical Apparatus and Supplies		Nonmetallic Mineral Products and Products of Petroleum and Coal[c]		Chemical Products[c]		Miscellaneous Manufacturing Industries	
		Employees	Paid Man-Hours	Employees	Paid Man-Hours	Employees	Paid Man-Hours	Employees	Paid Man-Hours
I	a	3.4	3.6	3.6	3.7	1.7	2.0	1.4	1.6
	b	3.3	3.6	3.6	3.7	1.8		1.4	1.6
	c	3.3	3.6	3.6	3.7	1.8	2.0	1.5	1.6
III	a	3.4	3.7	3.8	4.0	1.9	2.2	1.5	1.7
	b	3.4	3.7	3.8		1.9		1.5	1.7
	c	3.4	3.7	3.8	4.0	1.9	2.2	1.5	1.7
V	a	3.3	3.6	3.1	3.2	1.4	1.7	1.4	1.6
	b	3.3	3.6	3.1		1.4		1.4	1.6
	c	3.3	3.6	3.1	3.3	1.4	1.7	1.5	1.6

[a]Under each set of lives, rows labeled a, b, and c indicate change in rate of growth of total measured factor productivity when net income of unincorporated businesses is split 25:75, 50:50, 75:25 between labor and net capital input, respectively. Estimates in row b correspond to estimates presented in Part II.

[b]No net income of unincorporated businesses was shown in 1949 for the paper products major Group; see DBS 13-513, *Supplement to the Inter-Industry Flow of Goods and Services, Canada, 1949*, Table 1.

[c]Net unincorporated income was so small that all allocations yielded practically the same result.

TABLE SA-12

Revised Estimate:[a] Total Measured Factor Productivity (Gross Domestic Product Basis)

Total Manufacturing and Major Groups, 1946-56 and 1946-60

(continuous annual rates of change)

Set of Lives	Gross Domestic Product at Factor Cost[b]	Labor Input		Midyear Net Stock of Fixed Capital[b]	Midyear Inventories[b]	Capital Consumption Allowances[b]	Total Measured Factor Input		Total Measured Factor Productivity	
		Employees	Paid Man-Hours				Employees	Paid Man-Hours	Employees	Paid Man-Hours
Total Manufacturing										
1946-56										
I	5.7	2.5	2.0	5.8	4.3	2.8	3.2	2.9	2.5	2.8
III				5.3		2.2	3.1	2.8	2.7	3.0
V				6.4		4.7	3.4	3.1	2.3	2.6
1946-60										
I	4.6	1.4	1.0	5.6	3.8	3.4	2.5	2.2	2.1	2.4
III				5.1		3.0	2.4	2.1	2.1	2.5
V				5.9		4.9	2.7	2.3	1.9	2.2
Food and Beverages										
1946-56										
I	3.1	1.3	0.9	6.4	3.3	3.0	2.5	2.3	0.5	0.8
III				5.9		2.9	2.5	2.2	0.6	0.8
V				7.2		5.0	2.8	2.5	0.3	0.6
1946-60										
I	3.2	1.3	0.9	5.8	3.2	3.3	2.5	2.2	0.7	1.0
III				5.4		3.2	2.4	2.2	0.8	0.9
V				6.2		5.0	2.6	2.4	0.6	0.8

(continued)

TABLE SA-12 (continued)

Set of Lives	Gross Domestic Product at Factor Cost[b]	Labor Input		Midyear Net Stock of Fixed Capital[b]	Midyear Inventories[b]	Capital Consumption Allowances[b]	Total Measured Factor Input		Total Measured Factor Productivity	
		Employees	Paid Man-Hours				Employees	Paid Man-Hours	Employees	Paid Man-Hours
Tobacco, Rubber, and Leather Products										
1946-56	2.8	-0.9	-1.2		2.7					
I				3.5		3.6	0.1	-0.1	2.8	3.0
III				3.4		3.0	0.1	-0.2	2.8	3.0
V				3.1		4.9	0.1	-0.1	2.7	2.9
1946-60	2.9	-1.2	-1.4		1.9					
I				3.3		4.0	-0.2	-0.4	3.1	3.3
III				3.4		3.6	-0.2	-0.4	3.1	3.4
V				2.9		4.3	-0.3	-0.4	3.1	3.4
Textile Products (excl. Clothing and Fur)										
1946-56	3.4	0.5	0.1		12.3					
I				4.2		1.6	2.1	1.9	1.2	1.5
III				3.8		1.2	2.0	1.7	1.4	1.6
V				5.4		2.3	2.5	2.2	0.9	1.2
1946-60	3.0	-0.6	-1.0		9.4					
I				3.1		1.2	0.9	0.7	2.1	2.4
III				2.8		1.0	0.9	0.6	2.2	2.4
V				3.5		2.2	1.2	0.9	1.8	2.1
Clothing Products										
1946-56	2.4	0.5	0.4		2.2					
I				2.0		2.1	0.9	0.8	1.5	1.6
III				1.9		0.8	0.8	0.7	1.5	1.7
V				1.3		2.2	0.8	0.7	1.6	1.7

(continued)

TABLE SA-12 *(continued)*

Set of Lives	Gross Domestic Product at Factor Cost [b]	Labor Input		Midyear Net Stock of Fixed Capital [b]	Midyear Inventories [b]	Capital Consumption Allowances [b]	Total Measured Factor Input		Total Measured Factor Productivity	
		Employees	Paid Man-Hours				Employees	Paid Man-Hours	Employees	Paid Man-Hours
Clothing Products (continued)										
1946-60										
I	2.1	0.2	0.0	1.0	1.9	0.9	0.5	.03	1.6	1.8
III				1.1		1.0	0.5	.03	1.6	1.8
V				-0.2		1.8	0.3	0.2	1.8	1.9
Wood Products										
1946-56										
I	5.0	2.5	2.0	3.8	3.6	0.9	2.6	2.3	2.4	2.7
III				3.1		-0.7	2.4	2.1	2.6	2.9
V				4.3		3.1	2.8	2.5	2.2	2.5
1946-60										
I	3.6	0.9	0.5	3.4	2.8	1.2	1.3	1.0	2.2	2.6
III				2.9		0.2	1.2	0.9	2.4	2.7
V				3.4		3.1	1.5	1.2	2.1	2.4
Paper Products										
1946-56										
I	5.2	3.3	2.1	6.9	2.7	3.8	4.3	3.6	1.0	1.6
III				6.1		3.0	4.0	3.4	1.3	1.9
V				7.6		7.1	4.8	4.2	0.5	1.1
1946-60										
I	4.4	2.4	1.4	6.3	2.7	4.5	3.7	3.2	0.7	1.2
III				5.8		3.9	3.6	3.0	0.9	1.5
V				6.5		6.8	4.0	3.5	0.4	1.0

(continued)

TABLE SA-12 (continued)

Set of Lives	Gross Domestic Product at Factor Cost[b]	Labor Input		Midyear Net Stock of Fixed Capital[b]	Midyear Inventories[b]	Capital Consumption Allowances[b]	Total Measured Factor Input		Total Measured Factor Productivity	
		Employees	Paid Man-Hours				Employees	Paid Man-Hours	Employees	Paid Man-Hours
Printing, Publishing, and Allied Industries										
1946-56										
I	7.2	4.0	3.5	4.8	4.4	1.8	4.0	3.7	3.2	3.5
III				4.2		1.4	3.9	3.6	3.3	3.6
V				7.0		3.1	4.4	4.1	2.8	3.1
1946-60										
I	5.9	3.1	2.6	5.0	3.7	2.2	3.3	3.0	2.6	2.9
III				4.4		2.0	3.2	2.9	2.7	3.0
V				6.7		3.7	3.7	3.4	2.3	2.6
Iron and Steel Products										
1946-56										
I	6.4	2.6	2.2	5.8	5.4	2.4	3.3	3.0	3.1	3.4
III				5.3		2.3	3.2	2.9	3.2	3.5
V				6.1		3.7	3.4	3.1	3.0	3.3
1946-60										
I	4.3	1.7	1.2	5.8	4.4	3.5	2.7	2.3	1.7	2.0
III				5.5		3.6	2.6	2.3	1.7	2.0
V				6.1		4.7	2.8	2.4	1.6	1.9
Transportation Equipment										
1946-56										
I	6.8	3.4	3.1	4.2	1.5	-1.1	3.2	2.9	3.7	3.9
III				3.3		-1.5	3.0	2.7	3.8	4.1
V				5.5		1.7	3.5	3.2	3.4	3.6

(continued)

TABLE SA-12 (continued)

Set of Lives	Gross Domestic Product at Factor Cost^b	Labor Input		Midyear Net Stock of Fixed Capital^b	Midyear Inventories^b	Capital Consumption Allowances^b	Total Measured Factor Input		Total Measured Factor Productivity	
		Employees	Paid Man-Hours				Employees	Paid Man-Hours	Employees	Paid Man-Hours
Transportation Equipment (continued)										
1946-60										
I	3.8	0.6	0.4	3.9	0.4	-0.2	1.1	0.9	2.7	2.9
III				3.1		-0.2	1.0	0.8	2.8	3.0
V				4.6		2.0	1.3	1.1	2.5	2.7
Nonferrous Metal Products and Electrical Apparatus and Supplies										
1946-56										
I	7.8	5.0	4.5	3.4	4.5	1.1	4.2	3.9	3.6	3.9
III				3.3		0.5	4.1	3.8	3.7	4.0
V				2.7		2.3	4.3	4.0	3.5	3.8
1946-60										
I	5.9	2.6	2.3	3.6	5.3	2.3	2.8	2.6	3.1	3.3
III				3.6		1.9	2.8	2.5	3.1	3.4
V				3.0		3.2	2.9	2.6	3.0	3.3
Nonmetallic Mineral Products and Products of Petroleum and Coal										
1946-56										
I	10.3	4.6	4.3	10.4	7.6	6.9	6.6	6.4	3.7	3.8
III				9.5		6.1	6.3	6.2	3.9	4.1
V				11.7		9.0	7.1	6.9	3.2	3.4
1946-60										
I	8.6	3.5	3.2	9.8	6.9	7.0	5.8	5.6	2.8	2.9
III				9.1		6.2	5.6	5.4	3.0	3.1
V				10.7		8.5	6.1	5.9	2.5	2.6

(continued)

TABLE SA-12 (concluded)

Set of Lives	Gross Domestic Product at Factor Cost[b]	Labor Input		Midyear Net Stock of Fixed Capital[b]	Midyear Inventories[b]	Capital Consumption Allowances[b]	Total Measured Factor Input		Total Measured Factor Productivity	
		Employees	Paid Man-Hours				Employees	Paid Man-Hours	Employees	Paid Man-Hours
Chemical Products										
1946-56										
I	7.9	3.3	2.8	8.8	4.6	7.6	5.2	5.0	2.7	3.0
III				8.2		7.2	5.1	4.8	2.9	3.1
V				10.0		8.9	5.6	5.3	2.4	2.7
1946-60										
I	7.2	2.6	2.2	8.2	3.5	7.4	4.6	4.3	2.7	2.9
III				7.8		7.0	4.5	4.2	2.8	3.0
V				9.0		8.5	4.8	4.6	2.4	2.7
Miscellaneous Manufacturing Industries										
1946-56										
I	9.4	4.6	4.3	3.2	8.0	2.8	4.6	4.4	4.7	4.9
III				3.2		2.2	4.6	4.4	4.8	5.0
V				2.9		2.8	4.6	4.4	4.7	4.9
1946-60										
I	8.6	4.8	4.6	3.6	8.1	3.4	4.9	4.7	3.7	3.8
III				3.6		3.3	4.8	4.7	3.8	3.9
V				3.6		3.9	4.9	4.8	3.6	3.8

Source: See this appendix. The three different rates of change of midyear net stock and capital consumption allowances are based on the sets I, III, and V of average economic lives used by the DBS in the forthcoming reference paper, *Estimates of Fixed Capital Flows and Stocks, Manufacturing, Canada, 1926–1960*. For five of the combined major groups (foods and beverages; tobacco, rubber, and leather products; paper products; printing, publishing, and allied industries; and chemical products), the average economic lives used in sets I and II were the same. Continuous annual rates of change in this and subsequent tables are calculated as $\ln GDP_{56} - \ln GDP_{46} / 10$.

[a]This table is a revision of Table 6.

[b]Measured in constant 1949 dollars.

TABLE SA-13

Revised[a] Indexes of Constant 1949 Gross Domestic Product and Total Measured Factor Productivity, Total Manufacturing and Major Groups, 1946-60

(1949 = 1.000)

Year	Total Manufacturing GDP	Factor Productivity Employees	Factor Productivity Man-Hours	Food and Beverages GDP	Factor Productivity Employees	Factor Productivity Man-Hours	Tobacco, Rubber, and Leather Products GDP	Factor Productivity Employees	Factor Productivity Man-Hours	Textiles GDP	Factor Productivity Employees	Factor Productivity Man-Hours
1946	0.852	0.956	0.947	0.980	1.100	1.097	1.045	1.033	1.015	0.887	1.063	1.043
1947	0.932	0.989	0.983	0.972	1.043	1.048	1.124	1.099	1.090	0.940	1.025	1.017
1948	0.973	1.002	0.999	0.985	1.019	1.019	1.026	1.034	1.040	0.973	1.008	1.008
1949	1.000	1.000	1.000	1.000	1.000	1.000	1.000	1.000	1.000	1.000	1.000	1.000
1950	1.067	1.059	1.059	1.029	1.030	1.029	1.049	1.053	1.062	1.125	1.091	1.085
1951	1.159	1.083	1.092	1.065	1.035	1.042	1.039	1.048	1.072	1.151	1.074	1.099
1952	1.202	1.081	1.094	1.135	1.077	1.085	1.082	1.104	1.112	1.045	1.065	1.091
1953	1.289	1.106	1.124	1.166	1.077	1.095	1.192	1.180	1.196	1.111	1.028	1.051
1954	1.260	1.094	1.119	1.209	1.097	1.118	1.109	1.135	1.160	1.002	1.003	1.023
1955	1.383	1.181	1.203	1.257	1.125	1.148	1.254	1.271	1.280	1.200	1.159	1.167
1956	1.512	1.228	1.252	1.332	1.158	1.184	1.389	1.360	1.371	1.244	1.162	1.175
1957	1.509	1.187	1.219	1.385	1.151	1.184	1.381	1.351	1.377	1.254	1.183	1.208
1958	1.480	1.185	1.219	1.451	1.192	1.223	1.420	1.416	1.443	1.212	1.191	1.217
1959	1.590	1.250	1.278	1.523	1.219	1.249	1.554	1.528	1.552	1.370	1.367	1.367
1960	1.612	1.254	1.287	1.539	1.213	1.247	1.466	1.470	1.488	1.389	1.371	1.396

(continued)

TABLE SA-13 (continued)

Year	Clothing GDP	Clothing Factor Productivity Employees	Clothing Factor Productivity Man-Hours	Wood Products GDP	Wood Products Factor Productivity Employees	Wood Products Factor Productivity Man-Hours	Paper Products GDP	Paper Products Factor Productivity Employees	Paper Products Factor Productivity Man-Hours	Printing, Publishing, and Allied Industries GDP	Printing, Publishing, and Allied Industries Factor Productivity Employees	Printing, Publishing, and Allied Industries Factor Productivity Man-Hours
1946	0.953	1.068	1.058	0.868	0.981	0.956	0.810	0.962	0.948	0.769	0.952	0.938
1947	0.922	0.990	0.985	0.982	1.000	0.986	0.891	0.981	0.968	0.836	0.980	0.971
1948	0.976	1.004	1.010	1.006	1.004	1.007	0.949	0.995	0.987	0.926	1.030	1.030
1949	1.000	1.000	1.000	1.000	1.000	1.000	1.000	1.000	1.000	1.000	1.000	1.000
1950	1.013	1.023	1.022	1.082	1.050	1.049	1.083	1.075	1.072	1.098	1.068	1.072
1951	1.009	1.020	1.043	1.148	1.078	1.079	1.170	1.092	1.093	1.129	1.062	1.072
1952	1.110	1.103	1.107	1.169	1.088	1.084	1.123	1.005	1.025	1.148	1.075	1.093
1953	1.139	1.104	1.108	1.262	1.132	1.125	1.181	1.034	1.067	1.257	1.143	1.164
1954	1.090	1.123	1.150	1.253	1.151	1.156	1.222	1.039	1.083	1.355	1.192	1.209
1955	1.151	1.198	1.210	1.395	1.238	1.237	1.272	1.044	1.091	1.423	1.227	1.245
1956	1.238	1.267	1.270	1.435	1.251	1.260	1.368	1.055	1.101	1.574	1.306	1.329
1957	1.242	1.252	1.275	1.346	1.218	1.239	1.343	0.974	1.024	1.599	1.277	1.301
1958	1.216	1.271	1.288	1.358	1.285	1.302	1.335	0.955	0.997	1.572	1.270	1.302
1959	1.291	1.349	1.356	1.434	1.330	1.327	1.439	1.001	1.053	1.696	1.330	1.360
1960	1.280	1.336	1.356	1.436	1.338	1.357	1.509	1.040	1.093	1.762	1.357	1.395

(continued)

TABLE SA-13 (continued)

Year	Iron and Steel Products			Transportation Equipment			Nonferrous Metal Products and Electrical Apparatus and Supplies			Nonmetallic Mineral Products and Products of Petroleum and Coal		
	Factor Productivity			Factor Productivity			Factor Productivity			Factor Productivity		
	GDP	Employees	Man-Hours	GDP	Employees	Man-Hours	GDP	Employees	Man-Hours	GDP	Employees	Man-Hours
1946	0.808	0.888	0.879	0.806	0.802	0.806	0.752	0.820	0.815	0.729	0.929	0.932
1947	0.936	0.962	0.949	0.953	0.927	0.929	0.896	0.922	0.921	0.838	1.001	0.998
1948	1.015	0.996	0.988	0.972	0.975	0.979	0.956	0.966	0.968	0.913	1.001	1.000
1949	1.000	1.000	1.000	1.000	1.000	1.000	1.000	1.000	1.000	1.000	1.000	1.000
1950	1.027	1.031	1.037	1.079	1.086	1.081	1.080	1.058	1.062	1.114	1.069	1.069
1951	1.181	1.081	1.095	1.304	1.140	1.151	1.172	1.041	1.052	1.246	1.100	1.104
1952	1.206	1.045	1.062	1.494	1.124	1.140	1.173	1.005	1.022	1.328	1.109	1.121
1953	1.180	1.001	1.023	1.686	1.186	1.204	1.344	1.071	1.088	1.458	1.108	1.119
1954	1.109	0.978	1.007	1.381	1.060	1.088	1.338	1.064	1.092	1.540	1.100	1.114
1955	1.307	1.125	1.151	1.477	1.144	1.180	1.501	1.164	1.188	1.766	1.236	1.251
1956	1.536	1.212	1.237	1.592	1.158	1.193	1.644	1.187	1.212	2.029	1.326	1.346
1957	1.506	1.150	1.185	1.558	1.075	1.139	1.568	1.115	1.146	2.072	1.267	1.288
1958	1.354	1.103	1.143	1.370	1.069	1.111	1.531	1.119	1.157	2.126	1.248	1.268
1959	1.559	1.193	1.226	1.357	1.124	1.158	1.697	1.197	1.227	2.308	1.292	1.309
1960	1.515	1.126	1.164	1.369	1.146	1.177	1.721	1.265	1.295	2.284	1.247	1.269

(continued)

TABLE SA-13 *(concluded)*

Year	GDP	Factor Productivity		GDP	Factor Productivity	
		Employees	Man-Hours		Employees	Man-Hours
		Chemical Products			Miscellaneous Manufacturing Products	
1946	0.870	1.002	0.999	0.802	0.997	0.992
1947	0.908	1.017	1.020	0.841	0.962	0.968
1948	0.957	1.038	1.039	0.814	0.937	0.942
1949	1.000	1.000	1.000	1.000	1.000	1.000
1950	1.089	1.071	1.075	1.190	1.156	1.155
1951	1.239	1.119	1.126	1.311	1.223	1.234
1952	1.330	1.121	1.138	1.412	1.166	1.278
1953	1.487	1.111	1.127	1.752	1.448	1.455
1954	1.617	1.145	1.166	1.794	1.501	1.522
1955	1.753	1.241	1.264	1.854	1.542	1.559
1956	1.924	1.295	1.322	2.060	1.617	1.638
1957	2.086	1.311	1.342	2.211	1.643	1.671
1958	2.220	1.343	1.375	2.281	1.634	1.660
1959	2.287	1.365	1.396	2.488	1.693	1.711
1960	2.455	1.431	1.465	2.659	1.677	1.698

Source: Indexes of constant 1949 dollar gross domestic product at factor cost: From DBS 61-005, *Annual Supplement to the Monthly Index of Industrial Production,* May 1966. Indexes of total measured factor productivity: See this appendix. These indexes are based on Set I of the average economic lives of capital goods and correspond to row I in Table 6. The indexed total measured factor productivity is the gross-domestic-product-at-factor-cost version.

[a]This table is a revision of Table 7.

TABLE SA-14

Comparison of Revised[a] Indexes of Labor Input,

Total Manufacturing, 1946 - 60

(1949 = 100.0)

	Persons Employed			Man-Hours Worked DBS	Man-Hours Paid			
	DBS	Our Indexes				Our Indexes		
	(1)	(2)	(3)	(4)	(5)	(6)	(7)	(8)
1946	90.0	90.3	89.7	92.3	91.6	91.4	91.0	90.8
1947	96.3	96.6	95.9	97.7	97.4	97.6	96.6	96.7
1948	98.5	98.7	98.1	100.4	99.1	99.4	98.4	98.7
1949	100.0	100.0	100.0	100.0	100.0	100.0	100.0	100.0
1950	101.7	101.0	101.3	100.8	101.0	101.1	101.1	101.3
1951	107.9	107.4	107.7	104.9	106.0	104.4	106.3	104.9
1952	110.8	110.0	110.6	106.7	108.1	108.0	108.7	108.7
1953	114.2	113.3	114.0	110.5	110.6	109.2	111.4	110.1
1954	109.3	108.3	109.4	103.9	104.4	103.8	105.7	105.3
1955	112.1	110.9	112.1	107.1	107.6	107.4	109.0	108.9
1956	116.8	115.5	116.8	112.3	112.0	111.3	113.5	112.9
1957	117.3	116.0	117.7	111.4	111.0	108.9	112.9	111.0
1958	111.5	110.1	112.0	105.9	104.8	104.4	106.9	106.6
1959	112.9	111.3	113.1	107.8	107.0	106.2	108.9	108.3
1960	111.4	110.3	112.2	105.6	105.4	104.4	107.6	106.7
(continuous annual rates of change)								
1946-56	2.6	2.5	2.6	2.0	2.0	2.0	2.2	2.2
1946-60	1.5	1.4	1.6	1.0	1.0	1.0	1.2	1.2

Source: Columns (1) and (4): DBS 11-001, *Daily Bulletin,* June 7, 1966. This document provides data for 1946 which permit more useful comparisons than were possible in Tables SA-4 and SA-5. Column (2): Unweighted persons employed. Column (3): Persons employed with wages and salaries as weights. Column (5): See source note to column (1), Table SA-3. Column (6): See source note to column (2), Table SA-3. Column (7): See source note to column (3), Table SA-3. Column (8): See source note to column (4), Table SA-3.

[a]This table is a revision of Table SA-4.

TABLE SA-15

Revised[a] *Indexes of Output Per Labor Input,*

Total Manufacturing, 1946-60

(1949 = 1.000)

| | Output Per Person Employed | | | Output Per Man-Hour Worked | | Output Per Man-Hour Paid | | |
| | DBS | Our Indexes | | DBS | | | Our Indexes | |
	(1)	(2)	(3)	(4)	(5)	(6)	(7)	(8)
1946	0.947	0.944	0.950	0.923	0.930	0.932	0.936	0.938
1947	0.968	0.965	0.972	0.954	0.957	0.955	0.965	0.964
1948	0.988	0.986	0.992	0.969	0.982	0.979	0.989	0.986
1949	1.000	1.000	1.000	1.000	1.000	1.000	1.000	1.000
1950	1.049	1.056	1.053	1.059	1.056	1.055	1.055	1.053
1951	1.074	1.079	1.076	1.105	1.093	1.110	1.090	1.105
1952	1.084	1.093	1.087	1.127	1.112	1.113	1.106	1.106
1953	1.129	1.138	1.131	1.166	1.165	1.180	1.157	1.171
1954	1.152	1.163	1.152	1.213	1.207	1.214	1.192	1.197
1955	1.232	1.247	1.234	1.292	1.285	1.288	1.269	1.270
1956	1.295	1.309	1.295	1.347	1.350	1.358	1.330	1.339
1957	1.286	1.301	1.282	1.355	1.359	1.385	1.337	1.359
1958	1.328	1.344	1.321	1.399	1.412	1.418	1.384	1.388
1959	1.409	1.429	1.406	1.475	1.486	1.497	1.460	1.468
1960	1.447	1.461	1.437	1.527	1.529	1.544	1.498	1.511
	(continuous average annual rates of change)							
1946-56	3.1	3.3	3.1	3.8	3.7	3.8	3.5	3.6
1946-60	3.0	3.1	3.0	3.6	3.6	3.6	3.4	3.4

Source: Columns (1) and (4): DBS 11-001, *Daily Bulletin,* June 7, 1966.
Columns (2), (3), and (5)-(8) derived by dividing index of constant -1949- dollar gross domestic product at factor cost for total manufacturing, DBS 61-005, *Annual Supplement to the Monthly Index of Industrial Production,* May 1966, by respective indexes in Table SA-14.

[a]This table is a revision of Table SA-5.

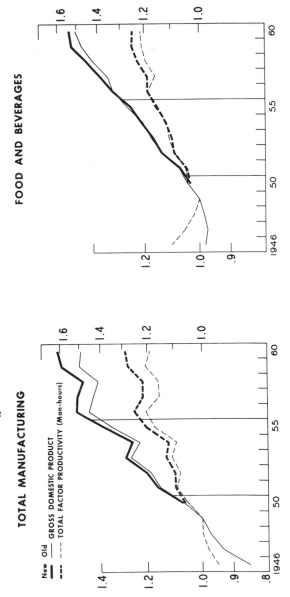

CHART SA-1

Indexes of Constant 1949 Gross Domestic Product and "Total Measured Factor Productivity," Total Manufacturing and Major Groups

(plotted on ratio scale; index, 1949 = 1.0)

TOTAL MANUFACTURING

FOOD AND BEVERAGES

New Old
GROSS DOMESTIC PRODUCT
TOTAL FACTOR PRODUCTIVITY (Man-hours)

CHART SA-1 (continued)

WOOD PRODUCTS

CLOTHING PRODUCTS

New Old
GROSS DOMESTIC PRODUCT
TOTAL FACTOR PRODUCTIVITY (Man-hours)

CHART SA-1 (continued)

TEXTILE PRODUCTS

TOBACCO, RUBBER AND LEATHER PRODUCTS

CHART SA-1 (continued)

TRANSPORTATION EQUIPMENT

IRON AND STEEL PRODUCTS

New Old
| | GROSS DOMESTIC PRODUCT
| | TOTAL FACTOR PRODUCTIVITY (Man-hours)

CHART SA-1 (continued)

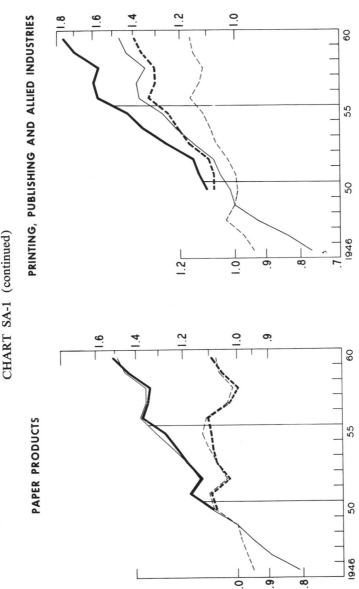

PAPER PRODUCTS

PRINTING, PUBLISHING AND ALLIED INDUSTRIES

CHART SA-1 (continued)

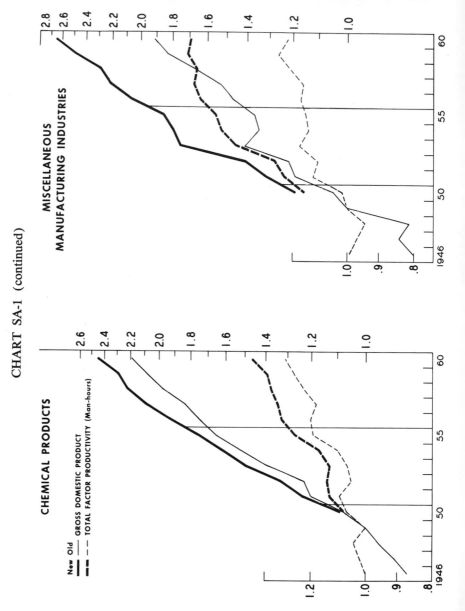

CHART SA-1 (concluded)

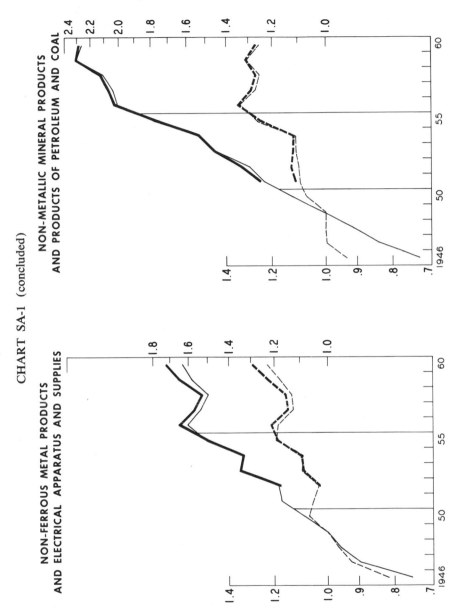

From the tables and Chart SA–1, it is clear that the old series seriously understates the growth of output and productivity in several of the major groups. The inexplicable decline in both output and productivity in clothing products is now reversed, and the rate of increase of these measures is substantially greater in printing, publishing, and allied industries, in chemical products, and in miscellaneous manufacturing. In the other major groups, the revisions are less substantial, but the impact on the total manufacturing measures is significant. The implications of these revisions in assessing the past performance of the Canadian economy are most important. Widespread concern about insufficient productivity growth as well as concern about the increase in unit labor costs must now be modified.

Technical Appendix

In this Technical Appendix to our paper, we set out more formally the format in which our various estimates of total measured factor productivity in Part II are presented, our reasons for the capital input measures we chose, and some comments about the various output versions of the productivity estimates presented. Finally, we make some brief comments upon the evaluation of commodity inputs (stocks and flows) in the estimation of total measured factor productivity.

Consider the social accounting *ex post* identity between the value of outputs and the value of inputs

1.1 $$\sum_i P_i Q_i \equiv \sum_j p_j q_j$$

for an activity, establishment, industry, or economy. Differentiation with respect to time yields

$$\sum_i (P_i \dot{Q}_i + Q_i \dot{P}_i) \equiv \sum_j (p_j \dot{q}_j + q_j \dot{p}_j)$$

with $\dot{Q}_i$ defined as dQ_i/dt, etc. Factoring and division by $\sum_i P_i Q_i$ yields

$$\sum_i \frac{P_i Q_i}{\Sigma P_i Q_i} \left(\frac{\dot{Q}_i}{Q_i} + \frac{\dot{P}_i}{P_i} \right) \equiv \sum_j \frac{p_j q_j}{\Sigma P_i Q_i} \left(\frac{\dot{q}_j}{q_j} + \frac{\dot{p}_j}{p_j} \right)$$

Rearrangement yields

1.2 $$\sum_i \frac{P_i Q_i}{\Sigma P_i Q_i} \left(\frac{\dot{Q}_i}{Q_i} \right) - \sum_j \frac{p_j q_j}{\Sigma P_i Q_i} \left(\frac{\dot{q}_j}{q_j} \right) \equiv \sum_j \frac{p_j q_j}{\Sigma P_i Q_i} \left(\frac{\dot{p}_j}{p_j} \right) - \sum_i \frac{P_i Q_i}{\Sigma P_i Q_i} \left(\frac{\dot{P}_i}{P_i} \right)$$

Identity 1.2 expresses the weighted proportionate rates of change of output(s) less the weighted proportionate rates of change of input(s) as being identically equal to the weighted proportionate rates of change of the price(s) of input(s) less the weighted proportionate rates of change of the price(s) of output(s). Much of the estimation of total measured factor productivity has been carried out, in one guise or another, within the context of the left-hand side of identity 1.2. Less frequently attempted is the estimation of the same phenomena within the context of the right-hand side of the identity.

Define

$$\sum_i \frac{P_i Q_i}{\Sigma P_i Q_i} \left(\frac{\dot{Q}_i}{Q_i}\right) - \frac{\dot{q}_j}{q_j} \equiv \frac{\dot{\lambda}_j}{\lambda_j}$$

as the proportionate rate of change of output per unit of the *j*th input and

$$\frac{\dot{p}_j}{p_j} - \sum_i \frac{P_i Q_i}{\Sigma P_i Q_i} \left(\frac{\dot{P}_i}{P_i}\right) \equiv \frac{\dot{r}_j}{r_j}$$

as the proportionate rate of change of the "own-product" price of the *j*th input. Then, identity 1.2 may be written as

$$1.3 \quad \sum_j \frac{p_j q_j}{\Sigma P_i Q_i} \left[\sum_i \frac{P_i Q_i}{\Sigma P_i Q_i} \left(\frac{\dot{Q}_i}{Q_i}\right) - \frac{\dot{q}_j}{q_j}\right] \equiv \sum_j \frac{p_j q_j}{\Sigma P_i Q_i} \left[\frac{\dot{p}_j}{p_j} - \sum_i \frac{P_i Q_i}{\Sigma P_i Q_i} \left(\frac{\dot{P}_i}{P_i}\right)\right]$$

Identity 1.3 expresses the weighted proportionate rates of change of output(s) per unit of input(s) as being identically equal to the weighted proportionate rates of change of the own-product prices of the input(s).

It is within the context of these identities that our estimation procedures in Part II of this paper have been conducted. What are the relevant input and output measures to use? In Part II of our paper, we have been primarily concerned with the capital input(s), and the reasons for our choice of the net stock and capital consumption allowances in preference to the gross stock are now outlined.

Suppose for the moment that the output concept chosen were net domestic product at factor cost. Corresponding to our basic social accounting identity 1.1, the value of net domestic product would be identically equal, *ex post*, to the wages and salaries bill and the *net* returns to capital. That is

$$1.4 \qquad\qquad PQ \equiv WL + rP^N N$$

where PQ is the value of net domestic product, WL is the wage bill, and $rP^N N$ is the net return to capital.[1] The net returns to capital are made up of the *ex post* net rate of return to capital multiplied by the value of the *net* stock of fixed capital (the net stock in terms of quantities times the

---

[1] For simplicity in exposition, we assume here that net output can be unambiguously conceived as one commodity, labor is homogeneous, and the capital input is represented solely by one fixed reproducible good.

price of the net stock).[2] When the customary algebraic manipulations are performed on identity 1.4, we have, as a variant of 1.2,[3]

1.5

$$\frac{\dot{Q}}{Q} - \left[\frac{WL}{PQ}\left(\frac{\dot{L}}{L}\right) + \frac{rP^N N}{PQ}\left(\frac{\dot{N}}{N}\right)\right] \equiv \left[\frac{WL}{PQ}\left(\frac{\dot{W}}{W}\right) + \frac{rP^N N}{PQ}\left(\frac{\dot{r}}{r} + \frac{\dot{P}^N}{P^N}\right)\right] - \frac{\dot{P}}{P}$$

Within the context of the net domestic product version of estimation of total measured factor productivity, we can find no place for the gross stock of capital—a proxy for capital input that is favored by some investigators in the area. It is clearly the net stock which gives rise to the nominal net returns to capital and the value of the net stock which is associated with the net rate of return to capital. In estimates of total measured factor productivity, changes in constant-dollar estimates of the net stock of capital reflect the value which the economic system, under the conditions of the base year whose constant net stock prices are selected, would place upon the changes in the fixed assets being used. In the estimation of total measured factor productivity, this valuation, which takes into account the changing age structure of the stock, is what we wish to approximate.

If the output concept chosen were gross domestic product at factor cost, then, again corresponding to our general social accounting identity 1.2, we would have

1.6 $$PQ \equiv WL + rP^N N + P^D D$$

where PQ is now the value of gross domestic product, $P^D D$ is the value of the capital consumption allowance, and the remaining terms are defined as before.

Corresponding to identity 1.2, we would have,

1.7 $$\frac{\dot{Q}}{Q} - \left[\frac{WL}{PQ}\left(\frac{\dot{L}}{L}\right) + \frac{rP^N N}{PQ}\left(\frac{\dot{N}}{N}\right) + \frac{P^D D}{PQ}\left(\frac{\dot{D}}{D}\right)\right]$$

$$\equiv \left[\frac{WL}{PQ}\left(\frac{\dot{W}}{W}\right) + \frac{rP^N N}{PQ}\left(\frac{\dot{r}}{r} + \frac{\dot{P}^N}{P^N}\right) + \frac{P^D D}{PQ}\left(\frac{\dot{P}^D}{P^D}\right)\right] - \frac{\dot{P}}{P}$$

where the proportionate rates of change of the two capital inputs are shown —namely, the net stock and capital consumption allowances. The former would appear again as the best measure of the value which the economic system, under base-period conditions, would place upon the augmentable

[2] Even in our simplified exposition, the net stock of capital would be composed of goods of many vintages. Market prices of the various vintages making up the net stock can be conceived of which permit the unambiguous valuation of the net stock.

[3] The terms in the right-hand side of the identity are discussed later in this appendix.

resources being used or held for productive purposes by the industry, while the latter would appear as the best proxy for the value which the economic system, again under base-period conditions, would place upon the resources "used up" from the processes of physical wear and tear, obsolescence, and aging. Again, in the estimation of total measured factor productivity, we would argue that these two evaluations rather than the gross stock permit the more satisfactory evaluation of the improvements made in transforming inputs into outputs.

Some investigators have expressed a preference for the use of the gross stock measure as the correct or more meaningful proxy for capital input on the grounds that, since capital goods retain their technical efficiency substantially unimpaired over their lifetimes, a measure of the capital input is required which moves with the contribution of capital to output.[4]

Changes in the composition of the stock of fixed capital and changes in the average age of the capital goods will set in motion changes in the net stock and capital consumption different from those recorded by the gross stock.[5]

For a hypothetical major group not subject to growth and possessed of a balanced age structure of capital goods, the value of the gross stock of capital will be, in competitive equilibrium, equal to the sum of the discounted flows of expected gross surpluses which would be accruing to each component of the stock if it were new. The value of the net stock would be the market's evaluation of the discounted flow of expected gross surplus accruing to each component of the stock and would appropriately take into account the different ages of the components. If the vintage composition of the stock remained unchanged over one year, then the sum of the changes in market values of each component of the stock as each component aged one period would be the capital consumption for the stock as a whole over the year.[6]

Consider now an equilibrium to equilibrium change in the composition of the stationary stock of capital goods such that the total current-period flow of returns and capital consumption allowances increase as compared to the

[4] It is, of course, admitted that capital goods nearing the end of their economic lives may suffer a decline in technical efficiency since the marginal rate of return to repair and maintenance expenditures declines and the more efficient associated inputs will be switched to newer and better capital goods. Thus it is not necessarily the case that technical efficiency of capital goods and capital's contribution to output, gross or net, will move together.

[5] See E. F. Denison, *The Sources of Economic Growth in the United States and the Alternatives Before Us,* Washington, D.C., 1962, Appendix D.

[6] For a balanced age stationary stock with finite lives and positive rates of interest (in competitive equilibrium with perfect foresight, equivalent to the net rate of return to capital), the value of the net stock will be greater than one-half of the value of the gross stock. Over one period of time, relatively new components of the stock will decline in value by smaller amounts than similar but older components.

base period with the total flow of net returns, the gross and net stock remaining unchanged.[7]

It appears appropriate to argue that the increased gross surplus accruing to capital goods has been obtained at a cost of shifting to a composition of capital goods involving a flow of capital consumption greater than before. In our view, any estimate of total measured factor productivity must take into account the increase in capital consumption which is associated with the increase in gross output. In this case, since the net returns accruing to the stock remain unchanged, it appears reasonable for the net stock to remain unchanged. Since the gross surplus accruing to the stock has increased because of the changed composition of the stock, there would appear to be little merit in using gross stock as representative of the capital input earning net surplus or gross surplus. The use of the net stock and capital consumption allowances (or the net stock) as the relevant capital input(s) in the gross (or net) domestic product version of the estimation of total measured factor productivity would appear to be appropriate.

When the equilibrium stock's age balance is disturbed by an increase in the rate of new additions, the fall in the average age of the stock and the greater rise in the net stock compared to the gross stock indicate, correctly in our view, the increase in value which society would have placed in the base period on the resources being used had their average age been lower.

Thus, we conclude that in assessing changes in total measured factor productivity on a gross domestic product basis, the more useful representations of the capital input are the net stock of capital and capital consumption allowances; and on a net domestic product basis, the net stock alone is to be used.

It follows from our way of looking at total measured factor productivity estimation that declines in activity legitimately show up as declines in the rate of advance in productivity. Yet, a major interruption in the rate of advance in output (or an absolute decline) will so adversely affect expectations as to profitable accumulation that the attempted measurement of capital inputs (however it is to be done) over such a decline in activity may well be impossible. If we wanted to adjust the capital inputs for underutilization, how do we construct an estimate of the base-period values which the economy would have placed upon current resources if there had been similar underutilization in the base period? Such values would, of course, be disequilibrium values par excellence, and there is doubt in our minds as to the usefulness (or even possibility) of such valuations. We do not suggest that the base-period values we have used are anything but crude approximations to market equilibrium values. The interruptions which occurred in manufacturing activity after 1957 were, however, so great in our view as to

---

[7] Here we attempt to follow Denison's advocacy (*ibid.*) of the gross stock as the appropriate measure of the capital input.

place serious doubts on the meaning of capital measurement, expressed in constant 1949 prices, for the years following 1957.

Where the estimation total measured factor productivity is performed at the industry level of detail, there are a number of output measures which are possible. One could use net or gross domestic product in constant dollars or two measures of gross output in constant dollars. With respect to the latter, the advantage for total measured factor productivity analysis is that intermediate inputs in constant dollars are treated as input rather than as negative output, as they are in the domestic product measures. We could include in both the gross output and intermediate inputs any intra-industry consumption which takes place in the industry. It would appear preferable to use as gross output a measure of the output of the industry which is *final to the industry* in question. In this case, the industry's intermediate inputs will not include intermediate inputs which were produced by other establishments within that same industry.[8]

Let us compare the gross output and gross domestic product measures of an industry's output from the point of view of total measured factor productivity estimation. The former measures would appear to be conceptually superior.[9] It is clear that intermediate inputs used to produce gross output final to an industry are, in every sense, as meaningfully conceived as inputs in the productive processes of the industry as are the labor and capital it uses.

There are difficulties [10] associated with the constant-dollar gross domestic product measure of output which are more readily apparent when examined within the context of the identity format of total measured factor productivity with which we work.

[8] In the text, it is assumed that no indirect taxes of subsidies prevail. With indirect taxes taken into account, the value of gross output must exclude indirect taxes (include subsidies) while the value of intermediate inputs must include indirect taxes (exclude subsidies) in order for the measures of domestic product to be on a factor cost basis. Thus, for the gross output variant of total measured factor productivity constant-dollar intermediate inputs will have a constant-dollar indirect tax component just as, in the gross domestic product variant, the constant-dollar net stock and capital consumption allowances will, if indirect taxes have been levied on capital goods, have a constant-dollar indirect tax component.

[9] There are no major difficulties in aggregating gross output final to each industry over all the industries concerned. Each time industries are added together, the measures of outputs and intermediate inputs are redefined to exclude any intra-industry consumption that arises as the aggregation process proceeds. For a closed economy, the last step in the aggregation procedure leads to a measure of final gross output equal to aggregate gross domestic product with intermediate inputs disappearing. Indirect taxes require special treatment. For an open economy, correct aggregation of intermediate inputs leads to flow of imports excluding those entering directly into components of final demand (see B. J. Emery and T. K. Rymes, "Price Indexes in a Social Accounting Framework," *Conferences on Statistics, 1962 and 1963,* Asimakopulos and Henripin, ed., Toronto, 1964).

[10] See P. A. David, "The Deflation of Value Added," *Review of Economics and Statistics,* May 1962, pp. 148–55.

Again, making certain simplifications for expositional purposes, we have

1.8 $$PQ \equiv WL + rP^N N + P^D D + P^M M$$

where PQ is the value of gross output final to an industry, $P^M M$ is the value of intermediate inputs employed by the industry, and the remaining terms are defined as before.

Again, we have, as a variant of 1.2,

1.9
$$\frac{\dot{Q}}{Q} - \left[\frac{WL}{PQ} \left(\frac{\dot{L}}{L} \right) + \frac{rP^N N}{PQ} \left(\frac{\dot{N}}{N} \right) + \frac{P^D D}{PQ} \left(\frac{\dot{D}}{D} \right) + \frac{P^M M}{PQ} \left(\frac{\dot{M}}{M} \right) \right] \equiv$$
$$\left[\frac{WL}{PQ} \left(\frac{\dot{W}}{W} \right) + \frac{rP^N N}{PQ} \left(\frac{\dot{r}}{r} + \frac{\dot{P^N}}{P^N} \right) + \frac{P^D D}{PQ} \left(\frac{\dot{P^D}}{P^D} \right) + \frac{P^M M}{PQ} \left(\frac{\dot{P^M}}{P^M} \right) \right] - \frac{\dot{P}}{P}$$

where
$$\dot{W}/W, \dot{r}/r, \dot{P^N}/P^N, \dot{P^D}/P^D, \text{ and } \dot{P^M}/P^M$$

are the proportionate rates of changes in the money price of labor, the nominal rate of return to augmentable capital, the price of the net stock of capital, the price of capital consumption allowances, and the price of intermediate inputs. When identities 1.8 and 1.9 are transformed into the gross domestic product version we have

2.0 $$PQ - P^M M \equiv WL + rP^N N + P^D D$$

2.1 $$\frac{PQ}{PQ - P^M M} \left(\frac{\dot{Q}}{Q} \right) - \frac{P^M M}{PQ - P^M M} \left(\frac{\dot{M}}{M} \right) - \left[\frac{WL}{PQ - P^M M} \left(\frac{\dot{L}}{L} \right) \right.$$
$$+ \frac{rP^N N}{PQ - P^M M} \left(\frac{\dot{N}}{N} \right) + \frac{P^D D}{PQ - P^M M} \left(\frac{\dot{D}}{D} \right) \right] \equiv \left[\frac{WL}{PQ - P^M M} \left(\frac{\dot{W}}{W} \right) \right.$$
$$+ \frac{rP^N N}{PQ - P^M M} \left(\frac{\dot{r}}{r} + \frac{\dot{P^N}}{P^N} \right) + \frac{P^D D}{PQ - P^M M} \left(\frac{\dot{P^D}}{P^D} \right) \right]$$
$$- \left[\frac{PQ}{PQ - P^M M} \left(\frac{\dot{P}}{P} \right) - \frac{P^M M}{PQ - P^M M} \left(\frac{\dot{P^M}}{P^M} \right) \right]$$

When identity 1.9 is transformed into the output per unit of input and "own-product price" of input format of identity 1.3, it follows that the proportionate rates of change of the own-product prices of the factor inputs will, if we assume for purposes of exposition that production is being carried on under perfectly competitive equilibrium conditions, be equal to the proportionate rates of changes of the marginal physical productivities of the factor inputs. For identity 2.1 however, the resulting proportionate rates of change in the own-product price of the factor inputs are difficult to interpret. Differences between the proportionate rates of change in the prices of gross output and intermediate inputs represent changes in the commodity terms of trade between the industry under examination and other sectors of the economy supplying it with intermediate inputs. Consider the proportionate rate of change in the wage rate, or the price of a standard labor input. In nominal terms, it is significant to the supplier and demander of labor. In "real" terms, it is presumably the consumption or total final goods value of the nominal wage rate which is of interest to the supplier of labor, whereas the demander of the labor input is presumably concerned with changes in the labor's marginal physical product in the production relationship in which it is engaged, that is, in changes in labor's own-product price. For analysis of changes in such price relationships, identity 1.9 would appear to be appropriate. The proportionate rate of change of the own-product price of labor which results from the use of identity 2.1 is, in fact, some intermediate position between the proportionate rate of change in the price of labor with which the demander of labor and the supplier of labor are concerned. The same difficulties of interpretation arise for the other own-product prices in identity 2.1. On the "real" output-input side of the identity, it must always be remembered that one is discussing the proportionate rates of change in output per unit of intermediate input. The weights that are attached to the proportionate rates of change of the gross output and the intermediate inputs transform the measure to the proportionate rate of change of the contribution to aggregate gross domestic product of the industry—a measure of output which is not necessarily the most useful for examining total measured factor productivity at the particular major group or industry level of detail.

Consider an industry producing a homogeneous product, which flows directly into final demand, with homogeneous labor, reproducible capital, and intermediate inputs. Technological change occurs in the industry producing the intermediate input, relative prices of the original industry's inputs change, so that the price of labor in terms of intermediate inputs rises. We should expect a switch in existing techniques used such that the gross output per unit of labor input would rise; output per unit of capital input and per unit of capital consumption allowances would (say) remain unchanged, and output per unit of intermediate input would fall. Elasticities of substitution are assumed such that the partial elasticities of gross output with respect to the inputs remain unchanged. The recorded changes in gross domestic product per unit of labor and reproducible capital inputs will, of course, be different from the recorded changes in gross output per unit of labor, reproducible capital, and intermediate inputs. The gross domestic product version of total measured factor productivity estimation will eliminate, for the industry under discussion, the influence of technological progress in the industry supplying it with its intermediate input. If one is concerned with assessing the changing efficiency with which direct and indirect primary inputs are contributing to the increased output of the industry in question, it is not clear that a measure of output which, in its method of construction, eliminates the effects of the increased efficiency of the indirect primary inputs is a measure which would be helpful in assessing that efficiency. That is, the unchanged efficiency of the primary inputs used in the industry under examination will possibly show up as a reduction in gross domestic product at factor cost (given the weights and changes in the primary inputs) which would appear to be correct. Yet it may well be that the gross output per unit of combined primary inputs in that industry and gross output per unit of total direct and indirect primary inputs have risen, whereas total measured factor productivity estimations will show no change because no allowance is made in the estimates, as they are presently formulated, for the reduced primary input content of the gross output of the industry supplying the intermediate inputs.

While this paper is concerned primarily with empirical results, there are further difficulties associated with the concept of output and the estimation of total measured factor productivity at the disaggregated level that we should like to touch upon briefly. Consider a two-sector economy that has long been in steady state growth equilibrium. Assume further that labor is homogeneous and that a steadily rising money wage rate prevails. Industry A is a fully integrated capital goods and intermediate-inputs-producing industry, and industry B is a consumption-goods-producing industry. Both industries are subject to rates of technological advance such that the consumption goods price of capital goods and intermediate inputs remains unchanged. The same unchanging rate of return to capital prevails in both industries. Techniques of production are such that different ratios of gross output per unit of primary and intermediate input prevail in the two industries. Then under such conditions, the rate of advance in total measured factor productivity in both sectors will be equal to the proportionate rates of change of wage rates (equal in both sectors) times the respective partial elasticities of output with respect to the labor input in both industries. As the definition of output for each sector is changed from gross output to gross or net domestic product, the respective measures of the rate of advance in total measured factor productivity will, of course, alter as the measured elasticities alter.

The example could easily be such that the deployment of factors over the two industries remained constant. In this case it is a drawback of our present methods of estimating total measured productivity that the resulting measures are not invariant to aggregation over major groups or industries whether the process of aggregation is by output final to industries or on the basis of gross or net domestic product. Indeed, if in the example the output of consumption goods and capital goods were growing at the same rate and the ratios of output per unit of net stock of capital, capital consumption allowances, and intermediate inputs remained unchanged in both industries, it would be hard to defend measures of proportionate rate of change of total measured factor productivity in both industries which yielded results that differed solely because of different partial production elasticities of labor. Parenthetically, it is interesting to note that in such a model, capital (i.e., all forms of commodity input) measured in terms of Robinsonian real capital would yield measures of total measured factor productivity which were equal in the two industries and invariant to the aggregation process.[11]

Secondly, if Professor Johnson is correct [12] in asserting that pure labor is an input concept appropriate to an earlier era and that an *increasing* share of net domestic income really represents net returns to capital, then in models of steady growth,[13] when commodity capital in all its stock and flow forms are growing at the same rate as output, the proportionate rate of change of total measured factor productivity, given our measurement procedures, would approach zero—a clearly meaningless result. Again, this dilemma would be surmounted by the utilization of the Robinsonian concept of real capital.

In conclusion, in this Technical Appendix we have argued the case for net stock and capital consumption allowances as the relevant measures of the capital inputs in total measured factor productivity estimation. We have noted certain difficulties in connection with the customary gross (or net) domestic product measures of constant-dollar output measures by industry, and suggest that some of the difficulties may be overcome by the transformation of the commodity inputs (stocks and flows) into estimates of their direct and indirect primary input reproduction requirements—a device which takes into account the changing efficiency with which commodity inputs are being produced.

Finally, for the direction of the reader, our estimates of total measured factor productivity in Part II of the paper in Tables 6, 7, 8, and 12 rest on an expanded version of identity 1.7 (or 2.1); in Table 9, on identity 1.5; and in Table 11, on identity 1.9. The expansion results simply from the introduction of inventories and the various measures of the labor inputs we have been able to derive.

[11] See L. M. Read, "The Measurement of Total Factor Productivity," DBS, June 1961 (mimeo.). Read's central thesis, in his attempt to make operational a variant of Joan Robinson's real capital input, is that changes in the commodity inputs (stocks and flows) in any activity in the economic system should, in total measured factor productivity measurement, be assessed not in terms of their base-period primary input requirements under conditions of base-period technology but rather in terms of current-period primary input requirements, under *current*-period conditions of technology, evaluated at base-period primary input prices. The problem of historical regress which is involved in Joan Robinson's real capital concept (see Joan Robinson, *The Accumulation of Capital*, p. 121) is overcome by a simultaneous solution for the changing direct and indirect primary input of all commodity inputs evaluated at base-period primary input prices.

[12] H. G. Johnson, "Towards a Generalized Capital Accumulation Approach to Economic Development," *The Canadian Quandary*, Toronto, 1963.

[13] See F. H. Hahn and R. C. O. Matthews, "The Theory of Economic Growth: A Survey," *Economic Journal*, September 1964, pp. 779–902.

COMMENT

DEREK A. WHITE

Since the Lithwick-Post-Rymes paper represents, perhaps, something of a landmark on the recent Canadian economic scene, a few words of introduction concerning its background may not be inappropriate. In Canada, the measurement of productivity and the estimation of production function relationships have lagged behind developments in these areas in the United States. Indeed, until quite recently, with one notable exception, very little domestically produced material pertaining to the measurement of Canadian productivity had been published or, for that matter, even developed, although some rough estimates had been used over the years for various purposes by different government departments. The notable exception referred to was the 1957 Hood and Scott study for the Royal Commission on Canada's Economic Prospects.[1] This study developed estimates of gross domestic product per man-hour for major economic sectors, covering the years 1926 to 1955. Projection of these trends to 1980 was used, in combination with labor input projections, to derive estimates of the aggregate supply capabilities of the Canadian economy over the twenty-five-year horizon from 1955 to 1980. A by-product of this work was the computation, at the major Standard Industrial Classification group level, using the perpetual inventory technique, of estimates of the net and gross capital stocks covering the period 1926 to 1955. These were used to calculate capital-output ratios by industry, which, in turn, were projected to yield estimates of gross capital stock and investment growth to 1980.

From 1957 until 1964, although development work was under way at the Dominion Bureau of Statistics, there was little significant further published material. Last year, however, after a prolonged period of gestation, the DBS published global indexes of real output per employee and per man-hour for the commercial nonagricultural industries, covering the years 1947 to 1963.[2] Also, in December 1964 the DBS released some limited details of the capital stock estimates prepared under the

[1] William C. Hood and A. D. Scott, *Output, Labour and Capital in the Canadian Economy,* Ottawa, 1957.

[2] *Indexes of Real Output Per Person Employed and Per Man-Hour, Canada, for 1947–63, Commercial Non-Agricultural Industries,* Dominion Bureau of Statistics, Cat. No. 14-501.

Fixed Capital Stock Project designed to extend and develop the work initiated by A. D. Scott.[3] Reasonably firm estimates of the net and gross stock were available for most of the two-digit manufacturing industries, and the full set of data were made available by the DBS to interested parties pending their release in detail in the forthcoming DBS publication, *Estimates of Fixed Capital Flows and Stocks, Manufacturing, 1926–60.* In addition to the estimates pertaining to manufacturing made available by the DBS, much more preliminary and tentative estimates covering most of the remaining major industry groups were released. Early in 1965, the Economic Council of Canada published, in a staff study, the estimates of output per man-hour in the agricultural and non-agricultural sectors of the economy underlying its potential output projections.[4] Another Economic Council Staff Study used industry output estimates consistent with its global output projections, together with industry gross capital-output ratio projections, to derive estimates of equilibrium values of invesment consistent with the steady growth of the Canadian economy to its potential level by 1970.[5] Mention should also be made of as yet unpublished work undertaken by two recent royal commissions which, it is understood, employed explicit production function models, and a recent paper by Y. Kotowitz.[6] A number of additional unpublished studies have been undertaken by Canadian university economists. The Lithwick-Post-Rymes paper before this conference represents an important addition to this now growing body of Canadian empirical studies of production function relationships, and presents what I believe are the first domestically produced published estimates of "total factor productivity."

The main thread linking the three sections of the paper appears to be their use of newly available capital stock estimates. It is perhaps a rather thin thread, since the estimates of capital stock actually used in Part III of the paper were apparently those developed independently by Lithwick in connection with the Ph.D. thesis referred to there. Presumably, the Lithwick estimates for manufacturing were broadly con-

[3] DBS, *Daily Bulletin Supplement 2,* December 22, 1964.

[4] B. J. Drabble, *Potential Output, 1946 to 1970,* Staff Study No. 2, Economic Council of Canada.

[5] Derek A. White, *Business Investment to 1970,* Staff Study No. 5, Economic Council of Canada.

[6] "Capital-Labour Substitution and Technological Change in Canadian Manufacturing, 1926–61," a paper presented to the meeting of the Canadian Political Science Association, June 10–12, 1965.

sistent with those used in the other two sections of the paper, although there is no direct discussion of this point.

The relation between Part I and the other two parts of the paper seems rather loose. The authors state that their purpose is to throw light indirectly on the role of the capital stock in Canadian manufacturing by studying the capital stock adjustment process, net investment. Net investment is related to output and net capital stock variables in the first regression equation, and in most industries the estimated relations reveal the expected positive sign for output and negative sign for the net capital stock. $\bar{R}^2$ values were low, however, and, in six cases out of fourteen, not significant at the 5 per cent level. The choices of the authors in specifying alternative hypotheses, in an attempt to explain a larger part of the variation in net investment, are somewhat difficult to understand. The choice of an interest rate variable appeared highly unlikely to yield significant coefficients in view of the known heavy reliance of Canadian corporations upon internal financing and likely low sensitivity to interest rate variations.[7] Of interest and relevance in the context of their paper would have been the introduction of gross stock variables in place of the net stock variables and of values of output lagged by more than one period, the latter in view of known substantial time lags between changes in output (or sales) and realized investment. Use of the gross stock is suggested by the authors' attribution of the poor fit of the first regression equation to "too mechanical" an estimation of replacement investment, which implies that the net stock estimates would suffer from similar defects.

The second set of regressions represents a considerable improvement on the first, although one suspects that part of the improvement results from serial correlation in gross investment and correlation between gross investment and the gross capital stock of the same period. Again, it would have been of interest if the authors had used gross capital stock estimates in the computation of capacity capital-output ratios and estimated excess capacity. Further, the introduction of excess capacity variables lagged more than one period would appear to have been desirable. Also, the use of fixed income share weights in Parts II and III of

---

[7] J. H. Young and J. F. Helliwell, assisted by W. A. McKay, "The Effects of Monetary Policy on Corporations," Royal Commission on Banking and Finance, *Appendix Volume,* Ottawa, 1964; also D. J. Daly, "The Scope for Monetary Policy—A Synthesis," in forthcoming Economic Council of Canada publication, *Conference on Stabilization Policies.*

the paper, implying unitary elasticity of substitution, suggests that it would have been appropriate for the authors to test a log-linear form of investment equation derived from the Cobb-Douglas function. In general, however, the influence of the business cycle upon annual investment data is such that high $\bar{R}^2$ values are not to be expected without the inclusion of cyclical variables; even then, of course, the use of annual data tends to obscure cyclical relationships.

Turning now to Part II of the paper, it is clear that, in a very general way, the evidence set forth in Parts II and III provides a useful addition to what Murray Brown has referred to as "an impressive set of evidence to indicate that, quantitatively, the labour and capital input components have been over-emphasized" in reference, specifically, to the results obtained by M. Abramovitz, R. Solow, M. Brown, and J. Popkin. Part II of the paper, together with the Statistical and Technical appendixes, is central in more than one sense. Since, as we have noted, it presents the first published estimates of the growth of total factor productivity in Canadian manufacturing using the new DBS capital stock estimates, it is perhaps appropriate for the authors to devote considerable attention to evaluating the effects of the different sets of average service lives assumed by DBS upon the growth of the capital stock over time and thus upon total weighted factor inputs and measured productivity.

The authors proceed to do this with great pessimistic zeal, as befits true devotees of the "dismal science." However, since one of the co-authors was responsible for supervising the preparation of the DBS capital stock estimates, it appears reasonable to conclude that the paper could have given somewhat firmer indications as to the growth estimates most likely to be accurate, that is, those based upon the capital stock estimates incorporating the most realistic service life assumptions. The authors do state that sets III and V were in general based respectively on the longest and shortest lives assumed, but we are not given any indication of the probabilities attached to these assumptions. The implied downgrading of the standard estimates thus appears to go beyond the requirements of detached objectivity, almost to the verge of masochism. Over the longer period 1926–56, the divergences between the total factor productivity estimates based upon the three sets of life assumptions at the total manufacturing level narrow substantially, but the authors are skeptical of this result and warn of the possible influence of secular changes in average economic lives.

While perhaps rather strong, the authors' caution is not without foundation and points to the need for continuing surveys of service lives in order both to establish their average current values and to keep abreast of changes in the rates of physical and technical obsolescence. Until such a firmer foundation for them exists, the capital stock estimates and the measures based upon them will continue to be open to some justified suspicion.

The authors' concern with capital stock measurement problems appears to have diverted their attention to some extent from other potentially serious questions relating to their results covering the 1946–56 period. One of these is the adequacy of the output data underlying the productivity estimates based upon data for gross domestic product at factor cost. In a number of industries, these have not been revised to census benchmarks since 1951. Since then, extrapolation has been on the basis of monthly data. Some 40 per cent of the monthly total industrial production index is based upon man-hours data adjusted for estimated trends in productivity. Variations in industry input requirements are not reflected in such estimates and in other projectors used in the estimates of GDP at factor cost. To the extent that unit input variations have been significant, the gross domestic product and factor productivity estimates will be subject to bias. Similar qualifications apply, of course, to the output data entering the regressions of Part I.

A further question relates to the corrections to the paid worker input series to eliminate hours paid for but not worked. DBS estimates based on Census of Industry data suggest that the allowances for hours paid for but not worked incorporated in Table SA–6 are considerably higher than is appropriate, producing a downward bias in labor inputs and an upward bias in total measured factor productivity. The DBS figures in fact suggest that the use of paid worker data over the period considered would not result in serious bias in the productivity estimates.

An additional major issue relates to the appropriateness of the period selected for the analysis of total factor productivity, apart from the shortness of the period covered by the estimates in Part II. The authors note the emergence of excess capacity from 1957 on and rightly restrict their measures to the 1946–56 period in preference to the longer period 1946–60 for which data were available. In 1946, however, the existing capital stock was depreciated to very low levels by the straight-line depreciation methods underlying the net stock computation. Subsequent growth rates for the net stock were therefore very large. In general, the net capital stock estimates reveal larger percentage swings than do the corresponding gross estimates, as is indicated by the following percentage changes in capital stock in Canadian manufacturing: [8]

	Gross Stock	*Net Stock*
1931–39	−8.8	−15.3
1946–56	+54.9	+78.8

Over the period 1946–56, gross domestic product at factor cost in manufacturing grew at 4.5 per cent per annum, the gross capital stock grew at 4.5 per cent per annum, and the net stock at 6 per cent per annum. It may be noted parenthetically that 1946 was a recession year in Canada, judged by the performance of industrial production, and manufacturing output was about 8 per cent lower than in 1945 and 9 per cent lower than in 1947. This has, of course, further implications for the choice of 1946 as a base year for the total factor productivity estimates. Here, I wish merely to observe that the calculation of the 1946–56 growth rate referred to earlier is based on the substitution of the average of the 1945 and 1947 values of manufacturing production in place of the actual estimated 1946 value.

While the authors indicate a preference for the net stock measure of capital on conceptual grounds, their illustration of its superiority assumes a change in the composition of the stock which leaves the net and gross stock unchanged but alters the level of output and capital consumption allowances. Empirical evidence suggests that changes in the average age of the stock are important and that disequilibrium relationships between the net and gross stock are the rule rather than the exception. This consideration appears to be of greater practical relevance than the hypothetical example used by the authors. It is not clear to me that the analysis of growth is usefully furthered by the introduction into the empirical measures of medium-term variations in the capital variable related to changes in the average lives of the assets comprising the capital stock.

In a more positive vein, the authors are, I feel, to be commended for their disaggregated approach to productivity measurement. As Part III shows, the effects of interindustry shifts in employment upon aggregate

[8] Based on Set I lives.

total factor productivity have been significant in the Canadian case, even within industry sectors such as manufacturing. The major influence has, however, been the shift out of agriculture, which occurred somewhat later in Canada than in the United States. The recent United Nations study of growth similarly reports important shift effects in some European countries during the 1949–59 decade,[9] and there are indications that the shift out of agriculture has been a significant influence on Japanese growth.

Here I should like to disagree mildly with the authors' statement that the productivity improvement resulting from the shift out of agriculture "has been a once and for all event." The decline in the agricultural labor force is still continuing at a rate of about 3 per cent per annum. While this rate is lower than in the earlier postwar years, and the size of the agricultural labor force itself has about halved over the postwar period, some further significant productivity improvements from the shift out of agriculture appear probable. The authors' contention that the past growth rate in aggregate productivity will not easily be attained in the future also requires some qualification to take account of the improvement in the quality of labor inputs arising from the high rate of entry of young persons with considerably improved educational standards into the labor force.

A further advantage of disaggregation lies in the additional knowledge that may be brought to bear upon the analysis of the sources of productivity change. The textile industry provides an interesting example of this. The authors note that if total factor productivity in this industry were measured from 1949, instead of 1946, its growth would appear much stronger. The different performance of the industry may be rather closely identified with economic changes between the two periods: from an immediate postwar situation of strongly rising demand and prices, extended by the effects of the Korean War, to a situation of slower demand growth, rising labor costs associated with the resource development and investment boom and increased foreign competition resulting from a shift in the exchange rate from a discount to a premium with resulting lower Canadian prices for imported manufactures. The second period was marked by increased specialization within the industry. In this case, it would appear that increased competition and forced speciali-

[9] *Some Factors in Economic Growth in Europe During the 1950s,* Geneva, 1964, Table 22, Chap. 3.

zation was a ratchet producing a higher rate of productivity growth. It is unfortunate, for the purposes of this sort of analysis that, because of capital stock data problems, such dissimilar industries as nonferrous metal products and electrical apparatus and supplies had to be amalgamated in the computation of the productivity measures.

In conclusion, I feel it appropriate to draw attention to a finding of Part III of the paper which appears to be an important one. In Tables 17 and 19, the authors point to the similarity of Canadian total factor productivity growth rates by industry between 1937 and 1961 and those for comparable industries in the United States over the period 1927–57. The similarity is indeed quite striking. The authors conclude from this evidence, as we have seen, that the different growth performance of the two economies is primarily attributable to "shift" effects, with similar technological changes occurring, industry by industry, in the two countries. A further implication to be drawn, however, is that since, notwithstanding dependence on different data sources and differences in the periods covered, the two sets of computations portray an essentially similar picture in the industries which can be compared directly, the data used, despite many shortcomings, appear to afford the basis for meaningful comparison and analysis of total factor productivity growth trends. There is an important crumb of comfort in this for those engaged in the uncertain task of productivity measurement.

THOMAS A. WILSON

In this interesting paper Lithwick, Post, and Rymes have incorporated a number of applications of measures of the capital stock recently released by the Dominion Bureau of Statistics. Incidentally, the availability of these estimates is due in large part to the painstaking work of Mr. Rymes.

The paper is really three papers bound together. The first deals with investment behavior. The second presents sector by sector estimates of "total factor productivity," and examines the sensitivity of these estimates to changes in the assumptions which underlie the capital stock figures. The third focuses on the aggregative growth performance of the Canadian economy, with explicit attention to what accounts for the observed differences between Canada and the United States in the rate of technical change.

I shall therefore divide my remarks accordingly, but shall discuss these topics in reverse order, as I want to devote most of my allotted time to the section dealing with investment behavior.

Let us first look at the aggregative study. The authors find that the rate of technical change over the 1926–56 period in Canada was considerably higher than the rate of technical change over the 1929–57 period in the United States, which accounted for nearly three-quarters of the observed growth in that country.[1] Their main contribution, however, is an examination of the sources of technical change to find out what accounts for the apparently higher rate of technical advance in Canada. Two sources are examined: changes in the quality of the labor force (as measured by changes in levels of educational attainment and by changes in the age-sex structure of the labor force), and movements of labor (and capital) between sectors or industries within the economy.

Surprisingly, the first source—improved quality of the labor force—actually contributed less to economic growth in Canada than it did in the United States. Whereas Denison found that in that country education was a particularly important source of economic growth,[2] in Canada the contribution of education to growth was much smaller, and was almost completely offset by unfavorable changes in the age-sex composition of the labor force.

Intersectoral movements of labor, on the other hand, are much more important in Canada, and largely account for the observed differences between the two countries in the rate of technical change. While this finding is somewhat influenced by the period analyzed (the important outmovement from agriculture was concentrated in the 1937–61 period), it is indicative of a fundamental difference between the two economies in the past. The much greater importance of agriculture in Canada, and the consequent greater relative importance of the shift of resources from agriculture to industry explain the larger relative importance of these intersectoral shifts for economic growth in Canada.

One thing that bothers me about these (and other) calculations of

[1] Technical change (including improvements in labor quality) accounted for 70 per cent of total growth in the United States, 1929–57 (E. F. Denison, *The Sources of Economic Growth in the United States and the Alternatives Before Us,* Washington, D.C., 1962, Table 32, p. 266).

[2] Denison (*loc. cit.*) estimates that education accounted for over one-fifth of total growth. If the correction for extra days of schooling per year of school completed is eliminated, this contribution is reduced to 12 per cent (Lithwick, Post, and Rymes, Table 16).

the effects of intersectoral shifts is that they only pick up the growth consequences of moving from a disequilibrium factor market position toward an equilibrium one. Paradoxically, in an economy with high labor mobility and well-functioning markets, the measured effect of interindustry labor movements will be small, because the interindustry mobility itself prevents situations with large wage or productivity differentials from emerging.

The authors point out that the contribution to growth of this out-movement from agriculture is likely to be less in the future than in the past, due largely to the decreased relative importance of the agricultural labor force. The depressing effect on the growth rate is likely to be more than offset by several favorable developments, however. The labor force is expected to grow at a very rapid rate over the next five years. If major wars and depression, which seriously retarded the capital formation rates in the past, are avoided, the capital stock will grow at a rate faster than that achieved over the past thirty years. These two factors together make the growth prospects of the Canadian economy particularly buoyant over the next five to ten years; to the extent that the educational level of the work force is improved and to the extent that shifts of workers occur from low- to high-productivity regions, the actual growth achieved will exceed even these buoyant prospects.

The estimates of total factor productivity presented in the second part of the paper are about as detailed as those published by Kendrick [3] for the United States. Future research involving comparisons of the estimates for Canada and the U.S. and the explanation of the observed differences in growth rates of total factor productivity might shed additional light on some of the issues discussed at this conference.

The authors find that their estimates of total factor productivity are somewhat sensitive to changes in the assumed lives of plant and equipment used in constructing the capital stock series. I think they are unduly disturbed by these findings. The changes are quite small, being of the order of one-tenth of 1 per cent per year over the 1926–56 period (or 7 per cent of the estimated growth of total factor productivity).

In any case this finding would suggest that DBS consider alternatives to the fixed lives approach now used. Under the present method

[3] John W. Kendrick, *Productivity Trends in the United States,* Princeton for NBER, 1961.

of estimating the capital stock, small changes in assumed lines may lead to fairly large changes in the gross stock for an industry which experienced an investment boom at some point in the past.

These changes would be much reduced if a survival curve approach (which is more realistic) were used—i.e., if the stocks were estimated on the assumption that the expected life of a specific machine is constant, but that its actual life is a probability function of its age.

Let us now turn to the analysis of investment behavior.

The basic model used is a simple accelerator type of capital stock adjustment model, with the desired stock this year dependent on last year's output, and with no role for variables reflecting liquidity or the availability of internal or external funds. A perusal of Table 1 indicates that this model does not perform particularly well. Economists are becoming used to unexpected signs on regression coefficients and other problems arising from the collinearity of the set of possible independent variables, but to have six out of thirteen time series R^2's statistically insignificant is not usually our lot!

A proponent of the Charles River theory of investment might argue that these results simply reflect the omission of liquidity or internal funds variables. However, in connection with some work I have carried out for the Royal Commission on Taxation, I fitted accelerator–residual funds models for industries at approximately the two-digit level in Canada. These results indicate that a capital stock adjustment model which incorporates residual funds as well as accelerator effects does not perform particularly well either.

I also have fitted forecasting and realization functions using the November forecasts of investment published by DBS. The forecasts work very well. When capital goods price changes are taken into account, roughly 90 per cent of the variation of *changes* in business fixed investment is accounted for by the forecasting functions at the aggregate level. While the disaggregated results are not that good, they are quite respectable. The realization functions, on the other hand, are very good at the aggregative level, but very poor at the two-digit level. For the economy as a whole, 80 per cent of the deviation of actual investment from forecast investment can be explained by changes in retained earnings, changes in sales, and changes in capital goods prices. At the two-digit level, it is rare that any significant improvement on the forecasts can be attained by a realization function.

What accounts for the generally poorer results obtained at the two-digit level in Canada as compared with the United States? (Compare, for example, the results of Lithwick, Post, and Rymes at the two-digit level with those recently published by Hickman.) [4]

One contributing factor may be the simple lumpiness of investment decisions by individual firms. The typical Canadian manufacturing industry is dominated by a few large firms, largely because the Canadian market is smaller than the American. Even at the two-digit level the investment decisions of a few large firms can noticeably affect the series for the industry as a whole.

Much more important, I believe, is the fact that the usual type of accelerator or accelerator–residual funds model is not suitable for industries in an open economy. The openness of the Canadian economy is great in two ways. First, exports and imports are 20 to 25 per cent of total GNP, and are even more important for the manufacturing sector. Second, roughly half of manufacturing industry is owned or controlled by foreigners; the typical foreign-controlled firm is a subsidiary of a United States firm.

Under these conditions, lagged domestic output will be a poor proxy for expected sales; retained earnings and Canadian interest rates will be inadequate measures of the availability and cost of funds. If relative prices are introduced, the relative costs of producing in Canada vis-à-vis the United States will probably be more important than the relative prices of Canadian inputs.

While some improvement may be possible with better specification of the conventional models, especially if new data series become available on a quarterly basis, I think that major improvements will be achieved only when we figure out a way of modifying the accelerator–residual funds model to handle the case of a very open economy. My first candidates for variables in such a modified model would include measures of sales expectations in foreign and domestic markets (weighting each market by its relative importance for the industry concerned), the inclusion of retained earnings of parent as well as subsidiary firms, particularly for industries such as autos where foreign ownership is very important, and measures reflecting the relative costs of production north and south of the border. Obtaining even proxy measures of these vari-

[4] Bert G. Hickman, *Investment Demand and U.S. Economic Growth,* Washington, D.C., 1965, Table 4, pp. 54–55.

ables will not be easy. But surely we can improve on models which predict, for example, that the devaluation of the dollar stimulates investment after output responds rather than before.

Another alternative worth trying might be to resurrect the old-fashioned profits theory. Given the aggregate amount of North American investment, the percentage allocated north rather than south of the forty-ninth parallel may well be explained (as conventional theory would suggest) by relative rates of return on capital.

These considerations also suggest that the aggregative results, while satisfactory at first glance, need to be interpreted with some caution, particularly for purposes of policy analysis. Given the links between the Canadian and the United States economies, the aggregate variables may move closely together so that a domestic variable (for example, Canadian output) is a reasonably good proxy for the correct variable (for example, North American sales).

Finally, let me turn to two issues dealt with by the authors where the methods used are inadequate.

They attempt to test the hypothesis that technical change is embodied in concrete capital goods in two ways. The first test is the introduction of a time trend into the capital requirements model. This does not test the hypothesis that technical change must be embodied in capital goods, since new techniques may be more or less capital-intensive than old, yet may still have to be embodied in new types of capital goods. The second test is a regression of changes in output per man-hour on changes in output and on lagged investment. However, a first-difference model, which emphasizes short-run changes in output per man-hour, will not likely be a good one for testing the effects of embodiment, which are presumably longer lasting. Some kind of distributed lag approach would seem to be in order. Furthermore, it is not clear that the inclusion of changes in output is an adequate method for eliminating the effects of cyclical fluctuations in productivity.

The authors also present estimates of the desired capital stock in manufacturing. Reversing the investment demand model, they obtain estimates of the desired stock by a procedure similar to that used by Hickman [5] to obtain capacity estimates. The Lithwick-Post-Rymes estimates of desired capital stock lie persistently *above* the actual capital stock

[5] *Ibid.*, pp. 94–104.

and are the counterpart of Hickman's estimates of capacity, being substantially *below* actual output. In the light of the sluggish performance of both the United States and the Canadian economies in the six years after 1957 these results are not particularly convincing. They confirm a suspicion of mine that the coefficient of the lagged capital stock in capital stock adjustment models is typically biased toward zero because of the likely positive serial correlation in the true error terms. If the coefficient on the lagged capital stock is biased toward zero the estimates of the desired stock will typically be upwardly biased, and the estimates of capacity downwardly biased.

To put matters more simply, the biased estimates of the coefficient on the lagged capital stock mean that too sluggish an adaptation rate is assumed. In a growing economy, this means that actual capital lags persistently behind the supposed desired capital stock.

REPLY by Lithwick, Post, and Rymes

It has been pointed out that the regressions in Part I are more successful in explaining aggregate investment than the capital expenditures of some major groups. This result is perhaps not surprising, since we specified relatively simple models of investment behavior and used them for all regressions. There are a number of factors which may have contributed to the poor performance of the models we chose and applied to all the data. A considerable amount of product and process heterogeneity may exist within the major groups. The answer to this problem lies in further disaggregation. If a major group includes plants with quite different capital-output coefficients and if the demand for the output of these different plants does not move together, then the required capital stock for the entire group will not be closely related to changes in total output for the group. A second explanation is that different industries may be subject to response lags of different length. The answer to this problem would have been to specify a model with lags tailored to the typical response pattern of each major group. Although we could have obtained better results by choosing different lags and variables for each industry, space limitations prevented us from so doing.

It was suggested by Professor Wilson that the dependence of many Canadian firms on export markets might influence their investment behavior. This will be the case if a decision maker when he is forecasting output and hence the need for capital inputs has different expectations about export sales than about domestic sales. This might, for example, be the case for a firm breaking into the export market for the first time and anticipating quite different quantities and elasticities than it has experienced in the domestic market. Our model, which assumes output expectations to depend on experienced patterns of output, is not capable of handling such a break with past patterns of behavior. Nor does our model attribute any role to the availability of financial capital; so inflows of long-term capital from abroad and direct investment in branch plants in Canada are also ignored. In the branch plant case the investment decision is made outside Canada, sometimes in the light of market possibilities outside Canada. A more complete analysis would need to take cognizance of the terms and availability of financing, as suggested by the discussants.

The emphasis in Part II of our paper on the variations in estimates of total measured factor productivity which arise because of an almost complete lack of reliable knowledge on the lives of capital goods, their survival curves, and realistic depreciation functions remains valid in our view. Clearly, in a disequilibrium world no unambiguous estimates will ever be obtained, but a great deal of work in the way of capital measurement remains to be done, in our view, before much confidence can be placed on estimates of total measured factor productivity in Canadian manufacturing. The Set I lives, which were the ones primarily used in our paper, represent the lives initially developed by DBS, and the different sets of lives were introduced by them in an attempt to see how sensitive capital stock estimates are to variations in assumed economic lives. Without further investigation it is not possible to say how appropriate the initial Set I lives are, nor would the application of crude survival curves, without first obtaining greatly improved data on actual survival patterns of capital goods, result in a reduction of the possible degree of error in the estimates.

We would have thought that our discussion in the Technical Appendix of the superiority of both the net stock and capital consumption allowances as the relevant capital inputs where the average age of the capital goods changes was quite pertinent to the points Mr. White raises in this connection. As Mr. White points out, our estimates of total measured factor productivity reflect the initial and terminal years chosen, and we drew explicit attention to this in our discussion of the cyclical sensitivity of the estimates and how they would have been altered had different initial and terminal years been chosen for analysis.

Mr. White criticizes our adjustment (in Table SA-6) of the labor series, from an hours-paid to an hours-worked basis. This correction involved only vacations with pay and other paid time off, and thus the large discrepancy between our adjustment and the preliminary work at DBS is not the result of a difference in concept. In fact, we suspect the latter series has some biases, but it would be inappropriate to discuss these unpublished materials. What we do conclude is that while our source is admittedly weak and our results biased thereby, there is strong evidence that a significant difference between hours paid and hours worked does exist, and that this must be explicitly taken into account.

PRODUCTION FUNCTIONS IN

MANUFACTURING:

SOME PRELIMINARY RESULTS

ZVI GRILICHES

UNIVERSITY OF CHICAGO

I. Introduction

THIS is a first progress report on a research program whose ultimate purpose is to account for the major sources of productivity growth in U.S. manufacturing industries in the post-World War II period. The analytical framework for this research endeavor was developed in my studies of technical change in agriculture, whose main substantive conclusions pointed to improvements in the quality of the labor force, economies of scale, and public investments in research and extension as the major sources of measured "residual" technical change in agriculture.[1] By extending this work to the manufacturing sector I hope to test the analytical framework and the broader relevance of the previous findings and to modify them in light of the different conditions prevailing in the industrial sector of the economy.

This paper, however, has a much narrower scope. It reports on a detailed analysis of cross-sectional data from the 1958 *Census of Manufactures* and the 1960 *Census of Population,* concentrating primarily on the construction and testing of quality-of-labor variables and an investigation of economies of scale.[2] The currently available data for analysis

NOTE: This work is a part of a larger study of the econometrics of technological change supported by grants from the National Science Foundation and the Ford Foundation. Parts of this paper were written during my tenure as a Ford Foundation Faculty Research Fellow at the Econometric Institute, Rotterdam.

[1] See Griliches (1963a) and (1964). Names and dates refer to the list of references at the end of this paper.

[2] The same data have been analyzed in somewhat similar fashion by Bell (1964) and Hildebrand and Liu (1965). Besides using somewhat different variables and procedures, the main difference between these studies and this paper is in purpose

are limited both in scope and quality and can answer only a few of the many interesting questions that could be explored within the production function framework. The work reported here is preliminary not only in the narrow scope of its questions, but also in the sense that it is based almost entirely on only one set of data. As such, it reports results that are an outcome of considerable "fishing" in these data. The findings of this analysis have to and will be eventually tested on new data (from the 1963 *Census of Manufactures*) which will become available shortly.

The major part of this article is devoted to reporting the results of estimating a production relation of the form

$$\log{(V/L)_{ij}} = a_0 + \alpha \log{(K/L)_{ij}} + h \log{L_{ij}} + \sum_h \beta_h Z_{hij} + d_i + d_j + u_{ij},$$

where V is value added, L is a measure of man-hours, K is a measure of capital services, the Z_{hij}'s are various measures of labor and capital quality, d_i and d_j are coefficients of industry and state dummy variables, and u_{ij} is a random disturbance. The index i varies over industries (two-digits, $i = 20, \ldots , 38$) and the index j over 49 states (including the District of Columbia but excluding Alaska and Hawaii). This form is convenient for the estimation of economies of scale, since the coefficient $h = a_k + a_l - 1$ provides a direct measure of it and a direct way of testing its "significance."

Note several old-fashioned aspects of this formulation: (1) I am estimating a Cobb-Douglas form, implicitly assuming that the elasticity of substitution is unity; (2) I will be using "naïve" simple least-squares estimation procedures; (3) I am imposing the *same* α and h coefficients on the whole universe of nineteen industries. Detailed estimates of the elasticity of substitution based both on the ACMS method [3] and on a direct approximation of the CES production function are presented in Section III of this paper. They indicate, overwhelmingly, that at least for these data the Cobb-Douglas assumption is not inappropriate.

It is harder to make an adequate allowance for the simultaneity

and scope. Bell did not test for economies of scale, nor allowed for any quality-of-labor variables. Hildebrand and Liu did try to use, unsuccessfully, a rather poor education variable. Their primary interest, however, was in defining and testing (with what I interpret to be negative results) a particular version of the embodiment-of-technical-change hypothesis. The main difference between this paper and their work is in the attempt that is made here to construct and test a series of specific industry-by-state quality-of-the-labor-force variables. See Griliches (1965) for a more detailed discussion of the Hildebrand and Liu results.

[3] See Arrow *et al.* (1961).

problem without constructing a complete production and input decision behavior model. Assuming profit maximization with random deviations but without any lags, one can estimate the coefficients by indirect least squares, which in this context is a full information method.[4] But this information, while "full," is apparently not very good, as it leads to unreasonable coefficients and very high standard errors. An alternative, and theoretically less demanding procedure, is to use the method of instrumental variables. Unfortunately, in aggregative cross sections of this type, the available instrumental variables such as lagged labor are "too good." They are so highly correlated with the variable they are replacing that there is almost no difference between the least squares and instrumental variables estimates of the major coefficients.[5] Either there is no simultaneity problem or it cannot be cured by the use of lagged endogenous variables as instruments. The possible magnitude of simultaneous equations bias is also somewhat reduced by the use of industry and state dummy variables, eliminating the systematic components of the correlation between the disturbance and the "independent" variables. But only the availability of several consistent cross sections over time will permit a more satisfactory treatment of the simultaneity problem.[6]

Perhaps the most unsatisfactory aspect of the estimates presented below is the imposition of the same coefficients on all two-digit subindustries. There are two answers to this criticism: (1) I have fitted the equations separately, and they are not significantly different from each other. This, however, is more a reflection of the lack of degrees of freedom and poorness of the data than of a true equality of coefficients. (2) I am not interested in individual industry effects but in average relations for manufacturing as a whole. If the coefficients are different, fitting one equation to them will in fact result in estimates that are averages of the corresponding individual industry coefficients.[7]

[4] See Hoch (1962) and Kmenta (1964) for a discussion of this method.

[5] This was also the case in the Hildebrand and Liu (1965) estimates for 1957 using essentially the same data and similar procedures. In none of the fifteen cases (industries) estimated by them is there any significant difference between their least squares and two-stage least squares estimates of the production function coefficients. See also Griliches (1963c).

[6] This would allow us to use Mundlak's (1963) covariance method and less highly serially correlated lagged variables as instruments.

[7] Things are a little bit more complicated than that. The statement in the text is strictly true only in the bivariate case (one independent variable) and in the multivariate case when the slope parameters are distributed independently of the values of the independent variables. More generally, each coefficient is a weighted

Whether these are the "right" averages having the "right" weights for eventual time series comparison is problematic. But clearly the procedure is superior to fitting the same equation to total manufacturing averages.[8] Allowing each industry to have a separate intercept will reduce somewhat the misspecification in the other coefficients. The alternative of using up an additional eighteen degrees of freedom and allowing also the a's to differ between industries leads to no appreciable improvement in the estimates. Again, as several cross sections with more degrees of freedom become available, one will also be able to relax this restriction.

The use of industry and state dummy variables is a mixed blessing. They do take care of various possible specification errors which are either industry or state specific. They also put the various hypotheses to a much more stringent test. On the other hand, they reduce the available variance of the various independent variables greatly, forcing us to estimate relations from the "within"-industry or state variance components. This is likely to lead to more unstable estimates with larger standard errors. Moreover, since it is quite likely that some of our measures are subject to substantial error, using only the "within" variance will magnify the error-to-systematic-component variance ratio and lead to downward bias in the estimated coefficients. Thus, while the equations including all the dummy variables have the highest R^2's, they do not necessarily yield the best estimates of the coefficients of interest.

The plan of the rest of the paper is as follows: Section II discusses data sources, the definitions of various variables and their possible shortcomings. Section III represents a digression devoted to a review of previous estimates of the elasticity of substitution in manufacturing and the presentation of a detailed set of new estimates. Section IV presents the major production function results, using also data from the 1954 *Census of Manufactures* for a further exploration of the problem of economies of scale. Section V indicates how some of the results of this study can be used to account for the growth of manufacturing output in the postwar period.

average of the corresponding microparameters plus a zero-weighted covariance correction term involving the noncorresponding parameters. If there is no particular correlation between the various parameters and the average deviations of the independent variables in the subindustries, the latter terms drop out. See Zellner (1962) and Theil (1954) for more details.

[8] Preliminary estimates using state average per establishment data for *total* manufacturing were presented in Griliches (1963c). The current results can be interpreted as a within-state disaggregation using two-digit industry detail.

The main results of this study can be summarized briefly: (1) There is no substantial evidence against the Cobb-Douglas assumption in manufacturing. (2) Differences in the quality of labor are an important factor in accounting for differences in labor productivity (holding capital-labor ratios constant). (3) There are some indications of mildly increasing returns to scale in manufacturing. The data used, however, are not the most suitable for an investigation of this question. More work and better data are required before the last finding can be considered to be definitive.

II. The Data and the Variables

The *Census of Manufactures, 1958,* presents, for the first time in decades, data on the gross book value of depreciable assets in manufacturing by states and two-digit industries.[9] This is the basic body of data defining the scope of this study and the number of available observations. In addition, the *Census of Manufactures* and the associated *Annual Surveys of Manufactures* provide data on value added, payrolls, man-hours, number of establishments, and other variables. The main limitation of this body of data, besides its being only a one-year cross section, is the extreme paucity of data on the characteristics of the labor force in the various states and industries. The largest expenditure of effort in this study was devoted to the construction of appropriate state-by-industry "quality-of-the-labor-force" variables from the 1960 *Census of Population.*[10]

The basic unit in this study is a per-establishment within-state industry average. Data are not available for all industries in all states. Preliminary investigations were carried out using a total of 440 observations in 49 states (including the District of Columbia) and 19 industries (excluding Industry 39, miscellaneous manufacturing). Most of the final computations were carried out using a reduced sample of 417 observations, excluding Industry 21, tobacco products, and Industry 29, petroleum and coal products. Industry 21 was excluded because I did not succeed in constructing the associated labor quality variables for it, and

---

[9] Vol. I, Chap. 9. These data were actually collected as part of the 1957 Annual Survey of Manufactures, but are part of the 1958 Census program.

[10] Vol. I, Chap. D, by State.

Industry 29 because the results for it proved to be extremely unstable in some of the preliminary calculations.

V—value added (adjusted) is the main dependent variable in this study and the measure of output used.[11]

K—the flow of capital services is defined as the sum of insurance premiums, rental payments, property taxes paid, depreciation and depletion charged in 1957, and .06 (6 per cent) of gross book value on December 31, 1957. Note that the first four items refer to 1957 instead of 1958. Since they are likely to be quite sticky and hence highly serially correlated, not much error is introduced by using one-year-lagged values (no comparable data are available for 1958).

L—total man-hours equals total payroll divided by the average wage rate per hour of *production* workers. Note that this converts the contribution of nonproduction workers into production worker hour-equivalents, allowing to some extent for quality differences due to a different mix of production and nonproduction workers in different industries or states.[12]

As noted above, all these variables are per establishment (i.e., the state totals are divided by the number of establishments in the industry in 1958).[13]

W—average wage rate of production workers is derived as the ratio of total wages to total man-hours of production workers.

Besides the capital service variable described above, two other capital measures were also tried: gross book value and a capital services concept as above except that the 6 per cent was taken of the net (depreciated) stock of capital rather than of the gross measure as in K above.[14] The first of these alternative measures gave similar but somewhat inferior

[11] This and all the other nonlabor-quality variables are taken from the *Census of Manufactures, 1958*, Vol. I, Chap. 9, the appropriate chapters of Vol. II, and the *Annual Survey of Manufactures, 1957*.

[12] One could have used two separate labor inputs here: production and nonproduction workers. The work of Hildebrand and Liu indicates, however, that there is little to be gained from such a division. There is no significant improvement in fit (or in other aspects of their results) when they disaggregate the labor input into these two components. Note, however, that implicitly we are assuming that the entire production-nonproduction wage difference is due to skill differences. But if, for example, the geographic dispersion of skilled worker wages is less than that of the unskilled, this will introduce a certain amount of bias into this labor measure.

[13] The 1957 data are also in per-1958 establishment units.

[14] Net stock was defined as gross book value minus accumulated depreciation to the end of 1956 and minus depreciation in 1957.

results in the preliminary runs. There was little to choose between the second alternative and the measure actually used.[15]

The flow formulation, whenever it is not proportional to the stock, is the more relevant measure of capital services. The variable I use approximates the idea of capital services—capital stock $(\delta + r)$, where δ is the depreciation rate and r is the interest rate. To the extent that the expected life of equipment differs between industries or establishments (either because of physical reasons or because of anticipated obsolescence), the use of current depreciation will approximate differences that are due to differences in δ.

The procedure used assumes, however, that capital services of different vintages are equally productive. This hypothesis can be tested by including R, the ratio of net to gross stock of capital, in the various regressions. R is a measure of the youngness of the capital stock. The higher is net stock relative to gross, the less it has depreciated, the more recent, presumably, is its vintage (on the average). Thus, to the extent that the "embodiment-of-technical-change-in-capital" hypothesis is important, it should show up in a significant and positive coefficient for R.[16] Unfortunately, this is a very weak test due to the main drawback of these capital data—they are all in historical costs rather than in current or constant prices. The embodiment hypothesis says that because of technical change, younger capital is more capital; but at the same time, because of price level changes it is also *less* capital. Thus, if the rate of embodied technical change is no greater than the average rate of inflation, not an unreasonable assumption, the two effects would cancel out. Also, the differences in R may reflect different depreciation policies more than they do age differences. Be that as it may, the R variable was never significant in any of the various combinations tried. Thus, I find no evidence for the embodiment hypothesis, which is consistent with the Hildebrand and Liu results and the Berglas (1965) time series investigation.[17]

The 1960 *Census of Population* provides data by state on the sex,

---

[15] The simple correlation between these two measures is .999. It is .990 between K as used and gross book value.

[16] In the form as introduced ($\log R = \log NK - \log GK$) it also allows the regression to "choose" a net capital stock concept if it were to fit better.

[17] Hildebrand and Liu introduced $\log R$ as an interaction term. I.e., they use $\log R \times \log K$ as their capital variable, and it is never significantly superior to just $\log K$ as a variable. By introducing $\log R$ separately we allow it a more general and independent role and a better chance at "significance," but with no greater success.

race, and age composition of the labor force by industry.[18] I have utilized the following variables constructed from this data:

Age—median age of employed males
P White—white as a fraction of the total employed males
P Female—females as a fraction of all employees

The Census does not provide a direct estimate of the educational distribution of the labor force by industry. Nor does it provide an education-by-occupation distribution at the state level. It does give, however, information on the occupational distribution of the labor force by industry by state, from which one can construct an occupational mix quality-of-the-labor-force variable. Such a variable will approximate and should be highly correlated with the education variables used in my previous studies. The occupational mix index is constructed as follows:

$$O_{ij} = \sum_k y_k O_{kij}$$

where k, i, and j are indexes for the occupation, industry, and state classifications respectively. O_{kij} is the fraction of total males in the ith industry in state j belonging to the kth occupation category. y_k is the mean income of *all* males , 25 years and over, in this occupational category in 1959. Two sets of y's were used, one for the northern and western states and another one for the southern states.[19] The resulting index can be

---

[18] Difficulties arise because the *Census of Population* industrial breakdown does not strictly equal the two-digit manufacturing Census classification. Where the population Census breakdown is more detailed, the results were aggregated using total employment in the subindustries as weights. In a few other cases, a population Census industry classification was attributed to several two-digit codes. For example, the *Census of Population* industry categories "primary ferrous" and "primary nonferrous" are added to yield the *Census of Manufactures* two-digit "primary metals" industry. Similarly, the *C of P* category "furniture, lumber, and wood products" is assigned to both the "lumber" and the "furniture" industries.

[19] Separate average-income-by-occupation figures were also computed for the North and West, but they differed only in the second or third place, and it was decided to average the two. The y_k used were

Occupation	North and West	South
Professional	$8,983	$8,577
Managerial	9,916	8,381
Clerical	5,536	5,205
Sales	7,374	6,149
Craftsmen	5,949	4,907
Operative	5,115	4,108
Service	4,423	3,721
Laborers	4,196	2,913
Occupation not reported	6,032	5,296

SOURCE: *Census of Population, 1960*, PC(2) 7B, Tables 2 and 3.

interpreted as the annual income predicted for this particular labor force given its occupational mix and national (or regional) average incomes by occupation.

Note that of the four labor quality variables, three (age, percentage white, and occupation mix) refer to the *male* labor force. That is, roughly speaking, we distinguish between the male and female labor force components and in addition allow for industry and state differences in the quality of the male labor force (only).[20]

Two types of dummy variables were used:

I_j—an industry dummy which takes the value of one for an observation from the corresponding industry and zero for all other industries. Eighteen such dummies were used, leaving out the dummy for Industry 20, and defining all industry effects as additive to or from the I_{20} level.

S_j—a similar dummy for states. Actually, I did not use a separate dummy for each state but combined several smaller states into quasi-regions. In preliminary investigations, forty such dummies were used. Since many of these did not differ significantly from each other, they were further combined into a total of twenty quasi-regional dummies.[21]

Using dummy variables forces the rest of the coefficients to be estimated from the variance around the respective class means. I.e., it takes out the between-class variance of all the variables. In some cases not much is left when this is taken out, and one should expect both a decline in the "significance" and in the numerical value of certain coefficients (because of an increase in the relative variance of measurement errors). Thus, much of the difference in capital-labor ratios is between industries. Introducing industry dummies is likely to reduce the apparent importance of this variable. Similarly, most of the labor force quality differences are geographical. Introducing state dummies is likely to eliminate much of their effect. Thus, it is not clear that the "dummies inclusive" estimates are necessarily the best. Moreover, since

[20] In principle one could construct also similar variables for the female labor force. This was not done both because of its costliness and because of the expectation that quality variation in the female *industrial* labor force is much narrower than among males.

[21] The "regions" used were: Maine; (rest of) New England; New York, New Jersey; Pennsylvania; Ohio, Indiana; Illinois; Michigan; Wisconsin; Minnesota; Iowa, Missouri, North Dakota, South Dakota, Nebraska, Kansas; Delaware, Maryland, District of Columbia, Virginia, West Virginia; North Carolina, South Carolina, Georgia, Florida; Kentucky; Tennessee, Alabama; Mississippi, Arkansas; Louisiana, Oklahoma, Texas; Colorado, Montana, Idaho, Wyoming; Arizona, New Mexico; Utah, Nevada; Washington, Oregon. California is the "left out" dummy, or the reference state.

much of the real wage differences that we count on to identify the production function are also geographical, we shall use the state dummies
only sparingly.[22]

The quality variables (and the wage rate) are in per-man or in
fraction-of-the-labor-force units. All the variables, except for the dummies and the percentage white and percentage female variables are
transformed into logarithms of the original units. The latter variables
are left in their original fraction form since it is thus easier to interpret
them as quality variables.[23]

One of the main shortcomings of these data has already been inti-
mated above: various variables refer to somewhat different points
of time. Perhaps the most important drawback is the unavailability of
capital figures in constant prices. In addition, the labor force quality data
is as of 1960. Also, I use 1957 data from the *Annual Survey of Manufactures* and 1958 data from the *Census of Manufactures* as if they relate
to the same universe and observations. Actually, there are some differences in coverage and the possibility of substantial sampling error.
Moreover, the year 1958 was a recession year (albeit mild), and some
of the industries may have been operating below capacity. To the extent
that this affects all establishments in an industry similarly, the use of
industry intercept dummies will allow for most of it. I am also relying on
the cross-sectional nature of the data and the rather slow changing nature
of geographic differentials to reduce the impact of the other shortcomings
discussed above.

---

[22] The state dummies are useful, however, against the hypothesis that there are
substantial regional price-of-output differentials which have not been eliminated
from our output measure.

[23] Consider two types of labor, which are convertible into each other at a fixed
exchange (premium) rate. Thus, the correct component of the total labor input
in the production function is, say:

$$(L_1 + cL_2)^\beta$$

This can be factored into

$$[L_1 + L_2 + (c - 1) L_2]^\beta = (L_1 + L_2)^\beta [1 + (c - 1)\pi]^\beta$$

where $\pi = L_2/(L_1 + L_2)$ is the fraction that class 2 workers are of the total.
Estimating this type of function we would need:

$$\beta \log (L_1 + L_2) + \beta \log (1 + m\pi_2)$$

Not knowing m ($m = c - 1$), it is hard to construct the second term satisfactorily.
But since π is a fraction, and m is also likely to be a fraction, we can approximate

$$\log (1 + x) \approx x, |x| < 1$$

and $\log (1 + m\pi)$ by a function of π alone, the m and β constants entering into
its estimated coefficient.

III. The Elasticity of Substitution
in Manufacturing: A Digression

From the point of view of production function estimation and the analysis of sources of productivity growth, the elasticity of substitution is a second-order parameter. Even if it were significantly different from unity, one would have to take this into account in an analysis of growth only if there were very substantial changes in the capital-labor ratio.[24] Nevertheless, by estimating a Cobb-Douglas-type production function we are assuming that this elasticity is equal to one in manufacturing. If this assumption is substantially incorrect, we will be committing a specification error of unknown magnitude and consequences. It is thus of some interest to review the previous evidence on this point and to conduct some additional tests with the data used in this study. Besides, the elasticity of substitution is a parameter of some general interest (particularly for theories of income distribution), and hence additional estimates of it are worth reporting for their own sake.

In reviewing the previous estimates of the elasticity of substitution in U.S. manufacturing industries we are faced with two conflicting sets of estimates. The studies based on cross-sectional data yield estimates which are on the whole not significantly different from unity. The time series studies report, on the average, substantially lower estimates. Almost all of these studies use the ACMS method of estimating the elasticity of substitution from the regression,

$$\log V/L = \sigma \log W + u$$

or a related form. At the two-digit industry level such an equation was fitted to cross-sectional data from the *Annual Survey of Manufactures*

---

[24] See Nelson (1964) for a more detailed analysis of this point. Roughly speaking, the percentage rate of growth of output can be approximated by the expression

$$y = t + \alpha n + (1 - \alpha)k + (1/2)\alpha(1 - \alpha)[(\sigma - 1)/\sigma](k - n)^2$$

where y, n, k, and t are the percentage rates of growth of output, labor, capital, and "productivity," respectively; α is the elasticity of output with respect to labor (at the particular point), and σ is the elasticity of substitution. The last term reflects the influence of $\sigma \neq 1$. Consider, for illustrative purposes, the following values for these variables: $\alpha = .7$, $\sigma = .5$, $k = .04$, $n = .01$. The halving of the elasticity of substitution would have a depressing effect on the rate of growth of output of only

$$-.5 \times .7 \times .3 \times 1.0\,(.04 - .01)^2 = -.105 \times .0009 = -.0001,$$

or one-hundredth of a percentage point.

by Minasian (1961) and Solow (1964), and for four-digit industries by Ferguson (1964), using data from the various Censuses of Manufactures.[25] Bell (1964) was the only one to use the capital-labor-ratio version of this equation. These estimates are briefly summarized in Table 1. The general impression from a more detailed look at these studies is that, accepting the ACMS model as correct, there is no strong evidence that σ is significantly different from unity. The estimates are often poor and erratic (particularly at the four-digit level), but they cluster around one, with a significant number of them exceeding unity by substantial amounts.

The time series estimates are summarized in Table 2.[26] In general they average below unity, though often not significantly so. In many cases the estimated relationships are also quite erratic and poor. For example, in 11 out of 18 cases the coefficient of log W_t estimated by McKinnon is not significantly different from zero. This implies either that σ is very small, or that the model or the data are not very good in accounting for the annual fluctuations in labor productivity. I shall come back to this point below. Suffice it to say here that in spite of the fact that the more recent Brown and Ferguson studies yield estimates which are closer to their cross-sectional counterparts, the over all impression from the time series results is that the estimates cluster around a σ which is significantly below unity.[27]

In a similar but more detailed recent survey Lucas examines these two conflicting bodies of evidence and concludes (with some reservations) in favor of the time series results. His argument is based on the existence of important biases in cross-sectional data, each of which would tend to bias the estimated elasticities towards unity. The two major sources of this bias are the disregard in these studies of regional price-of-output differentials and quality-of-labor differentials. It can be

[25] The summary of Ferguson's results is based on unpublished tables of the detailed results kindly supplied by him.

[26] These summaries are not really fair to the original papers, particularly those of Brown and Lucas, which contain much more material than is reported here. I have, however, limited myself to results which are comparable across studies.

[27] Ferguson's estimates are an exception to this statement, but given their undeflated nature and the consequent bias toward unity, I would attach less weight to them. Since this was first written the following additional studies have come to my attention: O'Neil (1965) and Sheshinski (1964) based on cross-sectional data and an additional time series study by McKinnon reviewed in Nerlove's survey in this volume. None of these studies is in strong conflict with the conclusions of this section.

TABLE 1

Cross-sectional Estimates of the Elasticity of Substitution in U.S. Manufacturing Industries

| Author | Period and Unit | Method | Number of Elasticities Estimated | | |
| | | | | Significantly (more than 2 standard errors) | |
			Total	Below 1	Above 1
Minasian (1961)	1957, states	ACMS	18	2	3
Solow (1964)	1956, regions	ACMS	18	0	1
Ferguson (1964)	1947, 1954, 1958 Selected *four-digit* industries, states	ACMS	129	13	8
Bell (1964)	1958, states	$\log \dfrac{WL}{V - WL} = a + \dfrac{(1-\sigma)}{\sigma} \log \dfrac{K}{L}$	18	0	11

ACMS: $\log V/L = a + \sigma \log W$. See Arrow *et al.* (1961)

TABLE 2

Time Series Estimates of the Elasticity of Substitution in U.S. Manufacturing Industries

| Author | Method | Period | Number of σ Coefficients Estimated | | |
| | | | | "Significantly" | |
			Total	Below 1	Above 1
McKinnon (1962)	$\log (V/L)_t = \sigma(1-\gamma) \log W_t + \gamma \log (V/L)_{t-1} + \lambda t$	1947–58	18	12[a]	0
Lucas (1963)	$\log (V/L)_t = \sigma \log W_t + \lambda t$	1931–58	14	13	0
Ferguson (1965)	$\log (V/L)_t = \sigma \log W_t + \lambda t$	1949–61	19	1	2
Brown (1965)[b]	$\log (V/L) = \sigma \log W^*_t + bC + \lambda t$	1948–60	13	3	0

[a] No exact test for σ is provided. The count here is approximate and impressionistic.

[b] W^* are different moving averages of past wage rates. C is a measure of capacity utilization.

shown that under reasonable assumptions each of these omissions will bias the estimate towards unity.[28] On the other hand, he considers the two sources of bias in the time series context—simultaneity and mis-specification of the lag structure—and concludes that these do not bias the time series estimates especially in some *particular* direction. The latter conclusion is supported by his finding that trying different lag schemes and a simultaneous equation model does not change his estimates by much.[29]

To my mind the choice is not all that clear-cut. First there is the puzzling frequency of *above*-unity estimates in the cross-sectional studies.

---

[28] Let the true equation be $\log V/L = \sigma \log W + u$. True W = total payroll/L, but actually we observe only N, the number of employees, while L, the effective labor input measure, is equal to $L = qN$, where q is a quality index. Then the true equation in the observed units can be rewritten as

$$\log V/L = \log V/N - \log q = \sigma \log \hat{W} - \sigma \log q + u$$

or

$$\log V/N = \sigma \log \hat{W} + (1 - \sigma) \log q + u$$

where $\hat{W}$ is the observed wage rate per incorrect unit $\hat{W}$ = Payroll/N, $\log \hat{W} = \log W + \log q$. Leaving out q from the regressions implies that the estimated σ is equal to

$$E\hat{\sigma} = \sigma + (1 - \sigma)b_{q\hat{w}}$$

where $b_{q\hat{W}}$ is the regression coefficient of $\log q$ on $\log \hat{W}$. It will always be positive, since quality as defined will be positively correlated with *measured* wage rates. If q is a random error,

$$b_{qW} = \frac{\text{Var}(\log q)}{\text{Var}(\log W)} < 1$$

is the fraction that error variance is of the total variance in the observed wage rates. The sign of the bias depends then on the sign of $(1 - \sigma)$, and the estimated $\hat{\sigma}$ is biased toward unity. The expression for bias due to ignored variations in the price of output is similar.

[29] Another possible source of difference between time series and cross-section estimates of σ, pointed out by Ferguson (1965), is the more restrictive definition of output (value added) in the OBE series. The *Census of Manufactures* data, the source of all cross-sectional estimates, includes in value added certain over-head expenses (mainly services) purchased from other industries, while the net-income-originating series of the OBE nets them out. If these inputs do belong in the production function with the same elasticity of substitution, then subtracting them from value added biases the estimated $\hat{\sigma}$ *away* from unity. If the elasticity of substitution of these overhead inputs is zero, which is the implicit assumption behind the subtraction procedure, including them (wrongly) in the value-added concept would reduce the fit but would not bias the estimate of σ (since by assumption these inputs are uncorrelated with differences in the wage level). The first formulation seems to be the more relevant one, which would lead to poorer and more erratic results in the time series estimates.

The significant-bias-toward-unity argument implies then that a number of these elasticities are *under*estimated and are in fact even further above unity. This contradicts the time series results, which rarely exceed unity. But more importantly, Lucas does not consider the major drawback of the time series data: the predominant influence of short-run business cycle phenomena. In cross sections one observes differences in labor productivity and capital intensity which are relatively long run and which change only slowly (this, of course, creates problems of its own). In time series estimates, partly because of the inclusion of the trend variable, almost all of the observations on the net relationship between V/L (labor productivity) and W are short run (deviations from trend) and are dominated by cyclical phenomena. By now it is well recognized that the cyclical behavior of labor productivity does not fit well the standard production function framework and requires a substantially more complicated model to explain it.[30] But it is from these same cyclical observations which are probably not on the production function at all that these studies attempt to derive the properties of the aggregate production function. No wonder the results are meager.

Another way of making this same criticism of the time series studies is to note that the coefficient of W is based on the variance of W net of trend (presumably its main systematic component) and often net of the previous labor productivity level. If, as is quite likely, the measured wage rate is subject to substantial measurement error, estimates that take out much of the systematic component of W magnify the relative error—variance—and result in downward-biased coefficients. Thus the time series estimates are biased toward zero. Since I do not believe that the usual time series data are really relevant to the question asked of them, I would prefer the cross-sectional estimates, particularly since there are ways of getting around their most obvious sources of bias.

In what follows we shall investigate the importance of these biases using three approaches: (1) introducing labor quality variables directly into the regression, (2) using separate regional dummy variables to take into account possible regional price-of-output and labor quality differentials, and (3) allowing for serial correlation in the disturbances due to persistence in the left-out variables.

Since we have observations for two years (1957 and 1958) on the

[30] There is a growing literature on this subject. For a recent view see Solow (1964b).

major variables, we can also investigate the possibility of a distributed lag model or other forms of time dependence in these data.

The standard Koyck-type distributed lag model,

$$\log (V/L)_t = \sigma(1 - \gamma) \log W_t + \gamma \log (V/L)_{t-1} + v_t,$$

when applied to this type of cross-sectional data yields usually very high γ's and implies a very slow rate of adjustment to wage changes.[31] But given only two years of data such a model would fit even if there were no disequilibrium or lagged adjustment problem with the estimated γ approaching unity, except for errors of measurement and other transitory variations. An alternative hypothesis, which would also explain the relatively good fit of the above form, is that the CES form holds without any appreciable lag

$$\log (V/L)_t = \sigma \log W_t + u_t,$$

but that there is a substantial first-order serial correlation in the residuals, due to the persistence of the various possible mis-specifications, such as regional quality-of-labor differentials. This correlation can be formalized as

$$u_t = \rho u_{t-1} + v_t$$

implying the estimation of

$$\log (V/L)_t = \sigma \log W_t + \rho \log (V/L)_{t-1} - \sigma\rho \log W_{t-1} + v_t$$

Thus, we can distinguish between the two models by adding the lagged wage rate term to the Koyck form of the CES function. The distributed lag model implies that the coefficient of the lagged wage rate should be zero or positive. The serial correlation model implies that it should be negative and of the same magnitude as the *product* of the coefficients of the current wage rate and the lagged productivity term.

Such a computation has been performed on the pooled seventeen-industry set of data for 1958, containing a total of 417 observations. A direct estimate of the elasticity of substitution gives

$$\log (V/L)_{58} = A_1 + 1.198 \log W_{58}; \; R^2 = .606$$

The partial adjustment model results in

$$\log (V/L)_{58} = A_2 + .233 \log W_{58} + .827 \log (V/L)_{57}; \; R^2 = .890$$

[31] E.g., see the labor-demand-equation results in Hildebrand and Liu.

with a "highly significant" coefficient for the lagged dependent variable and a much improved fit (the estimated σ is still above unity: $\sigma = .233/(1 - .827) = 1.35$. But it implies a distressingly low rate of adjustment of only 17 per cent per year. Adding the lagged wage rate term, we have

$$\log (V/L)_{58} = A_3 + 1.056 \log W_{58} + .855 \log (V/L)_{57}$$
$$\phantom{\log (V/L)_{58} = A_3 +} (.089) \phantom{\log W_{58} +} (.022)$$
$$- .900 \log W_{57}; R^2 = .918$$
$$(.022)$$

If the serial correlation model is right, the third coefficient should equal minus the product of the first two, which it does approximately ($1.056 \times .855 = .903 \approx .900$). Since there is no obvious alternative explanation for a significant negative coefficient of the lagged wage rate variable, I reject the partial adjustment model and accept the serial correlation one.[32]

Table 3 presents similar results for individual industries. The first set of σ estimates is comparable to, though substantially better than (in terms of fit and t ratios), the Minasian and Solow estimates and is generally of the same order of magnitude. Only one of these σ's (out of 17) is significantly different from unity, and that one is above unity.[33] The second set of σ estimates is based on the partial adjustment equation, while the third is based on the serial correlation model. In 12 out of the 17 cases the latter model is the one consistent with the data. In general, all the estimated σ's are not very (statistically) different from unity, the significant deviations if anything occurring above unity rather than below it.

[32] The matter should not rest here. "Serial correlation" does not explain anything. The next step is to find out what is the mis-specification that is causing it. A small attempt along these lines will be reported below, but the topic as a whole is outside the range of this paper.

Two more observations are worth making about these results: (1) In general one can interpret an equation of the form $y_t = ax_t + bx_{t-1} + cy_{t-1}$ as a distributed lag even if b is negative (assuming $a > 0$). But if $b \simeq -ac$, the implied lag is very short, and there is little gain from the more complicated interpretation. (2) Note (as pointed out to me by R. Solow) that *since* the estimated coefficient of w_t is about 1.0 and the others are about .9 (or $-.9$) the equation as a whole can be interpreted as saying that

$$\log (WL/V)_{58} = .9 \log (WL/V)_{57} + \text{random term.}$$

[33] This count excludes Industry 29, petroleum and coal products, for which no satisfactory estimates were obtained in either of the models. The regressions reported in this table and elsewhere in this section underwent almost no pretesting, and hence the estimated standard errors are applicable, subject to the conventional caveats.

TABLE 3

Estimates of the Elasticity of Substitution at the
Two-Digit Manufacturing Industries Level, 1958

(varying number of states as observations)

Industry and SIC Number	σ_1	R^2	N	σ_2 from Lag Function	σ_3 from Transformed Function	R_3^2
20. Food	0.908 (.097)	.694	41	1.014	c.	.861
22. Textile	0.938 (.170)	.615	21	1.113	1.094 (.540)	.748
23. Apparel	1.055 (.194)	.572	24	0.835	0.628 (.212)	.899
24. Lumber	1.069 (.055)	.948	23	1.107	1.175 (.202)	.963
25. Furniture	1.039 (.074)	.908	22	0.989	c.	.968
26. Paper	1.667 (.302)	.522	30	1.300	c.	.901
27. Printing	0.827 (.177)	.593	17	0.450	0.678 (.277)	.862
28. Chemicals	0.714 (.219)	.268	31	0.592	0.700 (.396)	.671
29. Petroleum	n.s.		17	n.s.	n.s.	
30. Rubber and plastics	1.281 (.416)	.422	15	2.208	0.902 (.434)	.847
31. Leather	0.839 (.257)	.470	14	1.603	1.164 (.401)	.852
32. Stone, clay, glass	0.908 (.187)	.496	26	0.774	1.877 (.494)	.780
33. Primary metals	1.407 (.422)	.299	28	3.491	2.374 (.473)	.891
34. Fabricated metals	0.849 (.144)	.530	33	1.167	1.203 (.283)	.740
35. Machinery, exc. electrical	1.240 (.383)	.272	30	2.400	2.004 (.294)	.866
36. Electrical machinery	0.662 (.314)	.162	25	0.397	1.533 (.529)	.592
37. Transportation equipment	0.961 (.547)	.110	27	1.087	c.	.617
38. Instruments	0.752 (.427)	.256	11	0.823	c.	.721

Notes to Table 3

Source: 1958 data from the *Census of Manufactures;* 1957 data from the *Annual Survey of Manufactures.*

Models:

1. $\log (V/L) = A + \sigma \log W$

2. $\log (V/L) = A + (1-\gamma) \sigma \log W + \gamma \log (V/L)_{t-1}$

3. $\log (V/L) = A + \sigma \log W + \rho \log (V/L)_{t-1} - \rho\sigma \log W_{t-1}$

c. — contradicts Model 3. The coefficient of $\log W_{t-1}$ is not significantly different from zero. In these cases R_3^2 is very close to R_2^2 .

n.s. — no significant relationships found in either of the models.

V/L — value added (adjusted) per man-hour.

W — wage per man-hour of production workers.

Total man-hours — total payroll divided by W.

The figures in parentheses are the estimated standard errors of the coefficients.

   Table 4 presents pooled estimates for total manufacturing, allowing for two possible sources of bias: (1) regional price variation through the introduction of regional dummies and (2) labor quality biases through the introduction of specific labor quality variables. Note that by pooling the data from all the industries we assume that elasticity of substitution is the same in all industries, an assumption which is not contradicted by the results presented in Table 2. But this does not imply that we have to assume the same CES form for the production function as a whole. By allowing different intercepts in this equation for different industries (using industry dummy variables) we can allow the distribution parameters in the CES form to differ between industries.[34]

   The same is true also of the exponents in the Cobb-Douglas form. A finding of a unitary elasticity of substitution does not imply that all industries are characterized by the *same* Cobb-Douglas form. That assumption we shall have to make in the next section, but it is not used

[34] If we write the CES production function as

$$V = A[\delta L^{-\rho} + (1 - \delta)K^{-\rho}]^{-1/\rho}$$

where $\sigma = 1/(1 + \rho)$, we can allow the A and δ parameters to differ between industries, by allowing the

$$\log (V/L) = I_i + \sigma \log W + u$$

equation to have different intercepts for different industries.

TABLE 4

Estimates of Elasticity of Substitution Equations in U.S. Manufacturing, 1958

(N = 417)

Coefficients of:	Regression Numbers							
	1	2	3	4	5	6	7	8
W_{58}	1.198 (.047)	1.056 (.089)	1.258 (.074)	.996 (.053)	1.035 (.096)	.993 (.095)	1.122 (.070)	1.039 (.099)
$(V/L)_{57}$		0.855 (.022)			0.661 (.029)	0.703 (.028)		0.634 (.030)
W_{57}		−0.900 (.090)			−0.686 (.094)	−0.698 (.097)		−0.677 (.095)
Occupation			0.043 (.129)		−0.067 (.058)			−0.213 (.114)
Age			−0.512 (.146)					−0.207 (.095)
P White			−0.156 (.062)		0.026 (.029)			
P Female			−0.015 (.036)		−0.024 (.042)			−0.046 (.039)
Industry dummies				yes	yes	yes	yes	yes
State dummies							yes	yes
R^2	.606	.916	.629	.843	.935	.931	.860	.941

Note: V/L is the dependent variable. All variables are logarithms of the original units except for P White, P Female, and the dummies. Regressions 6 and 7 are based on 440 observations.

here. Note also that if the labor quality variables are of a multiplicative nature in the original form, their coefficients will contain terms involving $(1 - \sigma)$ and thus we would not expect them to be significant if σ is close to unity.[35]

Table 4 shows clearly that the labor quality variables, which we shall find to be important in the production function framework in the next section, contribute little in the elasticity-of-substitution estimation context. This is as one would expect, given a σ close to unity. Moreover, their introduction or the introduction of state (quasi-region) dummies does not change the estimated elasticity of substitution significantly. It is still around unity. And now this result cannot be attributed to labor quality differentials or to other mis-specifications (such as price-of-output differences) which have a predominantly regional component. The only other alternative possible interpretation of these results is one which would deny entirely the possibility of estimating the elasticity of substitution from cross-sectional data, asserting that there are no real wage differences in the United States, all of the observed wage differentials reflecting "quality" differentials. This is unlikely, but cannot be disproved in the extreme form of the statement.[36]

All of the above estimates were based on estimates from a derived demand equation, using the hypothesis of profit maximization, rather than on estimates of the production function itself. Since the CES *production function* form is highly nonlinear in the parameters, it is rather difficult to estimate, and very few direct estimates of this function have been reported in the literature.[37] Recently, however, both Kmenta (1964b) and Nelson (1964) have shown that one can think of the Cobb-Douglas form as a first-order approximation to the CES, and that the second-order approximation can be written as

$$\log V = A + \alpha_1 \log K + \alpha_2 \log L - (1/2)\rho\alpha_1\alpha_2[\log K - \log L]^2,$$

where ρ is again related to $\sigma = 1/(1 + \rho)$. Thus if ρ is significantly different from zero (σ different from one) this should show up in a

---

[35] Among our quality-of-labor variables only the occupation mix is of this form.

[36] The quality variables used here can account for only about 66 per cent of the observed variance of wage rates. Allowing for industry differences raises this to 82 per cent. Even adding regional variables still leaves unexplained about 12 per cent of the observed wage rate variation.

[37] None, as far as I know, for manufacturing. In most of the other cases some of the parameters were estimated from other data, e.g., such as we explored above, using therefore the profit maximization assumption.

significant coefficient for the square of the (log) capital-labor ratio. This allows a direct test, one that does not depend on the correct specification of the maximization equations and the right expected input and output prices.[38] Using our data (for 417 observations) we estimate

$$\log\left(\frac{V}{L}\right) = .64 + .442 \log\frac{K}{L} + .050 \log L + .030 \left[\log\frac{K}{L}\right]^2;$$
$$\quad\quad (.03) \quad (.037) \quad\quad\quad (.014) \quad\quad\quad (.018)$$

$$R^2 = .550$$

The $[\log K/L]^2$ term is not significantly different from 0 at conventional significance levels, and this remains also true when industry dummies are added to the above equation. Given our data we cannot reject the hypothesis that the Cobb-Douglas form is an adequate representation up to a second-order approximation.[39] If anything, these results imply the possibility that the "true" σ is actually *above* unity, with a point estimate of $\hat{\sigma} = 1.29$ ($\rho = -.23$).[40]

I do not intend to argue that these results prove that the Cobb-Douglas is the right form for the manufacturing production function, only that there is no strong evidence against it. Until better evidence appears, there is no reason to give it up as the maintained hypothesis.

IV. Production Function Estimates

After the long digression on the form of the production function, we can summarize the main substantive results of this paper relatively briefly. The estimates using the combined set of observations over states

[38] It is, however, a fairly weak test. The expected coefficient of the $[\log K/L]^2$ term is quite small, e.g., if $\alpha_1 = .4$, $\alpha_2 = .6$, and $\rho = 1.0$ (i.e., $\sigma = .5$), this coefficient would be equal to $-.12$. For σ's closer to unity (e.g., $\sigma = .75$) this coefficient would be much smaller ($-.04$). Given the usual standard errors in such studies, it is not likely that these coefficients will be "significant." This is another reflection of the second-order nature of this question. Thus the results below should not surprise us. Unless one has much better data (in terms of the observed range of K/L) and more observations, one may not be able to detect by such procedures even substantial deviations of the true σ from unity.

[39] Since the estimates of the α_1 and α_2 coefficients are *not* invariant to the choice of units in which K and L are measured, the coefficients of $\log(K/L)$ should not be interpreted as the comparable Cobb-Douglas coefficients. These are given in the next section.

[40] Note that small differences in the estimated coefficient of $[\log K/L]^2$ imply large differences in the estimated σ. Thus this is not a very good way of estimating it, and one should not be surprised when rather wide swings result. This is an illustration of the point made by Domar at this conference.

and (two-digit) industries are presented in Table 5. As indicated in this table the estimated capital coefficient is always "highly significant." [41] It varies from about .39 in the "no dummies" regression to about .23 in the regressions which eliminate the between-industries differences in capital intensity.[42] These results are consistent with a priori notions about the order of magnitude of this coefficient and with estimates of factor shares at the aggregate level.[43] The coefficient of the labor variable, which indicates the excess of the sum of the coefficients over unity, and is thus a measure of economies of scale, is always significant and positive, albeit small. It indicates, roughly, that a 10 per cent expansion in the scale of the average enterprise in manufacturing would result in a 10.5 per cent increase in output. These results are consistent with the Hildebrand and Liu (1965) findings for 1957 for the separate two-digit industries using similar data. I shall say more about this finding below. The age of capital or embodiment variables is never significant and sometimes has even the wrong sign. The poor performance of this variable indicates that either it is a poor approximation to the relevant embodiment variable or that embodiment in capital is not an important force in manufacturing.

All the coefficients of the labor quality variables have the expected signs and are in general significant at the conventional levels, but the contribution of these variables becomes small if all the between-industry and between-regions variance is eliminated using the dummy variables procedure. This is as one would expect, since most of the important quality variations are likely to be associated with interregional or interindustry

[41] Since there was substantial pretesting of the estimates reported in this section, "significance" statements should be taken with more than usually large chunks of salt. In no case, however, are the statements in the text seriously in conflict with some of the preliminary results not reported here. For example, while the above statement about the numerical value of the capital coefficient is not exact for the other two versions of capital tried, the statement taken as an order of magnitude is correct. The alternative measures were also always "significant" at conventional significance levels. In what follows I shall drop the quotation marks around significant, assuming that they will be supplied by the reader.

[42] The decline in the capital coefficient arises from the introduction of the industry dummies rather than from the use of state dummies.

[43] Using the data provided in the October 1962 issue of the *Survey of Current Business* (pp. 6–18) on the share of payments to labor in total GNP originating in manufacturing (after an adjustment for indirect business taxes) gives .24 as the "share of capital" in 1958. However, 1958 is the low point for this variable in the postwar period. The "average" capital share for 1947–60 is .27 (from these same data).

TABLE 5

Production Function Estimates, U.S. Manufacturing, 1958

Coefficients of:	440 Observations		417 Observations								
	1	2	3	4	5	6	7	8	9	10	11
K/L	.358 (.023)	.297 (.023)	.392 (.018)	.388 (.018)	.382 (.075)	.351 (.019)	.252 (.022)	.258 (.021)	.261 (.020)	.235 (.021)	.229 (.021)
L	.058 (n.c.)			.056 (.013)	.070 (.012)	.078 (.012)	.032 (.015)	.047 (.015)	.055 (.016)	.058 (.016)	.054 (.015)
R (Age K)	.053 (.058)	.013 (.043)									
Occupation					.952 (.079)	.992 (.098)	.352 (.092)		.391 (.177)	.419 (.174)	.289 (.180)
Age						-.672 (.128)					.067 (.139)
P White						.092 (.056)	.196 (.046)				.134 (.047)
P Female						-.120 (.030)	-.261 (.069)			-.238 (.066)	-.245 (.059)
Industry dummies		yes					yes	yes	yes	yes	yes
State dummies							yes	yes	yes	yes	yes
R^2	n.c.	.781	.528	.547	.665	.697	.823	.852	.854	.860	.862
σ_u	.1090	.0772	.1073	.1052	.0907	.0865	.0672	.0629	.0626	.0616	.0611

n.c. – not computed. These estimates are from log V dependent regressions. While the coefficients are the same or related, the R^2's are not comparable with the log (V/L) forms.

See section II for definitions of the variables.

differentials. The coefficient of the occupation mix variable should be, if the variable were measured correctly, of the same order of magnitude as the coefficient of labor in the production function (about .7).[44] Its "nondummy" estimates are close (see especially the estimate in column 6 of Table 5), but the introduction of industry dummy variables reduces it substantially below this level, though not significantly so.[45] The introduction of regional dummies does not greatly affect the order of magnitude of this coefficient (or of the coefficients of the other quality variables) but substantially reduces its precision.

The age variable is significant in the simple regressions but does not survive the elimination of the interindustry and interregional variance. Its coefficient is negative, indicating a higher productivity in the establishments with a younger labor force. The differences in this variable may, however, be more a reflection of differences in the age of establishments or the age of (more finely defined) industries, rather than of the age of the labor force. Also, the median may be a poor measure for a variable whose effect is known to be u-shaped. Since we do not expect the average age distribution to change by much, and since the main purpose of this study is to derive conclusions which will be useful in an eventual analysis of aggregate time series, a more detailed analysis of the effects of this variable was not undertaken.

The race and sex variables are highly significant and have the expected signs. Since we are holding the occupational mix constant (though perhaps not in a completely satisfactory fashion), these coefficients reflect the well-known fact that women and Negroes are paid less even if one controls for differences in industrial and occupational composition. But these results also show that there are real productivity differences associated with these differentials. A finer occupational and educational breakdown would perhaps reduce these differentials, but is unlikely to eliminate them entirely.[46]

---

[44] This statement assumes that the correct labor measure to be entered into the production function is a quality-held-constant man-hours figure, constructed by weighting different classes (occupations) of workers by their relative prices (wages) in a base period. The occupation mix variable can be thought of as the result of factoring this measure into two components: number of workers and quality per worker, each entering the production function with the same coefficient (the coefficient of "correct" labor). The occupation mix variable is such a quality measure based on the division of the labor force into occupational categories and the use of 1959 prices (incomes) as weights.

[45] For closer estimates see pages 305 and 306, and footnote 57.

[46] For a detailed analysis of this problem in the income distribution context, see Hanoch (1965).

The industry dummies account for a substantial part of the residual variance. Their introduction reduces both the capital and occupational mix coefficients, leaving the other coefficients largely unchanged. Their significance implies either substantial interindustry differences in rates of return or more likely interindustry differences in the capital coefficients. Allowing for different industry intercepts reduces somewhat the mis-specification consequences of assuming that all the industry slopes are the same. This is illustrated in a highly exaggerated fashion in Figure 1. If the true production functions are different, forcing one line onto the data may result in a substantial upward bias in the estimated coefficient (this of course depends on the particular distribution of observations in the sample). Allowing for different intercepts both improves the fit of the

FIGURE 1

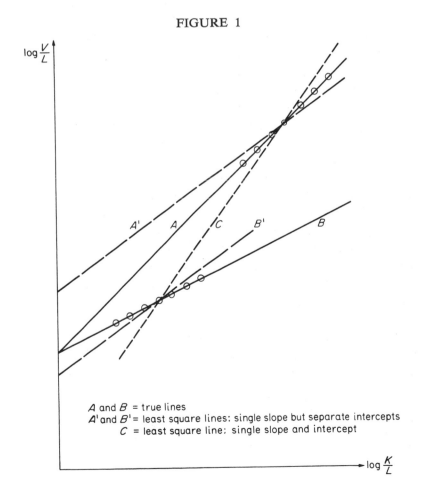

A and B = true lines
A' and B' = least square lines: single slope but separate intercepts
C = least square line: single slope and intercept

over-all relationship and brings the estimated slope relationship closer to the "average."

Attempts to allow for such interindustry differences in the slope coefficient were not particularly successful. Estimating the production functions (without the quality variables) separately for each of the industries resulted in "reasonable" coefficients (as far as order of magnitudes are concerned) in 15 out of the 18 possible cases. But only in 9 of these cases was the capital coefficient significantly different from zero at the conventional significance levels.[47] This is not surprising, since in most of these cases we were trying to identify this coefficient from the *within*-industry across-states variance in capital intensity, using only 20 or so degrees of freedom. To discover the effect of this variable we must either allow it to vary more (i.e., *across* industries) or obtain a much larger sample by pooling the data from different industries.

It is possible to pursue this subject a little bit further through the introduction of industry–capital-intensity interaction dummies. The use of such dummies allows for different slopes with respect to a particular variable while imposing the same coefficients on all the other variables. Table 6 provides an example of such an analysis, introducing an additional set of $19(K/L)_i$ variables, one for each two-digit industry. These variables take the value of the capital-labor ratio in the appropriate industry and state, and are zero for all noncorresponding industries. Two such regressions are presented in Table 6. The first one allows only for differences in the slope coefficient, imposing the same intercept on all industries but allowing separate regional effects. The results are "reasonable," and all the individual slope coefficients (except for Industry 29) are significantly different from zero. Introducing separate industry intercepts improves the over-all fit, but leads to much more erratic results. Generally it reduces the magnitude of most of the coefficients and increases their standard error.

The second set of results is similar to the results obtained by estimating these coefficients separately for each industry. The procedure used here differs only in imposing the same level of returns to scale on all the industries and utilizing the regional dummies (which is not possible

[47] It may be worth reporting that the capital coefficient appears to be above "average" in the food, lumber, pulp, and the stone, clay, glass industries, and below "average" in the textile, printing, leather, fabricated metals, and machinery industries. These results are roughly consistent with those obtained by Bell (1964) using similar data.

TABLE 6

Estimates of the Production Function, U.S. Manufacturing, 1958,
Allowing the Capital Coefficients to Differ Among Industries

	440 Observations			
	Coeffi-cient	Estimated Standard Error (1)	Coeffi-cient	Estimated Standard Error (2)
$(K/L)_i$ Variables by Industry				
20. Food	.329	(.056)	.384	(.139)
21. Tobacco	.136	(.061)	.818	(.125)
22. Textile	.650	(.046)	.135	(.151)
23. Apparel	.360	(.029)	.279	(.078)
24. Lumber	.729	(.059)	.363	(.076)
25. Furniture	.435	(.043)	.277	(.114)
26. Pulp and paper	.482	(.069)	.378	(.067)
27. Printing	.167	(.061)	.049	(.195)
28. Chemicals	.460	(.079)	.217	(.068)
29. Petroleum	.071	(.057)	-.198	(.110)
30. Rubber	.204	(.042)	.362	(.089)
31. Leather	.346	(.033)	.044	(.125)
32. Stone, clay, glass	.344	(.080)	.247	(.109)
33. Primary metals	.352	(.076)	.298	(.064)
34. Fabricated metals	.296	(.045)	.024	(.096)
35. Machinery	.349	(.056)	.009	(.084)
36. Electrical machinery	.197	(.032)	-.019	(.081)
37. Transportation equipment	.220	(.032)	.165	(.051)
38. Instruments	.248	(.049)	.047	(.162)
L	.028	(.014)	.039	(.014)
Industry dummies			yes	
State dummies		yes	yes	
R^2		.789	.873	
σ_u		.0782	.0622	

NOTE: $(K/L)_i$ equals K/L for the corresponding industry and zero for all others.

when they are estimated separately). One conclusion that I draw from this table is that the estimates not containing the industry dummies (in Table 5) may be the better ones, even if they do have a higher residual variance.

Another important conclusion which comes out of this table is that our estimate of economies of scale survives the industrial disaggregation. It is somewhat smaller but of the same order of magnitude as the estimates which impose the same slope in the output-capital relationship in Table 5. Thus, it is not a product of the disregard of industrial differences. Nevertheless, this finding of economies of scale is subject to an important reservation: we have very little relevant variation in scale in our data to determine this effect. We get it from interstate differences in the average size of establishment within industries. The average size does not differ much, and we do not have direct observations on large and small plants separately.[48] A definitive treatment of this issue awaits the availability of better data.[49]

Another difficulty arises from the fact that the Cobb-Douglas form of the production function is not very well suited to the analysis of economies-of-scale problems. It imposes one particular degree of economy over the whole range of sizes and observations. But this is not what one would expect either on theoretical grounds or on the basis of previous evidence. Most of the empirical evidence on cost functions seems to imply a slowing down of the rate of increasing returns with size.[50] To investigate this possibility one needs data, however, which can be separated into size classes.

Data of this sort are available from the 1954 *Census of Manufactures,* which provides a cross-tabulation by ten size-of-establishment classes, "size" being measured by the average number of employees. The main drawback of these data is the absence of relevant capital data. The Census does provide information on a variable, "aggregate horsepower of power equipment," which may be taken as a proxy for capital, but one should not expect very strong results using it. Nevertheless, since we are interested at this point mainly in scale relationships, we shall over-

---

[48] Data by establishment size (number of employees) are available in 1958 for value added and labor but not for the capital variable.

[49] If and when the Census Bureau completes its Time Series of Establishments project and provides some access to it, it will open up a new and very valuable set of data bearing directly on this question.

[50] See, for example, Johnston (1960) and Nerlove (1963).

look the possible poorness of this capital proxy variable, and carry out an analysis similar to the one performed on 1958 data, but using the size dimension instead of the interregional dimension to provide us with variation within industries.[51]

The results for 1954 are presented in Table 7. As expected, the horsepower coefficient is lower than the capital coefficient in 1958. But the size dummies are the interesting part of this table. Without any size dummies we get an estimate of economies of scale of about the same order of magnitude as in the 1958 data (.043). Substituting the size dummies for the economies-of-scale variable, allowing thereby nonlinear and abrupt changes in the size effect, we get the interesting finding of no significant size effect over the lower range of size classes, but a rising and significant size effect from about the 250–499 employees class and on. This result survives the introduction of industry dummies and $(HP/L)_i$ industry interaction dummies, both separately and together. The first four size coefficients are almost never significantly different from zero, while in all forms there is a consistent and significant increase in the size coefficients above the 100–249 employees class. This indicates that a constant rate of increasing returns is not a bad approximation for the upper size classes which account for most of the value added in manufacturing. But it does not fit the lowest size classes, which do not exhibit as large diseconomies as would be predicted by this constant rate assumption.[52] In any case, there is no evidence for a sharp J-shaped form. The implied average cost function is shaped more like half of a saucer with a relatively wide brim.

The third regression in Table 7 confirms this impression. It introduces both a constant economies-of-scale variable (L) *and* size class dummies. In this case the estimated average rate of increasing returns is higher, .089 instead of .043, but now the larger size class coefficients are all not significantly different from zero, while the smallest ones are significant and *positive*. This implies that the .089 rate reflects quite well the rate of increasing returns in the upper size classes, but under-

[51] The data are taken from *Census of Manufactures, 1954,* Vol. I, Chap. 3, Table 1. All the variables are defined as in Section II, except that installed horsepower is used instead of the various capital measures available in 1958. Data on ten size classes and twenty industries (including Industry 39) are used to generate a total of 182 observations. Since there were few observations in the largest-size class, the largest-size dummy is defined to correspond to the two largest-size classes.

[52] This finding may possibly reflect the distinctly poorer quality of data for the small establishments.

TABLE 7

Production Function, U.S. Manufacturing, 1954

(N = 182)

Coefficients of:	Regression Containing:					
	No Size Dummies	No Other Dummies		Industry Dummies	(HP/L)_i Interaction Dummies	Both Industry and Industry (HP/L)_i Interaction Dummies
HP/L	.104 (.015)	.102 (.016)	.100 (.016)	.029 (.018)	.025 (.022)	.055 (.064)
L	.043 (.007)		.089 (.038)			
Size dummies:						
1–4		−.009 (.032)	.126 (.076)	.024 (.021)		.015 (.046)
5–9		.040 (.032)	.131 (.058)	.017 (.020)	.020 (.020)	−.006 (.034)
10–19		.075 (.031)	.071 (.047)	−.003 (.020)	−.002 (.020)	−.012 (.022)
20–49		−.018 (.031)	.012 (.036)	−.019 (.019)	−.019 (.019)	
50–99		.000[a]	.000[a]	.000[a]	.000[a]	.000[a]
100–249		.029 (.031)	.000[b]	.037 (.019)	.038 (.020)	.042 (.022)
250–499		.060 (.031)	.000[b]	.070 (.019)	.072 (.020)	.089 (.032)
500–999		.078 (.031)	−.007 (.034)	.092 (.019)	.094 (.020)	.111 (.042)
1000 +		.127 (.028)	−.006 (.049)	.131 (.018)	.134 (.018)	.146 (.062)
R^2	.338	.387	.392	.788	.784	.854
σ_u	.0972	.0954	.0947	.0589	.0599	.0522

Note: $(HP/L)_i = (HP/L) \times I_i$ where I_i is the appropriate industry dummy.

[a] Assumed to be zero by definition.

[b] Not significantly different from zero. Actual coefficient not estimated, since the program did not enter this variable for failure to meet tolerance requirements.

predicts productivity in the lower size classes (overestimates average costs). Here the lower size dummies adjust for the imposition of a constant rate of scale economies. We conclude, therefore, that the rate of economies of scale is apparently not constant. Rather, it is approximately zero for the lower size classes, but significantly positive for the larger size classes. Imposing the *same* rate on the whole sample *underestimates* the economies of scale in the economically relevant range (in the size classes where most of the output is being produced).[53]

A similar phenomenon can be also detected in the 1958 data. Here we do not have separate data by establishment size, but we do know how many of the establishments, which comprise our averages within a state and industry, have more than 20 employees. A crude size mix variable is given by P Large (number of establishments with 20 or more employees)/(total number of establishments). A believer in economies of scale may anticipate a positive coefficient for this variable, implying a higher average productivity in the larger establishments. But we, having examined the 1954 results, are forewarned.

Introducing the P Large variable into the 1958 regression ($N = 417$) yields:

$$\log (V/L) = \underset{(.020)}{.374} \ \log (K/L) + \underset{(.019)}{.127} \ \log L - \underset{(.048)}{.157} \ \text{P Large}$$

$$- \underset{(.048)}{.066} \ \log R + \underset{(.106)}{.848} \ \text{Occup.} - \underset{(.131)}{.710} \ \text{Age} + \underset{(.055)}{.108} \ \text{P White}$$

$$- \underset{(.037)}{.049} \ \text{P Female;} \ R^2 = .706$$

and

$$\log (V/L) = \ldots \underset{(.019)}{.348} \ \log (K/L) + \underset{(.019)}{.109} \ \log L - \underset{(.047)}{.083} \ \text{P Large}$$

$$- \underset{(.047)}{.083} \ \log R + \underset{(.101)}{1.465} \ \text{Occup.} - \underset{(.150)}{.304} \ \text{Age} + \underset{(.056)}{.054} \ \text{P White}$$

$$- \underset{(.037)}{.069} \ \text{P Female} + \text{state dummies;} \ R^2 = .760$$

resulting in an increase in the estimate of the over-all economies of scale from .05 to above .10 and a *negative* coefficient for P Large. Since P

[53] In 1954 establishments with more than 100 employees comprised only 9 per cent of the total number of establishments, but accounted for over 78 per cent of total value added in manufacturing.

Large $= 1 - (P \text{ Small})$, this implies a positive coefficient for the below-20-employees size class. This is another indication that there may be no gains to be had from growing from a very small plant to a somewhat larger one. The economies of scale are largely in the medium- to large-scale plant range. If this is true, the estimates of economies of scale presented in Table 5 are probably too low.[54]

Two caveats are worth reiterating before we leave this section. (1) We have done nothing in this paper about the simultaneity problem. Since what we could have done (using W and lagged L as instrumental variables) would have made very little difference, it did not seem worth doing.[55] (2) The year 1958 was one of mild recession, and our results may be affected by differential underutilization of capacity.[56] But our results, to the extent that they are comparable, do not seem out of line with those of Hildebrand and Liu, who used data from the peak year of 1957.[57] Nevertheless, since all econometric results are no better than the data that went into them, these caveats should be kept in mind in evaluating the above findings.

V. Implications for the Measurement of Technical Change in Manufacturing

The conventional measure of residual technical change in an industry is given by

$$\lambda = y - w_k k - (1 - w_k)n$$

[54] Unfortunately, since the P Large variable does not survive the introduction of industry dummies, the above statement is not definitive.

[55] I have used the instrumental variable procedure in analyzing cross-sectional data for total manufacturing without any significant difference in the results. See Griliches (1964c). An attempt to use the indirect least-squares method led to nonsense results.

[56] This may explain the relatively poor performance of the petroleum products industry, which seems to have suffered the largest relative decline in value added from 1957 to 1958. That, however, may also be a reflection of certain incomparabilities between the 1957 Annual Survey and the 1958 Census.

[57] We have comparable data for 372 observations in 1957. They yield:

$$\log (V/L)_{57} = +.369 \log (K/L)_{57} + .074 \log L_{57} + .643 \text{ Occup.} + .155 \text{ P White}$$
$$\phantom{\log (V/L)_{57} = } (.017) \qquad\qquad (.012) \qquad\quad (.103) \qquad\qquad (.060)$$

$$- .105 \text{ P Female}; R^2 = .723, \sigma_u = .0838,$$
$$(.031)$$

which is not out of line with the more detailed results for 1958 presented in Table 5.

where y, k, n are percentage *rates* of growth in output, capital, and labor respectively, and w_k is the share of capital in total factor payments. This procedure assumes that all the variables are measured correctly, that all the relevant variables are included, and that factor prices represent adequately the marginal productivities of the respective inputs. The last assumption is equivalent to the assumption of competitive equilibrium and constant returns to scale. To analyze λ, the unexplained part of output growth, it is useful to rewrite this equation in terms of a more general underlying production function: [58]

$$\lambda = w_k(k^* - k) + (1 - w_k)(n^* - n) + (w_k^* - w_k)(k^* - n^*)$$
$$+ h[w^*k^* + (1 - w^*)n^* - f] + a_z z + u$$

where $w_k^* = a_k/(a_k + a_n) = a_k/(1 + h)$, with $h = a_k + a_n - 1$; a's are the true elasticities of output with respect to the various inputs; starred magnitudes are the correctly measured versions of the variables; f is the percentage rate of growth in the number of establishments; and z is the rate of growth in inputs which affect the production function but are not included in the standard accounting system. These could be services from the cumulated stock of past private research and development expenditures or services from the cumulated value of public (external) investments in research and extension in agriculture, or measurable disturbances such as weather or earthquakes. The first term measures the effect of errors in the conventional capital measures on the estimated "residual." The second term reflects errors in the definition and measurement of the labor input. The third term reflects errors in the measurement of the relative contribution of labor and capital to output growth. It would be zero if factor shares were in fact proportional to the respective production function elasticities. The fourth term is the economies-of-scale term. It would be zero if the sum of the coefficients were unity *or* if the rate of growth in the number of firms just equaled

---

[58] See Griliches (1964) and Griliches and Jorgenson (1965) for a more detailed exposition of this approach. The equation in the text can be derived from the production function-based statement

$$y = a_k k + a_n n + (1 - a_k - a_n)f + a_z z + u;$$

and the definitions $h = a_k + a_n - 1$ and $w_k^* = a_k/(1 + h)$. Here it is assumed that z is an external variable, and economies of scale are defined not to include it. It is easy to rewrite this, making the alternative assumption that y is homogeneous of degree $1 + h$ in k, n, *and* z.

the weighted rate of growth of total inputs.[59] The fifth term reflects the contribution of left-out variables, while the last term is the "pure" residual term—the amount of output growth not accounted for by this expanded list of possible sources.

Assuming that the a_i's are constant over time implies the assumption of a Cobb-Douglas form for the underlying production function and of neutral residual technical change. This equation can be also adapted to the CES form by introducing an additional $[k^* - n^*]^2$ term.

Given this framework, the purpose of econometric estimates of the production function is (1) to test or validate a particular way of measuring an input or adjusting it for quality change; (2) to test and estimate the role of left-out inputs such as research and development; (3) to estimate the rate of economies of scale; (4) to check on the possibility of disequilibrium and estimate the deviation of the "true" output elasticities from the observed factor shares; and (5) to check on the appropriateness of the assumed form of the production function and the related implicit assumptions used in constructing the various productivity indexes. In this paper we have only begun to approach some of these goals. We have some evidence on items (1), (3) and (5). We have done nothing about (2), and our evidence on (4)—the relative magnitude of capital and labor elasticities—is too weak to provide us with any useful conclusions at this point.

The effects of the findings we do have on the explanation of growth in U.S. manufacturing during 1947–60 can be illustrated using some figures derived in earlier work.[60] For this period the standard approach yields:

$$\lambda = y - w_k k - w_n n = 3.22 - .272 \times 3.33 - .728 \times .46 = 1.98$$

where .728 is the average share of payments to labor in total GNP originating in manufacturing (after an adjustment for indirect business taxes) during this period, n is a measure of man-hours, and k is a measure (of the rate of growth in) of the net stock of fixed capital in manufacturing.[61] Thus, the conventional productivity measure attributes more than

---

[59] This emphasis on plant or firm scale economies distinguishes this formulation from several other attempts to discuss this issue at the aggregate level. E.g., both Walters (1963) and Westfield (1964) proceed as if there were economies of nation or industry size, irrespective of the number of establishments over which the particular aggregate output is spread.

[60] See Griliches (1963c).

[61] See the Appendix for the sources and derivation of these and subsequent numbers.

60 per cent of the observed rate of growth in manufacturing output to the unexplained category of technical change.

What more can we say about this on the basis of our econometric results? First, on the basis of the results reported in Section III, the Cobb-Douglas assumption underlying the use of a fixed or average weight is not a bad approximation, though we have no evidence from the one cross section on whether this production function has shifted in a non-neutral way over time. Second, we have some evidence of mildly increasing returns to scale, to which we shall return after we discuss the problem of adjusting the inputs series for quality change. The third and major finding is that the quality-of-the-labor-force dimensions are important and that a base period income-weighted occupation mix variable enters into the production function with a coefficient that is not significantly different from the man-hours coefficient. Hence, it can be treated as a multiplier to the conventional labor force figures.

The other major labor force quality variables—percentage white, percentage female, and median age—changed very little in the aggregate over this time period, and will not be discussed further here.[62] At the aggregate level, however, we do have more detailed data not only on the occupation mix, but also on the educational level of each occupation. From these data we can construct a more detailed index of quality per man. From the data on "education by occupation" and on "occupation by industry" a distribution of employed males in manufacturing by number of school years completed was constructed using the second set as a source of weights for aggregating the first set. The resulting distributions (see Table 8) were weighted using 1959 mean incomes of *all* U.S. males by school years completed as weights to yield a weighted education-per-man index that rose from 100 in 1947 to about 113 in 1960, or at the approximate rate of 1.0 per cent per year.[63]

---

[62] Between 1950 and 1960, using *Census of Population* data, P Female increased from 24.9 to 25.3 in manufacturing, P White (of males) remained unchanged at 92.3, and the median age of employed males in manufacturing rose from 38.4 to 39.6 years.

[63] The principle behind this index is the same as for any other quality change adjustment. In some period we are able to observe a relationship between differences in some dimension(s) of a commodity and the price that these different dimension bundles fetch in the market place. From this information we are able to derive the "price(s)" of these dimensions, and we can then use these prices (incomes) to adjust for the changes that have occurred in the dimensions (education) of the commodity (labor) over time. That education enters into the production function in this particular form was shown for agriculture in Griliches (1963a). The 1947 figure in the text is based on an interpolation between the 1940 and 1950 values in Table 8.

TABLE 8

Schooling of the Labor Force: U.S. Manufacturing, Employed Males,
18 Years and Over, 1940, 1950, 1952, 1957, 1959, and 1962

Years of School Completed		Distribution by School Years Completed[a] (per cent)						Weights: Mean Income of Males 25 Years and Older, 1959[b]
		1940	1950	1952	1957	1959	1962	
Elementary	0	3.0	1.6	1.7	1.7	0.9		$2,092
	1-4	7.0	7.2	5.8	4.5	4.1		2,487
	5-7	15.9	15.8	14.1	12.2	10.9		3,552
	8	28.1	20.9	20.2	17.5	16.6		3,893
High school	1-3	19.1	20.9	21.4	22.1	22.7		5,412
	4	16.9	20.7	23.5	27.0	28.2		6,334
College	1-3	4.8	5.8	7.0	7.2	8.0		7,642
	4 +	4.3	5.6	6.3	7.8	8.6		10,222
n.r.		0.9	1.5					
Index of school years completed per man[c](1950=100)		94.7	100.0	103.3	107.7	110.5	113.1[d]	

n.r. = not reporting.

[a]The distributions are constructed by weighting the distributions of school years completed by occupation (usually 8 classes: professional, managers and proprietors, clerical, sales, craftsmen, operatives, service excluding domestic, and laborers excluding farm and mine) using occupation by industry weights. Education by occupation data are taken for 1940 and 1950 from the "Occupational Characteristics" volumes of the respective *Censuses of Population;* 1952 and 1957 from *Current Population Reports,* Series P-50, Nos. 49 and 78; 1959 and 1962 from *Special Labor Force Reports* Nos. 1 and 30. Weights are from the "Occupation by Industry" volumes of the respective *Censuses;* weights for other years interpolated on the bases of "occupation-by-industry" distributions for *all* workers (including female) from the annual *Labor Force Reports.* The "less than 5" class in 1940, 1952, and 1957 was broken down into 0 and 1-4 classes using the distribution by single years of school completed of all urban males, 25 years and over, given in the "Detailed Characteristics" volumes of the respective *Censuses* (1950 Census data were used to break down the 1952 distribution and 1960 Census data for the 1957 distribution.) The 7-8 class given in the 1940 distribution was similarly broken down using the 1940 Census data on school years completed (by single years) by urban males.

Notes to Table 8 (concluded)

[b]Average income of all U.S. males, 25 years old and over, by school years completed. Computed from *Census of Population, 1960*, PC(1)ID, Table 223, using the midpoints of the income classes and $20,000 for the $10,000 and over class.

[c]The product of the respective column with the weights (average income) column, divided by 100, adjusted for the nonreporting class by dividing through $(100 - \text{n.r.})$ /100, and expressed as an index to the base 1950 ($5,122).

[d]The 1959-1962 comparison is based on a somewhat different and more detailed occupational breakdown. The comparable distributions are:

School Years Completed

	Elementary				High School		College		
Year	0	1-4	5-7	8	1-3	4	1-3	4	5+
1959	.9	3.7	10.4	16.6	22.1	29.2	8.4	5.5	3.2
1962	.7	3.4	10.2	14.2	21.7	30.7	9.6	6.0	3.5

For the new classes the mean incomes are $9,386 for the four-year college class and $11,295 for the 5+ class. These were derived by interpolating the figures in the last column on the basis of more detailed data given by H. Miller, *Trends in Income Distribution in the U.S.* (forthcoming Census-Social Science Research Council monograph). The resulting estimate of a 2.3 per cent change in "education per man" in U.S. manufacturing between 1959 and 1962 was linked to the previous results leading to the 113.1 figure given in the body of the table.

Combining this with the man-hours index, we find that total labor inputs (quantity as well as quality) grew at the rate of 1.46 per cent per year.

No mention has yet been made of the very difficult problem of the correct measurement of capital services. Even though our work above throws little light on this subject, we shall digress at some length on this topic now, since it is of great importance to the correct accounting of output growth over time.

Conventional measures of capital, such as the one used in the numerical example above, suffer from several shortcomings: (1) they overdepreciate, that is, they assume that the services derived from a piece of capital equipment deteriorate too rapidly with age; (2) they measure the stock of capital rather than the flow of services from it; and (3), they overdeflate it; they use the wrong price indexes for converting capital in current prices to a measure "in constant prices."

What is needed from the production function point of view is a measure of the flow of services of capital in constant prices. One of the main problems to be faced in constructing such a measure is what assumption we are to make about how the services of a given machine behave as it ages. The usual assumption is that they decline rather rapidly, and this assumption is buttressed by the observation that the value (price) of a machine declines rapidly as it ages. But the value of old machines will decline because their expected life span is declining, because better new machines have become available, and because the quality of their services deteriorates as they age. Only the last one is a legitimate deduction to be made from a *service*-oriented measure of capital. It is true that there is less life left in an old machine, but that does not mean that its product during the current year is necessarily any worse for that. It is true that the availability of better new machines will result in capital losses by the owners of old machines, but this does not make the old machines any *worse;* it only makes the new ones better.

Instead of the usual sharp depreciation assumptions, I shall make the opposite assumption that the services of a machine do not decline at all (or very little) as long as it is in operation. To make this assumption a little bit more realistic, I shall use relatively conservative estimates of the length of life of machines. Given this assumption, the flow of capital services is proportional to the *gross* (undepreciated) stock of capital. During the 1947–60 period, the gross stock of capital in manufacturing grew at the rate of 4.2 per cent per year, as compared to the 3.3 per cent per year rate of growth in the net stock of capital.

While services are proportional to gross stock for a machine of a given length of life, this is not true if we want to add together machines with different lengths of life. A $100 machine that will last five years will have roughly twice as large an *annual* flow of services (in dollars) than another $100 machine whose expected length of life is ten years. Thus, the shorter the life expectancy, the higher is the ratio of services to stock. In manufacturing we can identify two major components of capital formation: equipment and structures. Structures have a much longer life than equipment and hence should be given a lower weight in compiling an index of capital *services*. Since the stock of equipment has grown more rapidly recently, this adjustment makes a substantial difference to our measurement of the growth in the total level of capital services. A service flow measure of capital in manufacturing grows at the rate of 4.7 per year, as compared to 4.2 for the gross stock and 3.3 per year for the net capital stock measure.

All of our capital measures are based on a cumulation of deflated investment figures. But some of the price indexes used to deflate investment goods are quite bad.[64] This is particularly true of the indexes used to deflate construction expenditures (our structure's component). These are not even "price" indexes. They are "cost" indexes (input rather than output price indexes), allowing for no improvements in the productivity of the construction industry. They do not price some well-specified factory buildings or houses, but simply average construction worker wage indexes, cement price indexes, lumber price indexes, and so forth. In this whole field there is only one decent price index available at the moment, the one computed by the Bureau of Public Roads, based on bid prices for federally supported highway construction. It prices such well-specified units as "a cubic yard of dirt excavated," "a square foot of concrete laid," and "a pound of structural steel put into place." If we use this index to deflate construction expenditures and recompute our estimate of service flows accordingly, we find that they grew at the rate of 5.6 per cent per year.[65]

Even though equipment price indexes do try to price output rather than inputs, they also do not take quality change into account very satisfactorily. Our equipment price indexes are all components of the Wholesale Price Index, on which much less resources are spent than on the Consumer Price Index, and whose quality change adjustments are much less frequent and looser. If we were to assume that both the rate of quality change and the forces determining the longer-run price levels have been roughly the same for consumer durables as for producer durables, we can get an idea about the possible magnitude of the quality bias in the WPI machinery price indexes by comparing them with the appropriate components of the CPI. From 1947 to 1960, the WPI index for machinery and motive products rose by 38 per cent *relative* to the consumer durables price index, or about 2.5 per cent per year.

[64] See Griliches (1963b) for more details.

[65] Ideally we would want an index pertaining to total construction rather than just to highway construction. An improved *price* index for all contract construction has been recently developed by Dacy (1964). Unfortunately, it covers only the 1947–61 period. During this period, however, it moves very much like the BPR index of highway construction prices.

I think that we are quite safe in making the assumption that the quality of producers equipment has been improving at the rate of *at least* 1.0 per cent per year.[66] If we were to incorporate this assumption into our measure of capital services, we would find that it grew at the rate of 6.2 per cent per year during the 1947–60 period. Nevertheless, since this last adjustment is not based on conclusive and direct evidence we will not use it in the final growth accounting to be presented below.

Having gone as far as we could in the direction of approaching the correct input measures, we can now return to the estimated role of economies of scale. It is quite small. Since we estimate h, the excess of the sum of the coefficients over unity, at about .05, and the rate of growth in the *number* of establishments (f) during this period at 1.2 per cent per year,[67] the total effect is

$$h(w_k k^* + w_n n^* - f) = .05(.27 \times 5.6 + .73 \times 1.46 - 1.2) = .07$$

or less than one-tenth of a percentage point.

These various adjustments are brought together in Table 9. It can be seen from this table that they reduce the contribution of the residual from about two-thirds to less than a fifth of the measured rate of growth in manufacturing output. The single largest adjustment is for the changing quality of labor, accounting for over a third of the measured residual. Thus by a more careful accounting we have been able to eliminate a substantial part of the unknown, assigning the bulk of it to improvements in the quality of labor and capital. This has been accomplished not by just renaming "technical change" as "quality change," but by actually going out and getting independent and nontautological estimates of the various components. This is a real gain in the explained fraction of growth.

Of course I may have overestimated the importance of some of the included factors, and left out some other important sources of growth.

[66] This is quite conservative. The scattered studies of quality change bias, in automobile and tractor prices indexes reviewed in Griliches (1963a and b), support this view. Note also that Solow (1962) estimates the rate of "quality improvement" in new capital at 3 per cent per year.

[67] This 1.2 per cent figure is based on the growth of the total number of establishments in manufacturing between 1947 and 1958 or the growth in the number of establishments with 20 or more employees between 1954 and 1963. The results of either computation are very much the same. The total number of establishments in manufacturing in 1963 was not yet available at the time this was being written.

TABLE 9

Output, Input, and Residual Measures of Technical Change:

U.S. Manufacturing, 1947 - 60

(per cent per year)

Category	Rate of Growth	Weighted Rate of Growth[a]	Residual "Technical Change"[b]	Residual as Per Cent of Output Growth
1. Output	3.22	3.220		
2. Man-hours	0.46	0.335		
3. Net stock of capital	3.33	0.906		
4. Residual (conventional)			1.98	61
5. Service flow, gross stock adjustment	1.36	0.370		
Residual (adjusted)			1.61	50
"Quality" adjustments:				
6. Schooling per man	1.00	0.728		
7. Bias in construction deflators	0.90	0.244		
Residual (adjusted)			0.64	20
8. Economies of scale	1.38	0.069		
Residual (adjusted)			0.57	18

Note: See Appendix for sources and derivations. The adjustments are cumulative; i.e., the gross service flow measures of capital in manufacturing grew at the rate of 4.69 per cent per year. What is recorded in the table is the excess over the rate of growth in the conventional measure: $4.69 - 3.33 = 1.36$.

Line 5: See Appendix for details.

Line 6: See Table 8 (1947 value interpolated from figures for 1940 and 1950).

Line 7: Line 5 concept recomputed using the Bureau of Public Roads construction price index to deflate the investment-in-structures component.

Line 8: The weighted rate of growth of total corrected inputs, from lines 2 through 7, is 2.583. Subtracting the estimated rate of growth in the number of establishments of 1.2 per cent per year, leaves 1.383 as the estimated rate of growth in the average scale of enterprises. Applying to it the 0.05 estimated rate of returns to scale,yields 0.069 as its contribution to the rate of growth of output.

[a]Labor measures multiplied by 0.728, capital measures multiplied by 0.272; their respective average factor shares during this period.

[b]Computed from appropriate entries in second column; e.g., residual (conventional) $= 3.220 - 0.335 - 0.906 = 1.979$.

In particular, I have done nothing in this paper about the possible effects of the growing level of research and development expenditures on output (except to the extent it has already reflected itself in the quality change measures).[68] This paper does not pretend to completeness or definitiveness. It is only a beginning, an attempt to illustrate the possibility and profitability of an alternative approach to the problem of sources of growth. Much hard work still remains to be done to pin down their individual contributions adequately.

The approach outlined above may not appear to be all that different from the conventional one. It also uses a Cobb-Douglas-type production function and the concept of embodiment, the main difference being in that we allow for "embodiment" of technical change in *both* capital and labor. But the use and purpose of the model are different. The Cobb-Douglas type framework (with or without embodiment) is usually used to *estimate* the rate of technical change. In our approach, it is used as an organizing device, as an accounting framework for putting together different *direct* estimates of technical change embodied in *particular* inputs. Thus, by focusing the question on where and how the quality (technical) changes occurred, it provides in some cases a handle for affecting the rate of technical change directly, while in others it at least points to areas where research on the particular sources of these quality changes is likely to pay off. For example, if one accepts the finding that growth in education per man (and not in some other variables that are correlated with education) is responsible for over a quarter of the observed rate of growth in output per man-hour, then we do in fact know how to affect this variable, what it may cost, and what the returns are likely to be (both in absolute terms and in their effect on the rate of

[68] A reasonable adjustment for the contribution of R&D would eliminate all of the remaining residual. The effect of R&D growth can be approximated from the formula

$$a_R \dot{R}/R = rs$$

where R is a measure of the *cumulative* amount of knowledge-capital arising out of R&D investments, a_r is the elasticity of output with respect to an increase in this knowledge measure, r is the gross rate of return to R&D investment, and s is the ratio of *net* investment in knowledge to output. The ratio of gross investment (R&D) in knowledge to output in 1958 was about .07. Assuming that half of it was for maintenance and replacement implies $s = .035$. Assuming $r = .2$, which is consistent with whatever scattered work there is on this subject [for the most important contribution and references to other work, see Mansfield (1964)] gives .007 as the contribution of R&D, or more than half of a percentage point of the observed rate of growth of output.

growth). Similarly, the adjustment for bias in capital deflators tells us that we may have been underestimating substantially the actual growth in capital that is the result of a given amount of saving. Moreover, by disaggregating further (beyond just structures and equipment) and finding out which are the items whose quality has been increasing, we may come closer to being able to affect the aggregate rate of productivity growth. This approach is, of course, very much more *ad hoc* and requires much and rather detailed data, but in economics as in most other fields it is difficult to get something for nothing.

VI. Concluding Remarks

The above is an installment from a relatively large and long-range research program. As such it has no clear beginning or end. Most of the findings must be interpreted as maintained hypotheses supported by data recently examined and to be tested further on additional data now being collected. Most of the production function work will be tested and expanded as soon as the complete results of the 1963 Census become available. The work on capital deflators and on the contribution of R&D require entirely different sets of data and possibly an entirely different approach.[69] In the meantime, there is a danger that here, as in much of other research, we may be looking for answers where the data are and not where the questions are important.

Appendix
Data: Sources and Adjustments

The data on manufacturing GNP in constant and current prices and the share of labor costs (after an adjustment for indirect business taxes) are all taken from the October 1962 issue of the *Survey of Current Business* (pp. 6–18).

The man-hours figures are taken from BLS Bulletin 1249, *Trends in Output Per Man-Hour,* and from subsequent BLS releases.

The "conventional" net stock estimates are from Wooden and Wasson, "Manufacturing Investment since 1929," *Survey of Current Business,* November 1956 and from subsequent issues of the *SCB.*

[69] On the contribution of R&D the major work is being done by Mansfield. I have done some work on the deflator problem [see Griliches (1963b)], but a definitive treatment awaits better data and is outside the scope of an individual research project.

The various capital series are derived from unpublished Department of Commerce data underlying the estimates presented in the November 1962 issue of *SCB* (pp. 9–18).

The lengths of life assumed here are the same as in the above cited source: seventeen years for equipment and forty years for structures. A constant 5 per cent per year rate of interest was assumed in converting the gross stock estimates into service flow. The conversion was accomplished using the "annuity" approach; i.e., first it was asked: What is the present value of a $1.00-per-year annuity that lasts for (say) seventeen years? If the discount rate is 5 per cent, the answer is $11.27. Next, one finds the number of such annuities that could be bought for (have the present value of) $100.00. It is 8.87 (100/11.27). Thus, the gross stock estimate for equipment was multiplied by 0.0887 and the gross stock of structures was multiplied by 0.0583 (which answers the same question for a forty-year annuity), and the two resulting series were summed to arrive at an estimate of the *flow* of capital services in constant prices.

The BPR price index of highway construction for 1922–60 is taken from U.S. Department of Commerce, *Price Trends for Federal Highway Construction,* various issues. It is extrapolated back to 1908 on the basis of the implicit GNP deflator.

The derivation of the education variable is given in greater detail in Table 8. It is the result of weighting the distribution of all employed males by school years completed, by the mean 1959 income of males (over 25) in the appropriate educational categories. The resulting variable can be thought of as the income predicted by the current educational distribution and the base period incomes for the respective educational subcategories. Actually, it is very close to a "mean school years per man" concept except for a nonzero weight for the zero education class and somewhat higher weights for the higher education categories.

References

Arrow, K. J., M. B. Chenery, B. S. Minhas, and R. M. Solow (1961), "Capital-Labor Substitution and Economic Efficiency," *Review of Economics and Statistics,* XLIII (3).

Bell, F. W. (1964), "The Role of Capital-Labor Substitution in the Economic Adjustment of an Industry Across Regions," *Southern Economic Journal,* XXXI (2).

Berglas, E. (1965), "Investment and Technological Change," *Journal of Political Economy,* LXXIII (2).

Brown, M. (1965), "The Share of Corporate Profits in the Postwar Period," unpublished U.S. Department of Commerce Staff Working Paper in Economics and Statistics, No. 11.

Dacy, D. C. (1964), "A Price and Productivity Index for a Non-Homogeneous Product," *Journal of the American Statistical Association,* 59 (306).

Ferguson, C. E. (1963), "Cross-Section Production Functions and the Elasticity of Substitution in American Manufacturing Industry," *Review of Economics and Statistics,* XLV (3).

——— (1965), "Time-Series Production Functions and Technological Progress in American Manufacturing Industry," *Journal of Political Economy,* LXXIII (2).

Griliches, Z. (1963a), "The Sources of Measured Productivity Growth: U.S. Agriculture, 1940–1960," *Journal of Political Economy,* LXXI (4).

——— (1963b), "Notes on the Measurement of Price and Quality Changes," in *Models of Income Determination,* Princeton for NBER.

——— (1963c), "Production Functions, Technical Change, and All That," unpublished Econometric Institute Report No. 6328, Rotterdam.

——— (1964), "Research Expenditures, Education, and the Aggregate Agricultural Production Function," *American Economic Review,* LIV (6).

——— (1965), Review of G. H. Hildebrand and T. C. Liu, "Manufacturing Production Functions in the U.S., 1957," *Journal of Political Economy,* LXXIV (1).

Griliches, Z., and D. W. Jorgenson (1966), "Sources of Measured Productivity Change: Capital Input," *American Economic Review,* LVI (2).

Hanoch, G. (1965), "Personal Earnings and Investment in Schooling," unpublished Ph.D. dissertation, University of Chicago.

Hildebrand, G. H., and T. C. Liu (1965), *Manufacturing Production Functions in the U.S., 1957,* Cornell Studies in Industrial and Labor Relations No. 15, Ithaca.

Hoch, I. (1958), "Simultaneous Equation Bias in the Context of the Cobb-Douglas Production Function," *Econometrica,* 26 (4).

Johnston, J. (1960), *Statistical Cost Analysis,* New York.

Kmenta, J. (1964), "Some Properties of Alternative Estimates of the Cobb-Douglas Production Function," *Econometrica,* 32 (1–2).

——— (1964), "On the Estimation of the CES Production Function," Social Systems Research Institute, University of Wisconsin (mimeo.).

Lucas, R. E., Jr. (1963), "Substitution between Labor and Capital in U.S. Manufacturing, 1929–58," unpublished Ph.D. dissertation, University of Chicago.

Mansfield, E. (1964), "Rates of Return from Industrial Research and Development," *American Economic Review,* LV (2).

Mundlak, Y. (1963), "Estimation of Production and Behavioral Functions from a Combination of Cross-Section and Time Series Data," in C. Christ *et al.* (ed.), *Measurement in Economics: Studies in Mathematical*

Economics and Econometrics in Memory of Yehuda Grunfeld, Stanford.

Nelson, R. R. (1964), "The CES Production Function and Economic Growth Projection," unpublished RAND Corporation paper P-2942, Santa Monica, Cal.

Nerlove, M. (1963), "Returns to Scale in Electricity Supply," in Christ, *et al.* (Mundlak, *op. cit.*).

O'Neill, D. (1965), "Estimating Elasticities of Substitution: Methodology and an Empirical Application to U.S. Manufacturing Industries," unpublished Ph.D. dissertation, Columbia University.

Sheshinski, E. (1964), "Estimation of Technical Changes with CES and Leontief Models," unpublished paper presented at the Chicago meeting of the Econometric Society.

Solow, R. M. (1962), "Technical Progress, Capital Formation, and Economic Growth," *American Economic Review*, LII (2).

———— (1964a), "Capital, Labor, and Income in Manufacturing," in *The Behavior of Income Shares*, Princeton for NBER.

———— (1964b), Presidential Address, 1964 Econometric Society Meeting, Chicago.

Theil, H. (1954), *Linear Aggregation of Economic Relations*, Amsterdam, Holland.

Walters, A. A. (1963a), "Production and Cost Functions: An Econometric Survey," *Econometrica*, 31 (1–2).

———— (1963b), "A Note on Economies of Scale," *Review of Economics and Statistics*, XLV (4).

Westfield, F. M. (1964), "Technical Progress and Returns to Scale," unpublished paper presented at the Chicago meeting of the Econometric Society.

Zellner, A. (1962), "Estimation of Cross-Section Relations: Analysis of a Common Specification Error," *Metroeconomica* (April–December).

COMMENT

RONALD G. BODKIN, University of Western Ontario

I would like to begin my comments by congratulating Professor Griliches on an excellent piece of scholarship. What in my view makes this an excellent paper is Griliches' discontent at allowing the large residual that has been termed "technical change" to go unanalyzed and his consequent attempt to provide some type of explanation for it, in terms of more adequate measures of the conventional inputs, unconventional inputs, and increasing returns to scale. In this paper, he largely confines his analysis of the unconventional inputs to education embodied in the labor force, although there is a suggestion that research and development outlays may explain a large part of the remaining residual, which itself is only 18 per cent (instead of 61 per cent) of the growth in U.S. manufacturing output over the period 1947–60. (Thus the role of research and development expenditures in manufacturing industry may parallel the effects of research and extension expenditures on agricultural productivity, which Griliches found to be of considerable quantitative importance in his recent *American Economic Review* paper on agricultural production functions.) In what follows, I shall, at particular junctures, be mildly critical of some of Professor Griliches' techniques or interpretations. These specific issues should be interpreted as merely mild differences of opinion, for I regard this paper, like his earlier *American Economic Review* article on agricultural production functions, as an excellent piece of research.

The first specific comment I would like to make concerns the size of the coefficients of the occupation variables in Table 5. Professor Griliches' discussion implies that he believes that the universe coefficient of this variable is approximately the same as that of the ordinary labor variable —that is, that quantity and quality of labor enter multiplicatively in the specification of the production function. Griliches asserts that this hypothesis is confirmed until the introduction of the industry and/or state dummies reduces the (relevant) variance of this variable to an amount too small to allow this effect to show up. An alternative hypothesis might be that not all of the improvement of the quality of labor represented by education and embodied in the work force is labor-augmenting technological progress. In the discussions this morning, it was pointed out that technological progress embodied in a factor of production need not result in technological progress that could be described as augmenting for that particular factor of production. Thus technological progress embodied in the labor force might not be labor-augmenting, or at least not all of its effects need show up as a multiplicative factor to quantities of "raw" labor. If this is so, then we have an alternative explanation of the lower coefficient of the occupation variable, which (if the standard errors be accepted at face value) is significantly different (or almost so) from the hypothetical equality with the implied coefficient of the (almost) entirely physical input of labor.

I have some reservations about one of the tests that Professor Griliches employed in deciding to fit a Cobb-Douglas production function, instead of the slightly more general constant-elasticity-of-substitution (CES) form. The regression of output (value added) per man-hour on the wage implies an equality, possibly disturbed by stochastic perturbations or lags in the adjustment process, between the marginal product of labor and its real wage. It seems to me that this sort of assumption is more appropriate in agriculture, the sector studied in Griliches' earlier *American Economic Review* paper, than in manufacturing, which is generally thought to be subject to imperfect competition and positions of market power in a number of subsectors. I personally would have preferred a test in which only cost minimization is assumed, that is, one in which the capital-labor ratio is regressed against the relative prices of these two factors, despite the fact that the data problems may be more severe with this kind of test. In any case, this shortcoming (if it be one) is not very severe, as Griliches also performs a direct test of the unitary elasticity of substitution implied by the Cobb-Douglas form, a test which is based not on a marginal productivity side condition but makes use of only a linear approximation to the CES form. Since the results of this test agree with those of the other test, one can agree that the Cobb-Douglas variant of the production function seems adequate to describe these data.[1]

Several other aspects of this very interesting paper deserve comment. Professor Griliches argues that time series studies of the production function deserve little weight in forming our considered view of what the world is "really" like, and this apart from the usual time series problems of autocorrelated residuals, errors of observation (including possible aggregation errors), and simultaneity of the relationships. Basically, the argument is that most time series studies of production functions remove the trend from the conventional variables, usually by including it (the time trend) as a separate explanatory variable to proxy for technical

---

[1] Griliches mentions that, because of the severe nonlinearity of the CES form, there are very few direct estimates of it that do not make use of a marginal productivity side condition. I cannot resist the opportunity to engage in a little self-advertising and mention that Professor Lawrence Klein and I will be presenting a paper at the meetings of the Econometric Society this winter in which we present some direct estimates of the parameters of this form, fitted to aggregative data for the U.S. economy. (This paper will be published in the *Review of Economics and Statistics*.) Professor Murray Brown has also obtained some direct estimates of the parameters of this type of production function, in a paper given at last winter's Econometric Society meetings, in which he tried to get directly at this thorny problem of the degree of monopoly power. But, again, one can hardly criticize Professor Griliches for failing to have knowledge of unpublished research.

change, and so the remaining relationship is dominated by short-term (cyclical) influences, which are likely to be quite different from those which are the subject of the standard production function model. I should like to emphasize that, if true, this conclusion would lead us to reject (or at least give very little weight to) most, if not all, of the studies of aggregate production functions of the past. As an invited discussant, I have felt an obligation to grapple with this conclusion, despite something of a self-preservative instinct to duck it. My present view is that Griliches is largely correct, although the situation may not be that bad when the sample period underlying the aggregative production function study is both long in term and homogeneous in character. It is also possible that the use of annual data may "wash out" some or most of the very short-term or transitory influences affecting the production relationships.

Another interesting feature of this paper is the attempt to test for technological progress that is embodied in capital goods of current (or recent) vintage, by including the ratio of the net stock of capital to the gross (a proxy for the average age of capital) as an explanatory variable in the production relations fitted. This variable was never statistically significant, thus providing little support for the embodiment hypothesis. However, the power of this test may not be very great, for reasons elucidated by Griliches. Still, it is interesting to note that Lithwick, Post, and Rymes, in their paper on Canadian production relations presented this morning, also tried a similar vintage variable (the average age of the net stock of capital) in attempting to explain investment behavior. They found no evidence of vintage effects on investment, which is of course not the same type of result as Griliches', but which is broadly consistent with his.

Professor Griliches also finds evidence of mild but statistically significant increasing returns to scale, which, as he notes, agrees rather well with the evidence on this point from aggregate production function studies. It is also interesting to observe that the evidence on this issue also survives a foray into data that are close to the individual establishments, although the Cobb-Douglas form of the production function does not appear to permit an adequate description of variations in returns to scale. (Here, as elsewhere, the Cobb-Douglas form would appear to be only an approximation, although better approximations are difficult to obtain!) If one accepts the existence of increasing returns to scale, especially in the range (that of the larger size classes) in which

Griliches found this phenomenon to be most important, this reinforces the view that pure competition is not likely to be very widespread in the manufacturing sector. Griliches also points out that the evidence from aggregate production functions with regard to increasing returns to scale in the individual firms or establishments (plants) of the economy is very indirect, as these aggregate production functions only measure (if they do that) changes in the scale of the economy, without making a correction for the number of firms or establishments operating within the economy. It is of course true that what Marshall used to call "internal technological economies" will be experienced (on average) only if the growth in the scale of the economy exceeds the growth in the number of producing units, i.e., only if the average producing unit grows in scale. However, to the extent that these aggregate production functions measure the Marshallian concept of "external [technological] economies," no correction for a changing number of producing units is necessary or even desirable.

Finally, I have some mild reservations about the "education per man" variable used in Table 9 to account for a portion of the "technical change" residual. The weighting of education classes by base-period income levels is appropriate only if these base-period income levels do actually measure relative (marginal) productivities among the groups so distinguished. But the correlation between education and income is rather tricky: those who have inherited large property incomes are also likely to have inherited a college education as a status right, which may have little to do with the bulk of the income that they receive. Even if one merely focuses on the correlation between education and earnings (labor income), it is not clear that we are dealing with a causal relationship. As Richard Nelson (following Burton Weisbrod) has argued in a paper to be given at tomorrow's session, education may merely serve to label an employee as possessing certain native characteristics that he required to complete his education (e.g., intelligence, docility, or industry) but may make little difference to his performance on the job. In this case, education simply serves to open up job opportunities which would have been closed if the individual did not possess the requisite number of years of formal schooling completed but which he presumably was capable of doing, nevertheless. The drift of these remarks might be an implication that Griliches has overestimated the growth of the relevant education variable for Table 9, and so the contribution of this factor to the explanation of "technical change," the growth in the residual, is too high.[2] (It might also be too high because the weight—taken to be the same as the labor coefficient—is too large, as I have discussed earlier.) On the other hand, this table takes no account of the external effects of education (that is, those that cannot be described as labor-augmenting effects), and these might well be substantial. Hence, I am unwilling to guess whether Griliches' estimate of the contribution of the education embodied in the manufacturing work force, to "technical change" in the manufacturing sector over the period examined, is too large or too small.

As I said at the outset, none of these remarks should be interpreted to mean that Professor Griliches' paper is anything other than excellent. My approach as a discussant has been the sandwich approach—a solid statement at the beginning, solid material at the end, with the Bologna in the middle.

JOEL POPKIN, Office of Business Economics [1]

In recent years, there has been a substantial increase in the resources we have devoted to attempting to quantify the factors causing technological change. We seem to have made considerable progress in the relatively short time since the appearance in 1958 of the studies of Niitamo and Wolfson, who first introduced into production analysis explicit measures of factors thought to underlie productivity change.[2] This excellent paper of Mr. Griliches, which focuses on manufacturing, together with his work in the agricultural sector undoubtedly represent an important contribution to this progress.

There are two brief points about this paper which I want to mention at the outset. First, I wish that Mr. Griliches could have shown more conclusively that the coefficient on his labor quality index did not differ significantly from estimates of labor's share. Certainly the introduction

[2] Edward F. Denison, in his *The Sources of Economic Growth in the United States and the Alternatives Before Us,* Washington, D.C., 1962, attempted to take a rough account of these factors by including only 60 per cent of the rise in a similar education variable as contributing directly to the growth of real output.

[1] These comments do not necessarily reflect the opinion of the Office of Business Economics.

[2] O. Niitamo, "The Development of Productivity in Finnish Industry, 1925–1952," *Productivity Measurement Review,* 1958, pp. 1–12; and R. J. Wolfson, "An Econometric Investigation of Regional Differentials in American Agricultural Wages," *Econometrica,* 1958, pp. 225–51.

of the dummy variables required for the analysis has served to reduce the coefficient below labor's share, but conclusive evidence that the coefficient would have taken on the appropriate value, in the absence of collinearity, has not been presented.

The second point is a conceptual one and probably does not bias Mr. Griliches' findings in any important way. From 1948 through 1960 there has been a net in-leasing of capital by manufacturers.[3] While slight, failure to account for this biases downward capital's contribution to the growth of output. In the time series analysis for certain manufacturing industries, failure to include changes in leased assets can lead to significant bias in the appraisal of the role of capital in the production process. Similarly, in cross-section work, bias can result from the substantial differences in the mix of leased and owned assets among industries. Perhaps, differences in asset leasing have partly contributed to the range of estimates of the elasticity of substitution which Mr. Mansfield has shown in his discussion of Mr. Nerlove's paper.

I would now like to focus the remainder of my discussion on Mr. Griliches' appraisal of the contribution of education to the growth of manufacturing output. Owing to the lack of suitable data, Mr. Griliches has had to use in his cross-section estimates an occupational mix variable as a proxy for educational mix. He feels that the two should be highly correlated but offers no evidence on the point. Data I have looked at cast some doubt on the strength of this correlation, certainly enough doubt to give us reason to suspect that the coefficient on the educational mix variable might not be close to labor's share. In 1959 the occupation "managers" had a mean income 7 per cent above that of "professionals," yet had 24 per cent less education (measured by the median) than professionals.[4] Craftsmen earned 13 per cent more than clerical workers, yet had 16 per cent less education. This last result suggests that other forms of education, such as apprenticeship programs, should be considered.

The ultimate point at issue here is the way in which formal education enters the production process. If one were to assume, quite conservatively, that rising educational levels influence the production process

[3] J. Popkin, "The Use of Wealth Data in Quantitative Economic Analysis," *1964 Proceedings of the Business and Economic Statistics Section, American Statistical Association,* pp. 346–51.

[4] Derived from *Census of Population, 1960,* PC(2)5B, Table 8, and *ibid.,* PC(1)1D, Table 208.

only through the changes which occur in the occupational mix—an assumption which Mr. Griliches' results clearly support since he used occupational mix as his quality variable—the influence of formal education on growth would be altered considerably. Indexes of occupational mix (percentage of employment accounted for by each occupation category weighted by 1959 mean income for that category) show only a 5 per cent shift toward higher skilled occupations between 1950 and 1960. These data are found in Table 1. This is less than half of the increase which Mr. Griliches found in his education index over time.

This apparently slower change in occupational mix than in the level of formal education has been recognized by other researchers. In particular, Folger and Nam find that an increasing amount of the rise in the level of formal education has been manifested in "within-occupation" educational advances, rather than in shifting the occupational mix toward

TABLE 1

Occupational Mix of Manufacturing Employees, 1950 and 1960,
and Mean Income by Occupation, 1959

Occupation	Per Cent of Manufacturing Employment		Mean Income
	1960 (1)	1950 (2)	1959 (3)
Professional, technical, and kindred workers	9.2	5.7	$8,601
Managers, officials, and proprietors, except farm	6.3	6.0	9,169
Clerical and kindred workers	6.5	6.6	4,926
Sales workers	4.5	3.6	6,337
Craftsmen, foremen, kindred workers	25.1	24.8	5,586
Operatives and kindred workers	37.2	39.5	4,396
Service workers, except private household	1.8	2.2	3,529
Laborers, except farm and mine	7.5	11.1	3,118
Occupation not reported	1.8	0.4	4,808

Source: Col. 1: *Census of Population, 1960*, PC(1)1D, Table 209; col. 2: *ibid., 1950*, P-C1, Table 134; col. 3: *ibid., 1960*, PC(1)1D, Table 208.

the higher skills. Obviously this finding need not weaken the hypothesis that all formal education abets economic growth if one can show that within-occupations income varies with formal educational achievement. However, this cannot be conclusively shown. In the 1960 population census, data were collected on the "within-occupation," "within-age-group" distribution of income by level of formal education.[5] These data show that the relationship between education and income is not as strong as might have been suspected from Griliches' Table 8, which is based on highly aggregative data. It is not uncommon to find, for instance, that within many occupations, workers who earn over $10,000 per year have less education than their occupational colleagues who earn $7,500 to $10,000. I was, also, quite surprised to find that the education-income relationship is weaker among salaried managers than among individual proprietors both of whom are in the managerial class. I originally had thought that the higher mean income of the managerial class than of the professional class reflected the influence of the individual entrepreneurs who pulled themselves up by their proverbial boot straps. Apparently the productivity of the captains of manufacturing industries, as reflected by their income, is not influenced by education to the degree to which the income of the owner of the corner store is.

The foregoing comments were not meant to question what Mr. Griliches feels is a major finding of his study—that differences in labor quality account for differences in labor productivity. Rather their purpose has been to point out that in the time series analysis of growth in Section V of his paper, the use of the growth of formal education may have resulted in an overestimation of the amount of economic growth explained by labor quality; and in a corresponding underestimate of the amount of growth rate residual which remains unaccounted for. Mr. Griliches has promised to tackle this residual in his future work, and it seems to me that it may be larger than he is willing to admit. I am sure that we all eagerly await future installments of this important research undertaking.

EVSEY D. DOMAR

Griliches claims that a part of the rate of growth of the residual can be explained by the improvements in the quality of capital left undetected by the deflation of capital formation in money terms by some conven-

[5] Derived from *ibid.*, PC(2)5B, Table 9.

tional price index of capital goods. A "correct" price index would rise less rapidly; hence the deflated capital formation and the capital stock would grow faster. I do not object to this procedure, except to point out that the resulting higher rate of growth of currently produced capital goods would increase the rate of growth of output as well. Of course, the textile industry does not produce its own capital goods; here Griliches is safe. But when his adjustment is applied to machine building the effect of the increase in the rate of growth of its output should be substantial and, I would expect, greater than that of the adjustment in its capital stock. So the unexplained part of the residual in this industry will increase rather than diminish. I do not know what the outcome might be in American manufacturing taken as a whole, but for the whole American economy (with a Cobb-Douglas function) the two adjustments (in capital formation and in the stock of capital) almost cancel each other, leaving a small difference with an uncertain sign.[1]

HANS NEISSER

The term "rental payment" as used by Griliches in Section II, in defining K, clearly is a net term, not the price of the service of the capital good, or "gross rental," as charged by the owner of the equipment piece to the user. This follows from Griliches' adding to the rental value the items depreciation and depletion, insurance premium, and property taxes. These three items would be covered in equilibrium by the market price of the service (gross rental), and the net rental would equal the interest on the capital value of the piece plus a risk premium.

It may be noted that there is a type of contract in which the stipulated rent is the net rental. I refer to the contracts between owner and tenant of a large agricultural estate, as they have been usual in Europe for many centuries. In such contracts the tenant has two obligations: (1) to pay a stipulated annual rent, and (2) at the end of the contract, say after twelve years, to return the property in the same state in which he received it. The second obligation does not refer only to the state of the soil, but to anything received when he took over the estate (livestock, equipment, seed, buildings, etc.). Since the obligation rarely could be fulfilled for buildings because of the depreciation during the contract's lifetime, meticulous accounting was necessary at the end of the contract,

[1] See E. D. Domar, "Total Productivity and the Quality of Capital," *Journal of Political Economy,* December 1963, pp. 586–88.

in which any improvements made by the tenant would find their place (see e.g., the German Civil Code of 1900, paragraphs 582, 586–589).

Griliches uses the gross rental also for measuring the contribution of the capital service to output in the production function. I consider this procedure erroneous. Griliches' formula would be correct only if (1) as mentioned above, the owner has to pay insurance premium and property taxes and (2) if the depreciation as charged precisely measured the actual wear and tear, as far as it affects performance. Possibly Griliches had this case in mind when he developed his model. But on page 314 we read: "Instead of the usual sharp depreciation assumptions, I shall make the opposite assumption that the services of a machine do not decline at all (or very little) as long as it is in operation." Nevertheless in the next paragraph he retains the "gross rental" approach: "A $100 machine that will last five years will have roughly twice as large an *annual* [Griliches' italics] flow of services (in dollars) than another $100 machine whose expected length of life is ten years." In the first quotation, Griliches assumes that the service of the machine in the technical sense is the same at the beginning and at the end of the year; in the second quotation he denies it. The first quotation develops the implications of an assumption concerning the behavior of the machine in rendering services year by year; hence, it is inconsistent with the second one. It scarcely needs proof that Ricardo's rent concept was a net term, but it referred only to the soil. In Walras, too, the necessity of distinguishing between the market price of the service (in equilibrium) and what we call the net rental is acknowledged. To obtain the equilibrium price for the machine, Walras deducts from the equilibrium price of the service the depreciation allowance and the insurance premium; the remainder is to be capitalized by the equilibrium rate of interest. Walras obviously refers to new machines; the price for second-hand machines will be influenced by the fact that the seller of the machine does not hand over to the buyer the accumulated depreciation reserve.

I do not assert, of course, that in reality the performance of a machine is constant over its lifetime. Leaving aside the complications arising for the production function from the possibility of maintaining it constant by putting in more maintenance labor, I suggest the following theoretical rule for the measurement of a machine's performance in the production function: market price of the service (gross rental) minus depreciation plus estimated wear and tear per unit of time. If there is no market price for the service, we may measure the contribution by current costs plus estimated wear and tear (as defined above); current costs are the sum of interest, property tax, insurance premium, and an estimated risk premium.

Murray Brown

1. There is difficulty in Professor Griliches' specification of the capital variable. It will be shown that his specification is a mixed embodied-disembodied model, and that it is impossible to specify a "service" concept of capital using gross stock without, at the same time, generating this inconsistency. This does not bias his results in Section IV, since the various specifications of capital are highly collinear, but it does affect his implementation of the results in Section V.

Let depreciation charges, calculated by declining balance, i.e., exponentially declining values over time, be

$$e^{-w}C_N = e^{-w} \int_{t-n}^{t} I(v)e^{w(v-t)} \, dv,$$

where w is the depreciation rate which includes *obsolescence, n* is the service life, and $I(v)$ is gross investment of vintage v.[1] Also, let

$$C_G = \int_{t-n}^{t} I(v) \, dv,$$

be gross stock. Then, ignoring the insurance and rental items, Griliches' capital variable K, in Section II, is

$$K = e^{-w}C_N + .06 \; C_G$$

$$= e^{-w} \int_{t-n}^{t} I(v)e^{w(v-t)} dv + .06 \int_{t-n}^{t} I(v) \, dv$$

His production model, stripped to the essentials, is

(1) $V = AL^\alpha G^\beta K^\gamma$

$$= AL^\alpha G^\beta \left(e^{-w} \int_{t-n}^{t} I(v)e^{w(v-t)} dv + .06 \int_{t-n}^{t} I(v)dv \right)^\gamma,$$

where G is, say, education.

---

[1] I have used the declining-balance method of writing off stocks, since this conforms more nearly to actual practice than the other major alternative, the straight-line method. Only if service lives are reduced below Bulletin F lives could one represent book value depreciation charges by the straight-line method. Cf. my "Depreciation and Corporate Profits," *Survey of Current Business,* October 1963, p. 12.

What is the marginal rate of substitution of new investment goods $I(T)$ to vintage investment goods $I(v)$ in (1)? It can be shown to be,

$$
(2) \qquad \frac{\partial V/\partial I(v)}{\partial V/\partial I(T)} = \frac{e^{w(v-t)-1} + .06}{e^{w(T-t)-1} + .06}
$$

This represents the increase in the Tth investment goods required to compensate for a reduction in the vth investment goods in order to keep output constant. Clearly, it is not unity, as Griliches maintains on page 281. ("The procedure used assumes, however, that capital services of different vintages are equally productive.") In fact, the more time that elapses between T and v, the smaller is (2).

It can be shown that w, the depreciation rate, which includes an obsolescence factor, is the same as Solow's productivity improvement factor in his embodied model, under the assumptions of competition and smooth deterioration of economic values.[2] Hence Griliches has specified a hybrid model, containing embodied and disembodied components.

His attempt to test what he terms the "embodied model" (*loc. cit.*) against his own specification is a misspent one, since he is comparing a hybrid embodied-disembodied model with another hybrid. Of course the proportions of the two components may differ between the two models, but the data is insufficiently precise to pick up that order of difference.

2. Griliches maintains that the estimated sigmas by industry in his Table 3 do not significantly differ from each other. There is insufficient data presented in the paper to perform an analysis of variance to test the assertion (could we request that he perform it) on his estimates of σ_3, but a casual inspection reveals to my eye that they may indeed differ. If they do, then his specification of the Cobb-Douglas production function yields biased estimates of the elasticities of production. In particular, if capital is growing more rapidly than labor, and the true sigma exceeds unity, then Griliches' estimated elasticity of production with respect to capital is biased upward.

3. On page 296, Griliches asserts: "The only other alternative possible interpretation of these results is one which would deny entirely

[2] R. Solow, "Investment and Technical Progress," in K. J. Arrow, S. Karlin and P. Suppes (ed.), *Mathematical Methods in the Social Sciences, 1959,* Stanford, 1960, p. 100; and my, "An Iconoclastic View of the New View of Investment," Econometric Institute Report, 1963.

the possibility of estimating the elasticity of substitution from cross-sectional data . . ." The assertion would be correct if his "serial correlation" model contains no specification error. There are several misspecifications that could yield the results in question: (1) the sigmas for each industry may indeed differ; (2) there is no utilization adjustment, a factor all of which would not be accounted for in the serial correlation terms; (3) not everyone agrees that cross-section estimates of sigma are identified; (4) value added is a misspecified output measure, which causes trouble in time series, but the misspecification may be compounded in cross-section data; (5) if w, the wage rate, is not deflated by the industry price, there is a problem because of the specification of the lag term in Griliches' model; the omission of the deflator could be justified only if prices were constant between 1957 and 1958 in all industries.

4. Griliches specifies the education variable, following Denison, as labor-augmenting. As a general specification, this cannot be correct, since education probably augments all factors.

5. It is well known that, unless certain conditions are met, the Cobb-Douglas production function is not identified in cross-section data; i.e., the estimated elasticities are functions of relative factor prices. Are these conditions satisfied in the Liu-Hildebrand–Griliches' data and in Griliches' model? In view of the importance of the problem, a brief discussion is certainly warranted.

REPLY by Griliches

Dr. Popkin raises several questions about the adequacy of the occupational mix index as a proxy for an education index and about the more general relevance of "education" to a quality-of-labor measure. The occupation index is not a very good approximation to the variable I really wanted but did not have. The correlation coefficient between such two measures for the urban population of forty-eight states is only about .8. It would probably be higher for better-defined groups and a more detailed occupational breakdown. But no doubt it is not as good a measure as I would wish. This, of course, may also explain why its ultimate coefficients are somewhat lower than expected (as noted by Professor Bodkin). Popkin also questions whether there is a net effect of education holding occupation constant. On this we now have the evidence of

Hanoch's (1965) dissertation based on the 1-in-a-1,000 sample from the 1959 Census. He shows unequivocally that there is a substantial, positive, and significant effect of school years completed on income, holding occupation constant (i.e., using the within-occupations variance).[1] The estimated education effect is larger when occupation is not held constant, but that is as one would expect. Since education affects occupation, the correct weight for it in an analysis such as I performed above is not its coefficient holding occupation constant, but its "reduced form" coefficient based on the solving out of the endogenous occupation variable.

This point can be illustrated by a very simple model. Let Y stand for income, O for occupation, E for education; and u and v are random variables representing such forces as ability and luck. Then we have *two* relations:

(1) $$O = \alpha E + u$$

(2) $$Y = \beta O + \gamma E + v$$

from which we can derive the reduced form:

(3) $$Y = (\beta \alpha + \gamma)E + v + \beta u$$

The last coefficient $(\beta \alpha + \gamma)$ is the one we are interested in. If it is estimated from (2) it will be underestimated. If, as I have done in the first part of my paper, it is estimated from a regression of Y on O, it will be underestimated if E and O are poorly correlated. Thus the coefficient may be too low, but the variable E used in the time series context is right, and does not overestimate its contribution.

Actually, the occupation-education dichotomy is an artifact of the data. The finer the occupational classification, the less difference it will make. What we really want is to allow for the changing mix of the labor force. This is a problem of aggregation error. In allowing for it what kinds of classes of workers should we distinguish? Given the data restrictions we want a classification which will maximize the between variance and minimize the within. None of these dimensions are perfect in this respect, but the educational one is better than the (major) occupational one. If and when the data come with enough detail, I will use both.

There is a certain inconsistency in the way capital is measured in the first and last parts of the paper, which has unfortunately led to some

---

[1] See his Table 1.

confusion and justifiable queries from Professors Brown and Neisser. This is partly the result of differences in data sources, but it also reflects the fact that much of the last part of the paper was written about two years earlier than the first. There are several different ways in which age and dating effects enter in and get mixed up in measuring services. First, there is the question of how the physical services of a machine age with calendar time. This is the question of what depreciation assumptions one should use. Second, there is the question of how one should aggregate *different* new machines (or their services) having different expected *life spans* (e.g., equipment and buildings). This leads to the distinction that I make between service flow (rental) and stock (purchase price) weights in aggregating the two types of capital that I can distinguish in the time series. Thirdly, there is the question of whether this year's *new* machine of the same type is as productive as last year's *new* machine. This can be viewed either as a question about the correctness of the price deflators for gross investment or as a question about embodied technical change, about the changing quality of *new* machines of roughly the same type (with similar expected life spans). Now these are three very different questions, though one can find examples where they all appear simultaneously. Thus it is not inconsistent as charged by Neisser to assume that (1) the annual flow of services from a given machine does not decline with age as long as the machine is alive (the one-hoss-shay assumption) and at the same time also to contemplate (2) the presence in the market of several types of machines having *different* life spans (10-year one-hoss shays and 100-year one-hoss shays). These are simply different questions.

In the time series data I assumed no deterioration in the service flow with age, and concentrated on the implications of different weights for construction and equipment and the possibility that the conventional deflators were wrong. When I came to the cross-section data I did not have the ingredients to construct the same type of measure. I chose to work with the rather strange measure of depreciation plus 6 per cent of gross stock plus insurance and rentals for the following reasons: I wanted to approximate my previous measure, but I did not have the structure-equipment breakdown. Hence I fell back on the depreciation data to help me along these lines. If, as was prevalent in 1957, the depreciation formula used is a straight-line one, the annual dollar flow will be proportional to gross stock for the same type of machine but will differ (in the right direction) for machines with different expected life spans. This is the difference I wanted to catch, and therefore I used this variable in spite of its questionable connection with the "truth." The next step was to apply the arbitrary (but hopefully reasonable) rate of interest of 6 per cent to the *gross* stock measure and add the result to the depreciation component. *If* the depreciation figures were in fact based on straight-line methods, and if the insurance and rentals component is ignored, the result is still proportional to gross stock and implies the same sort of no-declining-productivity-with-age assumption. It does, however, weight different gross stocks with different expected life spans differently. If there were only two types of capital on hand, the resulting measure would be approximately equal to

$$SK_t = \left(\frac{1}{n_1} + .06\right) K_1{}^G + \left(\frac{1}{n_2} + .06\right) K_2{}^G$$

where n_1 and n_2 are the expected life spans of machines of type 1 and 2 respectively. This is quite similar to the measure I use in the last part of the paper. Neither of these measures is subject to the embodiment objection raised by Brown.

An inconsistency may, however, arise here because the reported depreciation flows may not be based on straight-line assumptions or even if they were, the assumed life spans may include an allowance for obsolescence. Also, it is not really necessary to carry along at this stage the assumption of no deterioration of service quality with age. Either of these possibilities would suggest using the current value (net) of the stock (in constant prices) to compute the interest component of the capital service measure. By incorporating allowances for obsolescence, such a measure would contain some aspects of embodiment. Actually, as brought out in the text, I used such a measure also, but with almost no perceptible effect on the results.

While one can convert in some cases the problem of embodiment into the problem of what is the correct rate of depreciation to be used, what I had in mind under the embodiment label was the question: How many new machines of constant quality did a $100 in investment funds buy us this year as against the same amount spent on new machines last year? This is a question about the correctness of our estimate of gross *investment* in fixed prices, which logically precedes the question of what depreciation rates should be applied to it in constructing a capital stock or services measure. If my gross capital and depreciation data were in fixed prices, eliminating the general inflationary effects, the R measure used to catch the investment specific embodiment effect (net stock/gross stock) would be adequate for the job. Unfortunately, since these data are in historical prices, this measure is quite poor, and therefore the poor results obtained by using it are not conclusive.

Professor Domar makes the very important point that in considering embodiment or quality change in the context of productivity analysis one should be careful also to adjust the output side, since the mismeasured inputs are also outputs somewhere else in the economy. But he is wrong in applying the criticism to the computations presented in Table 9 of my paper and in his estimate of the order of magnitude of this adjustment for the economy at large. As far as this study is concerned, the only quality adjustment made is to the price deflator of gross investment in structures. Since structures are an output of the construction industry, the point made is not applicable to the analysis of sources of output growth in manufacturing to which I have restricted myself in this paper. Also, I believe that Domar reached the wrong general conclusion in his cited paper about the probability that the adjustments on the output and input side would tend to cancel out. If the rate of growth in the error of the investment deflator is constant, and the rate of growth of capital is constant, then the rate of growth of error in the measurement of investment is the same as the rate of growth of error in the measurement of capital. But in this case the adjustment on the output side is multiplied by the value share of gross investment in total output while on the input side it is multiplied by the share of capital in total costs. The second is usually significantly larger than the first (this is true for the entire 1929–64 period for the private domestic U.S. economy), and hence the two adjustments do *not* cancel out.[2] Thus there is merit and profit in pursuing the possibility that our investment deflators are not all that they should be.

The issue of whether the individual industry estimates of the elasticity of substitution are significantly different from each other, raised by Brown, is difficult to resolve because of the generally poor fit of the

[2] See D. W. Jorgenson, "The Embodiment Hypothesis," *Journal of Political Economy*, February 1966, for a more detailed exposition of this point and the above-cited Griliches and Jorgenson (1966) paper for an application to the total private domestic U.S. economy.

individual industry relations. Also I do not have exactly comparable results for the appropriate F tests (the aggregate I ran for the 17 industries contained 415 observations, 3 less than the 418 contained in the individual regressions for these industries). The results I have are roughly as follows: Allowing each industry in the aggregate equation to have a constant term of its own, we cannot reject the hypothesis that the slope coefficient (σ) is the same for all industries. In fact, the residual variance is the same to two decimal places (.0040) for the residuals from the 17 individual industry regressions (with 384 degrees of freedom) and the residuals from the aggregate equation (with 399 degrees of freedom). Switching to the serial correlation model, and testing now simultaneously the between-industry differences in the estimates of *three* parameters (σ, $\rho\sigma$, and ρ), we cannot reject at the 5 per cent level the hypothesis that as a *set* they are different for different industries. It is clear from inspection of the individual estimates that the difference arises from different estimates of ρ, the serial correlation coefficient. On the basis of our specification and data we can therefore reject the hypothesis that (1) the serial correlation properties of the disturbances are the same for all industries, and (2) that the distribution parameters are the same for all industries, but (3) we cannot reject the hypothesis that the elasticity of substitution is the same for all industries. Also, once (3) is accepted, we cannot reject the hypothesis that σ is equal to unity. An attempt to deal with the finding about significant differences in the distribution parameters is described in my paper in Table 6 and the associated text. This problem, and the simultaneity problem raised by Brown, are also discussed (perhaps unsatisfactorily) in the introduction to my paper.

THE INFLUENCE OF RESEARCH AND EDUCATION ON CES PRODUCTION RELATIONS

MURRAY BROWN

GEORGE WASHINGTON UNIVERSITY

ALFRED H. CONRAD

HARVARD UNIVERSITY

Introduction

THIS PAPER describes an experiment intended to reduce one part of the simultaneous equation bias usually encountered in the statistical estimation of production relationships. In the earliest, classic discussion of the simultaneity problem in production functions, by Marschak and Andrews,[1] changes in technology and differences in efficiency among the firms or industries were left among the random disturbances. In a more recent encounter with the problem, Irving Hoch [2] accounted for the differences in efficiency among agricultural units and the change in productivity over time by fitting individual time and firm intercepts in a generalized regression technique derived from the analysis of covariance.

As in our earlier paper,[3] we hypothesize that the "fundamental" variables, research and education, are influential in explaining inter- and intra-industry differences in efficiency. In this experiment, these variables are incorporated into the production function and their influ-

NOTE: This study was supported by a grant from the National Science Foundation. The authors gratefully acknowledge the assistance of Miss Hazel Elkington.

[1] J. Marschak and W. H. Andrews, "Random Simultaneous Equations and the Theory of Production," *Econometrica*, 1944.

[2] I. Hoch, "Estimation of Production Function Parameters Combining Time-Series and Cross-Section Data," *Econometrica*, 1962, p. 34.

[3] "Fundamental Variables in a Generalized System of Production," presented at Econometric Society meetings, Copenhagen, July 1963.

ence on labor productivity is measured in a pooled time series and cross-section set of observations for a limited group of manufacturing industries in the United States during the 1950s.

We develop a production model which generalizes previous attempts in two respects: first, it does not assume that the elasticity of substitution between labor and capital is equal to any specific constant, as, e.g., in the Cobb-Douglas production function; second, the model permits the fundamental variables to influence all parameters in the system, not simply those that have a neutral effect on technology. In unconstrained form, the model is capable of measuring the influence of the fundamental variables on output, productivity, labor demand, and capital demand, as well as measuring the elasticity of substitution.

The paper is organized as follows. A labor productivity equation is derived from the constant-elasticity-of-substitution (CES) production function in the next section. The parameters in the equation are identified, and the effects of their changes are noted. Most of the section is devoted to the specification of the fundamental variables in the CES labor productivity equation, and to a discussion of their influence on the parameters of the CES production function.

The variables and the data are described in the third section. Ten manufacturing industries in the United States, for the period 1950–60, constitute the basic set of observations. The following variables are specified: real corporate gross product, labor, capacity utilization, the wage rate, product price, education, and research—all at the industry level. An extensive discussion of education and research is warranted by virtue of the paucity of data and their intractability. In particular, it was necessary to devise a new procedure to *quantify* the interindustry flow of knowledge from research that affects productivity. This required an application of the 1958 input-output table that was prepared by the Office of Business Economics.

The fourth section discusses the estimation procedures. It is mainly concerned with an application of covariance analysis to our productivity equation in the context of pooled time series and cross-section observations.

Finally, the empirical results are given in the fifth section in two parts: the first shows the results obtained from pooling all industry data and not explicitly introducing the research variable; and the second part contains the results of the complete model.

A principal, though tentative, conclusion that emerges from our empirical investigation can be anticipated here. It derives from the disparate estimates of the labor productivity equation in the durable and nondurable industries: Education and research have a relatively larger impact on productivity in the group of durable goods industries than they do on labor productivity in the nondurable group. In order to rationalize this pattern we note that the industries in the durable group are more closely linked in an interindustry trading nexus than those in the nondurable group; the diffusion of the results of education and research is therefore more effective in durables than among the nondurable industries.

The Model

The constant-elasticity-of-substitution model of production forms the framework for the analysis. Since its properties have been explored in detail elsewhere, only a summary is given here. We write the production function of the two-factor case as follows:

$$(1) \qquad X_0 = \gamma[kX_1^{-\alpha} + (1 - k)X_2^{-\alpha}]^{-v/\alpha}$$

where X_0 is gross output, X_1 represents the services of labor, and X_2 denotes the services of capital as measured by net capital stock. The parameters of the function require more discussion.[4]

THE PARAMETERS

γ denotes the efficiency of a technology. Given the primary factors of production—labor and capital—and given the other characteristics of a technology, the efficiency characteristic determines the output that results. Changes in γ are neutral, i.e., they alter the relationship of the combined factor inputs to output but do not affect the marginal rate of substitution between labor and capital for given labor-capital ratios.

v is a homogeneity parameter, representing the degree of returns to scale. For $v \gtreqless 1$, there are economies of scale, constant returns, and diseconomies of scale, respectively. Changes in v have a neutral effect.

k is a capital intensity parameter. Degrees of capital intensity are reflected in the size of labor-capital ratios for given relative factor prices.

[4] A complete exposition of the function is given in M. Brown, *On the Theory and Measurement of Technological Change*, Cambridge, Eng., 1965, Chaps. 2, 4.

Thus, the larger is k, the larger is the labor-capital ratio for all values of the ratio of labor and capital prices. A change in k will have a non-neutral effect; an increase in the value of k is laborsaving, in the sense that the marginal rate of substitution of labor for capital rises at each labor-capital ratio. However, an increase in k augments the rate of growth of output only if the supply of capital is increasing relatively faster than the supply of labor.

α is a function of the elasticity of substitution between labor and capital; specifically, $\alpha = 1/\sigma - 1$. The elasticity of substitution measures the rate at which the marginal product of capital rises relative to the marginal product of labor as labor is substituted for capital. It can also be thought of as measuring the rate at which the marginal product of labor rises as the real wage rate rises. We know that if a change in technology generates an increase in the elasticity of substitution, there is a nonneutral effect: the increase in σ is laborsaving if the growth of capital exceeds the growth of labor. Moreover, changes in the elasticity of substitution due to technological progress are directly related to changes in the growth of output.[5]

THE PRODUCTIVITY EQUATION

We now want to specify the labor productivity relation in terms of the CES production function. We can start by considering the marginal productivity of labor derived from (1):

(2) $\delta X_0/\delta X_1 = h_0' X_0^{1+\alpha/v} X_1^{-1/\sigma}$, where $h_0' = (1 - k)v\gamma^{-\alpha/v}$.

The capital intensity affects the marginal productivity by way of the k parameter and the elasticity of substitution. A crucial assumption here is the independence of the empirical substitution relationship from the stock of capital.

Equating (2) to the deflated wage rate, P_1/P, and expressing the result in terms of the labor productivity index, X_0/X_1, we have

(3) $X_0/X_1 = h_0^*(P_1/P)^\sigma X_0^r$, where $r = 1 - \sigma + \dfrac{\sigma - 1}{v}$, and $h_0^* = (h_0')^{-\sigma}$.

The output term, X_0, brings returns to scale and variations in capacity utilization into the relationship. Clearly, when $v = 1$, that is, when there

---

[5] The proofs of the propositions that involve changes in the parameters of the CES production function are given in *loc. cit.*

are constant returns to scale, then $r = 0$, and variations in output have no effect on the productivity of labor. In the empirical tests, the output term on the right of (3) has been replaced by a capacity utilization index, denoted by S, so that we have

$$(4) \qquad X_0/X_1 = h_0*(P_1/P)^\sigma S^a,$$

where a is a parameter. One final adjustment should be noted before introducing the fundamental variables into the labor productivity equation. In (4) the real wage rate is assumed to influence output per unit of labor in the given period. But that assumption rests upon a dubious and unnecessary assumption that the observed data reflect equilibrium situations. The possibility that labor productivity is not in instantaneous equilibrium at the given real wage rate can be handled realistically by allowing the effects of changes in the wage rate to be spread over time. This requires that we write the deflated wage variable in distributed lag form. In this case, a Fisher distributed lag is specified.[6] It is written as $\rho'_{\eta, t-\delta}$, where η is the number of wage terms in the distributed lag expression and δ is the order of the lag. For example,

$$\rho'_{3, t-2} = [(P_1/P)_t^3 (P_1/P)_{t-1}^2 (P_1/P)_{t-2}]^{1/6}.$$

The labor productivity estimating form is now given by

$$(5) \qquad X_0/X_1 = h_0*(\rho'_{j, t-\delta})^\sigma S^a.$$

It should be noted that (5) is linear in logarithms and can be easily estimated by standard regression techniques.

We still have the problem of specifying the fundamental variables in the labor productivity equation. And, we want to accomplish this in such a way that the resulting econometric testing form is a simple one, in this case, one that is linear in logarithms. Data constraints are so severe, as we shall see below, that a simple form is required. Now suppose that our production function is the generalized CES function:

$$(6) \qquad X_0 = \gamma[k_1 X_1^{-\alpha} + k_2 X_2^{-\alpha} + k_3 X_3^{-\alpha} + k_4 X_4^{-\alpha}]^{-v/\alpha},$$

where X_3 is an educational attainments variable, X_4 represents the services of research and development, and the k's are intensity coefficients.

---

[6] The choice of the Fisher lag scheme in this setting is discussed in M. Brown and H. Wachtel, *The Share of Corporate Profits in the Postwar Period*, U.S. Department of Commerce Staff Working Paper No. 11, April 1965, pp. 66 ff.

Equation (6) is the first type of generalization proposed by H. Uzawa.[7] It assumes, *inter alia,* that the elasticities of substitution between all pairs of variables are the same. Now, taking the marginal product of labor from (6) gives us (2), as the reader can verify. This, of course, does not contain the fundamental variables in a simple manner, and hence we cannot accomplish our objectives by specifying the production function as in (6).

Consider another generalized CES function (also proposed by Uzawa):

$$(7) \qquad X_0 = \gamma[k_1 X_1^{-\alpha_1} + k_2 X_2^{-\alpha_1}]^{-v_1/\alpha_1}[k_3 X_3^{-\alpha_2} + k_4 X_4^{-\alpha_2}]^{-v_2/\alpha_2},$$

where α_1 is the partial elasticity of substitution between X_1 and X_2, and α_2 is the partial elasticity of substitution between X_3 and X_4; the other parameters are interpreted as above, with the modification that $v_1 + v_2 = v$. In this particular form of the generalized function, the ease of substitution between the fundamental variables is allowed to differ from the partial elasticity of substitution between labor and capital, which seems to be more reasonable than the assumption in (6). However, the elasticity of substitution between labor and education, say, is taken to be unity, an assumption that is subject to serious question. In any event, the marginal product of labor from (7) yields (2), and we have still failed to specify a productivity equation which includes research and education in a simple manner (as defined above).

Arguing as we did in the previous Brown-Conrad paper that the parameters of the production function are influenced by variations in the fundamental variables, we can return to (1) and specify the following:

$$(8) \qquad \gamma = \gamma(X_3, X_4) = \gamma_0 X_3^{\gamma_1} X_4^{\gamma_2},$$

$$(9) \qquad k = k(X_3, X_4) = k_0 X_3^{k_1} X_4^{k_2},$$

$$(10) \qquad \alpha = \alpha(X_3, X_4) = \alpha_0 X_3^{\alpha_1} X_4^{\alpha_2},$$

$$(11) \qquad v = v(X_3, X_4) = v_0 X_3^{v_1} X_4^{v_2}.$$

By inspection, it is seen that if we assume $\alpha_1 = \alpha_2 = 0$, then the substitution of (8)–(11) into (5) yields precisely what we are striving for:

[7] "Production Functions with Constant Elasticities of Substitution," *Review of Economic Studies,* October 1962, pp. 291–99.

a labor productivity form which both contains the fundamental variables and is linear in logarithms. Before specifying the relationship formally, however, we wish to indicate the directions of the effects of the fundamental variables on the parameters of the CES production function. In other words, what signs should be expected on the parameters in (8)–(11)?

THE INFLUENCE OF THE FUNDAMENTAL VARIABLES ON THE CES PARAMETERS

It is difficult to see how the γ_i ($i = 1, 2, 3$) could be anything but positive. That is, an increase in education and research should raise the productivity of each variable input in a neutral sense. A number of recent studies on the Cobb-Douglas function support this assertion.

As we pointed out earlier, an increase in k, the capital intensity parameter, is laborsaving in any event but will augment output only if the relative supply of capital is increasing. The effect of research on k, then, depends upon the success of research in reducing relative factor scarcity. If the innovational activity is directed toward saving labor, and if it is effective, then $k_2 > 0$. If long-term unit capital rents are increasing relative to wages, then k_2 may be negative when research has succeeded in reducing the relative scarcity. This argument rests upon a model of research activity in which the stock of technical information is reoriented by shifts in the composition and reductions in the service life of knowledge aimed at economizing in the face of different relative factor scarcities. In the present paper, the relationship between the service life of information and the long-run relative scarcities is avoided by treating X_4 as a flow rather than a stock. This involves some misspecification, however.

With respect to education, there should be a positive relation between that variable and the capital intensity of a technology. For if k rises, then a laborsaving technological change has occurred; and if education is doing its job well, then a labor force with a given stock of education and a given stock of facilities on which to operate should be more productive than a labor force with a smaller stock of educational attainments, *cet. par.* Hence a rise in X_3 should be laborsaving, and k_1 should be positive.

We note that the homogeneous functional form for k is a misspecification, since it is constrained in the interval, $0 < k < 1$. A form incorporating an asymptote for each of the fundamental variables would have been more appropriate. However, being interested only in the directions of the effects, it is unnecessary to pursue this here.

Although we are assuming that σ is constant in this paper, it may be useful to make a few remarks about the possible effects of the fundamental variables on the elasticity of substitution. Research directed toward reductions in factor scarcities should also be oriented toward making factor substitutions relatively easier. However, to the extent that innovation and education have the effect of increasing specialization, the elasticity of substitution may be reduced: A given machine may require a given complement of specific skills. One more anomaly follows from this suggestion: If increasing specialization means that more highly trained people achieve larger outputs with given stocks of equipment, then increasing education raises the elasticity of substitution. Obviously, more work is required on these questions.

To the extent that research and education increase the complexity of production processes, requiring control over increasingly larger amounts of resources for economical operations, there is a positive relation between the fundamental variables and the homogeneity parameter, v. Hence: $v_1, v_2 > 0$.

THE ADJUSTED PRODUCTIVITY EQUATION

The discussion of the relationships between the fundamental variables and the characteristics of the technology in a CES production system has raised many more problems of measurement than we are prepared to handle in the present paper. In order for us to make contact with the central issue of the relationship between the fundamental variables and productivity, it is necessary to treat the former set of relationships in a highly simplified manner. Thus, since it is known that the $h_0{}^*$ term in the labor productivity form, (5), is a conglomerate of parameters, each of which is a function of the fundamental variables, then $h_0{}^*$ must be a function of the fundamental variables, and can be specified as

$$(12) \qquad h_0{}^* = h_0 X_3{}^{h_1} X_4{}^{h_2}.$$

This specification treats the relationships between the fundamental variables and the technology as a package, a procedure which has the considerable advantage of permitting direct estimates of the influence of the fundamental variables on productivity. For, combining (12) and (5) yields:

$$(13) \qquad X_0/X_1 = h_0 X_3{}^{h_1} X_4{}^{h_2} (\rho'_{\eta,\,t-\delta})^\sigma S^\alpha,$$

which is linear in the logarithms and is relatively simple to estimate. The fundamental variables in (13) are expected to be directly related to labor productivity.

To sum up, labor productivity in (13) depends upon the following factors: the long-term substitution of capital for labor, as reflected by the lagged product-deflated wage rate; the utilization of capacity; the educational attainments of the work force; and the knowledge resulting from research and development activity. The form permits the fundamental variables to reflect the neutral as well as nonneutral characteristics of the technology within a constant-elasticity-of-substitution framework.

We now turn to a description of the procedures used to estimate (13).

The Variables and the Data

A basic set of data for ten industries is used in the present study. Although some of the series are available for longer periods, a reasonably matched set of data can only be developed for the period 1950–60. For the most part the data conform to the United States national income accounting system. The industries are given in the following table with their SIC codes.

Industry	SIC Code
Food and kindred products	20
Textile mill products plus apparel	22
Paper and allied products	26
Chemicals and allied products	28
Stone, clay, and glass products	32
Primary metal industries	33
Fabricated metal products, including ordnance and accessories	34
Machinery, except electrical	35
Electrical machinery	36
Automobiles and automobile equipment plus other transportation equipment	371

All major series are on an establishment basis. With the exception of the basic education data, all refer to the corporate sector in each industry.

REAL CORPORATE GROSS PRODUCT AT FACTOR COST FOR INDUSTRY j, $X_{0,j}$

This is obtained by summing profits (net of depreciation but including the inventory valuation adjustment), interest, employee compensation (wages and salaries plus supplements), and capital consumption allowance (depreciation plus accidental damage, and capital outlays charged to current expense).[8] By excluding such nonfactor costs as indirect business taxes, the corporate gross product series is conceptually closer to a factor cost than a market cost measure. The current-dollar corporate gross product series are deflated, using specific two-digit industry deflators developed in the National Economics Division of the Office of Business Economics.

As measured here, the corporate real gross product variable reflects advances in technology that result in reductions in costs; however, those reflected in new products, or in improvements in existing products which do not affect costs, are not included in the gross product series. To the extent that research inputs are directed toward new-product development, which is considerable, the estimated contribution of research will be biased downward in our model.

THE SERVICES OF LABOR, $X_{1,j}$

This is measured by the total annual man-hours worked in industry j, which is obtained by combining the total employed and an average hours series. The series for total employed is the same as that used by the National Income Division of the Office of Business Economics, which is based upon data compiled by the Bureau of Employment Security.[9] The industry series on production hours is from the Bureau of the Census.[10] The average hours series refers to production hours worked,

---

[8] The conceptual and methodological framework for developing a corporate gross product series by industry of origin is patterned after that used by the National Economics Division of the Office of Business Economics. See Martin L. Marimont, "GNP by Major Industries," *Survey of Current Business,* October 1962, pp. 13–18; and "GNP by Major Industries," Office of Business Economics, unpublished.

[9] *Employment and Wages,* U.S. Department of Labor, Bureau of Employment Security.

[10] *Annual Survey of Manufacturers.*

but the employment series includes both production and nonproduction workers. It is assumed that nonproduction workers work approximately the same hours as production workers.

THE WAGE RATE, $P_{1,j}$

The variable which measures the price of labor in equation (13) is derived by taking the ratio of employee compensation to total man-hours worked, $X_{1,j}$. Compensation of employees includes the sum of wages and salaries, plus such supplements to wages and salaries as employer contributions to social insurance funds, private pensions, health, and welfare funds. The source of the data is the Bureau of Employment Security. To obtain the product deflated wage rate, $P_{1,j}$ is divided by P_j, which is the same deflator that is used to obtain the constant-dollar corporate gross product series. The resulting deflated wage measure for each industry approximates the weighted average hourly product deflated wage in the industry, the weights being the total hours worked in each occupation.

It should be mentioned that the derivation of the hourly wage rate requires that employee compensation be divided by total man-hours worked, which is the same variable that forms the denominator in the labor productivity ratio. This does not introduce spurious correlation, however, since the productivity relationship is specified in terms of ratios; specifically, it relates labor productivity to the average wage rate.[11]

The distributed lag in the real wage rate was specified, as noted above, to reflect the long-run influences on productivity.[12] Due to data constraints, the order of the lags that were selected are typically low; for the most part, they are of order two and three. This limitation can be easily remedied, if necessary, as data points accumulate.

THE CAPACITY UTILIZATION INDEX, S_j

Two measures of capacity utilization were constructed at the industry level. One was patterned after the Wharton School methods; and the

[11] E. Kuh and J. R. Meyer, "Correlation and Regression Estimates When the Data Are Ratios," *Econometrica*, October 1955.

[12] The particular Fisher lag used in the present study was selected by criteria developed and presented in an earlier monograph: Brown and Wachtel, *op. cit.*, pp. 72–73.

other makes use of a method developed by Daniel Creamer.[13] The Wharton School measure requires that trend lines be constructed through output peaks which represent potential output series; the ratio of actual to potential output forms the measure of capacity utilization. The Creamer method uses a minimum capital-output ratio as a capacity benchmark, and then specifies the ratio of benchmark minimum capital-output ratio to each annual capital-output ratio as the measure of utilization. In the present applications, both methods are modified in certain respects which are detailed in the data appendix to the Brown-Wachtel study. The two utilization series are quite different for most industries. The criteria used to select the index for the productivity relationships are discussed also in the Brown-Wachtel study. Suffice it to say here that the construction of two indexes and the selection of the one which performed in a superior manner was motivated by a desire to reduce the specification error inherent in capacity utilization variables.

The specification of the output variable in the capacity utilization measures raises again the possibility of spurious correlation. Yet, recognizing this deficiency, we decided to use them in the present study in lieu of an acceptable alternative. Clearly, additional work is required on the problem of specifying the capacity utilization variable.

EDUCATION, $X_{3,j}$

The education variable is a measure of the average attainment of formal education in the employed work force of each industry over the sample period. Measured simply in years per worker, it is an average measure of the stock of educational capital embodied or objectified in the employees of the industry.

The basic data from which the variable was constructed were taken from the 1/1000 household sample, 1960 Census tape, and the 1950 Census, PE1-C, "Occupation by Industry," Table 2, and "Occupational Characteristics," Table 10.

The key figure in the computation, the median years of education in the industries in 1960, was obtained by aggregating over the medians of the detailed (297 individual titles) occupations within each industry. There is considerable variation in the years of education within single

[13] The methods are described in *Measures of Productive Capacity*, Report of the Subcommittee on Economic Statistics, Joint Economic Committee, 87th Cong., 2d Sess., 1962.

occupations, depending upon the industry, and for that reason it was decided to construct the industry estimates from the complete education-by-occupation-by-industry block of data.

Since comparable data were not available for 1950, however, the rate of change within each industry had to be computed from the medians for each of the occupations, given without regard to industry. For each industry in 1950 and 1960, the number of employees in each occupational category was multiplied by the median years of school completed for that occupation, to give a "stock" of education for the occupation in that industry. The stock figures were then aggregated for the two groups for which annual employment data were available—production workers and nonproduction workers—for each industry.

A set of median-stock-of-education series was then computed, using the decade trends for each industry's production and nonproduction workers separately and the annual employment proportions for the two groups. Finally, the year-to-year proportional changes from that series were applied to the 1960 detailed industry and education stock figure. The resulting education series is in units of average years of education per worker, unweighted by income differentials. The improvement in the "quality" of labor brought about by education is taken to be directly proportional to median school years completed.

RESEARCH AND DEVELOPMENT, $X_{4,j}$

The problem of finding an empirical specification for research and development that would fit the fundamental variable in the model and at the same time match the other variables dimensionally was one of the most difficult tasks of this study. (We are far from satisfied with the measures upon which we settled.) The model calls for an estimate of the knowledge that results from research activity, in the form that affects measured labor productivity. That is, since we use a productivity measure based upon national income concepts, which is therefore downward biased to the extent that technological changes are reflected in new products and new distribution systems, etc., the measure of research and development should have been confined, if possible, to cost-reducing activities.

Two upward biases can be identified in the research data we found available. The first, directly related to what has been said above, arises from the fact that much research activity in American industry is directed to the development of new products and is therefore not relevant to the explanation of labor productivity which is defined in gross product terms.[14] The second comes from the shift from unreported, unorganized research to organized and explicitly budgeted activities. However, in view of the short period covered in this study, this would be of negligible importance.

On the other side, there are downward biases in the data. Many innovations occur in the form of organizational knowledge—for example, as improved work-flow layouts. These result in productivity increases, but are not likely to be based on measured research and development activity. But this is of minor importance compared to the downward bias in the published series, attributable to the international and inter-industry nature of technological knowledge. Obviously, the total flow of technological information which can be utilized by a given industry is in no way limited to what is produced within the industry's research facilities.

There is a kind of temptation offered by the fact that we can balance the biases in terms of direction, even though we are otherwise almost totally ignorant of their quantitative effects. Without pretending that we can cancel them off against one another, we do assume that increments of technological knowledge are proportional to the resources used for industrial research and development.

A second major, maybe heroic, assumption underlies the identification of each industry's research level. The second assumption is addressed to the part of innovational activity that is relevant to an industry's productivity but is not conducted in the industry itself. The activity in question may be carried out in those sectors that supply the given industry with structures, equipment, and materials. Improved processes and products in supplying industries will have cost-reducing effects among their customer industries. It is natural, in this light, to search for an interindustry measure of the flow of knowledge, corresponding to the diffusion or reverberations of technological improvements through the economy, which a number of writers have examined before. The basic data will be described first and then the input-output procedure will be outlined.

The industry data on research and development expenditures are pro-

---

[14] See Nestor Terleckyj, *Research and Development, Its Growth and Composition,* National Industrial Conference Board, 1963, p. 54.

vided by the National Science Foundation. From 1952 to 1956 the Bureau of Labor Statistics developed the data for the NSF, and from 1956 to the present the Bureau of Census has been responsible for the compilation. Differences between the two series are due to different industry classifications, differences in reporting, variations in responses from the same reporting entity, and different sampling and estimating methods. These discrepancies have not deterred several investigators— including the present authors—from attempting to link the two sets of time series. Putting the two together allows us to test the model on industry observations drawn from the period 1952–60.

Attempting to mitigate the unreliability of the basic research and development data, several forms of the variable were constructed and tested. A third-order Fisher lag in real research expenditures and the unlagged real expenditure series were both tried. In addition, a research intensity variable was prepared by averaging the real gross product– real research expenditure ratios for 1952 and 1960 for each industry. From these averages, dummy variables were constructed which had the effect of grouping the industry observations into three sets according to their relative research commitments. None of these specifications provided a satisfactory measure of the relevant cost-reducing inputs of research and development. Finally, an interindustry research variable was constructed in the following manner.

For each industry in the data sample an interindustry research weight was estimated, reflecting the cost-reducing possibilities carried by the major intermediate flows of goods in 1958. From the column of inputs into each industry, purchases (from manufacturing industries) that exceeded 1.2 per cent of the column total were recorded. Then, the ratio of the recorded flow to the delivering industry's output was listed, and these proportions were then applied to the delivering industries' research and development expenditures. A similar division was made of the receiving industry's own research expenditure and the two—the direct expenditure and the indirect sum of expenditures—were summed to give the industry weight. An illustration, from the computation for food and kindred products, is given in Table 1. The interindustry flows are taken from the 1958 Input-Output Study.[15]

[15] M. R. Goldman, M. L. Marimont, and B. N. Vaccara, "The Interindustry Structure of the United States," *Survey of Current Business*, November 1964, pp. 10–29 (the SCB numbers in the table are those used in the article). An alternative proposed by Mr. Terleckyj—to include as the "own-expenditure" contribution

TABLE 1

Interindustry Research Weight for Food and Kindred Products (SCB 14)

(1) Purchases by SCB 14 from: SCB 39 — Metal containers	$23.88 mill.
SCB 25 — Paperboard containers	13.81 mill.
(2) Proportion of delivering industry outputs: SCB 39	72.80%
SCB 25	24.20%
(3) Delivering industry's research expenditures: SCB 39	$13 mill.
SCB 25	$11 mill.
(4) Proportions applied to Food, (2) × (3): SCB 39	9.46
SCB 25	2.66
	————
	12.12
(5) Receiving industry's research expenditure	$83 mill.
(6) Receiving industry's delivery to itself, proportion:	16.20%
(7) Proportion of (5) applied to Food:	$13.45 mill.
(8) Interindustry research weight, (4) + (7):	25.57

The next step involved the construction of a time series of research expenditures to which the interindustry weights could be applied. Again, a data constraint presented itself, for reasonably reliable research expenditure data by industry extend only back to 1952. This is inadequate for the time series analysis, since it is well recognized that research expenditures are related to productivity with a lag, and the available industry research data is of insufficient length to permit a lag specification and still have a minimally acceptable number of degrees of freedom. In addition, the length or order of the lag is difficult to specify. The first problem was treated by assuming that the trend in the growth of knowledge in each industry is proportional to the trend in the non-

all of the industry's research expenditure, instead of the internal deliveries only— involves considerable double-counting and inflation in some sectors. We tried it in the procedure used for the Table 3 estimates, with the following results: The coefficients on education were rendered completely insignificant in both groups, though R^2 was improved in the nondurables. When the symmetrical procedure (see our Reply to the Comment below) was used, there was no significant difference between the results with the two research variants.

farm private domestic sector, which permitted us to use total industry research and development expenditure data covering the period 1921–60, derived by Nestor Terleckyj,[16] but adjusted to exclude government and farm expenditures.[17] The final series were deflated by a cost-of-research index developed by Ellis A. Johnson and Helen S. Milton.[18]

The determination of the distributed lag in research expenditures was accomplished by trial and error: i.e., we experimented with various lag structures and orders and selected the one that performed in a superior manner. This gave us an inverted-V, fifteen-year Fisher lag which has the impacts of each annual, real expenditure on research and development increase at the rate of 20 per cent up to the fifth year and decrease by 20 per cent annually thereafter to the fifteenth year.[19] The application of the interindustry weights to the time series variable provided us with a research variable that has two important characteristics: a lag in the impact of real research and development expenditures, and interindustry differences that reflect the diffusion of technological knowledge among industries. We discuss this further below.

Estimation Procedures and the Analysis of Covariance

The logic of the technological progress relationship, the econometric specification derived from the CES function, and practical constraints imposed by the multicollinearity in our short time series require that we turn to pooled data in order to estimate the elasticities attached to research and education. Reasonably sufficient evidence is available for the estimation of the elasticity of substitution, σ, and the short-run capacity utilization effect, a, in the individual industries. But the fundamental variables in time series present us with serious statistical and conceptual problems. First, the series for research and education move closely together, and the short-run variations, especially for education, are dominated by strong trends. Since World War II, especially, there have been upward pressures on both series due largely to government

[16] *Op. cit.,* p. 39.

[17] Brown and Conrad, *op. cit.*

[18] "A Proposed Cost-of-Research Index," Operations Research Office, Johns Hopkins University, Staff Paper ORO-SP-142, February 1961.

[19] The justification for specifying the fifth year as the year of major impact is derived from a McGraw-Hill survey reported by Terleckyj, *op. cit.,* p. 55n. The fifteen-year service life assumption emerged from experiments in which different service lives were specified; the one we selected performed best.

support of a national policy for technological change and the continuing high level of activity. The resulting high correlation makes it extremely difficult to distinguish between the influences of the two variables or to estimate their parameters with much precision.

Secondly, it is difficult to conceive of the technological progress function (13) as representing the structure within which short-run choices are made among the alternatives facing an individual decision maker (whether the unit is a firm or establishment or even, stretching several points, an industry). Short-run variation in the production-worker–overhead–worker ratio is feasible, of course, and in most industries would cause the education index to vary. But that variation is more likely to be based upon exogenous cyclical swings in production levels than upon a real substitution decision. Changes in the amount of education "embodied" in the labor force reflect relatively long-run decisions rather than responses to short-term fluctuation in the relative price of formal training. Over a short period of time, then, we should expect levels of education to vary much more *among* industries than within single-industry time series.

There is more obvious evidence of year-to-year variation in expenditures on research and development. Research budgets, though they have been increasing at an increasing rate during the postwar years, tend to be tied, in the short run, to lagged gross profit levels, for reasons of capital supply, and to movements in relative factor prices, in a Hicksian or neoclassical response to cost pressures.[20] But, given the lags between (1) industrial research outlays, (2) innovational results, if any, and (3) subsequent embodiment in equipment or organizational change, we should not expect the appropriate evidence for innovational influence to show up in the short-run covariation between industrial development expenditures and an index of productivity change. Again, however, differences in the level and trend of the fundamental variables among industries, indicating differences in innovational activity, can be expected to vary with the long-run trends in productivity.

Given these constraints, we decided to use pooled time series and cross-section data in order to test the hypothesis that the fundamental variables affect the parameters of the CES production function. When

---

[20] See E. Mansfield, "Industrial Research and Development Expenditures: Determinants, Prospects, and Relations to Size of Firm and Inventive Output," *Journal of Political Economy,* August 1964, on the first reason, and Brown and Conrad, *op. cit.,* on the second.

the time and industry data were pooled, there was a sufficient number of observations for the test and considerably enriched variation to justify some hope of precision. But from the outset, it was obvious that the industries were heterogeneous in their productivity relationship and that some extraneous estimating procedures would be needed. Actually, two alternative statistical specifications of equation (13) were tried in a regression procedure derived from the analysis of covariance by S. S. Wilks. The difference between the two forms is in the method used to adjust labor productivity for the effects of short-run capacity utilization and for the substitution of capital for labor.

In the unconstrained model, derived directly from equation (13), the effects of the fundamental variables, the short-run capacity utilization variable, and the long-run factor substitution variable are estimated over the whole set of observations. Productivity is to be explained by all four variables; and estimates of the parameters, fitted by the usual regression procedures (under the usual assumptions), are undifferentiated as to industry.

In the "constrained" model, the factor price and cycle effects on productivity are accounted for by individual time series analyses. The productivity variable is then adjusted for these effects and the residual variation is explained by the fundamental variables in a time series of manufacturing cross sections. Consider the new variable,

$$(14) \qquad z_{jt} = \log\,(X_0/X_1)_{j,t} - \hat{\sigma}_j \log \rho'_{j,\eta,t-\delta} - \hat{a}_j \log S_{jt}$$

where the $\hat{\sigma}_j$ and $\hat{a}_j$ coefficients have been extraneously estimated from single-industry data.[21]

---

[21] See Brown and Wachtel, *op. cit.*, for the procedure that was used to fit the industry coefficients. There is some asymmetry in the "constrained" model, in that the productivity variable is adjusted for factor price and cycle effects, but the explanatory variables are not.

Professors Malinvaud and Griliches have noted that if the explanatory variables are uncorrelated with ρ' and S, then the coefficients should not be biased, though the standard errors may be underestimated. Two additional experiments have since been tried: (1) using a pooled residual procedure to get round the problem of insufficient significance in the regressions of the individual-industry education and research variables on ρ' and s; and (2) a completely symmetrical procedure. In the first experiment, there was improvement in the t ratios and R^2 (corrected) for the durables group, with some exaggeration of the difference between the coefficients; in the nondurables, the t ratios were reduced and the R^2 (corrected) much reduced, with no essential change in the magnitudes. In the second, fully symmetrical case, there was very little change in the durables statistics, but the significance on the nondurables research variable was obliterated, along with the R^2 (corrected). The estimates, and an intuitive argument for preferring the original procedure, will be found in our Reply.

Almost from the first appearance of a production function fitted across industry data, it has been argued that no economic meaning can be attached to a regression surface fitted to industry points in a three-dimensional—value added, labor, capital—space. Industries are not decision-making units, allocating homogeneous resource inputs under equivalent profit-maximizing conditions. Secondly, as technological conditions and the composition of aggregate value added both change, it is unlikely that industries will retain their relative positions on the production surface; the fitted elasticities in the production function will then be unstable, however stable the component (micro-) relationships might be. In the present case, the first problem, with respect to the homogeneity of inputs, is partially met. The education variable is defined so as to give considerable comparability among industries; research and development activity is unfortunately more specific to the individual sectors. The second difficulty is more effectively met in our data, however; relative research intensities and educational attainments remain stable among the industries in our sample over the period under examination.

In addition to the specific short-run industry production parameters, it is expected that there will be other omitted variables which differ among industries, but which may or may not differ over time. The manufacturing industries present a basically heterogeneous sample. The fitted time series elasticities, then, which define the response of output per unit of labor to the quality of that labor and to the research expenditures within single industries, may vary significantly from sector to sector. We argued earlier, however, that the technological progress relationships are not to be defined meaningfully in terms of short-run variations: the economic significance of heterogeneity among the time series regression coefficients is therefore limited and much less compelling with respect to the estimation of our model than the formal tallies of heterogeneity in the F tests would imply. The important short-term microrelationships do enter the econometric model explicitly: individual capacity utilization and elasticity of substitution terms are entered with each observed point in the array. After the short-run adjustments have been made, it is assumed that the remaining variation is similar from industry to industry, when the fundamental variables have been entered, *except for a constant*. Following Hoch, we experimented with the use of individual-industry intercepts to pick up the differences with respect to omitted influences which are peculiar to each industry and independent of the included variables. The effectiveness of these procedures and the plausibility of these arguments can be considered again when we present the covariance results.

The analysis of covariance enters the present study in the estimation of the regression coefficients as well as in the testing of the model, first, for stability over time, and then, for homogeneity among the industries. Kendall [22] pointed out the relationship between variance analysis and regression analysis, following Fisher and Wilks. Then he extended the discussion to the analysis of covariance. The testing procedure, derived from Kendall and Mood, has been described in an econometric time series and cross-section setting by Kuh.[23]

Let us consider the simplest version of the problem at hand. We are trying to estimate the response of adjusted output per unit of labor (z) to the logarithm of inputs of education in the labor force (x_3). The observations in given slices of time across industries will yield the following moments:

$$(15) \quad \sum_{jt} (z_{jt} - z_{..})(x_{3,jt} - x_{3,..}) = \sum_{jt} (z_{jt} - z_{.t})(x_{3,jt} - x_{3,.t})$$
$$+ \sum_{t} (z_{.t} - z_{..})(x_{3,.t} - x_{3,..})$$

from which the pooled regression coefficient

$$\hat{h}_1 = \frac{\Sigma(z_{jt} - z_{..})(x_{3,jt} - x_{3,..})}{\Sigma(x_{3,jt} - x_{3,..})^2}$$

may be derived. The sum of squares of the deviations from the pooled regression equation may then be partitioned as follows:

$$(16) \quad \sum_{jt} (z_{jt} - h_t - h_1 x_{3,jt}) = \sum_{jt} (z_{jt} - \hat{h}_t - \hat{h}_1 x_{3,jt})^2,$$
$$+ \sum_{jt} (h_1 - h_1)^2 (z_{jt} - z_{.t})^2 + J \sum_{t} (z_{.t} - \hat{h}_t - h_1 \bar{x}_{3,.t})^2$$

where h_t is a single constant, which will be replaced in the final estimates by the individual-industry constants, and J is the number of industries in the cross section.

[22] M. G. Kendall, *The Advanced Theory of Statistics*, London, 1951, II, 237.
[23] E. Kuh, *Capital Stock Growth: A Micro-economic Approach*, 1963, Chaps. 5 and 6.

From the pooled data and the moments defined in (15), it is possible to estimate the constant of regression and the coefficient on x_3, by ordinary least squares, under the assumption that the effect of time is not significant. Then, by taking deviations from the cross-section or cell means, we can estimate individual regressions for the annual cross sections, which are needed to test the pooled estimates for stability over time. Finally, we may use the analysis of covariance to fit individual-industry intercepts.

For each cross section, the residual sum of squares may be written as follows:

$$(17) \quad \sum_j (z_{jt} - h_t - h_{1,t}x_{3,jt})^2 = \sum_j (z_{jt} - \hat{h}_t - \hat{h}_{1,t}z_{jt})^2 + (\hat{h}_{1,t} - h_{1,t})^2$$
$$\sum_j (x_{3,jt} - \bar{x}_{3,.t})^2 + J(\bar{z}_{.t} - h_t - \hat{h}_{1,t}x_{3,.t})$$

The sum of these residuals (reduced by appropriate degrees of freedom) over the span of years for which we have cross sections, becomes the denominator in the over-all test for heterogeneity. The numerator is the difference between the residual variation from the pooled regression and the total of the sums of squares just defined, i.e., $\sum_t \sum_j (z_{jt} - h_t -$ $h_{1,t}x_{3,jt})^2$. That is, the F-test numerator measures the variation from the ordinary least squares regression not taken into account already by the unrestricted cross-section regressions.

Should the test indicate that there is no significant heterogeneity among the time slices (as it did) we are justified in concluding that the pooling over time is a legitimate procedure. Either time is not directly associated with the dependent variable or, more likely, we have corrected or allowed for the short-run differences in the relation of interest by introducing the index of capacity utilization and the "neoclassical" deflated wage effect. There is, in particular, no reason to introduce individual *time* constants, nor to attempt to estimate individual slopes for each cross section.

An analogous set of tests can be made in the time series direction, to test for heterogeneity among industries. As the second over-all test (across the industry series) indicated considerable departure from homogeneity, we were faced with the possibility that the heterogeneity might be due to the regression coefficients or, if the slopes are equal, due to heterogeneous intercepts. Kuh, following Mood, turns the test question first to the linearity of the regression coefficients and then, conditionally, to the homogeneity of the intercepts. In the present case, the over-all F-test in the industry time series direction indicated extreme heterogeneity. Visual inspection left no doubt as to the possible equality or linearity of the slopes. But, since we do not consider the progress function to be a short-run relationship over time, we concluded that no serious weight could be given to the single-industry slopes in these short time series, whatever the F-test might have shown. It followed, then, that the time series F-test result should not prohibit pooling in the adjusted productivity relation and need not be taken to indicate that individual slopes on the fundamental variables should be fitted within the pooled data. What remained, however, was the possibility that the residual variation might be considerably reduced if the differences among industries—apart from the short-run cyclical and substitution effects—were allowed to enter in the form of individual industry constants.

Returning to the pooled moment matrix, $\sum_{jt} (z_{jt} - z_{..})(x_{3,\,jt} - x_{3,\,..})$, individual dummy variables were introduced into the data set in the following form:

$$X_{bj} = \begin{cases} 1 \text{ for each observation on industry } j \\ 0 \text{ for each observation on industries not } -j \end{cases}$$

The coefficients of each x_j in the regression are estimates of the differences due to unspecified variation in the "industry" variate. The "correction," then, for industry j, is [24]

(18) $$h_j = (z_j - \bar{z}_{..}) - \hat{\beta}_3(\bar{x}_{3,j} - \bar{x}_{3,..}).$$

Empirical Results

ALL INDUSTRIES POOLED, NO EXPLICIT RESEARCH EFFECT

We begin with the hypothesis that productivity in each industry is influenced in a systematic manner by variations in the long-run real wage rate, by shifts in the degree of capacity utilization, and by changes in educational attainments—all peculiar to the given industry. The first two forces are permitted to affect productivity uniquely in each industry, whereas the effect of the education variable, though differing from

[24] I. Hoch, *op. cit.,* p. 40.

industry to industry, is represented by a single parameter fitted across all industries (the research and development variable in (13) will be added subsequently). The statistical specification of the model can be represented symbolically by

$$(19) \quad z_{j,t} = (x_{0,j,t} - x_{1,j,t}) - \hat{\sigma}_j \rho_{\eta,t-\delta} - \hat{a}_j s_{j,t} = h_0 + h_1 x_{3,j,t} + u_{j,t}.$$

Logarithms are denoted by lower-case letters and by omitting the prime on ρ, which is the Fisher distributed lag in the deflated wage rate; the $u_{j,t}$ is a stochastic term interpreted in the error-in-equation sense. The extraneous estimates of the elasticities of substitution, $\hat{\sigma}_j$, and the capacity utilization coefficient, $\hat{a}_j$, were derived previously on an industry-by-industry basis from the same set of data used in the present study.[25] Consequently, the estimating form (19) recognizes explicitly the heterogeneity of the industries with respect to the cyclical and factor price variables. The effect of education is represented by h_1, which in the present form is common to all industries.

For pooled data (eight industries and eight years), the least squares estimate is

$$(20) \qquad z_{j,t} = -1.639 + \underset{(4.127)}{1.923} \ x_{3,j,t} \qquad \bar{R}^2 = .190.$$

The number in parenthesis is the t ratio for the estimate of b. Even though the coefficient on education is highly significant and has the correct sign, the variable explains less than 20 per cent of the increase in productivity. In other words, the education attainments variable cannot, by itself, explain a major part of the inter- and intra-industry variation in productivity after adjustments have been made for the effects of shifts in factor substitution and capacity utilization.

Not only is (20) inadequate in its explanatory power, but as may be seen in Table 2, the residual disturbances appear not to be independently distributed with constant variance. The time-slice cross-section standard errors give a clear impression of upward drift.

The implication of this heteroscedasticity is that we have omitted a systematic variable (or variables) which can account for more of the variation in adjusted productivity through time, as well as the differences in adjusted productivity among the industries. It will be seen that a

[25] See Brown and Wachtel, *op. cit.*

TABLE 2

Standard Errors of Estimate of Cross-Section Estimates of Equation (20)

Year	Standard Errors of Estimate (Unbiased)
1953	.1464
1954	.1525
1955	.1460
1956	.1588
1957	.1613
1958	.1651
1959	.1582
1960	.1695

proper specification of the research variable can explain much of the remaining variance.

Before turning to the research variable, however, it is necessary to test the pooled estimate of equation (20), in the light of the suggested heteroscedasticity. The covariance analysis test described in the previous section was applied to the time slices. The result, as shown by the analysis of covariance for over-all homogeneity in cross-sections of equation (20), below does not permit the rejection of the homogeneity hypothesis:

Variance Ratio	*Degrees of Freedom*		*Approximate Significance Points on Null Hypothesis*
	Numerator	Denominator	
.44	14	48	$F_{.05} = 1.90$

Conclusion: Over-all homogeneity hypothesis definitely accepted.

In spite of the appearance of a trend in the relationship among the industries, the conclusion of over-all homogeneity among the regression coefficients is definitely acceptable. The relationships did not vary significantly over time and the pooling of cross sections is justified. In the previous section we presented the economic reasons for not accepting a time series covariance test on the present body of data. Thus, for the moment, we accept the assumptions that permit pooling through time and across industries.

Let us return to (20) and hypothesize that the large residual variation is attributable mainly to *inter*industry differences that are not associated with different levels of educational attainments. If the remaining, unexplained variance can be identified with industry-linked, but otherwise unspecified, variables, then (19) should be specified with dummy variables as described at the end of the last section: A value of 1 is assigned to the first industry and zeros for the others, the next dummy assumes a value of 1 for the second industry and zeros for the others, and so on. Their inclusion in (19) yields:

$$(21) \qquad z_{j,t} = -.193 + \underset{(2.043)}{.507} \; x_{3,j,t} + \text{industry dummies} \qquad \bar{R}^2 = .990$$

(It is unnecessary to list the regression parameters on the dummy variables, since the point we wish to make does not require their quantitative examination. All but one of the coefficients on the dummy variables is significant.) The importance of (21) is that the inclusion of the dummies reduces the coefficient on education, though it is still significant at the .05 level, and exhausts nearly all of the residual variation produced by (20). Hence, the industry constants, which represent differences in level, are effective in accounting for the residual variation in the productivity equation after we have allowed for the effects of educational attainments. We can infer at this point that if research and development are relevant at all, their relevance must be in explaining these interindustry differences in adjusted productivity.

Before introducing the research variable into the model, we present the unconstrained analogue of (20); from equation (13):

$$(22) \quad (x_0 - x_1)_{j,t} = -.475 + \underset{(3.728)}{.432} \; \rho_{j,t-\delta} + \underset{(1.492)}{.297} \; s + \underset{(3.918)}{.877} \; x_{3,j,t}$$

$$\bar{R}^2 = .313$$

This regression cannot easily be interpreted as a structural estimate, since we are not justified in assuming slope homogeneity among industries with respect to the relative wage expression and capacity utilization. Having said that, we are encouraged to note that the signs are intuitively correct and that the two main parameter estimates are highly significant. But the coefficients on the wage rate expression and on the education variable are smaller than those in (20): The average of the elasticities of substitution used in the constrained productivity relation is .780, while that fitted in (22) is .432; and the coefficient on education in (20) is more than twice that obtained in the unconstrained regression. These are not stunning differences if we take into consideration the data deficiencies. But the direction of the difference between the elasticity of substitution estimates is surprising, since we should expect the estimate on the unconstrained productivity relation to be larger than the average of the estimates used in the constrained relation to the extent that the former embodies a cross-section effect.[26] It appears that the time series estimates of σ, adjusted for disequilibrium effects by the Fisher lag scheme, are longer-run estimates of the elasticity of substitution than the combined cross-section and time series estimate. Although this is ancillary to the principal problem under discussion, it has important consequences for the interpretation of time series and cross-section estimates.

EXPLICIT EDUCATION AND RESEARCH EFFECTS,
SUBGROUPS OF INDUSTRIES

In the preceding subsection we introduced the education attainments variable into the adjusted productivity equation and drew the conclusion that the research effect, if it is present at all, would manifest itself primarily in interindustry differences in adjusted productivity. This has the implication that the time profile of the research variable is of ancillary importance to the specification in terms of varying industry intensities.

In order to obtain reasonable estimates of both the research and the education elasticities in the adjusted productivity equation, it is necessary to focus on subgroups of industries within our total pooled sample, since the estimates with every research variable we specified were unacceptable when fitted in the total pooled sample. As we shall see below, the subgrouping of industries, though forced upon us, in the sense that we did not initially expect to disaggregate, has the serendipitous consequence of permitting us to offer some very interesting propositions.

A host of criteria for subgrouping industries was considered; we finally selected the durability of the final product as the grouping criterion, since this is relatively independent of the model. The selection of such a broad categorizing principle has the further advantage of allocating a sufficient number of industries in each subgroup to provide the estimates with some probability content. Following the Bureau of

[26] See Kuh, *op. cit.*, pp 182–83.

Census definitions, the sample was divided into subgroups: durable and nondurable industries. However, smaller groups were also used in certain experiments in order to assure that our principal conclusion is not conditional upon an arbitrary grouping. In many respects, the chemical industry is an uncongenial member of the nondurable group: it has a relatively high concentration ratio; more important, the coincidence of high mean ρ and extreme research expenditures yields an essentially spurious correlation between those variables within the nondurable data set (see footnote 29, below).

The specification of the adjusted productivity equation in the present experiments is

$$(23) \qquad z_{j,t} = h_0 + h_1 x_{3,j,t} + h_2 x_{4,j,t} + u_{j,t},$$

where h_1 and h_2, the effects of education and research, respectively, are common to each industry in the subgroup, and $u_{j,t}$ denotes that the model is subject to error. It is useful to recall at this point that the research variable, $x_{4,\,j,\,t}$, is represented by a fifteen-year inverted V distributed lag in real research and development expenditures with weights assigned to each industry according to the inflow of research from its supplying industries, including the industry itself; the proportions being taken from the supplying industries' input-output rows and from the own-industry diagonal cell. Estimates of the two subgroups are contained in Table 3.

TABLE 3

Estimates of Adjusted Productivity Equation (23) for Selected Durable and Nondurable Goods Industries, 1950-60

	Education x_3	Research x_4	Constant	$\overline{R}^2$	Degrees of Freedom
Durable goods:					
Fabricated metals, machinery,	1.236	0.300	−1.892	.844	41
primary metals, automobiles	1.585	5.432			
Nondurable goods:					
Food, chemicals, paper,	0.182	0.200	−0.358	.580	41
textiles	2.905	7.033			

As before, the numbers in parentheses in Table 3 represent the t ratios for the respective coefficients. Except for the estimate of the education coefficient in the durable goods equation, which is significant only at the .15 level, the parameter estimates are highly significant, as are the coefficients of determination. Moreover, the cofficients bear intuitively correct signs, and the $\bar{R}^2$'s are quite respectable for pooled data, although a not inconsiderable amount of variation remains unexplained. However, the estimates are acceptable in providing orders of magnitude of the effects of the fundamental variables.

The most striking aspects of these results is the relative magnitude of the effects of the fundamental variables in the durable and nondurable groups. The sum of the elasticities (the coefficients are elasticities, since the estimating equation is homogeneous of degree, $h_1 + h_2$) in durable goods is 1.536, whereas it is 0.382 in the nondurable industry regression. In view of the shortcomings of the data and analysis, we do not feel justified in asserting that economies of scale to the fundamental variables were present in the durable goods industries while diseconomies existed in the other group. All we can say is that a given percentage increase in education and research in both sets of industries produces a substantially larger percentage increase in the adjusted productivity of durable goods than in the other set. Although there is some variation in the estimated elasticities when different groupings are specified, in general the same result emerges; e.g., the sum of the elasticities is significantly lower for chemicals and textiles, treated as a group, than the sum for fabricated metals, machinery, and primary metals, when those three industries are pooled. We conclude that this represents a persistent pattern in our data and that it is not an arbitrary artifact of our grouping procedure.[27]

How can we explain this pattern? Why do the fundamental variables tend to have larger elasticities in durable goods industries than in nondurable goods industries? The following consideration makes a considerable amount of sense to us, but nevertheless is offered in a tentative manner.

Suppose we have two groups of industries; in one group the industries are strongly coupled to each other, and in the other, they are less strongly coupled. Coupling strength is measurable by the size of the off-diagonal

---

[27] We did not run a covariance test to determine whether the estimates of the two groups differed from each other at a given significance level, since this is apparent by inspection.

elements in a matrix of input-output coefficients. For our present purposes there is no need to develop this further; suffice it to say that coupling strength represents the extent to which industries are "connected" to each other in a trading nexus. Now, the more strongly coupled are the industries in a group, *cet. par.*, the greater will be the percentage increase in productivity as a result of a given percentage change in the education and research in that group of industries.[28] For the stronger the coupling, the larger will be the *multiplier* of the fundamental variables, i.e., the research and education in one industry induce larger percentage increases in productivity in other industries in the group than if the coupling were weaker. Stated another way, the larger is the coupling, the more research and education will filter through the system to increase the time path of productivity in the highly coupled industries. Moreover, large diagonal coefficients work in the same direction, for the larger is the own research and education, the greater will be the impact on own measured productivity.

It is a straightforward matter now to rationalize the pattern of our results. We need only mention that our durable-nondurable goods distinction essentially conforms to a grouping of industries according to their degree of coupling: highly coupled industries in durables and less strongly coupled industries in nondurables.[29] Hence, the relatively large effect of the fundamental variables in the durable goods industries is probably attributable to the fact that they are more closely linked, and that the diffusion of the results of education and research is therefore more effective than among the industries in the nondurable category.[30]

When we turn to the relative sizes of the fundamental variables, we see that within the durables industries, the estimate of the education

[28] Analogous arguments have been put forward by R. M. Goodwin, "Dynamical Coupling with Especial Reference to Markets Having Production Lags," *Econometrica*, June 1947, pp. 181–204; in an international trade setting by M. Brown and R. Jones, "Economic Growth and the Theory of International Income Flows," *Econometrica*, 1962, p. 88; and to explain historical diffusion of technological change, in A. H. Conrad and J. R. Meyer, *The Economics of Slavery*, Chicago, 1965, Chap. 4, "Income Growth and Structural Change."

[29] By the coupling criterion, chemicals should have been included in the highly coupled group. When it is, the difference in the sums of elasticities of the fundamental variables between the two groups is augmented, thus lending support to our hypothesis. However, the estimates of the fundamental variables in the diminished nondurable group (food, paper, and textiles) have unacceptably high standard errors.

[30] The difference in degree of market imperfection between the two groups, raised in discussion by Mr. Weisbrod, is discussed briefly in our Reply to his Comment.

elasticity is four times as large as the research elasticity, whereas in the nondurables group the two elasticities are almost equal. Two explanations suggest themselves; both need further exploration. First, the education variable is specified as affecting only the own-industry's productivity. If it does have an interindustry effect, our failure to incorporate that effect into the model constitutes a misspecification and should, in particular, bias the elasticity estimate upward in direct relationship to the degree of coupling. Second, and perhaps more important, is the possibility that we are misspecifying by assuming that the two effects are additive. Some of the measured elasticity of response to education may in fact be due to the relationship between the two fundamental variables. Again, the degree of coupling would multiply the bias.

What are the marginal effects of the fundamental variables on adjusted productivity? These can be obtained from (23) and Table 3 by

$$\text{(24)} \qquad \partial z_{i,t}/\partial x_{3,j,t} = \hat{h}_1(\bar{z}_{j,t}/\bar{x}_{3,j,t})$$

$$\text{(25)} \qquad \partial z_{j,t}/\partial x_{4,j,t} = \hat{h}_2(\bar{z}_{j,t}/\bar{x}_{3,j,t}),$$

where the bars indicate geometric means (since the arithmetic mean of a variable in logarithms is the geometric mean of the variable). The expressions (24) and (25) represent the marginal productivities of the fundamental variables—i.e., they are estimates of the marginal returns in terms of adjusted productivity change resulting from the change in education or research. They are evaluated for both sets of industries in Table 4.

TABLE 4

Adjusted Marginal Productivities of Fundamental Variables in Two Groups of Industries

	Adjusted Marginal Productivities	
	Education	Research
Durable goods: Fabricated metals, machinery, primary metals, automobiles	.197	.053
Nondurable goods: Food, chemicals, paper, textiles	.046	.009

If, as these estimates indicate, the marginal productivities of education and research in durables exceeded the marginal productivities of the respective variables in the nondurable group, then—overlooking the possibility of significant monopoly gains—it would appear that resources devoted to these activities were malallocated in the period under consideration. A preferable allocation would have had resources in these activities shifted to the durable group from the nondurable group.

From this and our discussion of the elasticities in Table 3, a Bohm-Bawerkian implication emerges: that inputs of education and research will have greater yields among industries with more roundabout linkages than in the less closely coupled, in this case nondurables, sectors. Our conclusion holds, a fortiori, if research and development efforts in the nondurables group may be more closely directed to new-product development and promotion than to cost reduction.

The reference to shifting of resources moves us to advise, as a final note, that a shift in the direction of more work along the lines developed in the present paper would yield substantial returns, especially if the framework we developed were confronted with superior data. It may then be possible to measure the effects of the fundamental variables in the unconstrained model, just as we have made a first attempt to do so with the constrained model.

COMMENT

NESTOR E. TERLECKYJ, Bureau of the Budget

Brown and Conrad have constructed a model, built on a CES production function, which they propose for analysis of the relationship between productivity on the one hand, and education of the labor force and the amount of research and development activity on the other. They illustrate its use by applying it to a body of annual data for ten industries and ten years.

In my view, there are two particularly noteworthy features in the paper. One, of course, is the explicit treatment of education and research as variables affecting productivity, and the second is a novel specification of the R&D variable.

I will discuss first the results obtained within the framework which the authors set for themselves, then their framework itself, and finally the authors' specification of the R&D variable. The latter may well constitute a significant innovation, but probably for measuring the impact of outside R&D on an industry in addition to the industry's own R&D, and not as the authors use it to replace an industry's own research as a variable influencing its productivity.

The Authors' Results

The authors work with a productivity equation in which the value added per man-hour—with adjustment for the real wage rate together with the elasticity of substitution and for capacity utilization—depends in the following manner on the years of schooling of the labor force and the amount of R&D conducted by the industry's suppliers: [1]

$$\frac{X_0}{X_1} \cdot \frac{1}{W^\sigma} \cdot \frac{1}{S^a} = h_0 X_3{}^{h_1} X_4{}^{h_2}$$

The constant, h_0, represents a conglomerate of the various parameters of the CES production function. This form is linear in the logarithms. One question I have about this equation, is that it may be subject to distortions in the case of industries whose suppliers conduct very little or no R&D ($X_4 = 0$).

At first, Brown and Conrad estimate the equation with the educational variable only. In their initial attempt with both education and R&D, the authors report that they were not able to get reasonable estimates of the coefficient for the R&D variable fitted across the board.

They looked for groupings of industries which would give them more "acceptable" estimates of this parameter. After some exploration they settled on the grouping of industries by the durability of the product. This did give them statistically significant and presumably economically acceptable estimates of the parameter. Their solution was one way of handling the situation. There is no reason why the authors should have pursued all the possible alternatives. However, in the light of their earlier approach with the education variable only, I am puzzled why they did not at this stage use dummy variables for industries, which perhaps would have given them one acceptable estimate for the R&D coefficient.

[1] X_0 is output value added; X_1—man-hours; W—the real wage rate, Fisher-lagged; σ—the elasticity of substitution; S—capacity index; A—a parameter; X_3—median years of schooling of employees; and X_4—the amount of R&D as defined.

The authors stress the differences in the estimated magnitudes of the regression coefficients for research and education variables between the durable and nondurable goods industries. I think that they overstate the case. Actually the coefficients are not that different from each other. For the research variable, they are quite similar, and one of the coefficients for the educational variable is not significant at the .05 level. Aside from the various possible questions regarding errors in the data and the use of the annual figures for estimating these long-run relationships (the R&D variable is lagged over fifteen years) a formal test would evidently show that the 2σ intervals for both pairs of coefficients would overlap.

The Authors' Approach

I think the main limitation of the approach as finally [in estimating equation (23)] used by the authors, is that it does not lend itself well to analysis of changes in productivity over time, especially over longer periods, because it does not allow for a residual time trend, or change, in productivity. But it can be modified to serve that purpose, including some techniques explored by the authors elsewhere in the paper.

Essentially we are interested in explaining the unexplained residual in economic growth. Starting with the concept of inputs which include man-hours and services of the capital stock or some equivalent, and which leave a large residual, we add education and research (and maybe other variables), and reduce the residual. But we do not necessarily eliminate it completely. Also, the growth of output as conventionally measured is probably understated (in different degrees in different industries), and this bias is correlated with time (not necessarily in a simple manner). Therefore, it is important to have in the model an unexplained time residual in order better to estimate the effects of other factors.

For example, among the variables not included in the model there may be economies of scale at the plant or process level, and also economies of scale from the growth of industries which permit more efficient industrial specialization.

The data base is narrow. Given the authors' data and their final estimating form, the model is heavily oriented to the interindustry differences and not to changes over time.

The model also places a burden on the education and research variables as measured. For example, the authors argue for inclusion of R&D as a proxy variable for the flow of technologically relevant knowledge. I would prefer to view the flow of R&D expenditure as a form of capital investment. The organized and reported R&D probably cannot be stretched to cover all the technologically relevant knowledge but only a part of it.

Related to the data problem is a question of research strategy. While conceptually a CES formulation is preferable, it has at present a narrow data base and requires elaborate estimates (including those of elasticity of substitution) which are subject to errors. If CES estimates of productivity can be approximated by other procedures (e.g., using Cobb-Douglas functions or indexes of total factor productivity as developed by Kendrick), then a choice can be made between much more extensive coverage of real phenomena and the a priori preferable functional form.

Given a wider choice of data the approach of Brown and Conrad can be extended to cover longer periods. To be sure, some of the data, particularly those for research and development, are quite sketchy for earlier years, but the differences in the R&D level between industries have been very large (several orders of magnitudes), and the rates of growth in R&D have also been very high. Consequently, considerable lack of precision in the R&D estimates can be tolerated. Actually, I think that trading off the more precise but limited annual data covering a short period for perhaps less precise data for several periods [2] covering sufficient time for the underlying relationships to become manifest, is at least worth a try. Also the technique should allow for effects of factors not entered explicitly into the analysis. This could be done by various procedures allowing for separate equations (and/or intercepts) for the different periods and perhaps industries or sectors.

Brown and Conrad estimate large effects of education and R&D on adjusted productivity. A 1 per cent increase in the amount of research and development as measured is associated with a 0.2 or 0.3 per cent increase in the adjusted productivity. These estimates reflect primarily the interindustry variations.

I would like to cite here some of the estimates which I have obtained on an earlier occasion, relating research intensity to the rate of growth

[2] Or technological "epochs" as used by M. Brown and J. S. de Cani in "A Measure of Technological Employment," *Review of Economics and Statistics,* November 1963.

of industry productivity.[3] These estimates are also based on interindustry differences but cover a longer time period. Although the two formulations are not directly comparable, my estimates imply much smaller effects of R&D on productivity. These results also indicate the type of unexplained residuals associated with time periods that might be encountered in long-term analysis of the rate of growth in productivity.

Using Kendrick's data for nineteen two-digit manufacturing industries, I have calculated a number of regressions relating the average annual rate of growth in total factor productivity to the research intensity, defined as a ratio of research inputs to the total inputs. A measure of the amplitude of the cyclical fluctuations which these industries had experienced was also included in these equations. These in effect were cross-section regressions aimed at explaining the interindustry differences in the rate of productivity growth over the period 1919–1953, and two shorter subperiods. The results, shown in the tabulation below, suggests that a

Period	Constant	Log (R&D)/I (research intensity)	A (measure of cyclical amplitude)	R^2
1919–53	0.74	0.69 (4.85)	−0.06 (1.82)	.55
1919–37	2.49	0.77 (2.84)	−0.12 (1.97)	.30
1948–53	−2.96	1.26 (2.95)	−0.05 (0.44)	.28

tenfold difference in the research intensity was associated with a difference of roughly one percentage point in the annual rate of growth of industry productivity.[4] There were large differences in the constant of the regression, depending on the period, implying large effects of other factors.

The Specification of the R&D Variable

The novel treatment of the R&D variable introduced by the authors involves attributing the real R&D expenditures [5] as input not to the

---

[3] "Sources of Productivity Advance. A Pilot Study: Manufacturing Industries, 1899–1953," unpublished Ph.D. dissertation, Columbia University, 1960.

[4] The t values are in parentheses.

[5] Lagged over fifteen years. I am in perfect agreement with the authors regarding the lagging procedure.

industry which makes the outlays but to its customers (including itself) in proportion to purchases in the input-output matrix. This approach promises a possibility of measuring the benefits of R&D conducted elsewhere; however, this external effect should be counted in addition to the impact of own R&D on the industry's productivity, but not to replace the internal input, as was done by the authors.

The main reason why the authors undertake this adjustment is that in their view the research and development activities directed toward new or improved products do not find any reflection in the measured growth of output. While the output measures are probably biased, we have no evidence to assume that this bias is total. In fact, we do not even know whether the bias is more, or less, than one-half. Certainly, some of the new-product research finds its way into the value added in the form of higher profits and possibly higher wages. There is no need to assume a total bias. Eventually, the correct remedy should be to improve the output data rather than to eliminate new-product R&D from the input. We need more fundamental work on the "utility-oriented" measures of output. Noting this, of course, is not of much help in reviewing the present paper. Nevertheless, I think it is a valid point. Business-financed R&D, at least, is essentially no different from capital investment and, aside from possibly higher risk premiums, is decided upon by about the same set of considerations as any other investment. Consequently, the R&D expenditure should be treated similarly to fixed capital investment.

A few more technical points: While it provides a good starting point, the input-output matrix is a rather indiscriminate device to distribute R&D effects. It reflects all types of purchases. While the R&D conducted by suppliers of the intermediate materials too may influence productivity of the purchasing industry, its effect may be expected to be smaller than the effect of R&D conducted by suppliers of the industry's capital goods. Moreover, on the output side, the return to capital and profits enters into value added while the intermediate purchases do not. Also, the transformation carried out by the authors does not take into account R&D conducted outside of the manufacturing sector. Finally, there may also be a question about the use of the constant input-output weights taken from the 1958 matrix for the long periods, but I do not know how serious it may be.

Let me now state what I would consider a more complete treatment of R&D as a variable which affects output and productivity. I think it is very important to distinguish between the internal and the external R&D inputs. These two should enter as separate variables. One is a direct input and the other an external economy. Using the authors' notation, I would test the following productivity function

$$\frac{O}{I} = F(X_3, X_{4A}, X_{4B}; T)$$

with the productivity ratio as defined by the authors, or its empirically acceptable approximation estimated otherwise, and with time treated parametrically.

The first R&D variable, X_{4A}, would be the direct R&D undertaken by the industry in order to reduce unit cost or to develop new or better products, and should show up in properly measured real value added. If output measurement is deficient, it should be improved, but R&D undertaken by the industry is a valid investment input.[6] This, after some suitable time aggregation, I would consider direct input paid for by the sponsoring industry (possibly including the government-sponsored R&D done by the industry).

In addition to these internal inputs, I would consider external R&D inputs (X_{4B}). These, I would estimate as the authors estimated their X_3, but excluding the industry's own R&D part. This second variable would probably have a longer time lag. I would also like to test the hypothesis that the R&D conducted by the suppliers of capital goods has a different effect on productivity of an industry than the R&D done by the suppliers of intermediate goods.

In summary, I am inclined to see the principal contribution of the Brown and Conrad paper in the exploration of a series of techniques to deal with education and R&D as inputs, which the authors try, particularly the use of separate intercepts, and the specification for measuring the impact of outside R&D. The empirical results which the authors show, however, are to be considered of an exploratory nature, mainly because their time period is quite short and, consequently, the inter-industry variation is used to estimate time-process relationships. But

[6] Since the R&D data are reported on a company basis and all the other variables on an establishment basis, I would consider (for the more recent periods) making some use of the product line R&D data, published by the National Science Foundation, to obtain closer approximation to the establishment concept.

the paper does raise a number of meaningful questions which are subject to treatment by further research.

BURTON A. WEISBROD, University of Wisconsin

The resurgence of interest in the sources of economic growth has led to investigation of a number of variables other than traditional labor (man-hours), and capital that might explain the "unexplained residual" in observed U.S. economic growth. Among the variables receiving particularly augmented attention have been education and research.

A number of researchers have attempted to explore the impact of rising educational attainments on labor productivity by examining the differential earnings experience of persons similar in several respects but differing in level of educational attainment (LEA). Then, differential earnings—perhaps adjusted downward for the hypothesized effects of ability differentials which are believed to be correlated positively with LEA—can be taken as an approximate measure of the effects of education on labor productivity. Presumably in this way the effects of education on the value of a worker's *marginal* productivity are measured—if there are reasonably competitive labor and output markets and if equilibrium is approximated in these markets.

While this line of investigation has merit, alternative approaches are also needed. Professors Brown and Conrad utilize an aggregate production function model that incorporates education and also research inputs. With respect to education, this approach, as distinguished from the incremental earnings approach I briefly sketched above proceeds directly to the production function to seek the influence of education embodied in the labor force. After all, if schooling does contribute to labor productivity, then the effects of additional schooling of the labor force should appear in real output figures, whether or not it appears in the labor earnings data that serve the incremental earnings approach. Thus, in principle the Brown-Conrad approach appears to be superior to the incremental earnings approach, although we do not have to choose either one *or* the other.

Some of the comments that follow about this most stimulating paper deal with the model employed and its assumptions; some deal with the statistical results and their interpretation; but most of the comments deal with the ways that variables are measured. In raising some preliminary questions about the model's assumptions I do not intend to imply that "realism" of assumptions is a necessary condition of a useful model. However, without much evidence regarding the predictive accuracy of the behavioral and technological relationships that the model assumes, reference to the accuracy of assumptions seems warranted.

The Model

To begin with, the assumptions that perfect competition prevails in labor markets and in output markets, and that profit maximization is the goal of firms in each industry—assumptions implied by the hypothesized equalization of the marginal productivity of labor with the deflated wage rate (the ratio of factor price to output price)—must surely be subject to some eyebrow raising. Automobiles are one of the industries investigated: perfectly competitive? In addition, the degree of imperfection probably varies from industry to industry in both input and output markets, thus tending to affect differentially the input coefficients estimated for various industries. And since expenditures on research may well be related positively to the degree of monopoly power, a further bias is introduced.

In any event it is difficult to reconcile the perfect competition, profit maximization assumptions with the authors' statement of their principal conclusion—that the allocation of resources could have been improved had education and research resources been re-allocated from nondurable goods industries to durable goods industries during the 1950–60 decade. If perfect competition did prevail we would expect each resource to move until the values of its marginal product were equalized in all uses (and equalized with factor price). Why, then, would any misallocation remain? Although the authors did not take up this question, there appear to be three possible answers. (1) There might be differentials between durable goods and nondurable goods industries in the magnitudes of uncaptured real external benefits; (2) there might be differentials in extent of decreasing costs that tended to cause durable goods industries to operate at relatively suboptimal levels compared with nondurable goods industries; and (3) there might be differential lags in the adjustment process in the two types of industries.

These potential reasons for nonoptimalities are important; for, since there is no particular reason to believe that the interindustry distribution of externalities, or of decreasing costs, or of adjustment lags is very different today from what it was in 1950–60, the authors' conclusion that resources in education and research were misallocated in that decade suggests misallocation today. In short, Brown and Conrad are saying that a *systematic* tendency exists for relatively too little of these resources to flow into durable industries, and too much into nondurables.

Yet they offer no reason for believing that such a tendency exists. They do not argue that real externalities from education and research were and are generally more prominent in durable goods industries. Nor do they assert that durable goods industries have more generally decreasing costs than do nondurable goods industries. If they had, this would be a sufficient explanation for finding nonoptimal allocations—along traditional neoclassical lines. However, while this argument would suggest that the level of output should be expanded in these industries, it would not suggest that the level of any particular input, such as education or research, should be increased. There are obviously other means for inducing expansion in decreasing cost industries, and the presumption is still in favor of a lump-sum subsidy rather than a research or education subsidy.

If lags in adjustment to changing marginal value productivities of education and research varied systematically between durable and nondurable goods industries, this, too, would be a sufficient explanation for finding nonoptimalities, but neither is this argued by Brown and Conrad. In short, it is difficult to understand what economic theory underlies what seems to be their view that research and education are systematically underutilized in certain industries and overutilized in others.

There are a few other aspects of the model to which I would like to call brief attention.

1. Lags are assumed to exist in the process of adjustment to wage rate variation. However, the theoretical justification for the particular lag structure that is used is not clear, nor is it clear why adjustment lags, if they are relevant, should not also apply to the firm's employment of other inputs. Brown and Conrad note that labor productivity may not always be in instantaneous equilibrium at the given wage rate. Similarly, other productivities may not always be in equilibrium at their respective prices.

2. The model—or, at least, its current applied form—assumes implicitly that the levels of research and development expenditures and the (median) educational attainments of the labor force in each industry are

determined exogenously. Yet, the spirit of the decision-making process underlying the model—one of profit maximization—suggests that labor, capital, research, and education inputs should all be determined jointly. It seems that the authors' model which they select to estimate—namely, equation (13)—involves a questionable specification of economic behavior.

3. With regard to R&D, it is quite probably true, as the authors state, that the effect of R&D on labor productivity does depend upon the *stock* of knowledge; but since we know so little about the *durability* of productivity-increasing knowledge—or, in fact, about how to go about analyzing it—I can fully understand why they try to avoid estimating that stock. Thus they treat the relevant R&D measure as a current flow rather than as a stock. Yet one can only agree with their statement that "this involves some misspecification." And, unfortunately, one cannot avoid the issue, even if one can evade it by assuming, *implicitly,* that the stock is irrelevant.

4. One other aspect of the model merits particular emphasis, because it relates to some later remarks about the interpretation of the Brown-Conrad findings. Equation (3) and its subsequent description make it clear that the Brown-Conrad measure of "labor productivity" permits measured productivity to change *both* when a *shift* occurs in the production function for some commodity, *and* when a movement occurs *along* an unchanging production function that exhibits increasing returns— because of increasing returns to scale or increased capacity utilization. I shall suggest later that the use of a productivity measure that blends both kinds of effects may have led the authors to an unwarranted inference from their statistical findings.

5. Finally, it is worthwhile at least to raise the question of the appropriateness of a CES form of production function for every "industry"— no matter at what level of aggregation. Little attention to this question was given in the paper, although the empirical work implies that the authors feel the CES form is appropriate for the broadly conglomerate two-digit industries with which they dealt.

The Empirical Work

Moving from the conceptual form of the model to its empirical counterpart we face particularly intriguing questions about the proposed measures of $X_{3,j}$ and $X_{4,j}$, the educational input and R&D input, respectively.

The education variable, $X_{3,j}$, is a weighted average of median years of formal schooling per employee in industry j. The assumption that the median amount of schooling is the best measure of educational inputs is open to question on a variety of grounds. For one thing, a mean—arithmetic or perhaps geometric—would give a more accurate picture of total educational inputs than does a median. It is true that data availability may dictate using medians; however, their use may introduce a bias.

In addition the use of only a measure of central tendency, with no measure of dispersion, implies that *all* years of schooling—whether the fourth year, eleventh, or nineteenth—are perfect substitutes in production—i.e., have equal marginal value productivities. Two industries in a single year, or one industry in two different years, with the same median years of schooling per worker have, according to Brown and Conrad, the same educational inputs, although one industry might have all workers at the median while the other had some very highly educated workers and some workers with very limited schooling. To imply, as the authors do, that these two situations are equivalent seems very questionable. In fact, such an assumption flies in the face of the findings of other research, that substantial variation exists in the earnings differentials associated with various incremental years of schooling.

In addition, the productivity of a given incremental year of schooling is probably different according to when the education was received, as measured by the age of the worker. The expansion of knowledge alone tends to make more recent schooling more valuable. If one considers some sort of *value* weights for educational inputs, as an alternative to the simple median years of schooling, one probably comes to share my skepticism about the latter measure. For example, if the authors had considered *cost* (expenditure) weights—as they did implicitly for research—they would have recognized the considerable increase in cost of a year's schooling as the level of schooling rises.

Even apart from these questions about the homogeneity of years of schooling, that is, even if the function relating output per worker to median years of schooling per worker were log-linear within each firm —indicating that any year of schooling embodied in a worker is equivalent to any other year embodied in that or another worker—it would not follow that the *same* linear functions would apply to all firms in all of the component industries of the broad, two-digit industry groupings the authors treat. But unless each of the firms in each industry does have a similar production function a finding that the coefficients of the education (or research) input differs considerably among industries tells us nothing about whether these inputs should, for greater efficiency, have been re-allocated *among* industries rather than *within* industries. However, such a recommendation is precisely what Brown and Conrad make. They write: "A preferable allocation would have had resources in [education and research] shifted . . ." *to* the industries with high coefficients and *from* those with lower coefficients.

This noteworthy conclusion about efficient resource allocation is, according to the authors, an implication of the "main conclusion" of their empirical investigation. Yet, to repeat, for this conclusion to follow logically, a number of assumptions must be made. (1) It must be true that all years of schooling are perfect substitutes in production for all industries—i.e., all years of schooling have equal marginal value productivities; otherwise, it would be necessary to specify *which* years of schooling should have been shifted, and the Brown-Conrad model cannot specify this. (2) It must be true that all firms within the two-digit industrial classes must have approximately the same value of the marginal product (VMP) of education and VMP of research functions; otherwise internal shifts within industries might be preferable to shifts between industries. (3) It must be true—at least in the long run when the stock of education is a variable—that all years of schooling for workers in all industries must have the same cost of production; otherwise it would be wrong to reallocate resources in education so as to train more workers for the industries in which the VMP of a year of schooling is highest. However, the authors do not even mention the *cost* of producing educated people.

I turn now to the R&D variable, $X_{4,j}$. The measure of R&D proposed by the authors represents a most interesting and imaginative proxy for the flow of R&D effects between industries. It is quite clear that the research from which an industry benefits—in the sense that its average production costs are reduced—may bear little relationship to the research it performs. Therefore, Brown and Conrad sought to devise a research variable that would reflect this fact. Under certain conditions the measure they have produced—one which assumes that the benefits of research flow along with and in proportion to, the flow of industry sales to other industries—is appropriate and creative. This is the case, for example, when one industry performs research that it sells to another—either directly as research or advice, or indirectly, as when it sells goods in an improved form that makes the goods easier to handle or process. In such cases, which involve a change in the customer-industry's production function, the flow of transactions is a useful measure of the first industry's contribution to the customer-industry's labor productivity.

However, not all research expenditures have such effects in the customer industries. Some research is not effective at all; some research is not cost-reducing, but is, as Brown and Conrad recognize, quality-changing. Some research—such as that on improved processes—may be cost-reducing only for the supplying industry, having no effect whatsoever on costs in the customer industries. Thus, the authors have overstated when they assert that improved processes and products in supplying industries *will* have cost-reducing effects among their customer industries. There *may* be such effects, but there need not be. To the extent that less than 100 per cent of research expenditures is cost-reducing in customer industries, the Brown-Conrad method of allocating all research among industries in accordance with interindustry trading patterns allocates too much research expenditures to some industries and too little to others. The effect is to bias the industry research coefficients in some unspecified way. More study is needed of the degree to which research expenditures by one industry redound to the advantage of other industries with which it trades, or even of industries with which it does not trade. Yet, even if the Brown-Conrad research measure is not the last word, it is worthy of further consideration.[1]

A conceptual difficulty arises here in deciding what should be meant by the expression, "cost-reducing effects among customer industries." As the authors use the term "cost-reducing," they mean as noted previously, either that the production functions for customer industries shift outward, or that movement occurs along existing production functions that exhibit increasing returns—because of scale economies or excess

[1] It is interesting to note that what the authors term the "fundamental" variables, research and education, are not treated in parallel fashion. While each industry's research input is estimated to be net of its outflow of research embodied in sales to other industries, and gross of its inflow of research embodied in purchases from other industries, the education input is simply a function of each industry's own use of educated workers.

capacity. A potentially serious problem arises from their inclusion of the latter—movement along a production function—in their concept of "cost-reducing." To see why, consider the following two cases:

In case 1, industry A performs additional research, or employs better-educated workers, with the result that the production cost of the widgets that A sells to industry B falls. (I shall assume that the quality of widgets is unaffected.) In the first instance, labor productivity in industry A will rise, its production function having shifted. Productivity in industry B will also rise—provided that all of the following three conditions are met: (1) A must cut the price of widgets (which it may not do if competition is inadequate); (2) B must then proceed to cut the price of its output; and (3) the resulting expansion of B's output—assuming nonzero price elasticity—must bring either scale economies or use of excess capacity. If any of these three conditions fails to be met, productivity (as Brown and Conrad measure it) will not rise in industry B as a result of the measured rise in research or education inputs by A. Incidentally, as the authors measure research inputs (but for some unstated reason, not education inputs) the increased research expenditures by A would be partially allocated to industry B. Thus, if any of the three conditions just enumerated were not met, industry B would be shown by Brown and Conrad to have increased its research inputs but not its labor productivity.

Assume, however, that all three conditions are met, with the result that measured productivity in B, as well as in A, rises as a consequence of the initial increase in research by A. Note that in this case, productivity in A rises because of a *shifting* production function—although productivity might also be affected by a movement along the new function, if sales increased—but productivity in B rises only because of a movement along its original production function. Note also that depending on the price elasticity of demand for B's output, the expansion of B's output could bring a contraction in output in some other competing industry, C, with accompanying effects on its productivity.

Next, consider an alternative case in which A sells no output to other manufacturing industries like B, but sells only to retail stores or to the final-demand sector. As in the first case, real productivity in A would rise because of the production function shift. If we retain the assumption that industry A cuts its price, then, if price elasticity of demand is less than unity (in absolute value), consumers will spend less on A; and demand for products of some other industries—call them D—will rise correspondingly. Such an expansion of demand will bring increased productivity in D (as Brown and Conrad measure productivity) insofar as scale economies or unused capacity brings reduced unit costs even with a given production function. But recall that an expansion of output, rather than a shift in the production function, was also what brought the increased productivity in industry B in case 1.

In other words, a cost-reducing innovation in one industry can bring about a rise in average labor productivity in other industries if the industries are connected—whether via *trading* relationships or via *consumer budgets,* even when there are no real external effects. In the trading-connected industries, the productivity change in A may trigger a price reduction to B and, hence, a downward shift in B's marginal cost function, with a resulting expansion of output by B. Alternatively, in the budget-connected industries, the change in A may trigger a shift in demand for some other industry's output, and this, in conjunction with its declining cost curves, would tend to produce a falling price in B and a rising output. Thus, in both cases the result could be the same: falling price and rising output in some other industry as a consequence of the innovation in industry A. However, while the details of the Brown-Conrad computations are not in the paper, their estimation method seems to be one that would not treat these two cases—of budget-connected and trading-connected industries—as equivalent. As a result, while the estimated coefficients of the research and education variables in the Brown-Conrad model may well be greater in trading-connected industries, the appearance of a greater responsiveness of productivity to research and education in those industries may be an illusion.

As additional attention is devoted to this or related models, alternative specifications of the economy's behavior will, deservedly, receive hard study. At the moment we are hard-pressed to decide to what degree the author's operational model correctly portrays the responsiveness and adjustment opportunities of the economy—for to that extent the discovery of inequalities in marginal value productivities would indicate inefficiencies—and to what degree the model is incorrect in this regard, in which case the observed inequalities may be irrelevant. But this is a never-ending issue; it is no criticism of Brown and Conrad to suggest that they have not resolved it. Nonetheless, the boldness with which they conclude that educated workers and research inputs were malallocated in the 1950s suggests that they have greater confidence in their specification of the economy's behavior than many readers may have.

It seems to me, however, that the general aggregate production function approach to the understanding of the productivity effects of research and education is well worth pursuing. Additional study is particularly needed of the best measures of research and education inputs, and of the level of data aggregation that is most appropriate. Brown and Conrad should be congratulated, however, on their bold, imaginative, and thought-provoking effort. It should stimulate additional research on the contribution to output of education and research—two of the most rapidly expanding sectors of the economy.

ZVI GRILICHES

1. The stepwise procedure used by Brown and Conrad to estimate the coefficients of E and R (education and research) is inconsistent. The correct symmetrical procedure is to relate Z (which is a residual from regressions of y on w and t) to the *residuals* of E and R from similar regressions on w and t. As it stands, neither the coefficients nor the standard errors are correct (unless E and R are independent of w and t). In particular, the standard errors are underestimated. In light of this it is doubtful that their finding of different coefficients for the durable and nondurable groups is in fact significant (on top of the obvious biases introduced by pretesting). These coefficients could be estimated by fitting the whole set of industries jointly, allowing the coefficients of w and t to differ between industries but imposing the same coefficients on E and R. This procedure would be somewhat complicated, but it is entirely feasible.

2. It seems to me that the equation that Brown and Conrad finally estimate does not really depend much on the special assumed form for the production function. Thus, e.g., if L (labor) is not measured correctly and quality of labor is a function of E, E will enter the $Y/L = f(w)$ relation—where Y denotes output—even though it does not affect the parameters of the production function directly. Thus their reduced form cannot be distinguished from one derived from a "pure embodiment" model. In addition, the coefficient of E will be proportional to $(1 - \sigma)$ and hence will be small if σ is close to unity. Thus, this may

not be a very powerful procedure for testing hypotheses about E. (A similar argument can be also developed with respect to R.)

3. Since on their hypothesis E affects the distribution parameters, could not one test this more directly by looking at the relationship between factor shares and E?

REPLY by Brown and Conrad

The purpose of our paper was to report upon a series of experiments which was designed to test a way of treating the technological change "residual." Since our main interest was in the simple model we proposed, and in the possibility of estimating parameters for it, we accepted the data that were immediately available, excepting only our manipulation of the NSF research and development series in order to include some reflection of the interindustry flow of innovation. This being the case, we will not comment at length here upon the well-intentioned reminders that our data are faulty. There may well be bias in our results due to errors in our variables, but neither we nor our critics could assign a direction to the bias, and we felt it was sufficient to state our discomfort as clearly as possible.

Two problems with the data are worth some further comment, however, since both involve our handling of evidence, rather than its quality. Mr. Weisbrod complains that our use of a measure of central tendency for education, and an unweighted one at that, fails to reflect differences in the marginal value productivity over the range of years of schooling. We chose the simplest measure, first, because earnings differentials seem to us to reflect a great deal more than marginal productivity differentials, and second, because the *cost* of schooling probably contains a great many elements of consumption that are irrelevant to the productivity residual. Third, our own preliminary investigation of the relationship between the years of schooling and the earnings series, and Griliches' observations on the correlations among the quality-of-labor series derived with different weighting schemes, suggested that the increase in the quality of the data from more manipulation—with the additional load of assumptions—would be more apparent than real. Finally, the cost of education may have relevance for the remarks about reallocation of resources, but it can only have relevance for the estimation of the elasticity on education when it has been demonstrated that the increased cost of a specific year is directly related to the marginal increase in the quality of the graduated output. We have seen no convincing evidence on this question.

Both discussants suggest shortcomings in our interindustry research variable. It seems unnecessary to repeat that we are aware that not all research expenditures are cost-reducing in customer industries. With regard to Mr. Weisbrod's case 1, as long as A cuts the price of its deliveries to B, there will be an increase in labor productivity using our value-added measure of outputs, whether or not conditions (2) or (3) are met. The possible interindustry connection via consumer budgets—Mr. Weisbrod's second case—is an admitted oversight on our part. Over longer time periods than the one we had, the problem might have been encountered; in fact, the variations in industry mix were negligible in the period of our experiment. Since Hicks, in 1936, defined the role of the elasticity of product demand in factor demand relations, there have been no empirical applications (to our knowledge) outside of the zero-elasticity-of-substitution input-output case.

Mr. Terleckyj, especially, has suggested that the interindustry research and development variable might be constructed in other ways. We have tried one of the implied variations—attributing *all* of the industry's own expenditures, plus the proportional expenditures of its suppliers from the original formulation, to each industry in the sample [column (5) of Table 1 in this Reply]. Using the asymmetrical stepwise procedure of equation (23), the original formulation is better—in the sense of yielding a higher R^2 (corrected) and significant coefficients on both variables —in the durables group. In the nondurables, however, the R^2 (corrected) is improved, but the coefficient on education is rendered insignificant. When the symmetrical procedure is used as below, the equations with double counting in research in the nondurables have no explanatory power; in the durables the only notable change is a further widening of the difference between the elasticities on education and research. The new variable is shown in Table 1, column (5), which contains the decomposition of the interindustry research weights that Mr. Terleckyj requested.

We can only accept, with a seemly humility, the arching of Mr. Weisbrod's eyebrows at our assumption of competition. But, the distributed lag in the wage rate variable was specifically introduced to admit the

TABLE 1

Input-Output Research Variables

(dollars in millions)

Industry and SCB[a] Number	Receiving Industry Research Expenditure, 1958 (1)	Receiving Industry Research Expenditure Delivered to Itself (2)	Delivering Industry Research Expenditures to Receiving Industry (3)	(2) + (3) Weights Used for Table 4 (4)	(1) + (3) Weights Used for Reply (5)
(1) Food (14)	$83.0	$13.45	$12.12	25.57	95.12
(2) Textiles (16–18)	18.5	4.24	47.21	51.45	65.71
(3) Paper (24, 25)	42.0	6.20	14.86	21.06	56.86
(4) Chemicals (27–30)	792.0	91.74	6.89	98.63	798.89
(5) Primary metals (37, 38)	119.0	28.44	1.48	29.92	120.48
(6) Fabricated metals (39–42)	133.0	3.32	27.93	31.25	160.93
(7) Machinery except electrical, (43–52)	781.0	46.85	78.48	125.33	859.48
(8) Automobiles (59, 61)	831.0	215.23	75.20	290.43	906.20

[a]SBC refers to the industry numbers used in M.R. Goldman, M.L. Marimont, and B.N. Vaccara, "The Interindustry Structure of the United States," *Survey of Current Business*, November, 1964, pp. 10–29.

possibility of disequilibrium into the test, which is a far cry from a rigid assumption of perfect competition. Further, under plausible conditions, the presence of imperfect competition requires only proportionality between marginal products and factor prices, expressed in terms of the price of the product. A departure from the competitive assumption implies no fundamental changes in the specification of the model and no change at all in the estimating equations.

The estimation problems are immense. There were barely enough observations in our data to support the variables of direct interest; the possibility of adding demand and supply elasticities was unthinkable. Conscious of the unlikelihood of competition, or even of a comparable degree of imperfection in the several markets we were using in the cross sections, we engaged in some "ad hockery," or what Griliches might call "fishing." We looked for a pattern in the residuals and then in the industry dummies from the covariance procedure that might fall systematically along some array of market imperfections. Nothing convincing appeared. Finally, we tried other grouping criteria, a host of them, including capital intensity, research intensity, the relative size of the elasticity of substitution, and rough notions of concentration. The average concentration ratio is, in fact, higher in the durables than in the nondurables group. But observe that we ran our tests on the variance of the durables independently of the variance of the nondurables. And, since monopoly power is argued to be roughly homogeneous within the groups, we have effectively held the degree of monopoly power constant in our procedure. In the first stage, we were really using w/p $(1 - e)_i$ to correct the productivity index, where e is the elasticity of factor demand and i is an industry index. At least in the log-linear case, the effect of the e's could be to bias the intercept but not the coefficient. In the second stage, the industries were grouped in a manner such that the e's were roughly comparable within each group. Hence, the disparate estimates we obtained for these variables in the two groups could not be attributable to differences in monopoly power.

The Malinvaud-Griliches criticism correctly raises the issue of the error in the dependent education and research variables due to the asymmetry of the estimating procedure. In order to eliminate the primary-factor substitution effects and the short-run cyclical effects from our fitted relationship, we used an adjusted, or constrained, productivity variable, computed as the residual from regressions of output per unit of labor upon relative wage movements and a cyclical index. The independent variables in the final "constrained" equation—education and research—were not adjusted in a parallel fashion. To the extent that the resulting discrepancy or error in the variables is correlated with the true values, the estimated parameters will be biased and, furthermore, inconsistent.

If education and research are independent of the wage term and time (and capacity utilization, as well), the inconsistency will be minimized. In fact, there is considerable correlation in the nondurables between the research variables (in both the original and double-counting versions) and the wage term. Recall that the two variables are a deflated wage term, specified in terms of a second- or third-order distributed lag, and a fifteen-year inverted V, lagged research variable, the lagged observations stretching back in time from the date of the observation. The correlation in the nondurables is simply the result of the common trend. Removing the spurious wage "effect" from the lagged research expenditures (the regression on the cyclical term was never significant), reduced the explanatory power of research and depressed the R^2 to insignificance. In the symmetrical procedure for durables, the education coefficient suffers when the old research variable is used, and the differences between the elasticities increase when the new variable is used, as noted above.

When the residuals were taken from pooled regressions of research and education on the wage and cycle terms, which gives scope for the interindustry differences and depends less completely on the common trend, the results are those shown in Table 2 of this Reply. For the durable goods group, comparing our original and new regression, the education parameter is increased, as might have been expected, and the R^2 (corrected) is improved slightly. There is a redistribution of reliability, for in the symmetrical regression the education parameter as well as the research parameter are now significant at the .05 level. Moreover, the relationship between the sizes of the two parameters is roughly the same as in our original regression—or, at least is not reversed. In the nondurables group there is no significant change in the parameters, the t ratios decline, and the R^2 is reduced drastically. But even though the t ratios fall, they still hover around 2.0, and it is possible to infer

TABLE 2

Revised Estimates for Equation (23)

	Education E	Research R	Constant	R^2
Equation as in text, where $z = (x_0-x_1) - \sigma\rho - a^s$:				
Durable goods:	1.236	0.300	−1,892	.844
Fabricated metals, machinery, primary metals, automobiles	1.585	5.432		
Nondurable goods:	0.182	0.200	−0.358	.580
Food, chemicals, paper, textiles	2.905	7.033		
Symetrical stepwise procedure, where $z = (x_0-x_1) - \sigma\rho - a^s$ $E = x_3 - \beta\rho - \gamma s - a_1 t$ $R = x_4 - \beta\rho - \gamma s - a_1 t$				
Durable goods:	2.895	0.237	0.203	.872
Fabricated metals, machinery, primary metals, automobiles	2.865	3.158		
Nondurable goods:	0.176	0.173	0.350	.115
Food, chemicals, paper, textiles	1.930	2.054		

that the parameter estimates are significant. Hence, using the symmetrical procedure, which presumably does not underestimate the standard errors as our original procedure did, we find essentially the same pattern of results as before. Specifically, education and research have markedly different effects on productivity in the two groups of industries. We need not modify our conclusions in the text.

VINTAGE EFFECTS AND
THE TIME PATH OF INVESTMENT
IN PRODUCTION RELATIONS

MICHAEL GORT AND RAFORD BODDY
STATE UNIVERSITY OF NEW YORK AT BUFFALO

THE ROLE of capital stocks in empirical estimates of production relations is akin to that of a minor vice—we all know there is something wrong with it but persist in the practice for lack of a better substitute. The principal problem is that capital goods are aggregated as if they performed the same functions though they may be drawn from different production processes.

There are two principal ways in which aggregation has been carried out. On the one hand, there are those who combine all capital goods, regardless of their characteristics or the processes in which they are used, into a single conglomerate stock. On the other, there are those who assume that for each vintage of capital there is a separate production function, though, under certain conditions, the separable processes can be described by a single aggregate function. Thus Solow aggregated the activities of separate production units, each associated with a capital of a single vintage, into a single function for the economy as a whole. The difficulties of using a single conglomerate capital stock are well known and require little explanation. Those associated with the second approach are more subtle and need some elaboration.

The trouble with defining production units in a way that limits the scope of each to one vintage of capital is that, in fact, a large proportion of capital goods of differing vintages perform interdependent functions. Consequently, they are inputs in a common production process.

NOTE: The research on which this paper is based was carried out under a grant from the National Science Foundation. M. V. Chari and Thomas Hogarty assisted in the preparation of the data.

Hence, conceptual decomposition into independent production units overlooks what we call the interactions among investments. Since these interactions determine the nature of the services and the productivity of new capital goods, any attempt to aggregate investments without reference to them involves the aggregation of units that are nonhomogeneous in function even though of the same vintage.

The primary purpose of this paper is to explain the nature of interactions between various vintages of capital and to develop an analytical framework for taking into account the effects of alternative sequences of investment outlays. Part I presents our general approach to the problem. Part II gives the results of applying the analysis to one industry—namely, the electric utilities.

I

No one who works with economic data remains a purist for long. This is especially apparent when one focuses on the problem of identifying separate production processes. Production units are less observable entities in an objective reality than they are conveniences for organizing information in a useful way. From the standpoint of generating stable parameters, the best level of detail in the choice of production units depends upon two conditions: namely, the homogeneity of the physical process and the degree of interdependence among individual capital goods.

Since there is obviously greater homogeneity both in product structure and production methods at the level of individual plants than at the level of entire industries, this would argue for the measurement of production relations at the plant rather than at the industry level. Should the activities of a plant be further broken down into a set of functional relations for each equipment type? Obviously the technical process described by the production function would be far more homogeneous, but this homogeneity would be purchased at a price. For what the derived relation would miss are the interactions between the equipment types. The elasticity of output with respect to investment in turbines depends upon the boilers with which the turbines are combined, and the relation between output and investment in turbines and boilers depends upon the building in which both are placed. Indeed, production relations at the level of individual plants miss the interactions among the plants of a firm, and those at the level of firms miss the interactions among firms.

An implication of the above is that the choice of observations from the standpoint of the optimal level of detail depends not only on the homogeneity of processes but on the strength of interactions among the inputs of the various units into which the production process can be divided. This implies that the unit of observation which is analytically most relevant will vary among industries. Our intuition, however, is that it will most often be at the plant level. This is not to say that the boundaries that delineate a plant are not often arbitrary. In general, however, physical contiguity is not an accident, and the capital goods that are placed at given plant sites are likely to be functionally interrelated.

Those who have held that technical progress is largely "embodied" in tangible assets have taken one of two approaches to the definition of capital. Given the assumption that capital goods of differing vintages are not homogeneous, one approach (taken by Salter) is to examine production relations only for new plants. This means that all the tangible assets of each plant have approximately the same date of birth. A second approach (taken by Solow) is to aggregate capital across vintages where each vintage of investment is an input in a separate function.

Salter's position is conveniently summarized in his own words: [1]

> The bulk of output is produced with the aid of capital equipment already in existence and is the result of past techniques and investment decisions. . . . This simple but often neglected point is worth emphasizing. As Schumpeter has said "the production function is a planning function in a world of blueprints where every element that is technologically variable can be changed at will." . . . So far as the measurement problem is concerned this implies that capital in the production function must refer to new capital equipment or investment; the part-worn and part-obsolete capital comprising the capital stock cannot be relevant for this is the result of techniques and investment decisions already made.

In short, new investment is based exclusively on the most recent or "best-practice" technology. Technical change then is measured by the changes in investment and labor requirements per unit of output between the best practice investments of successive periods.

The difficulty with this approach is that new investment is made not only for new plants but also for "old" ones. Indeed, for the aggregate of

[1] W. E. G. Salter, "The Production Function and the Durability of Capital," *Economic Record,* April 1959.

manufacturing industries in the United States, over 90 per cent of all capital outlays are made for existing, as distinct from new, plants.[2] Substantially the same is probably true for the public utility industries; and even in the trade and service sectors most investment outlays are probably made in existing establishments rather than for new ones, at least when appropriate allowance is made for capital expenditures customarily charged to current account. The preponderance of investment for existing establishments is likely to be a characteristic of all but very new industries. Therefore, much the same conclusions should apply to any developed industrial economy as to the United States, for in all such economies new industries account for only a minor part of total investment.

Now it is reasonable to assume that decisions to spend on old as distinct from new plants are not arbitrary; they are made because they minimize the requirements of the variable inputs (including new investment) for a given level of output. This must, in turn, mean that the capital goods purchased by these outlays are functionally interrelated with those already in place, for only in this way can the input requirements be reduced below those of best-practice new plants. Consequently, the characteristics of new capital goods will depend upon those of the ones previously purchased; and the choices made today must, in this sense, depend upon yesterday's decisions. Thus, the term "best practice" need not refer only to new plants, and what is best practice for one plant need not be best practice for another. Instead there is a range of "best" alternatives, each contingent upon the endowments of particular plants—that is, upon the level and sequence of their past investments and the kinds of capital goods they already have. The input requirements per unit of output for new plants represent merely upper limits beyond which further investment will not be made on existing plants.

---

[2] The 1958 *Census of Manufactures* for the United States, I, 5–3, shows that 1958 capital expenditures for plants under construction (presumably unfinished as of the end of the year) were 5.2 per cent of total capital outlays for that year. For 1954, the comparable percentage was 4.7. If we assume an average gestation period of only one year and an even flow of capital outlays over time, expenditures for plants completed during the year will roughly equal those for plants still unfinished as of the end of the year. Under these assumptions, outlays for all plants that were under construction during any part of 1954 or 1958 were equal to about 10 per cent of the total outlays in these years. If, however, the average gestation period is two years, outlays for plants finished during the year would be one-third of those for plants listed as unfinished. On this basis, expenditures for new plants were less than 7 per cent of the total.

The difficulties in Salter's position are reflected in his empirical results. In his work on capital and labor requirements for several hundred Australian factories [3] he examined information for major additions as well as for new plants. The interdependence between old and new investments is perhaps less obvious for major than for minor additions. Nonetheless, the relation between investment and incremental output proved to be highly unstable for existing factories—there was no way of identifying the increments to output that flowed from the new investment alone—and Salter was able to present only his results for new plants.

Our principal objection to Salter's approach is that it leaves us with nothing to say about most capital outlays. However, even for new establishments, there may be no simple relation between investment and the expected or capacity output of a single period. The virtual certainty of subsequent additions is surely taken into account in planning new establishments. Since flexibility for future expansion is not costless, some part of the current investment cost is incurred for the purpose of reducing future capital requirements. In this sense, not all of the investment of a given period is related to the output level of a single interval of time. As an aspect of this, some components of a plant would not be operated at capacity except at an output that substantially exceeds the capacity of the plant as a whole. For reasons we explain later, such reserve capacity is likely to be far greater for new than for older plants and is, therefore, much likelier to bias parameter estimates for new plants.

We do not wish to imply that this problem is necessarily critical, nor to minimize the potential usefulness of estimating, as Salter has done, the capital coefficients of new plants. It is worth remembering, however, that data for new plants offer no simple solutions to estimating investment requirements per unit of output even for the limited segment of total investment to which such data are relevant.

Solow, through an ingenious analytical device, attempts to circumvent the obstacles to aggregating investments of varying vintages. Subject to three assumptions, his model aggregates investments into a capital stock even though capital goods are inputs in differing production processes. These assumptions are: (1) constant returns to scale; (2)

---

[3] W. E. G. Salter, "Marginal Labor and Investment Coefficients of the Australian Manufacturing Economy," *Economic Record*, June 1962.

substitution between capital and labor such that, at the margin, the productivity of labor is equal regardless of the vintage of capital with which
it is combined; and (3) production functions of various vintages differ
by a set of time-dependent multiplicative weights. The equation he
derives is: [4]

(1)
$$Q(t) = Be^{-\delta(1-\alpha)t}L^{\alpha}(t)\left[\int_{-\infty}^{t} I(v)e^{\sigma v}dv\right]^{1-\alpha}$$

where $Q(t)$ = aggregate output

    t = time

    δ = exponential decay rate of investment

    $L(t)$ = aggregate labor

    $I(v)$ = gross capital expenditures of period v

    $\sigma = \dfrac{1-\alpha}{\lambda} + \delta$, where λ is the time-dependent weight that
    relates production processes of successive vintages.

The difficulties involved in estimating improvement rates in the context of this model have been discussed by others. What concerns us
more are some theoretical implications. Since one unit of capital is
interchangeable with any other unit of the same age and vintage, one
cannot explain in terms of the model why most investment is made on
existing plants. Indeed, if one does not take into account the interdependence between old and new investment, the fact that a large proportion of outlays are made on additions to old plants is exceedingly puzzling since old capital goods are to some extent encumbrances that
reduce flexibility in the choice of new capital.

In our model, the time path of investment has a critical role, for it
determines the method by which technical change is introduced. Each
investment in an existing plant interacts with past investments. The
type of capital goods purchased depends, therefore, on the investment
history of each plant. Moreover, the input requirements for an incremental unit of output differ not only between new and old plants but
between old plants with differing birth dates and investment histories.
Stated in another way, the capital expenditures of yesterday enter as

[4] Robert M. Solow, "Investment and Technical Progress," in K. J. Arrow, S.
Karlin, and P. Suppes (ed.), *Mathematical Methods of the Social Sciences, 1959,*
Stanford, 1960.

factors in today's production function. Today's choice of capital goods therefore depends both upon current knowledge of the most efficient production process and upon the most effective way of adapting to it the capital goods purchased yesterday. This does not mean that each plant is unique and that one cannot infer from the input-output relations of one plant the input requirements of another. The range of variations in birth dates and investment histories over which any given parameter is applicable is an empirical question and has to be solved separately for each industry.

There are three sets of conditions that make it more efficient, most of the time, to spend on extensions and modifications of existing plants rather than on new plants. These conditions define the nature of the interactions between new and old investment. First, new investment may modify the way in which previously purchased capital goods function. This usually entails a smaller cost than the purchase of new assets alone and, in addition, involves a shorter gestation period than the construction of new plants. Second, old investment may raise the productivity of new investment by serving as a stage in the learning and adaptation process necessary for further expansion. Third, some components of old capital will always have spare capacity, with the result that not all of the tangible assets necessary to increase production need to be newly purchased when expanding existing plants.

It is a well-established fact that a large proportion of capital expenditures in the United States constitute outlays on "modernization" [5] —that is, on the adaptation of previously purchased capital goods to new technical processes. A principal variable in the economic life of plants is the adaptability to new production techniques of capital goods purchased by past investments. Expenditures for the replacement of components of plants are a form of interaction between new and old investment and one of the ways by which old processes are adapted to new techniques. Since one rarely replaces capital goods with others of the same specifications, replacement expenditures almost invariably lead to some modifications of earlier processes. As an aspect of this, most "replacement" outlays also affect a plant's capacity.[6] Indeed, because

[5] For example, according to the periodic surveys of business investment conducted by the McGraw-Hill Publishing Company, expenditures on "modernization and replacement" often account for well over half of all capital outlays.

[6] Presumably this is why the McGraw-Hill survey asks for expenditures on "modernization and replacement" rather than for replacement alone.

of this fact, the capital budgets of firms seldom distinguish between out-lays for replacement and for expansion and the concept of replacement is, itself, largely nonoperational from the standpoint of decision makers.[7]

Any organizational unit, whether a plant or firm (or even a uni-versity) has some maximum efficient growth rate which, if exceeded, leads to sharply rising costs per unit of output of constant quality. These internal diseconomies of high growth rates must be distinguished from diseconomies of scale. They stem from three sources. First, the com-ponents of a production unit need to be adapted to each other. The like-lihood of partially incompatible systems increases with rapid expansion. Second, it takes time to train managerial and technical personnel. One of the best training grounds is an established plant. In this way past tangible investment is instrumental in the acquisition of trained personnel and consequently exerts an influence on the productivity of new investment. Third, many improvements incorporated in new capital goods, or in the way new capital goods are used, arise from experience in the use of the old ones. This influence is strongest at the level of entire industries rather than of plants because one plant can borrow from the experience of another and, also, because the same equipment pro-ducers serve new as well as old plants. But even at the plant level the ability to borrow is important, particularly for the small and undramatic improvements which cumulatively may be quite important. Much of what is sometimes taken as disembodied technical change stems, in fact, from what we have called the interaction between successive streams of capital outlays.

Each plant when operated at its maximum output will have spare capacity in some of its components. This arises partly from indivisibilities in capital goods and partly from the uneven impact of economies of scale on the various parts of an establishment. The incremental cost of additional capacity is quite small for some components. Consequently, imbalances in the system are often the result of deliberate plans and not merely miscalculations. Though most additions to existing plants create some imbalances while reducing others, newly created imbalances are generally larger when entire plants are built. Therefore, additions to plants frequently cost less than building new plants. Indeed, some moderniza-tion outlays derive their high returns from the fact that improvements in

[7] Michael Gort, "The Planning of Investment: A Study of Capital Budgeting in the Electric Utilities, I," *Journal of Business,* April 1951.

some components of a plant often lead to a fuller utilization of the other parts.

We are now ready to present the interaction model for a plant with two distinct investment flows—an initial investment and a subsequent expansion or "renewal." In the Cobb-Douglas form, but without the assumption of constant returns to scale, the equation is:

$$(2) \quad O_{n,n-1}(t) = A(n,n-1)L(t)^{\phi(n,n-1)}M(t)^{\gamma(n,n-1)}I(n)^{\alpha_1(n,n-1)}$$
$$I(n-1)^{\alpha_2(n,n-1)}$$

where $O_{n,n-1}(t)$ = expected output in period t for a plant with investment in period n and with one previous investment in period $n-1$

$L(t)$ = expected labor in period t

$M(t)$ = expected materials use in period t

$I(n)$ = actual investment in period n

$I(n-1)$ = actual investment in period $n-1$.

One will note three distinguishing characteristics of this equation. First, *all* the parameters are made to depend upon *both* investment streams. This is because both contribute to determining the production process used. Second, the investment streams are assumed to have a multiplicative rather than an additive effect on output. Third, there is no implicit averaging of the elasticities of output with respect to particular investment streams. Instead, the exponents of the investment streams are allowed to vary.

Labor is assumed in the equation to be homogeneous though, in principle, this assumption is not necessary. Insofar as factor proportions are concerned, we assume that, *ex post,* they are determined by the nature of past investments. That is, once the capital goods have been put in place, factor proportions consistent with long-run equilibrium are fixed in the sense that they can be changed only through new outlays or through a reduction in the output generated by past investments as a result of the obsolescence of these investments. New investment, however, modifies existing plants and consequently can contribute to determining factor proportions on old as well as on new plants. New investment per unit of output, whether on existing or on new plants, can be varied. Moreover, its allocation between new and old plants and among old plants of different vintages should be such as to equate its

marginal product in all alternatives (subject, of course, to discontinuities).

Investment in our model is measured in gross rather than net terms
with the result that there are no negative values. Also, the equation
excludes all zero values (which, in an economic sense, are irrelevant).
Consequently, the successive investments do not necessarily relate to
consecutive periods.[8] Since the investments are not necessarily consecutive, their position in the sequence of capital flows does not automatically
date them. Inasmuch as an industry's technology continues to change
independently of whether any given plant has a capital outlay, the
expenditures need to be identified by their vintage as well as by their
position in the sequence of capital flows.

For n successive investments, the function is:

$$(3) \quad O_i(t) = A(i)L_i(t)^{\phi(i)}M_i(t)^{\gamma(i)}I(v_n)^{\alpha_1(i)}I(v_{n-1})^{\alpha_2(i)} \ldots I(v_1)^{\alpha_n(i)}$$

The letter v refers to the vintage of the investment. The letter i denotes
the technology of the plant and depends upon the birth date of the plant
and its pattern of subsequent investment streams, that is, the sequence
and magnitudes of the investments. Thus $O_i(t)$ is expected output for the
period t for a plant using process i, and i is a function of all investments
from vintage 1 to n. A strict interpretation of the model is that i is unique
to a specific investment history. As a practical matter, however, plants
can be grouped into technology classes, with each class encompassing
some variation in birth dates and subsequent investment flows. The
choice of grouping criteria is an empirical question and is discussed in
that context later. At this juncture we need only note that all the parameters depend upon i.

While the gross investment streams could be depreciated for physical
decay, assuming such information were available, this is not necessary.
The constant term and the exponents of the investments will reflect,
among other things, both the rate of physical decay and the differential
impact of technical change on the efficiencies of investments of different
vintages. Consequently, information on the economic life of assets is
not essential. This permits us to circumvent a somewhat tenuous estimat-

[8] If, however, maintenance expenditures were included in capital outlays, the
record would probably show a positive investment stream each year. Maintenance
expenditures that are expected to yield returns over more than one accounting
period are conceptually equivalent to other capital outlays.

ing procedure that is a crucial element in the application of all models in which the stock of capital is a variable. It can be shown that capital stock estimates are highly sensitive to assumptions about the economic life of assets and that all measures of economic life are subject to a largely unknown, and potentially serious, error. Moderate differences in measures of economic life can lead to significant differences in estimated growth rates of capital. Thus errors that stem from mismeasurement of the variables themselves are likely to be reduced if one can dispense with a capital stock variable.

In equation (3), technical change is reflected in the multiplicative term of the equation or, alternatively, in the partial elasticities, or in both. To the extent it affects the multiplicative term, it can be visualized as a force that affects the efficiencies of all the inputs of a plant uniformly. It is important to note, however, that the constant is not simply a trend term—that is, it depends not on time but on the technology of each plant, which, in turn, is a function of the plant's investment history. The parameter may be significantly different for a plant which has had no investment of vintage n from one for which $I(v_n)$ is a significant positive value. Technical change, in this context, can be envisaged as resulting from the introduction of new processes through tangible investment.

The second way in which both technical change and interactions are revealed is through the partial elasticities of output with respect to investments of different vintages and ages. There are four questions one can ask. First, what is the relation between the exponents for the same vintage of investment made on new and on old plants? Second, what is the relation between the exponents of investments of successive vintages within a given (single) production function and at one point in time? Third, how does the exponent of a given vintage of investment change over time (that is, as the investment ages)? Fourth, given two identically ordered sequences of investments but with one sequence n years later than the other, is there a predictable relation between the exponents of the two sequences?

In an interaction model, the relation between the successive partial elasticities for investments of differing vintages is complex. What is crucial is not the separate flow of productive services associated with any investment but the effect of new capital expenditures on the efficiency of the entire production process and thus on the incremental output of the plant as a whole. Because of interactions, it is usually cheaper to spend on existing rather than on new plants even when the partial elasticity of output with respect to the last investment on an existing plant is lower than the elasticity of investment in a new plant.

To clarify our analysis, let

$$(4) \qquad O_R(t) = A(R)\, I(v_n)^{\alpha_1(R)} I(v_{n-1})^{\alpha_2(R)} \ldots I(v_1)^{\alpha_n(R)} L_R(t)^{\gamma(R)}$$

where $O_R(t)$ is the output at time t of a plant with an initial investment and $n-1$ subsequent "renewals" or additions. Now let

$$(5) \qquad\qquad D = A(R)\, I(v_{n-1})^{\alpha_2(R)} \ldots I(v_1)^{\alpha_n(R)} L_R(t)^{\gamma(R)}$$

so that, $O_R(t) = DI(v_n)^{\alpha_1}$. Similarly for $O_{v_n}(t)$ the output of a newly created plant, with investment of vintage v_n, we have the equation

$$(6) \qquad\qquad O_{v_n}(t) = BI(v_n)^{\beta(v_n)} L_{v_n}(t)^{\gamma(v_n)}$$

If we define G such that

$$(7) \qquad\qquad\qquad G = BL_{v_n}(t)^{\gamma(v_n)}$$

then $O_{v_n}(t) = GI(v_n)^{\beta(v_n)}$. It is our conclusion that, usually, D is greater than G, α_1 is less than β (with both exponents greater than zero and less than 1), and $\alpha_1 D$ is greater than βG.

D will usually exceed G because modifications of an existing plant can greatly increase the efficiency of the plant as a whole, because of the presence of spare capacity in some components of the plant, etc. However, the constraints under which investment is carried out on existing plants are greater than those associated with plants under construction. For the latter, the plans are not encumbered by the limitations of old capital goods with the result that the number of feasible alternative designs and combinations of components is greater. Hence there is more flexibility to investment in new plants and this, in turn, leads to a greater elasticity for capital expenditures in new than in old plants. Indeed, as a plant ages, its technology becomes increasingly less adaptable to new techniques with the result that, beyond some point, no further investments are made on old plants. In most instances, however, the difference between D and G more than offsets the effects of a higher β than α_1, with the result that most investment is, in fact, carried out on existing plants.

In general, with each successive investment in a given plant, the flexibility in the planning of further renewals or additions should decline. However, this may be offset by developments in techniques which make new investment more adaptable to the old than it previously had been. Consequently, the exponents for successive renewals in a single production function can either rise or fall.

As a given vintage of investment becomes obsolete, its uses are degraded. To the extent that obsolete capital goods are held for special uses such as reserve capacity that goes on stream for only short intervals, small amounts of such capital goods are likely to find more uses, per dollar of past investment, than larger amounts. The volume of investment that was optimal for its original functions is more than would have been purchased for its new and less valued services. Thus, as capital goods age, the usefulness of increments to the total amount of such equipment placed in a given plant diminishes. This should have the effect of reducing elasticity. At the least, it is clear that as capital goods age, the exponent for an investment of a specified vintage is most unlikely to rise.

For two identically ordered sequences of investment, the entire process for the later one should be more productive. It is difficult, however, to say, a priori, what the effect will be on the exponents of the investments. The greater efficiency may be reflected in an increase in the elasticities of all the I's, but it may also generate some movements of the exponents in opposite directions.

An alternative way of representing technical change might be to weight the capital expenditures themselves, that is, to make the technical change capital augmenting. For example,

$$(8) \qquad\qquad I(v_n) = e^{\lambda n}I(v_0)$$

where λ is the rate of technical improvement. This would imply that there is a component to technical change that is dependent on time alone as distinct from the production process and investment history of a particular plant. Within the Cobb-Douglas production function such a redefinition of capital expenditures has the same effect as a time-dependent multiplicative trend.

Most of the characteristics of our model, as contrasted with the familiar trend relation in which K is a homogeneous capital stock, are apparent from the discussion above. One of these, however, warrants further elaboration. The simple trend model with constant returns to scale implies that each increment to the capital stock generates a proportionate increase in output provided the ratio K/L remains unchanged. In contrast, the interaction model with constant returns to scale indicates that, for a given set of past investment streams, increases in current investment accompanied by proportionate increases in all factors other than investment are associated with less than proportionate increases in output. This has several critical implications from the standpoint of economic planning. One implication is that as the growth rate of output rises, investment requirements per unit of additional capacity will also rise. Hence, for this reason alone, increases in the growth rate of output for the economy as a whole should be associated at least temporarily with successively higher values of $I/\Delta GNP$. Moreover, because of the same set of forces, the investment requirements for new capacity in a specified industry are greater in an economy in which the industry in question is itself new. Consequently, unless offset by differences in factor proportions, the investment cost per unit of new capacity should generally be higher in underdeveloped economies than in those with a mature industrial base.

Still another aspect of interactions between successive investment streams is that relatively small amounts of new investment can have large impacts on output. This may resolve a puzzle as to how "embodied" technical change can explain a significant proportion of technical advance in our economy, notwithstanding the fact that new investment is always small relative to the accumulated stock of capital. If new investment changes the efficiency of the entire process in which all past as well as current investments are inputs, the effect on technical change of even modest new capital expenditures can be very large. Moreover, if (as indicated earlier) tangible investment is instrumental in the learning process, capital expenditures will affect the rate of advance in our knowledge of techniques as well as the rate at which new techniques are applied to tangible assets.

The interaction model presented earlier needs to be modified to make it more generally applicable. First, not all new outlays interact with all past outlays. Second, while it is difficult to accelerate the learning process,[9] the implications of our equation with respect to continuously

---

[9] Partly for this reason, the isoquant for combinations of new and old investment is convex to the origin.

diminishing returns to new investment are too rigid. Apart from limitations in the supply of labor and materials, it is plausible that returns to successive increments of new investment will, beyond some point, approximate those associated with newly built plants in which interactions with past investments are irrelevant.

Consequently, a more general model is one with additive as well as interaction terms. Thus, leaving out labor and materials, the equation can be written as follows:

$$(9) \quad O_i(t) = B(v_n)I(v_n)^{\beta(v_n)} + B(v_{n-1})I(v_{n-1})^{\beta(v_{n-1})} \ldots + B(v_1)I(v_1)^{\beta(v_1)}$$
$$+ A(i)I(v_n)^{\alpha_1(i)}I(v_{n-1})^{\alpha_2(i)} \ldots I(v_1)^{\alpha_n(i)}$$

The terms are defined as before. The β's are shown to depend on vintage. The α's depend upon vintage and upon the position of the investments in the capital expenditure sequence. That is, they depend upon i where, as before, i is a function of all past investments. The above equation has only one interaction term. As a practical matter, this may be sufficient. In principle, however, there can be a separate interaction term for all combinations of n investments. We hope, however, that this degree of complexity is unnecessary.

The general interaction equation with additive terms encompasses as special cases both the "pure" interaction and the additive models. If the interactions are strong, the exclusion of additive terms may not seriously impair the usefulness of the equation for the purpose of estimating investment requirements.

II

In the statistical analysis that follows, we try to test an interaction model in which output depends upon the level and sequence of investments of successive vintages. One objective is to see if the individual investments are associated with significant differences in exponents. Another is to establish if the differences in exponents between investments of various vintages, both within a single production unit and among production units, are consistent with the analysis presented above. Thus our primary purpose is to examine the nature of interactions among investments rather than to "explain" variations in output.

With this objective in mind, we tried to select observations that are least affected by short-run deviations from equilibrium relations among the variables. The tests were carried out with cross-section data for individual plants in the electric power industry. Because the industry is characterized by steady growth with relatively few other-than-seasonal downturns in the outputs of individual plants, the problem of selecting points that correspond to "capacity" production is substantially reduced. Moreover, for most of the analysis, the measure of output we employed was peak demand—that is, the maximum production achieved for a single hour in the course of the year. This further reduced the likelihood that the observations related to nonequilibrium outputs.

As a simplification, additive terms were excluded from the equations tested. The relations tested were log-linear functions in which output or peak demand was expressed as a function of the individual investments only. Thus the parameters were estimated indirectly by means of a restricted reduced form equation where all the investments enter as predetermined variables. In this way we attempt to avoid some of the statistical biases and specification problems associated with a number of alternative approaches. In a reduced form equation of this type, labor and materials inputs have no role as independent variables.

For the electric utilities, given our purpose, there are compelling reasons for excluding labor and materials as variables on either side of an equation. First, there is no measure of a labor input that is relevant to peak demand. Annual or monthly data on labor (or materials) inputs are clearly inappropriate. Second, variations in the number of employees in electric power plants are largely attributable to construction work and, in this sense, are more germane to the measure of capital inputs than of labor engaged in current production. Moreover, for the electric power industry, statistical relations in which output is expressed as a function of capital (or investment), labor, and materials are subject to high collinearity among the factor inputs. For this reason, Komiya [10] found a single equation of the Cobb-Douglas type unsatisfactory and, as a result, sought to explain technical progress through equations each of which expressed a single input as a function of output.

One alternative to estimating production functions in which output is expressed as a function of all the factor inputs is to estimate a complete

[10] R. Komiya, "Technological Progress and the Production Function in the United States Steam Power Industry," *Review of Economics and Statistics,* May 1962.

demand equation for the factors. Nerlove [11] and Barzel [12] have used equations in which factor demand is expressed as a function of output, relative prices, and other indexes. This approach, however, suffers to some extent from the absence of reliable indexes of relative prices. Indeed, the cost of capital has thus far eluded an acceptable measure and the investigator is faced with the option of using an unsatisfactory measure or none.

If the proportions between investment and both labor and materials are fixed by a given technology, exclusion of the latter two variables should not bias the elasticities of output with respect to the individual investments. If, on the other hand, there is significant substitution among the factor inputs, the exponents will be biased upward. However, from the standpoint of our problem, the relevant question is whether the relative values of the exponents are changed materially. The equation with output as a function of the investments only can be interpreted as a restricted version of a reduced form equation in which the dependent variable is a function of the exogenous and predetermined variables. Thus, if our structural equations are all log-linear, we have the equation:

$$(10) \qquad O = GI(v_n)^{\gamma_1}I(v_{n-1})^{\gamma_2} \ldots I(v_1)^{\gamma_n}Z_1^{\phi_1}Z_2^{\phi_2} \ldots Z_m^{\phi_m},$$

where the Z's are the relevant exogenous variables (other than investment). If the vectors of exponents of the investments in all structural equations other than the production function are scalar multiples of the vector of investment exponents in the production function, then $\gamma_j = k\alpha_j$ where γ_j is the exponent of the jth investment in the reduced form equation, α_j is the exponent of that investment in the original production function, and k is a constant. The problem is to ascertain the impact on the relative values of the exponents of the I's if one or more of the exogenous variables are excluded. Assume that there is only one relevant exogenous variable, z. Then,

$$(11) \qquad E(\hat{\gamma}_R) = \gamma + [(X'X)^{-1}X' \log z] \phi,$$

where $E(\hat{\gamma}_R)$ is the expected value of the vector of exponents in the restricted equation, and $(X'X)^{-1}X' \log z$ is the vector of least squares

[11] Marc Nerlove, "Returns to Scale in Electricity Supply," in C. Christ *et al.* (ed.), *Measurement in Economics, Studies in Mathematical Economics and Econometrics in Memory of Yehuda Grunfeld,* Stanford, 1963.

[12] Y. Barzel, "The Production Function and Technical Change in the Steam Power Industry," *Journal of Political Economy,* April 1964.

estimates of the log of z on the logs of the capital expenditures. Consequently, if the regression coefficients for the regression of the log of z on the logs of I's do not differ markedly among the I's, the absolute differences between the exponents of the I's should not be materially affected by the exclusion of one or more Z's. That is,

$$E(\gamma_{1R}/\gamma_{2R}) \simeq (\gamma_1 + C/\gamma_2 + C).$$

There appears to be little reason to infer that the regression of any exogenous variable on the various I's is associated with coefficients that differ markedly among the I's. In fact, there is reason to doubt that the value of C is so large relative to the γ's as to alter significantly even the ratio between any two exponents. In this connection, our estimates of elasticity for plants with but a single investment do not differ much from those derived in the several other studies of the electric power industry (mentioned above) in which the estimating techniques differed from ours. Plants with but one investment do not involve problems of decomposition of capital; so our results for these plants can be readily compared with the earlier work of others.

While the lags used in the various equations we tested differed, in no case was the most recent investment allowed to lead output by less than one year. The long gestation period associated with investment projects in the electric utilities assures that the errors in decisions about investments are determined independently of the random component of current output or peak demand. This permits us to assume that the I's are predetermined variables. For most of our results, peak demand (the dependent variable) was measured at its maximum point over the period between the last investment and the next successive capital expenditure for the plant.

An alternative to peak demand as a measure of output is annual production of kilowatt-hours. One may expect important differences in the exponents of successive investments when output is measured by peak demand rather than by annual production. During peaks, older capital goods are used much more intensively than in off-peak intervals and the proportions in which new and old capital goods are used are relatively fixed. That is, all resources tend to be stretched as far as possible. In contrast, in off-peak periods there is substitution of the newer for the older capital goods in some of the functions performed by the old assets during peaks in production. As a result, the exponents for the later investments should rise markedly when output is measured by annual production and $\alpha_1(KWH)/\alpha_2(KWH)$, the ratio of the elasticities of KWH production with respect to $I(v_n)$ and $I(v_{n-1})$ should be greater than $\alpha_1(pd)/\alpha_2(pd)$, the ratio of the elasticities of peak demand with respect to the same two investments. Also, the correlation coefficients with output measured by KWH production should be lower than when output is measured by peak demand, since variables other than investment have a larger role in annual than in peak output.

Data for peak demand and kilowatt-hours were drawn from the annual issue of the Federal Power Commission's *Steam-Electric Plant Construction Cost and Annual Production Expenses*. Gross capital expenditures were derived from data on the gross book value of structures and of equipment (separately) as shown in the same source. Since retirements have been small and infrequent for most electric power plants,[13] the net change between consecutive years in the gross book value of structures and equipment is usually a valid measure of capital expenditures. In the few instances where it was appropriate, however, estimated retirements were added to the net change in book value.[14] When the derived capital expenditures were aggregated for the plants of individual companies, they were generally consistent with reported investment outlays of the companies.[15] However, the lag between expenditures and the time they were recorded differed between the two sources because of a difference in accounting practice. Capital expenditures for structures were deflated by a construction cost index, and those for equipment were deflated by an index derived from two wholesale price indexes, namely, for electrical machinery and for engines and turbines, with equal weights for the two.[16]

The specific subsamples used for each equation and the periods covered by the analysis are shown in the section below together with our results. These subsamples were drawn from a total sample of 198

[13] In the entire period 1948–63, retired capacity, measured in nameplate megawatts, was only 10 per cent of the nameplate capacity that existed in 1947 (Federal Power Commission, *Steam-Electric Plant Construction Cost and Annual Production Expenses,* 1962–63, Table 2, p. xix).

[14] Data for the value of retirements for individual plants were derived mainly from Federal Power Commission, *Statistics of Electric Utilities in the United States,* 1948–63. While the data in this source are classified by company, the information, when used in conjunction with available plant data, was sufficient to permit the allocation of retirements by plants.

[15] Company capital expenditures are reported annually since 1948 in *ibid.*

[16] Unpublished data of Office of Business Economics, Department of Commerce.

TABLE 1

Number of Plants in Each Year with Capital Expenditures,
1948-63[a]

(number of plants)

Year	Plants with First Investment Expenditures	Existing Plants with Investment Expenditures	
		Plants Built Since 1948	Plants Built Before 1948
1948	6		12
1949	10	2	25
1950	10	7	16
1951	16	6	19
1952	9	11	18
1953	11	13	16
1954	14	15	14
1955	8	14	12
1956	5	9	7
1957	6	12	8
1958	7	10	17
1959	5	17	8
1960	6	13	6
1961	7	13	6
1962	4	11	5
1963	1	14	1

Source: See accompanying text.

[a]Restricted to sample of 198 plants.

steam-electric plants, of which 74 existed before 1948 and 124 were built since 1948. The sample was selected with a view to covering a wide spectrum of plants of different ages. The plants selected, however, are somewhat newer and larger than the average for the industry. Table 1 shows the number of newly built plants in our sample in each year since 1948. For each year, it also shows the number of existing plants with capital expenditures. An interesting fact is that only a few of the plants built before 1948 had investment outlays after 1958. Apparently the adaptability to new capital goods of plants built before 1948 was largely exhausted by 1959. However, most of the expenditures after 1958 were made for *existing* plants born after 1948 rather than for completely new plants. Despite a growth rate in demand and production far above that for most industries, less than 30 per cent of the kilowatt capacity added by the steam-electric power industry in 1962–63 was in new plants completed in those two years.[17]

The statistical analysis was carried out on the basis of three classes of observations. First, we examined the investment-output relations for new plants built in 1948 or later. Second, we examined a subset of plants born in 1948 or later, namely those that had at least one "renewal" or expansion outlay. Third, we examined plants born in the pre-1948 period that had at least one outlay in 1948 or later. The composition of plants in the cross sections differed among the equations tested. The main selection criterion was the degree of homogeneity in investment history, but this criterion was constrained by the need for a sufficient number of observations.

We first present our results for newly built plants which, by definition, have but a single investment. For cross sections of plants built in each of three five-year periods, 1948–52, 1953–57, and 1958–62, the following equation was estimated:

(12) $$PD(v_1 + 1) = AI(v_1)^\pi$$

where v_1 denotes the birth year of the investment,[18] PD is peak demand measured in megawatts, and I is investment in thousands of dollars (deflated to 1954 prices). The results appear in Table 2 (the expressions in parentheses are the t ratios).

In general π appears not to differ much from the results obtained in other studies. For example, Barzel[19] reports a coefficient of .815 for capital as a function of kilowatt capacity, when the other explanatory variables are the load factor, the price of fuel, and the price of labor. The reciprocal, that is the measure of returns to scale for investment, is

---

[17] Federal Power Commission, *Steam-Electric Plant Construction Cost.* . . .

[18] New plants for which there appeared to be initial investment outlays extending over more than one year were excluded in these estimates.

[19] *Op. cit.*

TABLE 2

Results for Equation (12)

Period	A	π	R^2	n
1948-52	.0042	1.05 (13.6)	.840	37
1953-57	.0009	1.22 (17.9)	.917	31
1958-62	.0043	1.09 (10.7)	.838	25

then 1.23–a value that does not differ very much from our range of 1.05 to 1.22 for π.

For plants with at least one renewal or expansion outlay in the period beginning in 1948, the cross sections were also divided by period. The need for an adequate number of observations permitted only two periods defined by the year of the first renewal or expansion outlay after 1948.[20] The two periods were 1949–57 and 1958–62. With the variables measured in the same units as before, the following two equations were estimated for the plants born in 1948 or later:

$$(13) \qquad PD(v_2 + 1) = AI(v_2)^{\pi_1}I(v_1)^{\pi_2}$$

with $v_2 - v_1$ more than one and less than five years, and

$$(14) \qquad PD(v_2 + 1) = A[I(v_2) + I(v_1)]^{\beta}$$

with v_2 and v_1 the same as in equation (13). In equation (14) the impacts of the investments on output are additive, and $I(v_2) + I(v_1)$ is a form of capital stock. The results for the two equations are shown in Table 3.

For the post-1948 plants, Table 3 shows that π_2, the exponent for the initial investment, is greater than π_1 for both cross sections. As expected, the flexibility associated with the initial investment was apparently greater than that for the second investment, with the consequence that the exponent was higher. However, $(\pi_2 - \pi_1)$ is much smaller when the second investment comes later, reflecting possibly an improvement in

[20] To eliminate the possibly unstable effects of very small expenditures only outlays of $10.5 million or more were deemed to be renewals of expansions.

TABLE 3

Results for Equations (13) and (14)

Equation	Period[a] of v_2	A	π_1	π_2	β	R^2	n
(13)	1949-57	.360	.27 (3.1)	.63 (4.7)		.628	19
(14)	1949-57	.254			0.87 (5.2)	.617	19
(13)	1958-62	.031	.48 (8.2)	.69 (5.5)		.943	22
(14)	1958-62	.020			1.13 (17.4)	.938	22

[a]Period in which renewal or expansion outlays were made.

the techniques of adapting new to older capital goods. $(\pi_1 + \pi_2)$ differ only slightly from β, but because of the large difference between π_1 and π_2, the implications of the two equations for the planning of investment outlays are quite different. As an explanation of the variance in output, equation (14) does about as well as equation (13).

The above regressions excluded observations for plants with an initial or a second investment program that extended over more than one year. Hence, there were no observations for projects with a long gestation period. In addition, the assumed one-year lag in peak demand may be shorter than warranted. Accordingly, for the next set of estimates, we took sequences of investment expenditures cumulated over periods defined by the number of consecutive years with capital outlays. Peak demand was the highest peak attained from the last year of the second sequence to the next expenditure sequence. Where there was no third investment sequence, the maximum peak was taken at its highest point from the end of the second sequence to 1963. Actually, it usually occurred within the first several years following the last outlays. The following two equations were tested with results shown in Table 4.

(15) $\text{Max } PD(s_2, s_1) = AI(s_2)^{\pi_1} I(s_1)^{\pi_2}$

and the capital stock version of this equation:

TABLE 4

Results for Equations (15) and (16)

Equation	Period[a]	A	π_1	π_2	β	R^2	n
(15)	1950-57	11.3	.29 (4.0)	.81 (9.2)		.819	29
(16)	1950-57	5.6			1.09 (12.7)	.858	29
(15)	1958-62	20.2	.45 (4.1)	.50 (4.9)		.813	32
(16)	1958-62	8.4			0.92 (11.5)	.816	32

[a]Period which encompasses all $I(s_2)$ expenditures.

(16) $$\text{Max } PD(s_2, s_1) = A[I(s_2) + I(s_1)]^\beta$$

where

$I(s_1)$ = gross capital expenditures (in millions of dollars in 1954 prices) from the birth of the plant to the end of the first set of consecutive annual outlays.

$I(s_2)$ = second set of consecutive gross capital expenditures (in millions of dollars in 1954 prices).

Max $PD(s_2, s_1)$ = the maximum of peak demands (in megawatts) from the end of the second investment sequence to the beginning of the next one or to 1963.

Table 4 shows that for the 1950–57 period π_2 was much greater than π_1. The average age from birth to second expenditure sequence was higher for the plants with a second expenditure sequence in 1958–62 than for those with a second sequence in 1950–57. The aging of the initial investment appears to be reflected in a decline in π_2. On the other hand, the rise in π_1 may perhaps be attributed to increased flexibility of later investments as a consequence of technical advance. An awkward result from the standpoint of the interaction model is the somewhat higher R^2 for the equation with a capital stock variable, when estimated for the sample with renewals or expansions for 1950–57. This aspect of the problem is discussed later.

Estimates for equations with sequences of investments as variables were also made for the plants born before 1948. More than nine-tenths of these plants were in existence before 1938, the first year of Federal

TABLE 5

Results for Equations (17) and (18)

Equation	A	π_1	π_2	π_3	β	R^2	n
(17)	29.0	.258	.223	.360		.911	20
		(5.6)	(4.8)	(5.9)			
(18)	9.5				.87	.849	20
					(10.1)		

Power Commission data. As a result, our measure of what we call $I(s_1)$ is, in fact, a form of capital stock. It was derived by deflating the gross book value [21] of 1938 plant and equipment and adding to it gross capital expenditures (also deflated) for the period 1939–47. Actually, capital outlays in the 1939–47 period were not large, with the result that the stock of 1938 represented most of $I(s_1)$. After 1947, investment expenditures for these plants were very heavy until 1958, and thereafter fell abruptly. Only a few of the pre-1948 plants in our sample had capital outlays after 1958. Consequently, our analysis for these plants could not go beyond 1958, and for convenience, was carried out for plants with a third investment sequence that terminated in 1957 or earlier.

For the plants born before 1948, we estimated equations (17) and (18). The results are shown in Table 5.

(17) $$\text{Max } PD(s_3, s_2, s_1) = AI(s_3)^{\pi_1}I(s_2)^{\pi_2}I(s_1)^{\pi_3},$$

and the capital stock version of this equation is

(18) $$\text{Max } PD(s_3, s_2, s_1) = A[I(s_3) + I(s_2) + I(s_1)]^{\beta}$$

where Max $PD(s_3, s_2, s_1)$ = maximum peak demand (in megawatts) after the last year of $I(s_3)$ for a plant with $I(s_3)$, $I(s_2)$, and $I(s_1)$. The technique for determining the maximum peak was the same as described earlier.

$I(s_1)$ = gross capital in 1947 (millions of dollars in 1954 prices).

$I(s_2)$ = first investment sequence in 1948–57 period (millions of dollars in 1954 prices).

$I(s_3)$ = second investment sequence in 1948–57 period (millions of dollars in 1954 prices).

[21] Price indexes were taken from unpublished data of the Office of Business Economics, Department of Commerce.

Equation (17), the interaction model, does significantly better in explaining the variance in peak demand than equation (18). The exponent of the capital stock, π_3, is fairly low as compared with the exponent of the initial investment sequence, π_2, in equation (15). It is also less than the sum of π_2 and π_3 in equation (17). This reflects, in all likelihood, the adverse effects of age on the adaptability of old capital goods to the changing technology of existing plants.

Still another grouping criterion for plants of pre-1948 birth consisted of dividing the 1948–56 period into two arbitrarily chosen intervals, 1948–53 and 1954–56. The following two equations were then estimated with the dependent variable alternatively peak demand and kilowatt-hours. Table 6 indicates the results.

$$(19) \qquad Y(1957) = A\left(\sum_{'54}^{'56} I\right)^{\pi_1} \left(\sum_{'48}^{'53} I\right)^{\pi_2} \left(\sum_{v_1}^{'47} I\right)^{\pi_3}$$

$$(20) \qquad Y(1957) = A\left(\sum_{v_1}^{'56} I\right)^{\beta}$$

All the investments are measured in millions of dollars in 1954 prices. $\sum_{v_1}^{'47}$ and $\sum_{v_1}^{'56}$ are, respectively, the capital stocks of 1947 and 1956 (v_1 signifies the year of birth of the plant). $Y(1957)$ denotes alternatively megawatts of peak demand in 1957 and millions of kilowatt-hours produced in 1957.

TABLE 6

Results for Equations (19) and (20)

Equation	Dependent Variable	A	π_1	π_2	π_3	β	R^2	n
(19)	KWH	.0075	.25 (5.1)	.49 (6.5)	.54 (5.3)		.696	40
(20)	KWH	.0041				1.16 (7.4)	.590	40
(19)	PD	.0290	.15 (6.1)	.27 (7.3)	.54 (10.7)		.837	40
(20)	PD	.0126				0.92 (13.7)	.831	40

For reasons developed earlier, the partial elasticities for the later investments are substantially higher when the dependent variable is kilowatt-hours rather than peak demand. The R^2 is, however, higher for peak demand as the dependent variable, since variables other than the investments have a much larger role in determining kilowatt-hours than peak demand. With kilowatt-hours as the dependent variable, the interaction model, equation (19) explains more of the variance, than equation (20).

There remains still another methodological question. Suppose that $PD(s_2, s_1) = AI(s_2)^{\pi_1}I(s_1)^{\pi_2}$ [where both $I(s_2)$ and $I(s_1)$ are greater than zero] is a correct specification of the relation of peak demand to the investments. Under what conditions will

$$PD(s_2, s_1) = [BI(s_2) + I(s_1)]^\beta$$

yield a stable and meaningful β? The sufficient condition is that $I(s_1) = CI(s_2)$ for the investments of every plant. In that event

$$\beta = \pi_1 + \pi_2$$

that is, the exponent of the capital stock will equal the sum of the exponents of the individual investments in the "true" model. Statistically, correlations between $I(s_2)$ and $I(s_1)$ weaken the precision of the estimates of π_1 and π_2. The standard errors for the estimates of the exponents in the interaction equation will, under these conditions, be higher than the error for the exponent of the capital stock.

To sum up our results thus far, for plants born before 1948 the interaction equation is somewhat better as an explanation of the variance in output than an equation with a capital stock variable. For the newer plants, the two equations yield about the same R^2 in three out of four tests, with the capital stock version somewhat better in the fourth.[22] The level of R^2, however, is not the crucial test of the relative usefulness of the two alternative models. The specification of the interaction equation tested was somewhat arbitrary, especially insofar as it excluded all additive terms. The inclusion of additive terms along with interactive terms is probably a better description of the relevant process. Our primary purpose in this paper is not to defend a particular specification of

[22] The ratio of the highest to the lowest individual investment in each cross section was very high, and many times greater than, the ratio of largest to the smallest capital stock. This probably reduced the goodness of fit for the interaction equation.

the model but to explain certain relations among successive investments which need to be taken into account.

The decisive question is whether the elasticities of output with respect to the successive investments differ significantly from the elasticity of output with respect to a capital stock. Our results in general show marked differences among the exponents of successive investments and therefore between most of these exponents and that for a capital stock. If interactions are present, equations with a single capital stock variable can be seriously misleading from the standpoint of predicting the effects of new investment.

COMMENT

ANNE P. CARTER, Harvard Economic Research Project

When I told my ten-year-old son that I was going to New York to speak at a meeting, he was puzzled. He finally found a rationalization: "It must be one of those programs where they represent all walks of life!" You will have to forgive me if my remarks are not quite detached—if I tend to stress a few general articles of faith in place of detailed textual criticism. This is what you risk when you admit "all walks of life" to a conference on so serious a subject as production relations.

The paper is indeed serious, thoughtful—even provocative. It contains new and interesting ideas, not to be treated lightly. As the authors suggest, a lot of clever things have been said in this area, but there are important unsolved problems. If we do not learn to cope with them, empirically as well as theoretically, we shall be handicapped in dealing with the broader problems of economic growth and development, at home and abroad.

At the level of individual plant cross sections (I am not talking about broad aggregates. That's a "different game."), research in this area has not been very rewarding thus far. There are at least two major sources of difficulty: First, as Professors Gort and Boddy stress so carefully, capital goods of recent vintage may have very different effects on the operation of a plant or an industry, depending on the nature of the process and of the new investment. After all, there are many different kinds of processes to start with, many kinds of change in them, and as many kinds of new investment goods as you care to distinguish. Who could reasonably expect the installation of a computer to have the same effect on the production function as a new parking facility of the same cost? (It is hard to be factual and realistic without getting very specific.)

The old-fashioned "layering" approach—explaining changes in the average production function by weighting in strata of best-practice technique associated with new capacity and dropping out old strata associated with retired capacity is, admittedly, simple-minded. Nevertheless, even this approach works rather well in a few industries where the ties of process to capital are strong—notably in textiles (or it *used* to) and in electric power generation. (I shall return to this later.) These are especially rigid—simple-minded—industries. (It takes all kinds!) When I tested my faith in this approach in tin cans, and in ball and roller bearings, I emerged, as Kuh so aptly pointed out, an agnostic. No one really knows, as yet, just how well the layering approach or Gort-Boddy interaction, or any alternative approach, scores in the universe of roughly 500-odd four-digit SIC industries that make up the American economy.

Certainly there must be many industries, many innovations, many types of capital goods, many initial situations for which the layering approach is quite inadequate. Professors Gort and Boddy make an important contribution in emphasizing this. The dichotomy between "embodied" and "disembodied" change is too crude. Within the category of embodied change we have a spectrum of possibilities: New capital goods may remain aloof—may go about their business and produce as if old capital goods were not there, or, much more interesting, the old and new may interact. To allow for interaction of new and old capital goods, Gort and Boddy make the parameters of a plant's production function depend on its entire investment history. Good! The broader conception forces us to consider the many different ways in which new capital actually affects the productive process—and these ways vary from the inert to the catalytic. A new generating unit is inert: It just adds a layer of new capacity. Breaking a bottleneck, that is, correcting a state of initial imbalance in the capacities of different types of capital goods, activates idle capital, and thus yields a relatively rich return per dollar of new investment. Some types of new investment will accelerate an entire process, will multiply all old capacity by a predictable factor: Oxygen injection into blast furnaces and in open hearths boosts the productivity of all existing equipment; automated control of assembly processes may do the same. These last two seem to be the prototypes for the Gort and Boddy model—and well they might be—they are much the most exciting of the three types, to business, and to economists who are impatient with a pedestrian conception of progress. To implement what they call an "interaction model" in a given industry, however, one must know which kind of interaction predominates.

This brings me to the second major source of difficulty in this area of research: At the plant level very little data are readily available for studying these problems. And even though our profession puts a premium on ideas, on broadened conceptions, the bottleneck in this field is still information. I have had plans, for about five years, and even a small grant stashed away, for studying the impact of capital expenditures on input patterns of individual plants, using the Census individual-plant continuous time series records. Those records have been a long time in preparation. They seem to be just about ready now. When asking me to comment on this paper, Murray Brown said that it would be an investigation of vintage effects using Census data, and I frankly had high hopes of finding that Gort and Boddy had plunged into the work that Census (and I) had been so slow about. The fact that the empirical section deals with electric power generation tells us that the really interesting implementation of the Gort-Boddy model had to be postponed. The reasons are easy to guess: The Census tapes probably were not available in time. In any case, the individual-plant time series sample will be fraught with complicated problems of product mix, small samples in each sector, cumbersome arrangements for using the Census tapes. Materials inputs would have to be tabulated by hand.

Even with the best intentions, we are lost without our old standby: electric power generation. The man from Mars who scans the economic literature (strange idea?) may get the impression that electric power generation is our only real industry. For the empirical worker who requires adequate homogeneous samples for regressions, it is!

The situation is deplorable on general grounds, but particularly unfortunate for the Gort-Boddy interaction theory. Of all industries in the economy, electric power generation seems to be the one which is best described by the naïve layering approach, the one where the multiplicative interactions between new and old capital are least important. In 1959 Komiya and I, just as data-starved as Gort and Boddy, did a study of this industry, in which we projected fuel requirements from 1938 to 1956 using the layering thesis—assuming that all new capacity could be characterized by fuel requirements of a sample of new units. The results were generally within 1 per cent of actual fuel requirements! (The study was, irresponsibly, never published, although it was documented in a Harvard Economic Research Project Progress report. The reasons, I am afraid, were purely personal: Candidly, the theory was too simple-minded to enhance our reputations. I had been pushing this naïve hypothesis for years, and we both understood, a priori and a posteriori, that this industry is very special. Anyway, I had a new baby at home.)

If layering works so well in the power generation industry, how can the interaction model be appropriate? I am not sure it can. But, since "everything correlates" in electric power generation, I felt it necessary to do some further homework on the problem this week. This kind of homework, incidentally, is often very useful at the outset of an industry study: I spent a scant hour with a reputable industrial consultant in the field of electric power generation, a man who designs power networks, and posed my questions about interaction of old and new capital directly. In his opinion these interactions are negligible in this industry. His explanation was as follows: Existing steam capacity, with very minor exceptions, has been installed, in fully "optimized," that is, balanced, units (Engineers use jargon, too!) with boilers and turbogenerators paired—one to one—in carefully matched capacity. That fact is, incidentally, documented in a 1964 report of the Federal Power Commission. Above the $10.5 million cutoff point, which Gort and Boddy use, new capital expenditure means, mainly, more pairs of matched, balanced units, operated independently of existing capacity, except for some shared yard facilities of minor importance. (I think the problem of which units are used for peaking is not really relevant to the main point here.)

Why then, I asked, are new units added to old plants? Why is not all capital invested in new plants? The same factors which make the original site favorable for initial capacity may make it favorable for additional capacity: existing load distribution patterns and transmisson capacity, availability of space in crowded areas, adequate cooling water.

Capital charges contribute roughly 50 per cent of generating cost. The bulk of the remainder is fuel cost. In view of the problems of peak versus average production, of associating an appropriate output with the capital input, it would probably be preferable to concentrate on the fuel-output rather than the capital-output relation, if a single-input production function is to be used in this industry.

I do not understand the results of the Gort-Boddy regressions sufficiently to attempt to reconcile them with the frankly contradictory evidence which I have just mentioned. In all fairness to the central idea, one must remember that the authors did not really test the interaction theory in their empirical section. They fitted an exponential function distinguishing capital expenditures for different time periods. But the exponents are not made to depend explicitly on investment history. The regressions themselves are not production functions. I am not sure what they tell us.

I think the important ideas in this paper deserve a better "break." To give them a fair chance, however, it may be necessary to do more spadework along two closely related lines before submitting the program to the computer:

1. Industries, their technologies and types of capital, must first be screened qualitatively to locate bona fide, nontrivial interactions. Such interactions are common, but not universally important.

2. The interactions themselves must be surveyed, qualitatively, to identify the relevant input and output variables and to specify the forms of interactions. Are we talking about automation, with potential speedup of all existing capacity, or about adding balanced, independent lines of more conventional process equipment? How important are balancing and bottlenecks in a given industrial picture? Can they be related primarily to building expenditures alone?

I realize that there is grave danger in my recommendation of ignoring the forest for the trees. What I am really suggesting is that we follow a policy of informed, selective cutting. Otherwise, we will soon run out of wood, and we risk turning it all into pulp.

Our supply of individual plant input and investment data is expanding, but it is still very inadequate. Because we do not have ideal statistical materials, we must plan their use very carefully. Under the circumstances, perhaps under any circumstances, we must supplement the regression techniques we know and trust with outside technical information. The industrial specialist, or the literature, can help us to specify appropriate production functions for each industry. The specialist can help us to identify the important capital, input, and output variables, to anticipate specific kinds of interactions. Production functions, and changes in them, may be very dissimilar in different sectors. We cannot ignore the differences at a detailed level.

The engineer cannot, should not, do the whole job. The second, essential stage is to quantify the relationships which we have formulated, using economic statistics. But the more we know, concretely, before we run our regression programs, the better chance we have of getting meaningful answers to meaningful questions.

PETER A. DIAMOND

The authors raise a number of very interesting and extremely thorny questions in both production and investment theories on the way to developing the model they have estimated. I want to restate their general framework to see its relation to their specific model, and to point up certain alternative paths that might have been followed.

They are concerned with the interaction of present and future investment, an interaction which raises three fundamental questions: the effects of future additional investment on the current choice of technique and the future productivity of current investment and the effect of current investment on the productivity of future investment. Clearly the questions are interrelated, for the answers to the latter two contain essential information for the choice of technique.

Stated in terms of cost rather than production functions, the first question parallels the choice of technique faced by a firm with variable demand (or uncertainty about its level). For example the firm might have the two alternatives whose average cost curves are given in the diagram below.

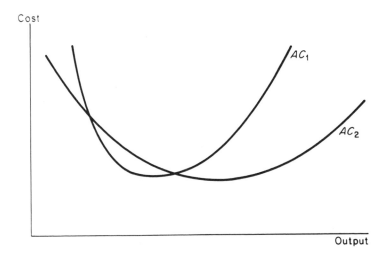

The choice between these techniques depends on the range of possible outputs. If future investment rather than, as the story is conventionally told, labor is viewed as the variable factor, we have a representation of the problem at hand. As the authors point out, the capital cost per unit output can differ when the economy is functioning normally from what might be achieved if, in a crash program, say, preparation for future possibilities are omitted. An empirical discussion of the choice of technique would be a difficult matter indeed, but one can, following the authors, assume a single available technique and still ask the remaining two questions.

When progressing from a general to a specific model, the view of the general model colors the choice of the specific model; and equivalent general models will, when viewed differently, lead to different specific models. The authors have viewed the interaction of new and old capital as analogous to the interaction of any two inputs into the production process. Alternatively, they could have concentrated on the modernization or replacement aspect of the interaction. An example may show the type of model to which this view might lead.

Output might be determined by the inputs of labor and two types of capital goods and by the vintages of the two capital goods. For example

$$O = F(L, K_1, K_2; V_1, V_1)$$

assuming both capital goods of vintage V_1. A modernization or replacement expenditure could convert one of the capital goods to a later vintage and thus alter the output level. A variety of capital goods would be necessary to permit sensitivity of output to small expenditures on key items.

In a more aggregated framework we could pursue this line and assume fixed coefficients. A new capital good might have particular output-capital and labor-capital ratios (perhaps with choice ex ante). Over time these coefficients could be changed with a cost of modernization. The cost of changing coefficients would decline over time with advancing technical knowledge but would probably rise with the increasing age of the original capital good (or perhaps with the age of the original good adjusted somewhat for modernization). Technical progress could then be viewed as embodiable; for, unlike embodied change, it affects old capital but unlike disembodied change only at a cost. Since with these assumptions new capital has greater improvement potential than improved capital and so probably a greater future quasi-rent stream, we would expect the marginal product of investment in new plants to be lower than in old plants if investment is carried on to equate the present values of the rental streams.

Now let us turn to the additional input approach to examine the setting of the authors' specific model. With future investment treated as an additional input, present and future output produced in the same plant are expressible by the same function of labor, present investment, and future investment.

$$O_1 = F(L, I_1, O)$$
$$O_2 = F(L, I_1, I_2).$$

By contrast, with homogeneous capital, present and future output would be written

$$O_1 = G(L, I_1)$$
$$O_2 = G(L, I_1 + I_2).$$

(With embodied technical change, the capital input in the future would be a weighted sum of the two investment streams.) In their general forms, the homogeneous capital approach is a special case of the additional input approach. However, this ceases to be true in general once the two functions are specified, as Cobb-Douglas functions for example.

Having selected the additional input approach, the authors chose to approximate the production function by two separate functions rather than a single function. For each plant there are two observations, at the points (I_1, O) and I_1, I_2. All the observations presumably lie along the same production function. The authors felt that the two types of observations differed sufficiently to warrant the use of two separate Cobb-Douglas functions, rather than a single function.

This discussion is my interpretation of the authors' view of the relation of their specific and general models. I hope that I have not done serious violence to their views.

REPLY by Gort and Boddy

It is true that the interactions among successive investments are weaker for the electric power industry than they are for most other industries. Our choice of industry was constrained by considerations that

Mrs. Carter explains all too well. However, she goes too far in saying that interactions for power-generating plants are negligible and that additions are normally made in combinations of perfectly balanced components.

A possible reason for Mrs. Carter's impression is the tendency to think of investment in terms of the purchase of the principal equipment units of a given production process—in the case of electric power, boilers and turbogenerators. In fact, however, investment expenditures are made on a large variety of items, many of them relatively small individually but large in the aggregate. For example, in electric power plants, there are outlays on transformers, switchgear, modifications of turbogenerators, the conversion of boilers from one fuel to another, improvements in structures, and many other items. Moreover, one form of interaction is the addition of new boilers and turbogenerators to an existing building.

The pattern of post-1947 outlays on plants built before 1948 is too distinctive to attribute to chance influences. If, for example, the principal reason why an outlay is made on an existing rather than on a new plant is the presence of unused yard space, the number of successive outlays made on a plant after its birth will depend on chance factors such as how much real estate was available at the time of a plant's construction. Accordingly, the number of successive after-birth outlays should vary widely among plants. Similarly, if successive outlays are made in the same location until the geographic pattern of demand shifts, variations in experience among plants should once again be great. As a matter of fact, there was a distinct modal category of two investment "programs" (sequences of consecutive years with outlays) after 1947 for plants built in or before 1947. Hardly any of these plants had investment outlays after 1958. Is it not more plausible that this pattern is explained by the character of interactions and the limits to interactions imposed by technical change rather than by chance factors such as the availability of yard space?

CAPITAL AND LABOR IN PRODUCTION: SOME DIRECT ESTIMATES

ROBERT EISNER

NORTHWESTERN UNIVERSITY

Introduction—New Data for Old and New Problems

ESTIMATES of critical parameters of the production function have been based frequently on special assumptions involving, most particularly, an equilibrium, perfectly competitive equivalence between wage rates and the marginal physical product of labor. They have also been bedeviled by difficulties in accounting for less-than-capacity utilization of capital. Further problems have originated in the uncertain biases introduced by the differing natures of variances and covariances in different sets of cross-sectional and time series observations. Disparate estimates have been obtained, for example, from cross sections of three-digit manufacturing industries, two-digit industries, states, and nations, and a variety of time series.

The data underlying the current analysis make possible, if not a head-on assault, a more direct attack upon a number of the problems which have become manifest in prior work. They may permit us eventually, with some effort, but without dependence upon assumptions of perfect competition and equality between the wage rate and the marginal product of labor, to estimate directly from output and capital and labor

NOTE: I am deeply indebted to a splendid group of young economists, research workers, and computer programers who have labored mightily with me in the collection and analysis of data and the preparation of this paper. They include: Margorie Bechtel, Betty Benson, Robert M. Coen, Joel Fried, Jon Joyce, Elsie Kurasch, Albert Morris, Hugh Pitcher, Judith Pitcher, Jon Rasmussen, Jay S. Salkin, Kenneth Smith, and Patricia Wishart. Particular credit should be given again to the McGraw-Hill Publishing Company Department of Economics and to Margaret K. Matulis of McGraw-Hill, who made available the original data. The research utilized the facilities of the Computing Center and the Econometrics Research Center of Northwestern University. It enjoyed the important financial support of a series of grants from the National Science Foundation.

inputs the parameters of constant elasticity of substitution production functions as formulated by Arrow, Chenery, Minhas, and Solow,[1] and by Brown and de Cani.[2] This paper, however, will constitute merely a tentative, preliminary report of results of analysis thus far.

Our basic data are literally thousands of individual-firm responses in McGraw-Hill Capital Expenditure Surveys over most of the period since World War II, especially from 1955 through 1962. These have been supplemented by accounting information collected to match the firms of the McGraw-Hill sample. Thus, while using code numbers to preserve anonymity of the respondents, it has been possible to combine the survey data with generally available financial statistics on an individual-firm basis over a substantial number of years.

The McGraw-Hill surveys themselves permit incorporation of variables reflecting explicit business evaluation of "per cent utilization of capacity" and per cent change in capacity. In addition, they offer a convenient compilation of year-by-year capital expenditures and the number of the firm's employees. In the current analysis, these data have been complemented by accounting statistics with regard to gross fixed assets, inventories, sales, and depreciation charges.

Price deflation of the basic data has been attempted where appropriate. Annual capital expenditures have been deflated uniformly by a single capital goods deflator, calculated as a weighted average of the implicit gross national product price deflators for "other new [nonresidential] construction" and "producers' durable equipment" weighted by the constant dollar volumes of these aggregates. Sales, inventories and, consequently, "output," defined as the sum of sales and inventory change, were deflated by one of eleven sets of price indexes constructed from Bureau of Labor Statistics price indexes and price relatives on the basis of the broad product or industry classes into which I was informed the McGraw-Hill firms could be categorized. Capital stock was in most instances measured as the "gross fixed assets" reported by "orginal cost" accounting. Attempts were also made, however, to deflate capital stock by a rather complicated scheme described briefly below.

[1] K. J. Arrow, H. B. Chenery, B. S. Minhas, and R. M. Solow, "Capital-Labor Substitution and Economic Efficiency," *Review of Economics and Statistics,* August 1961, pp. 225–50.

[2] Murray Brown and John S. de Cani, "Technological Change and the Distribution of Income," *International Economic Review,* September 1963, pp. 289–309.

The Variables and Methods of Analysis and Presentation

The results reported upon will stem from four sets of regressions involving individual firms: time series, cross sections, cross sections within industries, and over-all. Where there are sufficient observations, we shall also present three industry regressions: time series, cross sections, and over-all. In regard to the time series, which are pooled regressions of deviations about the means of observations for individual firms and for industries, respectively, a degree of freedom is lost for each firm or each industry included. In the case of the firm time series, where there was no more than one observation for a particular firm, that observation was excluded. Cross-section regressions were, in effect, pooled regressions of deviations about the means for each year, and a degree of freedom was hence lost for each year of observations.[3]

It should also be noted that, as in previous work, it has been deemed advisable to exclude observations containing extreme values of any of the variables. In variables requiring logarithmic transformations lower bounds were set to preclude the possibility of values relatively close or equal to zero. Upper and lower bounds of acceptable intervals were also established on the basis of preliminary analysis of means and standard deviations. Intervals were generally set so that inclusion of at least 99 per cent of the values on each variable might be expected.

No attempt was made to utilize information from incomplete observation vectors. A considerable number of observations were hence rejected because of missing information on only one or several variables. Table 1, "Definitions and Sources of Variables and Intervals for Acceptable Values," which follows shortly below, describes precisely the variables utilized and indicates the intervals for acceptable values. Subsequent tables report the number of observations (x) rejected because of extreme values of at least one of the variables in the observation vector.

The industry regressions are based on means of all of the observations included in the cross sections for each industry-year. There are eleven "industries" in all,[4] but in a number of cases lack of response or failure

---

[3] Appendix B states algebraically the precise nature of the deviations used in the various regressions.

[4] See Appendix Table A–1 for a tabulation of the total sample by industry.

to direct certain questions to an industry resulted in eliminating all observations for an industry for one or more years. Industry-year observations were in each case weighted by the number of individual firm observations. The regression results presented, therefore, involve several partitionings of the over-all sum of squares and cross products: firm cross section within industries plus industry cross section equal firm cross section; also, firm cross section within industries plus industry over-all equals firm over-all.

In the absence of information as to value added, "output" defined as sales plus inventory investment was frequently taken as the dependent variable. While this measure of "output" is generally conceptually more relevant to the production function than is sales itself, the absence of inventory statistics prior to 1957 in the body of data at our disposal caused us to use sales rather than output in several estimates over a longer period. It appears, however, that inventory investment, the difference between sales and output, is essentially a minor disturbance in the relation of sales to the arguments of the production function and does not markedly bias the estimates of parameters. In one set of relations the dependent variable was taken to be the change in the logarithm of "sales capacity," calculated as sales divided by the reported percentage utilization of capacity. In other relations the dependent variable was based upon firms' reports of their own "per cent change in capacity." More often, the reported figure for percentage utilization of capacity was introduced as an independent variable whose coefficient was estimated along with other variables introduced into the production function. The manner in which respondents' reports of utilization of capacity related to the production function was thus left open to estimation.

The data lend themselves obviously to estimates of "Cobb-Douglas-type" or log-linear production functions, and these have in most instances been estimated. The differing results stemming from utilization of differently structured sets of cross-sectional and time series data are presented below. In addition, however, direct estimates of constant elasticity-of-substitution production functions are being attempted, and a preliminary report on these attempts is offered in Appendix C.

TABLE 1

Definitions and Sources of Variables and Intervals for Acceptable Values

Variable[a]	Symbols and Definitions	Source[b]	Acceptable Interval[c]
Sales	S_t	FD	[20,000, .01]
Inventories (end of year)	H_t	FD	[∞, 0]
Output	$O_t = S_t + (H_t - H_{t-1})$	FD	[20,000, .01]
Utilization of capacity (end of year, ratio)	U_t	MH	[1.3, .3]
Sales capacity	$S_t^c = \dfrac{S_t}{U_t}$	FD/MH	[20,000, .01]
Change in capacity (ratio)	$\triangle C_t$	MH	[.5, -.25]
Gross fixed assets (end of year)	K_t	FD	[20,000, .01]
Employees (end of year)	E_t	MH	[2,000, .01]
Capital expenditures	I_t	MH	[2,000, .01]
Capital expenditures as ratio of 1957 gross fixed assets	$i_t = \dfrac{I_t}{K_{57}}$	MH/FD	[.6, .001]
Depreciation charge ratio, 1953	$d_{53} = \dfrac{D_{53}}{K_{53}}$	FD	[.2, .001]
Time trend integer, beginning with zero for first year of dependent variable	T		[7, 0]

[a]Sales, output, and gross capital expenditure (S, O, and I) but not depreciation charges (D) are price deflated. A further description of the procedure is found in Robert Eisner, "Capital Expenditures, Profits and the Acceleration Principle," in *Models of Income Determination,* Princeton for NBER, 1964, pp. 141-42. Where price-deflated values of gross fixed assets were used, they were calculated as the sum of the previous five years of deflated capital expenditures plus an estimate of the deflated value of gross fixed assets not acquired in these five years. Thus,

$$K_{pt} = \sum_{j=0}^{4} I_{pt-j} + \frac{K_t - \sum_{j=0}^{4} I_{t-j}}{\frac{1}{M} \sum_{h=1}^{M} P_{t-h-4}},$$

Notes to Table 1 (concluded)

Where P denotes a price deflator or (as a lower-case subscript) a price-deflated variable and M is the lesser of an estimate of the firm's length of life of capital

$\dfrac{1}{(D_{53}/K_{53})}$ and the number of years remaining back to 1946. (All gross fixed

assets acquired prior to 1946 were thus arbitrarily assigned the post-1945 mean price deflator calculated above.)

[b]MH = McGraw-Hill surveys.
  FD = financial data, generally from Moody's.
  FD/MH = numerator from financial data and denominator from McGraw-Hill.
  MH/FD = numerator from McGraw-Hill and denominator from financial data.

[c]All variables in millions of dollars except employees, which is in thousands; ratio variables, which are pure decimal numbers, and the time trend integer. Natural logarithms are used in all logarithmic transformations. $[U, L]$ = closed interval, including upper and lower bounds.

The Findings

A number of interesting results become apparent upon examination of Table 2. Here output is presented as a log-linear relation of utilization of capacity, gross fixed assets, and employment. Current and lagged values of each of the independent variables are introduced. This is important because the independent variables are defined at points of time as of the end of the year, while the dependent variable, output, is the integral of a rate over the entire year. It seems preferable to allow the regressions to indicate the relative weights to be attached to the two end-of-year points. Problems of collinearity for each couplet of variables can then be met by presenting the sums and standard errors of sums of coefficients.

The firm cross-section regression shows a not unsurprising result. Output varies most with end-of-current-year utilization of capacity, capital stock, and employment. The sum of the capital stock and employment coefficients is .991, with a standard error of .012. This suggests virtually constant returns to scale; and the sum of the labor coefficients is .651, approximately twice the sum of the capital coefficients. The elasticity of output with respect to capital stock seems relatively a bit too high but not very far off what might be taken, on a priori grounds, to be a reasonable value. The sum of the utilization of capacity coefficients does not pass the null hypothesis test, and this

TABLE 2

Logarithms of Output, 1959-62, as a Function of Logarithms of Utilization
of Capacity, Gross Fixed Assets and Employment, With and Without Time:
Firm Time Series, Cross Section, and Over-All Regressions

Variable or Statistic	Regression Coefficients and Standard Errors						Means and Standard Deviations[a]
	Firm Time Series		Firm Cross Section	Firm Cross Section Within Industries	Firm Over-All		
	With Time	Without Time			With Time	Without Time	
Constant term or $\ln O_t$					2.156 (.063)	2.212 (.059)	4.947 (1.470)
$\ln U_t$	.235 (.032)	.235 (.033)	.213 (.106)	.073 (.114)	.182 (.102)	.199 (.102)	−.257 (.183)
$\ln U_{t-1}$	.179 (.035)	.174 (.036)	−.112 (.105)	−.165 (.111)	−.081 (.102)	−.087 (.102)	−.253 (.186)
$\ln K_t$	.326 (.066)	.425 (.061)	.476 (.144)	.471 (.136)	.493 (.143)	.478 (.144)	4.404 (1.737)
$\ln K_{t-1}$	−.061 (.058)	.021 (.054)	−.136 (.145)	−.097 (.139)	−.154 (.144)	−.135 (.145)	4.342 (1.730)
$\ln E_t$	.188 (.031)	.178 (.032)	.390 (.098)	.367 (.093)	.375 (.095)	.378 (.096)	1.932 (1.342)
$\ln E_{t-1}$	.037 (.041)	.063 (.041)	.261 (.100)	.262 (.096)	.276 (.097)	.270 (.098)	1.915 (1.343)
T	.019 (.005)				.039 (.015)		1.527 (1.074)
$\Sigma \ln U$ coeffs.	.414 (.053)	.409 (.054)	.101 (.101)	−.093 (.102)	.101 (.100)	.111 (.101)	
$\Sigma \ln K$ coeffs.	.266 (.067)	.446 (.046)	.340 (.017)	.374 (.025)	.339 (.017)	.343 (.017)	
$\Sigma \ln E$ coeffs.	.275 (.050)	.242 (.050)	.651 (.022)	.629 (.028)	.652 (.022)	.648 (.022)	
$\Sigma \ln U + \Sigma \ln K$ coeffs.	.680 (.088)	.854 (.074)	.440 .100	.282 (.106)	.441 (.100)	.454 (.101)	

(continued)

TABLE 2 *(concluded)*

Variable or Statistic	Firm Time Series		Firm Cross Section	Firm Cross Section Within Industries	Firm Over-All	
	With Time	With-out Time			With Time	With-out Time
$\Sigma \ln K + \Sigma \ln E$ coeffs.	.541 (.071)	.687 (.059)	.991 (.012)	1.003 (.012)	.991 (.012)	.991 (.012)
$\Sigma \ln U + \Sigma \ln K$ $+ \Sigma \ln E$ coeffs.	.955 (.085)	1.096 (.077)	1.091 (.099)	.911 (.100)	1.092 (.099)	1.102 (.100)
$n (-17)$	606	606	674	674	674	674
r.d.f.	395	396	664	646	666	667
$\hat{R}^2$	.379	.359	.924	.926	.924	.923

n = number of observations; the figure following in parentheses is the number of individual firm observations eliminated because of extreme values for one of the variables.

r.d.f. = residual degrees of freedom.

$\hat{R}^2$ = adjusted or unbiased coefficient of determination.

[a]From firm over-all.

would suggest that differences between firms in reported utilization of capacity reflect rather interfirm differences in the measure than anything systematically related to output. Gross fixed assets and employment would seem to explain most of what there is to explain in differences in output between firms.

Partially contrasting results are found in the firm time series. Here we note, regarding the firm time series columns, that the employment coefficients are smaller than in the case of the cross section, but the utilization of capacity coefficients are high. The capital coefficients are somewhat higher, unless a time trend variance is included, but then are somewhat lower. It would appear that variation in output over time is accomplished in part by changing capital stock and changing the level of employment, but in part by varying their rates of utilization. This, of course, makes good sense in terms of our economic theory, old and new. Time series variations in output within the firm must be viewed in considerable part as short run or transitory in nature. They should not call for immediate equiproportionate changes in stocks of capital and labor.

Also of interest in Table 2 are the positive coefficients of the time trend variable. In the time series, the coefficient of .019 suggests that output tended to grow by 1.9 per cent per year during the period 1959–62, after taking into account changes in utilization of capacity, gross fixed assets, and employment. The even higher time trend coefficient of .039 in the firm over-all regression, in which cross sectional variance clearly dominated, similarly suggests substantial contributions to the growth of output not accounted for by the variables introduced into our relation.

What we have failed to include—increases in management skill, improvement in the quality of capital goods, greater productivity (or longer work weeks) of employees—we cannot presume to say. But it does appear that something is contributing to a growth in output beyond the factors we have introduced. And one may note that the higher capital coefficients when the time trend variable is excluded illustrate again the possibility that the true contribution of capital to output may be overestimated if a trend-like capital variable is allowed to act as a proxy for other, unspecified, trend-producing factors.

Table 3 offers some interesting confirmations of the findings of Table 2, along with information on the time profile of the capital and capital expenditures affecting output. Here, output is related to utilization of capacity, capital expenditures of the current and two previous years, the rate of depreciation, gross fixed assets in existence just prior to the beginning of the capital expenditure series, and employment. Each year's capital expenditures are found to be positively related to output in all of the regressions and the sums of the capital expenditure coefficients are in a statistical sense clearly significantly positive. On the other hand, the rate of depreciation, that is, the ratio of depreciation charges to gross fixed assets in 1953, before changing tax laws made this ratio a less reliable measure of replacement requirements, is negatively related to output.

As before, the contribution of the capital and labor variables is generally less in the time series than in the cross sections, except that the coefficient of $\ln K_{t-3}$ is high in the time series with the time trend

TABLE 3

Logarithms of Output, 1959-62, as a Function of Logarithms of Utilization of Capacity, Capital Expenditures, Depreciation Rate, Previous Gross Fixed Assets, and Employment, With and Without Time: Firm Time Series, Cross Sections and Over-All Regressions

Variable or Statistic	Regression Coefficients and Standard Errors						
	Firm Time Series		Firm Cross Section	Firm Cross Section Within Industries	Firm Over-All		Means and Standard Deviations
	With Time	Without Time			With Time	Without Time	
Constant term or $\ln O_t$					2.363 (.154)	2.437 (.151)	5.273 (1.377)
$\ln U_t$	.204 (.041)	.221 (.041)	.217 (.116)	.088 (.131)	.178 (.111)	.211 (.110)	-.252 (.175)
$\ln U_{t-1}$	.170 (.043)	.180 (.044)	-.070 (.118)	-.166 (.129)	-.032 (.113)	-.047 (.113)	-.245 (.175)
$\ln I_t$	.034 (.012)	.036 (.013)	.034 (.034)	.032 (.032)	.040 (.033)	.037 (.033)	1.745 (1.758)
$\ln I_{t-1}$	.003 (.011)	.012 (.011)	.056 (.039)	.049 (.037)	.052 (.039)	.054 (.039)	1.722 (1.747)
$\ln I_{t-2}$	.021 (.011)	.027 (.011)	.034 (.034)	.053 (.033)	.031 (.034)	.018 (.033)	1.787 (1.782)
$\ln d$			-.093 (.049)	-.035 (.047)	-.093 (.049)	-.081 (.049)	-2.930 (.390)
$\ln K_{t-3}$	.114 (.070)	.310 (.042)	.206 (.037)	.243 (.040)	.205 (.036)	.221 (.036)	4.557 (1.649)
$\ln E_t$	.148 (.033)	.144 (.033)	.401 (.104)	.335 (.100)	.388 (.102)	.397 (.102)	2.219 (1.281)
$\ln E_{t-1}$	.153 (.050)	.134 (.051)	.258 (.106)	.284 (.104)	.270 (.104)	.255 (.104)	2.202 (1.283)
T	.025 (.007)				.038 (.017)		1.712 (1.019)
$\Sigma \ln U$ coeffs.	.374 (.069)	.401 (.070)	.146 (.118)	-.077 (.118)	.146 (.118)	.165 (.118)	

(continued)

TABLE 3 *(concluded)*

Variable or Statistic	Regression Coefficients and Standard Errors					
	Firm Time Series		Firm Cross Section	Firm Cross Section Within Industries	Firm Over-All	
	With Time	Without Time			With Time	Without Time
$\Sigma \ln I$	.058	.075	.124	.134	.124	.109
coeffs.	(.022)	(.022)	(.034)	(.032)	(.033)	(.033)
$\Sigma \ln E$	.301	.278	.659	.619	.658	.652
coeffs.	(.059)	(.059)	(.025)	(.032)	(.025)	(.025)
$\Sigma \ln U + \Sigma \ln E$	.675	.679	.805	.542	.804	.817
coeffs.	(.084)	(.086)	(.121)	(.119)	(.121)	(.121)
$\Sigma \ln U + \ln K$	.790	.989	1.011	.785	1.010	1.038
$+ \Sigma \ln E$ coeffs.	(.111)	(.096)	(.127)	(.125)	(.127)	(.127)
n (-10)	425	425	500	500	500	500
r.d.f.	273	274	487	469	489	490
$\hat{R}^2$	.343	.317	.923	.929	.925	.925

variable excluded. And again, the coefficient of time is significantly positive.

Table 4 presents the results of regressions of changes in the logarithms of output on changes in the logarithms of utilization of capacity, gross fixed assets, and employment.[5] This, of course, makes most of the variance of our variables stem from changes over time in the cross sections as well as in the time series. One should now expect the coefficients of the various regressions to be less different; and, in fact, this is so. The coefficients of the change in the logarithms of gross fixed assets are indeed virtually identical in the time series and cross-section regressions. That the coefficients of $\Delta \ln U_t$ and $\Delta \ln E_t$ are somewhat higher in the time series may again involve a larger concentration of "noise" in the cross-section relation.

We may also note the substantial and statistically significant positive constant term in the firm over-all regression. This implies that output

[5] Acceptable intervals of [.5, $-$.5] were established for $\Delta \ln U$ and $\Delta \ln E$ and of [.693, $-$.693] for $\Delta \ln K$. These permit corresponding arithmetic ranges of [$+65$ per cent, -39 per cent] and [$+100$ per cent, -50 per cent].

TABLE 4

Changes in Logarithms of Output, 1959-62, as a Function of Changes in
Logarithms of Utilization of Capacity, Gross Fixed Assets and Employment:
Firm Time Series, Cross Sections and Over-All Regressions

	Regression Coefficients and Standard Errors					
Variable or Statistic	Firm Time Series	Firm Cross Section	Firm Cross Section Within Industries	Firm Over-All	Firm Over-All with Constant Term Constrained to Zero	Means and Standard Deviations
Constant term or $\Delta \ln O_t$				.031 (.006)		.063 (.134)
$\Delta \ln U_t$	.148 (.042)	.110 (.032)	.119 (.033)	.124 (.033)	.137 (.034)	.007 (.151)
$\Delta \ln K_t$	.384 (.105)	.407 (.061)	.408 (.061)	.416 (.064)	.621 (.051)	.062 (.076)
$\Delta \ln E_t$	.388 (.057)	.250 (.038)	.258 (.038)	.302 (.039)	.289 (.039)	.016 (.132)
$\Delta \ln U + \Delta \ln E$ coeffs.	.537 (.061)	.360 (.043)	.376 (.045)	.426 (.043)	.426 (.044)	
$\Delta \ln K + \Delta \ln E$ coeffs.	.772 (.111)	.657 (.063)	.665 (.064)	.718 (.066)	.910 (.056)	
$\Delta \ln U + \Delta \ln K$ coeffs.	.532 (.118)	.516 (.072)	.526 (.072)	.540 (.076)	.759 (.063)	
$\Delta \ln U + \Delta \ln K + \Delta \ln E$ coeffs.	.421 (.117)	.767 (.069)	.784 (.070)	.842 (.072)	1.047 (.061)	
$n\ (-37)$	555	622	622	622	622	
r.d.f.	357	615	597	618	618	
$\hat{R}^2$	.210	.185	.190	.214	.330	

would grow at some 3.1 per cent per year with utilization of capacity,
gross fixed assets, and employment all held constant. The results of a
firm over-all regression with time and with a constant term constrained
to zero is a markedly higher coefficient for the change in the logarithm
of gross fixed assets. It would appear that there are increases in output
essentially independent of capital stock and the other variables that are

attributed to increases in gross fixed assets when it is impossible to measure their causes elsewhere.

Table 5 differs from the previous tables in covering all the years from 1955 to 1962 but presenting the relation between the logarithms of sales and the logarithms of utilization of capacity and gross fixed assets. (Neither inventory investment nor employment figures were available for this study in the earlier years.) Again we note the coefficients of the factor input variables are distinctly lower in the firm time series than in the firm cross sections. We note also, however, that the role of utilization of capacity is apparently higher in the firm cross sections within industries than indicated in previous tables. This is perhaps accountable to the exclusion of employment from these regressions. The utilization-of-capacity variable within industries (where interfirm differences in measurement might account for less error than in the firm cross section between all firms) may be picking up some of the effect properly attributable to variance in employment. It may also be presumed that larger quantities of labor were associated with larger quantities of capital so that the "capital coefficient" in this regression reflects the effect of indeterminate covariances of capital and labor and of labor and output.

In Table 5, for the first time, we have a sufficient number of industry-year observations to warrant presentation of results of regressions on industry-year means. One might expect the variance over time in the experience of broad industry groups to be more "permanent" or long run in character than variance over time in the experience of individual firms. The regression coefficients in the industry time series are thus higher, as might be expected, although in fact a bit too high for plausible explanation. It would appear that variance in capital is more closely related to current and immediately subsequent output in the industry time series than in individual firm time series. The coefficients of utilization, however, are also higher than we should anticipate.

The introduction of a time trend variable did little to clarify the matter. Its coefficient was slightly negative ($-.021$) in the industry time series, trivially positive ($.006$) in the firm time series regression, in which the sum of the capital coefficients was then reduced from $.520$ to $.469$, but slightly negative ($-.014$) in the over-all regression.

Thus far all of the regressions discussed have included utilization of capacity as independent variables with coefficients to be estimated. We have also constructed a "sales capacity" variable, defined as actual sales

TABLE 5

Logarithms of Sales, 1955-62, as a Function of Logarithms of Utilization of Capacity and Gross Fixed Assets: Firm and Industry Time Series, Cross-Section, and Over-All Regressions

Variable or Statistic	Regression Coefficients and Standard Errors							Means and Standard Deviations
	Firm Time Series	Firm Cross Section	Firm Cross Section Within Industries	Firm Over-All	Industry Time Series	Industry Cross Section	Industry Over-All	
Constant term or $\ln S_t$				1.751 (.061)			2.757 (.298)	5.074 (1.392)
$\ln U_t$	.235 (.028)	.265 (.117)	0.324 (.109)	0.322 (.110)	0.814 (.191)	.174 (.493)	0.571 (.400)	-0.223 (.181)
$\ln U_{t-1}$	.260 (.029)	-.108 (.116)	0.072 (.105)	-0.056 (.110)	0.572 (.275)	-.493 (.571)	-0.026 (.508)	-.217 (.182)
$\ln K_t$	.341 (.043)	.793 (.162)	0.762 (.135)	0.889 (.160)	0.928 (.645)	.090 (1.644)	3.002 (1.228)	4.533 (1.670)
$\ln K_{t-1}$	.179 (.040)	-.054 (.162)	0.101 (.136)	-0.146 (.160)	0.009 (.656)	.408 (1.647)	-2.507 (1.227)	4.456 (1.662)
$\Sigma \ln U$ coeffs.	.516 (.041)	.157 (.113)	0.396 (.100)	0.266 (.109)	1.386 (.364)	-.318 (.625)	0.545 (.555)	
$\Sigma \ln K$ coeffs.	.520 (.019)	.739 (.010)	0.863 (.010)	0.744 (.010)	0.937 (.053)	.498 (.038)	0.495 (.040)	

(continued)

TABLE 5 (concluded)

Variable or Statistic	Regression Coefficients and Standard Errors							Means and Standard Deviations
	Firm Time Series	Firm Cross Section	Firm Cross Section Within Industries	Firm Over-All	Industry Time Series	Industry Cross Section	Industry Over-All	
$\ln U_t$ + $\ln K_t$ coeffs.	.596 (.052)	1.058 (.196)	1.086 (.169)	1.211 (.189)	1.742 (.605)	.264 (1.754)	3.573 (1.263)	
$\ln U_{t-1}$ + $\ln K_{t-1}$ coeffs.	.439 (.054)	-.162 (.208)	0.173 (.180)	-0.202 (.207)	0.581 (.851)	-.085 (1.715)	-2.533 (1.510)	
$\sum \ln U$ + $\sum \ln K$ coeffs.	1.036 (.051)	.896 (.111)	1.259 (.099)	1.009 (.107)	2.323 (.356)	.180 (.609)	1.039 (.538)	
n (-38)	1,299	1,352	1,352	1,352	48	48	48	
r.d.f.	1,012	1,340	1,300	1,347	38	36	43	
$\hat{R}^2$	.422	.803	.852	.809	.932	.835	.838	

divided by reported end-of-year utilization of capacity. The changes in the logarithm of this variable are then regressed on the changes in logarithms of gross fixed assets, current and lagged. In effect, therefore, the coefficient of the logarithm of utilization of capacity is constrained to unity. If reported utilization of capacity figures could be taken literally, we would thus be relating changes of capital stock to measures of changes in the rate of output which they are capable of producing.

As might be expected, with implicit constraints on the utilization-of-capacity coefficient and with first differences of the logarithms of our variables, the coefficients of determination are generally low. The large number of observations reported upon in Table 6 (1,210 in the firm cross section, even after eliminating 61 observations for extreme values [6]) permits estimates with reasonably low standard errors. It is to be noted, therefore, that the sum of the coefficients of the $\Delta \ln K_t$ coefficients ranges from .679 to .709 in the various individual firm regressions. Relative changes in sales capacity were thus some two-thirds of relative changes in gross fixed assets of the current and preceding years. This, of course, is not to argue that the elasticity of capacity with respect to capital stock is two-thirds. For we have not, in this regression, allowed for the effect of changes in employment. Employment now, perhaps like other factors in the other regressions, has been "embodied" in capital stock.

It will be recalled that we have included another variable from the McGraw-Hill surveys bearing on capacity. This is the annual change in capacity reported by respondents at the end of the year. The logarithm of this capacity change ratio (plus unity) has been regressed on the ratio of capital expenditures to 1957 gross fixed assets. Coefficients of current and lagged values of the logarithm of the capital expenditure ratios are positive, as shown in Table 7, but their magnitudes are deceptive. Since the geometric mean of the capital expenditure ratio was some 6.3 or 6.4 per cent, the sum of coefficients of, for example, 0.03, would imply that a 10 per cent increase in capital stock would bring about an increase in capacity of just under 5 per cent, which would be roughly consistent with our other results involving capital stock directly.

We have also introduced the depreciation ratio in Table 7. Its

---

[6] Intervals of [.47, −.23] and [.531, −.92] were established for $\Delta \ln K$ and $\Delta \ln S_t^c$, respectively. These permit corresponding arithmetic ranges of [+60 per cent, −20 per cent] and [+70 per cent, −60 per cent].

TABLE 6

Changes in Logarithms of Sales Capacity, 1955-62, as a Function of Changes in Logarithms of Gross Fixed Assets: Firm and Industry Time Series, Cross-Section, and Over-All Regressions

Variable or Statistic	Regression Coefficients and Standard Errors							Means and Standard Deviations
	Firm Time Series	Firm Cross Section	Firm Cross Section Within Industries	Firm Over-All	Industry Time Series	Industry Cross Section	Industry Over-All	
Constant term or $\Delta \ln S_t^c$				-.014 (.008)			.027 (.034)	.042 (.177)
$\Delta \ln K_t$	.519 (.081)	.456 (.065)	.433 (.064)	.536 (.066)	1.489 (.472)	.944 (.564)	1.482 (.428)	.079 (.079)
$\Delta \ln K_{t-1}$	.190 (.077)	.222 (.064)	.255 (.063)	.172 (.064)	-0.607 (.430)	-.291 (.482)	-0.599 (.402)	.080 (.081)
$\Sigma \Delta \ln K$ coeffs.	.709 (.109)	.679 (.076)	.688 (.075)	.708 (.075)	0.882 (.476)	.653 (.570)	0.882 (.412)	
n (-61)	1,165	1,210	1,210	1,210	48	48	48	
r.d.f.	896	1,200	1,160	1,207	40	38	45	
$\hat{R}^2$	.050	.064	.068	.074	.259	.020	.176	

TABLE 7

Logarithms of 1 Plus Change in Capacity, 1955-62, as a Function of Logarithms of
Capital Expenditure Ratios and Depreciation Ratios and of Time: Firm and
Industry Time Series, Cross-Section and Over-All Regressions

Variable or Statistic	Regression Coefficients and Standard Errors							Means and Standard Deviations
	Firm Time Series	Firm Cross Section	Firm Cross Section Within Industries	Firm Over-All	Industry Time Series	Industry Cross Section	Industry Over-All	
Constant term or $\ln(1+\Delta C)$				.150 (.016)			.255 (.046)	0.042 (.061)
$\ln i_t$	.031 (.004)	.025 (.004)	.024 (.004)	.027 (.004)	.050 (.008)	.049 (.019)	.047 (.011)	-2.767 (.690)
$\ln i_{t-1}$	.006 (.004)	.004 (.004)	.006 (.004)	.002 (.004)	-.012 (.008)	-.026 (.020)	-.018 (.011)	-2.745 (.652)
$\ln d_{53}$	.005 (.005)	.005 (.005)	.000 (.006)	.005 (.005)		.045 (.019)	.041 (.017)	-2.931 (.398)
T	-.0042 (.0010)			-.0033 (.0009)	-.0031 (.0007)		-.0029 (.0010)	4.000 (2.260)
$\sum \ln i$ coeffs.	.038 (.005)	.029 (.004)	.030 (.004)	.029 (.004)	.038 (.009)	.023 (.017)	.029 (.013)	
n (-15)	762	814	814	814	46	46	46	
r.d.f.	593	803	765	809	37	35	41	
$\hat{R}^2$	.140	.102	.093	.131	.670	.299	.511	

coefficient is, perhaps surprisingly, either zero or positive. Apparently, industries with more rapid rates of depreciation were those which, other things equal, reported more rapid growth in capacity. The absolutely small but negative coefficients of the time trend variable suggest that increases in capacity have been harder to come by as the years have progressed from 1955 to 1962.

In Table 8 we show the results of work with price-deflated capital stock and with output, capital stock, and employment all expressed as ratios of average sales of the 1956–58 period. While the latter transformation was intended to eliminate heteroscedasticity associated with the considerable differences in size of firms in the sample, it also had the effect of changing considerably the nature of the variance in the cross-section and over-all regressions. With each firm's observations normalized on its own sales base, the variance became essentially variance over time, as in the first-difference relations already discussed. The coefficient of lagged employment is strangely negative in the cross-section and over-all regressions, but the sum of the employment coefficients remains positive, if somewhat small. The coefficients of deflated, lagged capital stock are positive but small in the cross sections but quite high in the time series where the trend variable is excluded. The coefficient of the trend variable is positive and substantial, implying again a 3 to 5 per cent per annum increase in output with employment, capital, and utilization all held constant. Inclusion of trend, however, again reduces sharply the positive coefficient of lagged and deflated capital stock in the time series. This implies that the positive relation between capital stock and output involves a common trend element or that our relation again forces "embodiment" in capital of some other unspecified factors of production.

Summary and Conclusions

By way of summary we may indicate the following:

1. Log-linear relations of output with utilization of capacity, gross fixed assets, and the number of employees in individual firm cross sections prove consistent with many estimates suggesting relatively constant returns to scale. The elasticity of output with respect to capital stock is about one-third. Utilization of capacity does not enter significantly.

TABLE 8

Logarithms of Output/Sales,[a] 1959 - 62, as a Function of Logarithms of Utilization of Capacity, Price-Deflated-Capital-Stock/Sales[a] and Employment/Sales,[a] With and Without Time: Firm Time Series, Cross-Section and Over-All Regressions

Variable or Statistic	Regression Coefficients and Standard Errors						Means and Standard Deviations
	Firm Time Series		Firm Cross Section	Firm Cross Section Within Industries	Firm Over-All		
	With Time	Without Time			With Time	Without Time	
Constant term or $\ln O_t^s$					.609 (.058)	.682 (.059)	.118 (.222)
$\ln U_t$	.078 (.036)	.089 (.038)	.075 (.062)	.013 (.074)	.057 (.059)	.083 (.061)	-.254 (.191)
$\ln U_{t-1}$	.196 (.039)	.215 (.041)	.240 (.065)	.234 (.076)	.261 (.061)	.249 (.064)	-.252 (.183)
$\ln k_{p\,t-1}^s$	.088 (.072)	.381 (.057)	.061 (.012)	.064 (.019)	.061 (.012)	.059 (.013)	-.379 (.730)
$\ln e_t^s$	.469 (.046)	.455 (.049)	.472 (.078)	.498 (.080)	.471 (.077)	.476 (.080)	-2.933 (.515)
$\ln e_{t-1}^s$	.052 (.046)	-.001 (.048)	-.313 (.080)	-.309 (.081)	-.311 (.079)	-.319 (.082)	-2.941 (.501)
T	.030 (.005)				.051 (.009)		1.539 (1.063)
$\Sigma \ln U$ coeffs.	.274 (.059)	.305 (.063)	.315 (.056)	.247 (.062)	.317 (.056)	.332 (.058)	
$\Sigma \ln e$ coeffs.	.521 (.060)	.454 (.063)	.159 (.018)	.189 (.023)	.160 (.018)	.157 (.019)	
$\Sigma \ln U +$ $\ln k$ coeffs.	.362 (.102)	.686 (.093)	.376 (.057)	.311 (.067)	.378 (.057)	.392 (.059)	
$\Sigma \ln U +$ $\ln k +$ $\Sigma \ln e$ coeffs.	.883 (.096)	1.140 (.092)	.535 (.060)	.500 (.065)	.538 (.060)	.549 (.063)	
n (-10)	391	391	423	423	423	423	
r.d.f.	256	257	414	396	416	417	
$\hat{R}^2$	.490	.419	.262	.276	.308	.250	

[a] Average sales, 1956-58.

2. Pooled time series regressions of the same individual firm data for the years 1959–62 offer partially contrasting estimates. The utilization-of-capacity variable here looms large. Current changes in output of the firm are apparently accomplished partly by changing the "stocks" of employment and capital, and partly by altering their rates of utilization.

3. There is an upward movement of output of some 2 per cent to 5 per cent per annum not explained by the utilization, capital, and employment variables.

4. Current output is related to capital expenditures over a succession of previous years, and output is positively associated in time series with capital stock lagged several years. Much of this latter association is apparently accounted for by a linear trend in the 1959–62 period. The rate of depreciation is found to be negatively related to output.

5. Time series and cross-section regressions involving first differences (of logarithms) are more similar to each other, as might be expected from the nature of the variance and covariance involved. The sums of capital and labor coefficients are less than unity in all regressions. A positive constant term confirms again the contribution to growth of output of variables excluded from our relation. When the constant term is constrained to zero a large role is ascribed to changes in capital.

6. Exclusion of employment from relations over the years 1955–62 leads to generally higher coefficients for utilization of capacity and capital stock.

7. A positive relation is found between current and lagged ratios of capital expenditures to gross fixed assets and reported changes in capacity. One might infer, perhaps not too dangerously, that capital expenditures contribute to production because they contribute to the capacity to produce, and also that the McGraw-Hill data on year-to-year changes in capacity make some sense.

8. Comparison of firm time series regressions involving price-deflated capital stock, with and without inclusion of a time trend variable, suggests that capital can be constrained to "embody" the growth-producing effects of factors of production excluded from the relation estimated.

This is indeed a preliminary report. Much in the tables may merit further scrutiny and critical analysis. As new data are added, permitting more years of observations on several of the key variables, it should prove fruitful to devote further consideration to relations involving industry-year means. In particular, parameters should be estimated separately for different industries or industry groups. I am all too painfully aware of the specification errors and problems of aggregation involved in estimates of pooled regressions of a mythically unique production function for hundreds of different firms in many different industries with countless differences in technology.

Some broad outlines should, however, already be clear. Estimates will differ as between cross sections and time series of the same body of data, reflecting in large part, I would argue, differences in the nature of the variances which we seek to relate. Firms are not always, if ever, in equilibrium. They adjust differently to short-run changes in output, which dominate the time series variance, and long-run differences in output measured in cross sections, with short-run reactions involving significant alterations in the utilization of existing capacity.

These considerations would seem important to evaluation of estimates of critical parameters of the production function. Perhaps keeping them firmly in mind in further work will lead us a bit closer to Truth.

References

1. Arrow, K. J., H. B. Chenery, B. S. Minhas, and R. M. Solow, "Capital-Labor Substitution and Economic Efficiency," *The Review of Economics and Statistics,* Vol. XLIII, No. 3, August 1961, pp. 225–250.
2. Brown, Murray, and John S. de Cani, "Technological Change and the Distribution of Income," *International Economic Review,* Vol. 4, September 1963, pp. 289–309.
3. Eisner, Robert, "Capital Expenditures, Profits and the Acceleration Principle," in National Bureau of Economic Research, *Models of Income Determination* (Princeton, 1964).

Appendix A

TABLE A-1

Classification of Firms by Industry and Response
on Utilization-of-Capacity Questions

		Number of Firms	
		With Information on Utilization-of-Capacity Variable, 1955-62	
Industry	Total	Min.	Max.
Primary metals	38	15	32
Metalworking	230	113	188
Chemical processing	100	48	83
All other manufacturing	166	60	122
Mining	30	1	6
Utilities	43	0	0
Petroleum	33	10	16
Insurance and banks	44	0	0
Stores	71	0	0
Railroads	28	0	0
Transportation and communications other than railroads	19	0	0
All Industries	802	252	445

Appendix B

Algebraic Statement of Deviations
Used in the Various Regressions

Let X_{fnt} denote the observation vector of firm f in industry n for the year t.
Let F_{nt} denote the number of firms with observations in industry n in the year t.
Let τ_{fn} denote the number of years of observations for firm f in industry n.
Let N_t denote the number of industries containing observations in the year t.
Let τ denote the number of years for which observations are available.

Then, $\bar{X}_{fn} = \dfrac{1}{\tau_{fn}} \displaystyle\sum_{t=1}^{\tau_{fn}} X_{fnt} =$ the mean of observations of all years for firm f in industry n

and $X_{fnt} - \bar{X}_{fn}$ = the deviations used in firm time series, including only firms for which $\tau_{fn} > 1$.

$$\bar{X}_t = \frac{1}{\sum\limits_{n=1}^{N_t} F_{nt}} \sum_{n=1}^{N_t}\sum_{f=1}^{F_{nt}} X_{fnt}$$ = the mean of observations of all firms in all industries in year t

and $X_{fnt} - \bar{X}_t$ = the deviations used in firm cross sections.

$$\bar{X}_{nt} = \frac{1}{F_{nt}} \sum_{f=1}^{F_{nt}} X_{fnt}$$ = the mean of observations of all firms in industry n in year t (industry-year-mean)

and $X_{fnt} - \bar{X}_{nt}$ = the deviations used in firm cross sections within industries.

$$\bar{X} = \frac{1}{\sum\limits_{t=1}^{\tau}\sum\limits_{n=1}^{N_t} F_{nt}} \sum_{t=1}^{\tau}\sum_{n=1}^{N_t}\sum_{f=1}^{F_{nt}} X_{fnt}$$ = the mean of all observations of all industries in all years

and $X_{fnt} - \bar{X}$ = the deviations used in firm over-all regressions.

$$\bar{X}_n = \frac{1}{\sum\limits_{t=1}^{\tau} F_{nt}} \sum_{t=1}^{\tau}\sum_{f=1}^{F_{nt}} X_{fnt}$$ = the mean of all observations in industry n,

$\bar{X}_{nt} - \bar{X}_n$ = the deviations used in industry time series,

$\bar{X}_{nt} - \bar{X}_t$ = the deviations used in industry cross sections,

$\bar{X}_{nt} - \bar{X}$ = the deviations used in industry over-all regressions.

and $$\frac{F_{nt} \sum\limits_{t=1}^{\tau} N_t}{\sum\limits_{n=1}^{N_t}\sum\limits_{t=1}^{\tau} F_{nt}}$$ = the weight attached to the observation for industry n in the year t.

Appendix C

On CES Functions

It is hoped that the data available to us will permit direct estimates of parameters of the currently popular constant-elasticity-of-substitution production functions. Results obtained thus far do not appear to warrant more than a brief tentative report of what is being attempted.[1]

---

[1] I am particularly indebted to Jon Rasmussen for assistance in the preparation of this appendix.

Taking the somewhat more general form of Brown and de Cani, we may write the CES function as

$$(A1) \qquad Y = A[\delta K^{-\rho} + (1 - \delta)L^{-\rho}]^{-v/\rho},$$

where A is an "efficiency" or scale parameter, δ is the "distribution" parameter, ρ is the substitution parameter—the elasticity of substitution $= 1/(1+\rho)$ —and v defines the degree of the function, so that $v = 1$ implies homogeneity of the first degree and constant returns to scale and $v \gtrless 1$ imply increasing or decreasing returns to scale respectively.

The CES function, obviously, is not linear in either capital and labor or their logarithms. Following a suggestion of Murray Brown, however, it should be possible to form least-squares estimators of the CES function parameters by utilizing first-order Taylor series approximations.

Thus, letting A, δ, ρ, and v be designated respectively by C_i, $i = 1,2,3,4$, the CES function may be written:

$$(A2) \qquad Y = F(K, L, C_i),$$

and its first-order Taylor series approximation for assumed initial values, C_i^0, of the parameters, is

$$(A3) \qquad Y = F(K, L, C_i^0) + \sum_{i=1}^{4} F_i(K, L, C_i^0)(C_i - C_i^0),$$

where the F_i denote derivatives with respect to the C_i, and Y, K, and L are output, capital, and labor respectively. Transposing terms and letting the subscript j denote the jth observation, we may then form the statistical relation,

$$(A4) \quad Y_j - F(K_j, L_j, C_i^0) + \sum_{i=1}^{4} C_i^0 F_i(K_j, L_j, C_i^0) = \sum_{i=1}^{4} C_i F_i(K_j, L_j, C_i^0) + U_j.$$

Thus for each observation, j, for any assumed set of C_i^0, all of the terms are known values except the C_i on the right side of the equation, which are the parameters to be estimated, and the disturbance, U_j. We have a linear relation in which the unknown parameters can be estimated by direct least squares.

Initial values of the unknown parameters may be chosen on the basis of a priori knowledge or on the basis of prior estimates of the parameters of related linear or log-linear functions. Estimates of parameters secured from the Taylor-series formulation can then be used as assumed parameters in a second iteration. Successive iterations will reduce the variance of the dependent variable and, it is hoped, yield converging estimates of the parameters themselves.

The probability of achieving convergence would appear to depend considerably on initially assuming parameters not too far from the ultimate results of a possible convergence. This is made difficult, however, by the sensitivity of two of the parameters, A and δ, to the units of measurement of capital, labor and output.

For the estimates on which we are now able to report we used price deflated capital stock and divided each of our variables by average sales of the firm from 1956 to 1958, so that the variables would not be dominated by inter-firm size differences. We then defined

$$Y = 0_t{}^s$$

$$K = .5\,(k^s{}_{pt} + k^s{}_{p,t-1})$$

and

$$L = 10\,(e_t{}^s + e^s{}_{t-1})$$

thus setting a unit of employment as 50 employees, and assumed initial values of $A_o = 1.5$, $\delta_o = .25$, $\rho_o = .20$, and $v_o = 1.1$.

Attempts to achieve convergence in cross sectional estimates were unsuccessful. As indicated in Table C-1, after obtaining an acceptable first set of estimates we quickly exploded. By the fifth iteration not only had the estimates of ρ and v gone sky-high but, rather embarrassingly, those of A and δ turned negative. When we attempted to improve matters by constraining v at its estimated value after the first iteration, estimates still got out of

TABLE C-1

First-Order Taylor Series Estimates of Parameters,

Firm Cross Sections Within Industries[a]

Parameter or Statistic	Initial Assumed Value	Iterations				
		1	2	3	4	5
A	1.5	0.379 (.073)	.377 (.079)	0.269 (.480)	0.243 (.024)	−1.862 (2.227)
δ	0.25	0.263 (.011)	.312 (.047)	0.288 (.144)	0.369 (.031)	−.745 (.618)
ρ	0.20	0.178 (.035)	−.171 (.569)	−2.132 (1.784)	−1.453 (1.520)	8.149 (20.362)
v	1.1	1.050 (.030)	.369 (.504)	1.535 (1.266)	0.154 (.193)	9.222 (5.818)
$\hat{R}^2$		0.955	.296	0.202	0.692	0.181
σ dependent variable		1.080	.274	0.257	0.406	0.253

[a]646 Observations, 1959-62.

hand, with that of ρ going to -10.503 in the fifth iteration and 202.642 in the sixth. At this latter point δ was estimated as 1.319, thus implying a negative marginal product of labor!

We were able to secure apparent convergence in time-series estimates, however. It seemed clear within a dozen iterations, as may be seen in Table C-2, that all of our estimates were settling down. With a couple of "guided leaps" we were finally able to bring estimates of all of our parameters except A to within one unit at the fourth decimal place of their values at the previous iteration, at which point we terminated the laborious computations. And the estimates of A, albeit with large standard error, were apparently oscillating within a relatively narrow range.

Estimates of δ and ρ seemed plausible, the former not too far from the share of capital implied by our log-linear regressions and the latter suggesting an elasticity of substitution of 1.51. The time trend coefficient of about $.025$ is also consistent with our other estimates. The results of log-linear regressions with variables and observations identical to those employed here also argue for the reasonableness of the CES estimates of δ and the time trend, as seen in Table C-3.

What is troublesome, however, is the estimate of $.266$ for v, suggesting sharply decreasing returns to scale. It seemed that this might relate to the high covariance of F_A and F_v along with the substantial difference between the estimate of A and our a priori expectations based on the dimensions of the variables. We therefore undertook to constrain v at the estimate of $.865$ produced by the initial iteration. Apparent convergence was again attained as shown in Table C-4, with the estimates of $.311$ and $-.254$ for δ and ρ neither unreasonable nor far from those secured without constraining v. The estimate of $.918$ for A is sharper and more plausible, but the coefficient of determination is much lower and the standard error of the estimate of ρ is much higher. With v constrained at unity, iterations were continued to the point where the estimates of δ seemed to be settling about $.25$ and those of ρ were in à fairly narrow interval about zero.

The low unconstrained estimate of v from these data is perhaps not justly to be dismissed. It may well reflect the absence of a variable measuring utilization of capacity. (Attempts to introduce one raised formidable computational problems and convergence was not obtained, but the effort will be resumed in later work.) For if changes in inputs of capital and labor are associated with opposite movements in the rate of utilization, as would appear likely, output would move less than proportionately with capital and labor.

It was not feasible to iterate separately, but results of using as initial values in other regressions the penultimate estimates obtained in the unconstrained firm time series are fairly similar, as may be seen in Table C-5. This closeness of estimates of δ, ρ and v obtained from firm and industry cross-section and over-all regressions to those of the firm time series offers

TABLE C-2

First-Order Taylor Series Estimates of Parameters, Firm Time Series[a]

Parameter or Statistic	Initial Assumed Value	Iteration						Assumed Value	Iteration		Assumed Value	Iteration	
		1	2	3	4	11	12		3	4		1	2
A	1.5	1.358 (.213)	1.644 (.302)	2.141 (.516)	2.740 (.759)	3.935 (1.959)	3.962 (2.057)	4.093	4.017 (2.425)	4.018 (2.436)	4.020	4.019 (2.465)	4.026 (2.466)
δ	.25	.239 (.038)	.256 (.060)	.323 (.073)	.369 (.063)	.408 (.054)	.408 (.055)	.4105	.4110 (.059)	.4110 (.057)	.4111	.4112 (.059)	.4112 (.059)
ρ	.20	.203 (.117)	.132 (.192)	-.029 (.175)	-.130 (.105)	-.296 (.046)	-.305 (.046)	-.3492	-.3442 (.049)	-.3432 (.047)	-.3396	-.3397 (.049)	-.3397 (.049)
υ	1.1	.865 (.074)	.621 (.113)	.503 (.106)	.430 (.078)	.293 (.039)	.287 (.039)	.2705	.2682 (.040)	.2677 (.039)	.2665	.2664 (.041)	.2663 (.041)
T		.033 (.005)	.032 (.005)	.029 (.005)	.027 (.005)	.025 (.005)	.025 (.005)		.0248 (.005)	.0248 (.005)		.0248 (.005)	.0248 (.005)
$\hat{R}^2$		.892	.792	.782	.834	.929	.928		.924	.928		.923	.923
σ dependent variable		.295	.212	.207	.237	.360	.359		.349	.359		.347	.346

[a]609 Observations.

TABLE C-3

Log-Linear Estimates for Observations Used in CES First-Order Taylor Series Approximations

Variable or Statistic	Regression Coefficients and Standard Errors								Means and Standard Deviations	
	Firm Time Series	Firm Cross Section	Firm Cross Section Within Industries	Firm Over-All	Firm Over-All, Time Series Observations Only	Industry Time Series	Industry Cross Section	Industry Over-All	Firm Time Series	Firm Over-All
Constant term or dependent variable				.028 (.016)	.036 (.017)			.033 (.023)	.128 (.101)	.126 (.236)
$\ln K$	.232 (.061)	.016 (.010)	.041 (.017)	.017 (.010)	.015 (.010)	-.092 (.138)	-.009 (.017)	-.008 (.017)	-.407 (.084)	-.383 (.849)
$\ln L$	.517 (.054)	.152 (.016)	.191 (.019)	.153 (.016)	.157 (.016)	.152 (.136)	.020 (.044)	.024 (.043)	.053 (.077)	.062 (.525)
T	.0212 (.0044)			.0574 (.0079)	.0538 (.0082)	.0507 (.0071)		.0534 (.0111)	1.672 (1.145)	1.638 (1.063)
$\sum \ln K + \ln L$	.749 (.073)	.168 (.018)	.231 (.022)	.169 (.018)	.173 (.019)	.060 (.168)	.010 (.050)	.015 (.049)		
n	609	646	644	646	609	34	34	34		
r.d.f.	410	640	610	642	605	22	28	30		
$\hat{R}^2$	.336	.125	.175	.175	.178	.699	-.049	.384		

TABLE C-4

First-Order Taylor Series Estimates of Parameters, Firm Time Series, v Constrained to .865

Parameter or Statistic	Assumed Value	Iteration					Assumed Value	Iteration	Assumed Value	Iteration
		1	2	3	6	7				
A	1.358	.695 (.106)	.953 (.106)	.898 (.105)	.919 (.105)	.918 (.105)	.9177	.9189 (.105)	.9187	.9185 (.105)
δ	.239	.242 (.061)	.271 (.116)	.300 (.078)	.310 (.075)	.311 (.075)	.3116	.3113 (.075)	.3113	.3112 (.075)
ρ	.203	.118 (.195)	-.140 (.719)	-.185 (.337)	-.250 (.328)	-.253 (.325)	-.2566	-.2550 (.325)	-.2550	-.2544 (.325)
v	.865									
T		.032 (.005)	.031 (.005)	.030 (.005)	.030 (.005)	.030 (.005)		.0295 (.005)		.0295 (.005)
$\hat{R}^2$		.312	.347	.334	.344	.344		.345		.345
σ dependent variable		.118	.121	.120	.121	.121		.121		.121

TABLE C-5

First-Order Taylor Series Estimates of Parameters, Assumed Values from Firm Time Series,
Penultimate Iteration, Firm and Industry Time Series, Cross-Section, and Over-All Regressions

Parameter or Statistic	Assumed Value	Estimates and Standard Errors								Means and Standard Deviations	
		Firm Time Series	Firm Cross Section	Firm Cross Section Within Industries	Firm Over-All	Firm Over-All, Time Series Observations Only	Industry Time Series	Industry Cross Section	Industry Over-All	Firm Time Series	Firm Over-All
Constant term or dependent variable					.877 (.763)	.209 (.800)			-.244 (2.639)	1.030 (.346)	1.115 (2.195)
A	4.019	4.026 (2.466)	.194 (.771)	-1.066 (.890)	.140 (.770)	.820 (.806)	-15.426 (10.7)	1.402 (2.677)	1.275 (2.648)	.983 (.016)	.988 (.123)
δ	.412	.411 (.059)	.371 (.011)	.376 (.019)	.370 (.011)	.365 (.011)	.268 (.144)	.385 (.024)	.384 (.024)	-.411 (.103)	-.394 (1.002)
ρ	-.340	-.340 (.049)	-.377 (.016)	-.355 (.020)	-.376 (.016)	-.374 (.016)	-.284 (.126)	-.386 (.060)	-.387 (.059)	-.542 (.106)	-.542 (.647)
ν	.266	.266 (.041)	.275 (.013)	.301 (.015)	.276 (.013)	.265 (.014)	.520 (.171)	.249 (.042)	.252 (.042)	-.567 (.962)	-.266 (7.374)
T		.0248 (.0054)			.0705 (.0089)	.0671 (.0090)	.0723 (.0120)		.0662 (.0143)	1.672 (1.145)	1.638 (1.063)
n		609	646	644	646	609	34	34	34	Y 1.166 (.124)	Y 1.164 (.267)
r.d.f.		408	638	608	640	603	20	26	28	K .931 (.084)	K .974 (.908)
$\hat{R}^2$		.923	.988	.982	.988	.988	.951	.997	.996	L 1.201 (.092)	L 1.214 (.685)
σ dependent variable		.346	2.194	1.699	2.195	2.077	.227	1.524	1.462		

some hope for convergence to roughly common values in most of the regressions.

Finally, some attention may be given to the problem of our estimates of A, which vary so much from regression to regression, with high standard errors. The derivative of the CES function with respect to A is, of course,

$$(A5) \qquad F_A = [\delta K^{-\rho} + (1 - \delta)L^{-\rho}]^{-v/\rho},$$

and another estimate of A may thus be obtained by constraining δ, ρ and v at their final estimated values and regressing Y on F_A with the constant term constrained to zero. Employing the time series observations only, we thus estimate A as 1.178 (with a standard error of .088). This is, in a sense, the weighted average efficiency or scale parameter of the various firms in the sample. It may perhaps be compared with the value of 1.037, the anti-log of the constant term of .036 in the firm over-all log-linear regression of Table C-3 (column 6). Combining it with our estimates of the other parameters, we have

$$(A6) \qquad Y = 1.178[.411K^{.340} + .589L^{.340}]^{.784} + u$$

for which the coefficient of determination, relating back to deviations from the mean for each individual firm, is .158. Where the constant term is not constrained to zero, the estimate of A is again a high 4.686, but the coefficient of determination is .363, which compares favorably with the analogous $\hat{R}^2$ of .336 shown in the log-linear relation of Table C-3.

A number of refinements, including appropriate application of utilization variables, are called for. I hope that it will be possible to incorporate some of them in ongoing research. But it does appear now that there is a possibility of progress in direct estimation of CES production functions along the lines we have attempted.

COMMENT

BERT G. HICKMAN, The Brookings Institution

In this preliminary report on important research in progress, Robert Eisner uses micro data to estimate production functions of the Cobb-Douglas and CES types. The McGraw-Hill Capital Expenditure Surveys provide estimates of capacity utilization, employment, and capital expenditures, and these observations have been supplemented by matched accounting data on sales, inventories, gross fixed assets, and depreciation charges. The unit of observation is the individual firm, and annual observations are available for a broad range of industrial activities and for periods of four or more years. This body of data affords some unusual advantages in the estimation of production functions, and Eisner has exploited many of them in this report of his preliminary findings. I believe that he has not gone far enough in this direction, however, and I will have some, I hope constructive, suggestions to offer during my discussion of his preliminary results.

The basic Cobb-Douglas estimates are contained in Table 2 of the paper. The logarithm of output is regressed on the logarithms of capacity utilization, gross fixed assets, and employment. Results are presented for both cross sections and time series. The time series results are the pooled regressions of deviations about the means of observations for individual firms over periods of two to four years. The cross sections refer to deviations about the means of observations for all firms in each year, although the deviations for all years are pooled in the regressions.

Eisner notes in his introduction that estimates of the production function have been "bedeviled by difficulties in accounting for less-than-capacity utilization of capital," and one of the presumptive advantages of the McGraw-Hill data is the availability of a utilization variable. As they stand, Eisner's results suggest that this may be an illusory advantage insofar as the cross-section estimates are concerned, since the utilization variable is insignificant and therefore of little help in accounting for interfirm differences in the utilization of capital. As Eisner points out, this finding suggests that "differences between firms in reported utilization of capacity reflect rather interfirm differences in the measure than anything systematically related to output." It is hoped, however, that further work with the utilization variable may lead to better results.

One problem is that the utilization rates are reported on an end-of-year basis, whereas output is measured for the year as a whole. Thus the output differences among firms are free of seasonal influences, but this is not true of the utilization rates, which should be adjusted to an annual basis for comparability with the output variables. I have shown elsewhere that the disparity between the McGraw-Hill and other estimates of capacity utilization based on annual data can be substantially reduced by converting the former estimates to an annual basis. The correction is based on the ratio of, say, December production to that for the entire year, and while this information probably is not known for the individual firms in the McGraw-Hill sample, a uniform adjustment could be made for all firms in a given industry on the basis of independent production data.

Another problem is that the optimum or cost-minimizing rate of utilization may vary widely among firms, so that if two firms report, say, 80 per cent utilization of peak capacity, one may be operating to the right of the minimum point on its short-run cost curve, whereas the other is to the left of that point. The first firm would therefore possess less than the equilibrium amount of capital for the given output and the second firm, more than the equilibrium amount. Now, the firms in the McGraw-Hill sample are asked at least occasionally to report their preferred as well as their actual operating rates, and it seems reasonable to assume that the preferred rate is the cost-minimizing rate. This suggests that the ratio of the actual to the preferred utilization rate—which ratio implicitly expresses output as a percentage of optimum instead of peak capacity— would be a better indicator than the actual rate of the extent to which the existing capital stock falls short or exceeds the equilibrium stock corresponding to the existing level of output. The preferred rate for each firm may not be available for every year, but it probably does not change much over time and could be extrapolated or interpolated for the missing years.

I have discussed these measurement problems at some length because of the importance of the utilization adjustment for Eisner's avowed purpose of obtaining direct estimates of production function parameters from data on output, capital, and employment. He correctly observes that firms are not always, or ever, in equilibrium. Thus the measured labor and capital inputs of a given year are unlikely to be the equilibrium values corresponding to the measured output of the firm. Whereas I agree that cross sections are better able than short time series to reflect long-run adjustments of capital and labor to output, it is nonetheless likely that the capital stock variable in particular will be subject to large errors owing to disequilibrium conditions in each firm. The resulting bias in the estimate of the capital parameter could be reduced or eliminated by an adequate adjustment for under- or overutilization of capital in the various firms.

Incidentally, the utilization variable cannot properly be used to adjust both the capital and labor inputs. Despite the growing recognition of the fact that labor as well as capital inputs may adjust with a lag to short-term output movements, it would be surprising indeed if the speed of adjustment were not faster and the amount of disequilibrium smaller for labor than capital inputs. Ambiguous though it may be to employ a capacity utilization variable to adjust capital alone, the error is apt to be smaller than to neglect the adjustment entirely or to apply it to labor instead of capital.

This line of thought suggests that the utilization variable should not enter the regressions independently, but rather should be constrained so that its coefficient equals that of the capital variable to which it is conceptually attached; or, what amounts to the same thing, that the utilization ratio should simply be used to adjust the capital stock data prior to fitting the regressions. Conceptually, this adjustment would amount to converting the actual stock data into estimates of the equilibrium capital requirements corresponding to the observed outputs and labor inputs.

It may be objected that the foregoing procedure would place too much trust in the utilization variable as an indicator of the divergence between the actual and equilibrium capital stock. Eisner's practice of including the utilization variable separately could be regarded as a test of whether the variable is indeed a valid one for the purpose, in which case its independently estimated coefficient should differ insignificantly from that of the unadjusted capital variable. The two coefficients do appear to differ insignificantly in the time series results without trend, though not in the trend-adjusted results.

To turn to other aspects of the Cobb-Douglas estimates in Table 2, Eisner notes that the estimated cross-section elasticities of output with respect to capital and labor are respectively about one-third and two-thirds and that their sum is virtually equal to one, implying constant returns to scale. There are several reasons why these economic implications should not be taken at face value, however. (1) A radically smaller estimate of the labor coefficient is obtained when the variables are transformed to logarithmic first differences in the regressions presented by Eisner in Table 4, even though the parameters to be estimated are conceptually the same as in Table 2. (2) The dependent variable is output rather than value added, so that even if the capital and labor coefficients were equal to the true values, the unknown coefficient of the missing third factor—materials input—should properly enter the calculation of the degree of returns to scale. (3) The estimated coefficients are biased downward because of errors in the independent variables.

It should be possible to reduce some of the bias stemming from errors in the independent variables. Capacity utilization, capital stock, and employment are all measured on an end-of-year basis, whereas output refers to the entire year. Eisner therefore includes both the current- and preceding-year values of the independent variables in his regressions, and then sums the two coefficients for each variable to estimate its elasticity. This procedure, however, makes no allowance for different seasonal patterns in the labor and utilization variables as among firms in widely differing industries. Moreover, labor input is measured by number of employees rather than man-hours; so no account is taken of differences in hours of work between firms or over time. It should be feasible to devise correction factors to mitigate some of these observational errors, along the lines suggested above in my discussion of the utilization variable.

Capital stock in the regressions under discussion is measured by the book value of gross fixed assets at original cost. Price deflation to reduce the various vintages of capital goods to a constant-cost basis would be desirable and is attempted by Eisner in some additional regressions presented in Tables 3 and 8. How much difference this makes for the estimated elasticities is impossible to state, however, since the latter regressions differ from the earlier ones in other characteristics than the deflation of gross fixed assets.

Even when deflated to a constant-cost basis, the stock of gross fixed assets may comprise diverse vintages of capital goods with widely varying productivities. The simplest way to allow for the differing productivities of differing vintages is to measure the stock net of depreciation, on the assumption that technical change occurs smoothly and that the depreciation rate includes an obsolescence factor. If net stock data were not available for the firms in the sample, probably little could be done through other methods of allowing for embodied technical change, since these other methods would require knowledge of the past history of capital accumulation in each firm in order to weight the several vintages by the appropriate productivity improvement factors, even assuming that independent information existed about the latter.

So much for detailed comments on the data and the basic Cobb-Douglas results. Eisner also presents several regression experiments for which no theoretical justification is provided. The regressions in Table 3 are still avowedly production functions, in that they involve capital and labor inputs as explanatory variables, but they also include the depreciation rate as an independent variable, and the capital variable is furthermore broken into several vintages which enter independently. Neither of these departures from the conventional in production function specification is explained. Table 5 relates output to capacity utilization and capital stock, but includes no labor input. In Table 6 the utilization variable is used to convert observed output into a measure of the maximum output which the capital stock is presumptively capable of producing, and the corrected output is then regressed on capital stock alone. In Table 7, McGraw-Hill data on reported changes in capacity are regressed on the ratio of capital expenditures to gross fixed assets, the depreciation rate, and time. Whatever they may be, the regressions in Tables 5 to 7 are not complete production functions, and the reader may reasonably ask what meaning can be attributed to them as structural relationships and what purpose they are intended to serve.

In conclusion, I strongly endorse Eisner's proposal to make parameter estimates separately for different industries in future work. One of the principal advantages of the firm as the unit of observation is the opportunity it affords to allow for differing technologies among industries and to obtain greater homogeneity in the data, and thus far Eisner has neglected this opportunity. Another characteristic of his sample, which distinguishes it from most other cross-sectional data that has been used to estimate production functions, is the fact that time series observations are available for the firms. Thus it becomes possible to estimate a separate set of cross-section parameters for each year and to study the changes in the parameters over successive years, instead of pooling the cross-section observations as in the present work. A series of cross-section parameter estimates, preferably within well-defined industry groups, would permit study of changes in the constant term and input coefficients over time, possibly throwing important light on questions about the rate and neutrality of technical progress and about cyclical variations in apparent productivity.

DALE W. JORGENSON

I have only one objection to Eisner's very interesting paper. It seems to me that the paper lacks an explicit theoretical framework for interpreting the empirical results. We have some forty-eight regressions, yielding a wide variety of estimates. The coefficients associated with employment range from .157 to .659. Those associated with capital stock range from .266 to .937. It is difficult to see just what one is supposed to make of all these estimates.

The purpose of this comment is to supply a theoretical interpretation for Eisner's empirical findings. The basic theoretical model is only partly implicit in Eisner's regressions. When the model is made explicit, it becomes apparent that Eisner's statistical models could be improved. Nevertheless, the results obtained provide a clear and convincing picture of the underlying reality. I hope that the familiarity of the picture will not prevent a proper appreciation of it.

In constructing a theoretical framework for production one would like to have a single model that could be applied to all the different sets of data considered by Eisner—time series and cross section, firm and industry. Implicitly, Eisner takes the position that for the present this is asking too much. We are presented instead with a set of results based on a less comprehensive model. To fit this simpler model to the data a certain amount of legitimate doctoring of the data—taking out the variation associated with differences in firm or year or industry means—is required.

The basic theoretical model consists of a neoclassical production function,

$$Q^* = F(K^*, L^*),$$

where Q^* is the flow of output, K^* the flow of capital services, and L^* the flow of labor services. We may write each of these flows as the product of a stock and a rate of utilization of the stock:

$$Q^* = Q \cdot W,$$
$$K^* = K \cdot U,$$
$$L^* = L \cdot V,$$

where, for example, K is capital stock and U is the rate of utilization of that stock.

It may be noted that this model is essentially technological rather than economic. A model based on the economic theory of production would include not only a production function but also marginal productivity conditions for capital and labor services. Eisner disregards the possibility of obtaining information about the production function from the covariation of outputs and inputs on the one hand and price ratios on the other.

If the production function has Cobb-Douglas form we may write (ignoring the constant term):

$$\ln Q + \ln W = \alpha[\ln W + \ln U] + \beta[\ln L + \ln V],$$

where α and β are the elasticities of output with respect to capital and labor services, respectively. It is here that objections to Eisner's statistical model arise. Eisner has direct observations on the flow of output. He identifies K with the stock of capital and U with its rate of utilization. By analogy we must identify L with employment (the stock of labor). But V, the rate of utilization of labor, measured as man-hours per man employed, is missing from Eisner's initial empirical specification. Later in the paper the stock of labor itself is omitted from the empirical specification. One might also object to Eisner's omission of inventories and financial assets from capital and to errors of aggregation in both labor and capital.

In view of all the objections that can be raised to Eisner's implementation of the basic statistical model, it may be surprising to find that the model "works" at all. But it does work, as Eisner's empirical findings reveal.

Starting with the statistical model Eisner calls "firm over-all" in Tables 2 and 3 we find that the sum of coefficients associated with capital stock (Table 2) and lagged capital stock together with investment (Table 3) is .339 and .329, respectively, with a time variable included, and .343 and .330, respectively, with no time variable included. Turning to the coefficients associated with the stock of labor we find coefficients of .648 and .650 without time and .652 and .658 with time.

The disturbing feature of the firm over-all results is that the sum of coefficients associated with rates of utilization of capital is essentially zero, with or without a time variable. From the basic theoretical model it is clear that this variable should have exactly the same coefficient as capital stock, namely, .35 or thereabouts. As a statistical hypothesis, the equality of the coefficients of capital and its rate of utilization would be rejected at almost any level of significance.

The story told by Eisner's results for "firm cross section within industries" and "firm cross section" models is much the same. In these models "dummy variables" for years and industries and for years alone are included along with the explanatory variables. The coefficients of the explanatory variables are essentially unaffected. The results in Table 4 are similar to those in Tables 2 and 3 even though employment is excluded, provided that a time variable is included. Table 6 presents a somewhat different picture, but this is the result of Eisner's assumption for the statistical model underlying this table that the coefficient of the rate of utilization is unity. This assumption is so clearly contradicted by the evidence that these results may be disregarded.

The statistical model underlying the results labeled "firm time series" is different from Eisner's other statistical models in that dummy variables for individual firms are included along with the explanatory variables. No dummies for year or industry are included in these regressions. The results for firm time series are dramatically different from those for the other models. The sum of coefficients associated with the rate of utilization is .414 and .374 in Tables 2 and 3 with time included in the regression. With time excluded the sums are .409 and .401, respectively. On the other hand, the coefficients associated with capital stock are .266 and .172 with time included and .446 and .385 without time.

Turning to the results presented in Table 8, both output and capital stock are divided by sales for the individual firm. Not too surprisingly, this has essentially the same effect as removing "firm effects" in the firm time series model. The sum of coefficients associated with rates of utilization is .332 for the firm over-all model with no time variable included in the regression. Taking out year effects as well changes the coefficient to .315; removing both year and industry effects results in a coefficient of .247. Taking out firm effects yields a coefficient of .305 with no time variable included and .274 with time included. The sum of coefficients associated with capital stock is relatively small in most regressions— —.088, .381, .061, .064, .061, .059.

The switch in relative importance of employment and capital stock and their rate of utilization enables us to conclude with Eisner that inter-firm variations take the form of variations in "factor stock" while intra-firm variations take the form of variations in rates of utilization. However, the equality of the sum of coefficients of factor stock and utilization in the firm over-all regressions to the sum of coefficients of factor stocks and rates of utilization with firm effects removed enables us to draw a much stronger conclusion. The basic technological model with the flow of output as a function of flows of labor and capital inputs is strongly confirmed by the data.

We can suggest a further test of the basic theoretical model. Just as interfirm variations in capital input are largely variations in capital stock rather than its rate of utilization, so interfirm variations in labor input should be largely variations in employment. Turning to the empirical results we find this hypothesis strongly confirmed. With no firm effects removed the sum of coefficients of employment is always in the neighborhood of .65. The estimates from Tables 2 and 3 are .651, .659, .629, .619, .652, .658, .648 and .652. With firm effects removed this sum of coefficients drops to .275, .301, .242, and .278. Deflating output and employment by sales in Table 8, Eisner obtains further estimates of .521, .454, .159, .189, .160, and .157.

To test the basic theoretical model further, observations on the rate of utilization of labor would be required. The expected result would be a sum of coefficients of rates of utilization equal to approximately .65 with firm effects removed. The use of dummy variables for firms or deflation of output, employment, and capital stock by sales should produce approximately the same results.

My over-all conclusion is that the basic theoretical model is strongly confirmed by Eisner's empirical results. Interfirm variations in output are explained largely by interfirm variations in capital stock and employment. Variations in rates of utilization of productive capacity and stocks of capital and labor wash out because of errors of measurement. Intrafirm variations in output are explained largely by intrafirm variations in rates of utilization. Variations in productive capacity and stocks of inputs wash out. Both interfirm and intrafirm variations may be represented as movements along a production function of Cobb-Douglas form with an elasticity of labor services of .65 and an elasticity of capital services of .35. These results are, of course, precisely the results obtained by Douglas in the course of his research over the twenty-year period, 1927–47.

To sum up: Eisner has successfully extended the applicability of the basic Cobb-Douglas model to the level of the individual firm. By introducing the rate of utilization of capital explicitly, a new feature of the model has been uncovered. Eisner's findings should be followed up as quickly as possible by testing the implications of the model for the stock of labor and its rate of utilization. The implications of the model for both capital and labor should be further tested by direct measurement of capital and labor services.

EVSEY D. DOMAR

My question here is addressed to Mr. Eisner in particular, but also applies as well to several other authors. I wonder what has happened in all these studies to material inputs? If they are omitted because of the lack of required data, we have an answer, even if, to my mind, a regrettable one. But usually an author begins his paper with the model that he *would like to fit;* then he apologizes for the lack of data and fits a different one. I have not found any apologies for omitting material inputs from both sides of the equation and thus working with value added on the one side and with only labor and capital on the other. Is this then the desired method? And yet it seems to me that a production function is supposed to explain a productive process, such as the making of potato chips from potatoes (and other ingredients), labor and capital. It must take some ingenuity to make potato chips without potatoes. I do not mean that the omission of material inputs is necessarily wrong. Rather that it is not at all obvious that it is the preferred method. Among other things, it results in a larger residual, at least with a Cobb-Douglas function, and this remains true even when output and value added grow at exactly the same relative rate.

REPLY by Eisner

I may respond briefly to several related themes in the very useful comments which have been presented.

First, on the failure to include materials as an argument of the production function—the creation of potato chips without potatoes, as Domar has so aptly phrased it—I must of course plead guilty. I have boasted frequently about the nature of the data which we have built about the McGraw-Hill capital expenditure surveys; but these were put together originally in connection with work on the investment function and whether or not information as to materials purchased might have been solicited, I did not think of it at the time.

At some point it may indeed be well to graft on to this body of data individual-firm figures regarding materials, but I do wonder whether their use is likely to alter significantly our estimates of the relative contributions to output of labor and fixed capital. As matters stand, the omission of the materials variable may be expected to add considerably to the error term in our relations. But it is not clear that subtraction of materials purchased from our measure of "output," so that the dependent variable could be value added, would give us different parameter estimates for "labor" and "capital." [1]

---

[1] This may smack a bit of the Marxian notion of "constant capital," but is that likely to be far wrong in the case of materials? Fixed capital may well have some

Both Hickman and Jorgenson seem to believe that the coefficient of "utilization of capacity" should be the same as that of capital. I am not persuaded, either on conceptual grounds or by consideration of the nature of the data. First, I fail to see why, for example, a 10 per cent increase in utilization of existing capital stock should have the same effect upon output as a 10 per cent increase in the amount of capital utilized at the existing rate. Indeed, if this were so one might wonder why firms ever did alter their capital stock. It would appear that one could do just as well by utilizing existing capital more intensively, and think of the money one would save!

But further, it is hardly clear that the McGraw-Hill question, "At what rate of capacity were you operating?" relates exclusively to utilization of capital. "Capacity" means different things to different firms, but one might well imagine the concept to relate to what can be produced, without prohibitive cost, when utilizing fully *all* of the productive factors available to the firm. As has become increasingly well recognized in recent work, labor itself is a somewhat less than completely variable stock, the utilization of which varies markedly as the firm maintains a relatively stable level of employment in the face of fluctuating demand and output. Indeed, Jorgenson allows explicitly for varied utilization of labor in the "explicit model" which he provided for my paper. I fail to see why, in terms of *his* model, he then proceeds to interpret the utilization-of-capacity variable as relating only to capital.

I could not know a priori precisely what the utilization-of-capacity variable might reflect. If it did relate to the capacity provided by the stocks of both capital and labor and if diminishing returns to increased utilization of existing stocks were not of major importance over the range of variation of utilization experienced, the coefficient of the rate of utilization might even be unity.

In fact, as Jorgenson observes, the utilization-of-capacity variables in the firm time series (with firm effects removed, as Jorgenson puts it) do tend to have sums of coefficients of the same order of magnitude as the sums of the capital coefficients in the firm cross sections, which are based upon firm effects, and in the firm over-all regressions, where firm effects dominate. I would not carry the point as far as he, however. The

substantial "productivity" associated with the magnitude of its time dimension, as the socialist planners of Eastern Europe seem now to be perceiving more clearly, but should relatively short-lived inputs of materials be expected to contribute much more (or less) to output than their own value?

sum of the utilization coefficients of .414 shown in the "firm time series with time" in Table 2 is somewhat higher than the .340 estimate of the capital coefficients suggested in the cross-section and over-all regressions. What with the errors in variables due to seasonal factors of which Hickman reminds us and the general impreciseness of this utilization variable I remain skeptical of Jorgenson's inference that variations in capital stock and in utilization of capacity have precisely the same effect upon output.

I do probably owe the reader some further explanation, as Hickman has indicated, of the results reported in Tables 3 through 7. In Table 3, I was attempting to offer some measure of the time profile or lags relating capital and output. This was in part, I believe, successful. Rates of depreciation were included as an offset to the gross figures entering into the capital expenditure variables.

Table 4 involves the same theoretical relation as Table 2 but, put in first-difference form, removes any common trend effect from the parameter estimates. It also almost certainly reflects a relatively greater "noise" component in the variance of the independent variables, which tends to bias their parameter estimates downward. Table 5 seems worth noting because it includes a considerably larger body of data, relating to eight years instead of four. Unavailability of employment data for the early years forces the obvious misspecification in the exclusion of the labor variables.

Tables 6 and 7, while of only marginal value and again involving misspecifications because of the unavailability of employment data, might merit some consideration for the light they cast on the role and nature of the capacity variables in the McGraw-Hill series. It might of course also be observed that, to the extent that labor and capital stock are kept in a fairly stable equilibrium relation, the coefficients of capital variables will offer some at least rough measure of the joint contribution of capital and labor to output.

I am inclined to defend myself somewhat against the charge of presenting "a wide variety of estimates" without "an explicit theoretical framework for interpreting the empirical results." For one thing, Solow's paper is devoted to a major survey of the theoretical literature, and the implicit theory of the Cobb-Douglas function (or the CES function discussed in my Appendix B) is certainly well known to participants in this conference. As I have suggested above, Jorgenson's attempt to be more "explicit" than I felt I should or could be runs into difficulties both at the conceptual level, in the assumption that quantities of factors and their rates of utilization enter multiplicatively in the production function with identical parameters, and in the further interpretation of "capacity" as relating only to the stock of capital. (I may add that I am puzzled by Jorgenson's apparent view of output as the product of a stock of output and the rate of utilization of that stock.)

But the complaint of the wide variety of estimates is by now a familiar one. Nerlove has, I hope, made us all shudder with the weight of evidence of just how disparate many of the estimates are. That variety bears some consideration precisely in the light of my paper. For aside from certain differences which may be ignored because of the high standard errors attached to industry regressions based on relatively few observations, and further discounting differences relating to alternate specifications where data on all variables were not available, a point of stress in my findings may well be the explanation of the systematic differences in estimates which emerge. These, it may be reiterated, as both Jorgenson and I have stated them, relate to the different results to be obtained from cross sections and from time series. And these differences, I have stressed, are illuminated by the role of the utilization-of-capacity data fortunately available from the McGraw-Hill surveys. What can now be seen fairly clearly is that variation over time reflects in considerable part disequilibrium positions which, at least without appropriate adjustment, will give us biased and misleading estimates of the production surface. In the short run, firms alter their utilization of capacity, and changes in capital stock have relatively little to do with output, while the effects of changes in employment remain significant but are also sharply reduced. Interfirm variance, on the other hand, is apparently dominated by differences in equilibrium levels of capital stock and employment.

Exposure of these differences in estimates, and of their nature, would seem of considerable moment in explorations of the production function, and elsewhere as well.

PRODUCTION ANALYSIS
AND ECONOMIC POLICY

AGGREGATIVE PRODUCTION FUNCTIONS AND ECONOMIC GROWTH POLICY

RICHARD R. NELSON

THE RAND CORPORATION

AS the title of my paper indicates, I have narrowed the scope somewhat from the broader topic assigned to me. I have focused on the question: What guidance for economic growth policy is provided by our present knowledge of the relationship between various aggregative inputs and the production possibilities open to an economy. Further, I shall limit myself to the situation in the United States.

By economic growth policy I mean policy concerned with influencing the rate at which potential output will grow—the speed at which the frontier of production possibilities will push ahead. There are many and diverse kinds of knowledge inputs to economic growth policy making. Complementing or competing with the formal knowledge of professional economists is knowledge held by other disciplines, and hunches and inferences drawn by policy makers from experience, analogy, and *ad hoc* reasoning. The relative influence of the economist's formal knowledge about production relations depends, and rightly so, on its strength and scope. Perhaps even more important, the way knowledge is most fruitfully employed in decision-making depends on how reliable and complete that knowledge is.

The first parts of this paper will be concerned with assessing certain aspects of the strength and scope of existing knowledge. Then I shall attempt to assess in broad terms what real assistance to policy making is provided by present knowledge, and how that knowledge might most fruitfully be used.

Uncertainties About the Aggregate Production Function

By an aggregate production function I mean the constraint or set of constraints that determines the outer bounds of the set of production possibilities as a function of the quantity and quality of various inputs. Here I am interested in the dynamic aspects—the relationship between growth of potential output over time and increases or improvements in the inputs and changes in the nature of the constraints. Clearly, knowledge of this sort is a key input to growth policy making; it points out the variables on which to operate, and indicates the results of effecting various changes. Obviously the more complete and correct the list of influential variables, and the more accurate and reliable the estimates of exactly how and how much their changes will increase potential output, the greater the assistance to growth policy.

Several of the papers of this conference are concerned with examining the present state of knowledge regarding just this. I shall try to avoid too much overlapping or conflicting with these papers, but a brief assessment of the strength of existing knowledge about the dynamic aggregate production function is pivotal in examining the role of such knowledge in the making of growth policy.

Over the past several years the list of variables treated explicitly in aggregate production function theory has increased significantly. Not so long ago theory pointed to two variables—quantity of labor and quantity of physical capital—and wrung its hands that these alone appeared to be only half the story, increases in total factor productivity appearing about as important as increases in the variables dealt with explicitly. While sometimes increases in total factor productivity—measured as a residual or a time trend—were called technical progress, no one really believed this was all there was to it, and in any case such an implicit treatment of technological progress adds little to knowledge.[1]

Certainly today we have a much larger set of variables that we deal with explicitly. Denison works with at least a dozen variables.[2] Even

---

[1] For example, R. M. Solow, "Technical Change and the Aggregate Production Function," *Review of Economics and Statistics,* August 1957, or M. Abramowitz, "Resource and Output Trends in the United States," *American Economic Review,* May 1956.

[2] E. F. Denison, *The Sources of Economic Growth in the United States and the Alternatives Before Us,* Washington, D.C., 1962.

the more modest analyses generally attempt at the minimum to treat explicitly skills and knowledge embodied in the work force and deal at least in a semiexplicit way with the constraints imposed by the limits of man's technological knowledge, as well as examining the effects of different quantities of labor and capital.[3] Assuming these variables are important, over the past few years our growing knowledge of aggregate production relations has increased in usefulness to policymaking by providing a richer set of variables that policy can try to influence.

However, our knowledge still would appear to be quite weak with respect to the functional form of the relationships, and very weak with respect to the size of certain key parameters.

Problems probably are fewer with respect to the relationship between increased output potential and greater quantities of labor and capital inputs than with respect to other variables, but even here there are considerable uncertainties. Let me mention just a few. Denison has suggested that there is a strong negative relationship between average hours worked per week and the quality and intensity of work.[4] Clearly, the strength of this relationship (and the way it works) matters for growth policy, since one of the variables on which policy might act is trends in the average work week. Yet it is equally clear at the present time that the strength of the relationship is highly uncertain. With respect to physical capital, uncertainties still exist, for example, about the magnitude of the embodiment effect: the amount of gross investment that is really needed each year to keep the nation's capital stock from falling further out of date, and the extent to which more gross investment than this serves to achieve a fruitful updating of embodied technology.[5] The power of policies which increase the gross investment rate certainly depends on the answers to questions such as these. As another example, there is still some uncertainty with respect to the elasticity of substitution between capital and labor inputs, although over the short run this may not be very important.[6]

[3] For example, R. Nelson, "Aggregate Production Functions and Medium Range Growth Projections," *American Economic Review,* September 1964, or Z. Griliches, "Agricultural Production Functions," *American Economic Review,* December 1964.

[4] *Op. cit.* Of course, this notion has been long-standing in some of the economic literature.

[5] See, for example, E. F. Denison, "The Unimportance of the Embodied Question," *American Economic Review,* March 1964.

[6] The most recent results would appear to be those of P. A. David and Th. van de Klundert, "Biased Efficiency Growth in the U.S.," *American Economic Review,* June 1965. However, clearly a slightly different specification of the model can lead to different conclusions.

Our knowledge is far weaker regarding the effect of increasing the skills and knowledge possessed by the work force. Let us assume, for the moment, that years of educational attainment is an adequate proxy variable for this, and focus on the question of what the effect would be of an increase in average educational attainments, without worrying that we are using an input once removed from the production function. Presently we tend to treat educational attainment as a factor that multiplies the power of labor input; education makes a man a more efficient laborer —able to do more each hour than a person with less education. Undoubtedly this is part of what education does. At least the rudiments of education enable a man to make fewer mistakes in doing almost any job and to understand and follow instructions better. For certain jobs special courses and training programs likewise perform this function. However, one wonders how sharply diminishing returns set in to increases in average educational attainment, or in the number of people who go through certain occupational training programs, or in the length of these programs. Surely there are limits to what a man need know to do a certain job well, and to the number of jobs where a great deal of education or training is needed.[7]

The suspicion about sharply diminished returns becomes stronger when a second, and quite different, role of educational attainment is recognized: that of serving as an easily observable indicator to an employer of a person's intelligence and discipline. In this role the educational system serves not so much to impart useful knowledge and skills— but rather to put a different label on different kinds of people.[8] Assuming that the more intelligent and disciplined have more advantage in some jobs than others, improved ability of employers to discriminate in advance should result in an improvement in labor allocation, which should increase potential output. But in this role almost surely there would be little return from increasing average educational attainments; indeed such increases as would result from forcing early dropouts to remain in school would make the education screen a less useful quality-signaling device.

There is a third role that educational attainment plays that suggests

----

[7] For an elaboration of this and the following discussion, see R. Nelson, M. J. Peck, and E. Kalachek, *Technological Advance, Economic Growth, and Public Policy* (forthcoming).

[8] This is a point that has been much discussed orally. I have not been able to find a suitable written reference, however.

still another way it should fit into the aggregate production function. Obviously one of the principal things that education does is to increase the discriminating and the information-processing capacity of people; to enable a man better to assess the significance of different observations and to reduce the time and effort needed to comprehend additional knowledge generally (including more education).[9] In part this has its effect on the productivity of a man on a given task; thus a trained television repairman is much more likely to be able to diagnose a trouble, even if it is slightly different from those he has been trained to deal with, than someone with no knowledge of television sets. But in large part the principal effect is in adding flexibility to learn a new job fast and to understand and deal with things that are new. Thus in the early production operation of new chemical processes, chemical engineers often constitute a large fraction of the work force; their education and training gives them a comparative advantage both in rapidly acquiring any specialized knowledge needed for the job and in dealing with the unexpected things that are quite likely to happen. As the process becomes familiar and understood, special training programs can be set up to equip less well-educated persons to the task. As another example, the evidence suggests that well-educated farmers are better able to evaluate new agricultural products and processes than their less-educated peers, and tend therefore to adapt the high payoff innovations earlier.[10] Note that in this role education enters the production function as a variable determining how effectively the system adapts to change. Thus in agriculture average years of educational attainment may be an important variable determining the average lag between the introduction of productive new technology and its adaption.[11] In the chemical process industries the stock of educated people may determine how rapidly a new process can be adapted productively. This is very different than treating years of education as a variable multiplying productivity of labor.

In short, even though we may have considerable confidence that rising educational attainments have been a strong factor behind our growth,

[9] B. Wiesbrod has pointed this out in his "Education and Investment in Human Capital," *Journal of Political Economy,* October 1962.

[10] E. M. Rogers, *Diffusion of Innovations,* New York, 1962, particularly Chapter VI.

[11] R. Nelson and E. S. Phelps have developed such a model in "Investment in Humans, Technological Diffusion, and Economic Growth," *American Economic Review,* May 1966.

we must be quite modest about predicting the quantitative effects of policies which would increase educational attainments still further.

Of course, the greatest difficulties with the theory still lie in its treatment of technological progress. Clearly the treatment of technological progress as a residual or a time trend intrinsically is unsatisfactory, dealing neither with what technological advance is nor with its determinants. Technological advance is an increase in knowledge—an enrichment in the set of goods and processes man knows how to produce or use. In terms of its treatment in a production function, a technological advance is a relaxation of a constraint on what a given set of inputs can produce, often taking the form of a new activity that is open for use. It is true that technological advance in this sense will show up, as advances are implemented, as an increase in the productivity of various inputs, but increases in the productivity of inputs can result from a lot of other factors as well (in particular increases in other inputs not specified in the production function). Nor is incorporation of a variable like the rate of research and development (R&D) expenditures really very satisfactory, for the achievement of ouput increase through the expansion-of-knowledge route certainly involves both more and less than R&D inputs conventionally measured. A lot of technological progress results more from learning while doing—as a by-product of other activities—than from conscious R&D.

Further, even when a new product or process is largely the result of an R&D effort aimed at that objective, a lot more than R&D generally is required. Griliches may be on the right track when he incorporates both R&D and extension expenditures into his analysis of the factors behind productivity changes in agriculture, but he certainly would not claim he has the right functional form.[12] In a very real sense here the problem is similar to the use of years of educational attainment as a proxy for the skills and knowledge possessed by the labor force—the use of an input once removed whose connection with the variable which directly affects production potential is highly uncertain.

Relating to problems of dealing with technological progress, but actually a more general problem, is the basic inadequacy of our measurement of potential output. The production possibility frontier certainly does not shift out uniformly, and we have the familiar problem of try-

[12] *Op. cit.*

ing to characterize a changing vector with a scalor—the index number problem. I certainly do not want to open up a lengthy discussion of that general topic, but there is one point that is important in the context of this paper. The use of growth of GNP, as presently measured, probably leads to an understatement of the relative contribution of technological advance to economic growth.

Much of the economic growth we have experienced has involved the introduction of new consumer goods, like the airplane, penicillin, and the telephone. These goods are new in the sense that they enabled wants to be satisfied that could not be satisfied before. While in some situations the airplane is simply a less costly way to travel (counting time) than a train, prior to the modern airplane it was impossible to travel across the country in less than two days, much less five hours; not more difficult or expensive—impossible. Penicillin has made it possible—not just less costly—to save the lives of many people with certain infections. New products are measured in the GNP calculations by the amount people spend on them, but clearly many people would be willing to pay far more than that. If airplane service were eliminated from the spectrum of final products many consumers would require a significant increase in income to achieve a comparable level of satisfaction. For those for whom penicillin is the only thing that blocks death, the value of the new product clearly vastly exceeds what they pay for it. In general, a given increase in measured GNP tends to mean more in terms of increased utility when it is accompanied by an expansion of the range of consumer-produced choice than when it is not. Even without technological progress the near tripling of GNP per person we have experienced since 1900 would have been a boon. But it would have been a far less powerful liberating force if it had meant largely wider carriages, more coal for the kitchen stove, and more kerosene for the oil lamp. To the extent technological progress is the principal element behind the expansion of the kinds of product and services we know how to provide, its relative contribution to growth is underestimated by analyses using growth of measured GNP as an indicator of growth of potential output.

Again, it would appear that we are in much the same position as with respect to education. We have strong confidence with respect to the powerful role played by technological advance, but are in quite a weak position to estimate with confidence the impact of more or less rapid technological advance in the future.

The Scope of Theory; the Weak Links to Policy Instruments and Objectives

Of course, even if knowledge of aggregate production relations were very strong, this in itself would not provide full guidance for policy. This knowledge must be supplemented by a linkage to instruments under the control of government, by which the variables of the production function can be manipulated. Further, it must be possible to assess the welfare implications of different growth patterns and policies.

Presently the linkage downward to policy instruments is far from adequate. This is most striking in the case of technological progress. The delineation between the variables that enter the production function and the variables that influence these variables is, of course, somewhat arbitrary. Although I would prefer not to consider accumulated R&D expenditures as an input to the production function but rather as a variable once removed, this is in part at least a matter of taste. Further, I do not want to quibble here about the uncertain link between the pace of technological advance and R&D spending.

For the question of policy remains as to how the government can obtain increases in R&D spending. For certain kinds of R&D this is a simple matter; the government simply can increase its own R&D spending. But for other kinds of R&D—in particular applied research and development in most consumer goods fields and in many producer goods industries—the government presently does not spend any money. Experience of the past few years with proposals for the government to provide funds for R&D in housing and machine tools suggests that there are very great political obstacles to the direct approach. And there are questions as to whether direct provision of R&D grants and contracts would be the most efficient route. Rather, policy will, in large part, have to work through stimulating increases in private R&D spending. But how to do this? Theory of the determinants of private R&D spending is weak and at the present time provides little guidance in suggesting means of stimulation.[13] A tax credit has been proposed, and several suggestions have been made for increasing the incentives provided by the patent

---

[13] Pieces of a theory have been developed by E. Mansfield, "Industrial R&D Expenditures; Determinants, Prospects, and Relation to Size of Firm and Inventive Output," *Journal of Political Economy,* August 1964, and R. Nelson, "The Impact of Arms Reduction on R&D," *American Economic Review,* May 1963.

system. But it is quite uncertain how much effect these measures would have.

Similar questions exist with respect to how the government can reduce the gap between best and average practice through provision of better technical information services (like the extension service on agriculture). We shall examine this case in some detail later.

The situation is somewhat better for getting a policy handle on ways to influence growth of physical capital and educational attainments. While with respect to physical capital the government is even more limited than in the case of R&D regarding what it can procure directly (clearly there are very strong barriers to the government directly investing in industrial capital), existing theory of the determinants of private capital formulation, although weak, is better than existing knowledge of the determinants of private R&D spending. Further, some of these variables—in particular the tax rate on profit, allowable depreciation schedules, and interest rates—are directly at the influence of government. In stimulating education, the government is able to spend funds directly. With respect to higher education, to the extent the quantity and quality of the education provided is limited by the funds available to colleges and universities, and the number of talented people going to school is limited by the cost of attaining education, direct subsidies and scholarship assistance should work. Until just recently direct provision of federal funds for primary and secondary education was impossible politically, but now that obstacle seems to have been removed.

However, I doubt if we should have great confidence in our ability to predict exactly the effect of various government policies on the rate of physical capital formation and on growth of real educational attainments. Certainly the effect of interest rates and tax rates on private investment decisions is still uncertain quantitatively. With respect to education, the question remains: Will simply more money provided to educational institutions result in a real increase in relevant education imparted to students? The situation is better than the weak knowledge of the relationship between R&D input and output of technological advance, but we scarcely can be confident of our knowledge of the production function for education.

I could push the point further, but there should be no need; it is clear that present understanding of how to influence the variables that enter the aggregate production function is far from as strong as it might be.

Even if we know exactly how to influence growth, our knowledge still would not be complete. I do not wish to dwell here on the present state of theory and thinking with respect to the payoffs and costs of different growth patterns. Suffice it to say there still is some question even as to whose benefits and costs should be counted, and with what weights; I refer to the whole set of issues with respect to the treatment of future generations.[14] And it is evident we still are not quite clear with respect to the very nature of the benefits to be obtained from increased production potential. Let me recall again the problem of valuing new goods. And to what extent is utility a function of the difference between what one aspires to and what one has, rather than a function simply of increased consumption? What is the effect of an increase in one's neighbor's consumption upon one's own utility? What is the relationship of growth to a nation's prestige or security, and how should this be valued? And how about the process of growing; it is intrinsically unsettling, requiring changes in almost all aspects of the patterns of life. Is this a minus or a plus? Do, or should, people value or disvalue change per se?

These are very difficult questions. But so long as we cannot answer them with any real confidence we also cannot define with any confidence even what an optimum growth policy really means.

The Role of Theory in Growth Policy

It is clear that at the present time the role that growth theory can play in guiding growth policy is somewhat limited. In comparison, say, with employment theory, we can place less confidence on the basic model of the economic mechanisms involved, have less knowledge of how to influence the mechanisms in a predictable way, and are far less clear about what we want policy to achieve for us anyway. At the present time to formulate a Theil-like model and to use it to search for an optimal growth policy is utopian.

What use, then, is growth theory in policy making? In the first place it serves to identify relevant variables and the relevant directions of

[14] For example, S. Margolin, "The Social Rate of Discount and the Optimum Rate of Investment," *Quarterly Journal of Economics*, February 1963. E. S. Phelps, "The Golden Rule of Accumulation," *American Economic Review*, September 1961, and J. Tobin, "Economic Growth as an Objective of Government Policy," *American Economic Review*, May 1964.

change. When, for better or for worse, the United States joined with the other nations of the Organization for Economic Co-operation and Development in setting a growth rate target for the 1960s, theory pointed toward at least three variables that could be stimulated: physical investment, education, and technology. This is an important and useful function, assuming that the theory is correct about the variables. Recall how for many years unemployment policy was sorely handicapped by the belief that proper policy called for balancing the budget, rather than for providing an added fiscal stimulus. While identification of variables and their qualitative impact is far less useful than a more quantitative knowledge, this kind of knowledge is still worthwhile.

In the second place, theory provides a starting place for hunting for policy instruments. Thus the knowledge that investment decisions are, to a degree at least, sensitive to after-tax profit rates led to a focusing on corporate tax rates as a variable that might be manipulated. Knowledge of the importance of R&D expenditures and of information dissemination services to technological progress led to a search for various programs and policies by which the government could spend effectively on R&D, or stimulate companies to spend more. The idea of an industrial extension service evolved. Knowledge that many persons with low incomes were being deterred from college by high costs led to the search for an effective scholarship and fellowship program. Again, it would have been more helpful if theory had specified instruments and their effectiveness, but broader qualitative knowledge at least provides a convenient starting point.

Finally, theory provides a rough idea of the nature of some of the benefits and costs of more rapid growth and, also, helps to point out the kinds of objectives with which growth has little to do or which can be achieved without growth. This last role is quite interesting, I think. In the popular discussion of growth in the early 1960s, there was a tendency to argue that more rapid growth was needed if we were to solve the unemployment problem or the poverty problem; indeed, more rapid economic growth seemed to be thought of as the universal solvent. It was only with some difficulty that economists were able to get people to distinguish between growth of potential output and growth of effective demand, and to understand that, with sensible fiscal and monetary policies, unemployment could be reduced whether or not we decided to push for rapid growth of potential output. It took considerable work to show that by and large today's poor require special policies; growth alone is not enough. Theory has led us to stress that the issues of growth policy hinge largely around how much people were willing to give up today to get something more tomorrow. The nagging question remains: Are we right?

The Strategy of Policy Making in Situations Where Knowledge Is Mostly Qualitative

In short, existing growth theory seems capable of providing qualitative, but not quantitative, guidance; it points to the right variables and directions, but does not specify the details of what should be done, nor quantitatively how much should be done. Yet policy actions require specification of details and of quantity. How should we proceed under such conditions?

I suspect that the only sensible way to proceed is to acknowledge partial ignorance explicitly, and to view policy making as a sequential experimental decision process. What do I mean by this? The approach I am recommending has the following elements:

1. In assessing the promise of a particular proposed program the studies should not attempt to determine whether the expected return from the policy is high when the uncertainties are very great. Rather, the studies should ask: Is it quite possible that the rate of return will be high, what are the key uncertain variables that will determine whether the rate of return will be high or not, and how is it possible to find out more about these variables without very great cost? In a large number of instances I suspect the only way to get a significantly improved fix on the key uncertain variables is to try out an experimental program—this is the only way that history can be teased into creating the relevant data.

2. New programs should, where possible, be instituted on a modest scale and should be viewed as having two objectives—some alleviation of the problem the program is designed to deal with, and the creation of the data necessary to make a better analysis of the merit of the program. In other words, the program should be initiated as an experiment and should be organized so as to have a high chance of providing relevant data. A large part of the design of the program should involve a data-collecting scheme.

3. At the end of a specified number of years the experiment should be evaluated by a group who have no connection with the running of the program and no interest in it; and a study should be undertaken of the promise of a larger-scale program, utilizing the knowledge won in the experimental program. While it is quite possible that it still will be very difficult to estimate rates of return on a larger-scale program with any confidence (or even to estimate exactly what the rate of return was on the pilot program) it certainly should be possible to have a much better idea of the likely range of payoff: whether the idea is as promising as it seemed initially, whether some of the conditions which could cause the program to have a low rate of return materialized or not, what aspects of the design of the program proved most troublesome, etc.

An Example—The Proposed Industrial Extension Service

To make the discussion concrete let me cite an example—the proposed industrial extension service now undergoing hearings before Congress.

The basic policy idea is suggested by growth theory broadly defined. Recognition of the fact that the adoption of new technology takes time and that there is a gap between best and average practice leads rather naturally to a search for possible measures to increase the efficiency of the diffusion process. The data shows clearly that the rate of diffusion, even for extremely productive innovations, sometimes is extremely slow.[15] The significant differences in productivity which often exist between firms in the same industry, one would suspect, are in large part the reflection of the fact that the more productive firms are using more modern techniques.[16] While theory would suggest that there are added costs, as well as added benefits, from more rapid diffusion, the suspicion remains that in many cases the slowness of diffusion is inefficient; that if relatively low-cost measures could be found to accelerate diffusion the rate of return could be substantial.

However, existing knowledge is far from strong enough to point un-

[15] See, for example, E. Mansfield, "Technical Change and the Rate of Innovation," *Econometrics,* October 1961; Z. Griliches, "Hybrid Corn—an Exploration on the Economics of Technological Change," *Econometrica* 1957.

[16] This would appear to be the implication of the study by A. Grosse, "The Technological Structure of the Cotton Textile Industry," in L. Leontieff *et al., Studies in the Structure of the American Economy,* Oxford, 1953.

equivocally to particular policy instruments. While Mansfield and Griliches [17] have shown that such variables as the profitability of the innovation and its costs affect the rate of diffusion, our knowledge still is
limited, and does not indicate clearly how policy can influence the
process. One route would be to try to subsidize the purchase of new
equipment or the adoption of a new technique through some sort of
a special tax credit, but problems of differentiating between adoption of
something new and more routine investment decisions appear insuper-
able; further, such a policy has the strong risk of encouraging the adoption of uneconomic new technology.

Another route seems more promising. It would appear that the information dissemination system affects the diffusion process, at least in
some degree, by determining the time between the availability of new
technology and when various business firms feel they have enough reliable information to decide whether or not to try it out.[18] And information
services are a variable on which federal policy can operate rather
directly. One potentially interesting approach might be to try to beef
up the information services tailored to the needs of firms which do not
possess a strong in-house scientific and technical staff; it is these firms
that would appear to lag most in the diffusion process. A firm without
a strong in-house capability, to be sure, does at present have many
sources of technical and managerial information available to it; other
business firms (particularly its suppliers), trade journals, professional
consultants, contract research organizations, libraries, the Department
of Commerce, and the Small Business Administration, etc. But a firm
without an in-house capability often is untrustful of the sales pitch
of its suppliers, unable to understand and evaluate the technical literature, unfamiliar with and unable rationally to choose among professional consultants. In agriculture this same problem was recognized long
ago and a federal-state extension service designed to meet it. It might
be very interesting to try out a similar service for small business firms.

This is a reasonably accurate description of how growth theory, *ad hoc*
reasoning, and analogy played a role in generating a policy idea—at least
to the extent that economists at the Council of Economic Advisers contributed. Without going into further elaboration, I think a case can be

---

[17] Mansfield, *op. cit.,* and Griliches, *op. cit.*
[18] Much of this notion is implicit in Rogers, *op. cit.*

made that the returns to such a service could be quite high. However, it would appear completely impossible to provide a quantitative estimate and, further, there clearly are a large number of uncertainties. It is quite possible that such a service would be valueless. Also there are a number of different kinds of service that might be provided and it is extremely risky to judge in advance which would be the best.

The following are just a small sample of relevant questions:

1. To what extent will business firms using backward practice be willing to listen to and be persuaded by an industrial extension agent from the state university? Can the intercourse take place largely in short courses and conferences to which business firms are invited to send representatives, or must the extension service more aggressively reach out and force its attention on the firms most in need of help—if the latter, the cost of the service per firm influenced will be greater.

2. To what extent does useful advice depend on rather intimate knowledge of the specific problems of a particular firm, in contrast with the more general knowledge of best practices and typical practice in the industry? If the former, again a much more costly service will be required, or the advice will be of much less value and relevance.

3. Will the costs, in terms of increased need for personal consultation, be significantly larger for the really backward firm with almost no in-house technical competence than for the average or just subaverage firm, with perhaps a greater facility to learn from more impersonal and formal presentations, if a somewhat smaller amount to learn? If so, then perhaps the service should focus its efforts on the average firm rather than the most backward ones.

The answers to these rather specific questions, and others like them, will in large part determine whether any kind of an industrial extension program will have a high rate of return, and if so, what kind of a program. While a limited amount of knowledge regarding them can be obtained from the experience of the several industrial extension programs that presently exist, unfortunately these programs by and large have not been collecting the relevant data. However, it should be possible to get a much better feel for the answers by running pilot programs—with statistical collection controls—in several states. Each service could be asked to keep a complete set of case records. Changes in practice of these firms contacted personally could be compared with those not contacted.

Clearly, it would be no easy job to design an appropriate data collection scheme, but some of what should be collected is obvious.

The industrial extension idea is not presented in advocacy, but rather as an example of an approach to policymaking that I suspect is fruitful quite widely in the field of economic growth policymaking. While in some cases it will not be as easy to proceed by the experimental route as in the example above—even for such policies as a tax credit on investment or for R&D or the establishment of a petit patent with a short patent life for minor inventions—it is possible both to avoid posing the issue as a once and for all decision, and to establish a data collection and evaluation procedure which will facilitate re-evaluation of the issue at some later time. As professional economists our influence and our effectiveness should be enhanced, not diminished, if we explicitly recognize and communicate that while our present knowledge provides useful guidance for growth policy, much of our knowledge enables us more to identify the relevant uncertainties than to resolve them.

COMMENT

HOLLIS B. CHENERY

It is perhaps unfortunate that so much of the recent empirical work on production functions has dealt with aggregate time series for the United States economy. Because of the relatively steady growth in labor, capital, and productive capacity, we observe only a very limited range of input combinations. The growth of output is explained almost equally well by a great variety of functions.

The main policy conclusion drawn from these studies is the importance of factors other than the increase in the quantity of labor and capital. As Nelson rightly points out, the quantitative results of testing functions with additional inputs are useful mainly in providing a plausible listing of the other elements responsible for growth.

In limiting himself to aggregate functions and U.S. experience, Nelson has chosen the type of production function research whose policy implications are perhaps the least interesting. Since I have little quarrel with his conclusions, I should like to suggest a few samples of the much richer range of results that may be obtainable when these limitations are dropped.

Sector Production Functions

Although there is little to choose between Cobb-Douglas and more general production functions as applied to aggregate data, there are important differences on a sector basis. Variations among industries in the elasticity of substitution, for example, can lead to substantial changes in relative factor proportions as the price of labor rises in comparison to the price of capital. These changes in turn affect relative prices, international trade, and the distribution of employment by sector. All of these are important in planning for future growth.

In this area, too, research has been hampered by excessive attention to the United States, where the relative prices of labor and capital differ relatively little among regions. Intercountry analysis seems to hold much more promise of being able to estimate substitution possibilities more reliably, based on the much greater variation in relative factor prices.

Intercountry Analysis

The problems of using U.S. time series to identify and interpret the influence on output of various inputs would be greatly reduced if more attention were given to intercountry analysis. The U.S. studies, for example, suggest that the growth of capital plays a relatively small part in the growth of output, even under favorable assumptions about embodied technological change. A very different conclusion emerges from studies of rapidly growing economies such as Japan, Israel, or Greece, where the growth of the capital stock can be shown to account for a much higher proportion of the total growth than in the United States.

History is not likely to perform enough experiments on one economy to permit us to deduce all the relevant properties of production functions that are needed for policy purposes. I suspect that a comparison of the growth of the several inputs and corresponding output in the United States to comparable estimates for other countries may be the best way to acquire better insight into growth policy for the United States itself. The case for intercountry analysis becomes even stronger when we consider substantial departures from patterns of output and mixtures of inputs that have been experienced in the past. Intercountry analysis therefore becomes essential to the design of growth policies for underdeveloped countries, whose own experience is of very limited value for this purpose.

JAMES W. KNOWLES, Joint Economic Committee

Nelson's paper provides an exceptionally appropriate conclusion for the program of this conference on research into production functions. So far, we have been discussing what research has revealed about the theory of production functions and about the statistical determination of their parameters. This is all very well, but Nelson asks, "So what? What do we do with this knowledge?" He also asks what guidance can be derived from this knowledge that will help policymakers formulate public policies, particularly those aimed at improving the growth rate. By this he means what change in the outer limits of the production possibilities of the economy is set by the quality and quantity of inputs available or what can be done about the rate of growth in potential gross national output. He asks two questions about this: First, does our knowledge of the production function point to variables which public policy can work on to influence the rate of growth in potential output; second, does research enable technicians to predict well enough for policy purposes what the results will be of any changes that are made in public policies?

Nelson concludes that the present state of our knowledge of the production function provides us with qualitative knowledge; i.e., a sort of list of relevant variables, but knowledge is very incomplete about the form of the production function, the size of the parameters, and the links between policy instruments and the operation of the economy. He then goes on to give us some examples of how this qualitative knowledge has been applied in the Kennedy-Johnson administrations with some suggestions as to how it can be further applied.

Nelson's paper is excellent and deserves high praise as a pioneering effort. But some of its strengths are also its weaknesses, and a few comments upon these would perhaps be helpful to future workers. First, he is very correct in stressing the weakness of the growth of GNP as a measure of the growth in potential output and, further, in stressing that

NOTE: The views expressed are those of the writer and do not necessarily represent the views of the Joint Economic Committee or individual members thereof.

there are many things about the growth of the economy that cannot be comprehended in such a measure. This has been a matter of perennial concern, for example, to members of the Joint Economic Committee, as is evident to those who have attended our hearings. But the stress put upon this reveals, at the same time, a weakness among analysts. The incompleteness of GNP as a measure of growth is confused with the related problem of measuring the changing social utilities. In general, these are aspects of dynamic change in the economy, including changes in social valuations. They are not necessarily directly correlated with changes in output of goods and services.

Again, Nelson quite correctly stresses the importance for policy of differentiating between the growth of effective demand and the growth of potential output. Clearly, these are not the same thing. But Nelson makes an error which is common in the profession of assuming that this confusion is solely an error of nontechnical people which the economists have belatedly, and with some difficulty, tried to correct. I am embarrassed to say this, but the economists were major offenders in confusing changes in effective demand with changes in potential output, partly by stressing changes in the GNP as a measure of growth. I am afraid economists themselves have been lax at times in their policy advice by not distinguishing between demand and supply as our older mentors were wont to do.

Third, I think Nelson has fallen into a familiar trap in his praise for the state of so-called employment theory, or the theory of aggregate demand as developed in the Keynesian economics which he contrasts with the rather less satisfactory state of production theory. I think this is, unfortunately, a very general belief in the profession. As a policy adviser myself, I have been appalled at times to find that the state of this so-called employment theory is such as to lead to some very poor policy advice. For example, it has been the basis for some quite false and improper emphasis on the greater growth stimulation to be obtained from changes in public expenditures compared with that from tax changes. This stems from the emphasis on the so-called balanced budget theorem in modern Keynesian economics which rests on some very unlikely assumptions, among which is the unstated assumption that changes in the structure of the economy via tax changes have quite similar results to the changes in flows of incomes or expenditures within the existing structure.

It may be of some interest for me to give some other examples from my own experience at the Joint Economic Committee of the use of the production function in formulating economic policy advice. The committee's staff has made use of this tool for a number of purposes, the majority of which may be grouped together and called examples of its use as a tool to separate long-term from short-term influences in the economy. These studies revolved around using the production function to develop a long-term full employment estimate of potential output and then using the difference between this potential and the actual GNP as a measure of short-term changes in effective demand. With this as a basis, studies have been made of such issues as differences between short- and long-term marginal tax rates; differences between the short-term and long-term consumption functions; explorations into the role of money variables; and, finally, the relative role of long-term and short-term factors in determining the profitability of private enterprise.

From the studies we have made, many of which were published in connection with the committee's reports, we have learned some lessons which may be of value to others. There is much discussion, for example, about the accuracy with which we can determine production functions and whether the results are good enough. Nelson voices some doubt on this point. We made some tests to determine the answer to this question. We made a series of projections for a seventeen-year period between 1958 and 1975, using a number of different aggregate production functions, both with generally sensible parameters and then with some that incorporated ridiculous estimates such as inverted coefficients implying that an increase in labor input reduced output. The results showed that the maximum difference after seventeen years in the estimates of the potential output was only about 12 per cent, even using the most ridiculous functions. Within the calculation period 1909 to 1958, the difference for any of the more sensible functions was insignificant for practical policy purposes. The truth was that the most important factors were the assumptions about the input of labor and capital, how they would grow in the future, and what system of measurement was used.

Another lesson we learned was connected with what may be called the Denison effect, to which Nelson refers; that is, the negative correlation between average hours of work and labor productivity. Nelson indicates that the mere hypothesis of this negative relationship is in itself useful. In the early 1950s, I made some tests for the committee staff and found that we had to know fairly precisely the shape of this function, not just its slope. The reason is that it is almost certain that this curve is highly curvilinear. When average hours of work are sixty or eighty a week, a reduction in hours raises output per man-hour more than proportionate to the reduction of hours. But when hours of work get down to around forty per week, there seems to be barely a one-to-one effect, and at some lower point the relation becomes less than one-to-one. If this research could ever be confirmed, it would have substantial implications as to how far you could carry this policy, and probably would imply that it has been carried about as far as feasible in the United States.

I would like to close my remarks by a comment on the application of the production function to policy which is relative to a large area to which Nelson refers. The staff and members of the Joint Economic Committee have long been interested in the connection between education and training programs and the productivity of our economy. We have been particularly interested in whether or not substantial increases in the resources allocated to these programs would increase the rate of growth in potential output. However, large increases in the usual types of educational programs, such as elementary, secondary, and college education, if they are successful in increasing productivity, seem likely to bring about increments in aggregate output per man-hour twenty or thirty years after the program is started. I wonder how well an educational program could be sold now on the basis of a rather vague and indefinite estimate as to the benefits in the form of productivity increases that might be expected in 1980 or 1990? On the other hand, there must be a number of programs to train existing workers and managers which would have rather large effects within a much shorter time.

This emphasizes a point that our staff has run into time and time again in applying both production theory and other forms of economic analysis to public policy. It is of the utmost importance carefully to analyze, in each case, the sequence of events over time through which the proposed policy shifts will have their effects. It is very possible, if not indeed probable, that the lags involved between action and its consequences for the economy as a whole may be just as critical, if not more critical, than the magnitude or character of the policy change.

AUTHOR INDEX

SUBJECT INDEX